Golden Treasury of the Familiar

And the music's not immortal;
but the world has made it sweet.
        —Alfred Noyes, *The Barrel-Organ*

When Time, who steals our years away,
Shall steal our pleasures, too,
The mem'ry of the past will stay,
And half our joys renews.
        —Thomas Moore, *Song*

Let Fate do her worst; there are relics of joy,
Bright dreams of the past, which she cannot destroy;
Which come in the night-time of sorrow and care,
And bring back the features that joy used to wear.
Long; long be my heart with such memories fill'd!
Like the vase, in which roses have been distill'd—
You may break, you may shatter the vase, if you will,
But the scent of the roses will hang 'round it still.
        —Thomas Moore

Golden Treasury of the Familiar

Memorable and Beloved Selections Chosen
for Their Continuing Appeal to Old and New Readers
from the Three Famous Books,
A Treasury of the Familiar
A Second Treasury of the Familiar
and A Third Treasury of the Familiar

Edited by Ralph L. Woods

AVENEL BOOKS
New York

For Claire Michele Huot, a golden granddaughter

This 1983 edition is published by Avenel Books,
distributed by Crown Publishers, Inc., by arrangement with
Macmillan Publishing Co., Inc.

Manufactured in the United States of America

Library of Congress Cataloging in Publication Data
Main entry under title:

Golden treasury of the familiar.

"Memorable and beloved selections chosen for their
continuing appeal to old and new readers from the three
famous books, A treasury of the familiar (1942), A second
treasury of the familiar (1950), and A third treasury of the
familiar (1970)"
    Reprint. Originally published: New York : Macmillan
Pub. Co., c1980.
    Includes indexes.
    1. Literature—Collections.   I. Woods, Ralph Louis,
1904-   .
[PN6014.G58   1983]   808.8   82-20633
ISBN 0-517-40281-5
h g f e d c b a

CONTENTS

PREFACE

Readers may be pleased they are spared a long and unexciting preface.

I simply want to state that the hundreds of selections in this book have been chosen for reading pleasure from my three earlier anthologies, published in 1942, 1950, and 1970.

Inclusions in this book were made solely on the basis of their continuing appeal and familiarity to the American people, and because of their value and usefulness in the home, school, and library.

R. L. W.
Ramsey, New Jersey

TIME

Anonymous

Time is
Too slow for those who wait,
Too swift for those who Fear,
Too long for those who Grieve,
Too short for those who Rejoice;
But for those who Love
Time is
Eternity.

OCTOBER'S BRIGHT BLUE WEATHER

Helen Hunt Jackson

O suns and skies and clouds of June,
And flowers of June together,
Ye cannot rival for one hour
October's bright blue weather.

When loud the humblebee makes haste,
Belated, thriftless vagrant,
And Golden Rod is dying fast,
And lanes with grapes are fragrant;

When Gentians roll their fringes tight,
To save them for the morning,
And chestnuts fall from satin burrs
Without a sound of warning;

When on the ground red apples lie
In piles like jewels shining,
And redder still on old stone walls
Are leaves of woodbine twining;

When all the lovely wayside things
Their white-winged seeds are sowing,
And in the fields, still green and fair,
Late aftermaths are growing;

When springs run low, and on the brooks,
   In idle golden freighting,
Bright leaves sink noiseless in the hush
   Of woods, for winter waiting;

When comrades seek sweet country haunts,
   By twos and twos together,
And count like misers, hour by hour,
   October's bright blue weather.

O suns and skies and flowers of June,
   Count all your boasts together,
Love loveth best of all the year
   October's bright blue weather.

BILL NYE ACCEPTS APPOINTMENT AS POSTMASTER OF LARAMIE, WYOMING

Office of *Daily Boomerang*, Laramie City, Wy.
August 9, 1882

MY DEAR GENERAL:

I have received by telegraph the news of my nomination by the President and my confirmation by the Senate, as postmaster at Laramie, and wish to extend my thanks for same.

I have ordered an entirely new set of boxes and post office outfit, including new corrugated cuspidors for the lady clerks.

I look upon the appointment, myself, as a great triumph of eternal truth over error and wrong. It is one of the epochs, I may say, in the Nation's onward march toward political purity and perfection. I do not know when I have noticed any stride in the affairs of state which so thoroughly impressed me by its wisdom.

Now that we are co-workers in the same department, I trust that you will not feel shy or backward in consulting me at any time relative to matters concerning post office affairs. Be perfectly frank with me, and feel perfectly free to just bring anything of that kind right to me. Do not feel reluctant because I may at times appear haughty and indifferent, cold or reserved. Perhaps you do not think I know the difference between a general delivery and a three-m quad, but that is a mistake. My general information is far beyond my years.

With profound regard, and a hearty endorsement of the policy of the President and the Senate, whatever it may be,

I remain, sincerely yours,

BILL NYE, P. M.

Gen. Frank Hatton, Washington, D.C.

FOR EVERYTHING GIVE THANKS

Helena Isabella Tupper

For all that God in mercy sends,
For health and children, home and friends,
For comfort in the time of need,
For every kindly word and deed,
For happy thoughts and holy talk,
For guidance in our daily walk,
   'For everything give thanks!

For beauty in this world of ours,
For verdant grass and lovely flowers,
For song of birds, for hum of bees,
For refreshing summer breeze,
For hill and plain, for streams and wood,
For the great ocean's mighty flood,
   For everything give thanks!

For sweet sleep which comes with night,
For the returning morning light,
For the bright sun that shines on high,
For the stars glittering in the sky,
For these and everything we see,
O Lord, our hearts we lift to thee.
   For everything give thanks!

IS EPIMENIDES A LIAR?

Epimenides the Cretan says, "All Cretans are liars." But Epimenides is himself a Cretan; therefore he is a liar himself. But if he is a liar, his statements are lies, and consequently the Cretans are veracious. But Epimenides is a Cretan, and, since they are veracious, what he says is true; and it follows after all that all the Cretans are liars.

LOVE'S OLD SWEET SONG

G. Clifton Bingham

Once in the dear dead days beyond recall,
When on the world the mists began to fall,
Out of the dreams that rose in happy throng,
Low to our hearts love sang an old sweet song,
And in the dusk where fell the fire-light gleam,
Softly wove itself into our dream.

Chorus:

    Just a song at twilight, when the lights are low,
    And the flick'ring shadows softly come and go—
    Tho' the heart be weary, sad the day and long,
    Still to us at twilight comes love's old sweet song.

Even today we hear love's song of yore,
Deep in our hearts it dwells forever more;
Footsteps may falter, weary grow the way,
Still we can hear it at the close of day.
So to the end, when life's dim shadows fall,
Love will be found the sweetest song of all. (*Chorus.*)

PROTECTION FROM PROTECTORS

Henry David Thoreau

I went to the store the other day to buy a bolt for our front door, for as I told the storekeeper, the Governor was coming here. "Aye," said he, and the Legislature too." "Then I will take two bolts," said I. He said that there had been a steady demand for bolts and locks of late, for our protectors were coming.

POLITICS DEFINED

Oscar Ameringer

The art of obtaining money from the rich and votes from the poor, on the pretext of protecting each from the other.

4

ON PRINCE FREDERICK

Anonymous

Here lies Fred
Who was alive and is dead.
Had it been his father,
I had much rather;
Had it been his brother,
Still better than another;
Had it been his sister,
No one would have missed her;
Had it been the whole generation,
So much the better for the nation;
But since 'tis only Fred
Who was alive and is dead,
Why, there's no more to be said.

THE TOYS

Coventry Patmore

My Little Son, who look'd from thoughtful eyes
And moved and spoke in quiet grown-up wise,
Having my law the seventh time disobey'd,
I struck him and dismiss'd
With hard words and unkiss'd,
—His Mother, who was patient, being dead.
Then, fearing lest his grief should hinder sleep,
I visited his bed,
But found him slumbering deep,
With darken'd eyelids, and their lashes yet
From his late sobbing wet.
And I, with moan,
Kissing away his tears, left others of my own;
For, on a table drawn beside his head,
He had put, within his reach,
A box of counters and a red-vein'd stone,
A piece of glass abraded by the beach,
And six or seven shells,
A bottle with bluebells,
And two French copper coins, ranged there with careful art,
To comfort his sad heart.

5

So when that night I pray'd
To God, I wept, and said:
Ah, when at last we lie with trancèd breath,
Not vexing Thee in death,
And Thou rememberest of what toys
We made our joys,
How weakly understood
Thy great commanded good,
Then, fatherly not less
Than I whom Thou hast moulded from the clay,
Thou'lt leave Thy wrath, and say,
"I will be sorry for their childishness."

THERE IS A REALM WHERE THE RAINBOW NEVER FADES

George D. Prentice

It cannot be that the earth is man's only abiding place. It cannot be that our life is a mere bubble cast up by eternity to float a moment on its waves and then sink into nothingness. Else why is it that glorious aspirations which leap like angels from the temple of our hearts are forever wandering unsatisfied? Why is it that all the stars that hold festival around the midnight throne are set above the grasp of our limited faculties, forever mocking us with their unapproachable glory? And, finally, why is it that bright forms of human beauty presented to our view are taken from us, leaving the thousand streams of our affections to flow back in Alpine torrents upon our hearts? There is a realm where the rainbow never fades; where the stars will be spread out before us like islands that slumber in the ocean, and where the beautiful beings which now pass before us like shadows will stay in our presence forever.

* * *

You can fool some of the people all of the time and all of the people some of the time: but you can't fool all of the people all of the time.

—Attributed to Lincoln

FROM LINCOLN'S ANNUAL MESSAGE TO CONGRESS

The dogmas of the quiet past are inadequate to the stormy present. The occasion is piled high with difficulty, and we must rise with the occasion. As our case is new, so we must think anew and act anew. We must disenthrall ourselves, and then we shall save our country.

Fellow-citizens, we cannot escape history. We of this Congress and this administration will be remembered in spite of ourselves. No personal significance or insignificance can spare one or another of us. The fiery trial through which we pass will light us down, in honor or dishonor, to the latest generation. We say we are for the Union. The world will not forget that we say this. We know how to save the Union. The world knows that we know how to save it. We— even we here—hold the power and bear the responsibility. In giving freedom to the slave, we assure freedom to the free—honorable alike in what we give and what we preserve. We shall nobly save or meanly lose the last, best hope of earth. Other means may succeed; this could not fail. The way is plain, peaceful, generous, just—a way which, if followed, the world will forever applaud, and God must forever bless.

(1862)

OPPORTUNITY

Edward Rowland Sill

This I beheld, or dreamed it in a dream:—
There spread a cloud of dust along a plain;
And underneath the cloud, or in it, raged
A furious battle, and men yelled, and swords
Shocked upon swords and shields. A prince's banner
Wavered, then staggered backward, hemmed by foes.
A craven hung along the battle's edge,
And thought, "Had I a sword of keener steel—
That blue blade that the king's son bears,—but this
Blunt thing—!" he snapt and flung it from his hand,
And lowering crept away and left the field.
Then came the king's son, wounded, sore bestead,
And weaponless, and saw the broken sword,
Hilt-buried in the dry and trodden sand,
And ran and snatched it, and with battle-shout
Lifted afresh he hewed his enemy down,
And saved a great cause that heroic day.

PRAYER OF AN UNKNOWN CONFEDERATE SOLDIER

I asked God for strength, that I might achieve,
I was made weak, that I might learn humbly to obey . . .
I asked for health, that I might do greater things,
I was given infirmity, that I might do better things . . .
I asked for riches, that I might be happy,
I was given poverty that I might be wise . . .
I asked for power, that I might have the praise of men,
I was given weakness, that I might feel the need of God . . .
I asked for all things, that I might enjoy life,
I was given life, that I might enjoy all things . . .
I got nothing that I asked for—but everything that I had hoped for.
Almost despite myself, my unspoiled prayers were answered.
I am among all men, most richly blessed.

REST

John Sullivan Dwight

Rest is not quitting
   The busy career,
Rest is the fitting
   Of self to its sphere.

'Tis the brook's motion,
   Clear without strife,
Fleeing to ocean
   After its life.

'Tis loving and serving
   The Highest and Best!
'Tis onwards! unswerving,
   And that is true rest.

* * *

I never knew any man in my life who could not bear another's misfortune perfectly like a Christian.

—Alexander Pope

THE MOUNTAINS IN LABOR

The Mountains were said to be in labor, and uttered most dreadful groans. People came together far and near to see what birth would be produced; and, after they waited a considerable time in expectation, out crept a Mouse.

(From Aesop's Fables)

THE SECRET LIFE OF WALTER MITTY

James Thurber

"We're going through!" The Commander's voice was like thin ice breaking. He wore his full-dress uniform, with the heavily braided white cap pulled down rakishly over one cold gray eye. "We can't make it, sir. It's spoiling for a hurricane, if you ask me." "I'm not asking you, Lieutenant Berg," said the Commander. "Throw on the power lights! Rev her up to 8,500! We're going through!" The pounding of the cylinders increased: ta-pocketa-pocketa-pocketa-*pocketa-pocketa*. The Commander stared at the ice forming on the pilot window. He walked over and twisted a row of complicated dials. "Switch on No. 8 auxiliary!" he shouted. "Switch on No. 8 auxiliary!" repeated Lieutenant Berg. "Full strength in No. 3 turret!" shouted the Commander. "Full strength in No. 3 turret!" The crew, bending to their various tasks in the huge, hurtling eight-engined Navy hydroplane, looked at each other and grinned. "The Old Man ain't afraid of Hell!" . . .

"Not so fast! You're driving too fast!" said Mrs. Mitty. "What are you driving so fast for?"

"Hmm?" said Walter Mitty. He looked at his wife, in the seat beside him, with shocked astonishment. She seemed grossly unfamiliar, like a strange woman who had yelled at him in a crowd. "You were up to fifty-five," she said. "You know I don't like to go more than forty. You were up to fifty-five." Walter Mitty drove on toward Waterbury in silence, the roaring of the SN 202 through the worst storm in twenty years of Navy flying faded in the remote, intimate airways of his mind. "You're tensed up again," said Mrs. Mitty. "It's one of your days. I wish you'd let Dr. Renshaw look you over." Walter Mitty stopped the car in front of the building where his wife went to have her hair done. "Remember to get those overshoes while I'm having my hair done," she said. "I don't need

9

overshoes," said Mitty. She put her mirror back into her bag. "We've been all through that," she said, getting out of the car. "You're not a young man any longer." He raced the engine a little. "Why don't you wear your gloves? Have you lost your gloves?" Walter Mitty reached in a pocket and brought out the gloves. He put them on, but after she had turned and gone into the building and he had driven on to a red light, he took them off again. "Pick it up, brother!" snapped a cop as the light changed, and Mitty hastily pulled on his gloves and lurched ahead. He drove around the streets aimlessly for a time and then he drove past the hospital on his way to the parking lot.

"It's the millionaire banker, Wellington McMillan," said the pretty nurse. "Yes?" said Walter Mitty, removing his gloves slowly. "Who has the case?" "Dr. Renshaw and Dr. Benbow, but there are two specialists here, Dr. Remington from New York and Mr. Pritchard–Mitford from London. He flew over." A door opened down a long, cool corridor and Dr. Renshaw came out. He looked distraught and haggard. "Hello, Mitty," he said. "We're having the devil's own time with McMillan, the millionaire banker and close personal friend of Roosevelt. Obstreosis of the ductal tract. Tertiary. Wish you'd take a look at him." "Glad to," said Mitty.

In the operating room there were whispered introductions: "Dr. Remington, Dr. Mitty. Mr. Pritchard–Mitford, Dr. Mitty." "I've read your book on streptothricosis," said Pritchard–Mitford, shaking hands. "A brilliant performance, sir." "Thank you," said Walter Mitty. "Didn't know you were in the States, Mitty," grumbled Remington. "Coals to Newcastle, bringing Mitford and me up here for a tertiary." "You are very kind," said Mitty. A huge, complicated machine, connected to the operating table, with many tubes and wires, began at this moment to go pocketa-pocketa-pocketa. "The new anesthetizer is giving way!" shouted an interne. "There is no one in the east who knows how to fix it!" "Quiet, man!" said Mitty, in a low, cool voice. He sprang to the machine, which was going pocketa-pocketa-queep-pocketa-queep. He began fingering delicately a row of glistening dials. "Give me a fountain pen!" he snapped. Someone handed him a fountain pen. He pulled a faulty piston out of the machine and inserted the pen in its place. "That will hold for ten minutes," he said. "Get on with the operation." A nurse hurried over and whispered to Renshaw, and Mitty saw the man turn pale. "Coreopsis has set in," said Renshaw nervously. "If you would take over, Mitty?" Mitty looked at him and at the craven figure of Benbow, who drank, and at the grave, uncertain faces of the two great specialists. "If you wish," he said. They slipped a white gown on him; he adjusted a mask and drew on thin gloves; nurses handed him shining . . .

"Back it up, Mac! Look out for that Buick!" Walter Mitty jammed on the brakes. "Wrong lane, Mac," said the parking-lot attendant, looking at Mitty closely. "Gee. Yeh," muttered Mitty. He began cautiously to back out of the lane marked "Exit Only." "Leave her sit there," said the attendant. "I'll put her away." Mitty got out of the car. "Hey, better leave the key." "Oh," said Mitty, handing the man the ignition key. The attendant vaulted into the car, backed it up with insolent skill, and put it where it belonged.

They're so damn cocky, thought Walter Mitty, walking along Main Street; they think they know everything. Once he had tried to take his chains off, outside New Milford, and he had got them wound around the axles. A man had had to come out in a wrecking car and unwind them, a young, grinning garageman. Since then Mrs. Mitty always made him drive to a garage to have the chains taken off. The next time, he thought, I'll wear my right arm in a sling; they won't grin at me then. I'll have my right arm in a sling and they'll see I couldn't possibly take the chains off myself. He kicked at the slush on the sidewalk. "Overshoes," he said to himself, and he began looking for a shoe store.

When he came out into the street again, with the overshoes in a box under his arm, Walter Mitty began to wonder what the other thing was his wife had told him to get. She had told him, twice, before they set out from their house for Waterbury. In a way he hated these weekly trips to town—he was always getting something wrong. Kleenex, he thought, Squibb's, razor blades? No. Toothpaste, toothbrush, bicarbonate, cardorundumn, initiative and referendum? He gave it up. But she would remember it. "Where's the what-its-name." A newsboy went by shouting something about the Waterbury trial.

"Perhaps this will refresh your memory." The District Attorney suddenly thrust a heavy automatic at the quiet figure on the witness stand. "Have you ever seen this before?" Walter Mitty took the gun and examined it expertly. "This is my Webley–Vickers 50.80," he said calmly. An excited buzz ran around the courtroom. The Judge rapped for order. "You are a crack shot with any sort of firearms, I believe?" said the District Attorney, insinuatingly. "Objection!" shouted Mitty's attorney. "We have shown that the defendant could not have fired the shot. We have shown that he wore his right arm in a sling on the night of the fourteenth of July." Walter Mitty raised his hand briefly and the bickering attorneys were stilled. "With any known make of gun," he said evenly, "I could have killed Gregory Fitzhurst at three hundred feet *with my left hand*."

Pandemonium broke loose in the courtroom. A woman's scream rose above the bedlam and suddenly a lovely, dark-skinned girl was in Walter Mitty's arms. The District Attorney struck at her savagely. Without rising from his chair, Mitty let the man have it on the point of the chin. "You miserable cur!" . . .

"Puppy biscuit," said Walter Mitty. He stopped walking and the buildings of Waterbury rose up out of the misty courtroom and surrounded him again. A woman who was passing laughed. "He said 'Puppy Biscuit'," she said to her companion. "That man said 'Puppy Biscuit' to himself." Walter Mitty hurried on. He went into an A.&P., not the first one he came to but a smaller one farther up the street. "I want some biscuit for small, young dogs," he said to the clerk. "Any special brand, sir?" The greatest pistol shot in the world thought a moment. "It says 'Puppies Bark for It' on the box," said Walter Mitty.

His wife would be through at the hairdresser's in fifteen minutes, Mitty saw in looking at his watch, unless they had trouble drying it; sometimes they had trouble drying it. She didn't like to get to the hotel first; she would want him to be there waiting for her as usual. He found a big leather chair in the lobby, facing a window, and he put the overshoes and the puppy biscuit on the floor beside it. He picked up an old copy of *Liberty* and sank down into the chair. "Can Germany Conquer the World Through the Air?" Walter Mitty looked at the pictures of bombing planes and of ruined streets.

. . . "The cannonading has got the wind up in young Raleigh, sir," said the sergeant. Captain Mitty looked up at him through tousled hair. "Get him to bed," he said wearily. "With the others. I'll fly alone." "But you can't, sir," said the sergeant anxiously. "It takes two men to handle that bomber and the Archies are pounding hell out of the air. Von Richtman's circus is between here and Saulier." "Somebody's got to get that ammunition dump," said Mitty. "I'm going over. Spot of brandy?" He poured a drink for the sergeant and one for himself. War thundered and whined around the dugout and battered at the door. There was a rending of wood and splinters flew through the room. "A bit of a near thing," said Captain Mitty carelessly. "The box barrage is closing in," said the sergeant. "We only live once, sergeant," said Mitty with his faint, fleeting smile. "Or do we?" He poured another brandy and tossed it off. "I never see a man could hold his brandy like you, sir," said the sergeant. "Begging your pardon, sir." Captain Mitty stood up and strapped on his huge Webley–Vickers automatic. "It's forty kilometers through hell, sir," said the sergeant. Mitty finished one last brandy. "After all," he said softly, "what isn't?" The pounding of the cannon increased; there was the rat-tat-tatting of machine guns, and from somewhere came the menacing pocketa-pocketa-pocketa of the new flame-throwers. Walter Mitty walked to the door of the dugout humming "Auprès de Ma Blonde." He turned and waved to the sergeant. "Cheerio!" he said.

Something struck his shoulder. "I've been looking all over this hotel for you," said Mrs. Mitty. "Why do you have to hide in this old chair? How did you expect me to find you?" "Things close in," said Walter Mitty vaguely. "What?" Mrs. Mitty said. "Did you get the what's-its-name? The puppy biscuit? What's in that box?" "Over-shoes," said Mitty. "Couldn't you have put them on in the store?" "I was thinking," said Walter Mitty. "Does it ever occur to you that I am sometimes thinking?" She looked at him. "I'm going to take your temperature when I get you home," she said.

They went out through the revolving doors that made a faintly derisive whistling sound when you pushed them. It was two blocks to the parking lot. At the drugstore on the corner she said, "Wait here for me. I forgot something. I won't be a minute." Walter Mitty lighted a cigarette. It began to rain, rain with sleet in it. He stood up against the wall of the drugstore, smoking . . . He put his shoulders back and his heels together. "To hell with the handker-chief," said Walter Mitty scornfully. He took one last drag on his cigarette and snapped it away. Then with that faint, fleeting smile playing about his lips, he faced the firing squad; erect and motion-less, proud and disdainful, Walter Mitty the Undefeated, inscrutable to the last.

THE VALUE OF SILENCE

When someone twitted Calvin Coolidge for his habitual silence, he replied, "Well, I found out early in life that you didn't have to explain something you hadn't said."

*　　*　　*

Hypocrisy is a homage vice pays to virtue.—François, Duc de la Rochefoucauld

SWEET BETSEY FROM PIKE

Anonymous

Oh, don't you remember sweet Betsey from Pike,
Who crossed the big mountains with her lover Ike,
With two yoke of cattle, a large yellow dog,
A tall shanghai rooster and one spotted hog.

One evening quite early they camped on the Platte,
'Twas near by the road on a green shady flat,
Where Betsey, sore-footed, lay down to repose—
With wonder Ike gazed on that Pike County rose.

Their wagon broke down with a terrible crash,
And out on the prairie rolled all kinds of trash;
A few little baby clothes done up with care—
'Twas rather suspicious, though all on the *square*.

The shanghai ran off, and their cattle all died;
That morning the last piece of bacon was fried;
Poor Ike was discouraged, and Betsey got mad,
The dog drooped his tail and looked wondrously sad.

They stopped at Salt Lake to inquire the way,
When Brigham declared that sweet Betsey should stay;
But Betsey got frightened and ran like a deer,
While Brigham stood pawing the ground like a steer.

They soon reached the desert, where Betsey gave out,
And down in the sand she lay rolling about;
While Ike, half distracted, looked on with surprise,
Saying, "Betsey, get up, you'll get sand in your eyes."

Sweet Betsey got up in a great deal of pain,
Declared she'd go back to Pike County again;
But Ike gave a sigh, and they fondly embraced,
And they travelled along with his arm round her waist.

They suddenly stopped on a very high hill,
With wonder looked down upon old Placerville;
Ike sighed when he said, and he cast his eyes down,
"Sweet Betsey, my darling, we've got to Hangtown."

Long Ike and sweet Betsey attended a dance;
Ike wore a pair of his Pike County pants;
Sweet Betsey was covered with ribbons and rings;
Says Ike, "You're an angel, but where are your wings?"

A miner said, "Betsey, will you dance with me?"
"I will that, old hoss, if you don't make too free;
But don't dance me hard; do you want to know why?
Dog on you! I'm chock full of strong alkali!"

This Pike County couple got married of course,
And Ike became jealous—obtained a divorce;
Sweet Betsey, well satisfied, said with a shout,
"Good-by, you big lummox, I'm glad you've backed out!"

THERE IS AMERICA

Edmund Burke

Young man, there is America—which at this day serves for little
more than to amuse you with stories of savage men and uncouth
manners; yet shall, before you taste of death, show itself equal to the
whole of that commerce which now attracts the envy of the world.

(From a speech, 1775)

SLOW ME DOWN, LORD!

Orin L. Crane

Slow me down, Lord!
Ease the pounding of my heart by the quieting of my mind.
Steady my hurried pace,
With a vision of the eternal reach of time.
Give me, amidst the confusion of my day,
The calmness of the everlasting hills.
Break the tension of my nerves

With the soothing music of the singing streams
That live in my memory.
Help me to know the magical restoring power of sleep.
Teach me the art of taking minute vacations of slowing down.
To look at a flower;
To chat with an old friend or make a new one;
To pat a stray dog; to watch a spider build a web;
To smile at a child; or to read from a good book.
Remind me each day
That the race is not always to the swift;
That there is more to life
Than increasing its speed.

THE LIFE OF MAN ON EARTH

Anonymous

You remember, it may be, O king, that which sometimes happens in winter when you are seated at table with your earls and thanes. Your fire is lighted, and your hall warmed, and without is rain and snow and storm. Then comes a swallow flying across the hall; he enters by one door, and leaves by another. The brief moment while he is within is pleasant to him; he feels not rain nor cheerless winter weather; but the moment is brief—the bird flies away in the twinkling of an eye, and he passes from winter to winter. Such, me thinks, is the life of man on earth, compared with the uncertain time beyond. It appears for a while; but what is the time which comes after—the time which was before? We know not. If, then, this new doctrine may teach us somewhat of greater certainty, it were well that we should regard it.

(Attributed to a chief of the North-umbrians, speaking in the presence of nobles who had declared that the old gods were powerless. This took place at the turn of the seventh century, when Christian missionaries came to Great Britain after the Saxon invasion.)

THE DEATH OF JESUS

Holy Bible, Luke 23:1–46

1 And the whole multitude of them arose, and led him unto Pilate.

2 And they began to accuse him, saying, We found this fellow perverting the nation, and forbidding to give tribute to Caesar, saying that he himself is Christ a king.

3 And Pilate asked him, saying, Art thou the King of the Jews? And he answered him, and said, Thou sayest it.

4 Then said Pilate to the chief priests and to the people, I find no fault in this man.

5 And they were the more fierce, saying, He stirreth up the people, teaching, throughout all Jewry, beginning from Galilee to this place.

6 When Pilate heard of Galilee, he asked whether the man were a Galilean.

7 And as soon as he knew that he belonged unto Herod's jurisdiction, he sent him to Herod, who himself also was at Jerusalem at that time.

8 And when Herod saw Jesus, he was exceeding glad: for he was desirous to see him of a long season, because he had heard many things of him; and he hoped to have seen some miracles done by him.

9 Then he questioned with him in many words; but he answered him nothing.

10 And the chief priests and scribes stood and vehemently accused him.

11 And Herod with his men of war set him at nought, and mocked him, and arrayed him in a gorgeous robe, and sent him again to Pilate.

12 And the same day Pilate and Herod were made friends together: for before they were at enmity between themselves.

13 And Pilate, when he had called together the chief priests and the rulers and the people.

14 Said unto them, Ye have brought this man unto me, as one that perverteth the people; and, behold, I having examined him before you, have found no fault in this man, touching those things whereof ye accuse him:

15 No, nor yet Herod: for I sent you to him; and lo, nothing worthy of death is done unto him.

16 I will therefore chastise him, and release him.

17 (For of necessity he must release one unto them at the feast.)

18 And they cried out all at once, saying, Away with this man, and release unto us Barabbas:

19 (Who for a certain sedition made in the city, and for murder, was cast into prison.)

20 Pilate, therefore, willing to release Jesus, spake again to them.

21 But they cried, saying, Crucify him, crucify him.

22 And he said unto them the third time, Why, what evil hath he done? I have found no cause of death in him: I will therefore chastise him, and let him go.

23 And they were instant with loud voices, requiring that he might be crucified. And the voices of them and of the chief priests prevailed.

24 And Pilate gave sentence that it should be as they required.

25 And he released unto them him that for sedition and murder was cast into prison, whom they had desired; but he delivered Jesus to their will.

26 And as they led him away, they laid hold upon one Simon, a Cyrenian, coming out of the country, and on him they laid the cross, that he might bear it after Jesus.

27 And there followed him a great company of people, and of women, which also bewailed and lamented him.

28 But Jesus turning unto them, said, Daughters of Jerusalem, weep not for me, but weep for yourselves, and for your children.

29 For, behold, the days are coming, in the which they shall say, Blessed are the barren, and the wombs that never bare, and the paps which never gave suck.

30 Then shall they begin to say to the mountains, Fall on us; and to the hills, cover us.

31 For if they do these things in a green tree, what shall be done in the dry?

32 And there were also two other, malefactors, led with him to be put to death.

33 And when they were come to the place, which is called Calvary, there they crucified him, and the malefactors, one on the right hand, and the other on the left.

34 Then said Jesus, Father, forgive them; for they know not what they do. And they parted his raiment, and cast lots.

35 And the people stood beholding. And the rulers also with them derided him, saying He saved others; let him save himself, if he be Christ, the chosen of God.

36 And the soldiers also mocked him, coming to him, and offering him vinegar.

37 And saying, If thou be the king of the Jews, save thyself.

38 And a superscription also was written over him, in letters of Greek, and Latin, and Hebrew, THIS IS THE KING OF THE JEWS.

39 And one of the malefactors which were hanged railed on him, saying, If thou be Christ, save thyself and us.

40 But the other answering, rebuked him, saying, Dost not thou fear God, seeing thou art in the same condemnation?

41 And we indeed justly; for we receive the due reward of our deeds: but this man hath done nothing amiss.

42 And he said unto Jesus, Lord, remember me when thou comest into thy kingdom.

43 And Jesus said unto him, Verily I say unto thee, Today shalt thou be with me in paradise.

44 And it was about the sixth hour, and there was a darkness over all the earth until the ninth hour.

45 And the sun was darkened, and the veil of the temple was rent in the midst.

46 And when Jesus had cried with a loud voice, he said, Father, into thy hands I commend my spirit: and having said thus, he gave up the ghost.

"DO WHAT THY MANHOOD BIDS THEE DO"

Richard Burton

Do what thy manhood bids thee do, from none but self expect
  applause;
He noblest lives and noblest dies who makes and keeps his self-
  made laws.

All other living is living death, a world where none but phantoms
  dwell,
A breath, a wind, a sound, a voice, a tinkling of the camel-bell.

*   *   *

Where law ends tyranny begins.—William Pitt

WHAT FOLKS ARE MADE OF

Anonymous

What are little boys made of, made of?
What are little boys made of?
Piggins and pails and little puppy tails,
That's what little boys are made of.

What are little girls made of? etc.
Sugar and spice and all things nice
And that's what little girls are made of.

What's young men made of? etc.
Thorns and briars, they're all bad liars,
And that's what young men are made of.

What's young women made of? etc.
Rings and jings and all fine things
And that's what young women are made of.

What's old men made of? etc.
Whiskey and brandy and sugar and candy,
And that's what old men are made of.

THE DUEL

Eugene Field

The gingham dog and the calico cat
Side by side on the table sat;
'Twas half past twelve, and (what do you think!)
Nor one nor t'other had slept a wink!
   The old Dutch clock and the Chinese plate
   Appeared to know as sure as fate
There was going to be a terrible spat.
     (*I wasn't there; I simply state*
     What was told to me by the Chinese plate!)

The gingham dog went "Bow-wow-wow!"
And the calico cat replied "Mee-ow!"
The air was littered, an hour or so,
With bits of gingham and calico,

While the old Dutch clock in the chimney place
Up with its hands before its face,
For it always dreaded a family row!
   (*Now mind: I'm only telling you*
   What the old Dutch clock declares is true!)

The Chinese plate looked very blue,
And wailed, "Oh, dear! what shall we do!"
But the gingham dog and the calico cat
Wallowed this way and tumbled that,
   Employing every tooth and claw
   In the awfullest way you ever saw—
And, oh! how the gingham and calico flew!
   (*Don't fancy I exaggerate—*
   I got my news from the Chinese plate!)

Next morning where the two had sat
They found no trace of dog or cat:
And some folks think unto this day
That burglars stole that pair away!
   But the truth about the cat and pup
   Is this: they ate each other up!
Now what do you really think of that!
   (*The old Dutch clock it told me so,*
   And that is how I came to know.)

OUR LIPS AND EARS

Anonymous

If you your lips would keep from slips,
Five things observe with care:
Of whom you speak, to whom you speak,
And how and when and where.

If you your ears would save from jeers,
These things keep mildly hid:
Myself and I, and mine and my,
And how I do and did.

* * *

It is not possible to found a lasting power upon injustice.
                              —Demosthenes

ABRAHAM LINCOLN WALKS AT MIDNIGHT

Vachel Lindsay

It is portentous, and a thing of state
    That here at midnight, in our little town
A mourning figure walks, and will not rest
    Near the old court-house pacing up and down.

Or by his homestead, or in shadowed yards
    He lingers where his children used to play,
Or through the market, on the well-worn stones
    He stalks until the dawn-stars burn away.

A bronzed, lank man! His suit of ancient black,
    A famous high-top-hat and plain worn shawl
Make him the quaint great figure that men love,
    The prairie-lawyer, master of us all.

He cannot sleep upon his hillside now.
    He is among us, as in times before!
And we who toss and lie awake for long
    Breathe deep, and start, to see him pass the door.

His head is bowed. He thinks on men and kings.
    Yea, when the sick world cries, how can he sleep?
Too many peasants fight, they know not why,
    Too many homesteads in black terror weep.

The sins of all the war-lords burn his heart.
    He sees the dreadnaughts scouring every main.
He carries on his shawl-wrapt shoulders now
    The bitterness, the folly and the pain.

He cannot rest until a spirit-dawn
    Shall come;—the shining hope of Europe free;
The league of sober folk, the Workers' Earth
    Bringing long peace to Cornland, Alp and Sea.

It breaks his heart that kings must murder still,
    That all his hours of travail here for men
Seem yet in vain. And who will bring white peace
    That he may sleep upon his hill again?

ELEGY WRITTEN IN A COUNTRY CHURCH–YARD

Thomas Gray

The curfew tolls the knell of parting day,
The lowing herd winds slowly o'er the lea,
The ploughman homeward plods his weary way,
And leaves the world to darkness and to me.

Now fades the glimmering landscape on the sight,
And all the air a solemn stillness holds,
Save where the beetle wheels his droning flight,
And drowsy tinklings lull the distant folds;

Save that from yonder ivy-mantled tower
The moping owl does to the moon complain
Of such as, wandering near her secret bower,
Molest her ancient solitary reign.

Beneath those rugged elms, that yew-tree's shade,
Where heaves the turf in many a mouldering heap,
Each in his narrow cell for ever laid,
The rude forefathers of the hamlet sleep.

The breezy call of incense-breathing morn,
The swallow twittering from the straw-built shed,
The cock's shrill clarion, or the echoing horn,
No more shall rouse them from their lowly bed.

For them no more the blazing hearth shall burn,
Or busy housewife ply her evening care;
No children run to lisp their sire's return,
Or climb his knees the envied kiss to share.

Oft did the harvest to their sickle yield,
Their furrow oft the stubborn glebe has broke;
How jocund did they drive their team afield!
How bowed the woods beneath their sturdy stroke!

Let not ambition mock their useful toil,
Their homely joys, and destiny obscure;
Nor grandeur hear with a disdainful smile
The short and simple annals of the poor.

23

The boasts of heraldry, the pomp of power,
And all that beauty, all that wealth e'er gave,
Awaits alike th' inevitable hour:—
The paths of glory lead but to the grave.

Nor you, ye proud, impute to these the fault,
If memory o'er their tomb no trophies raise,
Where through the long-drawn aisle and fretted vault
The pealing anthem swells the note of praise.

Can storied urn or animated bust
Back to its mansion call the fleeting breath?
Can honor's voice provoke the silent dust,
Or flattery soothe the dull, cold ear of Death?

Perhaps in this neglected spot is laid
Some heart once pregnant with celestial fire;
Hands, that the rod of empire might have swayed,
Or waked to ecstasy the living lyre;

But knowledge to their eyes her ample page,
Rich with the spoils of time, did ne'er unroll;
Chill penury repressed their noble rage,
And froze the genial current of the soul.

Full many a gem of purest ray serene
The dark unfathomed caves of ocean bear;
Full many a flower is born to blush unseen,
And waste its sweetness on the desert air.

Some village Hampden, that with dauntless breast
The little tyrant of his fields withstood;
Some mute inglorious Milton here may rest,
Some Cromwell, guiltless of his country's blood.

Th' applause of listening senates to command,
The threats of pain and ruin to despise,
To scatter plenty o'er a smiling land,
And read their history in a nation's eyes,

Their lot forbade; nor circumscribed alone
Their growing virtues, but their crimes confined;
Forbade to wade through slaughter to a throne,
And shut the gates of mercy on mankind;

The struggling pangs of conscious truth to hide,
To quench the blushes of ingenuous shame,
Or heap the shrine of luxury and pride
With incense kindled at the Muse's flame.

Far from the madding crowd's ignoble strife,
Their sober wishes never learned to stray;
Along the cool sequestered vale of life
They kept the noiseless tenor of their way.

Yet e'en these bones from insult to protect
Some frail memorial still erected nigh,
With uncouth rhymes and shapeless sculpture decked,
Implores the passing tribute of a sigh.

Their name, their years, spelt by th' unlettered Muse,
The place of fame and elegy supply;
And many a holy text around she strews,
That teach the rustic moralist to die.

For who, to dumb forgetfulness a prey,
This pleasing anxious being e'er resigned,
Left the warm precincts of the cheerful day,
Nor cast one longing, lingering look behind?

On some fond breast the parting soul relies,
Some pious drops the closing eye requires;
E'en from the tomb the voice of Nature cries,
E'en in our ashes live their wonted fires.

For thee, who, mindful of th' unhonored dead,
Dost in these lines their artless tale relate;
If chance, by lonely contemplation led,
Some kindred spirit shall inquire thy fate,—

Haply some hoary-headed swain may say:
"Oft have we seen him, at the peep of dawn,
Brushing with hasty steps the dews away,
To meet the sun upon the upland lawn.

"There at the foot of yonder nodding beech
That wreathes its old fantastic roots so high,
His listless length at noontide would he stretch,
And pore upon the brook that babbles by.

"Hard by yon wood, now smiling as in scorn,
Muttering his wayward fancies, he would rove;
Now drooping, woeful-wan, like one forlorn,
Or craz'd with care, or cross'd in hopeless love.

"One morn I missed him on the customed hill,
Along the heath, and near his favorite tree;
Another came, nor yet beside the rill,
Nor up the lawn, nor at the wood was he;

"The next, with dirges due, in sad array
Slow through the church-way path we saw him borne;—
Approach and read (for thou canst read) the lay
Graved on the stone beneath yon aged thorn."

THE EPITAPH

Here rests his head upon the lap of earth
A youth, to fortune and to fame unknown;
Fair science frowned not on his humble birth
And melancholy marked him for her own.

Large was his bounty, and his soul sincere;
Heaven did a recompense as largely send:
He gave to misery all he had, a tear;
He gained from heaven ('twas all he wished) a friend.

No farther seek his merits to disclose,
Or draw his frailties from their dread abode,
(There they alike in trembling hope repose,)
The bosom of his Father and his God.

PARKINSON'S LAW, OR THIS RISING PYRAMID

C. Northcote Parkinson

Work expands so as to fill the time available for its completion. General recognition of this fact is shown in the proverbial phrase "It is the busiest man who has time to spare." Thus, an elderly lady of leisure can spend the entire day in writing and dispatching a postcard to her niece at Bognor Regis. An hour will be spent in finding the postcard, another in hunting for spectacles, half an hour in a search for the address, an hour and a quarter in composition, and twenty minutes in deciding whether or not to take an umbrella when going to the mailbox in the next street. The total effort that would occupy a busy man for three minutes all told may in this fashion leave another person prostrate after a day of doubt, anxiety, and toil.

Granted that work (and especially paperwork) is thus elastic in its demands on time, it is manifest that there need be little or no relationship between the work to be done and the size of the staff to which it may be assigned. A lack of real activity does not, of necessity, result in leisure. A lack of occupation is not necessarily revealed by a manifest idleness. The thing to be done swells in importance and complexity in direct ratio with the time to be spent. This fact is widely recognized, but less attention has been paid to its wider implications, more especially in the field of public administration. Politicians and taxpayers have assumed (with occasional phases of doubt) that a rising total in the number of civil servants must reflect a growing volume of work to be done. Cynics, in questioning this belief, have imagined that the multiplication of officials must have left some of them idle or all of them able to work for shorter hours. But this is a matter in which faith and doubt seem equally misplaced. The fact is that the number of officials and the quantity of the work are not related to each other at all. The rise in the total of those employed is governed by Parkinson's Law and would be much the same whether the volume of the work were to increase, diminish, or even disappear.

WHICHEVER WAY THE WIND DOTH BLOW

Caroline A. Mason

Whichever way the wind doth blow
Some heart is glad to have it so;
Then blow it east or blow it west,
The wind that blows, that wind is best.

My little craft sails not alone;
A thousand fleets from every zone
Are out upon a thousand seas;
And what for me were favoring breeze
Might dash another, with the shock
Of doom, upon some hidden rock.
And so I do not dare to pray
For winds to waft me on my way,
But leave it to a Higher Will
To stay or speed me; trusting still
That all is well, and sure that He
Who launched my bark, will sail with me
Through storm and calm, and will not fail
Whatever breezes may prevail
To land me, every peril past,
Within His sheltering Heaven at last.

Then whatsoever wind doth blow,
My heart is glad to have it so;
And blow it east or blow it west,
The wind that blows, that wind is best.

* * *

If you measure your shadow, you will find it no greater than
before the victory.

Archidamus to Philip of Macedon

28

THE EMPEROR'S NEW CLOTHES

Hans Christian Andersen

(Translator: Mrs. Edgar Lucas)

Many years ago there was an Emperor who was so excessively fond of new clothes that he spent all his money on them. He cared nothing about his soldiers, nor for the theatre, nor for driving in the woods except for the sake of showing off his new clothes. He had a costume for every hour in the day, and instead of saying as one does about any other King or Emperor, "He is in his council chamber," here one always said, "The Emperor is in his dressing-room."

Life was very gay in the great town where he lived; hosts of strangers came to visit it every day, and among them one day two swindlers. They gave themselves out as weavers, and said that they knew how to weave the most beautiful stuffs imaginable. Not only were the colours and patterns unusually fine, but the clothes that were made of these stuffs had the peculiar quality of becoming invisible to every person who was not fit for the office he held, or if he was impossibly dull.

"Those must be splendid clothes," thought the Emperor. "By wearing them I should be able to discover which men in my kingdom are unfitted for their posts. I shall distinguish the wise men from the fools. Yes, I certainly must order some of that stuff to be woven for me."

He paid the two swindlers a lot of money in advance so that they might begin their work at once.

They did put up two looms and pretended to weave, but they had nothing whatever upon their shuttles. At the outset they asked for a quantity of the finest silk and the purest gold thread, all of which they put into their own bags while they worked away at the empty looms far into the night.

"I should like to know how those weavers are getting on with the stuff," thought the Emperor; but he felt a little queer when he reflected that any one who was stupid or unfit for his post would not be able to see it. He certainly thought that he need have no fears for himself, but still he thought he would send somebody else first to see how it was getting on. Everybody in the town knew what wonderful power the stuff possessed, and every one was anxious to see how stupid his neighbour was.

"I will send my faithful old minister to the weavers," thought the Emperor. "He will be best able to see how the stuff looks, for he is a clever man and no one fulfills his duties better than he does!"

So the good old minister went into the room where the two swindlers sat working at the empty loom.

"Heaven preserve us!" thought the old minister, opening his eyes very wide. "Why, I can't see a thing!" But he took care not to say so.

Both the swindlers begged him to be good enough to step a little nearer, and asked if he did not think it a good pattern and beautiful coloring. They pointed to the empty loom, and the poor old minister stared as hard as he could, but he could not see anything, for of course there was nothing to see.

"Good heavens!" thought he, "is it possible that I am a fool. I have never thought so and nobody must know it. Am I not fit for my post? It will never do to say that I cannot see the stuffs."

"Well, sir, you don't say anything about the stuff," said the one who was pretending to weave.

"Oh, it is beautiful! quite charming!" said the old minister looking through his spectacles; "this pattern and these colours! I will certainly tell the Emperor that the stuff pleases me very much."

"We are delighted to hear you say so," said the swindlers, and then they named all the colours and described the peculiar pattern. The old minister paid great attention to what they said, so as to be able to repeat it when he got home to the Emperor.

Then the swindlers went on to demand more money, more silk, and more gold, to be able to proceed with the weaving; but they put it all into their own pockets—not a single strand was ever put into the loom, but they went on as before weaving at the empty loom.

The Emperor soon sent another faithful official to see how the stuff was getting on, and if it would soon be ready. The same thing happened to him as to the minister; he looked and looked, but as there was only the empty loom, he could see nothing at all.

"Is not this a beautiful piece of stuff?" said both the swindlers, showing and explaining the beautiful pattern and colours which were not there to be seen.

"I know I am not a fool!" thought the man, "so it must be that I am unfit for my good post! It is very strange though! however one must not let it appear!" So he praised the stuff he did not see, and assured them of his delight in the beautiful colours and the originality of the design. "It is absolutely charming!" he said to the Emperor. Everybody in the town was talking about this splendid stuff.

Now the Emperor thought he would like to see it while it was still on the loom. So, accompanied by a number of selected courtiers, among whom were the two faithful officials who had already seen the imaginary stuff, he went to visit the crafty impostors, who were working away as hard as ever they could at the empty loom.

"It is magnificent!" said both the honest officials. "Only see, your majesty, what a design! What colours!" And they pointed to the empty loom, for they thought that no doubt the others could see the stuff.

"What!" thought the Emperor; "I see nothing at all! This is terrible! Am I a fool? Am I not fit to be Emperor? Why, nothing worse could happen to me!"

"Oh, it is beautiful!" said the Emperor. "It has my highest approval!" and he nodded his satisfaction as he gazed at the empty loom. Nothing would induce him to say that he could not see anything.

The whole suite gazed and gazed, but saw nothing more than all the others. However, they all exclaimed with his majesty, "It is very beautiful!" and they advised him to wear a suit made of this wonderful cloth on the occasion of a great procession which was just about to take place. "It is magnificent! gorgeous! excellent!" went from mouth to mouth; they were all equally delighted with it. The Emperor gave each of the rogues an order of knighthood to be worn in their buttonholes and the title of "Gentlemen weavers."

The swindlers sat up the whole night before the day on which the procession was to take place, burning sixteen candles, so that people might see how anxious they were to get the Emperor's new clothes ready. They pretended to take the stuff off the loom. They cut it out in the air with a huge pair of scissors, and they stitched away with needles without any thread in them. At last they said: "Now the Emperor's new clothes are ready!"

The Emperor, with his grandest courtiers, went to them himself, and both the swindlers raised one arm in the air, as if they were holding something, and said: "See, these are the trousers, this is the coat, here is the mantle!" and so on. "It is as light as a spider's web. One might think one had nothing on, but that is the very beauty of it."

"Yes!" said all the courtiers, but they could not see anything, for there was nothing to see.

"Will your imperial majesty be graciously pleased to take off your clothes," said the impostors, "so that we may put on the new ones, along here before the great mirror."

The Emperor took off all his clothes, and the impostors pretended to give him one article of dress after the other of the new ones which they had pretended to make. They pretended to fasten something round his waist and to tie on something; this was the train, and the Emperor turned round and round in front of the mirror.

"How well his majesty looks in the new clothes! How becoming they are!" cried all the people round. "What a design, and what colours! They are the most gorgeous robes!"

"The canopy is waiting outside which is to be carried over your majesty in the procession," said the master of the ceremonies.

"Well, I am quite ready," said the Emperor. "Don't the clothes fit well?" and then he turned round again in front of the mirror, so that he should seem to be looking at his grand things.

The chamberlains who were to carry the train stooped and pretended to lift it from the ground with both hands, and they walked along with their hands in the air. They dared not let it appear that they could not see anything.

Then the Emperor walked along in the procession under the gorgeous canopy, and everybody in the streets and at the windows exclaimed, "How beautiful the Emperor's new clothes are! What a splendid train! And they fit to perfection!" Nobody would let it appear that he could see nothing, for then he would not be fit for his post, or else he was a fool.

None of the Emperor's clothes had been so successful before.

"But he has got nothing on," said a little child.

"Oh, listen to the innocent," said its father; and one person whispered to the other what the child had said. "He has nothing on, a child says he has nothing on!"

The Emperor writhed, for he knew it was true, but he thought "the procession must go on now." So he held himself stiffer than ever, and the chamberlains held up the invisible train.

* * *

Who killed Kildare? Who dared Kildare to kill?
Death killed Kildare—who dare kill whom he will.

Jonathan Swift

THE WORLD IS TOO MUCH WITH US

William Wordsworth

The world is too much with us; late and soon,
Getting and spending, we lay waste our powers:
Little we see in Nature that is ours;
We have given our hearts away, a sordid boon!
The Sea that bares her bosom to the moon;
The winds that will be howling at all hours,
And are up-gathered now like sleeping flowers;
For this, for everything, we are out of tune;
It moves us not.—Great God! I'd rather be
A Pagan, suckled in a creed outworn,
So might I, standing on this pleasant lea,
Have glimpses that would make me less forlorn;
Have sight of Proteus rising from the sea;
Or hear old Triton blow his wreathèd horn.

OLD SUPERSTITIONS

Anonymous

See a pin and pick it up,
All the day you'll have good luck.
See a pin and let it lay,
Bad luck you will have all day.

The maid who, on the first of May,
Goes to the fields at break of day,
And washes in dew from the hawthorn tree,
Will ever after handsome be.

Friday night's dream on a Saturday told,
Is sure to come true, be it never so old.

Monday's child is fair of face,
Tuesday's child is full of grace,
Wednesday's child is full of woe,
Thursday's child has far to go,
Friday's child is loving and giving,
Saturday's child works hard for its living,
And a child that is born on the Sabbath day
Is fair and wise and good and gay.

Marry Monday, marry for wealth;
Marry Tuesday, marry for health;
Marry Wednesday, the best day of all;
Marry Thursday, marry for crosses;
Marry Friday, marry for losses;
Marry Saturday, no luck at all.

They that wash on Monday
Have all the week to dry;
They that wash on Tuesday
Are not so much awry;
They that wash on Wednesday
Are not so much to blame;
They that wash on Thursday
Wash for shame;
They that wash on Friday
Wash for need;
And they that wash on Saturday
Oh, slovens are indeed!

Sneeze on a Monday, you sneeze for danger;
Sneeze on a Tuesday, you'll kiss a stranger;
Sneeze on a Wednesday, you sneeze for a letter;
Sneeze on a Thursday, for something better;
Sneeze on a Friday, you sneeze for sorrow;
Sneeze on a Saturday, your sweetheart tomorrow;
Sneeze on a Sunday, your safety seek,
For you will have trouble the whole of the week.

FREE TRADE IN IDEAS

Justice Oliver Wendell Holmes

But when men have realized that time has upset many fighting faiths,
they may come to believe even more than they believe the very
foundations of their own conduct that the ultimate good desired is
better reached by free trade in ideas—that the best test of truth is
the power of the thought to get itself accepted in the competition of
the market, and that truth is the only ground upon which their
wishes safely can be carried out. That at any rate is the theory of
our Constitution. It is an experiment, as all life is an experiment.

(1919)

THE SHOOTING OF DAN McGREW

Robert W. Service

A bunch of the boys were whooping it up in the
    Malamute saloon;
The kid that handles the music-box was hitting
    a jag-time tune;
Back of the bar, in a solo game, sat Dangerous
    Dan McGrew;
And watching his luck was his light-o'-love, the
    lady that's known as Lou.

When out of the night, which was fifty below,
    and into the din and the glare,
There stumbled a miner fresh from the creeks,
    dog-dirty, and loaded for bear.
He looked like a man with a foot in the grave
    and scarcely the strength of a louse,
Yet he tilted a poke of dust on the bar, and he
    called for drinks for the house.
There was none could place the stranger's face,
    though we searched ourselves for a clue;
But we drank his health, and the last to drink
    was Dangerous Dan McGrew.

There's men that somehow just grip your eyes,
    and hold them hard like a spell;
And such was he, and he looked to me like a
    man who had lived in hell;
With a face most hair, and the dreary stare of
    a dog whose day is done,
As he watered the green stuff in his glass, and
    the drops fell one by one.
Then I got to figgering who he was, and won-
    dering what he'd do,
And I turned my head—and there watching
    him was the lady that's known as Lou.

His eyes went rubbering round the room, and
    he seemed in a kind of daze,
Till at last that old piano fell in the way of his
    wandering gaze.

The rag-time kid was having a drink: there
was no one else on the stool,
So the stranger stumbles across the room, and
flops down there like a fool.
In a buckskin shirt that was glazed with dirt
he sat, and I saw him sway;
Then he clutched the keys with his talon hands
—my God! but that man could play.

Were you ever out in the Great Alone, when the
moon was awful clear,
And the icy mountains hemmed you in with a
silence you most could *hear;*
With only the howl of a timber wolf, and you
camped there in the cold,
A half-dead thing in a stark, dead world, clean
mad for the muck called gold;
While high overhead, green, yellow and red,
the North Lights swept in bars?—
Then you've a hunch what the music meant
. . . hunger and night and the stars.

And hunger not of the belly kind, that's banished with bacon and beans,
But the gnawing hunger of lonely men for a
home and all that it means:
For a fireside far from the cares that are, four
walls and a roof above;
But oh! so cramful of cosy joy, and crowned
with a woman's love—
A woman dearer than all the world, and true
as Heaven is true—
(God! how ghastly she looks through her
rouge,—the lady that's known as Lou.)

Then on a sudden the music changed, so soft
that you scarce could hear;
But you felt that your life had been looted clean
of all that it once held dear;
That someone had stolen the woman you loved;
that her love was a devil's lie;
That your guts were gone, and the best for you
was to crawl away and die.

'Twas the crowning cry of a heart's despair,
    and it thrilled you through and through—
"I guess I'll make it a spread misere," said
    Dangerous Dan McGrew.

The music almost died away . . . then it burst
    like a pent-up flood;
And it seemed to say, "Repay, repay," and my
    eyes were blind with blood.
The thought came back of an ancient wrong,
    and it stung like a frozen lash,
And the lust awoke to kill, to kill . . . then
    the music stopped with a crash,
And the stranger turned, and his eyes they
    burned in a most peculiar way;
In a buckskin shirt that was glazed with dirt
    he sat, and I saw him sway;
Then his lips went in a kind of grin, and he
    spoke, and his voice was calm,
And "Boys," says he, "you don't know me,
    and none of you care a damn;
But I want to state, and my words are straight,
    and I'll bet my poke they're true,
That one of you is a hound of hell . . . and
    that one is Dan McGrew."

Then I ducked my head, and the lights went
    out, and two guns blazed in the dark,
And a woman screamed, and the lights went up,
    and two men lay stiff and stark.
Pitched on his head, and pumped full of lead,
    was Dangerous Dan McGrew,
While the man from the creeks lay clutched to
    the breast of the lady that's known as Lou.
These are the simple facts of the case, and I
    guess you ought to know.
They say that the stranger was crazed with
    "hooch," and I'm not denying it's so.
I'm not so wise as the lawyer guys, but strictly
    between us two—
The woman that kissed him and—pinched his
    poke—was the lady that's known as Lou.

O MY LUVE'S LIKE A RED, RED ROSE

Robert Burns

O my Luve's like a red, red rose
   That's newly sprung in June:
O my Luve's like the melodie
   That's sweetly played in tune.

As fair art thou, my bonnie lass,
   So deep in luve am I;
And I will luve thee still, my dear,
   Till a' the seas gang dry:

Till a' the seas gang dry, my dear,
   And the rocks melt wi' the sun;
I will luve thee still, my dear,
   While the sands o' life shall run.

And fare thee weel, my only Luve!
   And fare thee weel awhile!
And I will come again, my Luve,
   Tho' it were ten thousand mile.

FATIGUE

Hilaire Belloc

I'm tired of Love: I'm still more tired of Rhyme.
But Money gives me pleasure all the time.

PIAZZA PIECE

John Crowe Ranson

—I am a gentleman in a dustcoat trying
To make you hear. Your ears are soft
                              and small
And listen to an old man not at all,
They want the young men's whispering
                              and sighing.
But see the roses on your trellis dying
And hear the spectral singing of the moon;
For I must have my lovely lady soon,
I am a gentleman in a dustcoat trying.

—I am a lady young in beauty waiting
Until my truelove comes, and then we kiss.
But what grey man among the vines is this
Whose words are dry and faint as
                              in a dream?
Back from my trellis, Sir, before I scream!
I am a lady young in beauty waiting.

MYSTERY ENGENDERS RELIGION

Albert Einstein

The most beautiful experience we can have is the mysterious. It is
the fundamental emotion which stands at the cradle of true art and
true science. Whoever does not know it and can no longer wonder,
no longer marvel, is as good as dead, and his eyes are dimmed. It was
the experience of mystery—even if mixed with fear—that engendered religion. A knowledge of the existence of something we cannot
penetrate, our perceptions of the profoundest reason and the most
radiant beauty, which only in their most primitive forms are accessi-
ble to our minds—it is this knowledge and this emotion that con-
stitute true religiosity; in this sense, and in this alone, I am a deeply
religious man.

PRESIDENT JOHN F. KENNEDY'S INAUGURAL ADDRESS

We observe today not a victory of party but a celebration of freedom—symbolizing an end as well as a beginning—signifying renewal as well as change. For I have sworn before you and Almighty God the same solemn oath our forebears prescribed nearly a century and three-quarters ago.

The world is very different now. For man holds in his mortal hands the power to abolish all forms of human poverty and all forms of human life. And yet the same revolutionary beliefs for which our forebears fought are still at issue around the globe—the belief that the rights of man come not from the generosity of the state but from the hand of God.

We dare not forget today that we are the heirs of that first revolution. Let the word go forth from this time and place, to friend and foe alike, that the torch has been passed to a new generation of Americans—born in this century, tempered by war, disciplined by a hard and bitter peace, proud of our ancient heritage—and unwilling to witness or permit the slow undoing of those human rights to which this nation has always been committed, and to which we are committed today at home and around the world.

Let every nation know, whether it wishes us well or ill, that we shall pay any price, bear any burden, meet any hardship, support any friend, oppose any foe to assure the survival and the success of liberty.

This much we pledge—and more.

To those old allies whose cultural and spiritual origins we share, we pledge the loyalty of faithful friends. United, there is little we cannot do in a host of new cooperative ventures. Divided, there is little we can do—for we dare not meet a powerful challenge at odds and split asunder.

To those new states whom we welcome to the ranks of the free, we pledge our word that one form of colonial control shall not have passed away merely to be replaced by a far more iron tyranny. We shall not always expect to find them supporting our view. But we shall always hope to find them strongly supporting their own freedom—and to remember that, in the past, those who foolishly sought power by riding the back of the tiger ended up inside.

To those peoples in the huts and villages of half the globe struggling to break the bonds of mass misery, we pledge our best efforts to help them help themselves, for whatever period is required—not because the Communists may be doing it, not because we seek their votes, but because it is right. If a free society cannot help the many who are poor, it cannot save the few who are rich.

To our sister republics south of our border, we offer a special pledge—to convert our good words into good deeds—in a new alliance for progress—to assist free men and free governments in casting off the chains of poverty. But this peaceful revolution of hope cannot become the prey of hostile powers. Let all our neighbors know that we shall join with them to oppose aggression or subversion anywhere in the Americas. And let every other power know that this hemisphere intends to remain the master of its own house.

To that world assembly of sovereign states, the United Nations, our last best hope in an age where the instruments of war have far outpaced the instruments of peace, we renew our pledge of support—to prevent it from becoming merely a forum for invective— to strengthen its shield of the new and the weak—and to enlarge the area in which its writ may run.

Finally, to those nations who would make themselves our adversary, we offer not a pledge but a request: that both sides begin anew the quest for peace, before the dark powers of destruction unleashed by science engulf all humanity in planned or accidental self-destruction.

We dare not tempt them with weakness. For only when our arms are sufficient beyond doubt can we be certain beyond doubt that they will never be employed.

But neither can two great and powerful groups of nations take comfort from our present course—both sides overburdened by the cost of modern weapons, both rightly alarmed by the steady spread of the deadly atom, yet both racing to alter that uncertain balance of terror that stays the hand of mankind's final war.

So let us begin anew—remembering on both sides that civility is not a sign of weakness, and sincerity is always subject to proof. Let us never negotiate out of fear. But let us never fear to negotiate.

Let both sides explore what problems unite us instead of belaboring those problems which divide us.

Let both sides, for the first time, formulate serious and precise proposals for the inspection and control of arms—and bring the absolute power to destroy other nations under the absolute control of all nations.

Let both sides seek to invoke the wonders of science instead of its terrors. Together let us explore the stars, conquer the deserts, eradicate disease, tap the ocean depths and encourage the arts and commerce.

41

Let both sides unite to heed in all corners of the earth the command of Isaiah—to "undo the heavy burdens . . . [and] let the oppressed go free."

And if a beachhead of cooperation may push back the jungles of suspicion, let both sides join in creating a new endeavor—not a new balance of power, but a new world of law, where the strong are just and the weak secure and the peace preserved.

All this will not be finished in the first 100 days. Nor will it be finished in the first 1,000 days, nor in the life of this Administration, nor even perhaps in our lifetime on this planet. But let us begin.

In your hands, my fellow citizens, more than mine, will rest the final success or failure of our course. Since this country was founded, each generation of Americans has been summoned to give testimony to its national loyalty. The graves of young Americans who answered the call to service surround the globe.

Now the trumpet summons us again—not as a call to bear arms, though arms we need—not as a call to battle, though embattled we are—but a call to bear the burden of a long twilight struggle year in and year out, "rejoicing in hope, patient in tribulation"— a struggle against the common enemies of man: tyranny, poverty, disease and war itself.

Can we forge against these enemies a grand and global alliance, north and south, east and west, that can assure a more fruitful life for all mankind? Will you join in that historic effort?

In the long history of the world, only a few generations have been granted the role of defending freedom in its hour of maximum danger. I do not shrink from this responsibility—I welcome it. I do not believe that any of us would exchange places with any other people or any other generation. The energy, the faith, the devotion which we bring to this endeavor will light our country and all who serve it—and the glow from that fire can truly light the world.

And so, my fellow Americans: ask not what your country can do for you—ask what you can do for your country.

My fellow citizens of the world: ask not what America will do for you, but what together we can do for the freedom of man.

Finally, whether you are citizens of America or citizens of the world, ask of us here the same high standards of strength and sacrifice which we ask of you. With a good conscience our only sure reward, with history the final judge of our deeds, let us go forth to lead the land we love, asking His blessing and His help, but knowing that here on earth God's work must truly be our own.

(January 20, 1961)

NOW THANK WE ALL OUR GOD

Martin Rinkart

(Translator: Catherine Winkworth)

Now thank we all our God,
    With heart, and hands and voices,
Who wondrous things hath done,
    In whom his world rejoices;
Who from our mother's arms
    Hath blessed us on our way
With countless gifts of love,
    And still is ours today.

O may this bounteous God
    Through all our life be near us!
With ever-joyful hearts
    And blessed peace to cheer us;
And keep us in his grace,
    And guide us when perplexed,
And free us from all ills
    In this world and the next.

HOW DOTH THE LITTLE BUSY BEE

Isaac Watts

How doth the little busy bee
Improve each shining hour,
And gather honey all the day
From every opening flower!

How skilfully she builds her cell!
How neat she spreads the wax!
And labors hard to store it well
With the sweet food she makes.

In works of labor or of skill
I would be busy too;
For Satan finds some mischief still
For idle hands to do.

43

In books, or work, or healthful play,
Let my first years be passed,
That I may give for every day
Some good account at last.

FOR WHOM THE BELL TOLLS

No man is an Iland, intire of it selfe; every man is a peece of
the Continent, a part of the maine; if a Clod bee washed away by
the Sea, Europe is the lesse, as well as if a Promontorie were, as
well as if a Mannor of thy friends or of thine owne were; any
mans death diminishes me, because I am involved in Mankinde;
and therefore never send to know for whom the bell tolls; It tolls
for thee.

(From John Donne's The Tolling Bell—A Devotion)

JULIUS CAESAR'S PREFERENCE

William Shakespeare

Let me have men about me that are fat,
Sleek-headed men, and such as sleep o' nights:
Yond Cassius has a lean and hungry look;
He thinks too much: such men are dangerous.

(From Julius Caesar)

GIVE ALL TO LOVE

Ralph Waldo Emerson

Give all to love;
Obey thy heart;
Friends, kindred, days,
Estate, good-fame,

Plans, credit and the Muse,—
Nothing refuse.

'Tis a brave master;
Let it have scope;
Follow it utterly,
Hope beyond hope;
High and more high
It dives into noon,
With wing unspent,
Untold intent;
But it is a god,
Knows its own path
And the outlets of the sky.

It was never for the mean;
It requireth courage stout.
Souls above doubt,
Valor unbending,
It will reward,—
They shall return
More than they were,
And ever ascending.

Leave all for love;
Yet, hear me, yet,
One word more thy heart behoved,
One pulse more of firm endeavor,—
Keep thee to-day,
To-morrow, forever,
Free as an Arab
Of thy beloved.

Cling with life to the maid;
But when the surprise,
First vague shadow of surmise
Flits across her bosom young,
Of a joy apart from thee,
Free be she, fancy-free;
Nor thou detain her vesture's hem,
Nor the palest rose she flung
From her summer diadem.

Though thou loved her as thyself,
As a self of purer clay,
Though her parting dims the day,
Stealing grace from all alive;
Heartily know,
When half-gods go,
The gods arrive.

CINDY

Anonymous

I wish I was an apple, a-hangin' on a tree,
And ev'ry time my Cindy passed, she'd take a bite of me.
She told me that she loved me, she called me sugar-plum,
She throwed 'er arms around me, I thought my time had come.

Chorus:
Get along home Cindy, Cindy, Get along home, Cindy, Cindy,
Get along home Cindy, Cindy, I'll marry you some time.

She took me to the parlor, she cooled me with her fan,
She swore that I's the purtiest thing in the shape of mortal man.
Oh where did you get your liquor, oh where did you get your
    dram?
I got it from a nigger, away down in Birmingham.

Cindy got religion, she had it once before,
When she heard my old banjo, she 'uz the first one on the floor.
I wish I had a needle, as fine as I could sew,
I'd sew that girl to my coat tail, and down the road we'd go.

Cindy in the springtime, Cindy in the fall,
If I can't have my Cindy girl, I'll have no girl at all.
Cindy went to the meetin', she swung around and around,
She got so full of glory, she knocked the parson down.

EPITAPH

Anonymous

Here lies a poor woman who always was tired,
She lived in a house where help wasn't hired.
The last words she said were: "Dear friends, I am going
Where washing ain't wanted, nor sweeping nor sewing;
And everything there is exact to my wishes,
For where folks don't eat there's no washing of dishes,
In heaven loud anthems forever are ringing,
But having no voice I'll keep clear of the singing.
Don't mourn for me now, don't mourn for me never;
I'm going to do nothing for ever and ever."

LOVE'S NOBILITY

Ralph Waldo Emerson

Not to scatter bread and gold,
Goods and raiment bought and sold;
But to hold fast his simple sense
And speak the speech of innocence;
And with hand and body and blood,
To make his bosom counsel good.
He that feeds men serveth few;
He serves all who dares be true.

A CHILD'S GRACE

Robert Herrick

Here a little child I stand
Heaving up my either hand;
Cold as paddocks though they be,
Here I lift them up to Thee,
For a benison to fall
On our meat and on us all, Amen.

ON TAKING UP ONE'S CROSS

Holy Bible, Luke 9:23–26

And he said to them all, If any man will come after me, let him deny himself, and take up his cross daily, and follow me.

For whosoever will save his life, shall lose it: but whosoever will lose his life for my sake, the same shall save it.

For what is a man advantaged, if he gain the whole world, and lose himself or be cast away?

For whosoever shall be ashamed of me and of my words, of him shall the Son of man be ashamed, when he shall come in his own glory, and in his Father's, and of the holy angels.

A LITTLE WORK, A LITTLE PLAY

George du Maurier

A little work, a little play
To keep us going—and so, good-day!

A little warmth, a little light
Of love's bestowing—and so, good-night!

A little fun, to match the sorrow
Of each day's growing—and so, to-morrow!

A little trust that when we die
We reap our sowing! And so—good-bye!

THE HEIGHTS

The heights by great men reached and kept
Were not attained by sudden flight,
But they, while their companions slept
Were toiling upward in the night.
(From Longfellow's
The Ladder of St. Augustine)

AFTER DUNKIRK

Winston Churchill

We shall not flag nor fail. We shall go on to the end. We shall fight in France and on the seas and oceans; we shall fight with growing confidence and growing strength in the air.

We shall defend our island whatever the cost may be; we shall fight on beaches, landing grounds, in fields, in streets and on the hills. We shall never surrender and even if, which I do not for the moment believe, this island or a large part of it were subjugated and starving, then our empire beyond the seas, armed and guarded by the British Fleet, will carry on the struggle until in God's good time the New World, with all its power and might, sets forth to the liberation and rescue of the Old.

(From the speech of June 4, 1940)

THE TIME TO STRIKE

William Shakespeare

There is a tide in the affairs of men
Which taken at the flood leads on to fortune;
Omitted, all the voyage of their life
Is bound in shallows and in miseries.
On such a full sea are we now afloat,
And we must take the current when it serves,
Or lose our ventures.

(From Julius Caesar)

BIGOTRY EXPLAINED

Daniel O'Connell

Bigotry has no head and cannot think, no heart and cannot feel. When she moves it is in wrath; when she pauses it is amid ruin. Her prayers are curses, her god is a demon, her communion is death, her vengeance is eternity, her decalogue is written in the blood of her victims, and if she stops for a moment in her infernal flight it is upon a kindred rock to whet her vulture fang for a more sanguinary desolation.

JESUS AND THE WOMAN AT THE WELL

Holy Bible, John 4:5–26

Then cometh he to a city of Samaria, which is called Sychar, near to the parcel of ground that Jacob gave to his son Joseph.

Now Jacob's well was there. Jesus therefore, being wearied with his journey, sat thus on the well: and it was about the sixth hour.

There cometh a woman of Samaria to draw water: Jesus saith unto her, Give me to drink.

(For his disciples were gone away unto the city to buy meat.)

Then saith the woman of Samaria unto him, How is it that thou, being a Jew, askest drink of me, which am a woman of Samaria? for the Jews have no dealings with the Samaritans.

Jesus answered and said unto her, If thou knewest the gift of God, and who it is that saith to thee, Give me to drink: thou wouldest have asked of him, and he would have given thee living water.

The woman saith unto him, Sir, thou hast nothing to draw with, and the well is deep: from whence then hast thou that living water?

Art thou greater than our father Jacob, which gave us the well, and drank thereof himself, and his children, and his cattle?

Jesus answered and said unto her, Whosoever drinketh of this water shall thirst again:

But whosoever drinketh of the water that I shall give him shall never thirst; but the water that I shall give him shall be in him a well of water springing up into everlasting life.

The woman saith unto him, Sir, give me this water, that I thirst not, neither come hither to draw.

Jesus saith unto her, Go, call thy husband and come hither.

The woman answered and said, I have no husband. Jesus said unto her, Thou hast well said, I have no husband:

For thou hast had five husbands; and he whom thou now hast is not thy husband: in that saidst thou truly.

The woman said unto him, Sir, I perceive that thou art a prophet.

Our fathers worshipped in this mountain; and ye say, that in Jerusalem is the place where men ought to worship.

Jesus saith unto her, Woman, believe me, the hour cometh, when ye shall neither in this mountain, nor yet at Jerusalem, worship the Father.

Ye worship ye know not what: we know what we worship: for salvation is of the Jews.

But the hour cometh, and now is, when the true worshippers shall worship the Father in spirit and in truth: for the Father seeketh such to worship him.

God is a Spirit: and they that worship him must worship him in spirit and in truth.

The woman saith unto him, I know that Messias cometh, which is called Christ: when he is come, he will tell us all things.

Jesus saith unto her, I that speak unto thee am he.

MUSIC AND POETRY

Charles Darwin

If I had my life to live over again, I would have made a rule to read some poetry and listen to some music at least once a week; for perhaps the parts of my brain now atrophied would thus have kept active through use.

The loss of these tastes is a loss of happiness, and may possibly be injurious to the intellect, and more probably the moral character, by enfeebling the emotional part of our nature.

From ALUMNUS FOOTBALL

Grantland Rice

You'll find the road is long and rough, with soft spots far apart,
Where only those can make the grade who have the Uphill Heart,
And when they stop you with a thud or jolt you with a crack,
Let Courage call the signals as you keep on coming back.
Keep coming back, and though the world may romp across your
 spine,
Let every game's end find you still upon the battling line:
For when the One Great Scorer comes to mark against your name,
He writes—not that you won or lost—but how you played the
 game.

*   *   *

No man e'er felt the halter draw
With good opinion of the law.
 John Trumbull's "M'Fingal"

WE ARE SEVEN

William Wordsworth

A simple child,
That lightly draws its breath,
And feels its life in every limb,
What should it know of death?

I met a little cottage girl:
She was eight years old, she said;
Her hair was thick with many a curl
That clustered round her head.

She had a rustic, woodland air,
And she was wildly clad;
Her eyes were fair, and very fair;-
Her beauty made me glad.

"Sisters and brothers, little maid,
How many may you be?"
"How many? Seven in all," she said,
And wondering looked at me.

"And where are they? I pray you tell."
She answered, "Seven are we;
And two of us at Conway dwell,
And two are gone to sea;

"Two of us in the churchyard lie,
My sister and my brother;
And, in the churchyard cottage, I
Dwell near them with my mother."

"You say that two at Conway dwell,
And two are gone to sea,
Yet ye are seven! I pray you tell,
Sweet maid, how this may be."

Then did the little maid reply,
"Seven boys and girls are we;
Two of us in the churchyard lie
Beneath the churchyard tree."

"You run about, my little maid;
  Your limbs they are alive;
If two are in the churchyard laid,
  Then ye are only five."

"Their graves are green, they may be seen,"
  The little maid replied:
"Twelve steps or more from my mother's door,
  And they are side by side.

"My stockings there I often knit;
  My kerchief there I hem;
And there upon the ground I sit,
  And sing a song to them.

"And often after sunset, sir,
  When it is light and fair,
I take my little porringer,
  And eat my supper there.

"The first that died was Sister Jane;
  In bed she moaning lay,
Till God released her of her pain;
  And then she went away.

"So in the churchyard she was laid;
  And, when the grass was dry,
Together round her grave we played,
  My brother John and I.

"And when the ground was white with snow,
  And I could run and slide,
My brother John was forced to go,
  And he lies by her side."

"How many are you, then," said I,
  "If they two are in heaven?"
Quick was the little maid's reply:
  "O Master! we are seven."

"But they are dead; those two are dead!
  Their spirits are in heaven!"—
'Twas throwing words away; for still
The little maid would have her will,
  And said, "Nay, we are seven!"

ROBERT E. LEE

Benjamin Harvey Hill

He was a foe without hate, a friend without treachery, a soldier without cruelty, and a victim without murmuring. He was a public officer without vices, a private citizen without wrong, a neighbor without reproach, a Christian without hypocrisy, and a man without guile. He was a Caesar without his ambition, a Frederick without his tyranny, a Napoleon without his selfishness, and a Washington without his reward.

"O, WOMAN!"

Sir Walter Scott

O, Woman! in our hours of ease,
Uncertain, coy, and hard to please,
And variable as the shade
By the light quivering aspen made;
When pain and anguish wring the brow,
A ministering angel thou!
(From *Marmion*)

VICTORY IN DEFEAT

Edwin Markham

Defeat may serve as well as victory
To shake the soul and let the glory out.
When the great oak is straining in the wind,
The boughs drink in new beauty and the trunk
Sends down a deeper root on the windward side.
Only the soul that knows the mighty grief
Can know the mighty rapture. Sorrows come
To stretch out spaces in the heart for joy.

TO THE FRINGED GENTIAN

William Cullen Bryant

Thou blossom, bright with autumn dew,
And colored with the heaven's own blue,
That openest when the quiet light
Succeeds the keen and frosty night;

Thou comest not when violets lean
O'er wandering brooks and springs unseen,
Or columbines, in purple dressed,
Nod o'er the ground bird's hidden nest.

Thou waitest late, and com'st alone,
When woods are bare and birds are flown,
And frosts and shortening days portend
The aged year is near his end.

Then doth thy sweet and quiet eye
Look through its fringes to the sky,
Blue—blue—as if that sky let fall
A flower from its cerulean wall.

I would that thus, when I shall see
The hour of death draw near to me,
Hope, blossoming within my heart,
May look to heaven as I depart.

PREAMBLE TO THE CONSTITUTION

We, the People of the United States, in order to form a more perfect union, establish justice, insure domestic tranquility, provide for the common defense, promote the general welfare, and secure the blessings of liberty to ourselves and our posterity, do ordain and establish this Constitution for the United States of America.

WORTH WHILE

Ella Wheeler Wilcox

It is easy enough to be pleasant,
When life flows by like a song,
But the man worth while is one who will smile,
When everything goes dead wrong.
For the test of the heart is trouble,
And it always comes with the years,
And the smile that is worth the praises of earth
Is the one that shines through tears.

It is easy enough to be prudent
When nothing tempts you to stray,
When without or within no voice of sin
Is luring your soul away;
But it's only a negative virtue
Until it is tried by fire,
And the life that is worth the honor of earth
Is the one that resists desire.

By the cynic, the sad, the fallen,
Who had no strength for the strife,
The world's highway is cumbered today;
They make up the sum of life.
But the virtue that conquers passion,
And the sorrow that hides in a smile,—
It is these that are worth the homage of earth,
For we find them but once in a while.

* * *

To err is human, to forgive divine.

* * *

The bookful blockhead, ignorantly read,
With loads of learned lumber in his head.

* * *

For fools rush in where angels fear to tread.
(From Pope's Essay on Criticism)

THE DYING CHRISTIAN TO HIS SOUL

Alexander Pope

Vital spark of heavenly flame!
Quit, O quit this mortal frame!
Trembling, hoping, lingering, flying,
O! the pain, the bliss of dying!
Cease, fond nature, cease thy strife,
And let me languish into life!

Hark! they whisper: angels say,
Sister spirit, come away!
What is this absorbs me quite?
Steals my senses, shuts my sight,
Drowns my spirit, draws my breath?
Tell me, my soul, can this be death?

The world recedes; it disappears!
Heaven opens on my eyes! my ears
With sounds seraphic ring!
Lend, lend your wings! I mount! I fly!
O Grave! where is thy victory?
O Death! where is thy sting?

* * *

Lord, reform thy world, beginning with me.
> (Prayer of a Chinese Christian, quoted
> by President Roosevelt in press confer-
> ence, Dec. 17, 1941)

TROUBLE

David Keppel

Better never trouble Trouble
Until Trouble troubles you;
For you only make your trouble
Double-trouble when you do;
And the trouble—like a bubble—
That you're troubling about,
May be nothing but a cipher
With its rim rubbed out.

THE TIGER

William Blake

Tiger! Tiger! burning bright
In the forests of the night,
What immortal hand or eye
Could frame thy fearful symmetry?

In what distant deeps or skies
Burnt the fire of thine eyes?
On what wings dare he aspire?
What the hand dare seize the fire?

And what shoulder, and what art,
Could twist the sinews of thy heart?
And when thy heart began to beat,
What dread hand? and what dread feet?

What the hammer? what the chain?
In what furnace was thy brain?
What the anvil? what dread grasp
Dare its deadly terrors clasp?

When the stars threw down their spears,
And watered heaven with their tears,
Did he smile his work to see?
Did he who made the Lamb make thee?

Tiger! Tiger! burning bright
In the forests of the night,
What immortal hand or eye
Dare frame thy fearful symmetry?

DREAM AND REALITY

Henry David Thoreau

If one advances confidently in the direction of his dreams, and endeavors to live the life which he imagined, he will meet with a success unexpected in common hours. . . . In proportion as he simplifies his life, the laws of the universe will appear less complex, and solitude will not be solitude, nor poverty poverty, nor weakness weakness. If you have built castles in the air, your work need not be lost; that is where they should be. Now put foundations under them.

THE SOLITARY REAPER

William Wordsworth

Behold her, single in the field,
Yon solitary Highland Lass!
Reaping and singing by herself;
Stop here, or gently pass!
Alone she cuts and binds the grain,
And sings a melancholy strain;
O listen! for the Vale profound
Is overflowing with the sound.

No Nightingale did ever chant
More welcome notes to weary bands
Of travellers in some shady haunt,
Among Arabian sands:
A voice so thrilling ne'er was heard
In spring-time from the Cuckoo-bird,
Breaking the silence of the seas
Among the farthest Hebrides.

Will no one tell me what she sings?—
Perhaps the plaintive numbers flow
For old, unhappy, far-off things,
And battles long ago:
Or is it some more humble lay,
Familiar matter of to-day?
Some natural sorrow, loss, or pain,
That has been, and may be again?

Whate'er the theme, the maiden sang
As if her song could have no ending;
I saw her singing at her work,
And o'er the sickle bending;—
I listened, motionless and still;
And, as I mounted up the hill,
The music in my ear I bore
Long after it was heard no more.

IN THE GARDEN

C. Austin Miles

I come to the garden alone,
While the dew is still on the roses;
   And the voice I hear,
   Falling on my ear;
The Son of God discloses.

Chorus:
And He walks with me, and He talks with me
And He tells me I am His own,
   And the joy we share
   As we tarry there,
None other has ever known.

He speaks, and the sound of His voice
Is so sweet the birds hush their singing
   And the melody,
   That He gave to me;
Within my heart is ringing.

I'd stay in the garden with Him
Though the night around me be falling,
   But He bids me go;
   Through the voice of woe,
His voice to me is calling.

I SOUGHT MY SOUL

Anonymous

I sought my soul,
   But my soul I could not see.
I sought my God,
   But my God eluded me.
I sought my brother,
   And I found all three.

60

LINCOLN TO COLONEL ELLSWORTH'S PARENTS

Washington, D.C., May 25, 1861

My Dear Sir and Madam: In the untimely loss of your noble son, our affliction here is scarcely less than your own. So much of promised usefulness to one's country, and of bright hopes for one's self and friends, have rarely been so suddenly dashed as in his fall. In size, in years, and in youthful appearance a boy only, his power to command men was surpassingly great. This power, combined with a fine intellect, an indomitable energy, and a taste altogether military, constituted in him, as seemed to me, the best natural talent in that department I ever knew.

And yet he was singularly modest and deferential in social intercourse. My acquaintance with him began less than two years ago; yet through the latter half of the intervening period it was as intimate as the disparity of our ages and my engrossing engagements would permit. To me he appeared to have no indulgences or pastimes; and I never heard him utter a profane or intemperate word. What was conclusive of his good heart, he never forgot his parents. The honors he labored for so laudably, and for which in the sad end he so gallantly gave his life, he meant for them no less than for himself.

In the hope that it may be no intrusion upon the sacredness of your sorrow, I have ventured to address you this tribute to the memory of my young friend and your brave and early fallen child.

May God give you that consolation which is beyond all earthly power.

A. Lincoln

GREAT THINGS

Thomas Hardy

Sweet cyder is a great thing,
   A great thing to me,
Spinning down to Weymouth town
   By Ridgway thirstily,
And maid and mistress summoning
   Who tend the hostelry;
O cyder is a great thing,
   A great thing to me!

The dance it is a great thing,
   A great thing to me,
With candles lit and partners fit
   For night-long revelry;
And going home when day-dawning
   Peeps pale upon the lea:
O dancing is a great thing,
   A great thing to me!

Love is, yea, a great thing,
   A great thing to me,
When having dreams across the lawn
   In darkness silently,
A figure flits like one a-wing
   Out from the nearest tree:
O love is, yea, a great thing,
   A great thing to me!

Will these be always great things,
   Great things to me? . . .
Let it befall that One will call,
   "Soul, I have need of thee":
What then? Joy-jaunts, impassioned flings,
   Love, and its ecstasy,
Will always have been great things,
   Great things to me!

COLUMBUS

Joaquin Miller

Behind him lay the gray Azores,
Behind the Gates of Hercules;
Before him not the ghost of shores,
Before him only shoreless seas.

The good mate said: "Now we must pray,
For lo! the very stars are gone.
Brave Admiral, speak, what shall I say?"
"Why, say, 'Sail on! sail on! and on!'"

"My men grow mutinous day by day;
My men grow ghastly wan and weak."
The stout mate thought of home; a spray
Of salt wave washed his swarthy cheek.
"What shall I say, brave Admiral, say,
If we sight naught but seas at dawn?"
"Why, you shall say at break of day,
'Sail on! sail on! and on!'"

They sailed and sailed, as winds might blow,
Until at last the blanched mate said:
"Why, now not even God would know
Should I and all my men fall dead.
These very winds forget their way,
For God from these dread seas is gone.
Now speak, brave Admiral, speak and say"—
He said, "Sail on! sail on! and on!"

They sailed. They sailed. Then spake the mate:
"This mad sea shows his teeth tonight.
He curls his lip, he lies in wait,
With lifted teeth, as if to bite!
Brave Admiral, say but one good word:
What shall we do when hope is gone?"
The words leapt like a leaping sword:
"Sail on! sail on! sail on! and on!"

Then pale and worn, he kept his deck,
And peered through darkness. Ah, that night
Of all dark nights! And then a speck—
A light! a light! at last a light!
It grew, a starlit flag unfurled!
It grew to be Time's burst of dawn.
He gained a world; he gave that world
Its grandest lesson: "On! sail on!"

FROM THE RUBÁIYÁT OF OMAR KHAYYÁM

Edward Fitzgerald

VII

Come, fill the Cup, and in the fire of Spring
Your Winter-garment of Repentance fling:
  The Bird of Time has but a little way
To flutter—and the Bird is on the Wing.

VIII

Whether at Naishápúr or Babylon,
Whether the Cup with sweet or bitter run,
  The Wine of Life keeps oozing drop by drop,
The Leaves of Life keep falling one by one.

XII

A Book of Verses underneath the Bough,
A Jug of Wine, a Loaf of Bread—and Thou
  Beside me singing in the Wilderness—
Oh, Wilderness were Paradise enow!

XIII

Some for the Glories of this World; and some
Sigh for the Prophet's Paradise to come;
  Ah, take the Cash, and let the Credit go,
Nor heed the rumble of a distant Drum!

XIX

I sometimes think that never blows so red
The Rose as where some buried Caesar bled;
  That every Hyacinth the Garden wears
Dropt in her Lap from some once lovely Head.

XXI

Ah, my Beloved, fill the Cup that clears
To-day of past Regrets and future Fears:
  To-morrow!—Why, To-morrow I may be
Myself with Yesterday's Sev'n thousand Years.

For some we loved, the loveliest and the best
That from his Vintage rolling Time hath prest,
  Have drunk their Cup a Round or two before.
And one by one crept silently to rest.

And we, that now make merry in the Room
They left, and Summer dresses in new bloom,
  Ourselves must we beneath the Couch of Earth
Descend—ourselves to make a couch—for whom?

Ah, make the most of what we yet may spend,
Before we too into the Dust descend;
  Dust into Dust, and under Dust to lie,
Sans Wine, sans Song, sans Singer, and—sans End!

Why, all the Saints and Sages who discuss'd
Of the Two Worlds so wisely—they are thrust
  Like Foolish Prophets forth; their Words to Scorn
Are scatter'd, and their Mouths are stopt with Dust.

With them the seed of Wisdom did I sow,
And with mine own hand wrought to make it grow;
  And this was all the Harvest that I reap'd—
"I came like Water, and like Wind I go."

Into this Universe, and *Why* not knowing
Nor *Whence*, like Water willy-nilly flowing;
  And out of it, as Wind along the Waste,
I know not *Whither*, willy-nilly blowing.

What, without asking, hither hurried *Whence?*
And, without asking, *whither* hurried hence?
  Oh, many a Cup of this forbidden Wine
Must drown the memory of that insolence!

LXVI

I sent my Soul through the Invisible,
Some letter of that After-life to spell:
   And by and by my Soul return'd to me,
And answered "I Myself am Heav'n and Hell:"

LXX

The Ball no question makes of Ayes and Noes,
But Here or There as strikes the Player goes;
   And He that toss'd you down into the Field,
He knows about it all—HE knows—HE knows!

LXXI

The Moving Finger writes; and, having writ,
Moves on: nor all your Piety nor Wit
   Shall lure it back to cancel half a Line,
Nor all your Tears wash out a Word of it.

LXXX

Oh Thou, who didst with pitfall and with gin
Beset the Road I was to wander in,
   Thou wilt not with Predestined Evil round
Enmesh, and then impute my Fall to Sin!

LXXXI

Oh Thou, who Man of baser Earth didst make,
And ev'n with Paradise devise the Snake:
   For all the Sin wherewith the Face of Man
Is blacken'd—Man's forgiveness give—and take!

XCI

Ah, with the Grape my fading Life provide,
And wash the Body whence the Life has died,
   And lay me, shrouded in the living Leaf,
By some not unfrequented Garden-side.

XCII

That ev'n my buried Ashes such as snare
Of Vintage shall fling up into the Air
   As not a True-believer passing by
But shall be overtaken unaware.

XCVI

Yet Ah, that Spring should vanish with the Rose!
That Youth's sweet-scented manuscript should close!
   The Nightingale that in the branches sang,
Ah whence, and whither flown again, who knows!

XCIX

Ah, Love! could you and I with Him conspire
To grasp this sorry Scheme of Things Entire,
   Would not we shatter it to bits—and then
Re-mould it nearer to the Heart's desire!

C

Yon rising Moon that looks for us again—
How oft hereafter will she wax and wane;
   How oft hereafter rising look for us
Through this same Garden—and for *one* in vain!

CI

And when like her, oh Sákí, you shall pass
Among the Guests Star-scatter'd on the Grass,
   And in your joyous errand reach the spot
Where I made One—turn down an empty Glass!

*   *   *

Variety's the very spice of life,
That gives it all its flavour.
—William Cowper

LINCOLN'S SECOND INAUGURAL ADDRESS

FELLOW-COUNTRYMEN:

At this second appearing to take the oath of the presidential office, there is less occasion for an extended address than there was at first. Then a statement, somewhat in detail, of a course to be pursued seemed very fitting and proper. Now, at the expiration of four years, during which public declarations have been constantly called forth on every point and phase of the great contest which still absorbs the attention and engrosses the energies of the nation, little that is new could be presented.

The progress of our arms, upon which all else chiefly depends, is as well known to the public as to myself, and it is, I trust, reasonably satisfactory and encouraging to all. With high hopes for the future, no prediction in regard to it is ventured.

On the occasion corresponding to this four years ago, all thoughts were anxiously directed to an impending civil war. All dreaded it, all sought to avoid it. While the inaugural address was being delivered from this place, devoted altogether to saving the Union without war, insurgent agents were in the city seeking to destroy it with war—seeking to dissolve the Union and divide the effects by negotiation. Both parties deprecated war, but one of them would make war rather than let the nation survive, and the other would accept war rather than let it perish, and the war came. One-eighth of the whole population were colored slaves, not distributed generally over the Union, but localized in the Southern part of it. These slaves constituted a peculiar and powerful interest. All knew that this interest was somehow the cause of the war. To strengthen, perpetuate, and extend this interest was the object for which the insurgents would rend the Union by war, while the government claimed no right to do more than to restrict the territorial enlargement of it.

Neither part expected for the war the magnitude or the duration which it has already attained. Neither anticipated that the cause of the conflict might cease when, or even before the conflict itself should cease. Each looked for an easier triumph. and a result less fundamental and astounding. Both read the same Bible and pray to the same God, and each invokes His aid against the other. It may seem strange that any men should dare to ask a just God's assistance in wringing their bread from the sweat of other men's faces, but let us judge not that we be not judged. The prayer of both could not be answered. That of neither has been answered fully. The Almighty has His own purposes. Woe unto the world because of offences, for it must needs be that offences come, but woe to that man by whom the offence cometh. If we shall suppose that American slavery is one of those offences which, in the providence of God, must needs come, but which having continued through His appointed time, He now wills to remove, and that He gives to both North and South this terrible war as the woe due to those by whom the offence came, shall we discern there any departure from those divine attributes which the believers in a living God always ascribe to Him? Fondly do we hope, fervently do we pray, that this mighty scourge of war may speedily pass away. Yet if God wills that it continue until all the wealth piled by the bondman's two hundred and fifty years of unrequited toil shall be sunk, and until every drop of blood drawn with the lash shall be paid by another drawn with the sword, as was said three thousand years ago, so still it must be said, that the judgments of the Lord are true and righteous altogether.

With malice toward none, with charity for all, with firmness in the right as God gives us to see the right, let us finish the work we are in, to bind up the nation's wounds, to care for him who shall have borne the battle, and for his widow and orphans, to do all which may achieve and cherish a just and lasting peace among ourselves and with all nations.

THE ARROW AND THE SONG

Henry Wadsworth Longfellow

I shot an arrow into the air,
It fell to earth, I knew not where;
For, so swiftly it flew, the sight
Could not follow it in its flight.

I breathed a song into the air,
It fell to earth, I knew not where;
For who has sight so keen and strong,
That it can follow the flight of song?

Long, long, afterward, in an oak
I found the arrow, still unbroke;
And the song, from beginning to end,
I found again in the heart of a friend.

A BAKER'S DUZZEN UV WIZE SAWZ

Edward Rowland Sill

Them ez wants, must choose.
Them ez hez, most lose.
Them ez knows, won't blab.
Them ez guesses, will gab.
Them ez borrows, sorrows.
Them ez lends, spends.
Them ez gives, lives.
Them ez keeps dark, is deep.
Them ez kin earn, kin keep.
Them ez aims, hits.
Them ez hez, gits.
Them ez waits, win.
Them ez *will, kin.*

AUTRES BÊTES, AUTRES MOEURS

Ogden Nash

The turtle lives 'twixt plated decks
Which practically conceals its sex.
I think it clever of the turtle
In such a fix to be so fertile.

* * *

When it shall be found that much is omitted, let it not be forgotten that much likewise is performed.
(From Samuel Johnson's Preface to his English Dictionary)

THE CHARGE OF THE LIGHT BRIGADE *

Alfred, Lord Tennyson

Half a league, half a league,
Half a league onward,
All in the valley of Death
   Rode the six hundred.
  "Forward, the Light Brigade!
Charge for the guns!" he said.
Into the valley of Death
   Rode the six hundred.

"Forward, the Light Brigade!"
Was there a man dismayed?
Not though the soldier knew
   Some one had blundered.
Theirs not to make reply,
Theirs not to reason why,
Theirs but to do and die.
Into the valley of Death
   Rode the six hundred.

Cannon to right of them,
Cannon to left of them,
Cannon in front of them
   Volleyed and thundered;
Stormed at with shot and shell,
Boldly they rode and well,
Into the jaws of Death,
Into the mouth of Hell
   Rode the six hundred.

Flashed all their sabres bare,
Flashed as they turned in air
Sabring the gunners there,
Charging an army, while
   All the world wondered:
Plunged in the battery-smoke
Right through the line they broke;
Cossack and Russian

* To commemorate the cavalry charge at Balaclava in the Crimean War.

71

Reeled from the sabre-stroke
　　Shattered and sundered.
Then they rode back, but not,
　　Not the six hundred.

Cannon to right of them,
Cannon to left of them,
Cannon behind them
　　Volleyed and thundered;
Stormed at with shot and shell,
While horse and hero fell,
They that had fought so well
Came through the jaws of Death,
Back from the mouth of Hell,
All that was left of them,
　　Left of six hundred.

When can their glory fade?
O the wild charge they made!
　　All the world wondered.
Honor the charge they made!
Honor the Light Brigade,
　　Noble six hundred!

THE PELICAN

Anonymous

A rare old bird is the Pelican;
His beak holds more than his belican.
He can take in his beak
Enough food for a week.
I'm darned if I know how the helican.

CASEY AT THE BAT

Ernest Lawrence Thayer

It looked extremely rocky for the Mudville nine that day;
The score stood two to four, with but one inning left to play.
So, when Cooney died at second, and Burrows did the same,
A pallor wreathed the features of the patrons of the game.

A straggling few got up to go, leaving there the rest,
With that hope which springs eternal within the human breast.
For they thought: "If only Casey could get a whack at that,"
They'd put even money now, with Casey at the bat.

But Flynn preceded Casey, and likewise so did Blake,
And the former was a pudd'n, and the latter was a fake.
So on that stricken multitude a deathlike silence sat;
For there seemed but little chance of Casey's getting to the bat.

But Flynn let drive a "single," to the wonderment of all.
And the much-despisèd Blakey "tore the cover off the ball."
And when the dust had lifted, and they saw what had occurred,
There was Blakey safe at second, and Flynn a-huggin' third.

Then from the gladdened multitude went up a joyous yell—
It rumbled in the mountaintops, it rattled in the dell;
It struck upon the hillside and rebounded on the flat;
For Casey, mighty Casey, was advancing to the bat.

There was ease in Casey's manner as he stepped into his place,
There was pride in Casey's bearing and a smile on Casey's face;
And when responding to the cheers he lightly doffed his hat,
No stranger in the crowd could doubt 'twas Casey at the bat.

Ten thousand eyes were on him as he rubbed his hands with dirt,
Five thousand tongues applauded when he wiped them on his
   shirt;
Then when the writhing pitcher ground the ball into his hip,
Defiance glanced in Casey's eye, a sneer curled Casey's lip.

And now the leather-covered sphere came hurtling through the air,
And Casey stood a-watching it in haughty grandeur there.
Close by the sturdy batsman the ball unheeded sped;
"That ain't my style," said Casey. "Strike one," the umpire said.

From the benches, black with people, there went up a muffled roar,
Like the beating of the storm waves on the stern and distant shore.
"Kill him! kill the umpire!" shouted someone on the stand;
And it's likely they'd have killed him had not Casey raised his hand.

With a smile of Christian charity great Casey's visage shone;
He stilled the rising tumult, he made the game go on;
He signaled to the pitcher, and once more the spheroid flew;
But Casey still ignored it, and the umpire said, "Strike two."

"Fraud!" cried the maddened thousands, and the echo answered
    "Fraud!"
But one scornful look from Casey and the audience was awed;
They saw his face grow stern and cold, they saw his muscles strain,
And they knew that Casey wouldn't let the ball go by again.

The sneer is gone from Casey's lips, his teeth are clenched in hate,
He pounds with cruel vengeance his bat upon the plate;
And now the pitcher holds the ball, and now he lets it go,
And now the air is shattered by the force of Casey's blow.

Oh, somewhere in this favored land the sun is shining bright,
The band is playing somewhere, and somewhere hearts are light;
And somewhere men are laughing, and somewhere children shout,
But there is no joy in Mudville—Mighty Casey has struck out.

CASEY'S REVENGE

Being a Reply to the Famous Baseball Classic, "Casey at the Bat"

James Wilson

There were saddened hearts in Mudville for a week or even more;
There were muttered oaths and curses—every fan in town was sore.
"Just think," said one, "how soft it looked with Casey at the bat!
And then to think he'd go and spring a bush-league trick like that."

All his past fame was forgotten; he was now a hopeless "shine,"
They called him "Strike-out Casey" from the mayor down the line,
And as he came to bat each day his bosom heaved a sigh,
While a look of helpless fury shone in mighty Casey's eye.

The lane is long, someone has said, that never turns again,
And Fate, though fickle, often gives another chance to men.
And Casey smiled—his rugged face no longer wore a frown;
The pitcher who had started all the trouble came to town.

All Mudville had assembled; ten thousand fans had come
To see the twirler who had put big Casey on the bum;
And when he stepped into the box the multitude went wild.
He doffed his cap in proud disdain—but Casey only smiled.

"Play ball!" the umpire's voice rang out, and then the game began;
But in that throng of thousands there was not a single fan
Who thought that Mudville had a chance; and with the setting sun
Their hopes sank low—the rival team was leading "four to one."

The last half of the ninth came round, with no change in the score;
But when the first man up hit safe the crowd began to roar.
The din increased, the echo of ten thousand shouts was heard
When the pitcher hit the second and gave "four balls" to the third.

Three men on base—nobody out—three runs to tie the game!
A triple meant the highest niche in Mudville's hall of fame;
But here the rally ended and the gloom was deep as night
When the fourth one "fouled to catcher" and the fifth "flew out to
    right."

A dismal groan in chorus came—a scowl was on each face—
When Casey walked up, bat in hand, and slowly took his place;
His bloodshot eyes in fury gleamed; his teeth were clinched in
    hate;
He gave his cap a vicious hook and pounded on the plate.

But fame is fleeting as the wind, and glory fades away;
There were no wild and woolly cheers, no glad acclaim this day.
They hissed and groaned and hooted as they clamored, "Strike
    him out!"
But Casey gave no outward sign that he had heard this shout.

The pitcher smiled and cut one loose; across the plate it spread;
Another hiss, another groan. "Strike one!" the umpire said.
Zip! Like a shot, the second curve broke just below his knee—
"Strike two!" the umpire roared aloud; but Casey made no plea.

No roasting for the umpire now—his was an easy lot;
But here the pitcher whirled again—was that a rifle shot!
A whack! a crack! and out through space the leather pellet flew,
A blot against the distant sky, a speck against the blue.

Above the fence in center field, in rapid whirling flight,
The sphere sailed on; the blot grew dim and then was lost to sight.
Ten thousand hats were thrown in air, ten thousand threw a fit;
But no one ever found the ball that mighty Casey hit!

Oh, somewhere in this favored land dark clouds may hide the sun,
And somewhere bands no longer play and children have no fun;
And somewhere over blighted lives there hangs a heavy pall;
But Mudville hearts are happy now—for Casey hit the ball!

*   *   *

As a goose is not frightened by cackling nor a sheep by bleating,
so do not let the clamor of a senseless multitude alarm you.
—Epictetus

A MORNING PRAYER

Robert Louis Stevenson

The day returns and brings us the petty round of irritating concerns
and duties. Help us to play the man, help us to perform them with
laughter and kind faces, let cheerfulness abound with industry. Give
us to go blithely on our business all this day, bring us to our resting
beds weary and content and undishonored, and grant us in the end
the gift of sleep.

THE SERMON ON THE MOUNT

Holy Bible, Matthew 5–7

5

1 And seeing the multitudes, he went up into a mountain: and when he was set, his disciples came unto him:

2 And he opened his mouth, and taught them, saying,

3 Blessed are the poor in spirit: for theirs is the kingdom of heaven.

4 Blessed are they that mourn: for they shall be comforted.

5 Blessed are the meek: for they shall inherit the earth.

6 Blessed are they which do hunger and thirst after righteousness: for they shall be filled.

7 Blessed are the merciful: for they shall obtain mercy.

8 Blessed are the pure in heart: for they shall see God.

9 Blessed are the peacemakers: for they shall be called the children of God.

10 Blessed are they which are persecuted for righteousness' sake: for theirs is the kingdom of heaven.

11 Blessed are ye, when men shall revile you, and persecute you and shall say all manner of evil against you falsely, for my sake.

12 Rejoice, and be exceeding glad: for great is your reward in heaven: for so persecuted they the prophets which were before you.

13 Ye are the salt of the earth: but if the salt have lost his savour, wherewith shall it be salted? it is thenceforth good for nothing, but to be cast out, and to be trodden under foot of men.

14 Ye are the light of the world. A city that is set on an hill cannot be hid.

15 Neither do men light a candle, and put it under a bushel, but on a candlestick; and it giveth light unto all that are in the house.

16 Let your light so shine before men, that they may see your good works, and glorify your Father which is in heaven.

17 Think not that I am come to destroy the law, or the prophets: I am not come to destroy, but to fulfil.

18 For verily I say unto you, Till heaven and earth pass, one jot or one tittle shall in no wise pass from the law, till all be fulfilled.

19 Whosoever therefore shall break one of these least command-

ments, and shall teach men so, he shall be called the least in the kingdom of heaven: but whosoever shall do and teach them, the same shall be called great in the kingdom of heaven.

20 For I say unto you, That except your righteousness shall exceed the righteousness of the scribes and Pharisees, ye shall in no case enter into the kingdom of heaven.

21 Ye have heard that it was said by them of old time, Thou shall not kill; and whosoever shall kill shall be in danger of the judgment:

22 But I say unto you, That whosoever is angry with his brother without a cause shall be in danger of the judgment: and whosoever shall say to his brother, Raca, shall be in danger of the council: but whosoever shall say, Thou fool, shall be in danger of hell fire.

23 Therefore if thou bring thy gift to the altar, and there rememberest that thy brother hath ought against thee;

24 Leave there thy gift before the altar, and go thy way; first be reconciled to thy brother, and then come and offer thy gift.

25 Agree with thine adversary quickly, whiles thou art in the way with him; lest at any time the adversary deliver thee to the judge, and the judge deliver thee to the officer, and thou be cast into prison.

26 Verily I say unto thee, Thou shalt by no means come out thence, till thou hast paid the uttermost farthing.

27 Ye have heard that it was said by them of old time, Thou shalt not commit adultery:

28 But I say unto you, That whosoever looketh on a woman to lust after her hath committed adultery with her already in his heart.

29 And if thy right eye offend thee, pluck it out, and cast it from thee: for it is profitable for thee that one of thy members should perish, and not that thy whole body should be cast into hell.

30 And if thy right hand offend thee, cut it off, and cast it from thee: for it is profitable for thee that one of thy members should perish, and not that thy whole body should be cast into hell.

31 It hath been said, Whosoever shall put away his wife, let him give her a writing of divorcement:

32 But I say unto you, That whosoever shall put away his wife, saving for the cause of fornication, causeth her to commit adultery: and whosoever shall marry her that is divorced committeth adultery.

33 Again, ye have heard that it hath been said by them of old time, Thou shalt not forswear thyself, but shalt perform unto the Lord thine oaths:

34 But I say unto you, Swear not at all; neither by heaven; for it is God's throne:

35 Nor by the earth; for it is his footstool: neither by Jerusalem; for it is the city of the great King.

36 Neither shalt thou swear by thy head, because thou canst not make one hair white or black.

37 But let your communication be, Yea, yea; Nay, nay: for whatsoever is more than these cometh of evil.

38 Ye have heard that it hath been said, An eye for an eye, and a tooth for a tooth:

39 But I say unto you, That ye resist not evil: but whosoever shall smite thee on thy right cheek, turn to him the other also.

40 And if any man will sue thee at the law, and take away thy coat, let him have thy cloke also.

41 And whosoever shall compel thee to go a mile, go with him twain.

42 Give to him that asketh thee, and from him that would borrow of thee turn not thou away.

43 Ye have heard that it hath been said, Thou shalt love thy neighbour, and hate thine enemy.

44 But I say unto you, Love your enemies, bless them that curse you, do good to them that hate you, and pray for them which despitefully use you, and persecute you;

45 That ye may be the children of your Father which is in heaven: for he maketh his sun to rise on the evil and on the good, and sendeth rain on the just and on the unjust.

46 For if ye love them which love you, what reward have ye? do not even the publicans the same?

47 And if ye salute your brethren only, what do ye more than others? do not even the publicans so?

48 Be ye therefore perfect, even as your Father which is in heaven is perfect.

6

1 Take heed that ye do not your alms before men, to be seen of them: otherwise ye have no reward of your Father which is in heaven.

2 Therefore when thou doest thine alms, do not sound a trumpet before thee, as the hypocrites do in the synagogues and

in the streets, that they may have glory of men. Verily I say unto you, They have their reward.

3 But when thou doest alms, let not thy left hand know what thy right hand doeth:

4 That thine alms may be in secret: and thy Father which seeth in secret himself shall reward thee openly.

5 And when thou prayest, thou shalt not be as the hypocrites are: for they love to pray standing in the synagogues and in the corners of the streets, that they may be seen of men. Verily I say unto you, They have their reward.

6 But thou, when thou prayest, enter into thy closet, and when thou hast shut thy door, pray to thy Father which is in secret; and thy Father which seeth in secret shall reward thee openly.

7 But when ye pray, use not vain repetitions, as the heathen do: for they think that they shall be heard for their much speaking.

8 Be not ye therefore like unto them: for your Father knoweth what things ye have need of, before ye ask him.

9 After this manner therefore pray ye: Our Father which art in heaven, Hallowed be thy name.

10 Thy kingdom come. Thy will be done in earth, as it is in heaven.

11 Give us this day our daily bread.

12 And forgive us our debts, as we forgive our debtors.

13 And lead us not into temptation, but deliver us from evil: For thine is the kingdom, and the power, and the glory, for ever. Amen.

14 For if ye forgive men their trespasses, your heavenly Father will also forgive you:

15 But if ye forgive not men their trespasses, neither will your Father forgive your trespasses.

16 Moreover when ye fast, be not, as the hypocrites, of a sad countenance: for they disfigure their faces, that they may appear unto men to fast. Verily I say unto you, They have their reward.

17 But thou, when thou fastest, anoint thine head, and wash thy face;

18 That thou appear not unto men to fast, but unto thy Father which is in secret: and thy Father, which seeth in secret, shall reward thee openly.

19 Lay not up for yourselves treasures upon earth, where moth and rust doth corrupt, and where thieves break through and steal:

20 But lay up for yourselves treasures in heaven, where neither moth nor rust doth corrupt, and where thieves do not break through nor steal:

21 For where your treasure is, there will your heart be also.

22 The light of the body is the eye: if therefore thine eye be single, thy whole body shall be full of light.

23 But if thine eye be evil, thy whole body shall be full of darkness. If therefore the light that is in thee be darkness, how great is that darkness!

24 No man can serve two masters: for either he will hate the one, and love the other; or else he will hold to the one, and despise the other. Ye cannot serve God and mammon.

25 Therefore I say unto you, Take no thought for your life, what ye shall eat, or what ye shall drink; nor yet for your body, what ye shall put on. Is not the life more than meat, and the body than raiment?

26 Behold the fowls of the air: for they sow not, neither do they reap, nor gather into barns; yet your heavenly Father feedeth them. Are ye not much better than they?

27 Which of you by taking thought can add one cubit unto his stature?

28 And why take ye thought for raiment? Consider the lilies of the field, how they grow, they toil not, neither do they spin:

29 And yet I say unto you, That even Solomon in all his glory was not arrayed like one of these.

30 Wherefore, if God so clothe the grass of the field, which to day is, and to morrow is cast into the oven, shall he not much more clothe you, O ye of little faith?

31 Therefore take no thought, saying, What shall we eat? or, What shall we drink? or, Wherewithal shall we be clothed?

32 (For after all these things do the Gentiles seek:) for your heavenly Father knoweth that ye have need of all these things.

33 But seek ye first the kingdom of God, and his righteousness; and all these things shall be added unto you.

34 Take therefore no thought for the morrow: for the morrow shall take thought for the things of itself. Sufficient unto the day is the evil thereof.

7

1 Judge not, that ye be not judged.

2 For with what judgment ye judge, ye shall be judged: and with what measure ye mete, it shall be measured to you again.

3 And why beholdest thou the mote that is in thy brother's eye, but considerest not the beam that is in thine own eye?

4 Or how wilt thou say to thy brother, Let me pull out the mote out of thine eye; and, behold, a beam is in thine own eye?

5 Thou hypocrite, first cast out the beam out of thine own eye; and then shalt thou see clearly to cast out the mote out of thy brother's eye.

6 Give not that which is holy unto the dogs, neither cast ye your pearls before swine, lest they trample them under their feet, and turn again and rend you.

7 Ask, and it shall be given you; seek, and ye shall find; knock, and it shall be opened unto you:

8 For every one that asketh receiveth; and he that seeketh findeth; and to him that knocketh it shall be opened.

9 Or what man is there of you, whom if his son ask bread, will he give him a stone?

10 Or if he ask a fish, will he give him a serpent?

11 If ye then, being evil, know how to give good gifts unto your children, how much more shall your Father which is in heaven give good things to them that ask him?

12 Therefore all things whatsoever ye would that men should do to you, do ye even so to them: for this is the law and the prophets.

13 Enter ye in at the strait gate: for wide is the gate, and broad is the way, that leadeth to destruction, and many there be which go in thereat:

14 Because strait is the gate, and narrow is the way, which leadeth unto life, and few there be that find it.

15 Beware of false prophets, which come to you in sheep's clothing, but inwardly they are ravening wolves.

16 Ye shall know them by their fruits. Do men gather grapes of thorns, or figs of thistles?

17 Even so every good tree bringeth forth good fruit; but a corrupt tree bringeth forth evil fruit.

18 A good tree cannot bring forth evil fruit, neither can a corrupt tree bring forth good fruit.

19 Every tree that bringeth not forth good fruit is hewn down, and cast into the fire.

20 Wherefore by their fruits ye shall know them.

21 Not every one that saith unto me, Lord, Lord, shall enter into the kingdom of heaven; but he that doeth the will of my Father which is in heaven.

22 Many will say to me in that day, Lord, Lord, have we not prophesied in thy name? and in thy name have cast out devils? and in thy name done many wonderful works?

23 And then will I profess unto them I never knew you: depart from me, ye that work iniquity.

24 Therefore whosoever heareth these sayings of mine, and doeth them, I will liken him unto a wise man, which built his house upon a rock:

25 And the rain descended, and the floods came, and the winds blew, and beat upon that house; and it fell not: for it was founded upon a rock.

26 And every one that heareth these sayings of mine, and doeth them not, shall be likened unto a foolish man, which built his house upon the sand:

27 And the rain descended, and the floods came, and the winds blew, and beat upon that house; and it fell: and great was the fall of it.

28 And it came to pass, when Jesus had ended these sayings, the people were astonished at his doctrine:

29 For he taught them as one having authority, and not as the scribes.

"IT IS A BEAUTEOUS EVENING"

William Wordsworth

It is a beauteous evening, calm and free,
The holy time is quiet as a Nun
Breathless with adoration; the broad sun
Is sinking down in its tranquillity;
The gentleness of heaven broods o'er the Sea:
Listen! the mighty Being is awake,
And doth with his eternal motion make
A sound like thunder—everlastingly.
Dear Child! dear Girl! that walkest with me here,
If thou appear untouched by solemn thought,
Thy nature is not therefore less divine:
Thou liest in Abraham's bosom all the year;
And worship'st at the Temple's inner shrine,
God being with thee when we know it not.

* * *

Lawyers are the only persons in whom ignorance of the law is not punished.

—Jeremy Bentham

CASEY JONES

Anonymous

Come all you rounders for I want you to hear
The story told of a brave engineer;
Casey Jones was the rounder's name
On a heavy six-wheeler he rode to fame.

Caller called Jones about half past four,
Jones kissed his wife at the station door,
Climbed into the cab with the orders in his hand,
Says, "This is my trip to the promised land."

Through South Memphis yards on the fly,
He heard the fireman say, "You've got a white eye."
All the switchmen knew by the engine's moans,
That the hogger at the throttle was Casey Jones.

Fireman says, "Casey, you're runnin' too fast,
You run the block signal the last station you passed."
Jones says, "Yes, I think we can make it, though,
For she steams much better than ever I know."

Jones says, "Fireman, don't you fret,
Keep knockin' at the firedoor, don't give up yet;
I'm goin' to run her till she leaves the rail
Or make it on time with the southbound mail."

Around the curve and a-down the dump,
Two locomotives were a-bound to bump,
Fireman hollered, "Jones, it's just ahead,
We might jump and make it but we'll all be dead."

'Twas around this curve he saw the passenger train,
Something happened in Casey's brain;
Fireman jumped off, but Jones stayed on,
He's a good engineer but he's dead and gone.

Poor Casey Jones was always all right,
He stuck to his post both day and night;
They loved to hear the whistle of old Number Three
As he came into Memphis on the old K.C.

Headaches and Heartaches and all kinds of pain
Are not apart from a railroad train;
Tales that are earnest, noble and gran'
Belong to the life of a railroad man.

REMEMBER

Christina Georgina Rossetti

Remember me when I am gone away,
   Gone far away into the silent land;
   When you can no more hold me by the hand,
Nor I half turn to go yet turning stay.
Remember me when no more day by day
   You tell me of our future that you plann'd:
   Only remember me; you understand
It will be late to counsel then or pray.
Yet if you should forget me for a while
   And afterwards remember, do not grieve:
   For if the darkness and corruption leave
   A vestige of the thoughts that once I had,
Better by far you should forget and smile
   Than that you should remember and be sad.

THE LOST SHEEP

Holy Bible, St. Luke 15:4–7

4 What man of you, having an hundred sheep, if he lose one of them, doth not leave the ninety and nine in the wilderness, and go after that which is lost, until he find it?

5 And when he hath found it, he layeth it on his shoulders, rejoicing.

6 And when he cometh home, he calleth together his friends and neighbours, saying unto them, Rejoice with me; for I have found my sheep which was lost.

7 I say unto you, that likewise joy shall be in heaven over one sinner that repenteth, more than over ninety and nine just persons which need no repentance.

POLITICAL PROMISES

Said Representative Charles S. Hartman of Montana, in 1896:
"It is true that the Populist party has a number of different remedies for the situation. And I am advised that they are about to add three additional planks to their platform. One of them is to make a cross between the lightning bug and the honeybee for the purpose of enabling the bee to work at night. Another, that of breeding the centipede with the hog, for the purpose of having a hundred hams to each animal. And I am told they have a further visionary scheme of budding strawberries into milkweeds, so that everybody can have strawberries and cream from the same plant."

THE BOOK OF BOOKS

Sir Walter Scott

Within this ample volume lies
The mystery of mysteries.
Happiest they of human race
To whom their God has given grace
To read, to fear, to hope, to pray,
To lift the latch, to force the way;
But better had they ne'er been born
That read to doubt or read to scorn.

WOMAN'S WILL

John G. Saxe

Men dying make their wills—but wives
    Escape a work so sad;
Why should they make what all their lives
    The gentle dames have had?

86

THE GOOD SAMARITAN

Holy Bible, Luke 10:25–37

25 And, behold, a certain lawyer stood up, and tempted him, saying, Master, what shall I do to inherit eternal life?

26 He said unto him, What is written in the law? how readest thou?

27 And he answering said, Thou shalt love the Lord thy God with all thy heart, and with all thy soul, and with all thy strength, and with all thy mind; and thy neighbour as thyself.

28 And he said unto him, Thou hast answered right: this do, and thou shalt live.

29 But he, willing to justify himself, said unto Jesus, And who is my neighbour?

30 And Jesus answering said, A certain man went down from Jerusalem to Jericho, and fell among thieves, which stripped him of his raiment, and wounded him, and departed, leaving him half dead.

31 And by chance there came down a certain priest that way: and when he saw him, he passed by on the other side.

32 And likewise a Levite, when he was at the place, came and looked on him, and passed by on the other side.

33 But a certain Samaritan, as he journeyed, came where he was: and when he saw him, he had compassion on him,

34 And went to him, and bound up his wounds, pouring in oil and wine, and set him on his own beast, and brought him to an inn, and took care of him.

35 And on the morrow when he departed, he took out two pence, and gave them to the host, and said unto him, Take care of him; and whatsoever thou spendest more, when I come again, I will repay thee.

A CHILD'S PRAYER

John Bannister Tabb

Make me, dear Lord, polite and kind
To every one, I pray.
And may I ask you how you find
Yourself, dear Lord, today?

THE SOLDIER

Rupert Brooke

If I should die, think only this of me:
That there's some corner of a foreign field
That is forever England. There shall be
In that rich earth a richer dust concealed;
A dust whom England bore, shaped, made aware,
Gave, once, her flowers to love, her ways to roam;
A body of England's, breathing English air,
Washed by the rivers, blest by suns of home.
And think, this heart, all evil shed away,
A pulse in the eternal mind, no less
Gives somewhere back the thoughts by England given;
Her sights and sounds; dreams happy as her day;
And laughter, learnt of friends, and gentleness,
In hearts at peace, under an English heaven.

HELPING THE HANDICAPPED

Emily Dickinson

If I can stop one heart from breaking,
I shall not live in vain;
If I can ease one life the aching
Or cool one pain,
Or help one fainting robin
Into its nest again,
I shall not live in vain.

* * *

A Philosopher is a fool who torments himself while he is alive,
to be talked of after he is dead.—Jean D'Alembert

* * *

I would rather sit on a pumpkin, and have it all to
myself, than to be crowded on a velvet cushion.
—Henry Thoreau

A MEDITATION UPON A BROOMSTICK

Jonathan Swift

This single stick, which you now behold ingloriously lying in that neglected corner, I once knew in a flourishing state in a forest; it was full of sap, full of leaves, and full of boughs; but now, in vain does the busy art of man pretend to vie with nature, by tying that withered bundle of twigs to its sapless trunk; it is now, at best, but the reverse of what it was, a tree turned upside down, the branches on the earth, and the root in the air; it is now handled by every dirty wench, condemned to do her drudgery, and by a capricious kind of fate, destined to make other things clean, and be nasty itself; at length worn to the stumps in the service of the maids, it is either thrown out of doors, or condemned to the last use, of kindling a fire. When I beheld this, I sighed, and said within myself, *Surely Man is a Broomstick!* Nature sent him into the world strong, and lusty, in a thriving condition, wearing his own hair on his head, the proper branches of this reasoning vegetable, until the ax of intemperance has lopped off his green boughs, and left him a withered trunk; he then flies to art, and puts on a periwig, valuing himself upon an unnatural bundle of hairs (all covered with powder) that never grew on his head; but now, should this our broomstick pretend to enter the scene, proud of those birchen spoils it never bore, and all covered with dust, though the sweepings of the finest lady's chamber, we should be apt to ridicule and despise its vanity. Partial judges that we are of our own excellencies, and other men's defaults!

But a broomstick, perhaps you will say, is an emblem of a tree standing on its head; and pray what is man, but a topsy-turvy creature, his animal faculties perpetually mounted on his rational, his head where his heels should be, groveling on the earth! And yet, with all his faults, he sets up to be a universal reformer and corrector of abuses, a remover of grievances, rakes into every slut's corner of nature, bringing hidden corruption to the light, and raises a mighty dust where there was none before; sharing deeply all the while in the very same pollutions he pretends to sweep away; his last days are spent in slavery to women, and generally the least deserving; till worn out to the stumps, like his brother's besom, he is either kicked out of doors, or made use of to kindle flames for others to warm themselves by.

DAFFODILS

William Wordsworth

I wandered lonely as a cloud
That floats on high o'er vales and hills,
When all at once I saw a crowd,—
A host, of golden daffodils,
Beside the lake, beneath the trees,
Fluttering and dancing in the breeze.

Continuous as the stars that shine
And twinkle on the Milky Way,
They stretched in never-ending line
Along the margin of a bay:
Ten thousand saw I at a glance,
Tossing their heads in sprightly dance.

The waves beside them danced; but they
Outdid the sparkling waves in glee:
A poet could not but be gay,
In such a jocund company!
I gazed—and gazed—but little thought
What wealth the show to me had brought:

For oft, when on my couch I lie
In vacant or in pensive mood,
They flash upon that inward eye
Which is the bliss of solitude;
And then my heart with pleasure fills,
And dances with the daffodils.

INNUENDO

Learned Hand

I had rather take my chance that some traitors will escape detection than spread abroad a spirit of general suspicion and distrust, which accepts rumor and gossip in place of undismayed and unintimidated inquiry.

(1952)

THE END OF A FAMOUS HISTORICAL WORK

Edward Gibbon

I have presumed to mark the moment of conception; I shall now commemorate the hour of my final deliverance. It was on the day, or rather night, of the 27th of June, 1787, between the hours of eleven and twelve, that I wrote the last lines of the last page [of *The Decline and Fall of the Roman Empire*] in a summer-house in my garden. After laying down my pen, I took several turns in a *berceau*, or covered walk of acacias, which commands a prospect of the country, the lake, and the mountains. The air was temperate, the sky was serene, the silver orb of the moon was reflected from the waters, and all nature was silent. I will not dissemble the first emotions of joy on recovery of my freedom, and, perhaps, the establishment of my fame. But my pride was soon humbled, and a sober melancholy was spread over my mind, by the idea that I had taken an everlasting leave of an old and agreeable companion, and that whatsoever might be the future date of my *History*, the life of the historian must be short and precarious.

LUCIFER IN STARLIGHT

George Meredith

On a starred night Prince Lucifer uprose.
Tired of his dark dominion swung the fiend
Above the rolling ball in cloud part screened,
Where sinners hugged their specter of repose.
Poor prey to his hot fit of pride were those.
And now upon his western wing he leaned,
Now his huge bulk o'er Afric's sands careened,
Now the black planet showed Arctic snows.
Soaring through wider zones that pricked his scars
With memory of the old revolt from Awe,
He reached a middle height, and at the stars,
Which are the brain of heaven, he looked, and sank.
Around the ancient track marched, rank on rank,
The arm of unalterable law.

ANTONY'S ORATION OVER CÆSAR'S BODY

William Shakespeare

Ant.   Friends, Romans, countrymen, lend me your ears;
I come to bury Cæsar, not to praise him.
The evil that men do lives after them;
The good is oft interred with their bones;
So let it be with Cæsar. The noble Brutus
Hath told you Cæsar was ambitious:
If it were so, it was a grievous fault,
And grievously hath Cæsar answer'd it.
Here, under leave of Brutus and the rest—
For Brutus is an honourable man;
So are they all, all honourable men—
Come I to speak in Cæsar's funeral.
He was my friend, faithful and just to me:
But Brutus says he was ambitious;
And Brutus is an honourable man.
He hath brought many captives home to Rome,
Whose ransoms did the general coffers fill:
Did this in Cæsar seem ambitious?
When that the poor have cried, Cæsar hath wept:
Ambition should be made of sterner stuff:
Yet Brutus says he was ambitious;
And Brutus is an honourable man.
You all did see that on the Lupercal
I thrice presented him a kingly crown,
Which he did thrice refuse: was this ambition?
Yet Brutus says he was ambitious;
And, sure, he is an honourable man.
I speak not to disprove what Brutus spoke,
But here I am to speak what I do know.
You all did love him once, not without cause:
What cause withholds you then, to mourn for him?
O judgement! thou art fled to brutish beasts,
And men have lost their reason. Bear with me,
My heart is in the coffin there with Cæsar,
And I must pause till it come back to me.
  First Cit.   Methinks there is much reason in his sayings.
  Sec. Cit.   If thou consider rightly of the matter,
Cæsar has had great wrong.

Third Cit.   Has he, masters?
I fear there will a worse come in his place.
  Fourth Cit.   Mark'd ye his words? He would not take the crown;
Therefore 'tis certain he was not ambitious.
  First Cit.   If it be found so, some will dear abide it.
  Sec. Cit.   Poor soul! his eyes are red as fire with weeping.
  Third Cit.   There's not a nobler man in Rome than Antony.
  Fourth Cit.   Now mark him, he begins again to speak.
  Ant.   But yesterday the word of Cæsar might
Have stood against the world; now lies he there,
And none so poor to do him reverence.
O masters, if I were disposed to stir
Your hearts and minds to mutiny and rage,
I should do Brutus wrong, and Cassius wrong,
Who, you all know, are honourable men:
I will not do them wrong; I rather choose
To wrong the dead, to wrong myself and you,
Than I will wrong such honourable men.
But here's a parchment with the seal of Cæsar;
I found it in his closet, 'tis his will:
Let but the commons hear this testament—
Which, pardon me, I do not mean to read—
And they would go and kiss dead Cæsar's wounds
And dip their napkins in his sacred blood,
Yea, beg a hair of him for memory,
And, dying, mention it within their wills,
Bequeathing it as a rich legacy
Unto their issue.
  Fourth Cit.   We'll hear the will: read it, Mark Antony.
  All.   The will, the will! we will hear Cæsar's will.
  Ant.   Have patience, gentle friends, I must not read it;
It is not meet you know how Cæsar loved you.
You are not wood, you are not stones, but men;
And, being men, hearing the will of Cæsar,
It will inflame you, it will make you mad:
'Tis good you know not that you are his heirs;
For, if you should, O, what would come of it!
  Fourth Cit.   Read the will; we'll hear it, Antony;
You shall read us the will, Cæsar's will.
  Ant.   Will you be patient? will you stay awhile?
I have o'ershot myself to tell you of it:
I fear I wrong the honourable men

Whose daggers have stabb'd Cæsar; I do fear it.

Fourth Cit. They were traitors: honourable men!

All. The will! the testament!

Sec. Cit. They were villains, murderers: the will! read the will.

Ant. You will compel me, then, to read the will?
Then make a ring about the corpse of Cæsar,
And let me show you him that made the will.
Shall I descend? and will you give me leave?

Several Cit. Come down.

Sec. Cit. Descend.

Third Cit. You shall have leave.

[*Antony comes down.*

Fourth Cit. A ring; stand round.

First Cit. Stand from the hearse, stand from the body.

Sec. Cit. Room for Antony, most noble Antony.

Ant. Nay, press not so upon me; stand far off.

Several Cit. Stand back; room; bear back.

Ant. If you have tears, prepare to shed them now.
You all do know this mantle: I remember
The first time ever Cæsar put it on;
'Twas on a summer's evening, in his tent,
That day he overcame the Nervii:
Look, in this place ran Cassius' dagger through:
See what a rent the envious Casca made:
Through this the well-beloved Brutus stabb'd;
And as he pluck'd his cursed steel away,
Mark how the blood of Cæsar follow'd it,
As rushing out of doors, to be resolved
If Brutus so unkindly knock'd, or no;
For Brutus, as you know, was Cæsar's angel:
Judge, O you gods, how dearly Cæsar loved him!
This was the most unkindest cut of all;
For when the noble Cæsar saw him stab,
Ingratitude, more strong than traitors' arms,
Quite vanquish'd him: then burst his mighty heart;
And, in his mantle muffling up his face,
Even at the base of Pompey's statua,
Which all the while ran blood, great Cæsar fell.
O, what a fall was there, my countrymen!
Then I, and you, and all of us fell down,
Whilst bloody treason flourish'd over us.
O, now you weep; and, I perceive, you feel

The dint of pity: these are gracious drops.
Kind souls, what, weep you when you but behold
Our Cæsar's vesture wounded? Look you here,
Here is himself, marr'd, as you see, with traitors.

First Cit. O piteous spectacle!

Sec. Cit. O noble Cæsar!

Third Cit. O woful day!

Fourth Cit. O traitors, villains!

First Cit. O most bloody sight!

Sec. Cit. We will be revenged.

All. Revenge! About! Seek! Burn! Fire! Kill! Slay! Let not a
traitor live!

Ant. Stay, countrymen.

First Cit. Peace there! hear the noble Antony.

Sec. Cit. We'll hear him, we'll follow him, we'll die with him.

Ant. Good friends, sweet friends, let me not stir you up
To such a sudden flood of mutiny.
They that have done this deed are honourable:
What private griefs they have, alas, I know not,
That made them do it: they are wise and honourable,
And will, no doubt, with reasons answer you.
I come not, friends, to steal away your hearts:
I am no orator, as Brutus is;
But, as you know me all, a plain blunt man,
That love my friend; and that they know full well
That gave me public leave to speak of him:
For I have neither wit, nor words, nor worth,
Action, nor utterance, nor the power of speech,
To stir men's blood: I only speak right on;
I tell you that which you yourselves do know;
Show you sweet Cæsar's wounds, poor poor dumb mouths,
And bid them speak for me: but were I Brutus,
And Brutus Antony, there were an Antony
Would ruffle up your spirits and put a tongue
In every wound of Cæsar that should move
The stones of Rome to rise and mutiny.

All. We'll mutiny.

First Cit. We'll burn the house of Brutus.

Third Cit. Away, then! come, seek the conspirators.

Ant. Yet hear me, countrymen; yet hear me speak.

All. Peace, ho! Hear Antony. Most noble Antony!

Ant. Why, friends, you go to do you know not what:

Wherein hath Cæsar thus deserved your loves?
Alas, you know not: I must tell you, then:
You have forgot the will I told you of.
    All.   Most true. The will! Let's stay and hear the will.
    Ant.   Here is the will, and under Cæsar's seal.
To every Roman citizen he gives,
To every several man, seventy five drachmas.
    Sec. Cit.   Most noble Cæsar! We'll revenge his death.
    Third Cit.   O royal Cæsar!
    Ant.   Hear me with patience.
    All.   Peace, ho!
    Ant.   Moreover, he hath left you all his walks,
His private arbours and new-planted orchards,
On this side Tiber; he hath left them you,
And to your heirs for ever, common pleasures,
To walk abroad, and recreate yourselves.
Here was a Cæsar! when comes such another?
    First Cit.   Never, never. Come, away, away!
We'll burn his body in the holy place,
And with the brands fire the traitors' houses.
Take up the body.
    Sec. Cit.   Go fetch fire.
    Third Cit.   Pluck down benches.
    Fourth Cit.   Pluck down forms, windows, anything.
                    [Exeunt Citizens with the body.
    Ant.   Now let it work. Mischief, thou art afoot,
Take thou what course thou wilt!
                      (From Julius Cæsar)

EPITAPH ON HIMSELF

Nobles and heralds, by your leave,
Here lies what once was Matthew Prior,
The son of Adam and Eve;
Can Bourbon or Nassau claim higher?

FROM DON JUAN

Lord Byron

Man's love is of man's life a thing apart,
'Tis woman's whole existence; man may range
The court, camp, church, the vessel, and the mart,
Sword, gown, gain, glory, offer in exchange
Pride, fame, ambition, to fill up his heart,
And few there are whom these can not estrange:
Men have all these resources, we but one,
To love again, and be again undone.

RICHARD CORY

Edwin Arlington Robinson

Whenever Richard Cory went down town,
    We people on the pavement looked at him:
He was a gentleman from sole to crown,
    Clean favored, and imperially slim.

And he was always quietly arrayed,
    And he was always human when he talked;
But still he fluttered pulses when he said,
    "Good-morning," and he glittered when he walked.

And he was rich—yes, richer than a king—
    And admirably schooled in every grace:
In fine, we thought that he was everything
    To make us wish that we were in his place.

So on we worked, and waited for the light,
    And went without the meat, and cursed the bread;
And Richard Cory, one calm summer night,
    Went home and put a bullet through his head.

*   *   *

A good constitution is infinitely better than the best despot.
                            —Thomas Babington Macaulay

THE BRIDGE OF SIGHS

Thomas Hood

One more Unfortunate,
Weary of breath,
Rashly importunate,
Gone to her death!

Take her up tenderly,
Lift her with care:
Fashion'd so slenderly,
Young, and so fair.

Look at her garments
Clinging like cerements;
Whilst the wave constantly
Drips from her clothing;
Take her up instantly,
Loving, not loathing.

Touch her not scornfully;
Think of her mournfully,
Gently and humanly;
Not of the stains of her,
All that remains of her
Now is pure womanly.

Make no deep scrutiny
Into her mutiny
Rash and undutiful:
Past all dishonour,
Death has left on her
Only the beautiful.

Still, for all slips of hers,
One of Eve's family—
Wipe those poor lips of hers
Oozing so clammily.

Loop up her tresses
Escaped from the comb,
Her fair auburn tresses;
Whilst wonderment guesses
Where was her home?

Who was her father?
Who was her mother?
Had she a sister?
Had she a brother?
Or was there a dearer one
Still, and a nearer one
Yet, than all others?

Alas! for the rarity
Of Christian charity
Under the sun!
O, it was pitiful!
Near a whole city full,
Home she had none!

Sisterly, brotherly,
Fatherly, motherly
Feelings had changed:
Love, by harsh evidence,
Thrown from its eminence;
Even God's providence
Seeming estranged.

Where the lamps quiver
So far in the river,
With many a light
From window and casement,
From garret to basement,
She stood, with amazement,
Houseless by night.

The bleak wind of March
Made her tremble and shiver;
But not the dark arch,
Or the black flowing river:
Mad from life's history,
Glad to death's mystery,
Swift to be hurl'd—
Anywhere, anywhere
Out of the world!

In she plunged boldly—
No matter how coldly
The rough river ran—
Over the brink of it,
Picture it—think of it,
Dissolute Man!
Lave in it, drink of it,
Then, if you can!

Take her up tenderly,
Lift her with care;
Fashion'd so slenderly,
Young, and so fair!

Ere her limbs frigidly
Stiffen too rigidly,
Decently, kindly,
Smooth and compose them;
And her eyes, close them,
Staring so blindly!

Dreadfully staring
Thro' muddy impurity,
As when with the daring
Last look of despairing
Fix'd on futurity.

Perishing gloomily,
Spurr'd by contumely,
Cold inhumanity,
Burning insanity,
Into her rest.—
Cross her hands humbly
As if praying dumbly,
Over her breast!

Owning her weakness,
Her evil behavior,
And leaving, with meekness,
Her sins to her Savior!

MAN

William Shakespeare

What a piece of work is a man! how noble in reason! how infinite in faculty! in form and moving how express and admirable! in action how like an angel! in apprehension how like a god! the beauty of the world! the paragon of animals!

(From Hamlet)

ON HIS SEVENTY-FIFTH BIRTHDAY

Walter Savage Landor

I strove with none, for none was worth my strife,
Nature I loved, and next to nature, art;
I warmed both hands before the fire of life,
It sinks, and I am ready to depart.

HOME, SWEET HOME

John Howard Payne

Mid pleasures and palaces though we may roam,
Be it ever so humble, there's no place like home;
A charm from the sky seems to hallow us there,
Which, seek through the world, is ne'er met with elsewhere.
Home, home, sweet, sweet home!
There's no place like home, oh, there's no place like home!

An exile from home, splendor dazzles in vain;
Oh, give me my lowly thatched cottage again!
The birds singing gayly, that came at my call—
Give me them—and the peace of mind, dearer than all!
Home, home, sweet, sweet home!
There's no place like home, oh, there's no place like home!

I gaze on the moon as I tread the drear wild,
And feel that my mother now thinks of her child,
As she looks on that moon from our own cottage door
Thro' the woodbine, whose fragrance shall cheer me no more.
Home, home, sweet, sweet home!
There's no place like home, oh, there's no place like home!

How sweet 'tis to sit 'neath a fond father's smile,
And the caress of a mother to soothe and beguile!
Let others delight mid new pleasures to roam,
But give me, oh, give me, the pleasures of home,
Home, home, sweet, sweet home!
There's no place like home, oh, there's no place like home!

To thee I'll return, overburdened with care;
The heart's dearest solace will smile on there;
No more from that cottage again will I roam;
Be it ever so humble, there's no place like home.
Home, home, sweet, sweet home!
There's no place like home, oh, there's no place like home!

LOCHINVAR

Sir Walter Scott

Oh, young Lochinvar is come out of the west:
Through all the wide border his steed was the best;
And save his good broadsword he weapons had none;
He rode all unarmed and he rode all alone.
So faithful in love, and so dauntless in war,
There never was knight like the young Lochinvar!

He stayed not for brake, and he stopped not for stone;
He swam the Esk River where ford there was none:
But ere he alighted at Netherby gate,
The bride had consented, the gallant came late;
For a laggard in love, and a dastard in war,
Was to wed the fair Ellen of brave Lochinvar.

So boldly he entered the Netherby Hall,
Among bridesmen, and kinsmen, and brothers, and all:
Then spoke the bride's father, his hand on his sword
(For the poor craven bridegroom said never a word),
"O come ye in peace here, or come ye in war,
Or to dance at our bridal, young Lord Lochinvar?"—

"I long wooed your daughter, my suit you denied;—
Love swells like the Solway, but ebbs like its tide!
And now am I come, with this lost love of mine,
To lead but one measure, drink one cup of wine:
There are maidens in Scotland more lovely by far,
That would gladly be bride to the young Lochinvar."

The bride kissed the goblet: the knight took it up,
He quaffed off the wine, and he threw down the cup.
She looked down to blush, and she looked up to sigh,
With a smile on her lips, and a tear in her eye.
He took her soft hand, ere her mother could bar,—
"Now tread we a measure!" said young Lochinvar.

So stately his form, and so lovely her face,
That never a hall such a galliard did grace:
While her mother did fret, and her father did fume,
And the bridegroom stood dangling his bonnet and plume;
And the bride-maidens whispered, " 'Twere better far
To have matched our fair cousin with young Lochinvar."

One touch to her hand, and one word in her ear,
When they reached the hall door, and the charger stood near;
So light to the croupe the fair lady he swung,
So light to the saddle before her he sprung!
"She is won! we are gone, over bank, bush, and scaur:
They'll have fleet steeds that follow," quoth young Lochinvar.

There was mounting 'mong Graemes of the Netherby clan:
Forsters, Fenwicks, and Musgraves, they rode and they ran;
There was racing and chasing on Canobie Lee,
But the lost bride of Netherby ne'er did they see.
So daring in love, and so dauntless in war,
Have ye e'er heard of gallant like young Lochinvar?

(From Marmion)

INVICTUS

William Ernest Henley

Out of the night that covers me,
Black as the Pit from pole to pole,
I thank whatever gods may be
For my unconquerable soul.

In the fell clutch of circumstance
I have not winced nor cried aloud.
Under the bludgeonings of chance
My head is bloody, but unbowed.

Beyond this place of wrath and tears
Looms but the horror of the shade,
And yet the menace of the years
Finds and shall find me unafraid.

It matters not how strait the gate,
How charged with punishments the scroll,
I am the master of my fate;
I am the captain of my soul.

* * *

If it wasn't for faith, there would be no living in this
world; we couldn't even eat hash with any safety.

—Josh Billings

A LETTER TO LORD CHESTERFIELD

February 7, 1755.

To the Right Honourable the Earl of Chesterfield.

My Lord,

I have been lately informed, by the proprietor of the World, that two papers, in which my Dictionary is recommended to the publick, were written by your Lordship. To be so distinguished, is an honour, which, being very little accustomed to favours from the great, I know not well how to receive, or in what terms to acknowledge.

When, upon some slight encouragement, I first visited your Lordship, I was overpowered, like the rest of mankind, by the enchantment of your address; and could not forbear to wish that I might boast myself *Le vainqueur du vainqueur de la terre;*—that I might obtain that regard for which I saw the world contending; but I found my attendance so little encouraged, that neither pride nor modesty would suffer me to continue it. When I had once addressed your Lordship in publick, I had exhausted all the art of pleasing which a retired and uncourtly scholar can possess. I had done all that I could; and no man is well pleased to have his all neglected, be it ever so little.

Seven years, my Lord, have now past, since I waited in your outward rooms, or was repulsed from your door; during which time I have been pushing on my work through difficulties, of which it is useless to complain, and have brought it, at last, to the verge of publication, without one act of assistance, one word of encouragement, or one smile of favour. Such treatment I did not expect, for I never had a Patron before.

The shepherd in Virgil grew at last acquainted with Love, and found him a native of the rocks.

Is not a Patron, my Lord, one who looks with unconcern on a man struggling for life in the water, and, when he has reached the ground, encumbers him with help? The notice which you have been pleased to take of my labours, had it been early, had been kind; but it has been delayed till I am indifferent, and cannot enjoy it; till I am solitary, and cannot impart it; till I am known, and do not want it. I hope it is no very cynical asperity not to confess obligations where no benefit has been received, or to be unwilling that the publick should consider me as owing that to a Patron, which Providence has enabled me to do for myself.

Having carried on my work thus far with so little obligation to any favourer of learning, I shall not be disappointed though I should conclude it, if less be possible, with less; for I have been long awakened from that dream of hope, in which I once boasted myself with so much exultation,

My Lord,

Your Lordship's most humble,

Most obedient servant,

S. Johnson.

I HAVE A RENDEZVOUS WITH DEATH

Alan Seeger

I have a rendezvous with Death
At some disputed barricade,
When Spring comes back with rustling shade
And apple-blossoms fill the air—
I have a rendezvous with Death
When Spring brings back blue days and fair.

It may be he shall take my hand
And lead me into his dark land
And close my eyes and quench my breath—
It may be I shall pass him still.
I have a rendezvous with Death
On some scarred slope of battered hill,
When Spring comes round again this year
And the first meadow-flowers appear.

God knows 'twere better to be deep
Pillowed in silk and scented down,
Where love throbs out in blissful sleep,
Pulse nigh to pulse, and breath to breath,
Where hushed awakenings are dear . . .
But I've a rendezvous with Death
At midnight in some flaming town,
When Spring trips north again this year,
And I to my pledged word am true,
I shall not fail that rendezvous.

* * *

All that I am or ever hope to be, I owe to my sainted mother.

—Abraham Lincoln

ROCK OF AGES

August M. Toplady

Rock of Ages, cleft for me,
Let me hide myself in Thee!
Let the water and the blood
From Thy riven side which flowed,
Be of sin the double cure,
Save from guilt and make me pure.

Could my tears forever flow;
Could my zeal no languor know;
These for sin could not atone,
Thou must save, and Thou alone.
Rock of Ages, cleft for me,
Let me hide myself in Thee.

PRAYER FOR A VERY NEW ANGEL

Violet Alleyn Storey

God, God, be lenient her first night there.
    The crib she slept in was so near my bed;
Her blue-and-white wool blanket was so soft,
    Her pillow hollowed so to fit her head.

Teach me that she'll not want small rooms or me
When she has You and Heaven's immensity!

I always left a light out in the hall.
    I hoped to make her fearless in the dark;
And yet, she was so small—one little light,
    Not in the room, it scarcely mattered. Hark!

No, no; she seldom cried! God, not too far
For her to see, this first night, light a star!

And in the morning, when she first woke up,
  I always kissed her on the left cheek where
The dimple was. And oh, I wet the brush,
  It made it easier to curl her hair.

Just, just tomorrow morning, God, I pray,
When she wakes up, do things for her my way!

WHEN I HEARD THE LEARN'D ASTRONOMER

Walt Whitman

When I heard the learn'd astronomer,
When the proofs, the figures, were ranged in columns before me,
When I was shown the charts and diagrams, to add, divide, and
  measure them,
When I sitting heard the astronomer where he lectured with much
  applause in the lecture-room,
How soon unaccountable I became tired and sick,
Till rising and gliding out I wander'd off by myself,
In the mystical moist night-air, and from time to time,
Look'd up in perfect silence at the stars.

CODA

Dorothy Parker

There's little in taking or giving,
There's little in water or wine;
This living, this living, this living
Was never a project of mine.
Oh, hard is the struggle, and sparse is
The gain of the one at the top,
For art is a form of catharsis,
And love is a permanent flop,
And work is the province of cattle,
And rest's for a clam in a shell,
So I'm thinking of throwing the battle—
Would you kindly direct me to hell?

THE LADY, OR THE TIGER

Frank R. Stockton

In the very olden time, there lived a semi-barbaric king, whose ideas, though somewhat polished and sharpened by the progressiveness of distant Latin neighbors, were still large, florid, and untrammeled, as became the half of him which was barbaric. He was a man of exuberant fancy, and, withal, of an authority so irresistible that, at his will, he turned his fancies into facts. He was greatly given to self-communing; and, when he and himself agreed upon anything, the thing was done. When every member of his domestic and political systems moved smoothly in its appointed course, his nature was bland and genial; but whenever there was a little hitch, and some of his orbs got out of their orbits, he was blander and more genial still, for nothing pleased him so much as to make the crooked straight, and crush down uneven places.

Among the borrowed notions by which his barbarism had become semified was that of the public arena, in which, by exhibitions of manly and beastly valor, the minds of his subjects were refined and cultured.

But even here the exuberant and barbaric fancy asserted itself. The arena of the king was built, not to give the people an opportunity of hearing the rhapsodies of dying gladiators, nor to enable them to view the inevitable conclusion of a conflict between religious opinions and hungry jaws, but for purposes far better adapted to widen and develop the mental energies of the people. This vast amphitheater, with its encircling galleries, its mysterious vaults, and its unseen passages, was an agent of poetic justice, in which crime was punished, or virtue rewarded, by the decrees of an impartial and incorruptible chance.

When a subject was accused of a crime of sufficient importance to interest the king, public notice was given that on an appointed day the fate of the accused person would be decided in the king's arena—a structure which well deserved its name; for, although its form and plan were borrowed from afar, its purpose emanated solely from the brain of this man, who, every barleycorn a king, knew no tradition to which he owed more allegiance than pleased his fancy, and who ingrafted on every adopted form of human thought and action the rich growth of his barbaric idealism.

When all the people had assembled in the galleries, and the king, surrounded by his court, sat high up on his throne of royal state on one side of the arena, he gave a signal, a door beneath him opened, and the accused subject stepped out into the amphitheater. Directly opposite him, on the other side of the enclosed space, were two doors, exactly alike and side by side. It was the duty and the privilege of the person on trial, to walk directly to these doors and open one of them. He could open either door he pleased; he was subject to no guidance or influence but that of the aforementioned impartial and incorruptible chance. If he opened the one, there came out of it a hungry tiger, the fiercest and most cruel that could be found, which immediately sprang upon him and tore him to pieces, as a punishment for his guilt. The moment that the case of the criminal was thus decided, doleful iron bells were clanged, great wails went up from the hired mourners posted on the outer rim of the arena, and the vast audience, with bowed heads and downcast hearts, wended slowly their homeward way, mourning greatly that one so young and fair, or so old and respected, should have merited so dire a fate.

But, if the accused person opened the other door, there came forth from it a lady, the most suitable to his years and station that His Majesty could select among his fair subjects; and to this lady he was immediately married, as a reward of his innocence. It mattered not that he might already possess a wife and family, or that his affections might be engaged upon an object of his own selection; the king allowed no such subordinate arrangements to interfere with his great scheme of retribution and reward. The exercise, as in the other instance, took place immediately and in the arena. Another door opened beneath the king, and a priest, followed by a band of choristers, and dancing maidens blowing joyous airs on golden horns and treading an epithalamic measure, advanced to where the pair stood, side by side; and the wedding was promptly and cheerily solemnized. Then the gay brass bells rang forth their merry peals, the people shouted glad hurrahs, and the innocent man, preceded by children strewing flowers on his path, led his bride to his home.

This was the king's semi-barbaric method of administering justice. Its perfect fairness is obvious. The criminal could not know out of which door would come the lady; he opened either he pleased, without having the slightest idea whether, in the next instant, he was to be devoured or married. On some occasions the tiger came out one door, and on some out of the other. The decisions of this tribunal were not only fair, they were positively determinate; the accused person was instantly punished if he found himself guilty; and, if innocent, he was rewarded on the spot, whether he liked it or not. There was no escape from the judgments of the king's arena.

The institution was a very popular one. When the people gathered together on one of the great trial days, they never knew whether they were to witness a bloody slaughter or a hilarious wedding. This element of uncertainty lent an interest to the occasion which it could not otherwise have attained. Thus, the masses were entertained and pleased, and the thinking part of the community could bring no charge of unfairness against this plan; for did not the accused person have the whole matter in his own hands?

This semi-barbaric king had a daughter as blooming as his most florid fancies, and with a soul as fervent and impervious as his own. As is usual in such cases, she was the apple of his eye, and was loved by him above all humanity. Among his courtiers was a young man of that firmness of blood and lowness of station common to the conventional heroes of romance who love royal maidens. This royal maiden was well satisfied with her lover, for he was handsome and brave to a degree unsurpassed in all this kingdom; and she loved him with an ardor that had enough of barbarism in it to make it exceedingly warm and strong. This love affair moved on happily for many months, until one day the king happened to discover its existence. He did not hesitate nor waver in regard to his duty in the premises. The youth was immediately cast into prison, and a day was appointed for his trial in the king's arena. This, of course, was an especially important occasion; and His Majesty, as well as all the people, was greatly interested in the workings and development of this trial. Never before had such a case occurred; never before had a subject dared to love the daughter of a king. In after-years such things became common-place enough; but then they were, in no slight degree, novel and startling.

The tiger-cages of the kingdom were searched for the most savage and relentless beasts, from which the fiercest monster might be selected for the arena; and the ranks of maiden youth and beauty throughout the land were carefully surveyed by competent judges in order that the young man might have a fitting bride in case fate did not determine for him a different destiny. Of course, everybody knew that the deed with which the accused was charged had been done. He had loved the princess, and neither he, she, nor anyone else thought of denying the fact; but the king would not think of allowing any fact of this kind to interfere with the working of the tribunal, in which he took such great delight and satisfaction. No matter how the affair turned out, the youth would be disposed of; and the king would take an aesthetic pleasure in watching the course of events, which would determine whether or not the young man had done wrong in allowing himself to love the princess.

The appointed day arrived. From far and near the people gathered, and thronged the great galleries of the arena; and crowds, unable to gain admittance, massed themselves against its outside walls. The king and his court were in their places, opposite the twin doors—those fateful portals, so terrible in their similarity.

All was ready. The signal was given. A door beneath the royal party opened, and the lover of the princess walked into the arena. Tall, beautiful, fair, his appearance was greeted with a low hum of admiration and anxiety. Half the audience had not known so grand a youth had lived among them. No wonder the princess loved him! What a terrible thing for him to be there!

As the youth advanced into the arena, he turned, as the custom was, to bow to the king; but he did not think at all of that royal personage; his eyes were fixed upon the princess who sat to the right of her father. Had it not been for the moiety of barbarism in her nature, it is probable that lady would not have been there; but her intense and fervid soul would not allow her to be absent on an occasion in which she was so terribly interested. From the moment that the decree had gone forth, that her lover should decide his fate in the king's arena, she had thought of nothing, night or day, but this great event and the various subjects connected with it. Possessed of more power, influence, and force of character than anyone who had ever before been interested in such a case, she had done what no other person had done—she had possessed herself of the secret of the doors. She knew in which of the two rooms that lay behind those doors stood the cage of the tiger, with its open front, and in which waited the lady. Through these thick doors, heavily curtained with skins on the inside, it was impossible that any noise or suggestion should come from within to the person who should approach to raise the latch of one of them; but gold, and the power of a woman's will, had brought the secret to the princess.

And not only did she know in which room stood the lady ready to emerge, all blushing and radiant, should her door be opened, but she knew who the lady was. It was one of the fairest and loveliest of the damsels of the court who had been selected as the reward of the accused youth, should he be proved innocent of the crime of aspiring to one so far above him, and the princess hated her.

Often had she seen, or imagined that she had seen, this fair creature throwing glances of admiration upon the person of her lover,
and sometimes she thought these glances were perceived and even
returned. Now and then she had seen them talking together; it
was but for a moment or two, but much can be said in a brief
space; it may have been on most unimportant topics, but how
could she know that? The girl was lovely, but she had dared to
raise her eyes to the loved one of the princess; and, with all the
intensity of the savage blood transmitted to her through long lines
of wholly barbaric ancestors, she hated the woman who blushed
and trembled behind the silent door.

When her lover turned and looked at her, and his eyes met hers
as she sat there paler and whiter than anyone in the vast ocean of
anxious faces about her, he saw, by that power of quick percep-
tion which is given to those whose souls are one, that she knew
behind which door crouched the tiger, and behind which stood
the lady. He had expected her to know it. He understood her
nature, and his soul was assured that she would never rest until
she had made plain to herself this thing, hidden to all other
lookers-on, even to the king. The only hope for the youth in which
there was any element of certainty was based upon the success
of the princess in discovering this mystery; and the moment he
looked upon her, he saw she had succeeded, as in his soul he
knew she would succeed.

Then it was his quick and anxious glance asked the question:
"Which?" It was as plain to her as if he shouted it from where he
stood. There was not an instant to be lost. The question was asked
in a flash; it must be answered in another.

Her right arm lay on the cushioned parapet before her. She
raised her hand, and made a slight, quick movement toward the
right. No one but her lover saw her. Every eye but his was fixed
on the man in the arena.

He turned, and with a firm and rapid step he walked across the
empty space. Every heart stopped beating, every breath was held,
every eye was fixed immovable upon that man. Without the slightest hesitation, he went to the door on the right, and opened it.

Now, the point of the story is this: Did the tiger come out of
that door, or did the lady?

The more we reflect upon this question the harder it is to
answer. It involves a study of the human heart which leads us
through devious mazes of passion, out of which it is difficult to
find our way. Think of it, fair reader, not as if the decision of
the question depended upon yourself, but upon that hot-blooded,

semi-barbaric princess, her soul at a white heat beneath the combined fires of despair and jealousy. She had lost him, but who should have him?

How often, in her waking hours and in her dreams, had she started in wild horror, and covered her face with her hands as she thought of her lover opening the door on the other side of which waited the cruel fangs of the tiger!

But how much oftener had she seen him at the other door! How in her grievous reveries had she gnashed her teeth, and torn her hair, when she saw his start of rapturous delight as he opened the door of the lady! How her soul had burned in agony when she had seen him rush to meet that woman, with her flushing cheek and sparkling eye of triumph; when she had seen him lead her forth, his whole frame kindled with the joy of recovered life; when she had heard the loud shouts from the multitude and the wild ringing of the happy bells; when she had seen the priest with his joyous followers advance to the couple, and make them man and wife before her very eyes; and when she had seen them walk away together upon their path of flowers, followed by the tremendous shouts of the hilarious multitude, in which her one despairing shriek was lost and drowned!

Would it not be better for him to die at once and go to wait for her in the blessed regions of semi-barbaric futurity?

And yet, that awful tiger, those shrieks, that blood!

Her decision had been indicated in an instant, but it had been made after days and nights of anguished deliberation. She had known she would be asked, she had decided what she would answer, and without the slightest hesitation, she had moved her hand to the right.

The question of her decision is not one to be lightly considered, and it is not for me to presume to set myself up as the one person able to answer it. And so I leave it all with you: Which came out of the opened door—the lady, or the tiger?

THE LAND OF COUNTERPANE

Robert Louis Stevenson

When I was sick and lay a-bed,
I had two pillows at my head,
And all my toys beside me lay
To keep me happy all the day.

And sometimes for an hour or so
I watched my leaden soldiers go,
With different uniforms and drills,
Among the bed-clothes, through the hills.

And sometimes sent my ships in fleets
All up and down among the sheets;
Or brought my trees and houses out,
And planted cities all about.

I was the giant great and still
That sits upon the pillow-hill,
And sees before him, dale and plain
The pleasant Land of Counterpane.

"BELIEVE ME, IF ALL THOSE ENDEARING YOUNG CHARMS"

Thomas Moore

Believe me, if all those endearing young charms,
Which I gaze on so fondly to-day,
Were to change by to-morrow, and fleet in my arms,
Like fairy-gifts fading away,
Thou wouldst still be adored, as this moment thou art,
Let thy loveliness fade as it will,
And around the dear ruin each wish of my heart
Would entwine itself verdantly still.

It is not while beauty and youth are thine own,
And thy cheeks unprofaned by a tear,
That the fervor and faith of a soul may be known,
To which time will but make thee more dear!
No, the heart that has truly loved never forgets,
But as truly loves on to the close,
As the sunflower turns on her god when he sets
The same look which she turned when he rose!

FROM THE VISION OF SIR LAUNFAL

James Russell Lowell

Earth gets its price for what Earth gives us;
  The beggar is taxed for a corner to die in,
The priest hath his fee who comes and shrives us,
  We bargain for the graves we lie in;
At the Devil's booth are all things sold,
Each ounce of dross costs its ounce of gold;
  For a cap and bells our lives we pay,
Bubbles we buy with a whole soul's tasking:
  'Tis heaven alone that is given away,
'Tis only God may be had for the asking;
There is no price set on the lavish summer;
And June may be had by the poorest comer.

And what is so rare as a day in June?
  Then, if ever, come perfect days;
Then Heaven tries earth if it be in tune,
  And over it softly her warm ear lays;
Whether we look, or whether we listen,
We hear life murmur, or see it glisten;
Every clod feels a stir of might,
  An instinct within it that reaches and towers,
And, groping blindly above it for light,
  Climbs to a soul in grass and flowers;
The flush of life may well be seen
  Thrilling back over hills and valleys;

The cowslip startles in meadows green,
  The buttercup catches the sun in its chalice,
And there's never a leaf nor a blade too mean
  To be some happy creature's palace;
The little bird sits at his door in the sun,
  Atilt like a blossom among the leaves,
And lets his illumined being o'errun
  With the deluge of summer it receives;
His mate feels the eggs beneath her wings,
And the heart in her dumb breast flutters and sings;
He sings to the wide world, and she to her nest,—
In the nice ear of Nature which song is the best?

"Lo, it is I, be not afraid!
In many climes, without avail,
Thou hast spent thy life for the Holy Grail;
Behold, it is here,—this cup which thou
Didst fill at the streamlet for me but now;
This crust is my body broken for thee,
This water His blood that died on the tree;
The Holy Supper is kept, indeed,
In whatso we share with another's need;
Not what we give, but what we share,—
For the gift without the giver is bare;
Who gives himself with his alms feeds three,
Himself, his hungering neighbor, and me."

NEW FRIENDS AND OLD FRIENDS

Joseph Parry

Make new friends, but keep the old;
Those are silver, these are gold.
New-made friendships, like new wine,
Age will mellow and refine.
Friendships that have stood the test—
Time and change—are surely best;
Brow may wrinkle, hair grow gray;
Friendship never knows decay.
For 'mid old friends, tried and true,
Once more we our youth renew.
But old friends, alas! may die;
New friends must their place supply.
Cherish friendship in your breast—
New is good, but old is best;
Make new friends, but keep the old;
Those are silver, these are gold.

THE PRODIGAL SON

Holy Bible, St. Luke 15:11-32

11 And he said, A certain man had two sons:

12 And the younger of them said to his father, Father, give me the portion of goods that falleth to me. And he divided unto them his living.

13 And not many days after the younger son gathered all together, and took his journey into a far country, and there wasted his substance with riotous living.

14 And when he had spent all, there arose a mighty famine in that land; and he began to be in want.

15 And he went and joined himself to a citizen of that country; and he sent him into his fields to feed swine.

16 And he would fain have filled his belly with the husks that the swine did eat: and no man gave unto him.

17 And when he came to himself, he said, How many hired servants of my father's have bread enough and to spare, and I perish with hunger!

18 I will arise and go to my father, and will say unto him, Father, I have sinned against heaven, and before thee,

19 And am no more worthy to be called thy son: make me as one of thy hired servants.

20 And he arose, and came to his father. But when he was yet a great way off, his father saw him, and had compassion, and ran, and fell on his neck, and kissed him.

21 And the son said unto him, Father, I have sinned against heaven, and in thy sight, and am no more worthy to be called thy son.

22 But the father said to his servants, Bring forth the best robe, and put it on him; and put a ring on his hand, and shoes on his feet:

23 And bring hither the fatted calf, and kill it; and let us eat, and be merry:

24 For this my son was dead, and is alive again; he was lost, and is found. And they began to be merry.

25 Now his elder son was in the field: and as he came and drew nigh to the house, he heard musick and dancing.

26 And he called one of the servants, and asked what these things meant.

27 And he said unto him, Thy brother is come; and thy father hath killed the fatted calf, because he hath received him safe and sound.

28 And he was angry, and would not go in: therefore came his father out, and intreated him.

29 And he answering said to his father, Lo, these many years do I serve thee, neither transgressed I at any time thy commandment: and yet thou never gavest me a kid, that I might make merry with my friends:

30 But as soon as this thy son was come, which hath devoured thy living with harlots, thou hast killed for him the fatted calf.

31 And he said unto him, Son, thou art ever with me, and all that I have is thine.

32 It was meet that we should make merry, and be glad: for this thy brother was dead, and is alive again; and was lost, and is found.

CARGOES

John Masefield

Quinquireme of Nineveh from distant Ophir,
Rowing home to haven in sunny Palestine,
With a cargo of ivory,
And apes and peacocks,
Sandalwood, cedarwood, and sweet white wine.

Stately Spanish galleon coming from the Isthmus,
Dipping through the Tropics by the palm-green shores,
With a cargo of diamonds,
Emeralds, amethysts,
Topazes, and cinnamon, and gold moidores.

Dirty British coaster with a salt-caked smoke stack,
Butting through the Channel in the mad March days,
With a cargo of Tyne coal,
Road-rails, pig-lead,
Firewood, iron-ware, and cheap tin trays.

NO TRUER WORD

Walter Savage Landor

No truer word, save God's, was ever spoken,
Than that the largest heart is soonest broken.

CATO'S SOLILOQUY

Joseph Addison

It must be so—Plato, thou reason'st well—
Else whence this pleasing hope, this fond desire,
This longing after immortality?
Or whence this secret dread, and inward horror
Of falling into nought? Why shrinks the Soul
Back on herself, and startles at destruction?
'Tis the Divinity, that stirs within us;
'Tis Heav'n itself, that points out a hereafter,
And intimates eternity to man.
Eternity! thou pleasing, dreadful thought!
Through what variety of untried being,
Through what new scenes and changes must we pass!
The wide, th' unbounded prospect lies before me;
But shadows, clouds, and darkness rest upon it.
Here will I hold. If there's a power above us,
(And that there is, all Nature cries aloud
Through all her works,) He must delight in virtue;
And that which He delights in must be happy.
But when or where? This world was made for Caesar.
I'm weary of conjectures—this must end 'em.
    Thus am I doubly arm'd—my death and life,
My bane and antidote are both before me.
This in a moment brings me to an end;
But this informs me I shall never die.
The Soul, secured in her existence, smiles
At the drawn dagger, and defies its point;
The stars shall fade away, the Sun himself
Grow dim with age, and Nature, sink in years;
But thou shalt flourish in immortal youth,
Unhurt amidst the war of elements,
The wreck of matter and the crash of worlds.

(From Cato, Act 5, Sc. 1)

QUOTES FROM HARRY TRUMAN

When Eisenhower was about to succeed Truman as President:
He'll sit there and he'll say, "Do this! Do that!" and nothing will
happen. Poor Ike—it won't be a bit like the Army.

When preparing to leave the Presidency, Mr. Truman said: If I had known there would be so much work leaving this place, I'd have run again.

Whenever the press quits abusing me, I know I'm in the wrong pew.

During a campaign speech, a woman listener called out to him, "Mr. Truman, you sound as if you have a cold." Mr. Truman replied: That's because I ride around in the wind with my mouth open.

If you can't stand the heat, get out of the kitchen.

When President, Mr. Truman kept this motto on his desk:

THE BUCK STOPS HERE.

SILENT NIGHT

Joseph Mohr

Silent Night! Holy Night!
All is calm, all is bright.
Round yon virgin mother and child!
Holy Infant so tender and mild,
Sleep in heavenly peace, sleep in heavenly peace.

Silent Night! Holy Night!
Shepherds quake at the sight!
Glories stream from heaven afar,
Heav'nly hosts sing Alleluia,
Christ, the Saviour, is born! Christ, the Saviour, is born!

Silent Night! Holy Night!
Son of God, love's pure light;
Radiant beams from Thy holy face,
With the dawn of redeeming grace,
Jesus, Lord, at Thy birth, Jesus, Lord, at Thy birth.

ON THE DEATH OF JOSEPH RODMAN DRAKE

Fitz-Greene Halleck

Green be the turf above thee,
  Friend of my better days!
None knew thee but to love thee,
  Nor named thee but to praise.

Tears fell when thou wert dying,
  From eyes unused to weep,
And long, where thou art lying,
  Will tears the cold turf steep.

When hearts, whose truth was proven,
  Like thine, are laid in earth,
There should a wreath be woven
  To tell the world their worth;

And I who woke each morrow
  To clasp thy hand in mine,
Who shared thy joy and sorrow,
  Whose weal and woe were thine;

It should be mine to braid it
  Around thy faded brow,
But I've in vain essayed it,
  And feel I cannot now.

While memory bids me weep thee,
  Nor thought nor words are free,—
The grief is fixed too deeply
  That mourns a man like thee.

AN HONEST MAN

A wit's a feather and a chief a rod;
An honest man's the noblest work of God.
        (From Pope's Essay on Man)

THE PLEASURE OF PAINTING

William Hazlitt

"There is a pleasure in painting which none but painters know. In writing, you have to contend with the world; in painting, you have only to carry on a friendly strife with Nature. You sit down to your task, and are happy. From the moment that you take up the pencil, and look Nature in the face, you are at peace with your own heart. No angry passions rise to disturb the silent progress of the work, to shake the hand, or dim the brow: no irritable humours are set afloat: you have no absurd opinions to combat, no point to strain, no adversary to crush, no fool to annoy—you are actuated by fear or favour to no man. There is "no juggling here," no sophistry, no intrigue, no tampering with the evidence, no attempt to make black white, or white black: but you resign yourself into the hands of a greater power, that of Nature, with the simplicity of a child, and the devotion of an enthusiast—"study with joy her manner, and with rapture taste her style." The mind is calm, and full at the same time. . . .

The painter thus learns to look at nature with different eyes. He before saw her "as in a glass darkly, but now face to face." He understands the texture and meaning of the visible universe, and "sees into the life of things," not by the help of mechanical instruments, but of the improved exercise of his faculties, and an intimate sympathy with nature. . . . He perceives form, he distinguishes character. He reads men and books with an intuitive eye. He is a critic as well as a connoisseur. The conclusions he draws are clear and convincing, because they are taken from the things themselves. He is not a fanatic, a dupe, or a slave; for the habit of seeing for himself also disposes him to judge for himself.

HOPE

Alexander Pope

Hope springs eternal in the human breast:
Man never is, but always to be blest.
The soul, uneasy, and confined from home,
Rests and expatiates in a life to come.
                    (From Essay on Man)

GOOD–BYE

Ralph Waldo Emerson

Good-bye, proud world! I'm going home:
Thou art my friend, and I'm not thine.
Long through thy weary crowds I roam;
A river-ark on the ocean brine,
Long I've been tossed like the driven foam;
But now, proud world! I'm going home.

Good-bye to Flattery's fawning face;
To Grandeur with his wise grimace;
To upstart Wealth's averted eye;
To supple Office, low and high;
To crowded halls, to court and street;
To frozen hearts and hasting feet;
To those who go, and those who come;
Good-bye, proud world! I'm going home.

I am going to my own hearth-stone,
Bosomed to yon green hills alone,—
A secret nook in a pleasant land,
Whose groves the frolic fairies planned;
Where arches green, the livelong day,
Echo the blackbird's roundelay,
And vulgar feet have never trod
A spot that is sacred to thought and God.

O, when I am safe in my sylvan home,
I tread on the pride of Greece and Rome;
And when I am stretched beneath the pines,
Where the evening star so holy shines,
I laugh at the lore and the pride of man,
At the sophist schools and the learned clan;
For what are they all, in their high conceit,
When man in the bush with God may meet?

"SAIL ON, O SHIP OF STATE!"

Henry Wadsworth Longfellow

Thou, too, sail on, O Ship of State!
Sail on, O Union, strong and great!
Humanity with all its fears,
With all its hopes of future years,
Is hanging breathless on thy fate!
We know what Master laid thy keel,
What Workmen wrought thy ribs of steel,
Who made each mast, and sail, and rope,
What anvils rang, what hammers beat,
In what a forge and what a heat
Were shaped the anchors of thy hope!
Fear not each sudden sound and shock,
'Tis of the wave and not the rock;
'Tis but the flapping of the sail,
And not a rent made by the gale!
In spite of rock and tempest's roar,
In spite of false lights on the shore,
Sail on, nor fear to breast the sea!
Our hearts, our hopes, are all with thee,
Our hearts, our hopes, our prayers, our tears,
Our faith, triumphant o'er our fears,
Are all with thee,—are all with thee!
              (From The Building of the Ship)

HOME–THOUGHTS, FROM ABROAD

Robert Browning

Oh, to be in England
  Now that April's there,
And whoever wakes in England
  Sees, some morning, unaware,
That the lowest boughs and the brush-wood sheaf
Round the elm-tree bole are in tiny leaf,
While the chaffinch sings on the orchard bough
In England—now!

And after April, when May follows,
And the whitethroat builds, and all the swallows!
Hark, where my blossomed pear-tree in the hedge
    Leans to the field and scatters on the clover
Blossoms and dewdrops—at the bent spray's edge—
    That's the wise thrush; he sings each song twice over,
Lest you should think he never could recapture
The first fine careless rapture!
And though the fields look rough with hoary dew,
All will be gay when noontide wakes anew
The buttercups, the little children's dower
—Far brighter than this gaudy melon-flower!

LIFE'S MIRROR

Madeline S. Bridges *

There are loyal hearts, there are spirits brave,
There are souls that are pure and true;
Then give to the world the best you have,
And the best will come back to you.

Give love, and love to your life will flow,
A strength in your utmost need;
Have faith, and a score of hearts will show
Their faith in your work and deed.

Give truth, and your gift will be paid in kind,
And honor will honor meet;
And the smile which is sweet will surely find
A smile that is just as sweet.

Give sorrow and pity to those who mourn;
You will gather in flowers again
The scattered seeds from your thought outborne
Though the sowing seemed but vain.

For life is the mirror of king and slave,
'Tis just what we are and do;
Then give to the world the best you have
And the best will come back to you.

* That is, Mary Ainge De Vere.

THE DEATH OF SOCRATES

(Socrates, an Athenian philosopher, was condemned to death by the authorities because of alleged impiety and innovation. His friends came to his prison to offer him an easy escape through the bribery of the officials. But the seventy-year-old leader of the revolting party refused, telling them "Be of good cheer, and say that you are burying my body only." In one of the great passages of the world's literature Plato tells the rest of the story.)

You, Simmias and Cebes, and all other men, will depart at some time or other. Me already, as the tragic poet would say, the voice of fate calls. Soon I must drink the poison; and I think that I had better repair to the bath first, in order that the women may not have the trouble of washing my body after I am dead.

When he had done speaking Crito said: And have you any commands for us, Socrates—anything to say about your children, or any other matter in which we can serve you?

Nothing particular, he said: only, as I have always told you, I would have you look to yourselves; that is a service which you may always be doing to me and mine as well as to yourselves. And you need not make professions; for if you take no thought for yourselves and walk not according to the precepts which I have given you, not now for the first time, the warmth of your professions will be of no avail.

We will do our best, said Crito. But in what way would you have us bury you?

In any way that you like; only you must get hold of me, and take care that I do not walk away from you. Then he turned to us, and added with a smile:—I cannot make Crito believe that I am the same Socrates who has been talking and conducting the argument; he fancies that I am the other Socrates whom he will soon see, a dead body—and he asks, How shall he bury me? And though I have spoken many words in the endeavour to show that when I have drunk the poison I shall leave you and go to the joys of the blessed,—these words of mine, with which I have comforted you and myself, have had, as I perceive, no effect upon Crito. And therefore I want you to be surety for me now, as he was surety for me at the trial. But let the promise be of another sort; for he was my surety to the Judges that I would remain, but you must be my surety to him that I shall not remain, but go away and depart; and then he will suffer less at my death, and not be grieved when he sees my body being burned or buried. I would not have him sorrow at my hard lot, or say at the burial, Thus we lay out Socrates, or, Thus we follow him to the grave or bury him; for false words are not only evil in themselves, but they infect the soul with evil. Be of good cheer, then, my dear Crito, and say that you are burying my body only, and do with that as is usual, and as you think best.

When he had spoken these words he arose and went into the bath-chamber with Crito, who bade us wait; and we waited, talking and thinking of . . . the greatness of our sorrow; he was like a father of whom we were being bereaved, and we were about to pass the rest of our lives as orphans. . . . Now the hour of sunset was near, for a good deal of time had passed while he was within. When he came out, he sat down with us again . . . but not much was said. Soon the jailer . . . entered and stood by him, saying: To you, Socrates, who I know to be the noblest and gentlest and best of all who ever came to this place, I will not impute the angry feelings of other men, who rage and swear at me when, in obedience to the authorities, I bid them drink the poison—indeed I am sure that you will not be angry with me; for others, as you are aware, and not I, are the guilty cause. And so fare you well, and try to bear lightly what must needs be; you know my errand. Then bursting into tears he turned away and went out.

Socrates looked at him and said: I return your good wishes and will do as you bid. Then turning to us, he said, How charming the man is; since I have been in prison he has always been coming to see me, and now see how generously he sorrows for me. But we must do as he says, Crito; let the cup be brought, if the poison is prepared; if not, let the attendant prepare some.

Yet, said Crito, the sun is still upon the hilltops, and many a one has taken the draught late; and after the announcement has been made to him he has eaten and drunk, and indulged in sensual delights; do not hasten then, there is still time.

Socrates said: Yes, Crito, and they of whom you speak are right in doing thus, for they think that they will gain by the delay; but I am right in not doing thus, for I do not think that I should gain anything by drinking the poison a little later; I should be sparing and saving a life which is already gone; I could only laugh at myself for this. Please then do as I say, and not to refuse me.

Crito, when he heard this, made a sign to the servant; and the servant went in, and remained for some time, and then returned with the jailer carrying the cup of poison. Socrates said, You, my good friend, who are experienced in these matters, shall give me directions how I am to proceed. The man answered: You have only to walk about until your legs are heavy, and then to lie down, and the poison will act. At the same time he handed the cup to Socrates, who in the easiest and gentlest manner, without the least fear or change of color or feature, looking at the man with all his eyes, as his manner was, took the cup and said: What do you say about making a libation out of this cup to any god? May I or not? The man answered: We only prepare, Socrates, just so much as we deem enough. I understand, he said; yet I may and must pray to the gods to prosper my journey from this to that of the other world—may this then, which is my prayer, be granted to me. Then, holding the cup to his lips, quite readily and cheerfully he drank the poison.

And hitherto most of us had been able to control our sorrow; but now when we saw him drinking, and saw too that he had finished the draught, we could no longer forbear, and in spite of myself my own tears were flowing fast; so that I covered my face and wept over myself; for certainly I was not weeping over him, but at the thought of my own calamity in having lost such a companion. Nor was I the first, for Crito, when he found himself unable to restrain his tears, had got up and moved away, and I followed; and at that moment Apollodorus, who had been weeping all the time, broke out into a loud cry which made cowards of us all. Socrates alone retained his calmness: What is this strange outcry? he said. I sent away the women mainly in order that they might not offend in this way, for I have heard that a man should die in peace. Be quiet, then, and have patience. When we heard that, we were ashamed, and restrained our tears; and he walked about until, as he said, his legs began to fail, and then he lay on his back, according to the directions, and the man who gave him the poison now and then looked at his feet and legs; and after a while he pressed his foot hard and asked him if he could feel; and he said No; and then his leg, and so upwards and upwards, and showed us that he was cold and stiff. And then Socrates felt them himself, and said, When the poison reaches the heart, that will be the end. He was beginning to grow cold about the groin, when he uncovered his face (for he had covered himself up) and said,—they were his last words,—Crito, I owe a cock to Asclepius; will you remember to pay the debt? The debt shall be paid, said Crito; is there anything else? There was no answer to this question; but in a minute or two a movement was heard, and the attendant uncovered him; his eyes were set, and Crito closed his eyes and mouth.

Such was the end of our friend, whom I may truly call the wisest, the justest, and best of all the men whom I have ever known.

(From Plato's Phaedo, transl. Benjamin Jowett)

EXCHANGE OF LETTERS BETWEEN LINCOLN AND McCLELLAN

President Abraham Lincoln
Washington, D. C.
 We have just captured six cows. What shall we do with them?
George B. McClellan

General George B. McClellan
Army of the Potomac
 As to the six cows captured—milk them.
A. Lincoln

*   *   *

The Puritans hated bear-baiting, not because it gave pain to the bear, but because it gave pleasure to the spectators.—Thomas Babington Macaulay

EPITAPH ON A DENTIST

Stranger, approach this spot with gravity;
John Brown is filling his last cavity.

O! SUSANNA

Stephen Foster

I came from Alabama
Wid my banjo on my knee;
I'm gwine to Louisiana,
My true love for to see.
It rained all night the day I left,
The weather it was dry,
The sun so hot I froze to death;
Susanna, don't you cry for me.

Chorus:

O! Susanna, O don't you cry for me;
I've come from Alabama
Wid my banjo on my knee.

I jumped aboard de telegraph
And trabbled down the ribber,
De 'lectric fluid magnified
And killed five hundred nigger;
De bullgine bust, de horse run off,
I really thought I'd die;
I shut my eyes to hold my breath;
Susanna, don't you cry. (*Chorus.*)

I had a dream de odder night
When ebery t'ing was still;
I thought I saw Susanna
A-coming down the hill;
The buckwheat cake was in her mouth,
The tear was in her eye;
Says I, "I'm coming from the South,
Susanna, don't you cry." (*Chorus.*)

I soon will be in New Orleans,
And den I'll look all round,
And when I find Susanna
I will fall upon the ground;
And if I do not find her
Dis darkie'll surely die,
And when I'm dead and buried,
Susanna, don't you cry. (*Chorus.*)

HAPPY IS THE MAN THAT FINDETH WISDOM

Holy Bible, Proverbs 3:11–18

11 My son, despise not the chastening of the Lord; neither be weary of his correction:

12 For whom the Lord loveth he correcteth; even as a father the son in whom he delighteth.

13 Happy is the man that findeth wisdom, and the man that getteth understanding.

14 For the merchandise of it is better than the merchandise of silver, and the gain thereof than fine gold.

15 She is more precious than rubies: and all the things thou canst desire are not to be compared unto her.

16 Length of days is in her right hand; and in her left hand riches and honour.

17 Her ways are ways of pleasantness, and all her paths are peace.

18 She is a tree of life to them that lay hold upon her: and happy is everyone that retaineth her.

THE VIOLET

Jane Taylor

Down in a green and shady bed
A modest violet grew;
Its stalk was bent, it hung its head,
As if to hide from view.

And yet it was a lovely flower,
   Its color bright and fair;
It might have graced a rosy bower,
   Instead of hiding there.

Yet there it was content to bloom,
   In modest tints arrayed;
And there diffused a sweet perfume,
   Within the silent shade.

Then let me to the valley go,
   This pretty flower to see,
That I may also learn to grow
   In sweet humility.

THERE WAS A LITTLE GIRL

Anonymous

There was a little girl,
And she had a little curl
Right in the middle of her forehead.
When she was good
She was very, very good,
And when she was bad she was horrid.

One day she went upstairs,
When her parents, unawares,
In the kitchen were occupied with meals
And she stood upon her head
In her little trundle-bed,
And then began hooraying with her heels.

Her mother heard the noise,
And she thought it was the boys
A-playing at a combat in the attic;
But when she climbed the stair,
And found Jemima there,
She took and she did spank her most emphatic.
            (Sometimes attributed to
            Henry Wadsworth Longfellow)

AMERICA THE BEAUTIFUL

Katharine Lee Bates

O beautiful for spacious skies,
For amber waves of grain,
For purple mountain majesties
Above the fruited plain!
America! America!
God shed His grace on thee
And crown thy good with brotherhood
From sea to shining sea!

O beautiful for pilgrim feet,
Whose stern, impassioned stress
A thoroughfare for freedom beat
Across the wilderness!
America! America!
God mend thine every flaw,
Confirm thy soul in self-control,
Thy liberty in law!

O beautiful for heroes proved
In liberating strife,
Who more than self their country loved,
And mercy more than life!
America! America!
May God thy gold refine
Till all success be nobleness
And every gain divine!

O beautiful for patriot dream
That sees beyond the years
Thine alabaster cities gleam
Undimmed by human tears!
America! America!
God shed His grace on thee
And crown thy good with brotherhood
From sea to shining sea!

* * *

All the world is queer save thee and me, and even thou art a
little queer.—Robert Owen (in letter to William Allen, 1828)

THE WAY OF THE WORLD

Ella Wheeler Wilcox

Laugh, and the world laughs with you,
Weep, and you weep alone,
For the brave old earth must borrow its mirth—
But has trouble enough of its own.
Sing and the hills will answer,
Sigh, it is lost on the air;
The echoes rebound to a joyful sound
And shrink from voicing care.

Rejoice, and men will seek you,
Grieve, and they turn and go;
They want full measure of your pleasure,
But they do not want your woe.
Be glad, and your friends are many,
Be sad, and you lose them all;
There are *none* to decline your nectared wine,
But *alone* you must drink life's gall.

Feast, and your halls are crowded,
Fast, and the world goes by.
Forget and forgive—it helps you to live,
But no man can help you to die;
There's room in the halls of pleasure
For a long and lordly train,
But one by one, we must all march on
Through the narrow isle of pain.

ARABIAN PROVERB

He who knows not and knows not that he knows not,
    He is a fool—shun him;

He who knows not and knows he knows not,
    He is simple—teach him;

He who knows and knows not he knows,
    He is alseep—wake him;

He who knows and knows he knows,
    He is wise; follow him.

I'LL TAKE YOU HOME AGAIN, KATHLEEN

Thomas P. Westendorf

I'll take you home again, Kathleen,
Across the ocean wild and wide,
To where your heart has ever been,
Since first you were my bonny bride.
The roses all have left your cheek,
I've watched them fade away and die;
Your voice is sad when e'er you speak,
And tears bedim your loving eyes.

Chorus:

    Oh! I will take you back, Kathleen,
    To where your heart will feel no pain;
    And when the fields are fresh and green,
    I'll take you to your home again.

I know you love me, Kathleen, dear,
Your heart was ever fond and true;
I always feel when you are near,
That life holds nothing dear but you.
The smiles that once you gave to me,
I scarcely ever see them now,
Though many, many times I see
A darkening shadow on your brow. (*Chorus.*)

To that dear home beyond the sea,
My Kathleen shall again return,
And when thy old friends welcome thee,
Thy loving heart will cease to yearn.
Where laughs the little silver stream,
Besides your mother's humble cot,
And brightest rays of sunshine gleam,
There all your grief will be forgot. (*Chorus.*)

THE BARGAIN

Sir Philip Sidney

My true love hath my heart, and I have his,
By just exchange one for another given:

I hold his dear. and mine he cannot miss
There never was a better bargain driven:
    My true love hath my heart, and I have his.

His heart in me keeps him and me in one,
    My heart in him his thoughts and senses guides:
He loves my heart, for once it was his own,
    I cherish his because in me it bides:
        My true love hath my heart, and I have his.

'TIS THE LAST ROSE OF SUMMER

Thomas Moore

'Tis the last rose of Summer,
Left blooming alone;
All her lovely companions
Are faded and gone;
No flower of her kindred,
No rosebud is nigh,
To reflect back her blushes,
Or give sigh for sigh!

I'll not leave thee, thou lone one,
To pine on the stem;
Since the lovely are sleeping,
Go sleep thou with them.
Thus kindly I scatter
Thy leaves o'er the bed
Where thy mates of the garden
Lie scentless and dead.

So soon may I follow,
When friendships decay,
And from Love's shining circle
The gems drop away!
When true hearts lie withered,
And fond ones are flown,
Oh! who would inhabit
This bleak world alone?

GOD, GIVE US MEN!

Josiah Gilbert Holland

God, give us Men! A time like this demands
Strong minds, great hearts, true faith and ready hands;
　Men whom the lust of office does not kill;
Men whom the spoils of office cannot buy;
　Men who possess opinions and a will;
Men who have honor; men who will not lie;
Men who can stand before a demagogue
　And damn his treacherous flatteries without winking!
Tall men, sun-crowned, who live above the fog
　In public duty and in private thinking;
For while the rabble, with their thumb-worn creeds,
Their large professions and their little deeds,
Mingle in selfish strife, lo! Freedom weeps,
Wrong rules the land and waiting Justice sleeps.

LINCOLN REVIEWS A BOOK

For those who like this kind of a book, this is the kind of a book they will like.

"WHERE IGNORANCE IS BLISS——"

Thomas Gray

To each his suffering; all are men,
Condemn'd alike to groan,
The tender for another's pain,
The unfeeling for his own.
Yet, ah! why should they know their fate,
Since sorrow never comes too late,
And happiness too swiftly flies?
Thought would destroy their paradise.
No more;—where ignorance is bliss,
'Tis folly to be wise.
(From On A Distant Prospect
of Eton College)

ABOU BEN ADHEM

James Henry Leigh Hunt

Abou Ben Adhem (may his tribe increase!)
Awoke one night from a deep dream of peace,
And saw, within the moonlight in his room,
Making it rich, and like a lily in bloom,
An Angel writing in a book of gold:
Exceeding peace had made Ben Adhem bold,
And to the Presence in the room he said,
"What writest thou?" The Vision raised its head,
And with a look made of all sweet accord
Answered, "The names of those who love the Lord."
"And is mine one?" said Abou. "Nay, not so,"
Replied the Angel. Abou spoke more low,
But cheerily still; and said, "I pray thee, then,
Write me as one that loves his fellow men."

The Angel wrote, and vanished. The next night
It came again with a great wakening light,
And showed the names whom love of God had blessed,
And lo! Ben Adhem's name led all the rest!

AS THE TWIG IS BENT

'Tis education forms the common mind;
Just as the twig is bent, the tree's inclined.
                    (From Pope's Moral Essays)

INTREAT ME NOT TO LEAVE THEE

Holy Bible, Ruth 1:16–17

16 And Ruth said, Intreat me not to leave thee, or to return from following after thee: for whither thou goest, I will go; and where thou lodgest, I will lodge: thy people shall be my people, and thy God my God:

17 Where thou diest, will I die, and there will I be buried: the Lord do so to me, and more also, if ought but death part thee and me.

FROM EVANGELINE

Henry Wadsworth Longfellow

PRELUDE

This is the forest primeval. The murmuring pines and the hemlocks,
Bearded with moss, and in garments green, indistinct in the twilight,
Stand like Druids of eld, with voices sad and prophetic,
Stand like harpers hoar, with beards that rest on their bosoms.
Loud from its rocky caverns, the deep-voiced neighboring ocean
Speaks, and in accents disconsolate answers the wail of the forest.

This is the forest primeval; but where are the hearts that beneath it
Leaped like the roe, when he hears in the woodland the voice of the huntsman?
Where is the thatched-roofed village, the home of Acadian farmers,—
Men whose lives glided on like rivers that water the woodlands,
Darkened by shadows of earth, but reflecting an image of heaven?
Waste are those pleasant farms, and the farmers forever departed!
Scattered like dust and leaves, when the mighty blasts of October
Seize them, and whirl them aloft, and sprinkle them far o'er the ocean.
Naught but tradition remains of the beautiful village of Grand-Pré.

Ye who believe in affection that hopes, and endures, and is patient,
Ye who believe in the beauty and strength of woman's devotion,
List to the mournful tradition still sung by the pines of the forest;
List to a Tale of Love in Acadie, home of the happy.

"WHEN, IN DISGRACE——"

William Shakespeare

When, in disgrace with fortune and men's eyes,
I all alone beweep my outcast state
And trouble deaf heaven with my bootless cries
And look upon myself and curse my fate,
Wishing me like to one more rich in hope,

Featured like him, like him with friends possess'd,
Desiring this man's art and that man's scope,
With what I most enjoy contented least;
Yet in these thoughts myself almost despising,
Haply I think on thee, and then my state,
Like to the lark at break of day arising
From sullen earth, sings hymns at heaven's gate;
   For thy sweet love remember'd such wealth brings
   That then I scorn to change my state with kings.

(From his Sonnets)

THE SECRET HORROR OF THE LAST

Samuel Johnson

There are few things, not purely evil, of which we can say, without some emotion of uneasiness, this is the last. Those who could never agree together shed tears when mutual discontent has determined them to final separation; of a place which has been frequently visited, though without pleasure, the last look is taken with heaviness of heart; and the Idler, with all his chilliness of tranquillity, is not wholly unaffected by the thought that his last essay is before him.

The secret of horror of the last is inseparable from a thinking being, whose life is limited, and to whom death is dreadful. We always make a secret comparison between a part and a whole; the termination of any period of life reminds us that life itself has likewise its termination; when we have done anything for the last time we involuntarily reflect that a part of the days allotted to us is past, and that as more is past there is less remaining.

ODE

Arthur O'Shaughnessy

We are the music-makers,
   And we are the dreamers of dreams,
Wandering by lone sea-breakers,
   And sitting by desolate streams;
World-losers and world-forsakers,
   On whom the pale moon gleams:
Yet we are the movers and shakers
   Of the world for ever, it seems.

With wonderful deathless ditties
  We build up the world's great cities,.
And out of a fabulous story
  We fashion an empire's glory:
One man with a dream, at pleasure,
  Shall go forth and conquer a crown;
And three with a new song's measure
  Can trample an empire down.

We, in the ages lying,
  In the buried past of the earth,
Built Nineveh with our sighing,
  And Babel itself with our mirth;
And o'erthrew them with prophesying
  To the old of the new world's worth;
For each age is a dream that is dying,
  Or one that is coming to birth.

THE MARINES' HYMN

Anonymous

From the Halls of Montezuma
To the shores of Tripoli
We fight our country's battles
On the land as on the sea.
First to fight for right and freedom
And to keep our honor clean;
We are proud to claim the title
Of United States Marine.

Our flag's unfurled to every breeze
From dawn to setting sun;
We have fought in every clime and place
Where we could take a gun;
In the snow of far-off Northern lands
And in sunny tropic scenes;
You will find us always on the job
The United States Marines.

Here's health to you and to our Corps
Which we are proud to serve;
In many a strife we've fought for life

And never lost our nerve;
If the Army and the Navy
Ever look on Heaven's scenes,
They will find the streets are guarded
By United States Marines.

PIPPA'S SONG

Robert Browning

The year's at the spring
The day's at the morn;
Morning's at seven;
The hillside's dew pearled;
The lark's on the wing;
The snail's on the thorn;
God's in his heaven—
All's right with the world!
(From Pippa Passes)

EXCELSIOR

Henry Wadsworth Longfellow

The shades of night were falling fast,
As through an Alpine village passed
A youth, who bore, 'mid snow and ice,
A banner with the strange device—
     Excelsior!

His brow was sad; his eye beneath
Flashed like a falchion from its sheath;
And like a silver clarion rung
The accents of that unknown tongue—
     Excelsior!

In happy homes he saw the light
Of household fires gleam warm and bright,
Above, the spectral glaciers shone,
And from his lips escaped a groan—
     Excelsior!

"Try not the pass," the old man said:
"Dark lowers the tempest overhead;
The roaring torrent is deep and wide."
And loud that clarion voice replied,
          Excelsior!

"Oh, stay," the maiden said, "and rest
Thy weary head upon this breast!"
A tear stood in his bright blue eye,
But still he answered with a sigh,
          Excelsior!

"Beware the pine-tree's withered branch!
Beware the awful avalanche!"
This was the peasant's last Good-night:
A voice replied, far up the height:
          Excelsior!

At break of day, as heavenward
The pious monks of Saint Bernard
Uttered the oft-repeated prayer,
A voice cried through the startled air,
          Excelsior!

A traveller, by the faithful hound,
Half-buried in the snow was found,
Still grasping in his hand of ice
That banner with the strange device,
          Excelsior!

There in the twilight cold and gray,
Lifeless, but beautiful, he lay,
And from the sky, serene and far,
A voice fell, like a falling star—
          Excelsior!

*   *   *

There is in every true woman's heart a spark of heavenly fire,
which lies dormant in the broad daylight of prosperity; but which
kindles up, and beams and blazes in the dark hour of adversity.
          —Washington Irving (The Sketch-Book)

A LAST WILL

IN THE NAME OF GOD, AMEN: I, Charles Lounsbery, being of sound and disposing mind and memory, do now make and publish this, my LAST WILL AND TESTAMENT, in order, as justly as I may, to distribute my interests in the world among succeeding men.

And first, that part of my interests which is known in the law and recognized in the sheep-bound volumes as my property, being inconsiderable and of no account, I make no account of it in this my will.

My right to live, it being but a life estate, is not at my disposal, but, these excepted, all else in the world I now proceed to devise and bequeath.

ITEM—And first, I give to good fathers and mothers, but in trust for their children, nevertheless, all good little words of praise and all quaint pet names, and I charge said parents to use them justly but generously, as the needs of their children shall require.

ITEM—I leave to children exclusively, but only for the life of their childhood, all and every, the dandelions of the fields and the daisies thereof, with the right to play among them freely, according to the custom of children, warning them at the same time against thistles. And I devise to children the yellow shores of creeks and the golden sands beneath the waters thereof, with the dragonflies that skim the surface of said waters, and the odors of the willows that dip into said waters, and the white clouds that float high over the giant trees.

And I leave to children the long days to be merry in, in a thousand ways, and the Night and the Moon and the Train of the Milky Way to wonder at, but subject, nevertheless, to the right thereinafter given to lovers; and I give to each child the right to choose a star that shall be his, and I direct that the child's father shall tell him the name of it, in order that the child shall always remember the name of that star after he has learned and forgotten astronomy.

ITEM—I devise to boys jointly all the useful idle fields and commons where ball may be played, and all the snow-clad hills where one may coast, and all the streams and ponds where one may skate, to have and to hold the same for the period of their boyhood.

And all meadows with the clover-blooms and the butterflies thereof; and all woods, with their appurtenances of squirrels and whirring birds and echoes and strange noises: And all distant places which may be visited, together with the adventures there found, I do give to said boys to be theirs; and I give to said boys each his own place at the fireside at night, with all the pictures that may be seen in the burning wood or coal, to enjoy it without let or hindrance, and without any encumbrance of cares.

ITEM—To lovers I devise their imaginary world, with whatever they may need, as the stars of the sky, the red, red roses by the wall, the snow of the hawthorn, the sweet strains of music, of aught else they may desire to figure to each other the lastingness and beauty of their love.

ITEM—To young men jointly, being joined in a brave, mad crowd, I devise and bequeath all boisterous, inspiring sports of rivalry. I give to them the disdain of weakness and undaunted confidence in their own strength. Though they are rude and rough, I leave to them alone the power of making lasting friendships and of possessing companions; and to them exclusively I give all merry songs and brave choruses to sing, with smooth voices to troll them forth.

ITEM—And to those who are no longer children or youths, or lovers, or young men, I leave a memory, and I leave to them the volumes of the poems of Shakespeare and Burns, and of other poets, if there are others, to the end that they may live over again the old days freely and fully, without tithe or diminution: and to those who are no longer children or youths or lovers I leave, too, the knowledge of what a rare, rare world it is.

(Actually written by Williston Fish, but often mistakenly believed to have been found among the effects of one deceased)

THE TREE OF LIBERTY

The tree of liberty only grows when watered by the blood of tyrants.

(From Bertrand Barère's speech in the
Convention Nationale, 1792)

BOY DEFINED

Anonymous

Nature's answer to that false belief that there is no such thing as perpetual motion. A boy can swim like a fish, run like a deer, climb like a squirrel, balk like a mule, bellow like a bull, eat like a pig, or act like a jackass, according to climatic conditions. He is a piece of skin stretched over an appetite; a noise covered with smudges. . . . He is a growing animal of superlative promise, to be fed, watered, and kept warm, a joy forever, a periodic nuisance, the problem of our times, the hope of a nation. Every boy born is evidence that God is not yet discouraged of man.

FOR, LO, THE WINTER IS PAST

Holy Bible, Song of Solomon 2:10–13

10 My beloved spake, and said unto me, Rise up, my love, my fair one, and come away.

11 For, lo, the winter is past, the rain is over and gone;

12 The flowers appear on the earth; the time of the singing of birds is come, and the voice of the turtle is heard in our land;

13 The fig tree putteth forth her green figs, and the vines with the tender grape give a good smell. Arise, my love, my fair one, and come away.

I HAVE SEEN A CURIOUS CHILD

William Wordsworth

I have seen
A curious child, who dwelt upon a tract
Of inland ground, applying to his ear
The convolutions of a smooth-lipped shell;
To which, in silence hushed, his very soul
Listened intensely; and his countenance soon

145

Brightened with joy; for from within were heard
Murmurings, whereby the monitor expressed
Mysterious union with its native sea.
Even such a shell the universe itself
Is to the ear of Faith; and there are times,
I doubt not, when to you it doth impart
Authentic tidings of invisible things;
Of ebb and flow, and ever-during power;
And central peace, subsisting at the heart
Of endless agitation.
                    (From The Excursion, Book Four)

MR. DOOLEY ON THE SUPREME COURT

Finley Peter Dunne

No matter whether th' constitution follows th' flag or not, th' supreme coort follows th' iliction returns.

THE PESSIMIST

Ben King

Nothing to do but work,
Nothing to eat but food,
Nothing to wear but clothes
To keep one from going nude.

Nothing to breathe but air,
Quick as a flash 'tis gone;
Nowhere to fall but off,
Nowhere to stand but on.

Nothing to comb but hair
Nowhere to sleep but in bed,
Nothing to weep but tears,
Nothing to bury but dead.

Nothing to sing but songs,
Ah, well, alas! alack!
Nowhere to go but out,
Nowhere to come but back.

Nothing to see but sights,
Nothing to quench but thirst,
Nothing to have but what we've got;
Thus thro' life we are cursed.

Nothing to strike but a gait;
Everything moves that goes.
Nothing at all but common sense
Can ever withstand these woes.

JESUS AND THE CHILDREN

Holy Bible, Mark 10:13–16

And they brought young children to him, that he should touch them: and his disciples rebuked those that brought them.

But when Jesus saw it, he was much displeased, and said unto them, Suffer the little children to come unto me, and forbid them not; for such is the kingdom of God.

Verily I say unto you, Whosoever shall not receive the kingdom of God as a little child, he shall not enter therein.

And he took them up in his arms, put his hands upon them, and blessed them.

DUTY

Robert Louis Stevenson

There is an idea abroad among moral people that they should make their neighbors good. One person I have to make good: myself. But my duty to my neighbor is much more nearly expressed by saying that I have to make him happy—if I may.

AFTER THE BALL

Charles K. Harris

A little maiden climbed an old man's knee,
Begged for a story, "Do, Uncle, please;
Why are you single, why live alone?
Have you no babies, have you no home?"
"I had a sweetheart, years, years ago,
Where she is now, pet, you will soon know.
List to the story, I'll tell it all,
I believed her faithless, after the ball.

Chorus:
"After the ball is over, after the break of morn,
After the dancers leaving, after the stars are gone;
Many a heart is aching, if you could read them all;
Many's the hopes that have vanished, after the ball.

"Bright lights were flashing in the grand ball room,
Softly the music, playing sweet tunes,
There came my sweetheart, my love, my own,
'I wish some water; leave me alone!'
When I returned, dear, there stood a man,
Kissing my sweetheart as lover can.
Down fell the glass, pet, broken, that's all,
Just as my heart was, after the ball. (*Chorus.*)

"Long years have passed, child, I've never wed,
True to my lost love, though she is dead,
She tried to tell me, tried to explain,
I would not listen, pleadings were vain;
One day a letter came, from that man,
He was her brother, the letter ran.
That's why I'm lonely, no home at all,
I broke her heart, pet, after the ball." (*Chorus.*)

JEANIE WITH THE LIGHT BROWN HAIR

Stephen Foster

I dream of Jeanie with the light brown hair,
Borne, like a vapor, on the summer air;
I see her tripping where the bright streams play,
Happy as the daisies that dance on her way.
Many were the wild notes her merry voice would pour,
Many were the blithe birds that warbled them o'er:
Oh! I dream of Jeanie with the light brown hair,
Floating, like a vapor, on the summer air.

I long for Jeanie with the day-dawn smile,
Radiant in gladness, warm with winning guile;
I hear her melodies, like joys gone by,
Sighing round my heart o'er the fond hopes that die:—

Sighing like the wind and sobbing like the rain,—
Wailing for the lost one that comes not again:
Oh! I long for Jeanie, and my heart bows low,
Never more to find her where the bright waters flow.

* * *

This house, where once a lawyer dwelt,
Is now a smith's, Alas!
How rapidly the iron age
Succeeds the age of brass!
                    —William Erskine

CHARTLESS

Emily Dickinson

I never saw a moor,
I never saw the sea;
Yet know I how the heather looks,
And what a wave must be.

I never spoke with God,
Nor visited in heaven;
Yet certain am I of the spot
As if the chart were given.

THE SONG OF THE UNGIRT RUNNERS

Charles Hamilton Sorley

We swing ungirded hips,
    And lightened are our eyes,
The rain is on our lips,
    We do not run for prize.
We know not whom we trust
    Nor whitherward we fare,
But we run because we must
    Through the great wide air.

The waters of the sea
    Are troubled as by storm.
The tempest strips the trees
    And does not leave them warm.
Does the tearing tempest pause?
    Do the tree-tops ask it why?
So we run without a cause
    'Neath the big bare sky.

The rain is on our lips,
    We do not run for prize.
But the storm the water whips
    And the wave howls to the skies.
The winds arise and strike it
    And scatter it like sand,
And we run because we like it
    Through the broad bright land.

THE WIT OF SYDNEY SMITH

Macaulay was a book in breeches; he not only overflowed with
learning but stood in the slops; he was laying society waste with his
waterspouts of talk; people in his company burst for want of an

opportunity of dropping in a word; he confounded soliloquy and colloquy. The great use of the raised center, revolving on a round table, would be to put Macaulay on it and distribute his talk fairly to the company. *When Smith called on Macaulay and found him ill in bed, he said later that he was* more agreeable than I have ever seen him. There were some gorgeous flashes of silence.

Luttrell is remarkably well, considering that he has been remarkably well for so many years.

Philosopher Malthus came here last week. I got an agreeable party for him of unmarried people. There was only one lady who had a child; but he is a good-natured man, and, if there are no appearances of approaching fertility, is civil to every lady.

The observances of the Church concerning feasts and fasts are tolerably well kept upon the whole, since the rich keep the feasts and the poor the fasts.

DOMINUS ILLUMINATIO MEA

R. D. Blackmore

In the hour of death, after this life's whim,
When the heart beats low, and the eyes grow dim,
And pain has exhausted every limb—
 The lover of the Lord shall trust in Him.

When the will has forgotten the lifelong aim,
And the mind can only disgrace its fame,
And a man is uncertain of his own name—
 The power of the Lord shall fill this frame.

When the last sigh is heaved, and the last tear shed,
And the coffin is waiting beside the bed,
And the widow and child forsake the dead—
 The angel of the Lord shall lift this head.

For even the purest delight may pall,
And power must fail, and the pride must fall,
And the love of the dearest friends grow small—
 But the glory of the Lord is all in all.

THESE ARE THE TIMES THAT TRY MEN'S SOULS

Thomas Paine

These are the times that try men's souls. The summer soldier and the sunshine patriot will, in this crisis, shrink from the service of their country; but he that stands it *now,* deserves the love and thanks of man and woman. Tyranny, like hell, is not easily conquered; yet we have this consolation with us, that the harder the conflict, the more glorious the triumph. What we obtain too cheap, we esteem too lightly; it is dearness only that gives everything its value. Heaven knows how to put a proper price upon its goods; and it would be strange, indeed, if so celestial an article as FREEDOM should not be highly rated. Britain, with an army to enforce her tyranny, has declared that she has a right (*not only to* TAX) but to "bind *us in* ALL CASES WHATSOEVER," and if being *bound in that manner,* is not slavery, then is there not such a thing as slavery upon earth. Even the expression is impious; for so unlimited a power can belong only to God.

Whether the independence of the continent was declared too soon, or delayed too long, I will not now enter into as an argument; my own simple opinion is, that had it been eight months earlier, it would have been much better. We did not make a proper use of last winter, neither could we, while we were in a dependent state. However, the fault, if it were one, was all our own; we have none to blame but ourselves. But no great deal is lost yet. All that Howe has been doing for this month past, is rather a ravage than a conquest, which the spirit of the Jerseys, a year ago, would have quickly repulsed, and which time and a little resolution will soon recover.

I have as little superstition in me as any man living, but my secret opinion has ever been, and still is, that God Almighty will not give up a people to military destruction, or leave them unsupported to perish, who have so earnestly and so repeatedly sought to avoid the calamities of war, by every decent method which wisdom could invent. Neither have I so much of the infidel in me, as to suppose that He has relinquished the government of the world, and given us up to the care of devils; and as I do not, I cannot see on what grounds the king of Britain can look up to heaven for help against us; a common murderer, a highwayman, or a housebreaker, has as good a pretence as he.

(From The American Crisis)

SOLITUDE

Henry David Thoreau

This is a delicious evening, when the whole body is one sense, and imbibes delight through every pore. I go and come with a strange liberty in Nature, a part of herself. As I walk along the stony shore of the pond in my shirt sleeves, though it is cool as well as cloudy and windy, and I see nothing special to attract me, all the elements are unusually congenial to me. The bullfrogs trump to usher in the night, and the note of the whippoorwill is borne on the rippling wind from over the water. Sympathy with the fluttering alder and poplar leaves almost takes away my breath; yet, like the lake, my serenity is rippled but not ruffled. The small waves raised by the evening wind are as remote from storm as the smooth reflecting surface. Though it is now dark, the wind still blows and roars in the wood, the waves still dash, and some creatures lull the rest with their notes. The repose is never complete. The wildest animals do not repose, but seek their prey now; the fox, and skunk, and rabbit now roam the fields and woods without fear. They are Nature's watchmen—links which connect the days of animated life.

When I return to my house I find that visitors have been there and left their cards, either a bunch of flowers, or a wreath of evergreen, or a name in pencil on a yellow walnut leaf or chip. They who come rarely to the woods take some little piece of the forest into their hands to play with by the way, which they leave, either intentionally or accidentally. One has peeled a willow wand, woven it into a ring, and dropped it on my table. I could always tell if visitors had called in my absence, either by the bended twigs or grass, or the print of their shoes, and generally of what sex or age or quality they were by some slight trace left, as a flower dropped, or a bunch of grass plucked and thrown away, even as far off as the railroad, half a mile distant, or by the lingering odor of a cigar or pipe. Nay, I was frequently notified of the passage of a traveler along the highway sixty rods off by the scent of his pipe.

There is commonly sufficient space about us. Our horizon is never quite at our elbows. The thick wood is not just at our door, nor the pond, but somewhat is always clearing, familiar and worn by us, appropriated and fenced in some way, and reclaimed from Nature. For what reason have I this vast range and circuit, some square miles of unfrequented forest, for my privacy, abandoned to me by men? My nearest neighbor is a mile distant, and no house is visible from any place but the hilltops within half a mile of my own. I have my horizon bounded by woods all to myself; a distant view of the railroad where it touches the pond on the one hand, and of the fence which skirts the woodland road on the other. But for the most part it is as solitary where I live as on the prairies. It is as much Asia or Africa as New England. I have, as it were, my own sun and moon and stars, and a little world all to myself. At night there was never a traveler passed my house, or knocked at my door, more than if I were the first or last man; unless it were in the spring, when at long intervals some came from the village to fish for pouts—they plainly fished much more in the Walden Pond of their own natures, and baited their hooks with darkness— but they soon retreated, usually with light baskets, and left "the world to darkness and to me," and the black kernel of the night was never profaned by any human neighborhood.

(From Walden)

MY HEART LEAPS UP WHEN I BEHOLD

William Wordsworth

My heart leaps up when I behold
A rainbow in the sky:
So was it when my life began;
So is it now I am a man;
So be it when I shall grow old,
Or let me die!
The Child is father of the Man;
And I could wish my days to be
Bound each to each by natural piety.

THE PURE HEART

My good blade carves the casques of men,
My tough lance thrusteth sure,
My strength is as the strength of ten,
Because my heart is pure.
(From Tennyson's Sir Galahad)

AMERICA

Samuel Francis Smith

My country, 'tis of thee,
Sweet land of liberty,
    Of thee I sing;
Land where my fathers died,
Land of the pilgrims' pride.
From every mountain-side
    Let Freedom ring.

My native country, thee,
Land of the noble free,—
    Thy name I love;
I love thy rocks and rills,
Thy woods and templed hills:
My heart with rapture thrills
    Like that above.

Let music swell the breeze,
And ring from all the trees,
    Sweet Freedom's song;
Let mortal tongues awake,
Let all that breathe partake,
Let rocks their silence break,—
    The sound prolong.

Our fathers' God, to Thee,
Author of liberty,
    To thee we sing;
Long may our land be bright
With Freedom's holy light;
Protect us by Thy might,
    Great God, our King.

*　*　*

Count that day lost whose low descending sun
Views from thy hand no worthy action done.
    (From Stamford's Art of Reading, 1803)

ONWARD, CHRISTIAN SOLDIERS

Sabine Baring-Gould

Onward, Christian soldiers,
Marching as to war,
With the cross of Jesus
Going on before!
Christ, the royal Master,
Leads against the foe;
Forward into battle,
See his banners go.
Onward, Christian soldiers,
Marching as to war,
With the cross of Jesus
Going on before!

At the sign of triumph
Satan's host doth flee;
On, then, Christian soldiers,
On to victory!
Hell's foundations quiver
At the shout of praise;
Brothers, lift your voices,
Loud your anthems raise!

Like a mighty army
Moves the Church of God;
Brother, we are treading
Where the saints have trod;
We are not divided,
All one Body we,
One in hope and doctrine,
One in charity.

Crowns and thrones may perish,
Kingdoms rise and wane,
But the Church of Jesus
Constant will remain;
Gates of hell can never
'Gainst that Church prevail;
We have Christ's own promise,
And that cannot fail.

Onward, then, ye people!
Join our happy throng!
Blend with ours your voices
In the triumph song!
Glory, laud, and honor,
Unto Christ the King;
This through countless ages
Men and angels sing.
Onward, Christian soldiers,
Marching as to war,
With the cross of Jesus
Going on before!

TIME, YOU OLD GIPSY MAN

Ralph Hodgson

Time, you old gipsy man,
    Will you not stay,
Put up your caravan
    Just for one day?

All things I'll give you
Will you be my guest,
Bells for your jennet
Of silver the best,
Goldsmiths shall beat you
A great golden ring,
Peacocks shall bow to you,
Little boys sing.
Oh, and sweet girls will
Festoon you with may,
Time, you old gipsy,
Why hasten away?

Last week in Babylon,
Last night in Rome,
Morning, and in the crush
Under Paul's dome;
Under Paul's dial
You tighten your rein—
Only a moment,
And off once again;

Off to some city
Now blind in the womb,
Off to another
Ere that's in the tomb.

Time, you old gipsy man,
   Will you not stay,
Put up your caravan
   Just for one day?

ACCORDING TO JOSH BILLINGS:

The quickest way to take the starch out of a man who is always blaming himself, is to agree with him. This ain't what he is looking for.

Q. How fast does sound travel?

A. This depends a good deal upon the nature of the noise you are talking about. The sound of a dinner horn, for instance, travels a half mile in a second, while an invitation to get up in the morning I have known to be three quarters of an hour going up two pairs of stairs, and then not have strength enough left to be heard.

I am a poor man, but I have this consolation: I am poor by accident, not design.

It is a wise man who profits by his own experience—but it is a good deal wiser one, who lets the rattlesnake bite the other fellow.

Take all the fools out of this world, and there wouldn't be any fun, nor profit, living in it.

Lasting reputations are of a slow growth; the man who wakes up famous some morning, is very apt to go to bed some night and sleep it all off.

Never take the bull by the horns, young man, but take him by the tail, then you can let go when you want to.

A WISE OLD OWL

Edward Hersey Richards

A wise old owl sat on an oak,
The more he saw the less he spoke;
The less he spoke the more he heard;
Why aren't we like that wise old bird?

SHAKESPEARE

Ben Jonson

I remember the players have often mentioned it as an honor to Shakespeare, that in his writing (whatsoever he penned) he never blotted out a line. My answer hath been, "Would he had blotted a thousand," which they thought a malevolent speech. I had not told posterity this but for their ignorance who chose that circumstance to commend their friend by wherein he most faulted; and to justify mine own candor, for I loved the man, and do honor his memory on this side of idolatry as much as any. He was, indeed, honest, and of an open and free nature; had an excellent phantasy, brave notions, and gentle expressions, wherein he flowed with that facility that sometimes it was necessary he should be stopped. "*Sufflaminandus enat*," as Augustus said of Haterius. His wit was in his own power; would the rule of it had been so, too! Many times he fell into those things, could not escape laughter, as when he said in the person of Caesar, one speaking to him, "Caesar, thou dost me wrong." He replied, "Caesar never did wrong but with just cause"; and such like, which were ridiculous. But he redeemed his vices with his virtues. There was ever more in him to be praised than to be pardoned.

LITTLE THINGS

Julia Carney

Little drops of water,
Little grains of sand,
Make the mighty ocean
And the pleasant land.

Little deeds of kindness,
Little words of love,
Make our world an Eden
Like the Heaven above.

HAMLET CONTEMPLATES SUICIDE

William Shakespeare

To be, or not to be; that is the question;
Whether 'tis nobler in the mind to suffer
The slings and arrows of outrageous fortune,
Or to take arms against a sea of troubles,
And by opposing end them. To die: to sleep;
No more; and by a sleep to say we end
The heart-ache and the thousand natural shocks
That flesh is heir to; 'tis a consummation
Devoutly to be wished. To die; to sleep;
To sleep: perchance to dream; aye, there's the rub;
For in that sleep of death what dreams may come
When we have shuffled off this mortal coil,
Must give us pause: there's the respect
That makes calamity of so long life;
For who would bear the whips and scorns of time,
The oppressor's wrong, the proud man's contumely,
The pangs of despised love, the law's delay,
The insolence of office, and the spurns
That patient merit of the unworthy takes,
When he himself might his quietus make
With a bare bodkin? Who would fardels bear,
To grunt and sweat under a weary life,
But that the dread of something after death—
The undiscover'd country from whose bourn
No traveler returns—puzzles the will
And makes us rather bear those ills we have
Than fly to others that we know not of?
Thus conscience does make cowards of us all,
And thus the native hue of resolution
Is sicklied o'er with the pale cast of thought,
And enterprises of great pith and moment
With this regard their currents turn awry,
And lose the name of action.

(From Hamlet)

AND THEY SHALL BEAT THEIR SWORDS INTO PLOWSHARES

Holy Bible, Micah 4:1–5

1 But in the last days it shall come to pass, that the mountain of the house of the Lord shall be established in the top of the mountains, and it shall be exalted above the hills; and people shall flow unto it.

2 And many nations shall come, and say, Come, and let us go up to the mountain of the Lord, and to the house of the God of Jacob; and he will teach us of his ways, and we will walk in his paths: for the law shall go forth of Zion, and the word of the Lord from Jerusalem.

3 And he shall judge among many people, and rebuke strong nations afar off; and they shall beat their swords into plowshares, and their spears into pruninghooks: nation shall not lift up a sword against nation, neither shall they learn war any more.

4 But they shall sit every man under his vine and under his fig tree; and none shall make them afraid: for the mouth of the Lord of hosts hath spoken it.

5 For all people will walk every one in the name of his god, and we will walk in the name of the Lord our God for ever and ever.

WE WILL SPEAK OUT

James Russell Lowell

We will speak out, we will be heard,
　Though all earth's systems crack;
We will not bate a single word,
　Nor take a letter back.
Let liars fear, let cowards shrink,
　Let traitors turn away;
Whatever we have dared to think
　That dare we also say.
We speak the truth, and what care we
　For hissing and for scorn,
While some faint gleamings we can see
　Of Freedom's coming morn?

SHE WALKS IN BEAUTY

Lord Byron

She walks in beauty, like the night
Of cloudless climes and starry skies,
And all that's best of dark and bright
Meet in her aspect and her eyes;
Thus mellow'd to that tender light
Which heaven to gaudy day denies.

One shade the more, one ray the less,
Had half impair'd the nameless grace
Which waves in every raven tress
Or softly lightens o'er her face,
Where thoughts serenely sweet express
How pure, how dear their dwelling-place.

And on that cheek and o'er that brow
So soft, so calm, yet eloquent,
The smiles that win, the tints that glow
But tell of days in goodness spent,
A mind at peace with all below,
A heart whose love is innocent.

AS THRO' THE LAND AT EVE

Alfred, Lord Tennyson

As thro' the land at eve we went,
    And pluck'd the ripen'd ears,
We fell out, my wife and I,

O we fell out I know not why,
    And kiss'd again with tears.
And blessings on the falling out
    That all the more endears,
When we fall out with those we love
    And kiss again with tears!
For when we came where lies the child
    We lost in other years,

There above the little grave,
O there above the little grave,
We kiss'd again with tears.
                    (From The Princess)

THE PURPLE COW

Gelett Burgess

Reflections on a Mythic Beast,
Who's Quite Remarkable, at Least.

I never saw a Purple Cow,
I never Hope to See One.
But I can Tell You Anyhow,
I'd rather See than Be One.

Years later Mr. Burgess added to the plethora of parodies of "The Purple Cow" by writing "Cinq Ans Après":

(Confession: and a Portrait, too,
Upon a Background that I Rue!)

Ah, Yes! I Wrote the Purple Cow—
I'm Sorry, now, I Wrote It!
But I can Tell You Anyhow,
I'll Kill You if You Quote It!

A MAN TO THE UNIVERSE

Stephen Crane

A man said to the universe:
"Sir, I exist!"
"However," replied the universe,
"The fact has not created in me
A sense of obligation."

I SHALL NOT PASS AGAIN THIS WAY

Anonymous

The bread that bringeth strength I want to give,
The water pure that bids the thirsty live:
I want to help the fainting day by day;
I'm sure I shall not pass again this way.

I want to give the oil of joy for tears,
The faith to conquer crowding doubts and fears.
Beauty for ashes may I give alway:
I'm sure I shall not pass again this way.

I want to give some measure running o'er,
And into angry hearts I want to pour
The answer soft that turneth wrath away;
I'm sure I shall not pass again this way.

I want to give to others hope and faith,
I want to do all that the Master saith;
I want to live aright from day to day;
I'm sure I shall not pass again this way.

CALVARY

Edwin Arlington Robinson

Friendless and faint, with martyred steps and slow,
Faint for the flesh, but for the spirit free,
Stung by the mob that came to see the show,
The Master toiled along to Calvary;
We gibed him, as he went, with houndish glee,
Till his dimmed eyes for us did overflow;
We cursed his vengeless hands thrice wretchedly—
And this was nineteen hundred years ago.

But after nineteen hundred years the shame
Still clings, and we have not made good the loss
That outraged faith has entered in his name.
Ah, when shall come love's courage to be strong!
Tell me, O Lord—tell me, O Lord, how long
Are we to keep Christ writhing on the cross!

164

A PRAYER

Max Ehrmann

Let me do my work each day; and if the darkened hours of despair overcome me, may I not forget the strength that comforted me in the desolation of other times.

May I still remember the bright hours that found me walking over the silent hills of my childhood, or dreaming, on the margin of the quiet river, when a light glowed within me, and I promised my early God to have courage amid the tempests of the changing years. Spare me from bitterness and from the sharp passions of unguarded moments. May I not forget that poverty and riches are of the spirit. Though the world know me not, may my thoughts and actions be such as shall keep me friendly with myself.

Lift my eyes from the earth, and let me not forget the uses of the stars. Forbid that I should judge others lest I condemn myself. Let me not follow the clamor of the world, but walk calmly in my path.

Give me a few friends who will love me for what I am; and keep ever burning before my vagrant steps the kindly light of hope. And though age and infirmity overtake me, and I come not within sight of the castle of my dreams, teach me still to be thankful for life, and for time's olden memories that are good and sweet; and may the evening's twilight find me gentle still.

FOR EVENING

Sabine Baring-Gould

Now the day is over,
   Night is drawing nigh;
Shadows of the evening
   Steal across the sky;

Jesus, give the weary
   Calm and sweet repose;
With Thy tenderest blessing
   May our eyelids close.

Grant to little children
  Visions bright of thee;
Guard the sailors tossing
  On the deep, blue sea.

Comfort every sufferer
  Watching late in pain;
Those who plan some evil
  From their sins restrain.

Through the long night watches,
  May thine angels spread
Their white wings above me,
  Watching round my bed.

When the morning wakens,
  Then may I arise
Pure, and fresh, and sinless
  In Thy holy eyes. Amen.

THE WIT OF JOHN F. KENNEDY

At a $100-a-plate Dinner, Salt Lake City, Utah, September, 1960:
I am deeply touched—not as deeply touched as you have been by coming to this dinner, but nevertheless, it is a sentimental occasion.

When asked by a little boy how he became a war hero:
It was absolutely involuntary. They sank my boat.

When he met Premier Khrushchev in Vienna and was told that the medal on the Russian's chest was the Lenin Peace Prize:
I hope you keep it.

During a White House Dinner honoring Nobel Prize Winners:
I think this is the most extraordinary collection of talent, of human knowledge, that has ever been gathered together at the White House—with the possible exception of when Thomas Jefferson dined alone.

May 27, 1961:
When we got into office, the thing that surprised me most was to find that things were just as bad as we'd been saying they were.

GOD OUR REFUGE

Richard Chenevix Trench

If there had anywhere appeared in space
    Another place of refuge where to flee,
Our hearts had taken refuge in that place,
    And not with Thee.

For we against creation's bars had beat
    Like prisoned eagles, through great worlds had sought
Though but a foot of ground to plant our feet,
    Where Thou were not.

And only when we found in earth and air,
    In heaven or hell, that such might nowhere be—
That we could not flee from Thee anywhere,
    We fled to Thee.

YOUTH'S IMMORTALITY

William Hazlitt

No young man believes he shall ever die. It was a saying of my brother's, and a fine one. There is a feeling of Eternity in youth which makes us amends for everything. To be young is to be as one of the Immortals. One half of time indeed is spent—the other half remains in store for us with all its countless treasures, for there is no line drawn, and we see no limit to our hopes and wishes. . . . We look round in a new world, full of life and motion, and ceaseless progress, and feel in ourselves all the vigour and spirit to keep pace with it, and do not foresee from any present signs how we shall be left behind in the race, decline into old age, and drop into a grave. . . . Like a rustic at a fair, we are full of amazement and rapture, and have no thought of going home, or that it will soon be night. We know our existence only by ourselves, and confound our knowledge with the objects of it. We and Nature are therefore one.

THE MOURNING BRIDE

William Congreve

**Thus grief still treads upon the heels of pleasure,
Married in haste, we may repent at leisure.**

THE CONCORD HYMN

Ralph Waldo Emerson

By the rude bridge that arched the flood,
Their flag to April's breeze unfurled,
Here once the embattled farmers stood,
And fired the shot heard round the world.

The foe long since in silence slept;
Alike the conqueror silent sleeps;
And Time the ruined bridge has swept
Down the dark stream which seaward creeps.

On this green bank, by this soft stream,
We set today a votive stone;
That memory may their deed redeem,
When, like our sires, our sons are gone.

Spirit, that made those spirits dare
To die, and leave their children free,
Bid Time and Nature gently spare
The shaft we raise to them and thee.

THE MORON

Anonymous

See the happy moron,
He doesn't give a damn!
I wish I were a moron—
My God! Perhaps I am!

LOST

Lost, yesterday, somewhere between sunrise and sunset, two
golden hours, each set with sixty diamond minutes. No reward is
offered for they are gone forever.

(Anonymous)

A LOST CHORD

Adelaide Anne Procter

Seated one day at the Organ,
I was weary and ill at ease,
And my fingers wandered idly
Over the noisy keys.

I do not know what I was playing,
Or what I was dreaming then;
But I struck one chord of music,
Like the sound of a great Amen.

It flooded the crimson twilight
Like the close of an angel's Psalm,
And it lay on my fevered spirit
With a touch of infinite calm.

It quieted pain and sorrow,
Like love overcoming strife;
It seemed the harmonious echo
From our discordant life.

It linked all perplexèd meanings
Into one perfect peace,
And trembled away into silence,
As if it were loath to cease.

I have sought, but I seek it vainly,
That one lost chord divine,
That came from the soul of the Organ
And entered into mine.

It may be that Death's bright angel
Will speak in that chord again,—
It may be that only in Heaven
I shall hear that grand Amen.

* * *

The cynic is one who knows the price of everything and the value of nothing.

—Oscar Wilde

ODE ON INTIMATIONS OF IMMORTALITY FROM RECOLLECTIONS OF EARLY CHILDHOOD

William Wordsworth

There was a time when meadow, grove, and stream,
The earth, and every common sight,
  To me did seem
  Apparelled in celestial light,
The glory and the freshness of a dream.
It is not now as it hath been of yore;—
  Turn whereso'er I may,
  By night or day,
The things which I have seen I now can see no more.
  The Rainbow comes and goes,
  And lovely is the Rose,
  The Moon doth with delight
Look round her when the heavens are bare;
  Waters on a starry night
  Are beautiful and fair;
  The sunshine is a glorious birth;
  But yet I know, where'er I go,
That there hath past away a glory from the earth.

* * *

Our birth is but a sleep and a forgetting:
The Soul that rises with us, our life's Star,
  Hath had elsewhere its setting,
  And cometh from afar:
  Not in entire forgetfulness,
  And not in utter nakedness,
But trailing clouds of glory do we come
  From God, who is our home:
Heaven lies about us in our infancy!
Shades of the prison-house begin to close
  Upon the growing Boy,
But he beholds the light, and whence it flows,
  He sees it in his joy;
The Youth, who daily farther from the east
  Must travel, still is Nature's Priest,
  And by the vision splendid
  Is on his way attended;

At length the Man perceives it die away,
And fade into the light of common day.

* * *

O joy! that in our embers
Is something that doth live,
That nature yet remembers
What was so fugitive!
The thought of our past years in me doth breed
Perpetual benediction: not indeed
For that which is most worthy to be blest—
Delight and liberty, the simple creed
Of Childhood, whether busy or at rest,
With new-fledged hope still fluttering in his breast:—
Not for these I raise
The song of thanks and praise;
But for those obstinate questionings
Of sense and outward things,
Fallings from us, vanishings;
Blank misgivings of a Creature
Moving about in worlds not realized,
High instincts before which our mortal Nature
Did tremble like a guilty Thing surprised:
But for those first affections,
Those shadowy recollections,
Which, be they what they may,
Are yet the fountain light of all our day,
Are yet a master light of all our seeing;
Uphold us, cherish, and have power to make
Our noisy years seem moments in the being
Of the eternal Silence: truths that wake,
To perish never;
Which neither listlessness, nor mad endeavour,
Nor Man nor Boy,
Nor all that is at enmity with joy,
Can utterly abolish or destroy!
Hence in a season of calm weather
Though inland far we be,
Our Souls have sight of that immortal sea
Which brought us hither,
Can in a moment travel thither,

And see the Children sport upon the shore,
And hear the mighty waters rolling evermore.

Then sing, ye Birds, sing, sing a joyous song!
    And let the young Lambs bound
    As to the tabor's sound!
We in thought will join your throng,
    Ye that pipe and ye that play,
    Ye that through your hearts to-day
    Feel the gladness of the May!
What though the radiance which was once so bright
Be now forever taken from my sight,
    Though nothing can bring back the hour
Of splendour in the grass, of glory in the flower;
    We will grieve not, rather find
    Strength in what remains behind;
    In the primal sympathy
    Which having been must ever be;
    In the soothing thoughts that spring
    Out of human suffering;
    In the faith that looks through death,
In years that bring the philosophic mind.

And O ye Fountains, Meadows, Hills, and Groves,
Forebode not any severing of our loves!
Yet in my heart of hearts I feel your might;
I only have relinquished one delight
To live beneath your more habitual sway.
I love the Brooks which down their channels fret,
Even more than when I tripped lightly as they;
The innocent brightness of a new-born Day
      Is lovely yet;
The Clouds that gather round the setting sun
Do take a sober colouring from an eye
That hath kept watch o'er man's mortality;
Another race hath been, and other palms are won.
Thanks to the human heart by which we live,
Thanks to its tenderness, its joys, and fears,
To me the meanest flower that blows can give
Thoughts that do often lie too deep for tears.

RENOUNCEMENT

Alice Meynell

I must not think of thee; and, tired yet strong,
I shun the thought that lurks in all delight—
The thought of thee—and in the blue Heaven's height,
And in the dearest passage of a song.
Oh, just beyond the fairest thoughts that throng
This breast, the thought of thee waits, hidden yet bright;
But it must never, never come in sight;
I must stop short of thee the whole day long.
But when sleep comes to close each difficult day,
When night gives pause to the long watch I keep,
And all my bonds I needs must loose apart,
Must doff my will as raiment laid away,—
With the first dream that comes with the first sleep
I run, I run, I am gathered to thy heart.

ABRAHAM LINCOLN ANNOUNCES HIS FIRST TRY FOR PUBLIC OFFICE

I have no wealth or popular relations to recommend me. My case is thrown exclusively upon the independent voters of this county, and if elected they will have conferred a favor upon me, for which I shall be unremitting in my labors to compensate. But if the good people in their wisdom shall see fit to keep me in the background, I have been too familiar with disappointments to be very much chagrined.

(Announcing his candidacy for the Illinois legislature in the columns of the Illinois *Sangamo Journal*, March 9, 1832)

WITH EVERY RISING OF THE SUN

Ella Wheeler Wilcox

With every rising of the sun
Think of your life as just begun.

The past has shrived and buried deep
All yesterdays—there let them sleep. . . .

Concern yourself with but today,
Woo it and teach it to obey,

Your wish and will. Since time began
Today has been the friend of man. . . .

You and today! a soul sublime
And the great pregnant hour of time.

With God between to bind the twain—
Go forth I say—attain—attain.

MR. DOOLEY ON OLD AGE

Finley Peter Dunne

"Manny a man that cudden't direct ye to th' dhrug store on th'
corner whin he was thirty will get a respectful hearin' whin age has
further impaired his mind. . . ."

"Why," said Mr. Hennessy, "ye'd give annythin' to be twinty-five
agin."

"I wuddn't," said Mr. Dooley. "Why shud I want to grow old
agin?"

ONE WORD IS TOO OFTEN PROFANED

Percy Bysshe Shelley

One word is too often profaned
    For me to profane it,
One feeling too falsely disdain'd
    For thee to disdain it;

One hope is too like despair
   For prudence to smother,
And Pity from thee more dear
   Than that from another.

I can give not what men call love;
   But wilt thou accept not
The worship the heart lifts above
   And the Heavens reject not,—
The desire of the moth for the star,
   Of the night for the morrow,
The devotion to something afar
   From the sphere of our sorrow?

POLONIUS' ADVICE TO HIS SON

William Shakespeare

These few precepts in thy memory
See thou character. Give thy thoughts no tongue,
Nor any unproportion'd thought his act.
Be thou familiar, but by no means vulgar:
The friends thou hast, and their adoption tried,
Grapple them to thy soul with hoops of steel;
But do not dull thy palm with entertainment
Of each new-hatch'd, unfledg'd comrade. Beware
Of entrance to a quarrel: but being in,
Bear't that th' opposed may beware of thee.
Give every man thine ear, but few thy voice:
Take each man's censure, but reserve thy judgment.
Costly thy habit as thy purse can buy,
But not express'd in fancy: rich, not gaudy;
For the apparel oft proclaims the man.
Neither a borrower nor a lender be;
For loan oft loses both itself and friend,
And borrowing dulls the edge of husbandry.
This above all: to thine own self be true;
And it must follow, as the night the day,
Thou canst not then be false to any man.
                              (From Hamlet)

BARBARA FRIETCHIE

John Greenleaf Whittier

Up from the meadows rich with corn,
Clear in the cool September morn,

The clustered spires of Frederick stand
Green-walled by the hills of Maryland.

Round about them orchards sweep,
Apple and peach-tree fruited deep,

Fair as a garden of the Lord
To the eyes of the famished rebel horde,

On that pleasant morn of the early fall
When Lee marched over the mountain wall;

Over the mountains winding down,
Horse and foot, into Frederick town.

Forty flags with their silver stars,
Forty flags with their crimson bars,

Flapped in the morning wind: the sun
Of noon looked down, and saw not one.

Up rose old Barbara Frietchie then,
Bowed with her fourscore years and ten;

Bravest of all in Frederick town,
She took up the flag the men hauled down;

In her attic window the staff she set,
To show that one heart was loyal yet.

Up the street came the rebel tread,
Stonewall Jackson riding ahead.

Under his slouched hat left and right
He glanced; the old flag met his sight.

"Halt!"—the dust-brown ranks stood fast.
"Fire!"—out blazed the rifle blast.

It shivered the window, pane and sash;
It rent the banner with seam and gash.

Quick, as it fell, from the broken staff
Dame Barbara snatched the silken scarf.

She leaned far out on the window-sill,
And shook it forth with a royal will.

"Shoot, if you must, this old grey head,
But spare your country's flag," she said.

A shade of sadness, a blush of shame,
Over the face of the leader came;

The nobler nature within him stirred
To life at that woman's deed and word;

"Who touches a hair of yon grey head
Dies like a dog! March on!" he said.

All day long through Frederick street
Sounded the tread of marching feet:

All day long that free flag tost
Over the heads of the rebel host.

Ever its torn folds rose and fell
On the loyal winds that loved it well;

And through the hill-gaps sunset light
Shone over it with a warm good-night.

Barbara Frietchie's work is o'er,
And the rebel rides on his raids no more.

Honor to her! and let a tear
Fall, for her sake, on Stonewall's bier.

Over Barbara Frietchie's grave,
Flag of freedom and union, wave!

Peace, and order, and beauty draw
Round thy symbol of light and law;

And ever the stars above look down
On thy stars below in Frederick town!

REQUIESCAT

Oscar Wilde

Tread lightly, she is near
　　Under the snow,
Speak gently, she can hear
　　The daisies grow.

All her bright golden hair
　　Tarnished with rust,
She that was young and fair
　　Fallen to dust.

Lily-like, white as snow,
　　She hardly knew
She was a woman, so
　　Sweetly she grew.

Coffin-board, heavy stone,
　　Lie on her breast,
I vex my heart alone,
　　She is at rest.

Peace, Peace, she cannot hear
　　Lyre or sonnet,
All my life's buried here,
　　Heap earth upon it.

* * *

Marriage resembles a pair of shears, so joined that they
can not be separated; often moving in opposite directions,
yet always punishing anyone who comes between them.
　　　　　　　　　　　　　　　　　　—Sydney Smith

TALL OAKS FROM LITTLE ACORNS GROW

David Everett

You'd scarce expect one of my age
To speak in public on the stage,
And if I chance to fall below
Demosthenes or Cicero,
Don't view me with a critic's eye,
But pass my imperfections by.
Large streams from little fountains flow,
Tall oaks from little acorns grow;
And though now I am small and young,
Of judgment weak and feeble tongue,
Yet all great, learned men, like me
Once learned to read their ABC.
But why may not Columbia's soil
Rear men as great as Britain's Isle,
Exceed what Greece and Rome have done
Or any land beneath the sun?
Mayn't Massachusetts boast as great
As any other sister state?
Or where's the town, go far or near,
That does not find a rival here?
Or where's the boy but three feet high
Who's made improvement more than I?
These thoughts inspire my youthful mind
To be the greatest of mankind:
Great, not like Caesar, stained with blood,
But only great as I am good.

WHAT IS GOOD?

John Boyle O'Reilly

"What is the real good?"
I ask in musing mood.

"Order," said the law court;
"Knowledge," said the school;
"Truth," said the wise man;
"Pleasure," said the fool;
"Love," said the maiden;
"Beauty," said the page;
"Freedom," said the dreamer;
"Home," said the sage;
"Fame," said the soldier;
"Equity," said the seer.
Spake my heart fully sad:
"The answer is not here."

Then within my bosom
Softly this I heard:
"Each heart holds the secret:
'Kindness' is the word."

THE BLUE AND THE GRAY

Francis Miles Finch

By the flow of the inland river,
Whence the fleets of iron have fled,
Where the blades of the grave-grass quiver,
Asleep are the ranks of the dead:—
Under the sod and the dew
Waiting the Judgment Day:—
Under the one, the Blue;
Under the other, the Gray.

These in the robings of glory,
Those in the gloom of defeat,
All with the battle-blood gory,
In the dusk of eternity meet;—
Under the sod and the dew
Waiting the Judgment Day:—
Under the laurel, the Blue;
Under the willow, the Gray.

From the silence of sorrowful hours
The desolate mourners go,
Lovingly laden with flowers,
Alike for the friend and the foe:—
Under the sod and the dew
Waiting the Judgment Day:—
Under the roses, the Blue;
Under the lilies, the Gray.

So with an equal splendor
The morning sun-rays fall,
With a touch impartially tender,
On the blossoms blooming for all;—
Under the sod and the dew
Waiting the Judgment Day:—
'Broidered with gold, the Blue;
Mellowed with gold, the Gray.

So when the summer calleth,
On forest and field of grain,
With an equal murmur falleth
The cooling drip of the rain;—

Under the sod and the dew
Waiting the Judgment Day:—
Wet with the rain, the Blue;
Wet with the rain, the Gray.

Sadly, but not with upbraiding
The generous deed was done.
In the storms of the years that are fading
No braver battle was won:—
Under the sod and the dew
Waiting the Judgment Day:—
Under the blossoms, the Blue;
Under the garlands, the Gray.

No more shall the war-cry sever,
Or the winding river be red;
They banish our anger forever
When they laurel the graves of our dead!
Under the sod and the dew
Waiting the Judgment Day:—
Love and tears for the Blue;
Tears and love for the Gray.

IN THE GOOD OLD SUMMER TIME

Ren Shields

There's a time each year that we always hold dear,
Good old summer time;
With the birds and the trees and the sweet scented breezes,
Good old summer time,
When your day's work is over then you are in clover,
And life is one beautiful rhyme.
No trouble annoying each one is enjoying,
The good old summer time.

Chorus:
    In the good old summer time,
    In the good old summer time,
    Strolling through the shady lanes,
    With your baby mine;
    You hold her hand, she holds yours.
    And that's a very good sign
    That she's your tootsey wootsey
    In the good old summer time.

To swim in the pool, you'd play "hookey" from school,
Good old summer time;
You'd play "ring-a-rosie" with Jim, Kate and Josie,
Good old summer time,
Those days full of pleasure we now fondly treasure,
When we never thought it a crime,
To go stealing cherries, with faces brown as berries,
Good old summer time. (*Chorus.*)

EVENING SONG

Sidney Lanier

Look off, dear Love, across the sallow sands,
  And mark yon meeting of the sun and sea,
How long they kiss in sight of all the lands,
  Ah, longer, longer, we!

Now in the sea's red vintage melts the sun,
  As Egypt's pearl dissolved in rosy wine,
And Cleopatra night drinks all. 'Tis done.
  Love, lay thine hand in mine.

Come forth, sweet stars, and comfort heaven's heart;
  Glimmer, ye waves, round else unlighted sands.
O night! divorce our sun and sky apart,
  Never our lips, our hands.

ON A CLERGYMAN'S HORSE BITING HIM

Anonymous

The steed bit his master;
How came this to pass?
He heard the good pastor
Cry "All flesh is grass."

A BAG OF TOOLS

R. L. Sharpe

Isn't it strange
That princes and kings,
And clowns that caper
In sawdust rings,
And common people
Like you and me
Are builders for eternity?

Each is given a bag of tools,
A shapeless mass,
A book of rules;
And each must make—
Ere life has flown—
A stumbling block
Or a steppingstone.

THE NOBLEST OCCUPATION

Montaigne

(TRANSLATOR: William Hazlitt)

What egregious fools are we! He hath passed his life in idleness, say we: "Alas, I have done nothing this day." What? have you not lived? It is not only the fundamental but the noblest of your occupation. "Had I been placed or thought fit for the managing of great affairs, I would have showed what I could have performed." Have you known how to meditate and manage your life? you have accomplished the greatest work of all. . . . Have you known how to compose your manners? you have done more than he who hath composed books. Have you known how to take rest? you have done more than he who hath taken Empires and Cities. The glorious masterpiece of man is to live to the purpose. All other things, as to reign, to govern, to hoard up treasure, to thrive and to build, are for the most part but appendixes and supports thereunto.

ALONG THE ROAD

Robert Browning Hamilton

I walked a mile with Pleasure;
    She chattered all the way,
But left me none the wiser
    For all she had to say.

I walked a mile with Sorrow
And ne'er a word said she;
But oh, the things I learned from her
When Sorrow walked with me!

WE ARE MADE FOR CO-OPERATION

Marcus Aurelius

(TRANSLATOR: Charles Long)

Begin the morning by saying to yourself, I shall meet with the busybody, the ungrateful, arrogant, deceitful, envious, unsocial. All these things happen to them by reason of their ignorance of what is good and evil. But I who have seen the nature of the good that it is beautiful, and of the bad that it is ugly, and the nature of him who does wrong, that it is akin to me, not only of the same blood and seed, but that it participates in the same intelligence and the same portion of divinity, I can neither be injured by any of them, for no one can fix on me what is ugly, nor can I be angry with my kinsman, nor hate him. For we are made for co-operation, like feet, like hands, like eyelids, like the rows of the upper and lower teeth. To act against one another is contrary to nature, and it is acting against one another to be vexed and to turn away.

THOU EASER OF ALL WOES

John Fletcher and Francis Beaumont

Care-charming sleep, thou easer of all woes,
Brother to Death, sweetly thyself dispose
On this afflicted prince. Fall, like a cloud,
In gentle showers; give nothing that is loud
Or painful to his slumbers; easy, sweet,
And as a purling stream, thou son of Night,
Pass by his troubled senses; sing his pain,
Like hollow murmuring wind, or silver rain;
Into this prince, gently, oh, gently slide,
And kiss him into slumbers, like a bride!

185

TEARS, IDLE TEARS

Alfred, Lord Tennyson

Tears, idle tears, I know not what they mean,
Tears from the depth of some divine despair
Rise in the heart, and gather to the eyes,
In looking on the happy autumn-fields,
And thinking of the days that are no more.

Fresh as the first beam glittering on a sail,
That brings our friends up from the underworld,
Sad as the last which reddens over one
That sinks with all we love below the verge;
So sad, so fresh, the days that are no more.

Ah, sad and strange as in dark summer dawns
The earliest pipe of half-awaken'd birds
To dying ears, when unto dying eyes
The casement slowly grows a glimmering square;
So sad, so strange, the days that are no more.

Dear as remember'd kisses after death,
And sweet as those by hopeless fancy feign'd
On lips that are for others; deep as love,
Deep as first love, and wild with all regret;
O Death in Life, the days that are no more!

(From The Princess)

IN TIME OF "THE BREAKING OF NATIONS"

Thomas Hardy

Only a man harrowing clods
  In a slow silent walk,
With an old horse that stumbles and nods
  Half asleep as they stalk.

Only thin smoke without flame
  From the heaps of couch grass:
Yet this will go onward the same
  Though Dynasties pass.

Yonder a maid and her wight
Come whispering by;
War's annals will fade into night
Ere their story die.

ULYSSES

Alfred, Lord Tennyson

There lies the port; the vessel puffs her sail:
There gloom the dark broad seas. My mariners,
Souls that have toil'd, and wrought, and thought with me—
That ever with a frolic welcome took
The thunder and the sunshine, and opposed
Free hearts, free foreheads—you and I are old;
Old age hath yet his honour and his toil;
Death closes all: but something ere the end,
Some work of noble note, may yet be done,
Not unbecoming men that strove with Gods.
The lights begin to twinkle from the rocks:
The long day wanes: the slow moon climbs: the deep
Moans round with many voices. Come, my friends
'Tis not too late to seek a newer world.
Push off, and sitting well in order smite
The sounding furrows; for my purpose holds
To sail beyond the sunset, and the baths
Of all the western stars, until I die.
It may be that the gulfs will wash us down:
It may be we shall touch the Happy Isles,
And see the great Achilles, whom we knew.
Tho' much is taken, much abides; and tho'
We are not now that strength which in old days
Moved earth and heaven; that which we are, we are;
One equal temper of heroic hearts,
Made weak by time and fate, but strong in will
To strive, to seek, to find, and not to yield.

ON A BAD SINGER

Samuel Taylor Coleridge

Swans sing before they die: 'twere no bad thing,
Should certain persons die before they sing.

HOME

Edgar A. Guest

It takes a heap o' livin' in a house t' make it home,
A heap o' sun an' shadder, an' ye sometimes have t' roam
Afore ye really 'preciate the things ye lef' behind,
An' hunger fer 'em somehow, with 'em allus on yer mind.
It don't make any differunce how rich ye get t' be,
How much yer chairs an' tables cost, how great yer luxury;
It ain't home t' ye, though it be the palace of a king,
Until somehow yer soul is sort o' wrapped round everything.

Home ain't a place that gold can buy or get up in a minute;
Afore it's home there's got t' be a heap o' livin' in it;
Within the walls there's got t' be some babies born, and then
Right there ye've got t' bring 'em up t' women good, an' men;
And gradjerly, as time goes on, ye find ye wouldn't part
With anything they ever used—they've grown into yer heart:
The old high chairs, the playthings, too, the little shoes they wore
Ye hoard; an' if ye could ye'd keep the thumb-marks on the door.

Ye've got t' weep t' make it home, ye've got t' sit an' sigh
An' watch beside a loved one's bed, an' know that Death is nigh;
An' in the stillness o' the night t' see Death's angel come,
An' close the eyes o' her that smiled, an' leave her sweet voice
    dumb.
For these are scenes that grip the heart, an' when yer tears are
    dried,
Ye find the home is dearer than it was, an' sanctified;
An' tuggin' at ye always are the pleasant memories
O' her that was an' is no more—ye can't escape from these.

Ye've got to sing an' dance fer years, ye've got t' romp an' play,
An' learn t' love the things ye have by usin' 'em each day;
Even the roses round the porch must blossom year by year
Afore they 'come a part o' ye, suggestin' someone dear
Who used t' love 'em long ago, and trained 'em just t' run
The way they do, so's they would get the early mornin' sun;
Ye've got to love each brick an' stone from cellar up t' dome:
It takes a heap o' livin' in a house t' make it home.

OLD IRONSIDES

Oliver Wendell Holmes

Ay, tear her tattered ensign down!
Long has it waved on high,
And many an eye has danced to see
That banner in the sky;
Beneath it rung the battle shout,
And burst the cannon's roar;—
The meteor of the ocean air
Shall sweep the clouds no more!

Her deck, once red with heroes' blood,
Where knelt the vanquished foe,
When winds were hurrying o'er the flood,
And waves were white below,
No more shall feel the victor's tread,
Or know the conquered knee;—
The harpies of the shore shall pluck
The eagle of the sea!

O, better that her shattered hulk
Should sink beneath the wave;
Her thunders shook the mighty deep,
And there should be her grave;
Nail to the mast her holy flag,
Set every threadbare sail,
And give her to the god of storms,
The lightning and the gale!

RETRIBUTION

Henry Wadsworth Longfellow

Though the mills of God grind slowly,
Yet they grind exceeding small;
Though with patience he stands waiting,
With exactness grinds he all.

* * *

Let us all be happy and live within our means, even if we have to borrow money to do it with.

—Artemus Ward

OH PROMISE ME

Clement Scott

Oh promise me, that some day you and I
Will take our love together to some sky
Where we can be alone and faith renew,
And find the hollows where those flowers grew,
Those first sweet violets of early Spring,
Which come in whispers, thrill us both and sing
Of love unspeakable that is to be;
Oh promise me! Oh promise me!

Oh promise me, that you will take my hand,
The most unworthy in this lonely land,
And let me sit beside you, in your eyes
Seeing the vision of our paradise,
Hearing God's message while the organ rolls
Its mighty music to our very souls;
No love less perfect than a life with thee;
Oh promise me! Oh promise me!

TO HELEN

Edgar Allan Poe

Helen, thy beauty is to me
    Like those Nicèan barks of yore
That gently, o'er a perfumed sea,
    The weary way-worn wanderer bore
    To his own native shore.

On desperate seas long wont to roam,
    Thy hyacinth hair, thy classic face,
Thy Naiad airs have brought me home
    To the glory that was Greece,
And the grandeur that was Rome.

Lo, in yon brilliant window-niche
    How statue-like I see thee stand,
    The agate lamp within thy hand,
Ah! Psyche, from the regions which
    Are holy land!

THE SUICIDE'S GRAVE

Sir W. S. Gilbert

On a tree, by a river, a little tom-tit
Sang "Willow, titwillow, titwillow!"
And I said to him, "Dicky-bird, why do you sit
Singing 'Willow, titwillow, titwillow?' "
"Is it weakness of intellect, birdie?" I cried,
"Or a rather tough worm in your little inside?"
With a shake of his poor little head, he replied,
"Oh, willow, titwillow, titwillow!"

He slapped at his chest as he sat on that bough,
Singing "Willow, titwillow, titwillow!"
And a cold perspiration bespangled his brow,
Oh, willow, titwillow, titwillow!
He sobbed and he sighed, and a gurgle he gave,
Then he threw himself into the billowy wave,
And an echo arose from the suicide's grave—
"Oh, willow, titwillow, titwillow!"

Now I feel just as sure as I'm sure that my name
Isn't Willow, titwillow, titwillow,
That 'twas blighted affection that made him exclaim,
"Oh, willow, titwillow, titwillow!"
And if you remain callous and obdurate, I
Shall perish as he did, and you will know why,
Though I probably shall not exclaim as I die,
"Oh, willow, titwillow, titwillow!"

* * *

They never taste who always drink;
They never talk who always think.
                    —Matthew Prior

* * *

In general, the art of government consists in taking as
much money as possible from one class of citizens to give
to the other.
                    —Voltaire

SILVER THREADS AMONG THE GOLD

Eben E. Rexford

Darling, I am growing old,
Silver threads among the gold,
Shine upon my brow today,
Life is fading fast away;
But, my darling, you will be
Always young and fair to me.
Yes! my darling, you will be
Always young and fair to me.

Chorus:

Darling, I am growing old,
Silver threads among the gold,
Shine upon my brow today;
Life is fading fast away.

When your hair is silver white,
And your cheeks no longer bright,
With the roses of the May,
I will kiss your lips and say;
Oh! my darling mine alone,
You have never older grown. (*Chorus.*)

Love can never more grow old,
Locks may lose their brown and gold,
Cheeks may fade and hollow grow,
But the hearts that love will know;
Never, never, winter's frost and chill,
Summer warmth is in them still. (*Chorus.*)

Love is always young and fair,
What to us is silver hair,
Faded cheeks or steps grown slow,
To the heart that beats below?
Since I kissed you mine alone,
You have never older grown. (*Chorus.*)

* * *

Wherever God erects a house of prayer,
The Devil always builds a chapel there;
And 'twill be found upon examination,
The latter has the largest congregation.
—Daniel Defoe

EASTER MORNING

Holy Bible, Matthew 28:1–10

1 In the end of the sabbath, as it began to dawn toward the first day of the week, came Mary Magdalene and the other Mary to see the sepulchre.

2 And, behold, there was a great earthquake: for the angel of the Lord descended from heaven, and came and rolled back the stone from the door, and sat upon it.

3 His countenance was like lightning, and his raiment white as snow:

4 And for fear of him the keepers did shake, and became as dead men.

5 And the angel answered and said unto the women, Fear not ye: for I know that ye seek Jesus, which was crucified.

6 He is not here: for he is risen, as he said. Come, see the place where the Lord lay.

7 And go quickly, and tell his disciples that he is risen from the dead; and, behold, he goeth before you into Galilee; there shall ye see him: lo, I have told you.

8 And they departed quickly from the sepulchre with fear and great joy; and did run to bring his disciples word.

9 And as they went to tell his disciples, behold, Jesus met them, saying, All hail. And they came and held him by the feet, and worshipped him.

10 Then said Jesus unto them, Be not afraid: go tell my brethren that they go into Galilee, and there shall they see me.

THE MAN HE KILLED

Thomas Hardy

"Had he and I but met
By some old ancient inn,
We should have sat us down to wet
Right many a nipperkin!

"But ranged as infantry,
And staring face to face,
I shot at him as he at me,
And killed him in his place.

"I shot him dead because—
 Because he was my foe,
Just so: my foe of course he was;
 That's clear enough; although

"He thought he'd 'list, perhaps,
 Off-hand like—just as I—
Was out of work—had sold his traps—
 No other reason why.

"Yes; quaint and curious war is!
 You shoot a fellow down
You'd treat, if met where any bar is,
 Or help to half-a-crown."

RAIN SONG

Robert Loveman

It isn't raining for me,
 It's raining daffodils;
In every dimpled drop I see
 Wild flowers on the hills.
The clouds of gray engulf the day
 And overwhelm the town;
It isn't raining rain to me,
 It's raining roses down.

It isn't raining rain to me,
 But fields of clover bloom,
Where any buccaneering bee
 Can find a bed and room.
A health unto the happy,
 A fig for him who frets!
It isn't raining rain to me,
 It's raining violets.

* * *

Orthodoxy is my doxy; heterodoxy is another man's
doxy.
                              —Bishop William Warburton

WAITING

John Burroughs

Serene, I fold my hands and wait,
Nor care for wind, or tide, or sea;
I rave no more 'gainst Time or Fate,
For, lo! my own shall come to me.

I stay my haste, I make delays,
For what avails this eager pace?
I stand amid the eternal ways,
And what is mine shall know my face.

Asleep, awake, by night or day,
The friends I seek are seeking me,
No wind can drive my bark astray,
Nor change the tide of destiny.

What matter if I stand alone?
I wait with joy the coming years;
My heart shall reap where it has sown,
And garner up its fruits of tears.

The waters know their own and draw
The brook that springs in yonder height;
So flows the good with equal law
Unto the soul of pure delights.

The stars come nightly to the sky;
The tidal wave unto the sea;
Nor time, nor space, nor deep, nor high,
Can keep my own away from me.

INSCRIPTION ON THE TOMB OF THE UNKNOWN SOLDIER

Here Rests in
Honored Glory
An American
Soldier
Known But to God

THE PASSIONATE SHEPHERD TO HIS LOVE

Christopher Marlowe

Come live with me and be my Love,
And we will all the pleasures prove
That valleys, groves, hills and fields,
Woods or steepy mountain yields.

And we will sit upon the rocks
Seeing the shepherds feed their flocks.
By shallow rivers, to whose falls
Melodious birds sing madrigals.

And I will make thee beds of roses
And a thousand fragrant posies,
A cap of flowers, and a kirtle
Embroidered all with leaves of myrtle.

A gown made of the finest wool,
Which from our pretty lambs we pull,
Fair linèd slippers for the cold,
With buckles of the purest gold.

A belt of straw and ivy buds,
With coral clasps and amber studs:
And if these pleasures may thee move,
Come live with me and be my Love.

The shepherd swains shall dance and sing
For thy delight each May-morning:
If these delights thy mind may move,
Then live with me and be my Love.

THE NYMPH'S REPLY TO THE SHEPHERD

Sir Walter Raleigh

If all the world and love were young,
And truth in every shepherd's tongue,
These pretty pleasures might me move
To live with thee and be thy love.

But time drives flocks from field to fold,
When rivers rage, and rocks grow cold;
And Philomel becometh dumb;
The rest complain of cares to come.

The flowers do fade, and wanton fields
To wayward Winter reckoning yields;
A honey tongue, a heart of gall,
Is fancy's spring, but sorrow's fall.

Thy gowns, thy shoes, thy beds of roses,
Thy cap, thy kirtle, and thy posies,
Soon break, soon wither, soon forgotten,
In folly ripe, in reason rotten.

Thy belt of straw and ivy buds,
Thy coral clasps and amber studs,
All these in me no means can move
To come to thee and be thy love.

But could youth last, and love still breed,
Had joys no date, nor age no need,
Then these delights my mind might move
To live with thee and be thy love.

THE DEAD

Rupert Brooke

Blow out, you bugles, over the rich Dead!
   There's none of these so lonely and poor of old,
   But, dying, has made us rarer gifts than gold.
These laid the world away; poured out the red
Sweet wine of youth; gave up the years to be
   Of work and joy, and that unhoped serene
   That men call age; and those who would have been,
Their sons, they gave, their immortality.
Blow, bugles, blow! They brought us, for our dearth,
   Holiness, lacked so long, and Love and Pain.
Honor has come back, as a king, to earth,
   And paid his subjects with a royal wage;
And Nobleness walks in our ways again;
   And we have come into our heritage.

THE GREATEST BATTLE THAT EVER WAS FOUGHT

Joaquin Miller

The greatest battle that ever was fought—
   Shall I tell you where and when?
On the maps of the world you will find it not:
   It was fought by the Mothers of Men.

Not with cannon or battle shot,
   With sword or nobler pen;
Not with eloquent word or thought
   From the wonderful minds of men;

But deep in a walled up woman's heart;
   A woman that would not yield;
But bravely and patiently bore her part;
   Lo! there is that battlefield.

No marshalling troops, no bivouac song,
   No banner to gleam and wave;
But Oh these battles they last so long—
   From babyhood to the grave!

But faithful still as a bridge of stars
   She fights in her walled up town;
Fights on, and on, in the endless wars;
   Then silent, unseen goes down!

Ho! ye with banners and battle shot,
   With soldiers to shout and praise,
I tell you the kingliest victories fought
   Are fought in these silent ways.

THE CANDID PHYSICIAN

John C. Lettsom

When people's ill, they come to I,
   I physics, bleeds, and sweats 'em;
Sometimes they live, sometimes they die.
   What's that to I? I lets 'em.

THE CREED OF OUR POLITICAL FAITH

Thomas Jefferson

Equal and exact justice to all men, of whatever state or persuasion, religious or political; peace, commerce, and honest friendship with all nations, entangling alliances with none. . . . Freedom of religion; freedom of the press, and freedom of person under the protection of the *habeas corpus*, and trial by juries impartially selected. These principles form the bright constellation which has gone before us, and guided our steps through an age of revolution and reformation. The wisdom of our sages and the blood of our heroes have been devoted to their attainment. They should be the creed of our political faith, the text of civil instruction, the touchstone by which we try the services of those we trust; and should we wander from them in moments of error or alarm, let us hasten to retrace our steps and to regain the road which alone leads to peace, liberty, and safety.

(From *First Inaugural Address*, 1801)

ELEGY IN A COUNTRY CHURCHYARD

G. K. Chesterton

The men that worked for England
They have their graves at home:
And bees and birds of England
About the cross can roam.

But they that fought for England,
Following a falling star,
Alas, alas for England
They have their graves afar.

And they that rule in England,
In stately conclave met,
Alas, alas for England
They have no graves as yet.

* * *

If I have seen further (than you and Descartes) it is by standing upon the shoulders of Giants.

(Sir Isaac Newton, in a letter to Robert Hooke, 1675)

THE MAD GARDENER'S SONG

Lewis Carroll

He thought he saw a Buffalo
    Upon the chimney-piece:
He looked again, and found it was
    His Sister's Husband's Niece.
"Unless you leave this house," he said,
    "I'll send for the Police!"

He thought he saw a Rattlesnake
    That questioned him in Greek:
He looked again, and found it was
    The Middle of Next Week.
"The one thing I regret," he said,
    "Is that it cannot speak!"

He thought he saw a Banker's Clerk
    Descending from the 'bus:
He looked again, and found it was
    A Hippopotamus.
"If this should stay to dine," he said,
    "There won't be much for us!"

He thought he saw a Kangaroo
    That worked a coffee-mill:
He looked again, and found it was
    A Vegetable-Pill.
"Were I to swallow this," he said,
    "I should be very ill!"

He thought he saw a Coach-and-Four
    That stood beside his bed:
He looked again, and found it was
    A Bear without a Head.
"Poor thing," he said, "poor silly thing!
    "It's waiting to be fed!"

He thought he saw an Albatross
    That fluttered round the lamp:
He looked again, and found it was
    A Penny-Postage Stamp.
"You'd best be getting home," he said:
    "The nights are very damp!"

WISE SAYINGS OF BENJAMIN FRANKLIN

Love your neighbors, but don't pull down your hedges.

Don't think to hunt two hares with one dog.

He that is rich need not live sparingly, and he than can live sparingly need not be rich.

None preaches better than the ant, and she says nothing.

A long life may not be good enough, but a good life is long enough.

God heals, and the doctor takes the fee.

If you'd have a good servant that you like, serve yourself.

A good example is the best sermon.

Search others for their virtues, thyself for thy vices.

Proclaim not all thou knowest, all thou owest, all thou hast, nor all thou canst.

If you would keep your secret from an enemy, tell it not to a friend.

GOD IS NOW

Henry David Thoreau

Men esteem truth remote, in the outskirts of the system, before Adam and after the last man. In eternity there is indeed something true and sublime. But all these time and places and occasions are now and here. God himself culminates in the present moment, and will never be more divine in the lapse of all the ages. And we are enabled to apprehend at all what is sublime and noble only by the perpetual instilling and drenching of the reality that surrounds us.

DETERMINATION

Anonymous

Sir Andrew Barton said, I'm hurt,
    I'm hurt, but I'm not slain.
I will lay me down and bleed awhile,
    Then rise and fight again.

ON A BAD SINGER

Samuel Taylor Coleridge

Swans sing before they die: 'twere no bad thing,
Should certain persons die before they sing.

THE GATE OF THE YEAR

M. Louise Haskins

And I said to the man who stood at the gate of the year:
"Give me a light, that I may tread safely into the unknown!"
And he replied:
"Go out into the darkness and put your hand into the Hand of
    God.
That shall be to you better than light and safer than a known
    way."
So, I went forth, and finding the Hand of God, trod gladly into
    the night.
And He led me toward the hills and the breaking of day in the
    lone East.
So, heart, be still!
What need our little life,
Our human life, to know,
If God hath comprehension?
In all the dizzy strife
Of things both high and low
God hideth His intention.

MY MIND TO ME A KINGDOM IS

Sir Edward Dyer

My mind to me a kingdom is;
    Such present joys therein I find
That it excels all other bliss
    That earth affords or grows by kind.
Though much I want which most would have,
Yet still my mind forbids to crave.

No princely pomp, no wealthy store,
    No force to win the victory,
No wily wit to salve a sore,
    No shape to feed a loving eye;
To none of these I yield as thrall—
For why? My mind doth serve for all.

I see how plenty surfeits oft,
  And hasty climbers soon do fall;
I see that those which are aloft
  Mishap doth threaten most of all;
They get with toil, they keep with fear—
Such care my mind could never bear.

Content to live, this is my stay;
  I seek no more than may suffice;
I press to bear no haughty sway;
  Look, what I lack my mind supplies.
Lo, thus I triumph like a king,
Content with that my mind doth bring.

Some have too much, yet still do crave;
  I little have, and seek no more.
They are but poor, though much they have,
  And I am rich with little store.
They poor, I rich; they beg, I give;
They lack, I leave; they pine, I live.

I laugh not at another's loss;
  I grudge not at another's pain;
No worldly waves my mind can toss;
  My state at one doth still remain.
I fear no foe, I fawn no friend;
I loathe not life, nor dread my end.

Some weigh their pleasure by their lust,
  Their wisdom by their rage of will;
Their treasure is their only trust;
  A cloakéd craft their store of skill.
But all the pleasure that I find
Is to maintain a quiet mind.

My wealth is health and perfect ease;
  My conscience clear my chief defense;
I neither seek by bribes to please
  Nor by deceit to breed offense,
Thus do I live; thus will I die;
Would all did so as well as I!

NO LONGER MOURN FOR ME WHEN I AM DEAD

William Shakespeare

No longer mourn for me when I am dead
Than you shall hear the surly sullen bell
Give warning to the world that I am fled
From this vile world, with vilest worms to dwell:
Nay, if you read this line, remember not
The hand that writ it; for I love you so,
That I in your sweet thoughts would be forgot,
If thinking on me then should make you woe.
O, if, I say, you look upon this verse
When I perhaps compounded am with clay,
Do not so much as my poor name rehearse,
But let your love even with my life decay;
    Lest the wise world should look into your moan,
    And mock you with me after I am gone.

                (From the *Sonnets*)

THE TWELVE MONTHS

Gregory Gander

Snowy, Flowy, Blowy,
Showery, Flowery, Bowery,
Hoppy, Choppy, Droppy,
Breezy, Sneezy, Freezy.

FREE SPEECH

Justice Oliver Wendell Holmes

The most stringent protection of free speech would not protect a man in falsely shouting fire in a theatre and causing a panic. . . The question in every case is whether the words used are used in such circumstances and are of such a nature as to create a clear and present danger that they will bring about the substantive evils that Congress has a right to prevent.

                (*Schenck* v. *U.S.*, 1919)

HYMN TO THE NIGHT

Henry Wadsworth Longfellow

I heard the trailing garments of the Night
  Sweep through her marble halls!
I saw her sable skirts all fringed with light
  From the celestial walls!

I felt her presence, by its spell of might,
  Stoop o'er me from above;
The calm, majestic presence of the Night,
  As of the one I love.

I heard the sounds of sorrow and delight,
  The manifold, soft chimes,
That fill the haunted chambers of the Night,
  Like some old poet's rhymes.

From the cool cisterns of the midnight air
  My spirit drank repose;
The fountain of perpetual peace flows there,—
  From those deep cisterns flows.

O holy Night! from thee I learn to bear
  What man has borne before!
Thou layest thy finger on the lips of Care,
  And they complain no more.

Peace! Peace! Orestes-like I breathe this prayer!
  Descend with broad-winged flight,
The welcome, the thrice-prayed for, the most fair,
  The best-beloved Night!

THE "KITTY"

Anonymous

There was a young man from the city,
Who met what he thought was a kitty;
He gave it a pat,
And said, "Nice little cat!"
And they buried his clothes out of pity.

"BE OF GOOD CHEER; I HAVE OVERCOME
THE WORLD"

Holy Bible, John 16:19–33

Now Jesus knew that they were desirous to ask him, and said unto them, Do ye inquire among yourselves of that I said, A little while, and ye shall not see me: and again, a little while, and ye shall see me? Verily, verily, I say unto you, That ye shall weep and lament, but the world shall rejoice: and ye shall be sorrowful, but your sorrow shall be turned into joy. A woman when she is in travail hath sorrow, because her hour is come: but as soon as she is delivered of the child, she remembereth no more the anguish, for joy that a man is born into the world. And ye now therefore have sorrow: but I will see you again, and your heart shall rejoice, and your joy no man taketh from you. And in that day ye shall ask me nothing. Verily, verily, I say unto you, Whatsoever ye shall ask the Father in my name, he will give it you. Hitherto have ye asked nothing in my name: ask, and ye shall receive, that your joy may be full. These things have I spoken unto you in proverbs: but the time cometh, when I shall no more speak unto you in proverbs, but I shall shew you plainly of the Father. At that day ye shall ask in my name: and I say not unto you, that I will pray the Father for you: For the Father himself loveth you, because ye have loved me, and have believed that I came out from God. I came forth from the Father, and am come into the world: again, I leave the world, and go to the Father. His disciples said unto him, Lo, now speakest thou plainly, and speakest no proverb. Now we are sure that thou knowest all things, and needest not that any man should ask thee: by this we believe that thou camest forth from God. Jesus answered them, Do ye now believe? Behold, the hour cometh, yea, is now come, that ye shall be scattered, every man to his own, and shall leave me alone: and yet I am not alone, because the Father is with me. These things I have spoken unto you, that in me ye might have peace. In the world ye shall have tribulation: but be of good cheer; I have overcome the world.

PROPHETIC WORDS BY WOODROW WILSON

A steadfast concert for peace can never be maintained except by a partnership of democratic nations. No autocratic government could be trusted to keep faith within it or observe its covenants. It must be a league of honor, a partnership of opinion. Intrigue would eat its vitals away; the plottings of inner circles who could plan what they would and render account to no one would be a corruption seated at its very heart. Only free peoples can hold their purpose and their honor steady to a common end and prefer the interests of mankind to any narrow interest of their own.

(From the Address to Congress asking for Declaration of War Against Germany, April 2, 1917)

THE CRY OF A DREAMER

John Boyle O'Reilly

I am tired of planning and toiling
In the crowded hives of men;
Heart-weary of building and spoiling,
And spoiling and building again.
And I long for the dear old river,
Where I dreamed my youth away;
For a dreamer lives forever,
And a toiler dies in a day.

I am sick of the showy seeming,
Of a life that is half a lie;
Of the faces lined with scheming
In the throng that hurries by.
From the sleepless thoughts' endeavour,
I would go where the children play;
For a dreamer lives forever,
And a thinker dies in a day.

I can feel no pride, but pity
For the burdens the rich endure;
There is nothing sweet in the city
But the patient lives of the poor.
Oh, the little hands too skillful
And the child mind choked with weeds!
The daughter's heart grown willful,
And the father's heart that bleeds!

No, no! from the street's rude bustle,
  From the trophies of mart and stage,
I would fly to the woods' low rustle
  And the meadow's kindly page.
Let me dream as of old by the river,
  And be loved for the dream alway;
For a dreamer lives forever,
  And a toiler dies in a day.

INWARD PEACE

Herman Melville

Consider the subtleness of the sea; how its most dreaded creatures
glide under water, unapparent for the most part, and treacherous
hidden beneath the loveliest tints of azure. Consider also the devilish
brilliance and beauty of many of its most remorseless tribes, as the
dainty embellished shape of many species of sharks. Consider, once
more, the universal cannibalism of the sea; all whose creatures prey
upon one another, carrying on eternal war since the world began.

Consider all this; and then turn to this green, gentle and most
docile earth; consider them both, the sea and the land; and do you
not find a strange analogy to something in yourself. For as this
appalling ocean surrounds the verdant land, so in the soul of man
there lies one insular Tahiti, full of peace and joy, but encompassed
by all the horrors of the half-known life. God keep thee! Push not
off from that isle, thou canst never return!

(From *Moby Dick*)

IN MEN WHOM MEN CONDEMN AS ILL

Joaquin Miller

In men whom men condemn as ill
I find so much of goodness still,
In men whom men pronounce divine
I find so much of sin and blot,
I do not dare to draw a line
Between the two, where God has not.

MISS YOU

David Cory

Miss you, miss you, miss you;
Everything I do
Echoes with the laughter
And the voice of you.
You're on every corner,
Every turn and twist,
Every old familiar spot
Whispers how you're missed.
Miss you, miss you, miss you.
Everywhere I go
There are poignant memories
Dancing in a row,
Silhouette and shadow
Of your form and face
Substance and reality
Everywhere displace.

Oh, I miss you, miss you!
How I miss you, Girl!
There's a strange, sad silence
'Mid the busy whirl,
Just as tho' the ordinary,
Daily things I do
Wait with me, expectant,
For a word from you.

Miss you, miss you, miss you!
Nothing now seems true,
Only that 'twas Heaven
Just to be with you.

MARRIAGE

Louis K. Anspacher

Marriage is that relation between man and woman in which the
independence is equal, the dependence mutual, and the obligation
reciprocal.

ON GROWING OLD

John Masefield

Be with me, Beauty, for the fire is dying,
My dog and I are old, too old for roving,
Man, whose young passion sets the spindrift flying,
Is soon too lame to march, too cold for loving.
I take the book and gather to the fire,
Turning old yellow leaves; minute by minute,
The clock ticks to my heart; a withered wire
Moves a thin ghost of music in the spinet.

I cannot sail your seas, I cannot wander,
Your cornland, nor your hill-land nor your valleys,
Ever again, nor share the battle yonder
Where the young knight the broken squadron rallies.
Only stay quiet while my mind remembers
The beauty of fire from the beauty of embers.

Beauty, have pity, for the strong have power,
The rich their wealth, the beautiful their grace,
Summer of man its sunlight and its flower,
Spring-time of man all April in a face.
Only, as in the jostling in the Strand,
Where the mob thrusts or loiters or is loud,
The beggar with the saucer in his hand
Asks only a penny from the passing crowd.
So, from this glittering world with all its fashion,
Its fire and play of men, its stir, its march,
Let me have wisdom, Beauty, wisdom and passion,
Bread to the soul, rain where the summers parch.
Give me but these, and though the darkness close
Even the night will blossom as the rose.

A PSALM OF LIFE

Henry Wadsworth Longfellow

Tell me not, in mournful numbers,
Life is but an empty dream!—
For the soul is dead that slumbers,
And things are not what they seem.

Life is real! Life is earnest!
And the grave is not its goal;
Dust thou art, to dust returnest,
Was not spoken of the soul.

Not enjoyment, and not sorrow
Is our destined end or way;
But to act, that each tomorrow
Find us farther than today.

Art is long, and Time is fleeting,
And our hearts, though stout and brave,
Still, like muffled drums, are beating
Funeral marches to the grave.

In the world's broad field of battle,
In the bivouac of life,
Be not like dumb, driven cattle!
Be a hero in the strife!

Trust no Future, howe'er pleasant
Let the dead Past bury its dead!
Act,—act in the living Present!
Heart within, and God o'erhead!

Lives of great men all remind us
We can make our lives sublime,
And, departing, leave behind us
Footprints on the sand of time—

Footprints, that perhaps another,
Sailing o'er life's solemn main,
A forlorn and shipwrecked brother,
Seeing, shall take heart again.

Let us, then, be up and doing,
With a heart for any fate;
Still achieving, still pursuing,
Learn to labor and to wait.

A VISIT FROM ST. NICHOLAS

Clement C. Moore

'Twas the night before Christmas, when all through the
    house
Not a creature was stirring, not even a mouse;
The stockings were hung by the chimney with care,
In hopes that St. Nicholas soon would be there;
The children were nestled all snug in their beds,
While visions of sugar-plums danced in their heads;
And mamma in her kerchief, and I in my cap,
Had just settled our brains for a long winter's nap,—
When out on the lawn there arose such a clatter,
I sprang from my bed to see what was the matter.
Away to the window I flew like a flash,
Tore open the shutters and threw up the sash.
The moon on the breast of the new-fallen snow
Gave a lustre of midday to objects below;
When, what to my wondering eyes should appear,
But a miniature sleigh and eight tiny reindeer,
With a little old driver, so lively and quick
I knew in a moment it must be St. Nick.
More rapid than eagles his coursers they came,
And he whistled and shouted, and called them by name:
"Now, Dasher! now, Dancer! now, Prancer and Vixen!
On, Comet! on, Cupid! on, Donder and Blitzen!
To the top of the porch, to the top of the wall!
Now dash away, dash away, dash away all!"
As dry leaves that before the wild hurricane fly,
When they meet with an obstacle, mount to the sky,
So up to the house-top the coursers they flew,
With the sleigh full of toys,—and St. Nicholas too.
And then in a twinkling I heard on the roof
The prancing and pawing of each little hoof.
As I drew in my head, and was turning around,
Down the chimney St. Nicholas came with a bound.
He was dressed all in fur from his head to his foot,
And his clothes were all tarnished with ashes and soot;
A bundle of toys he had flung on his back,
And he looked like a pedler just opening his pack.
His eyes how they twinkled! his dimples how merry!
His cheeks were like roses, his nose like a cherry;

His droll little mouth was drawn up like a bow,
And the beard on his chin was as white as the snow.
The stump of a pipe he held tight in his teeth,
And the smoke it encircled his head like a wreath.
He had a broad face and a little round belly
That shook, when he laughed, like a bowl full of jelly.
He was chubby and plump,—a right jolly old elf,
And I laughed, when I saw him, in spite of myself.
A wink of his eye and a twist of his head
Soon gave me to know I had nothing to dread.
He spoke not a word, but went straight to his work,
And filled all the stockings; then turned with a jerk,
And laying his finger aside of his nose,
And giving a nod, up the chimney he rose.
He sprang to his sleigh, to his team gave a whistle,
And away they all flew like the down of a thistle;
But I heard him exclaim, ere he drove out of sight,
"Happy Christmas to all, and to all a good-night!"

THE CONQUERED BANNER

Abram Joseph Ryan

Furl that Banner, for 'tis weary;
Round its staff 'tis drooping dreary;
Furl it, fold it, it is best;
For there's not a man to wave it,
And there's not a sword to save it,
And there's no one left to lave it
In the blood which heroes gave it;
And its foes now scorn and brave it;
Furl it, hide it—let it rest!

Take that Banner down! 'tis tattered;
Broken is its staff and shattered;
And the valiant hosts are scattered
Over whom it floated high.
Oh! 'tis hard for us to fold it;
Hard to think there's none to hold it;
Hard that those who once unrolled it
Now must furl it with a sigh.

Furl that Banner! furl it sadly!
Once ten thousand hailed it gladly,
And ten thousand wildly, madly,
Swore it should forever wave;
Swore that foeman's sword should never
Hearts like their entwined dissever,
Till that flag should float forever
O'er their freedom or their grave.

Furl it; for the hands that grasped it,
And the hearts that fondly clasped it,
Cold and dead are lying low;
And that Banner—it is trailing!
While around it sounds the wailing
Of its people in their woe.

For, though conquered, they adore it!
Love the cold, dead hands that bore it!
Weep for those who fell before it!
Pardon those who trailed and tore it!
But, oh! wildly they deplore it,
Now who furl and fold it so.

Furl that Banner! True, 'tis gory,
Yet 'tis wreathed around with glory,
And 'twill live in song and story,
Though its folds are in the dust:
For its fame on brightest pages,
Penned by poets and by sages,
Shall go sounding down the ages—
Furl its folds though now we must.

Furl that Banner, softly, slowly!
Treat it gently—it is holy—
For it droops above the dead.
Touch it not—unfold it never,
Let it droop there, furled forever,
For its peoples' hopes are dead!

* * *

One, with God, is always a majority, but
many a martyr has been burned at the stake
while the votes were being counted.
                    —Thomas B. Reed

FROM ABRAHAM LINCOLN'S
"HOUSE DIVIDED" SPEECH

If we could first know where we are, and whither we are tending, we could better judge what to do, and how to do it. We are now far into the fifth year since a policy was initiated with the avowed object and confident promise of putting an end to slavery agitation. Under the operation of that policy, that agitation has not only not ceased but has constantly augmented. In my opinion it will not cease until a crisis shall have been reached and passed. "A house divided against itself cannot stand." I believe this government cannot endure permanently, half-slave and half-free. I do not expect the Union to be dissolved,—I do not expect the house to fall—but I do expect it will cease to be divided. It will become all one thing, or all the other. Either the opponents of slavery will arrest the further spread of it, and place it where the public mind shall rest in the belief that it is in the course of ultimate extinction; or its advocates will push it forward till it shall become alike lawful in all the States, old as well as new, North as well as South.

(Springfield, Ill., June 17, 1858)

THE CURSE

(To A Sister Of An Enemy Of The Author's Who Disapproved Of "The Playboy")

J. M. Synge

Lord, confound this surly sister,
Blight her brow and blotch and blister,
Cramp her larynx, lung and liver,
In her guts a galling give her.

Let her live to earn her dinners
In Mountjoy with seedy sinners;
Lord, this judgment quickly bring,
And I'm your servant, J. M. Synge.

GUNGA DIN

Rudyard Kipling

You may talk o' gin and beer
When you're quartered safe out 'ere,
An' you're sent to penny-fights an' Aldershot it;
But when it comes to slaughter
You will do your work on water,
An' you'll lick the bloomin' boots of 'im that's got it.
Now in Injia's sunny clime,
Where I used to spend my time
A-servin' 'Er Majesty the Queen,
Of all them blackfaced crew
The finest man I knew
Was our regimental bhisti, Gunga Din.
     He was "Din! Din! Din!
  "You limpin' lump o' brick-dust, Gunga Din!
    "Hi! slippery *hitherao!*
    "Water, get it! *Panee lao!*
  "You squidgy-nosed old idol, Gunga Din."

The uniform 'e wore
Was nothin' much before,
An' rather less than 'arf o' that be'ind,
For a piece o' twisty rag
An' a goatskin water-bag
Was all the field-equipment 'e could find.
When the sweatin' troop-train lay
In a sidin' through the day,
Where the 'eat would make your bloomin' eyebrows crawl.
We shouted "Harry By!"
Till our throats were bricky-dry,
Then we wopped 'im 'cause 'e couldn't serve us all.
     It was "Din! Din! Din!
  "You 'eathen, where the mischief 'ave you been?
    "You put some *juldee* in it
    "Or I'll *marrow* you this minute
  "If you don't fill up my helmet, Gunga Din!"

'E would dot an' carry one
Till the longest day was done;
An' 'e didn't seem to know the use o' fear.

If we charged or broke or cut,
You could bet your bloomin' nut,
'E'd be waitin' fifty paces right flank rear.
With 'is mussick on 'is back,
'E would skip with our attack,
An' watch us till the bugles made "Retire"
An' for all 'is dirty 'ide
'E was white, clear white, inside
When 'e went to tend the wounded under fire!
     It was "Din! Din! Din!"
  With the bullets kickin' dust-spots on the green
    When the cartridges ran out,
    You could hear the front-ranks shout,
  "Hi! ammunition-mules an' Gunga Din!"

I shan't forgit the night
When I dropped be'ind the fight
With a bullet where my belt-plate should 'a' been.
I was chokin' mad with thirst,
An' the man that spied me first
Was our good old grinnin', gruntin' Gunga Din.
'E lifted up my 'ead,
An' he plugged me where I bled,
An' 'e guv me 'arf-a-pint of water green:
It was crawlin' and it stunk,
But of all the drinks I've drunk,
I'm gratefullest to one from Gunga Din.
     It was "Din! Din! Din!
  " 'Ere's a beggar with a bullet through 'is spleen;
   " 'E's chawin' up the ground,
   "An' 'e's kickin' all around:
  "For Gawd's sake git the water, Gunga Din!"

'E carried me away
To where a dooli lay,
An' a bullet come an' drilled the beggar clean.
'E put me safe inside,
An' just before he died,
"I 'ope you liked your drink," sez Gunga Din.
So I'll meet 'im later on
At the place where 'e is gone—
Where it's always double drill and no canteen;
'E'll be squattin' on the coals

Givin' drinks to poor damned souls,
An' I'll get a swig in hell from Gunga Din!
Yes, Din! Din! Din!
You Lazarushian-leather Gunga Din!
Though I've belted you and flayed you,
By the livin' Gawd that made you,
You're a better man than I am, Gunga Din!

JUST TELL THEM THAT YOU SAW ME

Paul Dresser

While strolling down the street one eve upon mere pleasure bent,
'Twas after business worries of the day,
I saw a girl who shrank from me in whom I recognized
My school mate in a village far away.
"Is that you, Madge?" I said to her. She quickly turned away.
"Don't turn away, Madge, I am still your friend.
Next week I'm going back to see the old folks and I thought
Perhaps some message you would like to send."

Chorus
　　"Just tell them that you saw me,"
　　She said; "they'll know the rest.
　　Just tell them I was looking well you know.
　　Just whisper if you get a chance to mother dear, and say
　　I love her as I did long, long ago."

"Your cheeks are pale, your face is thin, come tell me were you ill.
When last we met your eye shone clear and bright.
Come home with me when I go, Madge, the change will do you
　　good,
Your mother wonders where you are to-night!"
"I long to see them all again, but not just yet," she said.
" 'Tis pride alone that's keeping me away.
Just tell them not to worry, for I'm all right, don't you know,
Tell mother I am coming home some day."

THE LOST LEADER

Robert Browning

Just for a handful of silver he left us,
    Just for a riband to stick in his coat—
Found the one gift of which fortune bereft us,
    Lost all the others she lets us devote;
They, with the gold to give, doled him out silver,
    So much was theirs who so little allowed:
How all our copper had gone for his service!
    Rags—were they purple, his heart had been proud!
We that had loved him so, followed him, honored him,
    Lived in his mild and magnificent eye,
Learned his great language, caught his clear accents,
    Made him our pattern to live and to die!
Shakespeare was of us, Milton was for us,
    Burns, Shelley, were with us,—they watch from their graves!
He alone breaks from the van and the freemen,
    —He alone sinks to the rear and the slaves!

We shall march prospering,—not through his presence;
    Songs may inspirit us,—not from his lyre;
Deeds will be done,—while he boasts his quiescence,
    Still bidding crouch whom the rest bade aspire:
Blot out his name, then, record one lost soul more,
    One task more declined, one more footpath untrod,
One more devils'-triumph and sorrow for angels,
    One wrong more to man, one more insult to God!
Life's night begins: let him never come back to us!
    There would be doubt, hesitation and pain,
Forced praise on our part—the glimmer of twilight,
    Never glad confident morning again!
Best fight on well, for we taught him—strike gallantly,
    Menace our heart ere we master his own;
Then let him receive the new knowledge and wait us,
    Pardoned in heaven, the first by the throne!

DEMOCRACY

Abraham Lincoln

As I would not be a slave, so I would not be a master. This expresses
my idea of democracy. Whatever differs from this, to the extent of
the difference is no democracy.

THE NOBLEST ROMAN

William Shakespeare

This was the noblest Roman of them all:
All the conspirators, save only he,
Did that they did in envy of great Caesar;
He only, in a general honest thought
And common good to all, made one of them.
His life was gentle, and the elements
So mix'd in him that Nature might stand up
And say to all the world "This was a man!"
(From Julius Caesar)

THE SAD TALE OF MR. MEARS

Anonymous

There was a man who had a clock,
His name was Matthew Mears;
And every day he wound that clock
For eight and twenty years.

And then one day he found that clock
An eight-day clock to be;
And a madder man than Matthew Mears
You would not wish to see.

RENEWING FRIENDSHIP

Samuel Johnson

I have often thought, that as longevity is generally desired, and I believe, generally expected, it would be wise to be continually adding to the number of our friends, that the loss of some may be supplied by others. Friendship, "the vine of life," should, like a well-stocked cellar, be thus continually renewed.

* * *

Human history becomes more and more a race between education and catastrophe.
(H. G. Wells, 1920)

THE CHILDREN'S HOUR

Henry Wadsworth Longfellow

Between the dark and the daylight,
    When the night is beginning to lower,
Comes a pause in the day's occupations,
    That is known as the Children's Hour.

I hear in the chamber above me
    The patter of little feet,
The sound of a door that is opened,
    And voices soft and sweet.

From my study I see in the lamplight,
    Descending the broad hall stair,
Grave Alice, and laughing Allegra,
    And Edith with golden hair.

A whisper, and then a silence:
    Yet I know by their merry eyes
They are plotting and planning together
    To take me by surprise.

A sudden rush from the stairway,
    A sudden raid from the hall!
By three doors left unguarded
    They enter my castle wall!

They climb up into my turret
    O'er the arms and back of my chair;
If I try to escape, they surround me;
    They seem to be everywhere.

They almost devour me with kisses,
    Their arms about me entwine,
Till I think of the Bishop of Bingen
    In his Mouse-Tower on the Rhine!

Do you think, O blue-eyed banditti,
    Because you have scaled the wall,
Such an old mustache as I am
    Is not a match for you all!

I have you fast in my fortress,
  And will not let you depart,
But put you down into the dungeon
  In the round-tower of my heart.

And there will I keep you forever,
  Yes, forever and a day,
Till the walls shall crumble to ruin,
  And moulder in dust away!

OZYMANDIAS OF EGYPT

Percy Bysshe Shelley

I met a traveller from an antique land
Who said: Two vast and trunkless legs of stone
Stand in the desert . . . Near them, on the sand,
Half sunk, a shattered visage lies, whose frown,
And wrinkled lip, and sneer of cold command,
Tell that its sculptor well those passions read
Which yet survive, stamped on these lifeless things,
The hand that mocked them and the heart that fed:
And on the pedestal these words appear:
"My name is Ozymandias, king of kings:
Look on my works, ye Mighty, and despair!"
Nothing beside remains. Round the decay
Of that colossal wreck, boundless and bare,
The lone and level sands stretch far away.

TENDER-HEARTEDNESS

Harry Graham

Billy, in one of his nice new sashes,
Fell in the fire and was burnt to ashes;
Now, although the room grew chilly,
I haven't the heart to poke poor Billy.

* * *

A man who has committed a mistake and does not correct
it is committing another mistake.

—Confucius

"I TASTE A LIQUOR NEVER BREWED"

Emily Dickinson

I taste a liquor never brewed,
From tankards scooped in pearl;
Not all the vats upon the Rhine
Yield such an alcohol!

Inebriate of air am I,
And debauchee of dew,
Reeling, through endless summer days,
From inns of molten blue.

When landlords turn the drunken bee
Out of the foxglove's door,
When butterflies renounce their drams,
I shall but drink the more!

Till seraphs swing their snowy hats,
And saints to windows run,
To see the little tippler
Leaning against the sun!

*　　*　　*

She wears her clothes as if they were thrown on her with a pitch-fork.—Jonathan Swift

OUTWITTED

Edwin Markham

He drew a circle that shut me out—
Heretic, rebel, a thing to flout.
But Love and I had the wit to win;
We drew a circle that took him in!

PETER'S TEARS

Thomas Hood

After much dissension and strife,
Some wonder that Peter should weep for his wife;
But his tears on her grave are nothing surprising,
He's laying her dust, for fear of it rising.

A PEACEFUL LIFE, A LONG LIFE

Balthasar Gracian

To live, let live. Peacemakers not only live; they rule life. Hear,
see, and be silent. A day without dispute brings sleep without dreams.
Long life and a pleasant one is life enough for two: that is the fruit
of peace. He has all that makes nothing of what is nothing to him.
There is no greater perversity than to take everything to heart.
There is equal folly in troubling our heart about what does not
concern us and in not taking to heart what does.

MUSIC I HEARD

Conrad Aiken

Music I heard with you was more than music,
And bread I broke with you was more than bread;
Now that I am without you, all is desolate;
All that was once so beautiful is dead.

Your hands once touched this table and this silver
And I have seen your fingers hold this glass,
These things do not remember you, beloved,— .
And yet your touch upon them will not pass.

For it was in my heart you moved among them,
And blessed them with your hands and with your eyes;
And in my heart they will remember always,—
They knew you once, O beautiful and wise.

A DUTCH LULLABY

Eugene Field

Wynken, Blynken, and Nod one night
   Sailed off in a wooden shoe,—
Sailed on a river of crystal light
   Into a sea of dew.
"Where are you going, and what do you wish?"
   The old moon asked the three.
"We have come to fish for the herring fish
   That live in this beautiful sea;
   Nets of silver and gold have we!"
       Said Wynken,
       Blynken,
       And Nod.

The old moon laughed and sang a song,
   As they rocked in the wooden shoe;
And the wind that sped them all night long
   Ruffled the waves of dew.
The little stars were the herring fish
   That lived in that beautiful sea—
"Now cast your nets wherever you wish,—
   Never afeared are we!"
So cried the stars to the fishermen three,
       Wynken,
       Blynken,
       And Nod.

All night long their nets they threw
   To the stars in the twinkling foam,—
Then down from the skies came the wooden shoe,
   Bringing the fishermen home:
'Twas all so pretty a sail, it seemed
   As if it could not be;
And some folk thought 'twas a dream they'd dreamed
   Of sailing that beautiful sea;
   But I shall name you the fishermen three:
       Wynken,
       Blynken,
       And Nod.

Wynken and Blynken are two little eyes,
  And Nod is a little head,
And the wooden shoe that sailed the skies
  Is a wee one's trundle-bed;
So shut your eyes while Mother sings
  Of wonderful sights that be,
And you shall see the beautiful things
  As you rock in the misty sea
  Where the old shoe rocked the fishermen three:-
      Wynken,
      Blynken,
      And Nod.

CROSSING THE BAR

Alfred, Lord Tennyson

Sunset and evening star,
And one clear call for me!
And may there be no moaning of the bar,
When I put out to sea,

But such a tide as moving seems asleep,
Too full for sound and foam,
When that which drew from out the boundless deep
Turns again home.

Twilight and evening bell,
And after that the dark!
And may there be no sadness of farewell,
When I embark;

For tho' from out our bourne of Time and Place
The flood may bear me far,
I hope to see my Pilot face to face
When I have crossed the bar.

"SPEAK SOFTLY AND CARRY A BIG STICK"

Theodore Roosevelt

There is a homely adage which runs, "Speak softly and carry a big stick; you will go far." If the American nation will speak softly and yet build and keep at a pitch of the highest training a thoroughly efficient navy, the Monroe Doctrine will go far.

(1901)

BE NOT AFRAID OF LIFE

William James

These, then, are my last words to you: Be not afraid of life. Believe that life *is* worth living and your belief will help create the fact. The "scientific" proof that you are right may not be clear before the day of judgment (or some stage of being which that expression may serve to symbolize) is reached. But the faithful fighters of this hour, or the beings that then and there will represent them, may turn to the faint-hearted, who here decline to go on, with words like those with which Henry IV greeted the tardy Crillon after a great battle had been gained: "Hang yourself, brave Crillon! We fought at Arques, and you were not there!"

"HOW DO I LOVE THEE?"

Elizabeth Barrett Browning

How do I love thee? Let me count the ways.
I love thee to the depth and breadth and height
My soul can reach, when feeling out of sight
For the ends of Being and ideal Grace.
I love thee to the level of every day's
Most quiet need, by sun and candle-light.
I love thee freely, as men strive for Right;
I love thee purely, as men turn from Praise.
I love thee with the passion put to use
In my old griefs, and with my childhood's faith.
I love thee with a love I seemed to lose
With my lost saints,—I love thee with the breath,
Smiles, tears, of all my life!—and, if God choose,
I shall but love thee better after death.

(From Sonnets from the Portuguese)

SONG TO CELIA

Ben Jonson

Drink to me only with thine eyes,
    And I will pledge with mine;
Or leave a kiss but in the cup,
    And I'll not look for wine.

The thirst that from the soul doth rise
    Doth ask a drink divine;
But might I of Jove's nectar sup,
    I would not change for thine.

I sent thee late a rosy wreath,
    Not so much honoring thee
As giving it a hope, that there
    It could not withered be.
But thou thereon didst only breathe,
    And sent'st it back to me;
Since when it grows, and smells, I swear,
    Not of itself, but thee.

GIFTS

James Thompson

Give a man a horse he can ride,
Give a man a boat he can sail;
And his rank and wealth, his strength and health,
On sea nor shore shall fail.

Give a man a pipe he can smoke,
Give a man a book he can read:
And his home is bright with a calm delight,
Though the room be poor indeed.

Give a man a girl he can love,
As I, O my love, love thee;
And his heart is great with the pulse of Fate,
At home, on land, on sea.

IF—

Rudyard Kipling

If you can keep your head when all about you
Are losing theirs and blaming it on you;
If you can trust yourself when all men doubt you,
But make allowance for their doubting too;
If you can wait and not be tired by waiting,
Or being lied about, don't deal in lies,
Or, being hated, don't give way to hating,
And yet don't look too good, nor talk too wise;

If you can dream—and not make dreams your master
If you can think—and not make thoughts your aim;
If you can meet with triumph and disaster
And treat those two impostors just the same;
If you can bear to hear the truth you've spoken
Twisted by knaves to make a trap for fools,
Or watch the things you gave your life to, broken,
And stoop and build 'em up with wornout tools;

If you can make one heap of all your winnings
And risk it on one turn of pitch-and-toss,
And lose, and start again at your beginnings
And never breathe a word about your loss;
If you can force your heart and nerve and sinew
To serve your turn long after they are gone,
And so hold on when there is nothing in you
Except the Will which says to them: "Hold on";

If you can talk with crowds and keep your virtue,
Or walk with kings—nor lose the common touch;
If neither foes nor loving friends can hurt you;
If all men count with you, but none too much;
If you can fill the unforgiving minute
With sixty-seconds' worth of distance run—
Yours is the Earth and everything that's in it,
And—which is more—you'll be a Man, my son!

A WELCOME

Thomas O. Davis

Come in the evening, or come in the morning,
Come when you're looked for, or come without warning,
Kisses and welcomes you'll find here before you,
And the oftener you come here the more I'll adore you.

TAOISM

Lao Tzu

(TRANSLATOR: Lionel Giles)

When your work is done and fame has been achieved, then retire
into the background; for this is the Way of Heaven.

Those who follow the Way desire not excess; and thus without
excess they are for ever exempt from change.

All things alike do their work, and then we see them subside. When
they have reached their bloom, each returns to its origin. Returning
to their origin means rest or fulfilment of destiny. This reversion is
an eternal law. To know that law is to be enlightened. Not to know
it, is misery and calamity. He who knows the eternal law is liberal-
minded. Being liberal-minded, he is just. Being just, he is kingly.
Being kingly, he is akin to Heaven. Being akin to Heaven, he
possesses Tao. Possessed of Tao he endures for ever. Though his
body perish, yet he suffers no harm.

LIVES OF GREAT MEN

Anonymous

Lives of great men all remind us
As their pages o'er we turn,
That we're apt to leave behind us
Letters that we ought to burn.

POLLY WOLLY DOODLE

Anonymous

Oh, I went down South for to see my Sal,
Sing Polly-wolly-doodle all the day;
My Sally am a spunky girl,
Sing Polly-wolly-doodle all the day.
Fare thee well, fare thee well,
Fare thee well, my fairy fay,
For I'm going to Louisiana
For to see my Susyanna
Sing Polly-wolly-doodle all the day.

Oh, I came to a river, and I couldn't get across,
Sing Polly-wolly-doodle all the day;
So I jumped on a nigga' an' I thought he was a hoss.
Sing Polly-wolly-doodle all the day.

A grasshopper sitting on a railroad track,
Sing Polly-wolly-doodle all the day;
And picking his teeth with a carpet tack,
Sing Polly-wolly-doodle all the day.

Behind the barn down on my knees,
Sing Polly-wolly-doodle all the day,
I think I heard a chicken sneeze,
Sing Polly-wolly-doodle all the day.

He sneezed so hard with the whooping cough,
Sing Polly-wolly-doodle all the day,
He sneezed his head and his tail right off,
Sing Polly-wolly-doodle all the day.

* * *

Learning without wisdom is a load of books on an ass's back.
—Anonymous

TAKE BACK YOUR GOLD

Louis W. Paitzakow

I saw a youth and maiden on a lonely city street,
And thought them lovers at their meeting place;
Until, as I drew near, I heard the girl's sad voice entreat
The one who heeded not her tear-stained face.
"I only ask you, Jack, to do your duty, that is all,
You know you promised that we should be wed."
And when he said, "You shall not want, whatever may befall,"
She spurned the gold he offered her and said—

Chorus:

    "Take back your gold, for gold can never buy me;
    Take back your bribe and promise you'll be true;
    Give me the love, the love that you'd deny me;
    Make me your wife, that's all I ask of you."

He drew her close unto him and to soothe her then he tried,
But she in pride and sorrow turned away,
And as he sought to comfort her, she wept and softly sighed,
"You'll rue your cruel actions, Jack, some day."
"Now, little one, don't cry," he said, "for though tonight we part,
And though another soon will be my bride,
This gold will help you to forget"; but with a breaking heart,
She scorned his gift and bitterly replied: (*Chorus.*)

                 *   *   *

    Die when I may, I want it said by those who knew me best, that I always plucked a thistle and planted a flower where I thought a flower would grow.

                                     —Abraham Lincoln

RESOLUTION

Abraham Lincoln

I am not bound to win, but I am bound to be true. I am not bound to succeed but I am bound to live up to what light I have. I must stand with anybody that stands right: stand with him while he is right and part with him when he goes wrong.

THE PICTURE THAT IS TURNED TOWARD THE WALL

Charles Graham

Far away beyond the glamor of the city and its strife,
There's a quiet little homestead by the sea,
Where a tender loving lassie used to live a happy life
Contented in her home as she could be;
Not a shadow ever seemed to cloud the sunshine of her youth,
And they thought no sorrow could her life befall.
But she left them all one evening and their sad hearts knew the
     truth,
When her father turned her picture to the wall.

Chorus:
     There's a name that's never spoken and a mother's heart half
          broken,
     There is just another missing from the old home, that is all;
     There is still a memory living, there's a father unforgiving,
     And a picture that is turned toward the wall.

They have laid away each token of the one who ne'er returns,
Every trinket, every ribbon that she wore,
Though it seems so long ago now, yet the lamp of hope still burns,
And her mother prays to see her child once more,
Though no tidings ever reach them what her life or lot may be,
Though they sometimes think she's gone beyond recall,
There's a tender recollection of a face they never see,
In the picture that is turned toward the wall. (*Chorus.*)

O THOU WHO ART OUR AUTHOR AND OUR END

Sir John Beaumont

O Thou Who art our Author and our End,
On Whose large mercy chains of hope depend;
Lift me to Thee by Thy propitious hand:
For lower I can find no place to stand.

233

THE DIVINE OFFICE OF THE KITCHEN

God walks among the pots and pipkins—St. Teresa

Cecily Hallack

Lord of the pots and pipkins, I have no time to be
A saint by doing lovely things and vigiling with Thee,
By watching in the twilight dawn, and storming Heaven's gates,
Make me a saint by getting meals, and washing up the plates!

Lord of the pots and pipkins, please, I offer Thee my souls,
The tiresomeness of tea leaves, and the sticky porridge bowls!
Remind me of the things I need, not just to save the stairs,
But so that I may perfectly lay tables into prayers.

Accept my roughened hands because I made them so for Thee!
Pretend my dishmop is a bowl, which heavenly harmony
Makes on a fiddle frying pan; it is so hard to clean,
And, ah, so horrid! dear Lord, the music that I mean!

Although I must have Martha hands, I have a Mary mind,
And when I black the boots, I try Thy sandals, Lord, to find.
I think of how they trod our earth, what time I scrub the floor.
Accept this meditation when I haven't time for more!

Vespers and Compline come to pass by washing supper things.
And, mostly I am very tired; and all the heart that sings
About the morning's work, is gone, before me into bed.
Lend me, dear Lord, Thy Tireless Heart to work in me instead!

My matins are said overnight to praise and bless Thy Name
Beforehand for tomorrow's work, which will be just the same;
So that it seems I go to bed still in my working dress,
Lord make Thy Cinderella soon a heavenly Princess.

Warm all the kitchen with Thy Love and light it with Thy Peace!
Forgive the worrying, and make the grumbling words to cease.
Lord, who laid Breakfast on the shore, forgive the world which saith
"'Can any good thing come to God out of poor Nazareth?"

MOHAMMED AND THE MOUNTAIN

Francis Bacon

Mohammed indicated to the people that he would call a mountain to him, and from the top of it offer up his prayers for the observers of his law. The people assembled. Mohammed called the mountain to come to him, again and again; and when the mountain stood still he was never a whit abashed, but said, "If the mountain will not come to Mohammed, Mohammed will go to the mountain."

ENCOUNTERING GOD

Walt Whitman

Why should I wish to see God better than this day?
I see something of God each hour of the twenty-four,
    and each moment then,
In the faces of men and women I see God, and in my
    own face in the glass,
I find letters from God dropt in the street, and
    every one is sign'd by God's name,
And I leave them where they are, for I know that
    wheresoe'er I go,
Others will punctually come for ever and ever.

ABRIDGMENT OF FREEDOM

James Madison

I believe there are more instances of the abridgment of the freedom of the people by gradual and silent encroachments of those in power than by violent and sudden usurpations.

PAUL REVERE'S RIDE

Henry Wadsworth Longfellow

Listen, my children, and you shall hear
Of the midnight ride of Paul Revere,
On the eighteenth of April, in Seventy-five;
Hardly a man is now alive
Who remembers that famous day and year.

He said to his friend, "If the British march
By land or sea from the town tonight,
Hang a lantern aloft in the belfry arch
Of the North Church tower as a signal light,—
One, if by land, and two, if by sea;
And I on the opposite shore will be,
Ready to ride and spread the alarm
Through every Middlesex village and farm,
For the country folk to be up and to arm."

Then he said, "Good night!" and with muffled oar
Silently rowed to the Charlestown shore,
Just as the moon rose over the bay,
Where swinging wide at her moorings lay
The *Somerset*, British man-of-war;
A phantom ship, with each mast and spar
Across the moon like a prison bar,
And a huge black hulk, that was magnified
By its own reflection in the tide.

Meanwhile, his friend through alley and street
Wanders and watches, with eager ears,
Till in the silence around him he hears
The muster of men at the barrack door,
The sound of arms, and the tramp of feet,
And the measured tread of the grenadiers,
Marching down to their boats on the shore.

Then he climbed the tower of the Old North Church,
By the wooden stairs, with stealthy tread,
To the belfry-chamber overhead,
And startled the pigeons from their perch
On the sombre rafters, that round him made
Masses and moving shapes of shade,—

By the trembling ladder, steep and tall,
To the highest window in the wall,
Where he paused to listen and look down
A moment on the roofs of the town
And the moonlight flowing over all.

Beneath in the churchyard, lay the dead,
In their night-encampment on the hill,
Wrapped in silence so deep and still
That he could hear, like a sentinel's tread,
The watchful night-wind, as it went
Creeping along from tent to tent,
And seeming to whisper, "All is well!"
A moment only he feels the spell
Of the place and the hour, and the secret dread
Of the lonely belfry and the dead;
For suddenly all his thoughts are bent
On a shadowy something far away,
Where the river widens to meet the bay,—
A line of black that bends and floats
On the rising tide, like a bridge of boats.

Meanwhile, impatient to mount and ride,
Booted and spurred, with a heavy stride
On the opposite shore walked Paul Revere.
Now he patted his horse's side,
Now gazed at the landscape far and near,
Then, impetuous, stamped the earth,
And turned and tightened his saddle girth;
But mostly he watched with eager search
The belfry's tower of the Old North Church,
As it rose above the graves on the hill,
Lonely and spectral and sombre and still.
And lo! as he looks, on the belfry height
A glimmer, and then a gleam of light!
He springs to the saddle, the bridle he turns,
But lingers and gazes, till full on his sight
A second lamp in the belfry burns!

A hurry of hoofs in a village street,
A shape in the moonlight, a bulk in the dark,
And beneath, from the pebbles, in passing, a spark
Struck out by a steed flying fearless and fleet;

That was all! And yet, through the gloom and the light,
The fate of a nation was riding that night;
And the spark struck out by that steed, in his flight,
Kindled the land into flame with its heat.
He has left the village and mounted the steep,
And beneath him, tranquil and broad and deep,
Is the Mystic, meeting the ocean tides;
And under the alders that skirt its edge,
Now soft on the sand, now loud on the ledge,
Is heard the tramp of his steed as he rides.

It was twelve by the village clock,
When he crossed the bridge into Medford town.
He heard the crowing of the cock,
And the barking of the farmer's dog,
And he felt the damp of the river fog,
That rises after the sun goes down.

It was one by the village clock,
When he galloped into Lexington.
He saw the gilded weathercock
Swim in the moonlight as he passed,
And the meeting-house windows, blank and bare,
Gaze at him with a spectral glare,
As if they already stood aghast
At the bloody work they would look upon.

It was two by the village clock,
When he came to the bridge in Concord town.
He heard the bleating of the flock,
And the twitter of birds among the trees,
And felt the breath of the morning breeze
Blowing over the meadows brown.
And one was safe and asleep in his bed
Who at the bridge would be first to fall,
Who that day would be lying dead,
Pierced by a British musket-ball.

You know the rest. In books you have read,
How the British Regulars fired and fled,—
How the farmers gave them ball for ball,
From behind each fence and farmyard wall,
Chasing the redcoats down the lane,

Then crossing the fields to emerge again
Under the trees at the turn of the road,
And only pausing to fire and load.

So through the night rode Paul Revere;
And so through the night went his cry of alarm
To every Middlesex village and farm,—
A cry of defiance, and not of fear,
A voice in the darkness, a knock at the door,
And a word that shall echo for evermore!
For, borne on the night-wind of the Past,
Through all our history, to the last,
In the hour of darkness and peril and need,
The people will waken and listen to hear
The hurrying hoof-beats of that steed,
And the midnight message of Paul Revere.

WHAT YOU ARE SEEKING IS HERE

Horace

Whatever hour God has given for your weal, take it with grateful hand nor put off joys from year to year; so that in whatever place you have been you may say that you have lived happily. For if 'tis reason and wisdom that takes away cares and not a site commanding a wide expanse of sea, they change their clime, not their mind, who rush across the sea. 'Tis a busy idleness that is our bane; with yachts and cars we seek to make life happy. What you are seeking is here.

THE MAN WITH THE HOE

Edwin Markham

Written after seeing Millet's world-famous painting of
a brutalized toiler.
*God made man in his own image, in the image of God
made he him.*—Genesis.

Bowed by the weight of centuries he leans
Upon his hoe and gazes on the ground,
The emptiness of ages in his face,
And on his back the burden of the world.
Who made him dead to rapture and despair,
A thing that grieves not and that never hopes,
Stolid and stunned, a brother to the ox?
Who loosened and let down this brutal jaw?
Whose was the hand that slanted back this brow?
Whose breath blew out the light within this brain?

Is this the Thing the Lord God made and gave
To have dominion over sea and land;
To trace the stars and search the heavens for power;
To feel the passion of Eternity?
Is this the dream He dreamed who shaped the suns
And marked their ways upon the ancient deep?
Down all the caverns of Hell to their last gulf
There is no shape more terrible than this—
More tongued with censure of the world's blind greed—
More filled with signs and portents for the soul—
More packt with danger to the universe.

What gulfs between him and the seraphim!
Slave of the wheel of labor, what to him
Are Plato and the swing of Pleiades?
What the long reaches of the peaks of song,
The rift of dawn, the reddening of the rose?
Thru this dread shape the suffering ages look;
Time's tragedy is in that aching stoop;
Thru this dread shape humanity betrayed,
Plundered, profaned and disinherited,
Cries protest to the Judges of the world,
A protest that is also prophecy.

O masters, lords and rulers in all lands,
Is this the handiwork you give to God,
This monstrous thing distorted and soul-quenched?
How will you ever straighten up this shape;
Touch it again with immortality;
Give back the upward looking and the light;
Rebuild in it the music and the dream;
Make right the immemorial infamies,
Perfidious wrongs, immedicable woes?

O masters, lords and rulers in all lands,
How will the Future reckon with this Man?
How answer his brute question in that hour
When whirlwinds of rebellion shake all shores?
How will it be with kingdoms and with kings—
With those who shaped him to the thing he is—
When this dumb Terror shall rise to judge the world,
After the silence of the centuries?

KASHMIRI SONG

Laurence Hope

Pale hands I love beside the Shalimar,
   Where are you now? Who lies beneath your spell?
Whom do you lead on Rapture's Roadway, far,
   Before you agonize them in farewell?

Or, pale dispensers of my Joys and Pains,
   Holding the doors of Heaven and of Hell,
How the hot blood rushed wildly through the veins
   Beneath your touch, until you waved farewell.

Pale hands, pink-tipped, like Lotus buds that float
   On those cool waters where we used to dwell,
I would have rather felt you round my throat
   Crushing out life than waving me farewell!

OUT WHERE THE WEST BEGINS

Arthur Chapman

Out where the handclasp's a little stronger,
Out where the smile dwells a little longer,
That's where the West begins;
Out where the sun is a little brighter,
Where the snows that fall are a trifle whiter,
Where the bonds of home are a wee bit tighter,—
That's where the West begins.

Out where the skies are a trifle bluer,
Out where friendship's a little truer,
That's where the West begins;
Out where a fresher breeze is blowing,
Where there's laughter in every streamlet flowing,
Where there's more of reaping and less of sowing,—
That's where the West begins.

Out where the world is in the making,
Where fewer hearts in despair are aching,
That's where the West begins;
Where there's more of singing and less of sighing,
Where there's more of giving and less of buying,
And a man makes friends without half trying—
That's where the West begins.

* * *

Here lies my wife; here let her lie!
Now she's at rest, and so am I.
                    —John Dryden

EPIGRAM

Sir William Watson

'Tis human fortune's happiest height, to be
    A spirit melodious, lucid, poised, and whole;
Second in order of felicity
    I hold it, to have walk'd with such a soul.

THE RAVEN

Edgar Allan Poe

Once upon a midnight dreary, while I pondered, weak and weary,
Over many a quaint and curious volume of forgotten lore—
While I nodded, nearly napping, suddenly there came a tapping,
As of some one gently rapping, rapping at my chamber door.
" 'Tis some visitor," I muttered, "tapping at my chamber door:
  Only this, and nothing more."

Ah, distinctly I remember, it was in the bleak December,
And each separate dying ember wrought its ghost upon the floor.
Eagerly I wished the morrow; vainly I had sought to borrow
From my books surcease of sorrow—sorrow for the lost Lenore—
For the rare and radiant maiden whom the angels named Lenore—
  Nameless here for evermore.

And the silken, sad, uncertain rustling of each purple curtain,
Thrilled me—filled me with fantastic terrors never felt before;
So that now, to still the beating of my heart, I stood repeating,
" 'Tis some visitor entreating entrance at my chamber door—
Some late visitor entreating entrance at my chamber door:
  This it is, and nothing more."

Presently my soul grew stronger: hesitating then no longer,
"Sir," said I, "or Madam, truly your forgiveness I implore;
But the fact is, I was napping, and so gently you came rapping,
And so faintly you came tapping, tapping at my chamber door,
That I scarce was sure I heard you"—here I opened wide the
  door;—
  Darkness there, and nothing more!

Deep into that darkness peering, long I stood there, wondering,
  fearing,
Doubting, dreaming dreams no mortal ever dared to dream before;
But the silence was unbroken, and the darkness gave no token,
And the only word there spoken was the whispered word, "Le-
  nore!"
This I whispered, and an echo murmured back the word "Le-
  nore!"
  Merely this, and nothing more.

Back into the chamber turning, all my soul within me burning,
Soon again I heard a tapping, somewhat louder than before.

"Surely," said I, "surely that is something at my window-lattice;
Let me see then what thereat is, and this mystery explore—
Let my heart be still a moment, and this mystery explore;—
        'Tis the wind, and nothing more!"

Open here I flung the shutter, when, with many a flirt and flutter,
In there stepped a stately Raven of the saintly days of yore.
Not the least obeisance made he; not an instant stopped or stayed
    he;
But, with mien of lord or lady, perched above my chamber door—
Perched upon a bust of Pallas, just above my chamber door—
        Perched, and sat, and nothing more.

Then this ebony bird beguiling my sad fancy into smiling,
By the grave and stern decorum of the countenance it wore,
"Though thy crest be shorn and shaven, thou," I said, "art sure no
    craven,
Ghastly, grim, and ancient Raven, wandering from the nightly
    shore!
Tell me what thy lordly name is on the night's Plutonian shore!"
        Quoth the Raven, "Nevermore!"

Much I marveled this ungainly fowl to hear discourse so plainly,
Though its answer little meaning—little relevancy bore:
For we cannot help agreeing that no living human being
Ever yet was blessed with seeing bird above his chamber door—
Bird or beast upon the sculptured bust above his chamber door,
        With such name as "Nevermore!"

But the Raven, sitting lonely on the placid bust, spoke only
That one word, as if his soul in that one word he did outpour.
Nothing further then he uttered—not a feather then he fluttered—
Till I scarcely more than muttered, "Other friends have flown be-
    fore—
On the morrow *he* will leave me, as my hopes have flown before."
        Then the bird said, "Nevermore!"

Startled at the stillness broken by reply so aptly spoken,
"Doubtless," said I, "what it utters is its only stock and store,
Caught from some unhappy master, whom unmerciful Disaster
Followed fast and followed faster, till his songs one burden bore—
Till the dirges of his Hope one melancholy burden bore
        Of 'Never—nevermore.' "

But the Raven still beguiling all my sad soul into smiling,
Straight I wheeled a cushioned seat in front of bird, and bust, and
door;
Then, upon the velvet sinking, I betook myself to linking
Fancy unto fancy, thinking what this ominous bird of yore—
What this grim, ungainly, ghastly, gaunt, and ominous bird of
yore—
Meant in croaking "Nevermore!"

This I sat engaged in guessing, but no syllable expressing
To the fowl whose fiery eyes now burned into my bosom's core;
This and more I sat divining, with my head at ease reclining
On the cushion's velvet lining that the lamplight gloated o'er,
But whose velvet violet lining, with the lamplight gloating o'er,
She shall press, ah! nevermore!

Then methought the air grew denser, perfumed from an unseen
censer,
Swung by seraphim, whose footfalls tinkled on the tufted floor.
"Wretch," I cried, "thy God hath lent thee—by these angels he
hath sent thee
Respite—respite and nepenthe from the memories of Lenore!
Quaff, Oh, quaff this kind nepenthe, and forget this lost Lenore!"
Quoth the raven, "Nevermore!"

"Prophet!" said I, "thing of evil!—prophet still, if bird or devil!
Whether tempter sent, or whether tempest tossed thee here ashore,
Desolate yet all undaunted, on this desert land enchanted—
On this home by horrors haunted—tell me truly, I implore—
Is there—*is* there balm in Gilead?—tell me—tell me, I implore!"
Quoth the raven, "Nevermore!"

"Prophet!" said I, "thing of evil!—prophet still, if bird or devil!
By that heaven that bends above us—by that God we both adore,
Tell this soul with sorrow laden if, within the distant Aidenn,
It shall clasp a sainted maiden, whom the angels name Lenore—
Clasp a fair and radiant maiden, whom the angels named Lenore!"
Quoth the raven, "Nevermore!"

"Be that word our sign of parting, bird or fiend!" I shrieked, up-
starting—
"Get thee back into the tempest and the night's Plutonian shore!
Leave no black plume as a token of that lie thy soul hath spoken!
Leave my loneliness unbroken!—quit the bust above my door!

Take thy beak from out my heart, and take thy form from off my
    door!"
            Quoth the raven, "Nevermore!"

And the raven, never flitting, still is sitting, still is sitting
On the pallid bust of Pallas, just above my chamber door;
And his eyes have all the seeming of a demon that is dreaming,
And the lamplight o'er him streaming throws his shadow on the
    floor;
And my soul from out that shadow that lies floating on the floor
            Shall be lifted—*nevermore!*

INSCRIPTION ON GENERAL POST OFFICE, NEW YORK, N. Y.

**Neither Snow, Nor Rain, Nor Heat, Nor Gloom
of Night Stops These Couriers From the
Swift Completion of Their Appointed Rounds.**
                        (From Herodotus)

WHITE HOUSE BLESSING*

John Adams

I pray Heaven to bestow the best of blessings on this house, and
all that shall hereafter inhabit it. May none but honest and wise men
ever rule under this roof.

                (In a letter from the White House, 1800.)

* Engraved on the fireplace of the White House State Dining Room by President Franklin D. Roosevelt.

THE WRECK OF THE HESPERUS

Henry Wadsworth Longfellow

It was the schooner Hesperus,
That sailed the wintry sea;
And the skipper had taken his little daughter,
To bear him company.

Blue were her eyes as the fairy flax,
Her cheeks like the dawn of day,
And her bosom white as the hawthorn buds
That ope in the month of May.

The skipper he stood beside the helm,
His pipe was in his mouth,
And he watched how the veering flaw did blow
The smoke now West, now South.

Then up and spake an old Sailor,
Had sailed to the Spanish Main,
"I pray thee, put into yonder port,
For I fear a hurricane.

"Last night, the moon had a golden ring,
And to-night no moon we see!"
The skipper, he blew a whiff from his pipe,
And a scornful laugh laughed he.

Colder and louder blew the wind,
A gale from the Northeast;
The snow fell hissing in the brine,
And the billows frothed like yeast.

Down came the storm, and smote amain
The vessel in its strength;
She shuddered and paused, like a frightened steed,
Then leaped her cable's length.

"Come hither! come hither! my little daughter,
And do not tremble so;
For I can weather the roughest gale
That ever wind did blow."

He wrapped her warm in his seaman's coat
Against the stinging blast;
He cut a rope from a broken spar,
And bound her to the mast.

"O father! I hear the church-bells ring,
Oh say, what may it be?"
" 'Tis a fog-bell on a rock-bound coast!"
And he steered for the open sea.

"O father! I hear the sound of guns,
Oh say, what may it be?"
"Some ship in distress, that cannot live
In such an angry sea!"

"O father! I see a gleaming light,
Oh say, what may it be?"
But the father answered never a word,—
A frozen corpse was he.

Lashed to the helm, all stiff and stark,
With his face turned to the skies,
The lantern gleamed through the gleaming snow
On his fixed and glassy eyes.

Then the maiden clasped her hands and prayed
That saved she might be;
And she thought of Christ, who stilled the waves
On the Lake of Galilee.

And fast through the midnight dark and drear,
Through the whistling sleet and snow,
Like a sheeted ghost, the vessel swept
Towards the reef of Norman's Woe.

And ever the fitful gusts between
A sound came from the land;
It was the sound of the trampling surf,
On the rocks and the hard sea-sand.

The breakers were right beneath her bows,
She drifted a dreary wreck,
And a whooping billow swept the crew
Like icicles from her deck.

She struck where the white and fleecy waves
Looked soft as carded wool,
But the cruel rocks, they gored her side
Like the horns of an angry bull.

Her rattling shrouds, all sheathed in ice,
With the masts went by the board;
Like a vessel of glass, she stove and sank,
Ho! Ho! the breakers roared!

At daybreak, on the bleak sea-beach,
A fisherman stood aghast,
To see the form of a maiden fair,
Lashed close to a drifting mast!

The salt sea was frozen on her breast,
The salt tears in her eyes;
And he saw her hair, like the brown sea-weed,
On the billows fall and rise.

Such was the wreck of the Hesperus,
In the midnight and the snow!
Christ save us all from a death like this,
On the reef of Norman's Woe!

"MY YOKE IS EASY"

Holy Bible, Matthew 11:28–30

Come unto me, all ye that labour and are heavy laden, and I
will give you rest. Take my yoke upon you, and learn of me; for I
am meek and lowly in heart; and ye shall find rest unto your souls.
For my yoke is easy, and my burden is light.

THE LAST LEAF

Oliver Wendell Holmes

I saw him once before,
As he passed by the door,
   And again
The pavement stones resound
As he totters o'er the ground
   With his cane.

They say that in his prime,
Ere the pruning-knife of Time
   Cut him down,
Not a better man was found
By the crier on his round
   Through the town.

But now he walks the streets,
And he looks at all he meets
   Sad and wan,
And he shakes his feeble head,
That it seems as if he said,
   "They are gone."

The mossy marbles rest
On the lips that he has pressed
   In their bloom,

And the names he loved to hear
Have been carved for many a year
   On the tomb.

My grandmamma has said—
Poor old lady, she is dead
   Long ago—
That he had a Roman nose,
And his cheek was like a rose
   In the snow.

But now his nose is thin,
And it rests upon his chin
    Like a staff,
And a crook is in his back,
And a melancholy crack
    In his laugh.

I know it is a sin
For me to sit and grin
    At him here;
But the old three-cornered hat,
And the breeches, and all that,
    Are so queer!

And if I should live to be
The last leaf upon the tree
    In the spring,
Let them smile, as I do now,
At the old forsaken bough
    Where I cling.

SEA FEVER

John Masefield

I must go down to the seas again, to the lonely sea and the sky,
And all I ask is a tall ship and a star to steer her by,
And the wheel's kick and the wind's song and the white sail's
    shaking,
And a gray mist on the sea's face, and a gray dawn breaking.

I must go down to the seas again, for the call of the running tide
Is a wild call and a clear call that may not be denied;
And all I ask is a windy day with the white clouds flying,
And the flung spray and the blown spume, and the sea-gulls crying.

I must go down to the seas again, to the vagrant gypsy life,
To the gull's way and the whale's way, where the wind's like a
    whetted knife;
And all I ask is a merry yarn from a laughing fellow-rover,
And quiet sleep and a sweet dream when the long trick's over.

LIGHT SHINING OUT OF DARKNESS

William Cowper

God moves in a mysterious way
   His wonders to perform;
He plants his footsteps in the sea,
   And rides upon the storm.

Deep in unfathomable mines
   Of never-failing skill
He treasures up his bright designs,
   And works his sovereign will.

Ye fearful saints, fresh courage take!
   The clouds ye so much dread
Are big with mercy, and shall break
   In blessings on your head.

Judge not the Lord by feeble sense,
   But trust him for his grace;
Behind a frowning providence
   He hides a smiling face.

His purposes will ripen fast,
   Unfolding every hour;
The bud may have a bitter taste,
   But sweet will be the flower.

Blind unbelief is sure to err,
   And scan his work in vain;
God is his own interpreter,
   And he will make it plain.

NON SUM QUALIS ERAM BONAE SUB REGNO CYNARAE

Ernest Dowson

Last night, ah, yesternight, betwixt her lips and mine
There fell thy shadow, Cynara! thy breath was shed
Upon my soul between the kisses and the wine;
And I was desolate and sick of an old passion,
    Yea, I was desolate and bowed my head:
I have been faithful to thee, Cynara! in my fashion.

All night upon mine heart I felt her warm heart beat,
Night-long within mine arms in love and sleep she lay;
Surely the kisses of her bought red mouth were sweet;
But I was desolate and sick of an old passion,
    When I awoke and found the dawn was grey:
I have been faithful to thee, Cynara! in my fashion.

I have forgot much, Cynara! gone with the wind,
Flung roses, roses riotously with the throng,
Dancing, to put thy pale, lost lilies out of mind;
But I was desolate and sick of an old passion,
    Yea, all the time, because the dance was long:
I have been faithful to thee, Cynara! in my fashion.

I cried for madder music and for stronger wine,
But when the feast is finished and the lamps expire,
Then falls thy shadow, Cynara! the night is thine;
And I am desolate and sick of an old passion,
    Yea, hungry for the lips of my desire:
I have been faithful to thee, Cynara! in my fashion.

DUTY

Ralph Waldo Emerson

So nigh is grandeur to our dust,
So near is God to man,
When Duty whispers low, "Thou must,"
The youth replies, "I can."

LANDING OF THE PILGRIM FATHERS

Felicia Dorothea Hemans

The breaking waves dashed high
On a stern and rock-bound coast;
And the woods against a stormy sky,
Their giant branches tossed;
And the heavy night hung dark
The hills and waters o'er—
When a band of exiles moored their bark
On a wild New England shore.

Not as the conqueror comes,
They, the true-hearted, came;—
Not with the roll of stirring drums,
And the trumpets that sing of fame;—
Not as the flying come,
In silence and in fear;
They shook the depths of the desert's gloom
With their hymns of lofty cheer.

Amidst the storm they sang,
And the stars heard, and the sea!
And the sounding aisles of the dim woods rang
To the anthem of the free;
The ocean eagle soared
From his nest by the white wave's foam,
And the rocking pines of the forest roared:—
This was their welcome home!

There were men with hoary hair
Amidst that pilgrim band;
Why had they come to wither there,
Away from their childhood's land?
There was woman's fearless eye,
Lit by her deep love's truth;
There was manhood's brow serenely high,
And the fiery heart of youth.

What sought they thus afar?
Bright jewels of the mine?
The wealth of seas? the spoils of war?
They sought a faith's pure shrine!

Ay, call it holy ground,
The soil where first they trod!
They left unstained what there they found
Freedom to worship God!

THE LAMB

William Blake

Little lamb, who made thee?
Dost thou know who made thee,
Gave thee life and bade thee feed
By the stream and o'er the mead;
Gave thee clothing of delight,
Softest clothing, woolly, bright;
Gave thee such a tender voice,
Making all the vales rejoice?
    Little lamb, who made thee?
    Dost thou know who made thee?

Little lamb, I'll tell thee;
Little lamb, I'll tell thee.
He is callèd by thy name,
For He calls himself a Lamb;
He is meek and He is mild,
He became a little child.
I a child and thou a lamb,
We are callèd by His name.
    Little lamb, God bless thee!
    Little lamb, God bless thee!

LOVE ONE ANOTHER

Holy Bible, John 13:33–35

Little children, yet a little while I am with you. Ye shall seek me: and as I said unto the Jews, Whither I go, ye cannot come: so now I say to you.

A new commandment I give unto you, That ye love one another; as I have loved you, that ye also love one another.

By this shall all men know that ye are my disciples, if ye love one to another.

THE CLOUD

Percy Bysshe Shelley

I bring fresh showers for the thirsting flowers,
    From the seas and the streams;
I bear light shade for the leaves when laid
    In their noonday dreams.
From my wings are shaken the dews that waken
    The sweet buds every one,
When rocked to rest on their mother's breast,
    As she dances about the sun.
I wield the flail of the lashing hail,
    And whiten the green plains under,
And then again I dissolve it in rain,
    And laugh as I pass in thunder.

I sift the snow on the mountains below,
    And their great pines groan aghast,
And all the nights 'tis my pillow white,
    While I sleep in the arms of the blast.
Sublime on the towers of my skiey bowers,
    Lightning, my pilot, sits,
In a cavern under is fettered the thunder,
    It struggles and howls at fits;
Over earth and ocean, with gentle motion,
    This pilot is guiding me,
Lured by the love of the genii that move
    In the depths of the purple sea;
Over the rills, and the crags, and the hills,
    Over the lakes and the plains,
Wherever he dream, under mountain or stream,
    The Spirit he loves remains;
And I all the while bask in heaven's blue smile,
    Whilst he is dissolving in rains.

The sanguine sunrise, with his meteor eyes,
    And his burning plumes outspread,
Leaps on the back of my sailing rack,
    When the morning star shines dead,
As on the jag of a mountain crag,
    Which an earthquake rocks and swings,

An eagle alit one moment may sit
   In the light of its golden wings.
And when sunset may breathe, from the lit sea beneath,
   Its ardours of rest and of love,
And the crimson pall of eve may fall
   From the depth of heaven above,
With wings folded I rest, on mine airy nest,
   As still as a brooding dove.

That orbèd maiden with white fire laden,
   Whom mortals call the moon,
Glides glimmering o'er my fleece-like floor,
   By the midnight breezes strewn:
And wherever the beat of her unseen feet,
   Which only the angels hear,
May have broken the woof of my tent's thin roof,
   The stars peep behind her and peer;
And I laugh to see them whirl and flee,
   Like a swarm of golden bees,
When I widen the rent in my wind-built tent,
   Till the calm rivers, lakes, and seas,
Like strips of the sky fallen through me on high,
   Are each paved with the moon and these.

I bind the sun's throne with a burning zone,
   And the moon's with a girdle of pearl;
The volcanoes are dim, and the stars reel and swim,
   When the whirlwinds my banner unfurl.
From cape to cape, with a bridge-like shape,
   Over a torrent sea,
Sunbeam-proof, I hang like a roof,
   The mountains its columns be.
The triumphal arch through which I march
   With hurricane, fire, and snow,
When the powers of the air are chained to my chair,
   Is the million-coloured bow;
The sphere-fire above its soft colours wove,
   While the moist earth was laughing below.

I am the daughter of earth and water,
   And the nursling of the sky;
I pass through the pores of the ocean and shores;
   I change, but I cannot die.

For after the rain, when with never a stain
    The pavilion of heaven is bare,
And the winds and sunbeams, with their convex gleams,
    Build up the blue dome of air,
I silently laugh at my own cenotaph,
    And out of the caverns of rain,
Like a child from the womb, like a ghost from the tomb,
    I arise and unbuild it again.

NOT BY BREAD ALONE

James Terry White

If thou of fortune be bereft,
And thou dost find but two loaves left
To thee—sell one, and with the dole
Buy hyacinths to feed thy soul.

But not alone does beauty bide
Where bloom and tint and fragrance hide;
The minstrel's melody may feed
Perhaps a more insistent need.

But even beauty, howe'er blent
To ear and eye, fails to content;
Only the heart, with love afire,
Can satisfy the soul's desire.
                    (From *The Greek Anthology*)

"THE CRIME OF BEING A YOUNG MAN"

William Pitt

The atrocious crime of being a young man, which the honourable gentleman has, with such spirit and decency charged upon me, I shall neither attempt to palliate nor deny; but content myself with wishing that I may be one of those whose follies may cease with their youth, and not of those who continue ignorant in spite of age and experience.
            (From a speech, March 3, 1741, in reply to Walpole)

SILVER

Walter de la Mare

Slowly, silently, now the moon
Walks the night in her silver shoon;
This way, and that, she peers, and sees
Silver fruit upon silver trees;
One by one the casements catch
Her beams beneath the silvery thatch;
Couched in his kennel, like a log,
With paws of silver sleeps the dog;
From their shadowy cote the white breasts peep
Of doves in a silver-feathered sleep;
A harvest mouse goes scampering by,
With silver claws and a silver eye;
And moveless fish in the water gleam,
By silver reeds in a silver stream.

CASABIANCA

Felicia Dorothea Hemans

In the battle of the Nile, thirteen-year-old Casabianca,
son of the Admiral of the Orient, remained at his post
after the ship had taken fire and all the guns had been
abandoned. He perished when the vessel exploded.

The boy stood on the burning deck,
Whence all but he had fled;
The flame that lit the battle's wreck,
Shone round him o'er the dead.

Yet beautiful and bright he stood,
As born to rule the storm;
A creature of heroic blood,
A proud though childlike form.

The flames rolled on; he would not go
Without his father's word;
That father, faint in death below,
His voice no longer heard.

259

He called aloud, "Say, Father, say,
If yet my task is done!"
He knew not that the chieftain lay
Unconscious of his son.

"Speak, Father!" once again he cried,
"If I may yet be gone!"
—And but the booming shots replied,
And fast the flames rolled on.

Upon his brow he felt their breath,
And in his waving hair;
And looked from that lone post of death
In still yet brave despair;

And shouted but once more aloud,
"My Father! must I stay?"
While o'er him fast, through sail and shroud,
The wreathing fires made way.

They wrapt the ship in splendor wild,
They caught the flag on high,
And streamed above the gallant child,
Like banners in the sky.

There came a burst of thunder sound;
The boy—Oh! where was *he?*
—Ask of the winds, that far around
With fragments strewed the sea;—

With shroud, and mast, and pennon fair,
That well had borne their part,—
But the noblest thing that perished there
Was that young, faithful heart.

* * *

Speech is the index of the mind.
                                    —Seneca

TRY, TRY AGAIN

Anonymous

'Tis a lesson you should heed,
    Try, try again;
If at first you don't succeed,
    Try, try again;
Then your courage should appear,
For, if you will persevere,
You will conquer, never fear;
    Try, try again.

Once or twice though you should fail,
    Try, try again;
If you would at last prevail,
    Try, try again;
If we strive, 'tis no disgrace
Though we do not win the race;
What should you do in the case?
    Try, try again.

THE BALLAD OF READING GAOL

Oscar Wilde

I

He did not wear his scarlet coat,
    For blood and wine are red,
And blood and wine were on his hands
    When they found him with the dead,
The poor dead woman whom he loved,
    And murdered in her bed.

He walked amongst the Trial Men
    In a suit of shabby gray;
A cricket cap was on his head,
    And his step seemed light and gay;
But I never saw a man who looked
    So wistfully at the day.

I never saw a man who looked
   With such a wistful eye
Upon that little tent of blue
   Which prisoners call the sky,
And at every drifting cloud that went
   With sails of silver by.

I walked, with other souls in pain,
   Within another ring,
And was wondering if the man had done
   A great or little thing,
When a voice behind me whispered low,
"That fellow's got to swing."

Dear Christ! the very prison walls
   Suddenly seemed to reel,
And the sky above my head became
   Like a casque of scorching steel;
And, though I was a soul in pain,
   My pain I could not feel.

I only knew what hunted thought
   Quickened his step, and why
He looked upon the garish day
   With such a wistful eye;
The man had killed the thing he loved,
   And so he had to die.

Yet each man kills the thing he loves,
   By each let this be heard,
Some do it with a bitter look,
   Some with a flattering word,
The coward does it with a kiss,
   The brave man with a sword!

Some kill their love when they are young,
   And some when they are old;
Some strangle with the hands of Lust,
   Some with the hands of Gold:
The kindest use a knife, because
   The dead so soon grow cold.

Some love too little, some too long,
　　Some sell, and others buy;
Some do the deed with many tears,
　　And some without a sigh:
For each man kills the thing he loves,
　　Yet each man does not die.

He does not die a death of shame
　　On a day of dark disgrace,
Nor have a noose about his neck,
　　Nor a cloth upon his face,
Nor drop feet foremost through the floor
　　Into an empty space.

He does not sit with silent men
　　Who watch him night and day;
Who watch him when he tries to weep,
　　And when he tries to pray;
Who watch him lest himself should rob
　　The prison of its prey.

He does not wake at dawn to see
　　Dread figures throng his room,
The shivering Chaplain robed in white,
　　The Sheriff stern with gloom,
And the Governor all in shiny black,
　　With the yellow face of Doom.

He does not rise in piteous haste
　　To put on convict-clothes,
While some coarse-mouthed Doctor gloats, and notes
　　Each new and nerve-twitched pose,
Fingering a watch whose little ticks
　　Are like horrible hammer-blows.

He does not know that sickening thirst
　　That sands one's throat, before
The hangman with his gardener's gloves
　　Slips through the padded door,
And binds one with three leathern thongs
　　That the throat may thirst no more.

He does not bend his head to hear
   The Burial Office read,
Nor, while the terror of his soul
   Tells him he is not dead,
Cross his own coffin, as he moves
   Into the hideous shed.

He does not stare upon the air
   Through a little roof of glass:
He does not pray with lips of clay
   For his agony to pass;
Nor feel upon his shuddering cheek
   The kiss of Caiaphas.

II

Six weeks our guardsman walked the yard
   In the suit of shabby gray:
His cricket cap was on his head,
   And his step seemed light and gay,
But I never saw a man who looked
   So wistfully at the day.

I never saw a man who looked
   With such a wistful eye
Upon that little tent of blue
   Which prisoners call the sky.
And at every wandering cloud that trailed
   Its ravelled fleeces by.

He did not wring his hands, as do
   Those witless men who dare
To try to rear the changeling Hope
   In the cave of black Despair:
He only looked upon the sun,
   And drank the morning air.

He did not wring his hands nor weep,
   Nor did he peek or pine,
But he drank the air as though it held
   Some healthful anodyne;
With open mouth he drank the sun
   As though it had been wine!

And I and all the souls in pain
  Who tramped the other ring,
Forgot if we ourselves had done
  A great or little thing,
And watched with gaze of dull amaze
  The man who had to swing.

And strange it was to see him pass
  With a step so light and gay,
And strange it was to see him look
  So wistfully at the day,
And strange it was to think that he
  Had such a debt to pay.

For oak and elm have pleasant leaves
  That in the spring-time shoot:
But grim to see is the gallows-tree,
  With its adder-bitten root,
And, green or dry, a man must die
  Before it bears its fruit.

The loftiest place is that seat of grace
  For which all worldlings try:
But who would stand in hempen band
  Upon a scaffold high,
And through a murderer's collar take
  His last look at the sky?

It is sweet to dance to violins
  When Love and Life are fair:
To dance to flutes, to dance to lutes
  Is delicate and rare:
But it is not sweet with nimble feet
  To dance upon the air!

So with curious eyes and sick surmise
  We watched him day by day,
And wondered if each one of us
  Would end the self-same way,
For none can tell to what red Hell
  His sightless soul may stray.

At last the dead man walked no more
  Amongst the Trial Men,
And I knew that he was standing up
  In the black dock's dreadful pen,
And that never would I see his face
  In God's sweet world again.

Like two doomed ships that pass in storm
  We had crossed each other's way:
But we made no sign, we said no word,
  We had no word to say;
For we did not meet in the holy night,
  But in the shameful day.

A prison wall was round us both,
  Two outcast men we were:
The world had thrust us from its heart,
  And God from out His care:
And the iron gin that waits for Sin
  Had caught us in its snare.

III

In Debtors' Yard the stones are hard,
  And the dripping wall is high,
So it was there he took the air
  Beneath the leaden sky.
And by each side a Warder walked,
  For fear the man might die.

Or else he sat with those who watched
  His anguish night and day;
Who watched him when he rose to weep,
  And when he crouched to pray;
Who watched him lest himself should rob
  Their scaffold of its prey.

The Governor was strong upon
  The Regulations Act:
The Doctor said that Death was but
  A scientific fact:
And twice a day the Chaplain called,
  And left a little tract.

And twice a day he smoked his pipe,
    And drank his quart of beer:
His soul was resolute, and held
    No hiding-place for fear;
He often said that he was glad
    The hangman's hands were near.

But why he said so strange a thing
    No Warder dared to ask:
For he to whom a watcher's doom
    Is given as his task,
Must set a lock upon his lips,
    And make his face a mask.

Or else he might be moved, and try
    To comfort or console:
And what should Human Pity do
    Pent up in Murderers' Hole?
What word of grace in such a place
    Could help a brother's soul?

With slouch and swing around the ring
    We trod the Fools' Parade!
We did not care: we knew we were
    The Devil's Own Brigade:
And shaven head and feet of lead
    Make a merry masquerade.

We tore the tarry rope to shreds
    With blunt and bleeding nails;
We rubbed the doors, and scrubbed the floors,
    And cleaned the shining rails:
And, rank by rank, we soaped the plank,
    And clattered with the pails.

We sewed the sacks, we broke the stones.
    We turned the dusty drill:
We banged the tins, and bawled the hymns,
    And sweated on the mill:
But in the heart of every man
    Terror was lying still.

So still it lay that every day
    Crawled like a weed-clogged wave:
And we forgot the bitter lot
    That waits for fool and knave,
Till once, as we tramped in from work,
    We passed an open grave.

With yawning mouth the yellow hole
    Gaped for a living thing;
The very mud cried out for blood
    To the thirsty asphalt ring:
And we knew that ere one dawn grew fair
    Some prisoner had to swing.

Right in we went, with soul intent
    On Death and Dread and Doom:
The hangman, with his little bag,
    Went shuffling through the gloom:
And each man trembled as he crept
    Into his numbered tomb.

That night the empty corridors
    Were full of forms of Fear,
And up and down the iron town
    Stole feet we could not hear,
And through the bars that hide the stars
    White faces seemed to peer.

He lay as one who lies and dreams
    In a pleasant meadow-land,
The watchers watched him as he slept,
    And could not understand
How one could sleep so sweet a sleep
    With a hangman close at hand.

But there is no sleep when men must weep
    Who never yet have wept:
So we—the fool, the fraud, the knave—
    That endless vigil kept,
And through each brain on hands of pain
    Another's terror crept.

Alas! it is a fearful thing
    To feel another's guilt!
For, right within, the sword of Sin
    Pierced to its poisoned hilt,
And as molten lead were the tears we shed
    For the blood we had not spilt.

The Warders with their shoes of felt
    Crept by each padlocked door,
And peeped and saw, with eyes of awe,
    Gray figures on the floor,
And wonder why men knelt to pray
    Who never prayed before.

All through the night we knelt and prayed,
    Mad mourners of a corse!
The troubled plumes of midnight were
    The plumes upon a hearse:
And bitter wine upon a sponge
    Was the savor of Remorse.

The gray cock crew, the red cock crew,
    But never came the day:
And crooked shapes of Terror crouched,
    In the corners where we lay:
And each evil sprite that walks by night
    Before us seemed to play.

They glided past, they glided fast,
    Like travelers through a mist:
They mocked the moon in a rigadoon
    Of delicate turn and twist,
And with formal pace and loathsome grace
    The phantoms kept their tryst.

With mop and mow, we saw them go,
    Slim shadows hand in hand:
About, about, in ghostly rout
    They trod a saraband:
And the damned grotesques made arabesques,
    Like the wind upon the sand!

With the pirouettes of marionettes,
    They tripped on pointed tread:
But with flutes of Fear they filled the ear,
    As their grisly masque they led,
And loud they sang, and long they sang,
    For they sang to wake the dead.

"Oho!" they cried, "The World is wide,
    But fettered limbs go lame!
And once, or twice, to throw the dice
    Is a gentlemanly game;
But he does not win who plays with Sin
    In the secret House of Shame."

No things of air these antics were,
    That frolicked with such glee:
To men whose lives were held in gyves,
    And whose feet might not go free,
Ah! wounds of Christ! they were living things,
    Most terrible to see.

Around, around, they waltzed and wound;
    Some wheeled in smirking pairs;
With the mincing step of a demirep
    Some sidled up the stairs:
And with subtle sneer, and fawning leer,
    Each helped us at our prayers.

The morning wind began to moan,
    But still the night went on:
Through its giant loom the web of gloom
    Crept till each thread was spun:
And, as we prayed, we grew afraid
    Of the Justice of the Sun.

The moaning wind went wandering round
    The weeping prison-wall:
Till like a wheel of turning steel
    We felt the minutes crawl:
O moaning wind! what had we done
    To have such a seneschal?

At last I saw the shadowed bars,
   Like a lattice wrought in lead,
Move right across the whitewashed wall
   That faced my three-plank bed,
And I knew that somewhere in the world
   God's dreadful dawn was red.

At six o'clock we cleaned our cells,
   At seven all was still,
But the sough and swing of a mighty wing
   The prison seemed to fill,
For the Lord of Death with icy breath
   Had entered in to kill.

He did not pass in purple pomp,
   Not ride a moon-white steed.
Three yards of cord and a sliding board
   Are all the gallows' need:
So with rope of shame the Herald came
   To do the secret deed.

We were as men who through a fen
   Of filthy darkness grope:
We did not dare to breathe a prayer,
   Or to give our anguish scope:
Something was dead in each of us,
   And what was dead was Hope.

For Man's grim Justice goes its way,
   And will not swerve aside:
It slays the weak, it slays the strong,
   It has a deadly stride:
With iron heel it slays the strong,
   The monstrous parricide!

We waited for the stroke of eight:
   Each tongue was thick with thirst:
For the stroke of eight is the stroke of **Fate**
   That makes a man accursed,
And Fate will use a running noose
   For the best man and the worst.

We had no other thing to do,
  Save to wait for the sign to come:
So, like things of stone in a valley lone,
  Quiet we sat and dumb:
But each man's heart beat thick and quick,
  Like a madman on a drum!

With sudden shock the prison clock
  Smote on the shivering air,
And from all the gaol rose up a wail
  Of impotent despair,
Like the sound that frightened marshes hear
  From some leper in his lair.

And as one sees most fearful things
  In the crystal of a dream,
We saw the greasy hempen rope
  Hooked to the blackened beam,
And heard the prayer the hangman's snare
  Strangled into a scream.

And all the woe that moved him so
  That he gave that bitter cry,
And the wild regrets, and the bloody sweats,
  None knew so well as I:
For he who lives more lives than one
  More deaths than one must die.

IV

There is no chapel on the day
  On which they hang a man:
The Chaplain's heart is far too sick,
  'Or his face is far too wan,
Or there is that written in his eyes
  Which none should look upon.

So they kept us close till nigh on noon,
  And then they rang the bell,
And the Warders with their jingling keys
  Opened each listening cell,
And down the iron stair we tramped,
  Each from his separate Hell.

Out into God's sweet air we went,
    But not in wonted way,
For this man's face was white with fear,
    And that man's face was gray,
And I never saw sad men who looked
    So wistfully at the day.

I never saw sad men who looked
    With such a wistful eye
Upon that little tent of blue
    We prisoners called the sky,
And at every careless cloud that passed
    In happy freedom by.

But there were those amongst us all
    Who walked with downcast head,
And knew that, had each got his due,
    They should have died instead:
He had but killed a thing that lived,
    Whilst they had killed the dead.

For he who sins a second time
    Wakes a dead soul to pain,
And draws it from its spotted shroud,
    And makes it bleed again,
And makes it bleed great gouts of blood,
    And makes it bleed in vain!

Like ape or clown, in monstrous garb
    With crooked arrows starred,
Silently we went round and round
    The slippery asphalt yard;
Silently we went round and round,
    And no man spoke a word.

Silently we went round and round,
    And through each hollow mind
The Memory of dreadful things
    Rushed like a dreadful wind,
And Horror stalked before each man,
    And Terror crept behind.

The Warders strutted up and down,
    And kept their herd of brutes,
Their uniforms were spick and span,
    And they wore their Sunday suits,
But we knew the work they had been at,
    By the quicklime on their boots.

For where a grave had opened wide,
    There was no grave at all:
Only a stretch of mud and sand
    By the hideous prison-wall,
And a little heap of burning lime,
    That the man should have his pall.

For he has a pall, this wretched man,
    Such as few men can claim:
Deep down below a prison-yard,
    Naked for greater shame,
He lies, with fetters on each foot,
    Wrapt in a sheet of flame!

And all the while the burning lime
    Eats flesh and bone away;
It eats the brittle bone by night,
    And the soft flesh by day,
It eats the flesh and bone by turns,
    But it eats the heart away.

For three long years they will not sow
    Or root or seedling there:
For three long years the unblessed spot
    Will sterile be and bare,
And look upon the wondering sky
    With unreproachful stare.

They think a murderer's heart would taint
    Each simple seed they sow.
It is not true! God's kindly earth
    Is kindlier than men know,
And the red rose would but blow more red,
    The white rose whiter blow.

Out of his mouth a red, red rose!
   Out of his heart a white!
For who can say by what strange way,
   Christ brings His will to light,
Since the barren staff the pilgrim bore
   Bloomed in the great Pope's sight?

But neither milk-white rose nor red
   May bloom in prison air;
The shard, the pebble, and the flint,
   Are what they give us there:
For flowers have been known to heal
   A common man's despair.

So never will wine-red rose or white,
   Petal by petal, fall
On that stretch of mud and sand that lies
   By the hideous prison-wall,
To tell the men who tramp the yard
   That God's Son died for all.

Yet though the hideous prison-wall
   Still hems him round and round,
And a spirit may not walk by night
   That is with fetters bound,
And a spirit may but weep that lies
   In such unholy ground.

He is at peace—this wretched man—
   At peace, or will be soon:
There is no thing to make him mad,
   Nor does Terror walk at noon,
For the lampless Earth in which he lies
   Has neither Sun nor Moon.

They hanged him as a beast is hanged:
   They did not even toll
A requiem that might have brought
   Rest to his startled soul,
But hurriedly they took him out,
   And hid him in a hole.

They stripped him of his canvas clothes,
  And gave him to the flies;
They mocked the swollen purple throat,
  And the stark and staring eyes;
And with laughter loud they heaped the shroud
  In which their convict lies.

The Chaplain would not kneel to pray
  By his dishonored grave:
Nor mark it with that blessed Cross
  That Christ for sinners gave,
Because the man was one of those
  Whom Christ came down to save.

Yet all is well; he has but passed,
  To Life's appointed bourne:
And alien tears will fill for him
  Pity's long-broken urn,
For his mourners will be outcast men,
  And outcasts always mourn.

v

I know not whether Laws be right,
  Or whether Laws be wrong;
All that we know who lie in gaol
  Is that the wall is strong;
And that each day is like a year,
  A year whose days are long.

But this I know, that every Law
  That men have made for Man,
Since first Man took his brother's life,
  And the sad world began,
But straws the wheat and saves the chaff
  With a most evil fan.

This too I know—and wise it were
  If each could know the same—
That every prison that men build
  Is built with bricks of shame,
And bound with bars lest Christ should see
  How men their brothers maim.

With bars they blur the gracious moon,
And blind the goodly sun:
And they do well to hide their Hell,
For in it things are done
That Son of God nor Son of Man
Ever should look upon!

The vilest deeds like poison weeds
Bloom well in prison-air:
It is only what is good in Man
That wastes and withers there:
Pale Anguish keeps the heavy gate,
And the Warder is Despair.

For they starve the little frightened child
Till it weeps both night and day:
And they scourge the weak, and flog the fool,
And gibe the old and gray,
And some grow mad, and all grow bad,
And none a word may say.

Each narrow cell in which we dwell
Is a foul and dark latrine.
And the fetid breath of living Death
Chokes up each grated screen,
And all, but Lust, is turned to dust
In Humanity's machine.

The brackish water that we drink
Creeps with a loathsome slime,
And the bitter bread they weigh in scales
Is full of chalk and lime,
And Sleep will not lie down, but walks
Wild-eyed, and cries to Time.

But though lean Hunger and green Thirst
Like asp with adder fight,
We have little care of prison fare,
For what chills and kills outright
Is that every stone one lifts by day
Becomes one's heart by night.

With midnight always in one's heart,
    And twilight in one's cell,
We turn the crank, or tear the rope,
    Each in his separate Hell,
And the silence is more awful far
    Than the sound of a brazen bell.

And never a human voice comes near
    To speak a gentle word:
And the eye that watches through the door
    Is pitiless and hard:
And by all forgot, we rot and rot,
    With soul and body marred.

And thus we rust Life's iron chain
    Degraded and alone:
And some men curse, and some men weep,
    And some men make no moan:
But God's eternal Laws are kind
    And break the heart of stone.

And every human heart that breaks,
    In prison-cell or yard,
Is as that broken box that gave
    Its treasure to the Lord,
And filled the unclean leper's house
    With the scent of costliest nard.

Ah! happy they whose hearts can break
    And peace of pardon win!
How else may man make straight his plan
    And cleanse his soul from Sin?
How else but through a broken heart
    May Lord Christ enter in?

And he of the swollen purple throat,
    And the stark and staring eyes
Waits for the holy hands that took
    The Thief to Paradise;
And a broken and a contrite heart
    The Lord will not despise.

The man in red who reads the Law
  Gave him three weeks of life,
Three little weeks in which to heal
  His soul of his soul's strife,
And cleanse from every blot of blood
  The hand that held the knife.

And with tears of blood he cleansed the hand,
  The hand that held the steel:
For only blood can wipe out blood,
  And only tears can heal:
And the crimson stain that was of Cain
  Became Christ's snow-white seal.

VI

In Reading gaol by Reading town
  There is a pit of shame,
And in it lies a wretched man
  Eaten by teeth of flame,
In a burning winding-sheet he lies,
  And his grave has got no name.

And there, till Christ call forth the dead,
  In silence let him lie:
No need to waste the foolish tear,
  Or heave the windy sigh:
The man had killed the thing he loved,
  And so he had to die.

And all men kill the thing they love,
  By all let this be heard,
Some do it with a bitter look,
  Some with a flattering word,
The coward does it with a kiss,
  The brave man with a sword!

KISS ME AGAIN

Henry Blossom

Sweet summer breeze,
Whispering trees,
Stars shining above;
Roses in bloom, wafted perfume,
Sleepy birds dreaming of love.
Safe in your arms, far from alarms,
Daylight shall come but in vain.
Tenderly pressed close to your breast,
Kiss me, kiss me again.
Kiss me again! Kiss me!
Kiss me again!

BENJAMIN DISRAELI'S ESTIMATE OF WILLIAM E. GLADSTONE

A sophisticated rhetorician inebriated with the exuberance of his own verbosity, and gifted with an egotistical imagination that can at all times command an interminable and inconsistent series of arguments to malign an opponent and to glorify himself.

MEMORY

Thomas Bailey Aldrich

My mind lets go a thousand things,
Like dates of wars and deaths of kings,
And yet recalls the very hour—
'T was noon by yonder village tower,
And on the last blue noon in May—
The wind came briskly up this way,
Crisping the brook beside the road;
Then, pausing here, set down its load
Of pine-scents, and shook listlessly
Two petals from that wild-rose tree.

MY OLD KENTUCKY HOME

Stephen Foster

The sun shines bright in our old Kentucky home;
  'Tis summer, the darkeys are gay;
The corn top's ripe and the meadow's in the bloom,
  While the birds make music all the day;
The young folks roll on the little cabin floor,
  All merry, all happy, all bright;
By'm by hard times come a knockin' at the door,—
  Then, my old Kentucky home, good night!

Chorus:
    Weep no more, my lady; O, weep no more today!
    We'll sing one song for my old Kentucky home,
    For our old Kentucky home far away.

They hunt no more for the possum and the coon,
  On the meadow, the hill, and the shore;
They sing no more by the glimmer of the moon,
  On the bench by the old cabin door;
The day goes by, like a shadow o'er the heart,
  With sorrow where all was delight;
The time has come, when the darkeys have to part,
  Then, my old Kentucky home, good night!
    Weep no more, my lady, &c.

The head must bow, and the back will have to bend,
  Wherever the darkey may go;
A few more days, and the troubles all will end,
  In the field where the sugar-cane grow;
A few more days to tote the weary load,
  No matter it will never be light;
A few more days till we totter on the road,
  Then, my old Kentucky home, good night!
    Weep no more, my lady, &c.

ST. PAUL ON CHARITY

Holy Bible, I Corinthians 13

1 Though I speak with the tongues of men and of angels, and have not charity, I am become as sounding brass, or a tinkling cymbal.

2 And though I have the gift of prophecy, and understand all mysteries, and all knowledge; and though I have all faith, so that I could remove mountains, and have not charity, I am nothing.

3 And though I bestow all my goods to feed the poor, and though I give my body to be burned, and have not charity, it profiteth me nothing.

4 Charity suffereth long, and is kind; charity envieth not; charity vaunteth not itself, is not puffed up.

5 Doth not behave itself unseemly, seeketh not her own, is not easily provoked, thinketh no evil;

6 Rejoiceth not in iniquity, but rejoiceth in the truth.

7 Beareth all things, believeth all things, hopeth all things, endureth all things.

8 Charity never faileth: but whether there be prophecies, they shall fail; whether there be tongues, they shall cease; whether there be knowledge, it shall vanish away.

9 For we know in part, and we prophesy in part.

10 But when that which is perfect is come, then that which is in part shall be done away.

11 When I was a child, I spake as a child, I understood as a child, I thought as a child; but when I became a man, I put away childish things.

12 For now we see through a glass, darkly; but then face to face: now I know in part; but then shall I know even as also I am known.

13 And now abideth faith, hope, charity, these three; but the greatest of these is charity.

* * *

Not to go back is somewhat to advance,
And men must walk, at least, before they dance,
—Alexander Pope

ODE ON A GRECIAN URN

John Keats

Thou still unravish'd bride of quietness,
  Thou foster-child of silence and slow time,
Sylvan historian, who canst thus express
  A flowery tale more sweetly than our rhyme:
What leaf-fring'd legend haunts about thy shape
  Of deities or mortals, or of both,
    In Tempe or the dales of Arcady?
What men or gods are these? What maidens loth?
  What mad pursuit? What struggle to escape?
    What pipes and timbrels? What wild ecstasy?

Heard melodies are sweet, but those unheard
  Are sweeter; therefore, ye soft pipes, play on;
Not to the sensual ear, but, more endear'd,
  Pipe to the spirit ditties of no tone:
Fair youth, beneath the trees, thou canst not leave
  Thy song, nor ever can those trees be bare;
    Bold Lover, never, never canst thou kiss
Though winning near the goal—yet, do not grieve;
  She cannot fade, though thou hast not thy bliss,
    For ever wilt thou love, and she be fair!

Ah, happy, happy boughs! that cannot shed
  Your leaves, nor ever bid the Spring adieu;
And, happy melodist, unwearied,
  For ever piping songs for ever new;
More happy love! more happy, happy love!
  For ever warm and still to be enjoy'd,
    For ever panting, and for ever young;
All breathing human passion far above,
  That leaves a heart high-sorrowful and cloy'd,
    A burning forehead, and a parching tongue.

Who are these coming to the sacrifice?
  To what green altar, O mysterious priest,
Lead'st thou that heifer lowing at the skies,
  And all her silken flanks with garlands dressed?
What little town by river or sea shore,
  Or mountain-built with peaceful citadel,
    Is emptied of this folk, this pious morn?

And, little town, thy streets for evermore
  Will silent be; and not a soul to tell
  Why thou art desolate, can e'er return.

O Attic shape! Fair attitude! with brede
  Of marble men and maidens overwrought,
With forest branches and the trodden weed;
  Thou, silent form, dost tease us out of thought
As doth eternity: Cold Pastoral!
  When old age shall this generation waste,
    Thou shalt remain, in midst of other woe
Than ours, a friend to man, to whom thou say'st,
  "Beauty is truth, truth beauty,"—that is all
  Ye know on earth, and all ye need to know.

* * *

Everyone is as God made him and oftentimes a good deal worse.
                                              —Cervantes

LOVE'S NOT TIME'S FOOL

William Shakespeare

Let me not to the marriage of true minds
Admit impediments. Love is not love
Which alters when it alteration finds,
Or bends with the remover to remove:
O, no! it is an ever-fixed mark
That looks on tempests and is never shaken;
It is the star to every wandering bark,
Whose worth's unknown, although his height be taken.
Love's not Time's fool, though rosy lips and cheeks
Within his bending sickle's compass come;
Love alters not with his brief hours and weeks,
But bears it out even to the edge of doom.
  If this be error and upon me proved,
  I never writ, nor no man ever loved.
                                    (From the Sonnets)

MONEY

Richard Armour

Workers earn it,
Spendthrifts burn it,
Bankers lend it,
Women spend it,
Forgers fake it,
Taxes take it,
Dying leave it,
Heirs receive it,
Thrifty save it,
Misers crave it,
Robbers seize it,
Rich increase it,
Gamblers lose it . . .
I could use it.

THE MAD HATTER'S TEA-PARTY

Lewis Carroll

There was a table set out under a tree in front of the house, and the March Hare and the Hatter were having tea at it: a Dormouse was sitting between them fast asleep, and the other two were using it as a cushion, resting their elbows on it, and talking over its head. 'Very uncomfortable for the Dormouse,' thought Alice; 'only as it's asleep, I suppose it doesn't mind.'

The table was a large one, but the three were all crowded together at one corner of it. 'No room! No room!' they cried out when they saw Alice coming. 'There's *plenty* of room!' said Alice indignantly, and she sat down in a large arm-chair at one end of the table.

'Have some wine,' the March Hare said in an encouraging tone.

Alice looked all round the table, but there was nothing on it but tea. 'I don't see any wine,' she remarked.

'There isn't any,' said the March Hare.

'Then it wasn't very civil of you to offer it,' said Alice angrily.

'It wasn't very civil of you to sit down without being invited,' said the March Hare.

'I didn't know it was *your* table,' said Alice; 'it's laid for a great many more than three.'

'Your hair wants cutting,' said the Hatter. He had been looking at Alice for some time with great curiosity, and this was his first speech.

'You shouldn't make personal remarks,' Alice said with some severity; 'it's very rude.'

The Hatter opened his eyes very wide on hearing this; but all he *said* was: 'Why is a raven like a writing-desk?'

'Come, we shall have some fun now!' thought Alice. 'I'm glad they've begun asking riddles.—I believe I can guess that,' she added aloud.

'Do you mean that you think you can find out the answer to it?' said the March Hare.

'Exactly so,' said Alice.

'Then you should say what you mean,' the March Hare went on.

'I do,' Alice hastily replied; 'at least—at least I mean what I say —that's the same thing, you know.'

'Not the same thing a bit!' said the Hatter. 'You might just as well say that "I see what I eat" is the same thing as "I eat what I see"!'

'You might just as well say,' added the March Hare, 'that "I like what I get" is the same thing as "I get what I like"!'

'You might just as well say,' added the Dormouse, which seemed to be talking in its sleep, 'that "I breathe when I sleep" is the same thing as "I sleep when I breathe"!'

'It *is* the same thing with you,' said the Hatter, and here the conversation dropped, and the party sat silent for a minute, while Alice thought over all she could remember about ravens and writing-desks, which wasn't much.

The Hatter was the first to break the silence. 'What day of the month is it?' he said, turning to Alice: he had taken his watch out of his pocket, and was looking at it uneasily, shaking it every now and then, and holding it to his ear.

Alice considered a little, and then said: 'The fourth.'

'Two days wrong!' sighed the Hatter, 'I told you butter wouldn't suit the works!' he added, looking angrily at the March Hare.

'It was the *best* butter,' the March Hare meekly replied.

'Yes, but some crumbs must have got in as well,' the Hatter grumbled: 'you shouldn't have put it in with the bread-knife.'

The March Hare took the watch and looked at it gloomily: then he dipped it into his cup of tea, and looked at it again: but he could think of nothing better to say than his first remark: 'It was the *best* butter, you know.'

Alice had been looking over his shoulder with some curiosity.

'What a funny watch!' she remarked. 'It tells the day of the month, and doesn't tell what o'clock it is!'

'Why should it?' muttered the Hatter. 'Does *your* watch tell you what year it is?'

'Of course not,' Alice replied very readily: 'but that's because it stays the same year for such a long time together.'

'Which is just the case with *mine*,' said the Hatter.

Alice felt dreadfully puzzled. The Hatter's remark seemed to her to have no sort of meaning in it, and yet it was certainly English. 'I don't quite understand you,' she said, as politely as she could.

'The Dormouse is asleep again,' said the Hatter, and he poured a little hot tea upon its nose.

The Dormouse shook its head impatiently, and said, without opening its eyes: 'Of course, of course; just what I was going to remark myself.'

'Have you guessed the riddle yet?' the Hatter said, turning to Alice again.

'No, I give it up,' Alice replied: 'what's the answer?'

'I haven't the slightest idea,' said the Hatter.

'Nor I,' said the March Hare.

Alice sighed wearily. 'I think you might do something better with the time,' she said, 'than waste it in asking riddles with no answers.'

'If you knew Time as well as I do,' said the Hatter, 'you wouldn't talk about wasting *it*. It's *him*.'

'I don't know what you mean,' said Alice.

'Of course you don't!' the Hatter said, tossing his head contemptuously. 'I dare say you never even spoke to Time!'

'Perhaps not,' Alice cautiously replied: 'but I know I have to beat time when I learn music.'

'Ah! that accounts for it,' said the Hatter. 'He won't stand beating. Now, if you only kept on good terms with him, he'd do almost anything you liked with the clock. For instance, suppose it were nine o'clock in the morning, just time to begin lessons: you'd only have to whisper a hint to Time, and round goes the clock in a twinkling! Half-past one, time for dinner!'

('I only wish it was,' the March Hare said to itself in a whisper.)

'That would be grand, certainly,' said Alice thoughtfully: 'but then—I shouldn't be hungry for it, you know.'

'Not at first, perhaps,' said the Hatter: 'but you could keep it to half-past one as long as you liked.'

'Is that the way *you* manage?' Alice asked.

The Hatter shook his head mournfully. 'Not I!' he replied. 'We quarrelled last March—just before *he* went mad, you know—' (pointing with his teaspoon at the March Hare) '—it was at the great concert given by the Queen of Hearts, and I had to sing

> Twinkle, twinkle, little bat!
> How I wonder what you're at!

You know the song, perhaps?'

'I've heard something like it,' said Alice.

'It goes on, you know,' the Hatter continued, 'in this way:

> Up above the world you fly,
> Like a tea-tray in the sky.
>   Twinkle, twinkle—'

Here the Dormouse shook itself, and began singing in its sleep: 'Twinkle, twinkle, twinkle, twinkle—' and went on so long that they had to pinch it to make it stop.

'Well, I'd hardly finished the first verse,' said the Hatter, 'when the Queen jumped up and bawled out: "He's murdering the time! Off with his head!" '

'How dreadfully savage!' exclaimed Alice.

'And ever since that,' the Hatter went on in a mournful tone, 'he won't do a think I ask! It's always six o'clock now.'

A bright idea came into Alice's head. 'Is that the reason so many tea-things are put out here?' she asked.

'Yes, that's it,' said the Hatter with a sigh: 'it's always tea-time, and we've no time to wash the things between whiles.'

'Then you keep moving round, I suppose?' said Alice.

'Exactly so,' said the Hatter: 'as the things get used up.'

'But what happens when you come to the beginning again?' Alice ventured to ask.

'Suppose we change the subject,' the March Hare interrupted, yawning. 'I'm getting tired of this. I vote the young lady tells us a story.'

'I'm afraid I don't know one,' said Alice, rather alarmed at the proposal.

'Then the Dormouse shall!' they both cried. 'Wake up, Dormouse!' And they pinched it on both sides at once.

The Dormouse slowly opened its eyes. 'I wasn't asleep,' it said in a hoarse, feeble voice: 'I heard every word you fellows were saying.'

'Tell us a story!' said the March Hare.

'Yes, please do!' pleaded Alice.

'And be quick about it,' added the Hatter, 'or you'll be asleep again before it's done.'

'Once upon a time there were three little sisters,' the Dormouse began in a great hurry; 'and their names were Elsie, Lacie, and Tillie; and they lived at the bottom of a well—'

'What did they live on?' said Alice, who always took a great interest in questions of eating and drinking.

'They lived on treacle,' said the Dormouse, after thinking a minute or two.

'They couldn't have done that, you know,' Alice gently remarked; 'they'd have been ill.'

'So they were,' said the Dormouse: '*very* ill.'

Alice tried to fancy to herself what such an extraordinary way of living would be like, but it puzzled her too much, so she went on: 'But why did they live at the bottom of a well?'

'Take some more tea,' the March Hare said to Alice, very earnestly.

'I've had nothing yet,' Alice replied in an offended tone, 'so I can't take more.'

'You mean you can't take *less*,' said the Hatter: 'it's very easy to take *more* than nothing.'

'Nobody asked *your* opinion,' said Alice.

'Who's making personal remarks now?' the Hatter asked triumphantly.

Alice did not quite know what to say to this: so she helped herself to some tea and bread-and-butter, and then turned to the Dormouse, and repeated her question: 'Why did they live at the bottom of a well?'

The Dormouse again took a minute or two to think about it, and then said: 'It was a treacle-well.'

'There's no such thing!' Alice was beginning very angrily, but the Hatter and the March Hare went 'Sh! sh!' and the Dormouse sulkily remarked: 'If you can't be civil, you'd better finish the story for yourself.'

'No, please go on!' Alice said. 'I won't interrupt again. I dare say there may be *one*.'

'One, indeed!' said the Dormouse indignantly. However, it consented to go on. 'And so, these three little sisters—they were learning to draw, you know—'

'What did they draw?' said Alice, quite forgetting her promise.

'Treacle,' said the Dormouse, without considering at all this time.

'I want a clean cup,' interrupted the Hatter: 'let's all move one place on.'

He moved on as he spoke, and the Dormouse followed him: the March Hare moved into the Dormouse's place, and Alice rather unwillingly took the place of the March Hare. The Hatter was the only one who got any advantage from the change: and Alice was a good deal worse off, as the March Hare had just upset the milk-jug into his plate.

Alice did not wish to offend the Dormouse again, so she began very cautiously: 'But I don't understand. Where did they draw the treacle from?'

'You can draw water out of a water-well,' said the Hatter; 'so I should think you could draw treacle out of a treacle-well—eh, stupid?'

'But they were *in* the well,' Alice said to the Dormouse, not choosing to notice this last remark.

'Of course they were,' said the Dormouse; '—well in.'

This answer so confused poor Alice that she let the Dormouse go on for some time without interrupting it.

'They were learning to draw,' the Dormouse went on, yawning and rubbing its eyes, for it was getting very sleepy: 'and they drew all manner of things—everything that begins with an M—'

'Why with an M?' said Alice.

'Why not?' said the March Hare.

Alice was silent.

The Dormouse had closed its eyes by this time, and was going off into a doze; but, on being pinched by the Hatter, it woke up again with a little shriek, and went on: '—that begins with an M, such as mouse-traps, and the moon, and memory, and muchness— you know you say things are "much of a muchness"—did you ever see such a thing as a drawing of a muchness?'

'Really, now you ask me,' said Alice, very much confused, 'I don't think—'

'Then you shouldn't talk,' said the Hatter.

This piece of rudeness was more than Alice could bear: she got up in great disgust, and walked off; the Dormouse fell asleep instantly, and neither of the others took the least notice of her going, though she looked back once or twice, half hoping that they would call after her: the last time she saw them, they were trying to put the Dormouse into the teapot.

'At any rate I'll never go *there* again!' said Alice as she picked her way through the wood. 'It's the stupidest tea-party I ever was at in all my life!'

(From Alice's Adventures in Wonderland)

LIBERTY

John Milton

Give me the liberty to know, to utter and to argue freely according to conscience above all liberties. And though all the winds of doctrine were let loose to play upon the earth, so Truth be in the field, we do injuriously, by licensing and prohibiting, to misdoubt her strength. Let her and Falsehood grapple; who ever knew Truth put to the worse, in a free and open encounter?

PRAYER

Hartley Coleridge

Be not afraid to pray—to pray is right.
Pray, if thou canst, with hope; but ever pray,
Though hope be weak, or sick with long delay;
Pray in the darkness, if there be no light. . . .
Whate'er is good to wish, that ask of Heaven,
Though it be what thou canst not hope to see:
Pray to be perfect, though material leaven
Forbid the spirit so on earth to be:
But if for any wish thou darest not pray,
Then pray to God to cast that wish away.

THE GIFT OF A LOVELY THOUGHT

Anonymous

If instead of a jewel, or even a flower, we could cast the gift of a lovely thought into the heart of another, that would be giving as the angels must give.

FOLLOW THE GLEAM

Alfred, Lord Tennyson

Not of the sunlight,
Not of the moonlight,
Not of the starlight!
O young Mariner,
Down to the haven,
Call your companions,
Launch your vessel,
And crowd your canvas,
And, ere it vanishes
Over the margin,
After it, follow it,
Follow the Gleam.

NEW ENGLAND SPRING

Mark Twain

There is a sumptuous variety about the New England weather that compels the stranger's admiration—and regret. The weather is always doing something there; always attending strictly to business; always getting up new designs and trying them on people to see how they will go. But it gets through more business in Spring than in any other season. In the Spring I have counted one hundred and thirty-six different kinds of weather inside of twenty-four hours. Probable nor'-east to sou'-west winds, varying to the southard and westard and eastard and points between; high and low barometer, sweeping round from place to place; probable areas of rain, snow, hail, and drought, succeeded or preceded by earthquakes with thunder and lightning.

THANATOPSIS

William Cullen Bryant

To him who, in the love of Nature, holds
Communion with her visible forms, she speaks
A various language: for his gayer hours
She has a voice of gladness, and a smile
And eloquence of beauty; and she glides
Into his darker musings with a mild
And gentle sympathy, that steals away
Their sharpness, ere he is aware. When thoughts
Of the last bitter hour come like a blight
Over thy spirit, and sad images
Of the stern agony, and shroud, and pall,
And breathless darkness, and the narrow house,
Make thee to shudder, and grow sick at heart,
Go forth under the open sky, and list
To Nature's teachings, while from all around—
Earth and her waters, and the depths of air—
Comes a still voice,—Yet a few days, and thee
The all-beholding sun shall see no more
In all his course; nor yet in the cold ground,
Where thy pale form was laid, with many tears,
Nor in the embrace of ocean, shall exist
Thy image. Earth, that nourished thee, shall claim
Thy growth, to be resolved to earth again;
And, lost each human trace, surrendering up
Thine individual being, shalt thou go
To mix forever with the elements;
To be a brother to the insensible rock,
And to the sluggish clod, which the rude swain
Turns with his share, and treads upon. The oak
Shall send his roots abroad, and pierce thy mould.

Yet not to thine eternal resting-place
Shalt thou retire alone,—nor couldst thou wish
Couch more magnificent. Thou shalt lie down
With patriarchs of the infant world,—with kings,
The powerful of the earth,—the wise, the good,
Fair forms, and hoary seers of ages past,
All in one mighty sepulchre. The hills,
Rock-ribbed, and ancient as the sun; the vales
Stretching in pensive quietness between;

The venerable woods; rivers that move
In majesty, and the complaining brooks,
That make the meadows green; and, poured round all,
Old ocean's gray and melancholy waste,—
Are but the solemn decorations all
Of the great tomb of man! The golden sun,
The planets, all the infinite host of heaven,
Are shining on the sad abodes of death,
Through the still lapse of ages. All that tread
The globe are but a handful to the tribes
That slumber in its bosom. Take the wings
Of morning, traverse Barca's desert sands,
Or lose thyself in the continuous woods
Where rolls the Oregon, and hears no sound
Save his own dashings,—yet the dead are there!
And millions in those solitudes, since first
The flight of years began, have laid them down
In their last sleep,—the dead reign there alone!
So shalt thou rest; and what if thou withdraw
In silence from the living; and no friend
Take note of thy departure? All that breathe
Will share thy destiny. The gay will laugh
When thou art gone, the solemn brood of care
Plod on, and each one, as before, will chase
His favorite phantom; yet all these shall leave
Their mirth and their employments, and shall come
And make their bed with thee. As the long train
Of ages glide away, the sons of men—
The youth in life's green spring, and he who goes
In the full strength of years, matron and maid,
The speechless babe, and the gray-headed man—
Shall, one by one, be gathered to thy side
By those who in their turn shall follow them.

So live, that when thy summons comes to join
The innumerable caravan that moves
To the pale realms of shade, where each shall take
His chamber in the silent halls of death,
Thou go not, like the quarry-slave at night,
Scourged to his dungeon, but, sustained and soothed
By an unfaltering trust, approach thy grave
Like one who wraps the drapery of his couch
About him, and lies down to pleasant dreams.

CHICAGO

Carl Sandburg

Hog Butcher for the World,
Tool Maker, Stacker of Wheat,
Player with Railroads and the Nation's Freight Handler;
Stormy, husky, brawling,
City of the Big Shoulders:
They tell me you are wicked, and I believe them; for I have seen
    your painted women under the gas lamps luring the farm boys.
And they tell me you are crooked, and I answer: Yes, it is true
    I have seen the gunman kill and go free to kill again.
And they tell me you are brutal, and my reply is: On the faces
    of women and children I have seen the marks of wanton
    hunger.
And having answered so I turn once more to those who sneer
    at this my city, and I give them back the sneer and say to them:
Come and show me another city with lifted head singing so
    proud to be alive and coarse and strong and cunning.
Flinging magnetic curses amid the toil of piling job on job, here
    is a tall bold slugger set vivid against the little soft cities;
Fierce as a dog with tongue lapping for action, cunning as a sav-
    age pitted against the wilderness,
    Bareheaded,
    Shoveling,
    Wrecking,
    Planning,
    Building, breaking, rebuilding,
Under the smoke, dust all over his mouth, laughing with white
    teeth,
Under the terrible burden of destiny laughing as a young man
    laughs,
Laughing even as an ignorant fighter laughs who has never lost
    a battle,
Bragging and laughing that under his wrist is the pulse, and
    under his ribs the heart of the people,
                    Laughing!
Laughing the stormy, husky, brawling laughter of youth; half-
    naked, sweating, proud to be Hog-butcher, Tool-maker, Stacker
    of Wheat, Player with Railroads, and Freight Handler to the
    Nation.

BRUTUS EXPLAINS WHY HE MURDERED CAESAR

William Shakespeare

Romans, countrymen, and lovers! hear me for my cause, and be silent, that you may hear: believe me for mine honor, and have respect to mine honor, that you may believe: censure me in your wisdom, and awake your senses, that you may the better judge. If there be any in this assembly, any dear friend of Caesar's, to him I say that Brutus' love to Caesar was no less than his. If then that friend demand why Brutus rose against Caesar, this is my answer: not that I loved Caesar less, but that I loved Rome more. Had you rather Caesar were living, and die all slaves, than that Caesar were dead, to live all freemen? As Caesar loved me, I weep for him; as he was fortunate, I rejoice at it; as he was valiant, I honor him; but as he was ambitious, I slew him. There is tears for his love; joy for his fortune; honor for his valor; and death for his ambition. Who is here so base that would be a bondman? If any, speak; for him have I offended. Who is here so rude that would not be a Roman? If any, speak; for him have I offended. Who is here so vile that will not love his country? If any, speak; for him have I offended. I pause for a reply.

(From *Julius Caesar*)

DE PROFUNDIS

Holy Bible, Psalm 130

1 Out of the depths have I cried unto thee, O Lord.

2 Lord, hear my voice: let thine ears be attentive to the voice of my supplications.

3 If thou, Lord, shouldest mark iniquities, O Lord, who shall stand?

4 But there is forgiveness with thee, that thou mayest be feared.

5 I wait for the Lord, my soul doth wait, and in his word do I hope.

6 My soul waiteth for the Lord more than they that watch for the morning; I say, more than they that watch for the morning.

7 Let Israel hope in the Lord: for with the Lord there is mercy, and with him is plenteous redemption.

8 And he shall redeem Israel from all his iniquities.

BREDON HILL

A. E. Housman

In summertime on Bredon
   The bells they sound so clear;
Round both the shires they ring them
   In steeples far and near,
   A happy noise to hear.

Here of a Sunday morning
   My love and I would lie,
And see the coloured counties,
   And hear the larks so high
   About us in the sky.

The bells would ring to call her
   In valleys miles away:
"Come all to church, good people;
   Good people, come and pray."
   But here my love would stay.

And I would turn and answer
   Among the springtime thyme,
"Oh, peal upon our wedding,
   And we will hear the chime,
   And come to church in time."

But when the snows at Christmas
   On Bredon top were strown,
My love rose up so early
   And stole out unbeknown
   And went to church alone.

They tolled the one bell only,
   Groom there was none to see,
The mourners followed after,
   And to church went she,
   And would not wait for me.

The bells they sound on Bredon,
   And still the steeples hum.
"Come all to church, good people,"—
   Oh, noisy bells, be dumb;
   I hear you, I will come.

IN THE BEGINNING WAS THE WORD

Holy Bible, John 1:1–17

1 In the beginning was the Word, and the Word was with God, and the Word was God.

2 The same was in the beginning with God.

3 All things were made by him; and without him was not any thing made that was made.

4 In him was life; and the life was the light of men.

5 And the light shineth in darkness; and the darkness comprehended it not.

6 There was a man sent from God, whose name was John.

7 The same came for a witness, to bear witness of the Light, that all men through him might believe.

8 He was not that Light, but was sent to bear witness of that Light.

9 That was the true Light, which lighteth every man that cometh into the world.

10 He was in the world, and the world was made by him, and the world knew him not.

11 He came unto his own, and his own received him not.

12 But as many as received him, to them gave he power to become the sons of God, even to them that believe on his name:

13 Which were born, not of blood, nor of the will of the flesh, nor of the will of man, but of God.

14 And the Word was made flesh, and dwelt among us, (and we beheld his glory, the glory as of the only begotten of the Father,) full of grace and truth.

15 John bare witness of him, and cried, saying, This was he of whom I spake, He that cometh after me is preferred before me: for he was before me.

16 And of his fulness have all we received, and grace for grace.

17 For the law was given by Moses, but grace and truth came by Jesus Christ.

EPIGRAM

Samuel Taylor Coleridge

Sir, I admit your general rule,
That every poet is a fool,
But you yourself may serve to show it,
That every fool is not a poet.

WHEN I WAS ONE-AND-TWENTY

A. E. Housman

When I was one-and-twenty
I heard a wise man say,
"Give crowns and pounds and guineas
But not your heart away;
Give pearls away and rubies
But keep your fancy free."
But I was one-and-twenty,
No use to talk to me.

When I was one-and-twenty
I heard him say again,
"The heart out of the bosom
Was never given in vain;
'Tis paid with sighs a-plenty
And sold for endless rue."
And I am two-and-twenty,
And oh, 'tis true, 'tis true.

MR. VALIANT–FOR–TRUTH CROSSES THE RIVER

John Bunyan

After this, it was noised abroad that Mr. *Valiant-for-truth* was taken with a Summons, by the same *Post* as the other, and had this for a Token that the Summons was true, *That his Pitcher was broken at the fountain.* When he understood it, he called for his Friends, and told them of it. Then said he, I am going to my Fathers, and though with great difficulty I am got hither, yet now I do not repent me of all the Trouble I have been to arrive where I am. *My Sword,* I give to him that shall succeed me in my Pilgrimage, and my *Courage* and *Skill,* to him that can get it. My *Marks* and *Scars* I carry with me, to be a Witness for me, that I have fought his Battles who now will be my Rewarder. When the Day that he must go hence, was come, many accompanied him to the River side, into which, as he went, he said, *Death, where is thy Sting?* And as he went down deeper, he said, *Grave, where is thy Victory?* So he passed over, and the Trumpets sounded for him on the other side.

(From Pilgrim's Progress)

MINIVER CHEEVY

Edwin Arlington Robinson

Miniver Cheevy, child of scorn,
  Grew lean while he assailed the seasons;
He wept that he was ever born,
  And he had reasons.

Miniver loved the days of old
  When swords were bright and steeds were prancing;
The vision of a warrior bold
  Would set him dancing.

Miniver sighed for what was not,
  And dreamed, and rested from his labors;
He dreamed of Thebes and Camelot,
  And Priam's neighbors.

Miniver mourned the ripe renown
  That made so many a name so fragrant;
He mourned Romance, now on the town,
  And Art, a vagrant.

Miniver loved the Medici,
  Albeit he had never seen one;
He would have sinned incessantly
  Could he have been one.

Miniver cursed the commonplace
  And eyed a khaki suit with loathing;
He missed the mediaeval grace
  Of iron clothing.

Miniver scorned the gold he sought,
  But sore annoyed was he without it;
Miniver thought, and thought, and thought,
  And thought about it.

Miniver Cheevy, born too late,
  Scratched his head and kept on thinking;
Miniver coughed, and called it fate,
  And kept on drinking.

WHEN THE SON OF MAN SHALL COME
IN HIS GLORY

Holy Bible, Matthew 25:31–46

31 When the Son of man shall come in his glory, and all the holy angels with him, then shall he sit upon the throne of his glory:

32 And before him shall be gathered all nations: and he shall separate them one from another, as a shepherd divideth his sheep from the goats:

33 And he shall set the sheep on his right hand, but the goats on the left.

34 Then shall the King say unto them on his right hand, Come, ye blessed of my Father, inherit the kingdom prepared for you from the foundation of the world:

35 For I was an hungred, and ye gave me meat: I was thirsty, and ye gave me drink: I was a stranger, and ye took me in:

36 Naked, and ye clothed me: I was sick, and ye visited me: I was in prison, and ye came unto me.

37 Then shall the righteous answer him, saying, Lord, when saw we thee an hungred, and fed thee? or thirsty, and gave thee drink?

38 When saw we thee a stranger, and took thee in? or naked, and clothed thee?

39 Or when saw we thee sick, or in prison, and came unto thee?

40 And the King shall answer and say unto them, Verily I say unto you, Inasmuch as ye have done it unto one of the least of these my brethren, ye have done it unto me.

41 Then shall he say also unto them on the left hand, Depart from me, ye cursed, into everlasting fire, prepared for the devil and his angels:

42 For I was an hungred, and ye gave me no meat: I was thirsty, and ye gave me no drink:

43 I was a stranger and ye took me not in: naked, and ye clothed me not: sick and in prison, and ye visited me not.

44 Then shall they also answer him, saying, Lord, when saw we thee an hungred, or athirst, or a stranger, or naked, or sick, or in prison, and did not minister unto thee?

45 Then shall he answer them, saying, Verily I say unto you, Inasmuch as ye did it not to one of the least of these, ye did it not to me.

46 And these shall go away into everlasting punishment: but the righteous into life eternal.

TO AN ATHLETE DYING YOUNG

A. E. Housman

The time you won your town the race
We chaired you through the market-place;
Man and boy stood cheering by,
And home we brought you shoulder-high.

To-day, the road all runners come,
Shoulder-high we bring you home,
And set you at your threshold down,
Townsman of a stiller town.

Smart lad, to slip betimes away
From fields where glory does not stay
And early though the laurel grows,
It withers quicker than the rose.

Eyes the shady night has shut
Cannot see the record cut,
And silence sounds no worse than cheers
After earth has stopped the ears:

Now you will not swell the rout
Of lads that wore their honours out,
Runners whom renown outran
And the name died before the man.

So set, before its echoes fade,
The fleet foot on the sill of shade,
And hold to the low lintel up
The still-defended challenge-cup.

And round that early-laurelled head
Will flock to gaze the strengthless dead,
And find unwithered on its curls
The garland briefer than a girl's.

* * *

You can always get the truth from an American statesman after
he has turned seventy, or given up all hope for the Presidency.
                                                —Wendell Phillips

DO NOT GO GENTLE INTO THAT GOOD NIGHT

Dylan Thomas

Do not go gentle into that good night,
Old age should burn and rave at close of day;
Rage, rage against the dying of the light.

Though wise men at their end know dark is right,
Because their words had forked no lightning they
Do not go gentle into that good night.

Good men, the last wave by, crying how bright
Their frail deeds might have danced in a green bay,
Rage, rage against the dying of the light.

Wild men who caught and sang the sun in flight,
And learn, too late, they grieved it on its way,
Do not go gentle into that good night.

Grave men, near death, who see with blinding sight
Blind eyes could blaze like meteors and be gay,
Rage, rage against the dying of the light.

And you, my father, there on the sad height,
Curse, bless, me now with your fierce tears, I pray.
Do not go gentle into that good night.
Rage, rage against the dying of the light.

BASEBALL'S SAD LEXICON

Franklin P. Adams

These are the saddest of possible words:
    "Tinker to Evers to Chance."
Trio of bear cubs, and fleeter than birds,
    Tinker and Evers and Chance.
Ruthlessly pricking our gonfalon bubble,
Making a Giant hit into a double—
Words that are heavy with nothing but trouble:
    "Tinker to Evers to Chance."

THE STAR-SPANGLED BANNER

Francis Scott Key

O! say can you see by the dawn's early light,
What so proudly we hail'd at the twilight's last gleaming,
Whose broad stripes and bright stars, through the perilous figh
O'er the ramparts we watched were so gallantly streaming?
And the rocket's red glare, the bombs bursting in air,
Gave proof through the night that our flag was still there;
O! say does that star-spangled banner yet wave,
O'er the land of the free, and the home of the brave?

On the shore dimly seen through the mists of the deep,
Where the foe's haughty host in dread silence reposes,
What is that which the breeze, o'er the towering steep,
As it fitfully blows, half conceals, half discloses?
Now it catches the gleam of the morning's first beam,
In full glory reflected now shines in the stream.
'Tis the star-spangled banner, O! long may it wave
O'er the land of the free, and the home of the brave.

And where is that band who so vauntingly swore
That the havoc of war and the battle's confusion,
A home and a country, shall leave us no more?
Their blood has wash'd out their foul footsteps pollution;
No refuge could save the hireling and slave,
From the terror of flight, or the gloom of the grave;
And the star-spangled banner in triumph doth wave,
O'er the land of the free, and the home of the brave.

O, thus be it ever when freemen shall stand,
Between their lov'd home and the war's desolation,
Blest with vict'ry and peace, may the heav'n-rescued land,
Praise the Power that hath made and preserved us a nation.
Then conquer we must, when our cause it is just,
And this be our motto,—"In God is our trust,"
And the star-spangled banner in triumph shall wave,
O'er the land of the free, and the home of the brave.

* * *

'Tis more brave to live than to die.
—Meredith

AS BROTHERS LIVE TOGETHER

Henry Wadsworth Longfellow

Down the rivers, o'er the prairies,
Came the warriors of the nations,
Came the Delawares and Mohawks,
Came the Choctaws and Camanches,
Came the Shoshonies and Blackfeet,
Came the Pawnees and Omahas,
Came the Mandans and Dacotahs,
Came the Hurons and Ojibways,
All the warriors drawn together
By the signal of the Peace-Pipe,
To the Mountains of the Prairie,
To the great Red Pipe-stone Quarry
   And they stood there on the meadow,
With their weapons and their war-gear,
Painted like the leaves of Autumn,
Painted like the sky of morning,
Wildly glaring at each other;
In their faces stern defiance,
In their hearts the feuds of ages,
The hereditary hatred,
The ancestral thirst of vengeance.
   Gitche Manito, the mighty,
The creator of the nations,
Looked upon them with compassion,
With paternal love and pity;
Looked upon their wrath and wrangling
But as quarrels among children,
   Over them he stretched his right hand
To subdue their stubborn natures,
To allay their thirst and fever,
By the shadow of his right hand;
Spake to them with voice majestic
As the sound of far-off waters,
Falling into deep abysses,
Warning, chiding, spake in this wise:—
   "O my children! my poor children!
Listen to the words of wisdom,
Listen to the words of warning,

From the lips of the Great Spirit,
From the Master of Life, who made you!
   "I have given you lands to hunt in,
I have given you streams to fish in,
I have given you bear and bison,
I have given you roe and reindeer,
I have given you brant and beaver,
Filled the marshes full of wild-fowl,
Filled the river full of fishes;
Why then are you not contented?
Why then will you hunt each other?
   "I am weary of your quarrels,
Weary of your wars and bloodshed,
Weary of your prayers for vengeance,
Of your wranglings and dissensions;
All your strength is in your union,
All your danger is in discord;
Therefore be at peace henceforward
And as brothers live together.
   "I will send a prophet to you,
A Deliverer of the nations,
Who shall guide you and shall teach you,
Who shall toil and suffer with you.
If you listen to his counsels,
You will multiply and prosper;
If his warnings pass unheeded,
You will fade away and perish!
   "Bathe now in the stream before you,
Wash the war-paint from your faces,
Wash the blood-stains from your fingers,
Bury your war-clubs and your weapons,
Break the red stone from this quarry,
Mould and make it into Peace-Pipes,
Take the reeds that grow beside you,
Deck them with your brightest feathers,
Smoke the calumet together,
And as brothers live henceforward!"
   Then upon the ground the warriors
Threw their cloaks and shirts of deer-skin,
Threw their weapons and their war-gear,
Leaped into the rushing river,
Washed the war-paint from their faces.
Clear above them flowed the water,

Clear and limpid from the footprints
Of the Master of Life descending;
Dark below them flowed the water,
Soiled and stained with streaks of crimson,
As if blood were mingled with it!
    From the river came the warriors,
Clean and washed from all their war-paint;
On the banks their clubs they buried,
Buried all their warlike weapons,
Gitche Manito, the mighty,
The Great Spirit, the Creator,
Smiled upon his helpless children!
    And in silence all the warriors
Broke the red stone of the quarry,
Smoothed and formed it into Peace-Pipes,
Broke the long reeds by the river,
Decked them with their brightest feathers,
And departed each one homeward,
While the Master of Life, ascending,
Through the opening of cloud-curtains,
Through the doorways of the heaven,
Vanished from before their faces,
In the smoke that rolled about him,
The Pulwana of the Peace-Pipe!
                    (From *The Song of Hiawatha*)

HOPE

Oliver Goldsmith

Hope, like a gleaming taper's light,
    Adorns and cheers our way;
And still, as darker grows the night,
    Emits a brighter ray.

*   *   *

Let us endeavor so to live that when we come to die even the undertaker will be sorry.—Mark Twain

DANIEL WEBSTER IN REPLY TO HAYNE

When my eyes shall be turned to behold for the last time the sun in heaven, may I not see him shining on the broken and dishonored fragments of a once glorious Union; on States dissevered, discordant, belligerent; on a land rent with civil feuds, or drenched, it may be, in fraternal blood! Let their last feeble and lingering glance rather behold the gorgeous ensign of the Republic, now known and honored throughout the earth, still full high advanced, its arms and trophies streaming in their original lustre, not a stripe erased or polluted, not a single star obscured. Bearing for its motto, no such miserable interrogatory as "What is all this worth?" nor those other words of delusion and folly, "Liberty first and Union afterward"; but everywhere, spread all over in characters of living light, blazing on all its ample folds, as they float over the sea and over the land, and in every wind under the whole heavens, that other sentiment, dear to every true American heart,—Liberty and Union, now and forever, one and inseparable!

(United States Senate, January 26, 1830)

ARITHMETIC

Multiplication is vexation,
Division is as bad;
The Rule of Three doth puzzle me,
And Practice drives me mad.

JENNY KISS'D ME

James Henry Leigh Hunt

Jenny kissed me when we met,
Jumping from the chair she sat in.
Time, you thief! who love to get
Sweets into your list, put that in.
Say I'm weary, say I'm sad;
Say that health and wealth have missed me;
Say I'm growing old, but add—
Jenny kissed me.

DAYBREAK

Henry Wadsworth Longfellow

A Wind came up out of the sea,
And said, "O mists, make room for me."

It hailed the ships, and cried, "Sail on,
Ye mariners, the night is gone."

And hurried landward far away,
Crying, "Awake! it is the day."

It said unto the forest, "Shout!
Hang all your leafy banners out!"

It touched the wood-bird's folded wing,
And said, "O bird, awake and sing."

And o'er the farms, "O chanticleer,
Your clarion blow; the day is near."

It whispered to the fields of corn,
"Bow down, and hail the coming morn."

It shouted through the belfry-tower,
"Awake, O bell! proclaim the hours."

It crossed the churchyard with a sigh,
And said, "Not yet! in quiet lie."

*   *   *

It is the common fate of the indolent to see their rights become a prey to the active. The condition upon which God hath given liberty to man is eternal vigilance, which condition if he break, servitude is at once the consequence of his crime and the punishment of his guilt.—John Philpot Curran (from Speech, 1790)

BURIAL OF SIR JOHN MOORE

Charles Wolfe

Not a drum was heard, not a funeral note,
  As his corse to the rampart we hurried;
Not a soldier discharged his farewell shot
  O'er the grave where our hero we buried.

We buried him darkly, at dead of night,
  The sods with our bayonets turning;
By the struggling moonbeams' misty light,
  And the lantern dimly burning.

No useless coffin inclosed his breast,
  Not in sheet nor in shroud we wound him;
But he lay, like a warrior taking his rest,
  With his martial cloak around him.

Few and short were the prayers we said,
  And we spoke not a word of sorrow;
But we steadfastly gazed on the face that was dead,
  And we bitterly thought of the morrow.

We thought, as we hollowed his narrow bed,
  And smoothed down his lonely pillow,
That the foe and the stranger would tread o'er his head,
  And we far away on the billow!

Lightly they'll talk of the spirit that's gone,
  And o'er his cold ashes upbraid him;
But little he'll reck, if they let him sleep on,
  In the grave where a Briton has laid him!

But half of our heavy task was done,
  When the clock struck the hour for retiring,
And we heard the distant and random gun
  That the foe was sullenly firing.

Slowly and sadly we laid him down,
  From the field of his fame fresh and gory!
We carved not a line, we raised not a stone,
  But we left him alone with his glory.

ABIDE WITH ME

Henry F. Lyte

Abide with me: fast falls the eventide;
The darkness deepens; Lord, with me abide:
When other helpers fail, and comforts flee,
Help of the helpless, oh, abide with me!

Swift to its close ebbs our life's little day;
Earth's joys grow dim, its glories pass away;
Change and decay in all around I see:
O Thou Who changeth not, abide with me!

Not a brief glance, I beg, a passing word,
But, as Thou dwell'st with Thy disciples, Lord,
Familiar, condescending, patient, free,—
Come, not to sojourn, but abide with me!

Come not in terrors, as the King of kings;
But kind and good, with healing in Thy wings:
Tears for all woes, a heart for every plea;
Come, Friend of sinners, and abide with me!

Thou on my head in early youth didst smile,
And, though rebellious and perverse meanwhile
Thou hast not left me, oft as I left Thee;
On to the close, O Lord, abide with me!

I need Thy presence every passing hour:
What but Thy grace can foil the tempter's power?
Who like Thyself my guide and stay can be?
Through cloud and sunshine, oh, abide with me!

I fear no foe with Thee at hand to bless;
Ills have no weights, and tears no bitterness;
Where is death's sting? where, grave thy victory?
I triumph still, if Thou abide with me.

Hold then Thy cross before my closing eyes;
Shine through the gloom, and point me to the skies:
Heaven's morning breaks, and earth's vain shadows flee—
In life and death, O Lord, abide with me!

THE ONE–HOSS SHAY

(THE DEACON'S MASTERPIECE)

Oliver Wendell Holmes

Have you heard of the wonderful one-hoss shay,
That was built in such a logical way
It ran a hundred years to a day,
And then, of a sudden, it—ah, but stay,
I'll tell you what happened without delay,
Scaring the parson into fits,
Frightening people out of their wits,—
Have you ever heard of that, I say?

Seventeen hundred and fifty-five.
Georgius Secundus was then alive,—
Snuffy old drone from the German hive.
That was the year when Lisbon-town
Saw the earth open and gulp her down,
And Braddock's army was done so brown,
Left without a scalp to its crown.
It was on the terrible Earthquake-day
That the Deacon finished the one-hoss shay.

Now in building of chaises, I tell you what,
There is always *somewhere* a weaker spot,—
In hub, tire, felloe, in spring or thill,
In panel, or crossbar, or floor, or sill,
In screw, bolt, thoroughbrace,—lurking still,
Find it somewhere you must and will,—
Above or below, or within or without,—
And that's the reason, beyond a doubt,
A chaise *breaks down*, but doesn't *wear out*.

But the Deacon swore (as Deacons do),
With an "I dew vum," or an "I tell yeou,"
He would build one shay to beat the taown
'N' the keounty 'n' all the kentry raoun';
It should be so built that it *couldn'* break daown:
—"Fur," said the Deacon, " 't's mighty plain
Thut the weakes' place mus' stan' the strain;
'N' the way t' fix it, uz I maintain,
                                    Is only jest
T' make that place uz strong uz the rest."

So the Deacon inquired of the village folk
Where he could find the strongest oak,
That couldn't be split nor bent nor broke,—
That was for spokes and floor and sills;
He sent for lancewood to make the thills;
The crossbars were ash, from the straightest trees,
The panels of white-wood, that cuts like cheese,
But lasts like iron for things like these;
The hubs of logs from the "Settler's ellum,"—
Last of its timber,—they couldn't sell 'em,
Never an axe had seen their chips,
And the wedges flew from between their lips,
Their blunt ends frizzled like celery tips;
Step and prop-iron, bolt and screw,
Spring, tire, axle, and linchpin too,
Steel of the finest, bright and blue;
Thoroughbrace bison-skin, thick and wide;
Boot, top, dasher, from tough old hide
Found in the pit when the tanner died.
That was the way he "put her through."—
"There!" said the Deacon, "naow she'll dew!"

Do! I tell you, I rather guess
She was a wonder, and nothing less!
Colts grew horses, beards turned gray,
Deacon and Deaconess dropped away,
Children and grandchildren—where were they?
But there stood the stout old one-hoss shay
As fresh as on Lisbon-earthquake-day!

EIGHTEEN HUNDRED;—it came and found
The Deacon's masterpiece strong and sound.
Eighteen hundred increased by ten;—
"Hahnsum kerridge" they called it then.
Eighteen hundred and twenty came;—
Running as usual; much the same.
Thirty and forty at last arrive,
And then come fifty, and FIFTY-FIVE.

Little of all we value here
Wakes on the morn of its hundredth year
Without both feeling and looking queer.
In fact, there's nothing that keeps its youth,
So far as I know, but a tree and truth.

(This is a moral that runs at large;
Take it.—You're welcome.—No extra charge.)
FIRST OF NOVEMBER—the-Earthquake-day,—
There are traces of age in the one-hoss-shay,
A general flavor of mild decay,
But nothing local, as one may say.
There couldn't be,—for the Deacon's art
Had made it so like in every part
That there wasn't a chance for one to start.
For the wheels were just as strong as the thills,
And the floor was just as strong as the sills,
And the panels just as strong as the floor,
And the whipple-tree neither less nor more,
And the back-cross bar as strong as the fore,
And spring and axle and hub *encore.*
And yet, as *a whole,* it is past a doubt
In another hour it will be *worn out!*

First of November, 'Fifty-five!
This morning the parson takes a drive.
Now, small boys, get out of the way!
Here comes the wonderful one-hoss shay,
Drawn by a rat-tailed, ewe-necked bay.
"Huddup!" said the parson. Off went they.
The parson was working his Sunday text,—
Had got to *fifthly,* and stopped perplexed
At what the—Moses—was coming next.
All at once the horse stood still,
Close by the meet'n'-house on the hill.
—First a shiver, and then a thrill,
Then something decidedly like a spill,—
And the parson was sitting up on a rock,
At half-past nine by the meet'n'-house clock,—
Just the hour of the Earthquake shock!
—What do you think the parson found,
When he got up and stared around?
The poor old chaise in a heap or mound,
As if it had been to the mill and ground!
You see, of course, if you're not a dunce,
How it went to pieces all at once,—
All at once, and nothing first,—
Just as bubbles do when they burst.

End of the wonderful one-hoss shay,
Logic is logic. That's all I say.

PERFECT WOMAN

William Wordsworth

She was a Phantom of delight
When first she gleamed upon my sight;
A lovely Apparition sent
To be a moment's ornament;
Her eyes as stars of Twilight fair;
Like Twilight's, too, her dusky hair;
But all things else about her drawn
From May-time and the cheerful Dawn;
A dancing Shape, an Image gay,
To haunt, to startle, and way-lay.

I saw her upon nearer view,
A Spirit, yet a Woman too!
Her household motions light and free,
And steps of virgin-liberty;
A countenance in which did meet
Sweet records, promises as sweet;
A Creature not too bright or good
For human nature's daily food;
For transient sorrows, simple wiles,
Praise, blame, love, kisses, tears and smiles.

And now I see with eye serene
The very pulse of the machine;
A Being breathing thoughtful breath,
A Traveler between life and death;
The reason firm, the temperate will,
Endurance, foresight, strength, and skill;
A perfect Woman, nobly planned,
To warn, to comfort, and command;
And yet a Spirit still, and bright
With something of angelic light.

BENJAMIN FRANKLIN

He snatched the lightning from heaven, and the sceptre from tyrants.

(Turgot's inscription on Houdon's bust)

REQUIEM

Robert Louis Stevenson

Under the wide and starry sky
Dig the grave and let me lie.
Glad did I live and gladly die,
And I laid me down with a will.

This be the verse that you grave for me:
Here he lies where he longed to be,
Home is the sailor, home from sea,
And the hunter home from the hill.

GOOD AND BAD CHILDREN

Robert Louis Stevenson

Children, you are very little,
And your bones are very brittle;
If you would grow great and stately,
You must try to walk sedately.

You must still be bright and quiet,
And content with simple diet;
And remain, through all bewild'ring,
Innocent and honest children.

Happy hearts and happy faces,
Happy play in grassy places—
That was how, in ancient ages,
Children grew to kings and sages.

But the unkind and the unruly,
And the sort who eat unduly,
They must never hope for glory—
Theirs is quite a different story!

Cruel children, crying babies,
All grow up as geese and gabies,
Hated, as their age increases,
By their nephews and their nieces.

316

UPON JULIA'S CLOTHES

Robert Herrick

Whenas in silks my Julia goes,
Then, then, methinks, how sweetly flows
The liquefaction of her clothes.

Next, when I cast mine eyes, and see
That brave vibration, each way free,
O, how that glittering taketh me!

A PERFECT DAY

Carrie Jacobs-Bond

When you come to the end of a perfect day,
And you sit alone with your thought,
While the chimes ring out with a carol gay,
For the joy that the day has brought,
Do you think what the end of a perfect day
Can mean to a tired heart,
When the sun goes down with a flaming ray
And the dear friends have to part.

Well this is the end of a perfect day,
Near the end of a journey too,
But it leaves a thought that is big and strong,
With a wish that is kind and true,
For mem'ry has painted this perfect day
With colors that never fade,
And we find at the end of a perfect day,
The soul of a friend we've made.

HAPPINESS

Happy the man, and happy he alone,
He who can call to-day his own;
He who, secure within, can say,
Tomorrow, do thy worst, for I have liv'd today.
                    (From Dryden's Imitation of Horace)

JABBERWOCKY

Lewis Carroll

'Twas brillig, and the slithy toves
  Did gyre and gimble in the wabe;
All mimsy were the borogoves,
  And the mome raths outgrabe.

"Beware the Jabberwock, my son!
  The jaws that bite, the claws that catch!
Beware the Jubjub bird, and shun
  The frumious Bandersnatch!"

He took his vorpal sword in hand:
  Long time the manxome foe he sought,—
So rested he by the Tumtum tree,
  And stood awhile in thought.

And as in uffish thought he stood,
  The Jabberwock, with eyes of flame,
Came whiffling through the tulgey wood,
  And burbled as it came!

One, two! One, two! And through and through
  The vorpal blade went snicker-snack!
He left it dead, and with his head
  He went galumphing back.

"And hast thou slain the Jabberwock?
  Come to my arms, my beamish boy!
O frabjous day! Callooh! Callay!"
  He chortled in his joy.

'Twas brillig, and the slithy toves
  Did gyre and gimble in the wabe;
All mimsy were the borogoves,
  And the mome raths outgrabe.

* * *

Life is a tragedy wherein we sit as spectators awhile, and then act our own part in it.

    —Jonathan Swift

Edit

THE WIT OF ADLAI STEVENSON

Man does not live by words alone, despite the fact that sometimes he has to eat them.

On Taxes: There was a time when a fool and his money were soon parted, but now it happens to everybody.

Do you know the difference between a beautiful woman and a charming one? A beauty is a woman you notice, a charmer is one who notices you.

The relationship of the toastmaster to speaker should be the same as that of the fan to the fan dancer. It should call attention to the subject without making any particular effort to cover it.

Eggheads unite—you have nothing to lose but your yolks.

I have sometimes said that flattery is all right—if you don't inhale.

You know how it is in an election year. They pick a President and then for four years they pick on him.

I have finally figured out what the Republican orators mean by what they call "moderate progressivism." All they mean is: "Don't just do something. Stand there."

In 1956, after losing a Presidential election for the second time: I think I missed my calling. As a matter of fact, I think I missed it twice.

* * *

After reading the epitaphs in the cemetery, you wonder where they bury the sinners.

—Anonymous

* * *

Winter lingered so long in the lap of Spring that it occasioned a great deal of talk.

—Bill Nye

THE LISTENERS

Walter de la Mare

"Is there anybody there?" said the Traveller,
   Knocking on the moonlit door;
And his horse in the silence champed the grasses
   Of the forest's ferny floor:
And a bird flew up out of the turret,
   Above the Traveller's head:
And he smote upon the door again a second time;
   "Is there anybody there?" he said.
But no one descended to the Traveller;
   No head from the leaf-fringed sill
Leaned over and looked into his grey eyes,
   Where he stood perplexed and still.
But only a host of phantom listeners
   That dwelt in the lone house then
Stood listening in the quiet of the moonlight
   To that voice from the world of men:
Stood thronging the faint moon beams on the dark stair,
   That goes down to the empty hall,
Hearkening in an air stirred and shaken
   By the lonely Traveller's call.
And he felt in his heart their strangeness,
   Their stillness answering his cry,
While his horse moved, cropping the dark turf,
   'Neath the starred and leafy sky;
For he suddenly smote on the door, even
   Louder, and lifted his head:—
"Tell them I came, and no one answered,
   That I kept my word," he said.
Never the least stir made the listeners,
   Though every word he spake
Fell echoing through the shadowiness of the still house
   From the one man left awake:
Ay, they heard his foot upon the stirrup,
   And the sound of iron on stone
And how the silence surged softly backward
   When the plunging hoofs were gone.

* * *

There is always room at the top—after the investigation.
                     —Oliver Herford

TO A WATERFOWL

William Cullen Bryant

Whither, midst falling dew,
While glow the heavens with the last steps of day,
Far through their rosy depths dost thou pursue
    Thy solitary way?

Vainly the fowler's eye
Might mark thy distant flight, to do thee wrong,
As, darkly painted on the crimson sky,
    Thy figure floats along.

Seek'st thou the plashy brink
Of weedy lake, or marge of river wide,
Or where the rocking billows rise and sink
    On the chafed ocean-side?

There is a Power whose care
Teaches thy way along that pathless coast—
The desert and illimitable air—
    Lone wandering, but not lost.

All day thy wings have fanned,
At that far height, the cold, thin atmosphere;
Yet stoop not, weary, to the welcome land,
    Though the dark night is near.

And soon that toil shall end;
Soon shalt thou find a summer home, and rest,
And scream among thy fellows; reeds shall bend
    Soon o'er thy sheltered nest.

Thou'rt gone; the abyss of Heaven
Hath swallowed up thy form; yet on my heart
Deeply hath sunk the lesson thou hast given,
    And shall not soon depart.

He, who from zone to zone
Guides through the boundless sky thy certain flight,
In the long way that I must tread alone,
    Will lead my steps aright.

THE SUGAR-PLUM TREE

Eugene Field

Have you ever heard of the Sugar-Plum Tree?
'Tis a marvel of great renown!
It blooms on the shore of the Lollypop Sea
In the garden of Shut-Eye Town;
The fruit that it bears is so wondrously sweet
(As those who have tasted it say)
That good little children have only to eat
Of that fruit to be happy next day.

When you've got to the tree, you would have a hard time
To capture the fruit which I sing;
The tree is so tall that no person could climb
To the boughs where the sugar-plums swing!
But up in that tree sits a chocolate cat,
And a gingerbread dog prowls below—
And this is the way you contrive to get at
Those sugar-plums tempting you so:

You say but the word to that gingerbread dog
And he barks with such a terrible zest
That the chocolate cat is at once all agog,
As her swelling proportions attest.
And the chocolate cat goes cavorting around
From this leafy limb unto that,
And the sugar-plums tumble, of course, to the ground—
Hurrah for that chocolate cat!

There are marshmallows, gumdrops, and peppermint canes
With stripings of scarlet and gold,
And you carry away of the treasure that rains,
As much as your apron can hold!
So come, little child, cuddle closer to me
In your dainty white nightcap and gown,
And I'll rock you away to that Sugar-Plum Tree
In the garden of Shut-Eye Town.

* * *

Knowledge comes but wisdom lingers.
—Tennyson

EVOLUTION

John Bannister Tabb

Out of the dusk a shadow,
Then a spark;
Out of the cloud a silence,
Then a lark;

Out of the heart a rapture,
Then a pain;
Out of the dead, cold ashes,
Life again.

MY SHADOW

Robert Louis Stevenson

I have a little shadow that goes in and out with me,
And what can be the use of him is more than I can see.
He is very, very like me, from the heels up to the head;
And I see him jump before me, when I jump into bed.

The funniest thing about him is the way he likes to grow—
Not at all like proper children, which is always very slow;
For he sometimes shoots up taller, like an india-rubber ball,
And he sometimes gets so little that there's none of him at all.

He hasn't got a notion of how children ought to play,
And can only make a fool of me in every sort of way.
He stays so close beside me, he's a coward you can see;
I'd think shame to stick to nursie as that shadow sticks to me!

One morning, very early, before the sun was up,
I 'rose and found the shining dew on every buttercup;
But my lazy little shadow, like an arrant sleepy head,
Had stayed at home behind me and was fast asleep in bed.

* * *

Count that day lost whose low descending sun
Views from thy hand no worthy action done.
(From Stamford's Art of Reading, 1803)

323

HANUKKAH HYMN

Anonymous

Rock of Ages, let our song
Praise Thy saving power;
Thou, amidst the raging foes,
Wast our sheltering tower.
Furious, they assailed us,
But Thine arm availed us,
And Thy word
Broke their sword
When our own strength failed us.

Kindling new the holy lamps,
Priest approved in suffering,
Purified the nation's shrine,
Brought to God their offering.
And His courts surrounding,
Hear, in joy abounding,
Happy throngs
Singing songs
With a mighty sounding.

Children of the martyr race,
Whether free or fettered,
Wake the echoes of the songs
Where ye may be scattered.
Yours the message cheering
That the time is nearing
Which will see
All men free,
Tyrants disappearing.

QUANDARY

Mrs. Edward Craster

The centipede was happy quite
  Until a toad in fun
Said, "Pray, which leg goes after which?"
That worked her mind to such a pitch,
She lay distracted in a ditch,
  Considering how to run.

O CAPTAIN! MY CAPTAIN!

Walt Whitman

1

O Captain! my Captain! our fearful trip is done;
The ship has weather'd every rack, the prize we sought is won;
The port is near, the bells I hear, the people all exulting,
While follow eyes the steady keel, the vessel grim and daring:
        But O heart! heart! heart!
        O the bleeding drops of red,
        Where on the deck my Captain lies,
        Fallen cold and dead.

2

O Captain! my Captain! rise up and hear the bells;
Rise up—for you the flag is flung—for you the bugle trills;
For you bouquets and ribbon'd wreaths—for you the shores
    a-crowding;
For you they call, the swaying mass, their eager faces turning:
        Here Captain! dear father!
          The arm beneath your head!
          It is some dream that on the deck,
           You've fallen cold and dead.

3

My Captain does not answer, his lips are pale and still;
My father does not feel my arm, he has no pulse nor will;
The ship is anchor'd safe and sound, its voyage closed and done;
From fearful trip, the victor ship comes in with object won:
        Exult, O shores, and ring, O bells!
        But I, with mournful tread,
          Walk the deck my Captain lies,
          Fallen cold and dead.

* * *

When I was a boy of fourteen, my father was so ignorant I could
hardly stand to have the old man around. But when I got to be
twenty-one I was astonished at how much the old man had learned
in seven years.
                        —Mark Twain

PRAYER

John Greenleaf Whittier

Dear Lord and Father of mankind,
　Forgive our foolish ways!
Reclothe us in our rightful mind,
In purer lives Thy service find,
　In deeper reverence, praise.

Drop Thy still dews of quietness,
Till all our strivings cease;
Take from our souls the strain and stress,
And let our ordered lives confess
　The beauty of Thy peace.

TWO VIEWS OF THE SAME SHIP

Midrash

I am standing upon the seashore; a ship at my side spreads her white sails to the morning breeze and starts for the blue ocean. She is an object of beauty and strength, and I stand and watch her until —at length—she hangs like a speck of white cloud just where the sea and sky come down to mingle with each other. Then someone at my side says, "There! She's gone!" Gone where? Gone from my sight—that is all. She is just as large in mast and hull and spar as she was when she left my side and is just as able to bear her load of living freight to the place of destination. Her diminished size is in me, not in her; and just at the moment when someone at my side says, "There! She's gone!", there are other eyes watching her coming and other voices ready to take up the glad shout, "There she comes!" And that is dying.

* * *

Liquor talks mighty loud when it gets loose from the jug.
　　　　　　　　　　　　—Joel Chandler Harris

NATURE

Henry Wadsworth Longfellow

As a fond mother, when the day is o'er,
　　Leads by the hand her little child to bed,
　　Half willing, half reluctant to be led,
　　And leaves his broken playthings on the floor,
Still gazing at them through the open door,
　　Nor wholly reassured and comforted
　　By promises of others in their stead,
　　Which, though more splendid, may not please him more:
So Nature deals with us, and takes away
　　Our playthings one by one, and by the hand
　　Leads us to rest so gently, that we go
Scarce knowing if we wish to go or stay,
　　Being too full of sleep to understand
　　How far the unknown transcends the what we know.

THE MOUNTAINS ARE A LONELY FOLK

Hamlin Garland

The mountains they are silent folk,
　　They stand afar—alone;
And the clouds that kiss their brows at night
　　Hear neither sign nor groan.
　　Each bears him in his ordered place
　　As soldiers do, and bold and high
They fold their forests round their feet
　　And bolster up the sky.

* * *

He's the kind of politician who follows you through a revolving door and then comes out ahead of you.

—Anonymous

* * *

Perched on the loftiest throne in the world, man is still sitting on his own behind.

—Michel de Montaigne

DAISY BELL

Harry Dacre

There is a flower within my heart,
Daisy, Daisy!
Planted one day by a glancing dart,
Planted by Daisy Bell!
Whether she loves me or loves me not
Sometimes it's hard to tell;
Yet I am longing to share the lot
Of beautiful Daisy Bell!

Chorus:

> Daisy, Daisy, Give me your answer, do!
> I'm half crazy, All for the love of you!
> It won't be a stylish marriage,
> I can't afford a carriage,
> But you'll look sweet on the seat
> Of a bicycle built for two!

We will go "tandem" as man and wife,
Daisy, Daisy!
"Ped'ling" away down the road of life,
I and my Daisy Bell!
When the road's dark we can both despise
P'licemen and "lamps" as well;
There are "bright lights" in the dazzling eyes
Of beautiful Daisy Bell!   (*Chorus.*)

I will stand by you in "wheel" or woe,
Daisy, Daisy!
You'll be the bell(e) which I'll ring, you know!
Sweet little Daisy Bell!
You'll take the "lead" in each "trip" we take,
Then, if I don't do well
I will permit you to use the brake,
My beautiful Daisy Bell!   (*Chorus.*)

* * *

The highest and most lofty trees have the most reason to dread
the thunder.

—Charles Rollin

MY WILD IRISH ROSE

Chauncey Olcott

If you listen, I'll sing you a sweet little song
Of a flower that's now drooped and dead,
Yet dearer to me, yes, than all of its mates,
Though each holds aloft its proud head.
'Twas given to me by a girl that I know;
Since we've met, faith, I've known no repose,
She is dearer by far than the world's brightest star,
And I call her my wild Irish rose.

Chorus
My wild Irish rose,
The sweetest flower that grows,
You may search everywhere,
But none can compare
With my wild Irish rose.
My wild Irish rose,
The dearest flower that grows,
And some day for my sake
She may let me take
The bloom from my wild Irish rose.

They may sing of their roses which by other names,
Would smell just as sweetly, they say,
But I know that my Rose would never consent
To have that sweet name taken away.
Her glances are shy when e'er I pass by
The bower where my true love grows.
And my one wish has been that some day I may win
The heart of my wild Irish rose.

SOCRATES' PRAYER

(TRANSLATOR: Benjamin Jowett)

Beloved Pan, and all ye other gods who haunt this place, give me
beauty in the inward soul; and may the outward and inward man
be at one. May I reckon the wise to be the wealthy, and may I have
such a quantity of gold as a temperate man and he only can bear.
(From Plato's *Phaedrus*)

THUS PITEOUSLY LOVE CLOSED

George Meredith

Thus piteously Love closed what he begat:
The union of this ever-diverse pair!
These two were rapid falcons in a snare,
Condemned to do the flitting of the bat.
Lovers beneath the singing sky of May
They wandered once; clear as the dew on flowers:
But they fed not on the advancing hours:
Their hearts held cravings for the buried day.
Then each applied to each that fatal knife,
Deep questioning, which probes to endless dole.
Ah, what a dusty answer gets the soul
When hot for certainties in this our life!—
In tragic hints here see what evermore
Moves dark as yonder midnight ocean's force,
Thundering like ramping hosts of warrior horse,
To throw that faint thin line upon the shore!

ADLAI STEVENSON AT CHICAGO, JULY 26, 1952

When the tumult and shouting die, when the bands are gone and the lights are dimmed, there is the stark responsibility in an hour of history haunted with those gaunt, grim specters of strife, dissension, and ruthless, inscrutable, and hostile powers abroad.

The ordeal of the twentieth century—the bloodiest, most turbulent era of the Christian age—is far from over. Sacrifice, patience, understanding, and implacable purpose must be our lot for years to come. . . .

The victory to be won in the twentieth century mocks the pretensions of individual acumen and ingenuity. For it is a citadel guarded by thick walls of ignorance and mistrust which do not fall before the trumpets' blast or the politicians' imprecations or even the generals' baton. They are, my friends, walls that must be directly stormed by the hosts of courage, morality, and of vision, standing shoulder to shoulder, unafraid of ugly truth, contemptuous of lies, half-truths, circuses, and demagoguery.

LIFE

Anna Letitia Barbauld

Life! I know not what thou art,
But know that thou and I must part;
And when, or how, or where we met,
I own to me's a secret yet.
But this I know, when thou art fled,
Where'er they lay these limbs, this head,
No cloud so valueless shall be
As all that then remains of me.

*　*　*

Life! we've been long together,
Through pleasant and through cloudy weather;
　'Tis hard to part when friends are dear;
　Perhaps 'twill cost a sigh, a tear;—
　Then steal away, give little warning,
　　Choose thine own time;
Say not Good-night, but in some brighter clime
　　Bid me Good-morning!

FLATTERY

Jonathan Swift

'Tis an old maxim in the schools,
That flattery's the food of fools;
Yet now and then your men of wit
Will condescend to take a bit.

BEFORE SLEEPING

Anonymous

Matthew, Mark, Luke and John
Bless the bed that I lie on!
Four corners to my bed,
Four angels round my head,
One at head and one at feet,
And two to guard my soul asleep.

SELF-DEPENDENCE

Matthew Arnold

Weary of myself, and sick of asking
What I am, and what I ought to be,
At this vessel's prow I stand, which bears me
Forwards, forwards, o'er the starlit sea.

And a look of passionate desire
O'er the sea and to the stars I send:
"Ye who from my childhood up have calm'd me,
Calm me, ah, compose me to the end!

"Ah, once more," I cried, "ye stars, ye waters,
On my heart your mighty charm renew;
Still, still let me, as I gaze upon you,
Feel my soul becoming vast like you!"

From the intense, clear, star-sown vault of heaven,
Over the lit sea's unquiet way,
In the rustling night-air came the answer:
"Wouldst thou *be* as these are? *Live* as they.

"Unaffrighted by the silence round them,
Undistracted by the sights they see,
These demand not that the things without them
Yield them love, amusement, sympathy.

"And with joy the stars perform their shining,
And the sea its long moon-silver'd roll;
For self-poised they live, nor pine with noting
All the fever of some differing soul.

NEEDLESS WORRY

Ralph Waldo Emerson

Some of your hurts you have cured,
   And the sharpest you still have survived,
But what torments of grief you endured
   From evils which never arrived!

GRACE BEFORE MEALS

Jewish
Lift up your hands toward the sanctuary and bless the Lord. Blessed art Thou, O Lord our God, King of the universe, who bringest forth bread from the earth. Amen.

Protestant
Bless, O Lord, this food to our use, and us to Thy services, and make ·us ever mindful of the needs of others, in Jesus' Name. Amen.

Roman Catholic
Bless us, O Lord, and these Thy gifts which we are about to receive from Thy bounty. Through Christ our Lord. Amen.

Eastern Orthodox
The Hungry shall eat and shall be satisfied, and those who seek out the Lord shall praise Him; their hearts shall live forever. Glory to the Father, and to the Son, and to the Holy Ghost, both now and ever, and unto ages of ages. Amen.

HOW TO GUESS YOUR AGE

Corey Ford

It seems to me that they are building staircases steeper than they used to. The risers are higher, or there are more of them, or something. Maybe this is because it is so much farther today from the first to the second floor, but I've noticed it is getting harder to make two steps at a time any more. Nowadays it is all I can do to make one step at a time.

Another thing I've noticed is the small print they're using lately. Newspapers are getting farther and farther away when I hold them, and I have to squint to make them out. The other day I had to back halfway out of a telephone booth in order to read the number on the coin box. It is obviously ridiculous to suggest that a person my

333

age needs glasses, but the only other way I can find out what's going on is to have somebody read aloud to me, and that's not too satisfactory because people speak in such low voices these days that I can't hear them very well.

Everything is farther than it used to be. It's twice the distance from my house to the station now, and they've added a fair-sized hill that I never noticed before. The trains leave sooner too. I've given up running for them, because they start faster these days when I try to catch them. You can't depend on timetables any more, and it's no use asking the conductor. I ask him a dozen times a trip if the next station is where I get off, and he always says it isn't. How can you trust a conductor like that? Usually I gather up my bundles and put on my hat and coat and stand in the aisle a couple of stops away, just to make sure I don't go past my destination. Sometimes I make doubly sure by getting off at the station ahead.

A lot of other things are different lately. Barbers no longer hold up a mirror behind me when they've finished, so I can see the back of my head, and my wife has been taking care of the tickets lately when we go to the theater. They don't use the' same material in clothes any more, either. I've noticed that all my suits have a tendency to shrink, especially in certain places such as around the waist or in the seat of pants, and the laces they put in shoes nowadays are harder to reach.

Revolving doors revolve much faster than they used to. I have to let a couple of openings go past me before I jump in, and by the time I get up nerve enough to jump out again I'm right back in the street where I started. It's the same with golf. I'm giving it up because these modern golf balls they sell are so hard to pick up when I stoop over. I've had to quit driving, too; the restrooms in filling stations are getting farther and farther apart. Usually I just stay home at night and read the papers, particularly the obituary columns. It's funny how much more interesting the obituary columns have been getting lately.

Even the weather is changing. It's colder in winter and the summers are hotter than they used to be. I'd go away, if it wasn't so far. Snow is heavier when I try to shovel it, and I have to put on rubbers whenever I go out, because rain today is wetter than the rain we used to get. Draughts are more severe too. It must be the way they build windows now.

People are changing too. For one thing, they're younger than they used to be when I was their age. I went back recently to an alumni reunion at the college I graduated from in 1943—that is,

1933—I mean, 1923—and I was shocked to see the mere tots they're admitting as students these days. The average age of the freshman class couldn't have been more than seven. They seem to be more polite than in my time, though; several undergraduates called me "Sir," and one of them asked if he could help me across the street.

On the other hand, people my own age are so much older than I am. I realize that my generation is approaching middle age (I define middle age roughly as the period between 21 and 110) but there is no excuse for my classmates tottering into a state of advanced senility. I ran into my old roommate at the bar, and he'd changed so much that he didn't recognize me. "You've put on a little weight, George," I said.

"It's this modern food," George said. "It seems to be more fattening."

"How about another martini?" I said. "Have you noticed how much weaker the martinis are these days?"

"Everything is different," said George. "Even the food you get. It's more fattening."

"How long since I've seen you, George?" I said. "It must be several years."

"I think the last time was right after the election," said George.

"What election was that?"

George thought for a moment. "Harding."

I ordered a couple more martinis. "Have you noticed these martinis are weaker than they used to be?" I said.

"It isn't like the old days," George said. "Remember when we'd go down to the speak, and order some Orange Blossoms, and maybe pick up a couple of flappers? Boy, could they neck! Hot diggety!"

"You used to be quite a cake-eater, George," I said. "Do you still do the Black Bottom?"

"I put on too much weight," said George. "This food nowadays seems to be more fattening."

"I know," I said, "you mentioned that just a minute ago."

"Did I?" said George.

"How about another martini?" I said. "Have you noticed the martinis aren't as strong as they used to be?"

"Yes," said George, "you said that twice before."

"Oh," I said. . . .

I got to thinking about poor old George while I was shaving this morning, and I stopped for a moment and looked at my own reflection in the mirror. They don't seem to use the same kind of glass in mirrors any more.

ON LADY POLTAGRUE, A PUBLIC PERIL

Hilaire Belloc

The Devil, having nothing else to do,
Went off to tempt My Lady Poltagrue.
My Lady, tempted by a private whim,
To his extreme annoyance, tempted him.

THE QUEEN INTRODUCES ALICE TO A
FACT OF MODERN LIFE

Lewis Carroll

Alice never could quite make out, in thinking it over afterwards, how it was that they began; all she remembers is that they were running hand in hand, and the Queen went so fast that it was all she could do to keep up with her; and still the Queen kept crying "Faster! Faster!" but Alice felt she *could not* go faster, though she had no breath left to say so.

The most curious part of the thing was, that the trees and other things round them never changed their places at all; however fast they went, they never seemed to pass anything. "I wonder if all the things move along with us?" thought poor, puzzled Alice. And the Queen seemed to guess her thoughts, for she cried, "Faster! Don't try to talk!"

Not that Alice nad any idea of doing *that*. She felt as if she would never be able to talk again, she was getting so much out of breath; and still the Queen cried "Faster! Faster!" and dragged her along. "Are we nearly there?" Alice managed to pant out at last.

"Nearly there?" the Queen repeated. "Why, we passed it ten minutes ago! Faster!" And they ran on for a time in silence, with the wind whistling in Alice's ears, and almost blowing her hair off her head, she fancied.

"Now! Now!" cried the Queen. "Faster! Faster!" And they went so fast that at last they seemed to skim through the air, hardly touching the ground with their feet, till suddenly, just as Alice was getting quite exhausted, they stopped, and she found herself sitting on the ground, breathless and giddy.

The Queen propped her up against a tree, and said kindly, "You may rest a little now."

Alice looked around her in great surprise. "Why, I do believe we've been under this tree the whole time! Everything's just as it was!"

"Of course it is," said the Queen; "What would you have it?"

"Well, in *our* country," said Alice, still panting a little, "you'd generally get to somewhere else—if you ran very fast for a long time, as we've been doing."

"A slow sort of country!" said the Queen. "Now, *here*, you see, it takes all the running *you* can do, to keep in the same place. If you want to get somewhere else you must run at least twice as fast as that!"

ODE ON SOLITUDE

Alexander Pope

Happy the man whose wish and care
   A few paternal acres bound,
Content to breathe his native air
    In his own ground.

Whose herds with milk, whose fields with bread,
   Whose flocks supply him with attire,
Whose trees in summer yield him shade,
    In winter fire.

Bless'd who can unconcern'dly find
   Hours, days, and years slide soft away,
In health of body, peace of mind,
    Quiet by day;

Sound sleep by night: study and ease
   Together mix'd; sweet recreation;
And innocence, which most does please,
    With meditation.

Thus let me live, unseen, unknown,
   Thus unlamented let me die;
Steal from the world, and not a stone
    Tell where I lie.

GO, LOVELY ROSE!

Edmund Waller

Go, lovely rose!
Tell her that wastes her time and me,
That now she knows,
When I resemble her to thee,
How sweet and fair she seems to be.

Tell her that's young,
And shuns to have her graces spied,
That hadst thou sprung
In deserts, where no men abide,
Thou must have uncommended died.

Small is the worth
Of beauty from the light retired;
Bid her come forth,
Suffer herself to be desired,
And not blush so to be admired.

Then die! that she
The common fate of all things rare
May read in thee;
How small a part of time they share
That are so wondrous sweet and fair!

THEODORE ROOSEVELT STANDS AT ARMAGEDDON

What happens to me is not of the slightest consequence; I am
to be used, as in a doubtful battle any man is used, to his hurt or
not, so long as he is useful and is then cast aside and left to die.
I wish you to feel this. I mean it; and I shall need no sympathy
when you are through with me. . . . It would be far better to fail
honorably for the cause we champion than it would be to win by
foul methods the foul victory for which our opponents hope. But
the victory shall be ours, and it shall be . . . clean and honest
fighting for the loftiest of causes. We fight in honorable fashion
for the good of mankind; unheeding of our individual fates; with
unflinching hearts and undimmed eyes; we stand at Armageddon,
and we battle for the Lord.

(Before the Republican National
Convention, Chicago, 1912)

338

ONE HOUR OF LIFE

Sir Walter Scott

One hour of life, crowded to the full with glorious action, and filled with noble risks, is worth whole years of those mean observances of paltry decorum, in which men steal through existence, like sluggish waters through a marsh, without either honour or observation.

PRAYER FOR SERENITY

Reinhold Niebuhr

O God, grant us the serenity to accept
What cannot be changed;
The courage to change what can be changed,
And the wisdom to know the one from the other.

A BIRD IN A GILDED CAGE

Arthur J. Lamb

The ball-room was filled with fashion's throng,
It shone with a thousand lights,
And there was a woman who passed along,
The fairest of all the sights.
A girl to her lover then softly sighed
"There's riches at her command";
"But she married for wealth, not for love," he cried,
"Though she lives in a mansion grand."

Chorus
She's only a bird in a gilded cage,
A beautiful sight to see,
You may think she's happy and free from care;
She's not, though she seems to be.
'Tis said when you think of her wasted life,
For youth cannot mate with age,
And her beauty was sold for an old man's gold,
She's a bird in a gilded cage.

I stood in a church-yard just at eve,
When sunset adorned the west,
And looked at the people who'd come to grieve,
For loved ones now laid at rest.
A tall marble monument marked the grave
Of one who'd been fashion's queen,
And I thought, "She is happier here at rest,
Than to have people say when seen":

(*Chorus.*)

JESUS EATS WITH SINNERS

Holy Bible, Mark 2:15–17

And it came to pass, that, as Jesus sat at meat in his house, many publicans and sinners sat also together with Jesus and his disciples: for there were many, and they followed him.

And when the scribes and Pharisees saw him eat with publicans and sinners, they said unto his disciples, How is it that he eateth and drinketh with publicans and sinners?

When Jesus heard it, he saith unto them, They that are whole have no need of the physician, but they that are sick: I came not to call the righteous, but sinners to repentance.

A FAMOUS TOAST

Richard Brinsley Sheridan

Here's to the maiden of bashful fifteen;
Here's to the widow of fifty;
Here's to the flaunting, extravagant queen,
And here's to the housewife that's thrifty.
Let the toast pass;
Drink to the lass;
I'll warrant she'll prove an excuse for the glass.
(From School for Scandal)

ARMED FORCES SLOGAN—WORLD WAR II

If it moves, salute it.
If it doesn't move, pick it up.
If you can't pick it up, paint it.

340

THE KING'S RING

Theodore Tilton

Once in Persia reigned a king,
Who upon his signet ring
Graved a maxim true and wise,
Which, if held before his eyes,
Gave him counsel, at a glance,
Fit for every change or chance:
Solemn words, and these are they:
"Even this shall pass away!"

Trains of camels through the sand
Brought him gems from Samarcand;
Fleets of galleys through the seas
Brought him pearls to rival these.
But he counted little gain
Treasures of the mine or main.
"What is wealth?" the king would say;
"Even this shall pass away."

Fighting on a furious field,
Once a javelin pierced his shield.
Soldiers with a loud lament
Bore him bleeding to his tent.
Groaning from his tortured side,
"Pain is hard to bear," he cried,
"But with patience day by day,
'Even this shall pass away.'"

Towering in the public square
Twenty cubits in the air,
Rose his statue carved in stone,
Then the king, disguised, unknown,
Gazing at his sculptured name,
Asked himself, "And what is fame?
Fame is but a slow decay:
'Even this shall pass away.'"

In the revels of his court,
At the zenith of his sport,
When the palms of all his guests
Burned with clapping at his jests,
He, amid his figs and wine,
Cried, "O loving friends of mine!
Pleasure comes, but does not stay;
'Even this shall pass away.' "

Lady fairest ever seen
Was the bride he crowned his queen.
Pillowed on the marriage-bed,
Whispering to his soul, he said,
"Though a bridegroom never pressed
Dearer bosom to his breast,
Mortal flesh must come to clay:
'Even this shall pass away.' "

Struck with palsy, sere and old,
Waiting at the Gates of Gold,
Spake he with his dying breath,
"Life is done, but what is Death?"
Then, in answer to the king,
Fell a sunbeam on his ring,
Showing by a heavenly ray—
"Even this shall pass away."

PRAYER AT NIGHT

From The Book of Common Prayer

O Lord, support us all the day long, until the shadows lengthen and the evening comes, and the busy world is hushed, and the fever of life is over, and our work is done. Then in thy mercy grant us a safe lodging, and a holy rest, and peace at the last. Amen.

O God, who art the life of mortal men, the light of the faithful, the strength of those who labour, and the repose of the dead; We thank thee for the timely blessings of the day, and humbly supplicate thy merciful protection all this night. Bring us, we beseech thee, in safety to the morning hours; through him who died for us and rose again, thy Son, our Saviour Jesus Christ. Amen.

ONE WORLD

Johann Amos Comenius

We are all citizens of one world, we are all of one blood. To hate a man because he was born in another country, because he speaks a different language, or because he take a different view on this subject or that, is a great folly. Desist, I implore you, for we are all equally human. . . . Let us have but one end in view, the welfare of humanity.

WHO WALKS WITH BEAUTY

David Morton

Who walks with Beauty has no need of fear;
The sun and moon and stars keep pace with him,
Invisible hands restore the ruined year,
And time, itself, grows beautifully dim.
One hill will keep the footprints of the moon,
That came and went a hushed and secret hour;
One star at dusk will yield the lasting boon;
Remembered Beauty's white, immortal flower.
Who takes of Beauty wine and daily bread,
Will know no lack when bitter years are lean;
The brimming cup is by, the feast is spread,—
The sun and moon and stars his eyes have seen,
Are for his hunger and the thirst he slakes:
The wine of Beauty and the bread he breaks.

THE SURRENDER OF GENERAL ROBERT E. LEE

General U. S. Grant

I found Lee at the house of a Mr. McLean, at Appomattox Court House, with Colonel Marshall, one of his staff officers, awaiting my arrival. The head of his column was occupying a hill, on a portion of which was an apple orchard, beyond a little valley which sepa-rated it from that on the crest of which Sheridan's forces were drawn up in line of battle to the south.

343

I had known General Lee in the old army, and had served with him in the Mexican War; but did not suppose, owing to the difference in our age and rank that he would remember me; while I would more naturally remember him distinctly, because he was the chief of staff of General Scott in the Mexican War.

When I had left camp that morning, I had not expected so soon the result that was then taking place, and consequently was in rough garb. I was without a sword, as I usually was when on horseback in the field, and wore a soldier's blouse for a coat, with the shoulder straps of my rank to indicate to the army who I was. When I went into the house I found General Lee. I had my staff with me, a good portion of whom were in the room during the whole of the interview.

What General Lee's feelings were I do not know. As he was a man of much dignity, with an impassible face, it was impossible to say whether he felt inwardly glad that the end had finally come, or felt sad over the result, and was too manly to show it. Whatever his feelings, they were entirely concealed from my observation; but my own feelings, which had been quite jubilant on the receipt of his letter, were sad and depressed. I felt like anything rather than rejoicing at the downfall of a foe who had fought so long and valiantly.

General Lee was dressed in a full uniform which was entirely new, and was wearing a sword of considerable value, very likely the sword which had been presented by the State of Virginia; at all events, it was an entirely different sword from the one that would ordinarily be worn in the field. In my rough traveling suit, the uniform of a private with the straps of a lieutenant-general, I must have contrasted very strangely with a man so handsomely dressed, six feet high and of faultless form. But this was not a matter that I thought of until afterwards.

We soon fell into a conversation about old army times. He remarked that he remembered me very well in the old army; and I told him that as a matter of course I remembered him perfectly, but from the difference in our ranks and years (there being about sixteen years difference in our ages), I had thought it very likely that I had not attracted his attention sufficiently to be remembered by him after such a long interval. Our conversation grew so pleasant that I almost forgot the object of our meeting. After the conversation had run on in this style for some time, General Lee called my attention to the object of our meeting, and said he had asked for this interview for the purpose of getting from me the terms I had proposed to give his army. I said that I meant merely that his army should lay down its arms, not to take them up again during the continuance of the war unless duly and properly exchanged. He said that he had so understood my letter.

Then we gradually fell off again into conversation about matters foreign to the subject which had brought us together. This continued for some little time, when General Lee again interrupted the course of the conversation by suggesting that the terms I proposed to give his army ought to be written out. I called to General Parker, secretary on my staff, for writing materials, and commenced writing out the terms.

When I put my pen to the paper I did not know the first word that I should make use of in writing the terms. I only knew what was in my mind, and I wished to express it clearly, so that there could be no mistaking it. As I wrote on, the thought occurred to me that the officers had their own private horses and effects, which were important to them, but of no value to us; also that it would be an unnecessary humiliation to call upon them to deliver their side arms.

No conversation, not one word, passed between General Lee and myself, either about private property, side arms or kindred subjects. He appeared to have no objections to the terms first proposed; or if he had a point to make against them he wished to wait until they were in writing to make it. When he had read over that part of the terms about side arms, horses, and private property of the officers, he remarked, with some feeling, I thought, that this would have a happy effect upon his army.

Then, after a little further conversation, General Lee remarked to me again that their army was organized a little differently from the army of the United States (still maintaining by implication that we were two countries); that in their army the cavalry-men and artillerists owned their own horses; and he asked if he was to understand that the men who so owned their horses were to be permitted to retain them. I told him that as the terms were written they would not; that only the officers were permitted to take their private property. He then, after reading over the terms a second time, remarked that that was clear.

I then said to him that I thought this would be about the last battle of the war—I sincerely hoped so; and I said further I took it that most of the men in the ranks were small farmers. The whole country had been so raided by the two armies that it was doubtful whether they would be able to put in a crop to carry themselves and their families through the next winter without the aid of the horses they were then riding. The United States did not want them and I would, therefore, instruct the officers I left behind to receive the paroles of his troops to let every man of the Confederate army who claimed to own a horse or mule take the animal to his home. Lee remarked again that this would have a happy effect upon his army.

The much talked of surrendering of Lee's sword and my handing it back, this and much more that has been said about it is the purest romance. The word sword or side arms was not mentioned by either of us until I wrote it in the terms. There was no premeditation, and it did not occur to me until the moment I wrote it down. If I had happened to omit it, and General Lee had called my attention to it, I should have put it in the terms precisely as I acceded to the provision about the soldiers retaining their horses.

General Lee, after all was completed and before taking his leave, remarked that his army was in a very bad condition for want of food, and they were without forage; that his men had been living for some days on parched corn exclusively, and that he would have to ask me for rations and forage. I told him "certainly" and asked for how many men he wanted rations. His answer was "about twenty-five thousand"; and I authorized him to send his own commissary and quartermaster to Appomattox Station, two or three miles away, where he could have, out of the trains we had stopped, all the provisions wanted. As for forage, we had ourselves depended almost entirely upon the country for that.

When news of the surrender first reached our lines our men commenced firing a salute of a hundred guns in honor of the victory. I at once sent word, however, to have it stopped. The Confederates were now our prisoners, and we did not want to exult over their downfall.

I determined to return to Washington at once, with a view to putting a stop to the purchase of supplies, and what I now deemed other useless outlay of money. Before leaving, however, I thought I would like to see General Lee again; so next morning I rode out beyond our lines toward his headquarters, preceded by a bugler and a staff-officer carrying a white flag.

Lee soon mounted his horse, seeing who it was, and met me. We had there between the lines, sitting on horseback, a very pleasant conversation of over half an hour, in the course of which Lee said to me that the South was a big country and that we might have to march over it three or four times before the war entirely ended, but that we would now be able to do it as they could no longer resist us. He expressed it as his earnest hope, however, that we would not be called upon to cause more loss and sacrifice of life;

but he could not foretell the result. I then suggested to General Lee that there was not a man in the Confederacy whose influence with the soldiery and the whole people was as great as his, and that if he would now advise the surrender of all the armies I had no doubt his advice would be followed with alacrity. But Lee said, that he could not do that without consulting the President first. I knew there was no use to urge him to do anything against his idea of what was right.

AN OLD WOMAN OF THE ROADS

Padraic Colum

O, to have a little house!
    To own the hearth and stool and all!
The heaped-up sods upon the fire,
    The pile of turf against the wall!

To have a clock with weights and chains
    And pendulum swinging up and down!
A dresser filled with shining delph,
    Speckled and white and blue and brown!

I could be busy all the day
    Clearing and sweeping hearth and floor,
And fixing on their shelf again
    My white and blue and speckled store!

I could be quiet there at night
    Beside the fire and by myself,
Sure of a bed and loath to leave
    The ticking clock and the shining delph!

Och! but I'm weary of mist and dark,
    And roads where there's never a house or bush,
And tired I am of bog and road
    And the crying wind and the lonesome hush!

347

And I am praying to God on high,
　And I am praying Him night and day,
For a little house—a house of my own—
　Out of the wind's and the rain's way.

IDEALS

Carl Schurz

Ideals are like stars; you will not succeed in touching them with your hands. But like the seafaring man on the desert of waters, you choose them as your guides, and following them you will reach your destiny.

LIGHT IN DARKNESS

Talmud

When Adam saw for the first time the sun go down, and an ever-deepening gloom enfold creation, his mind was filled with terror. God then took pity on him, and endowed him with the divine intuition to take two stones—the name of one was Darkness and the name of the other Shadow of Death—and rub them against each other, and so discover fire. Thereupon Adam exclaimed with grateful joy: "Blessed be the Creator of Light."

LIMERICK

Anonymous

There was once a maiden of Siam
　Who said to her lover, young Kiam,
　　If you kiss me, of course,
　　You will have to use force,
　But God knows you are stronger than I am.

A BOOK

Emily Dickinson

There is no frigate like a book
　To take us lands away,
Nor any coursers like a page
　Of prancing poetry.

This traverse may the poorest take
　Without oppress of toll;
How frugal is the chariot
　That bears a human soul!

STUPIDITY STREET

Ralph Hodgson

I saw with open eyes
Singing birds sweet
Sold in the shops
For the people to eat,
Sold in the shops of
Stupidity Street.

I saw in a vision
The worm in the wheat,
And in the shops nothing
For people to eat:
Nothing for sale in
Stupidity Street.

THE FATEFUL CHOICE

Bernard M. Baruch

We are here to make a choice between the quick and the dead.
That is our business. Behind the black portent of the new atomic
age lies a hope which, seized upon with faith, can work out salvation.
If we fail, then we have damned every man to be the slave of fear.
Let us not deceive ourselves; we must elect world peace or world
destruction.

(From an address to the United Nations, June 14, 1946)

ENJOY THE GOOD

Holy Bible, Ecclesiastes 5:18–20

Behold that which I have seen: it is good and comely for one to eat and to drink, and to enjoy the good of all his labor that he taketh under the sun all the days of his life, which God giveth him; for it is his portion.

Every man also to whom God hath given riches and wealth, and hath given him power to eat thereof, and to take his portion, and to rejoice in his labor: this is the gift of God.

For he shall not much remember the days of his life; because God answereth him in the joy of his heart.

UNITE AS ONE PEOPLE

Abraham Lincoln

Let us discard all this quibbling about this man and the other man, this race and that race and the other race being inferior, and therefore they must be placed in an inferior position. Let us discard all these things, and unite as one people throughout this land, until we shall once more stand up declaring that all men are created equal.

(1858)

OLD AGE

Edmund Waller

The seas are quiet when the winds give o'er;
So calm are we when passions are no more.
For then we know how vain it was to boast
Of fleeting things, so certain to be lost.
Clouds of affection from our younger eyes
Conceal that emptiness which age descries.

The soul's dark cottage, batter'd and decay'd,
Lets in new light through chinks that Time hath made
Stronger by weakness, wiser men become
As they draw near to their eternal home.
Leaving the old, both worlds at once they view
That stand upon the threshold of the new.

GREATER LOVE HATH NO MAN

Holy Bible, John 15:13–16

Greater love hath no man than this, that a man lay down his life for his friends.

Ye are my friends, if ye do whatsoever I command you.

Henceforth I call you not servants; for the servant knoweth not what his lord doeth: but I have called you friends . . .

Ye have not chosen me, but I have chosen you.

TEWKESBURY ROAD

John Masefield

It is good to be out on the road, and going one knows not where,
    Going through meadow and village, one knows not whither nor
      why;
Through the grey light drift of the dust, in the keen, cool rush of
    the air,
    Under the flying white clouds, and the broad blue lift of the sky.

And to halt at the chattering brook, in the tall green fern at the brink
    Where the harebell grows, and the gorse, and the fox-gloves purple
      and white;
Where the shy-eyed delicate deer troop down to the brook to drink
    When the stars are mellow and large at the coming on of night.

O, to feel the beat of the rain, and the homely smell of the earth,
    Is a tune for the blood to jig to, a joy past power of words;
And the blessed green comely meadows are all a-ripple with mirth
    At the noise of the lambs at play and the dear wild cry of the birds.

THE BABY

Sir William Jones

On parent knees, a naked, new-born child,
Weeping thou sat'st when all around thee smiled;
So live that, sinking to thy last long sleep,
Thou then mayst smile while all around thee weep.
                  (From the Sanskrit of Kalidasa)

THE GOLDEN RULE

Mahabharata, c. 800 B.C.: Deal with others as thou wouldst thyself be dealt by. Do nothing to thy neighbor which thou wouldst not have him to thee hereafter.

Dadistan-I dinik, Zend-Avesta, c. 700 B.C.: That nature only is good when it shall not do unto another whatever is not good for its own self.

Undana Varga, c. 500 B.C.: Hurt not others with that which pains yourself.

Confucius, 5th century B.C.: Tuan-mu Tzv said, "What I do not wish others to do unto me I also wish not to do unto others." Do not unto others what you would not they should do unto you.

Panchatantra, c. 200 B.C.: Ponder well the maxim: Never do to other persons what would pain thyself.

Hillel Ha-Babli, c. 30 B.C.: Whatsoever thou wouldst that men should not do to thee, do not do that to them. This is the whole law. The rest is only explanation.

St. Luke, c. A.D. 75: As ye would that men should do to you, do ye also to them likewise.

St. Matthew, c. A.D. 75: All things whatsoever ye would that men should do to you, do ye even so to them; for this is the law and the prophets.

Mohammed, 7th century A.D.: Say not, if people are good to us, we will do good to them, and if people oppress us we will oppress them: but resolve that if people do good to you, you will do good to them, and if they oppress you, oppress them not again.

PROPOSAL

Anonymous

"Go ask Papa," the maiden said.
The young man knew Papa was dead;
He knew the life Papa had led;
He understood when the maiden said,
"Go ask Papa."

SCHOOL DAYS

Will D. Cobb

Nothing to do, Nellie Darling;
Nothing to do, you say.
Let's take a trip on memory's ship,
Back to the by-gone days.
Sail to the old village school house,
Anchor outside the school door,
Look in and see, there's you and there's me,
A couple of kids once more.

Chorus
School days, school days, dear old golden rule days;
Readin' and 'ritin' and 'rithmetic,
Taught to the tune of a hick'ry stick,
You were my queen in calico,
I was your bashful, barefoot beau,
And you wrote on my slate,
"I love you, Joe,"
When we were a couple of kids.

'Member the hill, Nellie Darling,
And the oak tree that grew on its brow?
They've built forty stories upon that old hill
And the oak's an old chestnut now.
'Member the meadows so green, dear,
So fragrant with clover and maize?
Into new city lots and preferred business plots,
They've cut them up since those days.

A GOOD NAME

William Shakespeare

Iago. Good name in man and woman, dear my lord,
Is the immediate jewel of their souls:
Who steals my purse steals trash; 'tis something, nothing;
'Twas mine, 'tis his, and has been slave to thousands.
But he that filches from me my good name
Robs me of that which not enriches him
And makes me poor indeed.

(From Othello)

353

FRIENDS

George W. Childs

Do not keep the alabaster box of your love and tenderness sealed up until your friends are dead. Fill their lives with sweetness. Speak approving, cheering words while their ears can hear them, and while their hearts can be thrilled and made happier. The kind things you mean to say when they are gone, say before they go. The flowers you mean to send for their coffin, send to brighten and sweeten their homes before they leave them. If my friends have alabaster boxes laid away, full of fragrant perfumes of sympathy and affection, which they intend to break over my body, I would rather they would bring them out in my weary and troubled hours and open them, that I may be refreshed and cheered while I need them. I would rather have a plain coffin without flowers, a funeral without a eulogy, than a life without the sweetness and love emanating from sympathy. Let us learn to anoint our friends while they are yet among the living. Post-mortem kindness does not cheer the burdened heart; flowers on the coffin cast no fragrance backward over the weary way.

AN EPITAPH UPON HUSBAND AND WIFE WHO DIED AND WERE BURIED TOGETHER

Richard Crashaw

To these whom death again did wed
This grave's the second marriage-bed.
For though the hand of Fate could force
'Twixt soul and body a divorce,
It could not sever man and wife,
Because they both lived but one life.
Peace, good reader, do not weep;
Peace, the lovers are asleep.
They, sweet turtles, folded lie
In the last knot that love could tie.
Let them sleep, let them sleep on,
Till the stormy night be gone,
And the eternal morrow dawn;
Then the curtains will be drawn,
And they wake into a light
Whose day shall never die in night.

LOCH LOMOND

Lady John Scott

By yon bonnie banks and by yon bonnie braes,
Where the sun shines bright on Loch Lomond,
Where me and my true love were ever wont to be,
On the bonnie, bonnie banks of Loch Lomond.

Chorus:
Oh, you'll take the high road
And I'll take the low road,
And I'll be in Scotland before you:
But me and my true love will never meet again,
On the bonnie, bonnie banks of Loch Lomond.

I mind where we parted in yon shady glen,
On the steep, steep side of Ben Lomond,
Where in deep purple hue the Highland hills we view,
And the moon coming out in the gloaming.

The wee birdies sing and the wild flowers spring,
And in sunshine the waters are sleeping,
But the broken heart will ken no second spring again,
And the world does not know how we are greeting.

MARY'S A GRAND OLD NAME

George M. Cohan

My mother's name was Mary, she was so good and true;
Because her name was Mary, she called me Mary, too.
She wasn't gay or airy, but plain as she could be;
I'd hate to be contrary, and call myself Marie.

Chorus
For it is Mary, Mary, plain as any name can be;
But with propriety, society will say Marie.
But it was Mary, Mary, long before the fashions came;
And there is something there that sounds so fair,
It's a grand old name!

Now, when her name is Mary, there is no falseness there;
When to Marie she'll vary, she'll surely bleach her hair.
Though Mary's ordinary, Marie is fair to see;
Don't ever fear sweet Mary, beware of sweet Marie!

CASSIUS POISONS BRUTUS' MIND

William Shakespeare

Well, honour is the subject of my story.
I cannot tell what you and other men
Think of this life, but, for my single self,
I had as lief not be as live to be
In awe of such a thing as I myself.
I was born free as Caesar; so were you:
We both have fed as well, and we can both
Endure the winter's cold as well as he:
For once, upon a raw and gusty day,
The troubled Tiber chafing with her shores,
Caesar said to me "Darest thou, Cassius, now
Leap in with me into this angry flood,
And swim to yonder point?" Upon the word,
Accoutred as I was, I plunged in
And bade him follow: so indeed he did.
The torrent roar'd, and we did buffet it
With lusty sinews, throwing it aside
And stemming it with hearts of controversy;
But ere we could arrive the point proposed,
Caesar cried "Help me, Cassius, or I sink!"
I, as Aeneas our great ancestor
Did from the flames of Troy upon his shoulder
The old Anchises bear, so from the waves of **Tiber**
Did I the tired Caesar. And this man
Is now become a god, and Cassius is
A wretched creature, and must bend his body
If Caesar carelessly but nod on him.
He had a fever when he was in Spain,
And when the fit was on him, I did mark
How he did shake: 'tis true, this god did shake;
His coward lips did from their colour fly,
And that same eye whose bend doth awe the world
Did lose his lustre: I did hear him groan:
Ay, and that tongue of his that bade the Romans
Mark him and write his speeches in their books,
Alas, it cried "Give me some drink, Titinius,"
As a sick girl. Ye gods, it doth amaze me
A man of such a feeble temper should
So get the start of the majestic world
And bear the palm alone. . . .

Why, man, he doth bestride the narrow world
Like a Colossus, and we petty men
Walk under his huge legs and peep about
To find ourselves dishonourable graves.
Men at some time are masters of their fates:
The fault, dear Brutus, is not in our stars,
But in ourselves, that we are underlings.
Brutus, and Caesar: what should be in that Caesar?
Why should that name be sounded more than yours?
Write them together, yours is as fair a name;
Sound them, it doth become the mouth as well;
Weigh them, it is as heavy; conjure with 'em,
Brutus will start a spirit as soon as Caesar.
Now, in the names of all the gods at once,
Upon what meat doth this our Caesar feed,
That he is grown so great?

(From Julius Caesar)

THE GOOD SHEPHERD

Holy Bible, John 10:7–18

Then said Jesus unto them again, Verily, verily, I say unto you, I am the door of the sheep. All that ever came before me are thieves and robbers: but the sheep did not hear them. I am the door: by me if any man enter in, he shall be saved, and shall go in and out, and find pasture. The thief cometh not, but for to steal, and to kill, and to destroy: I am come that they might have life, and that they might have it more abundantly. I am the good shepherd: the good shepherd giveth his life for the sheep. But he that is an hireling, and not the shepherd, whose own the sheep are not, seeth the wolf coming, and leaveth the sheep, and fleeth; and the wolf catcheth them, and scattereth the sheep. The hireling fleeth, because he is an hireling, and careth not for the sheep. I am the good shepherd, and know my sheep, and am known of mine. As the Father knoweth me, even so know I the Father: and I lay down my life for the sheep. And other sheep I have, which are not of this fold: them also I must bring, and they shall hear my voice; and there shall be one fold, and one shepherd. Therefore doth my Father love me, because I lay down my life, that I might take it again. No man taketh it from me, but I lay it down of myself. I have power to lay it down, and I have power to take it again. This commandment have I received of my Father.

LET DOGS DELIGHT TO BARK AND BITE

Isaac Watts

Let dogs delight to bark and bite,
 For God hath made them so;
Let bears and lions growl and fight,
 For 'tis their nature, too.

But, children, you should never let
 Such angry passions rise;
Your little hands were never made
 To tear each other's eyes.

SOUND THE CLARION

Sir Walter Scott

Sound, sound the clarion, fill the fife!
 To all the sensual world proclaim,
One crowded hour of glorious life
 Is worth an age without a name.

A BRIEF SERMON

Anonymous

Man's ingress into the world is naked and bare;
His progress through the world is trouble and care;
His egress out of the world is nobody knows where;
 If we do well here we shall do well there;
 I can tell you no more if I preach for a year.

* * *

The man who has not anything to boast of but his illustrious ancestors is like a potato—the only good belonging to him is underground.—Sir Thomas Overbury

ADDRESS TO THE OCEAN

Lord Byron

Roll on, thou deep and dark blue Ocean—roll!
Ten thousand fleets sweep over thee in vain:
Man marks the earth with ruin—his control
Stops with the shore;—upon the watery plain
The wrecks are all thy deed, nor doth remain
A shadow of man's ravage, save his own,
When for a moment, like a drop of rain,
He sinks into thy depths with bubbling groan,
Without a grave, unknell'd, uncoffin'd and unknown.

His steps are not upon thy paths—thy fields
Are not a spoil for him—thou dost arise
And shake him from thee; the vile strength he wields
For earth's destruction thou dost all despise,
Spurning him from thy bosom to the skies,
And send'st him, shivering in thy playful spray,
And howling, to his Gods, where haply lies
His petty hope in some near port or bay,
And dashest him again to earth—there let him lay.

The armaments which thunderstrike the walls
Of rock-built cities, bidding nations quake,
And monarchs tremble in their capitals,
The oak leviathans, whose huge ribs make
Their clay creator the vain title take
Of lord of thee, and arbiter of war—
These are thy toys, and, as the snowy flake,
They melt into thy yeast of waves, which mar
Alike the Armada's pride, or spoils of Trafalgar.

Thy shores are empires, changed in all save thee—
Assyria, Greece, Rome, Carthage, what are they?
Thy waters washed them power while they were free,
And many a tyrant since: their shores obey
The stranger, slave or savage; their decay
Has dried up realms to deserts:—not so thou,
Unchangeable save to thy wild waves' play—
Time writes no wrinkle on thine azure brow—
Such as creation's dawn beheld, thou rollest now.

Thou glorious mirror, where the Almighty's form
Glasses itself in tempests: in all time,
Calm or convulsed—in breeze, or gale, or storm,
Icing the pole, or in the torrid clime
Dark-heaving;—boundless, endless, and sublime—
The image of Eternity—the throne
Of the Invisible; even from out thy slime
The monsters of the deep are made; each zone
Obeys thee; thou goest forth, dread, fathomless, alone.

And I have loved thee, Ocean! and my joy
Of youthful sports was on thy breast to be
Borne, like thy bubbles, onward: from a boy
I wanton'd with thy breakers—they to me
Were a delight; and if the freshening sea
Made them a terror—'twas a pleasing fear,
For I was as it were a child of thee,
And trusted to thy billows far and near,
And laid my hand upon thy mane—as I do here.
                    (From Childe Harold's Pilgrimage)

"I'M NOBODY! WHO ARE YOU?"

Emily Dickinson

I'm nobody! Who are you?
Are you nobody, too?
Then there's a pair of us—don't tell!
They'd banish us, you know.

How dreary to be somebody!
How public, like a frog
To tell your name the livelong day
To an admiring bog!

WHEN LOVE RULES ON EARTH

Martin Buber

When senseless hatred reigns on earth, and men hide their faces
from one another, then heaven is forced to hide its face. But when
love comes to rule on earth, and men reveal their faces to one
another, then the splendor of God will be revealed.

INDIAN SERENADE

Percy Bysshe Shelley

I arise from dreams of thee
  In the first sweet sleep of night,
When the winds are breathing low,
  And the stars are shining bright.
I arise from dreams of thee,
  And a spirit in my feet
Hath led me—who knows how?—
  To thy chamber-window, Sweet!

The wandering airs they faint
  On the dark, the silent stream,—
The Champak odors fail
  Like sweet thoughts in a dream;
The nightingale's complaint,
  It dies upon her heart;—
As I must die on thine,
  Oh, beloved as thou art!

Oh, lift me from the grass!
  I die! I faint! I fail!
Let thy love in kisses rain
  On my lips and eyelids pale.
My cheek is cold and white, alas!
  My heart beats loud and fast;—
Oh! press it to thine own again,
  Where it will break at last!

* * *

If all our misfortunes were laid in one common heap, whence every one must take an equal portion, most people would be contented to take their own and depart.

—Solon

* * *

When a true genius appears in the world you may know him by this sign: that the dunces are all in confederacy against him.

—Jonathan Swift

LINCOLN'S FAREWELL

MY FRIENDS:

No one not in my position can appreciate the sadness I feel at this parting. To this people I owe all that I am. Here I have lived more than a quarter of a century; here my children were born, and here one of them lies buried. I know not how soon I shall see you again. A duty devolved upon me which is, perhaps, greater than that which has devolved upon any other man since the days of Washington. He never could have succeeded except for the aid of Divine Providence, upon which he at all times relied. I feel that I cannot succeed without the same Divine Aid which sustained him; and in the same Almighty Being I place my reliance for support; and I hope you, my friends, will all pray that I may receive that Divine Assistance, without which I cannot succeed, but with which success is certain. Again I bid you all an affectionate farewell.

WHATEVER IS—IS BEST

Ella Wheeler Wilcox

I know, as my life grows older,
 And mine eyes have clearer sight,
That under each rank wrong somewhere
 There lies the root of Right;
That each sorrow has its purpose,
 By the sorrowing oft unguessed;
But as sure as the sun brings morning,
 Whatever is—is best.

I know that each sinful action,
 As sure as the night brings shade,
Is somewhere, sometime punished,
 Though the hour be long delayed.
I know that the soul is aided
 Sometimes by the heart's unrest,
And to grow means often to suffer—
 But whatever is—is best.

I know there are no errors,
 In the great Eternal plan,

And all things work together
   For the final good of man.
And I know when my soul speeds onward,
   In its grand Eternal quest,
I shall say as I look back earthward,
   Whatever is—is best.

THE FOX AND THE GRAPES

A Fox, very hungry, chanced to come into a vineyard, where there hung branches of charming ripe grapes; but nailed up to a trellis so high, that he leaped till he quite tired himself, without being able to reach one of them. At last—"Let who will take them!" says he, "they are but green and sour; so I will even let them alone."

(From Aesop's Fables)

THE USES OF ADVERSITY

William Shakespeare

Now, my co-mates and brothers in exile,
Hath not old custom made this life more sweet
Than that of painted pomp? Are not these woods
More free from peril than the envious court?
Here feel we but the penalty of Adam,
The season's difference, as the icy fang
And churlish chiding of the winter's wind,
Which, when it bites and blows upon my body,
Even till I shrink with cold, I smile and say
"This is no flattery: these are counsellors
That feelingly persuade me what I am."
Sweet are the uses of adversity,
Which, like the toad, ugly and venomous,
Wears yet a precious jewel in his head,
And this our life exempt from public haunt
Finds tongues in trees, books in the running brooks,
Sermons in stones and good in every thing.
I would not change it.

(From As You Like It)

HARK! THE HERALD ANGELS SING

Charles Wesley

Hark! the herald angels sing,
"Glory to the new-born King;
Peace on earth, and mercy mild,
God and sinners reconciled!"
Joyful all ye nations rise,
Join the triumph of the skies;
With the angelic host proclaim,
"Christ is born in Bethlehem!"

Christ, by the highest heaven adored;
Christ, the everlasting Lord;
Come, Desire of Nations, come,
Fix in us Thy humble home.
Veiled in flesh the God-head see;
Hail the Incarnate Deity,
Pleased as man with men to dwell,
Jesus, our Emmanuel.

Mild He lays His glory by,
Born that man no more may die;
Born to raise the sons of earth,
Born to give them second birth.
Ris'n with healing in His wings,
Light and life to all He brings,
Hail, the Son of Righteousness!
Hail, the heav'n-born Prince of Peace!

OATH TAKEN BY NATURALIZED CITIZENS OF THE UNITED STATES

I hereby declare, on oath, that I absolutely and entirely renounce and abjure all allegiance and fidelity to any foreign prince, potentate, state, or sovereignty of whom or which I have heretofore been a subject or citizen; that I will support and defend the Constitution and laws of the United States of America against all enemies, foreign and domestic; that I will bear true faith and allegiance to the same; and that I take this obligation freely without any mental reservation or purpose of evasion; so help me God. In acknowledgment whereof I have hereunto affixed my signature.

364

SAIL, DON'T DRIFT

Oliver Wendell Holmes, M.D.

I find the greatest thing in this world not so much where we stand, *as in what direction we* are moving. To reach the port of heaven, we must sail sometimes with the wind, and sometimes against it, but we sail, and not drift, nor live at anchor.

IN MEMORIAM
Margaritae Sorori

William Ernest Henley

A late lark twitters from the quiet skies;
And from the west,
Where the sun, his day's work ended,
Lingers as in content,
There falls on the old, grey city
An influence luminous and serene,
A shining peace.

The smoke ascends
In a rosy-and-golden haze. The spires
Shine, and are changed. In the valley
Shadows rise. The lark sings on. The sun,
Closing his benediction,
Sinks, and the darkening air
Thrills with a sense of the triumphing night—
Night with her train of stars
And her great gift of sleep.

So be my passing!
My task accomplished and the long day done,
My wages taken, and in my heart
Some late lark singing,
Let me be gathered to the quiet west,
The sundown splendid and serene,
Death.

365

THE HAPPIEST HEART

John Vance Cheney

Who drives the horses of the sun
    Shall lord it but a day;
Better the lowly deed were done,
    And kept the humble way.

The rust will find the sword of fame,
    The dust will hide the crown;
Aye, none shall nail so high his name
    Time will not tear it down.

The happiest heart that ever beat
    Was in some quiet breast
That found the common daylight sweet,
    And left to Heaven the rest.

OLD SUSAN

Walter de la Mare

When Susan's work was done, she would sit,
With one fat guttering candle lit,
And window opened wide to win
The sweet night air to enter in.
There, with a thumb to keep her place,
She would read, with stern and wrinkled face,
Her mild eyes gliding very slow
Across the letters to and fro,
While wagged the guttering candle flame
In the wind that through the window came.
And sometimes in the silence she
Would mumble a sentence audibly,
Or shake her head as if to say,
"You silly souls, to act this way!"
And never a sound from night I would hear,
Unless some far-off cock crowed clear;
Or her old shuffling thumb should turn
Another page; and rapt and stern,
Through her great glasses bent on me,
She would glance into reality;
And shake her round old silvery head,

With—"You!—I thought you was in bed!"—
Only to tilt her book again,
And rooted in Romance remain.

OUT IN THE FIELDS

Anonymous

The little cares that fretted me,
  I lost them yesterday
Among the fields above the sea,
  Among the winds that play,
Among the lowing of the herds,
  The rustling of the trees,
Among the singing of the birds,
  The humming of the bees.

The foolish fears of what might pass,
  I cast them all away
Among the clover-scented grass,
  Among the new-mown hay,
Among the hushing of the corn,
  Where drowsy poppies nod,
Where ill thoughts die and good are born—
  Out in the fields of God.

LOVE CONCEALED

William Shakespeare

                    She never told her love,
But let concealment, like a worm i' the bud,
Feed on her damask cheek: she pined in thought;
And with a green and yellow melancholy
She sat like patience on a monument,
Smiling at grief. Was not this love indeed?
We men may say more, swear more: but indeed
Our shows are more than will; for still we prove
Much in our vows, but little in our love.
                    (From Twelfth Night)

* * *

A man is in general better pleased when he has a good
dinner upon his table than when his wife talks Greek.
                    —Samuel Johnson

WE NEVER SPEAK AS WE PASS BY

Anonymous

The spell is past, the dream is o'er,
And tho' we meet, we love no more!
One heart is crushed to droop and die,
And for relief must heav'nward fly!
The once bright smile has faded, gone;
And given way to looks forlorn!
Despite her grandeur's wicked flame,
She stoops to blush beneath her shame.

Chorus:

> We never speak as we pass by,
> Altho' a tear bedims her eye;
> I know she thinks of her past life,
> When we were loving man and wife!

In guileless youth I sought her side,
And she became my virtuous bride,
Our lot was peace, so fair, so bright.
One sunny day, no gloomy night;
No life on earth more pure than ours,
In that dear home, 'midst fields and flowers,
Until the tempter came to her,
It dazzled her, alas, she fell!

In gilded halls 'midst wealth she dwells,
How her heart aches, her sad face tells,
She fain would smile, seem bright and gay,
But Conscience steals her peace away;
And when the flatterer casts aside
My fallen dishonored bride,
I'll close her eyes, in death forgive,
And in my heart her name shall live.

STILL THE WONDER GREW

Oliver Goldsmith

While words of learned strength and thundering sound
Amazed the gazing rustics gathered round,
And still they gazed, and still the wonder grew
That one small head could carry all he knew.

AN OLD STORY

Edwin Arlington Robinson

Strange that I did not know him then,
　That friend of mine!
I did not even show him then
　One friendly sign;

But cursed him for the ways he had
　To make me see
My envy of the praise he had
　For praising me.

I would have rid the earth of him
　Once in my pride. . . .
I never knew the worth of him
　Until he died.

SONG

Christina Georgina Rossetti

When I am dead, my dearest,
　Sing no sad songs for me;
Plant thou no roses at my head,
　Nor shady cypress tree:
Be the green grass above me
　With showers and dewdrops wet;
And if thou wilt, remember,
　And if thou wilt, forget.

I shall not see the shadows,
　I shall not feel the rain;
I shall not hear the nightingale
　Sing on, as if in pain;
And dreaming through the twilight
　That doth not rise or set,
Haply I may remember,
　And haply may forget.

ROBINSON CRUSOE DISCOVERS
FRIDAY'S FOOTPRINT

Daniel Defoe

It happened one day, about noon, going towards my boat, I was exceedingly surprised with the print of a man's naked foot on the shore, which was very plain to be seen in the sand. I stood like one thunderstruck, or as if I had seen an apparition. I listened, I looked round me, I could hear nothing, nor see anything. I went up to a rising ground, to look farther. I went up the shore, and down the shore, but it was all one; I could see no other impression but that one. I went to it again to see if there were any more, and to observe if it might not be my fancy; but there was no room for that, for there was exactly the very print of a foot—toes, heel and every part of a foot. How it came thither I knew not, nor could in the least imagine. But after innumerable fluttering thoughts, like a man perfectly confused and out of myself, I came home to my fortification, not feeling, as we say, the ground I went on, but terrified to the last degree, looking behind me at every two or three steps, mistaking every bush and tree, and fancying every stump at a distance to be a man; nor is it possible to describe how many various shapes affrighted imagination represented things to me in, how many wild ideas were found every moment in my fancy, and what strange, unaccountable whimsies came into my thought by the way.

When I came to my castle, for so I think I called it ever after this, I fled into it like one pursued. Whether I went over by the ladder, as first contrived, or went in at the hole in the rock, which I called a door, I cannot remember; no, nor could I remember the next morning, for never frighted hare fled to cover, or fox to earth, with more terror of mind than I to this retreat.

(From Robinson Crusoe)

BATTLE-HYMN OF THE REPUBLIC

Julia Ward Howe

Mine eyes have seen the glory of the coming of the Lord:
He is trampling out the vintage where the grapes of wrath are
    stored;

He hath loosed the fateful lightning of his terrible swift sword.
　　His truth is marching on.

I have seen him in the watch-fires of a hundred circling camps;
They have builded him an altar in the evening dews and damps;
I can read his righteous sentence by the dim and flaring lamps.
　　His day is marching on.

I have read a fiery gospel, writ in burnished rows of steel:
"As ye deal with my contemners, so with you my grace shall deal;
Let the Hero, born of woman, crush the serpent with his heel,
　　Since God is marching on."

He has sounded forth the trumpet that shall never call retreat;
He is sifting out the hearts of men before his judgment-seat:
O, be swift, my soul, to answer him! be jubilant my feet!
　　Our God is marching on.

In the beauty of the lilies Christ was born across the sea,
With a glory in his bosom that transfigures you and me;
As he died to make men holy, let us die to make men free,
　　While God is marching on.

SONG

William Watson

April, April,
Laugh thy girlish laughter;
Then, the moment after,
Weep thy girlish tears,
April, that mine ears
Like a lover greetest,
If I tell thee, sweetest,
All my hopes and fears.
April, April,
Laugh thy golden laughter,
But, the moment after,
Weep thy golden tears!

371

WHAT MUST GOD THINK?

Abraham Lincoln

We, on our side, are praying to Him to give us victory, because we believe we are right; but those on the other side pray to Him, look for victory, believing they are right. What must He think of us?

YOUR MISSION

Ellen M. H. Gates

If you cannot on the ocean,
  Sail among the swiftest fleet,
Rocking on the highest billows,
  Laughing at the storms you meet,
You can stand among the sailors,
  Anchored yet within the bay;
You can lend a hand to help them,
  As they launch their boats away.

If you are too weak to journey
  Up the mountain, steep and high,
You can stand within the valley,
  While the multitude go by.
You can chant in happy measure,
  As they slowly pass along;
Though they may forget the singer,
  They will not forget the song.

If you have not gold and silver
  Ever ready to command,
If you cannot toward the needy
  Reach an ever-open hand,
You can visit the afflicted,
  O'er the erring you can weep;
You can be a true disciple,
  Sitting at the Saviour's feet.

If you cannot in a conflict
  Prove yourself a soldier true,
If where the fire and smoke are thickest
  There's no work for you to do,
When the battle field is silent,
  You can go with careful tread;
You can bear away the wounded,
  You can cover up the dead.

Do not stand then idly waiting
  For some greater work to do;
Fortune is a lazy goddess,
  She will never come to you.
Go and toil in any vineyard,
  Do not fear to do or dare;
If you want a field of labor,
  You can find it anywhere.

BREATHES THERE THE MAN WITH SOUL SO DEAD

Sir Walter Scott

Breathes there the man with soul so dead
Who never to himself hath said,
This is my own, my native land!
Whose heart hath ne'er within him burned,
As home his footsteps he hath turned
From wandering on a foreign strand?
If such there breathe, go, mark him well;
For him no minstrel raptures swell;
High though his titles, proud his name,
Boundless his wealth as wish can claim,
Despite those titles, power, and pelf,
The wretch, concentred all in self,
Living, shall forfeit fair renown,
And, doubly dying, shall go down
To the vile dust from whence he sprung,
Unwept, unhonored, and unsung.
    (From The Lay of the Last Minstrel)

THE KILKENNY CATS

Anonymous

There wanst was two cats of Kilkenny,
Each thought there was one cat too many,
So they quarreled and they fit,
They scratch'd and they bit,
Till, barrin' their nails,
And the tips of their tails,
Instead of two cats, there warnt any.

STEALING

James Russell Lowell

In vain we call old notions fudge,
    And bend our conscience to our dealing;
The Ten Commandments will not budge,
    And stealing will continue stealing.

METHUSELAH

Anonymous

Methuselah ate what he found on his plate,
And never, as people do now,
Did he note the amount of the calory count:
He ate it because it was chow.
He wasn't disturbed as at dinner he sat,
Devouring a roast or a pie,
To think it was lacking in granular fat
Or a couple of vitamins shy.
He cheerfully chewed each species of food,
Unmindful of troubles or fears
Lest his health might be hurt
By some fancy dessert;
And he lived over nine hundred years.

"THE RIGHT IS MORE PRECIOUS THAN PEACE"

Woodrow Wilson

It is a fearful thing to lead this great peaceful people into war, into the most terrible and disastrous of wars, civilization itself seeming to be in the balance. But the right is more precious than peace, and we shall fight for the things which we have always carried nearest our hearts—for democracy, for the right of those who submit to authority to have a voice in their own governments, for the rights and liberties of small nations, for a universal dominion of right by such a concert of free peoples as shall bring peace and safety to all nations and make the world itself at last free. To such a task we can dedicate our lives and our fortunes, everything that we are and everything that we have, with the pride of those who know that the day has come when America is privileged to spend her blood and her might for the principles that gave her birth and the peace which she has treasured. God helping her, she can do no other.

> (From a message to Congress, April 2, 1917, asking for Declaration of War Against Germany)

THERE IS PLEASURE IN THE PATHLESS WOODS

Lord Byron

There is a pleasure in the pathless woods,
There is a rapture on the lonely shore,
There is society where none intrudes,
By the deep Sea, and music in its roar:
I love not man the less, but Nature more,
From these our interviews, in which I steal
From all I may be, or have been before,
To mingle with the Universe, and feel
What I can ne'er express, yet cannot all conceal.
> (From Childe Harold)

ON CONSISTENCY

Ralph Waldo Emerson

A foolish consistency is the hobgoblin of little minds, adored by little statesmen and philosophers and divines. With consistency a great soul has simply nothing to do. He may as well concern himself with his shadow on the wall. Out upon your guarded lips! Sew them up with pack thread, do. Else, if you would be a man, speak what you think today in words as hard as cannon balls, and tomorrow speak what tomorrow thinks in hard words again, though it contradict everything you said today. . . . Fear never but what you shall be consistent in whatever variety of actions, so they be each honest and natural in their hour. For of one will, the actions will be harmonious, however unlike they seem. These varieties are lost sight of when seen at a little distance, at a little height of thought. One tendency unites them all. The voyage of the best ship is a zigzag line of a hundred tacks. This is only a microscopic criticism. See the line from a sufficient distance, and it straightens itself to the average tendency, your genuine action will explain itself and will explain your other genuine actions.

(From the essay, Self-Reliance)

OPPORTUNITY

John James Ingalls

Master of human destinies am I!
Fame, love, and fortune on my footsteps wait.
Cities and fields I walk; I penetrate
Deserts and seas remote, and passing by
Hovel and mart, and palace—soon or late
I knock unbidden once at every gate!

If sleeping, wake—if feasting, rise before
I turn away. It is the hour of fate,
And they who follow me reach every state
Mortals desire, and conquer every foe
Save death; but those who doubt or hesitate,
Condemned to failure, penury and woe,
Seek me in vain and uselessly implore.
I answer not, and I return no more.

THE BANKS O' DOON

Robert Burns

Ye banks and braes o' bonnie Doon,
   How can be bloom sae fresh and fair!
How can ye chant, ye little birds,
   And I sae weary fu' o' care!
Thou'lt break my heart, thou warbling bird,
   That wantons thro' the flowering thorn:
Thou minds me o' departed joys,
   Departed—never to return.

Thou'lt break my heart, thou bonnie bird,
   That sings beside thy mate,
For sae I sat, and sae I sang,
   And wist na o' my fate.
Aft hae I rov'd by bonnie Doon,
   To see the rose and woodbine twine;
And ilka bird sang o' its luve,
   And fondly sae did I o' mine.

Wi' lightsome heart I pu'd a rose,
   Fu' sweet upon its thorny tree;
And my fause luver stole my rose,
   But ah! he left the thorn wi' me.
Wi' lightsome heart I pu'd a rose
   Upon a morn in June;
And sae I flourish'd on the morn,
   And sae was pu'd on noon.

A MIND DISEASED

William Shakespeare

Macbeth: How does your patient, doctor?
Doctor: Not so sick, my lord,
As she is troubled with thick-coming fancies,
That keep her from her rest.
Macbeth: Cure her of that.
Canst thou not minister to a mind diseased,

Pluck from the memory a rooted sorrow,
Raze out the written troubles of the brain,
And with some sweet oblivious antidote
Cleanse the stuff'd bosom of that perilous stuff
Which weighs upon the heart?
Doctor: Therein the patient
Must minister to himself.

(From *Macbeth*)

ON FLEAS

The vermin only tease and pinch
Their foes superior by an inch;
So. naturalists observe a flea
Has smaller fleas that on him prey,
And these have smaller still to bite 'em,
And so proceed *ad infinitum*.

Jonathan Swift

Great fleas have little fleas upon their backs to bite 'em,
And little fleas have lesser fleas, and so ad infinitum.
The great fleas themselves in turn have greater fleas to go on,
While those again have greater still, and greater still, and so on.

Augustus De Morgan

THE SEA GYPSY

Richard Hovey

I am fevered with the sunset,
I am fretful with the bay,
For the wander-thirst is on me
And my soul is in Cathay.

There's a schooner in the offing,
With her topsails shot with fire,
And my heart has gone aboard her
For the Islands of Desire.

I must forth again to-morrow!
With the sunset I must be
Hull down on the trail of rapture
In the wonder of the sea.

LINCOLN CHALLENGES ROBERT ALLEN

New Salem, June 21, 1836

Dear Colonel: I am told that during my absence last week you passed through this place, and stated publicly that you were in possession of a fact or facts which, if known to the public, would entirely destroy the prospects of N. W. Edwards and myself at the ensuing election; but that, through favor to us, you should forbear to divulge them. No one has needed favors more than I, and, generally, few have been less unwilling to accept them; but in this case favor to me would be injustice to the public, and therefore I must beg your pardon for declining it. That I once had the confidence of the people of Sangamon, is sufficiently evident; and if I have since done anything, either by design or misadventure, which if known would subject me to a forfeiture of that confidence, he that knows of that thing, and conceals it, is a traitor to his country's interest.

I find myself wholly unable to form any conjecture of what fact or facts, real or supposed, you spoke; but my opinion of your veracity will not permit me for a moment to doubt you at least believed what you said. I am flattered with the personal regard you manifested for me; but I do hope that, on more mature reflection, you will view the public interest as a paramount consideration, and therefore determine to let the worst come. I here assure you that the candid statement of facts on your part, however low it may sink me, shall never break the tie of personal friendship betweer. us. I wish an answer to this, and you are at liberty to publish both, if you choose.

A. Lincoln

YOU NEVER CAN TELL

Ella Wheeler Wilcox

You never can tell when you send a word
  Like an arrow shot from a bow
By an archer blind, be it cruel or kind,
  Just where it may chance to go.
It may pierce the breast of your dearest friend,
  Tipped with its poison or balm,
To a stranger's heart in life's great mart
  It may carry its pain or its calm.

379

You never can tell when you do an act
  Just what the result will be,
But with every deed you are sowing a seed,
  Though the harvest you may not see.
Each kindly act is an acorn dropped
  In God's productive soil;
You may not know, but the tree shall grow
  With shelter for those who toil.

You never can tell what your thoughts will do
  In bringing you hate or love,
For thoughts are things, and their airy wings
  Are swifter than carrier doves.
They follow the law of the universe—
  Each thing must create its kind,
And they speed o'er the track to bring you back
  Whatever went out from your mind.

GOD GOVERNS IN THE AFFAIRS OF MEN

Benjamin Franklin

I have lived, sir, a long time. And the longer I live, the more convincing proofs I see of this truth—that God governs in the affairs of men. And if a sparrow cannot fall on the ground without his notice, is it probable that an empire can rise without his aid? We have been assured, sir, in the sacred writings that except the Lord build the house, they labor in vain that build it. I firmly believe this; and I also believe that without his concurring aid we shall succeed in this political building no better than the builders of Babel; our projects will be confounded and we ourselves shall become a reproach and a byword down to future ages.

INSCRIPTION ON THE NATIONAL ARCHIVES BUILDING, WASHINGTON, D.C.

The heritage of the past is the seed that brings forth
the harvest of the future.

HIGH FLIGHT

John Gillespie Magee, Jr.

Oh! I have slipped the surly bonds of Earth
And danced the skies on laughter-silvered wings;
Sunward I've climbed, and joined the tumbling mirth
Of sun-split clouds—and done a hundred things
You have not dreamed of—wheeled and soared and swung
High in the sunlit silence. Hov'ring there,
I've chased the shouting wind along, and flung
My eager craft through footless halls of air. . . .

Up, up the long, delirious, burning blue
I've topped the wind-swept heights with easy grace,
Where never lark, or even eagle, flew;
And, while with silent, lifting mind I've trod
The high untrespassed sanctity of space,
Put out my hand, and touched the face of God.

>   (Written by a 19-year-old American volunteer with
>   the Royal Canadian Air Force, who was killed in
>   training December 11, 1941)

THE CELESTIAL SURGEON

Robert Louis Stevenson

If I have faltered more or less
In my great task of happiness;
If I have moved among my race
And shown no glorious morning face;
If beams from happy human eyes
Have moved me not; if morning skies,
Books, and my food, and summer rain
Knocked on my sullen heart in vain:—
Lord, thy most pointed pleasure take
And stab my spirit broad awake;
Or, Lord, if too obdurate I,
Choose thou, before that spirit die,
A piercing pain, a killing sin,
And to my dead heart run them in!

THE DEATH OF COWARDS

William Shakespeare

Cowards die many times before their deaths;
The valiant never taste of death but once.
Of all the wonders that I yet have heard,
It seems to me most strange that men should fear;
Seeing that death, a necessary end,
Will come when it will come.

(From Julius Caesar)

SAMUEL JOHNSON ANSWERS A CHALLENGE

(Johnson had said that some poems, which MacPherson claimed
to have translated, were forgeries. MacPherson sent Johnson a
challenge)

Mr. James MacPherson,—I received your foolish and impudent
letter. Any violence offered me I shall do my best to repel, and what
I cannot do for myself, the law shall do for me. I hope I shall never
be deterred from detecting what I think a cheat, by the menaces
of a ruffian.

What would you have me retract? I thought your book an imposture; I think it an imposture still. For this opinion I have given
my reasons to the publick which I here dare you to refute. Your
rage I defy. Your abilities, since your Homer, are not so formidable; and what I hear of your morals, inclines me to pay regard
not to what you shall say, but to what you shall prove. You may
print this if you will.

SAM. JOHNSON

SONG

James Thomson

Let my voice ring out and over the earth,
  Through all the grief and strife,
With a golden joy in a silver mirth:
  Thank God for life!

Let my voice swell out through the great abyss
   To the azure dome above,
With a chord of faith in the harp of bliss:
   Thank God for Love!

Let my voice ring out beneath and above,
   The whole world through,
O my Love and Life, O my Life and Love,
   Thank God for you!

MY CHOICE

Robert G. Ingersoll

I would rather go to the forest, far away, and build me a little cabin—build it myself—and daub it with clay, and live there with my wife and children; and have a winding path leading down to the spring where the water bubbles out, day and night, whispering a poem to the white pebbles, from the heart of the earth; a little hut with some hollyhocks at the corner, with their bannered bosoms open to the sun, and a thrush in the air like a winged joy —I would rather live there and have some lattice work across the window so that the sun-light would fall checkered on the babe in the cradle—I would rather live there, with my soul erect and free, than in a palace of gold, and wear a crown of imperial power, and feel that I was superstition's cringing slave, and dare not speak my honest thought.

TO BOSTON

John Collins Bossidy

And this is good old Boston,
   The home of the bean and the cod,
Where the Lowells talk only to Cabots
And the Cabots talk only to God.
(Toast, Midwinter Dinner, Holy Cross Alumni, 1910)

TO NEW HAVEN

Frederick Scheetz Jones

Here's to the town of New Haven,
The home of the Truth and the Light,
   Where God talks to Jones
   In the very same tones
That he uses with Hadley and Dwight.

> (Toast, dinner of the Yale Alumni Association, Waterbury, Conn., 1915)

TO NEW HAVEN AND BOSTON

Walter Foster Angell

Here's to New Haven and Boston,
And the turf that the Puritans trod,
In the rest of mankind little virtue they find,
But they feel quite chummy with God.

> (Toast, Brown University)

THE AMERICANS AND THE RUSSIANS

Alexis de Tocqueville

There are at the present time two great nations in the world which seem to tend toward the same end, although they started from different points. I allude to the Russians and the Americans. . . . All other nations seem to have nearly reached their natural limits; but these are still in the act of growth. All the others are stopped, or continue to advance with extreme difficulty; these are proceeding with ease and celerity along a path to which the human eye can assign no term. . . .

The Anglo-American relies upon personal interest to accomplish his ends, and gives free scope to the unguided exertions and common sense of the citizens. The Russian centers all the authority of society in a single arm. The principal instrument of the former is freedom; of the latter, servitude. Their starting points are different and their courses are not the same; yet each of them seems to be marked out by the will of Heaven to sway the destinies of half the globe.

(1835)

THE BLIND MEN AND THE ELEPHANT

John G. Saxe

It was six men of Indostan
To learning much inclined,
Who went to see the elephant
(Though all of them were blind),
That each by observation
Might satisfy his mind.

The first approached the elephant,
And, happening to fall
Against his broad and sturdy side,
At once began to bawl,
"God bless me! but the elephant
Is very like a wall!"

The second feeling of the tusk
Cried: "Ho! what have we here
So very round and smooth and sharp?
To me 'tis mighty clear
This wonder of an elephant
Is very like a spear!"

The third approached the animal,
And, happening to take
The squirming trunk within his hands,
Thus boldly up and spake:
"I see," quoth he, "the elephant,
Is very like a snake!"

The fourth reached out his eager hand,
And felt about the knee;
"What most this wondrous beast is like
Is mighty plain," quoth he;
" 'Tis clear enough the elephant
Is very like a tree."

The fifth, who chanced to touch the ear,
Said: "E'en the blindest man
Can tell what this resembles most.
Deny the fact who can,
This marvel of an elephant
Is very like a fan!"

The sixth no sooner had begun
About the beast to grope,
Than, seizing on the swinging tail
That fell within his scope,
"I see," quoth he, "the elephant
Is very like a rope!"

And so these men of Indostan
Disputed loud and long,
Each in his own opinion
Exceeding stiff and strong,
Though each was partly in the right,
And all were in the wrong!

So, oft in theologic wars
The disputants, I ween,
Rail on in utter ignorance
Of what each other mean,
And prate about an elephant
Not one of them has seen!

*　*　*

This is the final test of a gentleman: his respect for those who
can be of no possible service to him.

—William Lyon Phelps

DEATH OF THE AGED

Robert G. Ingersoll

After all, there is something tenderly appropriate in the serene
death of the old. Nothing is more touching than the death of the
young, the strong. But when the duties of life have all been nobly
done; when the sun touches the horizon; when the purple twilight
falls upon the past, the present, and the future; when memory, with
dim eyes, can scarcely spell the blurred and faded records of the
vanished days—then, surrounded by kindred and friends, death
comes like a strain of music. The day has been long, the road weary,
and the traveler gladly stops at the welcome inn.

Nearly forty-eight years ago, under the snow, in the little town of
Cazenovia, my poor mother was buried. I was but two years old. I
remember her as she looked in death. That sweet, cold face has kept
my heart warm through all the changing years.

LITTLE ANNIE ROONEY

Michael Nolan

A winning way, a pleasant smile,
Dress'd so neat but quite in style,
Merry chaff your time to while,
Has little Annie Rooney;

Ev'ry ev'ning, rain or shine,
I make a call twixt eight and nine,
On her who shortly will be mine,
Little Annie Rooney.

Chorus:
>   She's my sweetheart, I'm her beau,
>   She's my Annie, I'm her Joe,
>   Soon we'll marry, never to part,
>   Little Annie Rooney is my sweetheart.

The parlor's small but neat and clean,
And set with taste so seldom seen,
And you can bet the household queen
Is little Annie Rooney!
The fire burns cheerfully and bright,
As a family circle round, each night
We form and every one's delight
Is little Annie Rooney. (*Chorus.*)

We've been engaged close on a year,
The happy time is drawing near,
I'll wed the one I love so dear,
Little Annie Rooney!
My friends declare I am in jest,
Until the time comes will not rest,
But one who knows its value best,
Is little Annie Rooney. (*Chorus.*)

When married we'll so happy be,
I love her and she loves me,
Happier wife you'll never see,
Than Little Annie Rooney.
In a little cozy home,
No more from her I'll care to roam;
She'll greet you all when-e'er you come,
My Little Annie Rooney. (*Chorus.*)

THE DAY IS DONE

Henry Wadsworth Longfellow

The day is done, and the darkness
Falls from the wings of Night,
As a feather is wafted downward
From an eagle in his flight.

I see the lights of the village
Gleam through the rain and the mist,
And a feeling of sadness comes o'er me
That my soul cannot resist:

A feeling of sadness and longing,
That is not akin to pain,
And resembles sorrow only
As the mist resembles the rain.

Come, read to me some poem,
Some simple and heartfelt lay,
That shall soothe this restless feeling,
And banish the thoughts of the day.

Not from the grand old masters,
Not from the bards sublime,
Whose distant footsteps echo
Through the corridors of Time.

For, like strains of martial music,
Their mighty thoughts suggest
Life's endless toil and endeavor;
And tonight I long for rest.

Read from some humbler poet,
Whose songs gushed from his heart,
As showers from the clouds of summer,
Or tears from the eyelids start:

Who, through long days of labor,
And nights devoid of ease,
Still heard in his soul the music
Of wonderful melodies.

Such songs have power to quiet
The restless pulse of care,
And come like the benediction
That follows after prayer.

Then read from the treasured volume
The poem of thy choice,
And lend to the rhyme of the poet
The beauty of thy voice.

And the night shall be filled with music,
And the cares, that infest the day,
Shall fold their tents, like Arabs,
And as silently steal away.

LUCY

William Wordsworth

She dwelt among the untrodden ways
   Beside the springs of Dove;
A maid whom there were none to praise,
   And very few to love.

A violet by a mossy stone
   Half hidden from the eye!
Fair as a star, when only one
   Is shining in the sky.

She lived unknown, and few could know
   When Lucy ceased to be;
But she is in her grave, and O,
   The difference to me!

LIZZIE BORDEN

Anonymous

Lizzie Borden took an axe
And gave her mother forty whacks;
When she saw what she had done,
She gave her father forty-one.

FANCY

William Shakespeare

Tell me where is fancy bred,
Or in the heart or in the head?
How begot, how nourished?
  Reply, reply,
It is engender'd in the eyes,
With gazing fed; and fancy dies
In the cradle where it lies.
    Let us all ring fancy's knell;
    I'll begin it,—Ding, dong, bell.
        (From The Merchant of Venice)

REQUIESCAT

Matthew Arnold

Strew on her roses, roses,
  And never a spray ot yew.
In quiet she reposes:
  Ah! would that I did too.

Her mirth the world required:
  She bathed it in smiles of glee.
But her heart was tired, tired,
  And now they let her be.

Her life was turning, turning,
  In mazes of heat and sound.
But for peace her soul was yearning,
  And now peace laps her round.

Her cabin'd, ample spirit,
  It flutter'd and fail'd for breath.
Tonight it doth inherit
  The vasty Hall of Death.

THE SEVEN WONDERS OF THE ANCIENT WORLD

Anonymous

The Pyramids first, which in Egypt were laid;
Next Babylon's Garden, for Amytis made;
Then Mausolos' Tomb of affection and guilt;
Fourth, the Temple of Dian in Ephesus built;
The Colossus of Rhodes, cast in brass, to the Sun;
Sixth, Jupiter's Statue, by Phidias done;
The Pharos of Egypt comes last, we are told,
Or the Palace of Cyrus, cemented with gold.

GO TO THE ANT, THOU SLUGGARD

Holy Bible, Proverbs 6:6–11

Go to the ant, thou sluggard: consider her ways and be wise:
Which having no guide, overseer, or ruler,
Provideth her meat in the summer, and gathereth her food in the
    harvest.
How long wilt thou sleep, O sluggard? when wilt thou arise out of
    thy sleep?
Yet a little sleep, a little slumber, a little folding of the hands to
    sleep:
So shall thy poverty come as one that travelleth, and thy want as an
    armed man.

WITH RUE MY HEART IS LADEN

A. E. Housman

With rue my heart is laden
  For golden friends I had,
For many a rose-lipt maiden
  And many a lightfoot lad.

By brooks too broad for leaping
The lightfoot boys are laid;
The rose-lipt girls are sleeping
In fields where roses fade.

BROKEN FRIENDSHIP

Samuel Taylor Coleridge

Alas! they had been friends in youth,
But whispering tongues can poison truth!
And constancy lives in realms above!
And life is thorny, and Youth is vain!
And to be wroth with one we love,
Doth work like madness in the brain!
They parted—ne'er to meet again!
But never either found another
To free the hollow heart from paining!
They stood aloof, the scars remaining;
Like cliffs which had been rent asunder!
A dreary sea now flows between;
But neither heat, nor frost, nor thunder,
Shall wholly do away, I ween,
The marks of that which once had been.

THE VILLAGE BLACKSMITH

Henry Wadsworth Longfellow

Under a spreading chestnut-tree
The village smithy stands;
The smith, a mighty man is he,
With large and sinewy hands;
And the muscles of his brawny arms
Are strong as iron bands.

His hair is crisp, and black, and long,
His face is like the tan;
His brow is wet with honest sweat,
He earns whate'er he can,
And looks the whole world in the face,
For he owes not any man.

Week in, week out, from morn till night,
You can hear his bellows blow;
You can hear him swing his heavy sledge,
With measured beat and slow,
Like a sexton ringing the village bell,
When the evening sun is low.

And children coming home from school
Look in at the open door;
They love to see the flaming forge,
And hear the bellows roar,
And catch the burning sparks that fly
Like chaff from a threshing-floor.

He goes on Sunday to the church,
And sits among his boys;
He hears the parson pray and preach,
He hears his daughter's voice
Singing in the village choir,
And it makes his heart rejoice.

It sounds to him like her mother's voice,
Singing in Paradise!
He needs must think of her once more,
How in the grave she lies;
And with his hard, rough hand he wipes
A tear out of his eyes.

Toiling—rejoicing—sorrowing,
Onward through life he goes;
Each morning sees some task begin,
Each evening sees it close;
Something attempted, something done,
Has earned a night's repose.

Thanks, thanks to thee, my worthy friend,
For the lesson thou hast taught!
Thus at the flaming forge of life
Our fortunes must be wrought;
Thus on its sounding anvil shaped
Each burning deed and thought

BLUE GIRLS

John Crowe Ransom

Twirling your blue skirts, traveling the sward
Under the towers of your seminary,
Go listen to your teachers old and contrary
Without believing a word.

Tie the white fillets then about your lustrous hair
And think no more of what will come to pass
Than bluebirds that go walking on the grass
And chattering on the air.

Practice your beauty, blue girls, before it fail;
And I will cry with my loud lips and publish
Beauty which all our power shall never establish,
It is so frail.

For I could tell you a story which is true:
I know a lady with a terrible tongue,
Blear eyes fallen from blue,
All her perfections tarnished—and yet it is not long
Since she was lovelier than any of you.

A MAN'S HOME

William Pitt

The poorest man may in his cottage bid defiance to all the forces
of the Crown. It may be frail; its roof may shake; the wind may
blow through it; the storms may enter, the rain may enter,—but the
King of England cannot enter; all his forces may not dare cross the
threshold of the humblest home.

THE SECRET ISOLATED JOY OF THE THINKER

Oliver Wendell Holmes, Jr.

No man has earned the right to intellectual ambition until he has learned to lay his course by a star which he has never seen—to dig by the divining rod for springs which he may never reach. In saying this, I point to that which will make your study heroic. For I say unto you in all sadness of conviction, that to think great thoughts you must be heroes as well as idealists. Only when you have worked alone—when you have felt around you a black gulf of solitude more isolating than that which surrounds the dying man, and in hope and in despair have trusted to your own unshaken will,—then only can you gain the secret isolated joy of the thinker, who knows that, a hundred years after he is dead and forgotten, men who had never heard of him will be moving to the measure of his thought,—the subtle rapture of a postponed power, which the world knows not because it has no external trappings, but which to his prophetic vision is more real than that which commands an army. And if this joy should not be yours, still it is only thus that you can know that you have done what lay in you to do,—can say that you have lived, and be ready for the end.

GOD IS OUR REFUGE AND STRENGTH

Holy Bible, Psalm 46:1–6, 10–11

God is our refuge and strength, a very present help in trouble.

Therefore will we not fear, though the earth be removed, and though the mountains be carried into the midst of the sea;

Though the waters thereof roar and be troubled, though the mountains shake with the swelling thereof. Selah.

There is a river, the streams whereof shall make glad the city of God, the holy place of the tabernacles of the Most High.

God is in the midst of her; she shall not be moved: God shall help her, and that right early. . . .

Be still, and know that I am God; I will be exalted among the heathen, I will be exalted in the earth.

The Lord of hosts is with us; the God of Jacob is our refuge. Selah.

OH, MY DARLING CLEMENTINE

Anonymous

In a cavern, in a canyon,
Excavating for a mine,
Dwelt a miner, 'Forty-Niner,
And his daughter Clementine.

Chorus:
Oh, my darling, Oh, my darling,
Oh, my darling Clementine,
You are lost and gone forever,
Dreadful sorry, Clementine.

Light she was and like a fairy,
And her shoes were number nine;
Herring boxes, without topses
Sandals were for Clementine. (*Chorus.*)

Drove she ducklings to the water,
Every morning just at nine;
Hit her foot against a splinter,
Fell into the foaming brine. (*Chorus.*)

Ruby lips above the water,
Blowing bubbles soft and fine;
Alas for me! I was no swimmer,
So I lost my Clementine. (*Chorus.*)

In a churchyard, near the canyon,
Where the myrtle doth entwine,
There grow roses and other posies,
Fertilized by Clementine. (*Chorus.*)

Then the miner, 'Forty-Niner,
Soon began to peak and pine,
Thought he oughter jine his daughter,
Now he's with his Clementine. (*Chorus.*)

In my dreams she still doth haunt me,
Robed in garments soaked in brine,
Though in life I used to hug her,
Now she's dead, I'll draw the line. (*Chorus.*)

LINCOLN'S LETTER TO MRS. BIXBY

November 21, 1864

DEAR MADAM:

I have been shown in the files of the War Department a statement of the Adjutant General of Massachusetts that you are the mother of five sons who have died gloriously on the field of battle. I feel how weak and fruitless must be any words of mine which should attempt to beguile you from the grief of a loss so overwhelming, but I cannot refrain from tendering to you the consolation that may be found in the thanks of the Republic that they died to save. I pray that the Heavenly Father may assuage the anguish of your bereavement, and leave you only the cherished memory of the loved and lost, and the solemn pride that must be yours to have laid so costly a sacrifice upon the altar of freedom.

Yours very sincerely and respectfully,
Abraham Lincoln

* * *

A man is rich in proportion to the number of things which he can afford to let alone.

—Henry David Thoreau

PILGRIMAGE

Sir Walter Raleigh

Give me my scallop-shell of quiet,
My staff of faith to walk upon,
My scrip of joy, immortal diet,
My bottle of salvation,
My gown of glory, hope's true gage,
And thus I'll take my pilgrimage.

THE WALLOPING WINDOW-BLIND

Charles E. Carryl

A capital ship for an ocean trip
Was the Walloping Window-Blind!
No wind that blew dismayed her crew,
Or troubled the Captain's mind.
The man at the wheel was made to feel
Contempt for the wildest blow,
Tho' it often appeared when the gale had cleared
That he'd been in his bunk below.

Chorus:
>   Then blow ye winds, heigh-ho!
>   A-roving I will go!
>   I'll stay no more on this bright shore,
>   So let the music play,
>   I'm off for the morning train,
>   I'll cross the raging main!
>   I'm off to my love with a boxing glove,
>   Ten thousand miles away.

The bo'swain's mate was very sedate,
Yet fond of amusement too;
He played hopscotch with the starboard watch
While the Captain, he tickled the crew,
And the gunner we had was apparently mad,
For he sat on the after rail,
And fired salutes with the Captain's boots,
In the teeth of the booming gale!

The Captain sat on the Commodore's hat,
And dined in a royal way,
Off toasted pigs and pickles and figs,
And gunnery bread each day.
And the cook was Dutch, and behaved as such,
For the diet he gave the crew
Was a number of tons of hot cross buns
Served up with sugar and glue!

All nautical pride we laid aside,
And we ran the vessel ashore
On the Gullibly Isles, where the Poo-poo smiles,

And the Rubly Ubdugs roar.
And we sat on the edge of a sandy ledge
And shot at the whistling bee;
And the cinnamon bats wore wet-proof hats
As they dipped in the shiny sea.

On Rugbug bark, from morn till dark,
We dined till we all had grown
Uncommonly shrunk; when a Chinese junk
Came up from the Torribly Zone.
She was chubby and square,
But we didn't much care,
So we cheerily put to sea;
And we left all the crew of the junk to chew
On the bark of the Rugbug tree.

ALL TIMES ARE HIS SEASONS

John Donne

We ask our daily bread, and God never says, You should have
come yesterday. He never says, You must come again tomorrow.
But "today if you will hear His voice," today He will hear you. If
some king of the earth have so large an extent of dominion in north
and south as that he hath winter and summer together in his dominions, so large an extent of east and west as that he hath day and
night together in his dominions, much more hath God mercy and
judgment together. He brought light out of darkness, not out of a
lesser light. He can bring thy summer out of winter though thou
have no spring. Though in the ways of fortune, or misunderstand-
ing, or conscience, thou have been benighted till now, wintered and
frozen, clouded and eclipsed, damp and benumbed, smothered and
stupefied till now, now God comes to thee, not as in the dawning
of the day, not as in the bud of the spring, but as the sun at noon,
to banish all shadows; as the sheaves in harvest, to fill all penuries.
All occasions invite His mercies, and all times are His seasons.

God made sun and moon to distinguish seasons, and day and
night; and we cannot have the fruits of the earth but in their seasons.
But God hath made no decrees to distinguish the seasons of His
mercies. In Paradise the fruits were ripe the first minute, and in
Heaven it is always autumn, His mercies are ever in their maturity.

THE ARAB TO HIS FAVORITE STEED

Caroline Norton

My Beautiful! my beautiful! that standest meekly by,
With thy proudly arched and glossy neck, and dark and fiery eye,
Fret not to roam the desert now, with all thy wingèd speed;
I may not mount on thee again,—thou'rt sold, my Arab steed!
Fret not with that impatient hoof—snuff not the breezy wind,—
The farther that thou fliest now, so far am I behind;
The stranger hath thy bridle-rein,—thy master hath *his* gold,—
Fleet-limbed and beautiful, farewell; thou'rt sold, my steed, thou'rt
 sold.

Farewell! those free, untired limbs full many a mile must roam,
To reach the chill and wintry sky which clouds the stranger's
 home;
Some other hand, less fond, must now thy corn and bed prepare,
The silky mane, I braided once, must be another's care!
The morning sun shall dawn again, but nevermore with thee
Shall I gallop through the desert paths, where we were wont to be;
Evening shall darken on the earth, and o'er the sandy plain
Some other steed, with slower step, shall bear me home again.

Yes, thou must go! the wild, free breeze, the brilliant sun and sky,
The master's house,—from all of these my exiled one must fly;
The proud dark eye will grow less proud, thy step become less fleet,
And vainly shalt thou arch thy neck, thy master's hand to meet.
Only in sleep shall I behold that dark eye, glancing bright;—
Only in sleep shall hear again that step so firm and light;
And when I raise my dreaming arm to check or cheer thy speed,
Then must I, starting, wake to feel,—thou'rt *sold*, my Arab steed!

Ah! rudely then, unseen by me, some cruel hand may chide,
Till foam-wreaths lie, like crested waves, along thy panting side:
And the rich blood that's in thee swells, in thy indignant pain,
Till careless eyes, which rest on thee, may count each starting vein.
Will they ill-use thee? If I thought—but no, it cannot be,—
Thou art so swift, yet easy curbed; so gentle, yet so free:
And yet, if haply, when thou'rt gone, my lonely heart should
 yearn,—
Can the hand which casts thee from it now command thee to
 return?

400

Return! alas! my Arab steed! what shall thy master do,
When thou, who wast his all of joy, hast vanished from his view?
When the dim distance cheats mine eye, and through the gathering
    tears
Thy bright form, for a moment, like the false mirage appears;
Slow and unmounted shall I roam, with weary step alone,
Where, with fleet step and joyous bound, thou oft hast borne me
    on;
And sitting down by that green well, I'll pause and sadly think,
"It was here he bowed his glossy neck when last I saw him drink!"

When last I saw thee drink!—Away! the fevered dream is o'er,—
I could not live a day, and *know* that we should meet no more!
They tempted me, my beautiful!—for hunger's power is strong,—
They tempted me, my beautiful! but I have loved too long.
Who said that I had given thee up? who said that thou wast sold?
'Tis false,—'tis false, my Arab steed! I fling them back their gold!
Thus, *thus,* I leap upon thy back, and scour the distant plains;
Away! who overtakes us now shall claim thee for his pains!

NOW THE LABORER'S TASK IS O'ER

John Ellerton

Now the laborer's task is o'er;
   Now the battle day is past;
Now upon the farther shore
   Lands the voyager at last.
Father, in thy gracious keeping
Leave we now thy servant sleeping.

There the tears of earth are dried;
   There its hidden things are clear;
There the work of life is tried
   By a juster Judge than here.
Father, in thy gracious keeping
Leave we now thy servant sleeping.

There the sinful souls, that turn
   To the cross their dying eyes,
All the love of Christ shall learn
   At his feet in Paradise.
Father, in thy gracious keeping
Leave we now thy servant sleeping.

BOOKS

Richard de Bury

Books delight us when prosperity smiles upon us; they comfort us inseparably when stormy fortune frowns on us. They lend validity to human compacts, and no serious judgments are propounded without their help. Arts and sciences, all the advantages of which no mind can enumerate, consist in books. How highly must we estimate the wondrous power of books, since through them we survey the utmost bounds of the world and time, and contemplate the things that are as well as those that are not, as it were in the mirror of eternity. In books we climb mountains and scan the deepest gulfs of the abyss; in books we behold the finny tribes that may not exist outside of their native waters, distinguish the properties of streams and springs and of various lands; from books we dig out gems and metals and the materials of every kind of mineral, and learn the virtues of herbs and trees and plants, and survey at will the wholy progeny of Neptune, Ceres, and Pluto.

Books are masters who instruct us without words of anger, without bread or money. If you approach them they are not asleep. If you seek them, they do not hide, if you blunder they do not scold, if you are ignorant, they do not laugh at you.

MY FINANCIAL CAREER

Stephen Leacock

When I go into a bank I get rattled. The clerks rattle me; the wickets rattle me; the sight of the money rattles me; everything rattles me.

The moment I cross the threshold of a bank and attempt to transact business there, I become an irresponsible idiot.

I knew this beforehand, but my salary had been raised to fifty dollars a month and I felt that the bank was the only place for it.

So I shambled in and looked timidly round at the clerks. I had an idea that a person about to open an account must needs consult the manager.

I went up to a wicket marked "Accountant." The accountant was a tall, cool devil. The very sight of him rattled me. My voice was sepulchral.

"Can I see the manager?" I said, and added solemnly, "alone." I don't know why I said "alone."

"Certainly," said the accountant, and fetched him.

The manager was a grave, calm man. I held my fifty-six dollars clutched in a crumpled ball in my pocket.

"Are you the manager?" I said. God knows I didn't doubt it.

"Yes," he said.

"Can I see you," I asked, "alone?" I didn't want to say "alone" again, but without it the thing seemed self-evident.

The manager looked at me in some alarm. He felt that I had an awful secret to reveal.

"Come in here," he said, and led the way to a private room. He turned the key in the lock.

"We are safe from interruption here," he said; "sit down."

We both sat down and looked at each other. I found no voice to speak.

"You are one of Pinkerton's men, I presume," he said.

He had gathered from my mysterious manner that I was a detective. I knew what he was thinking, and it made me worse.

"No, not from Pinkerton's," I said, seeming to imply that I came from a rival agency.

"To tell the truth," I went on, as if I had been prompted to lie about it, "I am not a detective at all. I have come to open an account. I intend to keep all my money in this bank."

The manager looked relieved but still serious; he concluded now that I was a son of Baron Rothschild or a young Gould.

"A large account, I suppose," he said.

"Fairly large," I whispered. "I propose to deposit fifty-six dollars now and fifty dollars a month regularly."

The manager got up and opened the door. He called to the accountant.

"Mr. Montgomery," he said unkindly loud, "this gentleman is opening an account, and he will deposit fifty-six dollars. Good morning."

I rose.

A big iron door stood open at the side of the room.

"Good morning," I said, and stepped into the safe.

"Come out," said the manager coldly, and showed me the other way.

I went up to the accountant's wicket and poked the ball of money at him with a quick convulsive movement as if I were doing a conjuring trick.

My face was ghastly pale.

"Here," I said, "deposit it." The tone of the words seemed to mean, "Let us do this painful thing while the fit is on us."

He took the money and gave it to another clerk.

He made me write the sum on a slip and sign my name in a book I no longer knew what I was doing. The bank swam before my eyes.

"Is it deposited?" I asked in a hollow, vibrating voice.

"It is," said the accountant.

"Then I want to draw a cheque."

My idea was to draw out six dollars of it for present use. Some one gave me a cheque book through a wicket and some one else began telling me how to write it out. The people in the bank had the impression that I was an invalid millionaire. I wrote something on the cheque and thrust it in at the clerk. He looked at it.

"What! Are you drawing it all out again?" he asked in surprise. Then I realized I had written fifty-six instead of six. I was too far gone to reason now. I had a feeling that it was impossible to explain the thing. All the clerks had stopped writing to look at me.

Reckless with misery, I made a plunge.

"Yes, the whole thing."

"You withdraw your money from the bank?"

"Every cent of it."

"Are you not going to deposit any more?" said the clerk, astonished.

"Never."

An idiot hope struck me that they might think something had insulted me while I was writing the cheque and that I had changed my mind. I made a wretched attempt to look like a man with a fearfully quick temper.

The clerk prepared to pay the money.

"How will you have it?" he said.

"What?"

"How will you have it?"

"Oh—I caught his meaning and answered without even trying to think—in fifties."

He gave me a fifty dollar bill.

"And the six?" he asked dryly.

"In sixes," I said.

He gave it to me and I rushed out.

As the big door swung behind me I caught the echo of a roar of laughter that went up to the ceiling of the bank. Since then I bank no more. I keep my money in cash in my trousers and my savings in silver dollars in a sock.

A PROPHETIC UTTERANCE

Leo Szilard

The first bomb that is detonated over Japan will be spectacular enough to start a race in atomic armaments between us and other nations . . . The strong position of the United States in the world in the past thirty years has been due to the fact that the U. S. could out-produce every other country in heavy armaments. The existence of the atomic bomb means the end of the strong position of the United States in this respect.

(From a letter to President Roosevelt, written on April 12, 1945, the day the President died.)

THE COMMON PEOPLE

Walt Whitman

The genius of the United States is not best or most in its executives or legislatures, nor in its ambassadors or authors or colleges or churches or parlors, nor even in its newspapers or inventors . . . but always most in the common people. Their manners, speech, dress, friendships,—the freshness and candor of their physiognomy—the picturesque looseness of their carriage . . . their deathless attachment to freedom—their aversion to anything indecorous or soft or mean—the practical acknowledgment of the citizens of one state by the citizens of all other states—the fierceness of their roused resentment—their curiosity and susceptibility to a slight—the air they have of persons who never knew how it felt to stand in the presence of superiors—the fluency of their speech—their delight in music, the sure symptom of manly tenderness and native elegance of soul . . . their good temper and open-handedness—the terrible significance of their elections—the President's taking off his hat to them and not they to him—these too are unrhymed poetry.

(From the preface to Leaves of Grass)

STRANGE MEETING

Wilfred Owen

It seemed that out of battle I escaped
Down some profound dull tunnel, long since scooped
Through granites which titanic wars had groined.
Yet also there encumbered sleepers groaned,
Too fast in thought or death to be bestirred.
Then, as I probed them, one sprang up, and stared
With piteous recognition in fixed eyes,
Lifting distressful hands as if to bless.
And by his smile, I knew that sullen hall,
By his dead smile I knew we stood in Hell.
With a thousand pains that vision's face was grained;
Yet no blood reached there from the upper ground,
And no guns thumped, or down the flues made moan.
"Strange friend," I said, "here is no cause to mourn."
"None," said the other, "save the undone years,
The hopelessness. Whatever hope is yours,
Was my life also; I went hunting wild
After the wildest beauty in the world,
Which lies not calm in eyes, or braided hair,
But mocks the steady running of the hour.
And if it grieves, grieves richlier than here.
For by my glee might many men have laughed,
And of my weeping something had been left,
Which must die now. I mean the truth untold,
The pity of war, the pity war distilled.
Now men will go content, with what we spoiled.
Or, discontent, boil bloody, and be spilled.
They will be swift with swiftness of the tigress,
None will break ranks, though nations trek from progress.
Courage was mine, and I had mystery,
Wisdom was mine, and I had mastery;
To miss the march of this retreating world
Into vain citadels that are not walled.
Then, when much blood had clogged their chariot-wheels,
I would go up and wash them from sweet wells,
Even with truths that lie too deep for taint.
I would have poured my spirit without stint
But not through wounds; not on the cess of war.
Foreheads of men have bled where no wounds were.

I am the enemy you killed, my friend.
I knew you in this dark; for so you frowned
Yesterday through me as you jabbed and killed.
I parried; but my hands were loath and cold.
Let us sleep now . . ."

ONE YEAR

William Drummond of Hawthorden

One year is sufficient to behold all the Magnificence of Nature,
nay, even one Day and Night; for more is but the same brought
again. This Sun, that Moon, these Stars, the varying Dance of the
Spring, Summer, Autumn, Winter, is that very same which the
Golden Age did see. They which have the longest time lent them to
live in, have almost no Part of it at all, measuring it either by the
Space of Time which is past, when they were not, or by that which
is to come. Why shouldst thou then care, whether thy Days be many
or few, which, when prolonged to the uttermost, prove, paralleled
with Eternity, as a Tear is to the Ocean? To die young, is to do that
soon, and in some fewer days, which once thou must do; it is but the
giving over of a Game, that after never so many Hazards, must be
lost.

O WORLD, THOU CHOOSEST NOT THE BETTER PART!

George Santayana

O World, thou choosest not the better part!
It is not wisdom to be only wise,
And on the inward vision close the eyes,
But it is wisdom to believe the heart.
Columbus found a world, and had no chart,
Save one that faith deciphered in the skies;
To trust the soul's invisible surmise

Was all his science and his only art.
Our knowledge is a torch of smoky pine
That lights the pathway but one step ahead
Across a void of mystery and dread.
Bid, then, the tender light of faith to shine
By which alone the mortal heart is led
Unto the thinking of the thought divine.

IT COULDN'T BE DONE

Edgar A. Guest

Somebody said it couldn't be done,
    But he with a chuckle replied
That "maybe it couldn't," but he would be one
    Who wouldn't say so until he had tried.
So he buckled right in with a trace of a grin
    On his face. If he worried he hid it.
He started to sing as he tackled the thing
    That couldn't be done, and he did it.

Somebody scoffed: "Oh, you'll never do that;
    At least no one ever has done it";
But he took off his coat and he took off his hat,
    And the first thing we knew he'd begun it.
With a lift of his chin and a bit of a grin,
    Without any doubting or quiddit,
He started to sing as he tackled the thing
    That couldn't be done, and he did it.

There are thousands to tell you it cannot be done,
    There are thousands to prophesy failure;
There are thousands to point out to you, one by one,
    The dangers that wait to assail you.
But just buckle in with a bit of a grin,
    Just take off your coat and go to it;
Just start to sing as you tackle the thing
    That "cannot be done," and you'll do it.

REASON

Anonymous

He that will not reason is a bigot,
He that cannot reason is a fool,
He that does not reason is a slave.

*   *   *

The Right Honorable Gentleman is indebted to his memory
for his jests and to his imagination for his facts.
          (R. B. Sheridan's reply to Mr. Dundas)

BROADCAST ON HIS NINETIETH BIRTHDAY

Oliver Wendell Holmes, Jr.

In this symposium my part is only to sit in silence. To express one's feelings as the end draws near is too intimate a task.

But I may mention one thought that comes to me as a listener-in. The riders in a race do not stop short when they reach the goal. There is a little finishing canter before coming to a standstill. There is time to hear the kind voice of friends and to say to one's self: "The work is done."

But just as one says that, the answer comes: "The race is over, but the work never is done while the power to work remains."

The canter that brings you to a standstill need not be only coming to rest. It cannot be while you still live. For to live is to function. That is all there is in living.

And so I end with a line from a Latin poet who uttered the message more than fifteen hundred years ago:

"Death plucks my ears and says, Live—
I am coming."

(March 7, 1931)

REPARTEE

Anonymous

Loud brayed an ass. Quoth Kate, "My dear,"
(To spouse with scornful carriage)
"One of your relations I hear."
"Yes, love," said he, "by marriage."

* * *

Was this the face that launched a thousand ships
And burnt the topless towers of Ilium?
Sweet Helen, make me immortal with a kiss.
(From Marlowe's Tragedy of Dr. Faustus)

409

GROWING OLD

R. J. Wells

A little more tired at the close of day,
A little less anxious to have our way;
A little less anxious to scold and blame,
And so we are nearing the journey's end,
Where Time and Eternity meet and blend.

A little less care for bonds and gold,
A little more zest in the days of old;
A broader view and a saner mind,
And a little more love for all mankind;
And so we are faring adown the way
That leads to the gates of a better day.

A little more love for the friends of youth,
A little less zeal for established truth;
A little more charity in our views,
A little less thirst for the daily news;
And so we are folding our tents away
And passing in silence, at close of day.

A little more leisure to sit and dream,
A little more real the things unseen;
A little nearer to those ahead,
With visions of those long-loved and dead;
And so we are going, where all must go,
To the place the living may never know.

A little more laughter, a few more tears,
And we shall have told our increasing years;
The book is closed, and the prayers are said,
And we are a part of the countless dead.
Thrice happy, if then some soul can say,
"I live because he has passed my way."

* * *

All sorts of allowances are made for the illusions of
youth; and none, or almost none, for the disenchantment of
age.

—Robert Louis Stevenson

THE DEATH OF STONEWALL JACKSON

Lieut.-Col. George F. R. Henderson

About noon, when Major Pendleton came into the room, he [Stonewall Jackson] asked, "Who is preaching at headquarters today?" He was told that Mr. Lacy was, and that the whole army was praying for him. "Thank God," he said; "they are very kind to me." Already his strength was fast ebbing, and although his face brightened when his baby was brought to him, his mind had begun to wander. Now he was on the battle-field, giving orders to his men; now at home in Lexington; now at prayers in the camp. Occasionally his sense came back to him, and about half-past one he was told that he had but two hours to live. Again he answered, feebly but firmly, "Very good; it is all right." These were almost his last coherent words. For some time he lay unconscious, and then suddenly he cried out: "Order A. P. Hill to prepare for action! Pass the infantry to the front! Tell Major Hawks—" then stopped, leaving the sentence unfinished. Once more he was silent; but a little while after he said very quietly and clearly, "Let us cross over the river, and rest under the shade of the trees," and the soul of the great captain passed into the peace of God.

"SIGH NO MORE, LADIES"

William Shakespeare

Sigh no more, ladies, sigh no more,
  Men were deceivers ever,
One foot in sea and one on shore,
  To one thing constant never:
Then sigh not so, but let them go,
  And be you blithe and bonny,
Converting all your sounds of woe
  Into Hey nonny, nonny.

*   *   *

I'm lonesome. They are all dying. I have hardly a warm personal enemy left.—James McNeill Whistler

411

THE OCEAN OF LIFE

Henry Wadsworth Longfellow

Ships that pass in the night, and speak
    each other in passing;
Only a signal shown and a distant
    voice in the darkness;
So in the ocean of life we pass and
    speak one another,
Only a look and a voice; then darkness
    again and a silence.

ADMIRATION AND AWE

Immanuel Kant

Two things fill the mind with ever new and increasing admiration
and awe, the oftener and more steadily we reflect on them: *the starry
heavens above and the moral law within.* I have not to search for
them and conjecture them as though they were veiled in darkness or
were in the transcendent region beyond my horizon; I see them
before me and connect them directly with the consciousness of my
existence.

A PRAYER

Frank Dempster Sherman

It is my joy in life to find
At every turning of the road
The strong arm of a comrade kind
To help me onward with my load.

And since I have no gold to give,
And love alone must make amends,
My only prayer is, while I live—
God make me worthy of my friends.

From IS LIFE WORTH LIVING?

Alfred Austin

Is life worth living? Yes, so long
    As there is wrong to right,
Wail of the weak against the strong,
    Or tyranny to fight;
Long as there lingers gloom to chase,
    Or streaming tear to dry,
One kindred woe, one sorrowing face
    That smiles as we draw nigh;
Long as a tale of anguish swells
    The heart, and lids grow wet,
And at the sound of Christmas bells
    We pardon and forget;
So long as Faith with Freedom reigns,
    And loyal Hope survives,
And gracious Charity remains
    To leaven lowly lives;
While there is one untrodden tract
    For Intellect or Will,
And men are free to think and act
    Life is worth living still.

ON TAKING A WIFE

Thomas Moore

"Come, come," said Tom's father, "at your time of life,
There's no longer excuse for thus playing the rake—
It is time you should think, boy, of taking a wife."—
"Why, so it is, father—whose wife shall I take?"

*   *   *

One of the things we have to be thankful for is that we
don't get as much government as we pay for.
                             —C. H. Kettering

THAT ENERGY EQUALS MASS TIMES THE SPEED OF LIGHT SQUARED

Albert Einstein

$E=mc^2$, where E is the energy in ergs, m the mass in grams and c the velocity of light (that is 3×10^{10} cm. per second).

THE POWER OF SPIRIT

When Svetaketu, at his father's bidding, had brought a ripe fruit from the banyan tree, the father said to him,
    "Split the fruit in two, dear son."
    "Here you are. I have split it in two."
    "What do you find there?"
    "Innumerable tiny seeds."
    "Then take one of the seeds and split it."
    "I have split the seed."
    "And what do you find there?"
    "Why, nothing, nothing at all."
    "Ah, dear son, but this great tree cannot possibly come from nothing. Even if you cannot see with your eyes that subtle something in the seed which produces this mighty form it is present nonetheless. That is the power, that is the spirit unseen which pervades everywhere and is in all things. Have faith! That is the spirit which lies at the root of all existence, and that also art thou, O Svetaketu."
                            (From the *Chandogya Upanishad*)

OLD LESSON

Anonymous

God made bees, and bees made honey,
God made man, and man made money;
Pride made the devil, and the devil made sin;
So God made a cole-pit to put the devil in.

414

SAILING TO BYZANTIUM

William Butler Yeats

That is no country for old men. The young
In one another's arms, birds in the trees,
—Those dying generations—at their song,
The salmon-falls, the mackerel-crowded seas,
Fish, flesh, or fowl, commend all summer long
Whatever is begotten, born, and dies.
Caught in that sensual music all neglect
Monuments of unageing intellect.

An aged man is but a paltry thing,
A tattered coat upon a stick, unless
Soul clap its hands and sing, and louder sing
For every tatter in its mortal dress,
Nor is there singing school but studying
Monuments of its own magnificence;
And therefore I have sailed the seas and come
To the holy city of Byzantium.

O sages standing on God's holy fire
As in the gold mosaic of a wall,
Come from the holy fire, perne in a gyre,
And be the singing-masters of my soul.

Consume my heart away; sick with desire
And fastened to a dying animal
It knows not what it is; and gather me
Into the artifice of eternity.

Once out of nature I shall never take
My bodily form from any natural thing,
But such a form as Grecian goldsmiths make
Of hammered gold and gold enamelling
To keep a drowsy Emperor awake;
Or set upon a golden bough to sing
To lords and ladies of Byzantium
Of what is past, or passing, or to come.

REMEMBER NOW THY CREATOR

Holy Bible, Ecclesiastes 12

1 Remember now thy Creator in the days of thy youth, while the evil days come not, nor the years draw nigh, when thou shalt say, I have no pleasure in them;

2 While the sun, or the light, or the moon, or the stars, be not darkened, nor the clouds return after the rain:

3 In the day when the keepers of the house shall tremble, and the strong men shall bow themselves, and the grinders cease because they are few, and those that look out of the windows be darkened.

4 And the doors shall be shut in the streets, when the sound of the grinding is low, and he shall rise up at the voice of the bird, and all the daughters of musick shall be brought low;

5 Also when they shall be afraid of that which is high, and fears shall be in the way, and the almond tree shall flourish, and the grasshopper shall be a burden, and desire shall fail: because man goeth to his long home, and the mourners go about the streets:

6 Or ever the silver cord be loosed, or the golden bowl be broken, or the pitcher be broken at the fountain, or the wheel broken at the cistern.

7 Then shall the dust return to the earth as it was: and the spirit shall return unto God who gave it.

8 Vanity of vanities, saith the preacher; all is vanity.

9 And moreover, because the preacher was wise, he still taught the people knowledge; yea, he gave good heed, and sought out, and set in order many proverbs.

10 The preacher sought to find out acceptable words: and that which was written was upright, even words of truth.

11 The words of the wise are as goads, and as nails fastened by the masters of assemblies, which are given from one shepherd.

12 And further, by these, my son, be admonished: of making many books there is no end; and much study is a weariness of the flesh.

13 Let us hear the conclusion of the whole matter: Fear God, and keep his commandments: for this is the whole duty of man.

14 For God shall bring every work into judgment, with every secret thing, whether it be good, or whether it be evil.

THE SEA

Bryan Waller Procter (Barry Cornwall)

The sea! the sea! the open sea!
The blue, the fresh, the ever free!
Without a mark, without a bound,
It runneth the earth's wide regions round;
It plays with the clouds; it mocks the skies;
Or like a cradled creature lies.

I'm on the sea! I'm on the sea!
I am where I would ever be;
With the blue above, and the blue below,
And silence wheresoe'er I go;
If a storm should come and awake the deep,
What matter? *I* shall ride and sleep.

I love, O, how I love to ride
On the fierce, foaming, bursting tide,
When every mad wave drowns the moon
Or whistles aloft his tempest tune,
And tells how goeth the world below,
And why the sou'west blasts do blow.

I never was on the dull, tame shore,
But I loved the great sea more and more,
And backwards flew to her billowy breast,
Like a bird that seeketh its mother's nest;
And a mother she *was,* and *is,* to me;
For I was born on the open sea!

The waves were white, and red the morn,
In the noisy hour when I was born;
And the whale it whistled, the porpoise rolled,
And the dolphins bared their backs of gold;
And never was heard such an outcry wild
As welcomed to life the ocean-child!

I've lived since then, in calm and strife,
Full fifty summers, a sailor's life,
With wealth to spend and power to range,
But never have sought nor sighed for change;
And Death, whenever he comes to me,
Shall come on the wild, unbounded sea!

SCIENCE'S LESSON

Thomas Huxley

Science seems to me to teach in the highest and strongest manner the great truth which is embodied in the Christian conception of entire surrender to the will of God. Sit down before a fact as a little child, be prepared to give up every preconceived notion, follow humbly wherever and to whatever abyss nature leads, or you shall learn nothing. I have only begun to learn content and peace of mind since I have resolved at all risks to do this.

PROSPERO ENDS THE REVELS

William Shakespeare

Our revels now are ended. These our actors,
As I foretold you, were all spirits and
Are melted into air, into thin air:
And, like the baseless fabric of this vision,
The cloud-capp'd towers, the gorgeous palaces,
The solemn temples, the great globe itself,
Yea, all which it inherit, shall dissolve
And, like this insubstantial pageant faded,
Leave not a rack behind. We are such stuff
As dreams are made on, and our little life
Is rounded with a sleep.

                              (From The Tempest)

THE WOMAN TAKEN IN ADULTERY

Holy Bible, John 8:2–11

And early in the morning he came again into the temple, and all the people came unto him; and he sat down, and taught them.

And the scribes and Pharisees brought unto him a woman taken in adultery; and when they had set her in the midst,

They say unto him, Master, this woman was taken in adultery, in the very act.

Now Moses in the law commanded us that such should be stoned: but what sayest thou?

This they said, tempting him, that they might have to accuse him. But Jesus stooped down, and with his finger, wrote on the ground, as though he heard them not.

So when they continued asking him, he lifted up himself, and said unto them, He that is without sin among you, let him first cast a stone at her.

And again he stooped down, and wrote on the ground.

And they which heard it, being convicted by their own conscience, went out one by one, beginning at the eldest, even unto the last: and Jesus was left alone, and the woman standing in the midst.

When Jesus had lifted up himself, and saw none but the woman, he said unto her, Woman, where are those thine accusers? hath no man condemned thee?

She said, No man, Lord. And Jesus said unto her, Neither do I condemn thee: go, and sin no more.

DUTY

Ellen S. Hooper

I slept and dreamed that life was Beauty:
I woke and found that life was Duty:
Was my dream then a shadowy lie?
Toil on, sad heart, courageously,
And thou shalt find thy dream to be
A noonday light and truth to thee.

ST. TERESA'S BOOK-MARK

(TRANSLATOR: Henry Wadsworth Longfellow)

Let nothing disturb thee,
Nothing affright thee;
All things are passing;
God never changeth;
Patient endurance
Attaineth to all things;
Who God possesseth
In nothing is wanting;
Alone God sufficeth.

A REASONABLE AFFLICTION

Matthew Prior

On his death-bed poor Lubin lies;
   His spouse is in despair;
With frequent sobs and mutual cries,
   They both express their care.

"A different cause," says Parson Sly,
   "The same effect may give:
Poor Lubin fears that he may die;
   His wife, that he may live."

THE VICAR OF BRAY

Thomas Fuller, in his *Worthies of England* (1662), tells the story of the legendary Vicar of Bray, in Berkshire county, during the reigns of Henry VIII, Edward VI, Queen Mary, and Queen Elizabeth.

This particular Vicar adroitly adjusted his religious loyalties to those of the reigning monarch, as a consequence of which he was first a Catholic, then a Protestant, again a Catholic, and finally a Protestant.

When charged with being a chronic turncoat, an unconstant changeling, and a man without principle, the Vicar replied: "Not so. I have always kept my principle, which is to live and die the Vicar of Bray."

EPITAPH

Remember man, that passeth by,
As thou is now so once was I;
And as I am now so must thou be:
Prepare thyself to follow me.
Under this someone wrote:
To follow you I'm not content,
Until I learn which way you went.
(Churchyard;
Linton, England, 1825)

MAKE BIG PLANS

Daniel Burnham

Make no little plans; they have no magic to stir men's blood and probably in themselves will not be realized. Make big plans; aim high in hope and work, remembering that a noble, logical diagram once recorded will never die, but long after we are gone will be a living thing, asserting itself with ever-growing intensity. Remember that our sons and grandsons are going to do things that would stagger us. Let your watchword be order and your beacon beauty.

A MAN OF WORDS

Anonymous

A man of words and not of deeds,
Is like a garden full of weeds;
And when the weeds begin to grow,
It's like a garden full of snow;
And when the snow begins to fall,
It's like a bird upon the wall;
And when the bird away does fly,
It's like an eagle in the sky;
And when the sky begins to roar,
It's like a lion at the door;
And when the door begins to crack,
It's like a stick across your back;
And when your back begins to smart,
It's like a penknife in your heart;
And when your heart begins to bleed,
You're dead, and dead, and dead indeed.

THE CHILD'S WORLD

William Brighty Rands

Great, wide, beautiful, wonderful World,
With the wonderful water round you curled,
And the wonderful grass upon your breast,
World, you are beautifully dressed.

The wonderful air is over me,
And the wonderful wind is shaking the tree—
It walks on the water, and whirls the mills,
And talks to itself on the top of the hills.

You friendly Earth, how far do you go,
With the wheat-fields that nod and the rivers that flow,

With cities and gardens and cliffs and isles,
And the people upon you for thousands of miles?

Ah! you are so great, and I am so small,
I hardly can think of you, World, at all;
And yet, when I said my prayers to-day,
My mother kissed me, and said, quite gay,

"If the wonderful World is great to you,
And great to father and mother too,
You are more than the Earth, though you are such a dot!
You can love and think, and the Earth cannot!"

THE MONARCH

William Cowper

I am monarch of all I survey,
    My right there is none to dispute,
From the center all round to the sea,
    I am lord of the fowl and the brute.

PROPHECY

Alfred, Lord Tennyson

For I dipt into the future, far as human eye could see,
Saw the Vision of the world, and all the wonder that would be;

Saw the heavens fill with commerce, argosies of magic sails,
Pilots of the purple twilight, dropping down with costly bales;

Heard the heavens fill with shouting, and there rain'd a ghastly
    dew
From the nations' airy navies grappling in the central blue;

Far along the world-wide whisper of the south-wind rushing warm,
With the standards of the peoples plunging thro' the thunder-
storm;

Till the war-drum throbb'd no longer, and the battle-flags were
furl'd
In the Parliament of man, the Federation of the world.

There the common sense of most shall hold a fretful realm in awe,
And the kindly earth shall slumber, lapt in universal law.

(From Locksley Hall)

THE TERROR OF THE INFINITE

Blaise Pascal

When I consider the shortness of my life, lost in an eternity
before and behind, "passing away as the remembrance of a guest
who tarrieth but a day," the little space I fill or behold in the
infinite immensity of spaces, of which I know nothing and which
know nothing of me—when I reflect on this, I am filled with terror,
and wonder why I am *here* and not *there*, for there was no reason
why it should be the one rather than the other; why *now* rather
than *then*. Who set me here? By whose command and rule were this
time and place appointed me? How many kingdoms know nothing
of us! The eternal silence of those infinite spaces terrifies me.

FIVE REASONS FOR DRINKING

Dean Henry Aldrich

If all be true that I do think,
There are five reasons we should drink:
Good wine—a friend—or being dry—
Or lest we should be by and by—
Or any other reason why.

THE LARGER HOPE

Alfred, Lord Tennyson

Oh yet we trust that somehow good
  Will be the final goal of ill,
  To pangs of nature, sins of will,
Defects of doubt, and taints of blood;

That nothing walks with aimless feet;
  That not one life shall be destroy'd,
  Or cast as rubbish to the void,
When God hath made the pile complete;

That not a worm is cloven in vain;
  That not a moth with vain desire
  Is shrivell'd in a fruitless fire,
Or but subserves another's gain.

Behold, we know not anything;
  I can but trust that good shall fall
  At last—far off—at last, to all,
And every winter change to spring.

So runs my dream; but what am I?
  An infant crying in the night;
  An infant crying for the light,
And with no language but a cry.
                 (From In Memoriam)

MACBETH LEARNS OF HIS WIFE'S DEATH

William Shakespeare

Tomorrow, and tomorrow, and tomorrow,
Creeps in this petty pace from day to day
To the last syllable of recorded time,
And all our yesterdays have lighted fools
The way to dusty death. Out, out, brief candle!
Life's but a walking shadow, a poor player
That struts and frets his hour upon the stage
And then is heard no more; it is a tale
Told by an idiot, full of sound and fury,
Signifying nothing.

TO AN ANXIOUS FRIEND

William Allen White

You tell me that law is above freedom of utterance. And I reply that you can have no wise laws nor free enforcement of wise laws unless there is free expression of the wisdom of the people—and, alas, their folly with it. But if there is freedom, folly will die of its own poison, and the wisdom will survive. That is the history of the race. It is proof of man's kinship with God. You say that freedom of utterance is not for time of stress, and I reply with the sad truth that only in time of stress is freedom of utterance in danger. No one questions it in calm days, because it is not needed. And the reverse is true also; only when free utterance is suppressed it is needed, and when it is needed, it is most vital to justice.

Peace is good. But if you are interested in peace through force and without free discussion—that is to say, free utterance decently and in order—your interest in justice is slight. And peace without justice is tyranny, no matter how you may sugar-coat it with expedience. This state today is in more danger from suppression than from violence, because, in the end, suppression leads to violence. Violence, indeed, is the child of suppression. Whoever pleads for justice helps to keep the peace; and whoever tramples on the plea for justice temperately made in the name of peace only outrages peace and kills something fine in the heart of man which God put there when we got our manhood. When that is killed, brute meets brute on each side of the line.

So, dear friend, put fear out of your heart. This nation will survive, this state will prosper, the orderly business of life will go forward if only men can speak in whatever way given them to utter what their hearts hold—by voice, by posted card, by letter, or by press. Reason has never failed men. Only force and repression have made the wrecks in the world.

(Emporia Gazette, July 27, 1922)

* * *

If we could read the secret history of our enemies we should find in each man's life sorrow and suffering enough to disarm all hostility.

—Henry Wadsworth Longfellow

THE SHEPHERDESS

Alice Meynell

She walks—the lady of my delight—
  A shepherdess of sheep.
Her flocks are thoughts. She keeps them white;
  She guards them from the steep;
She feeds them on the fragrant height,
  And folds them in for sleep.

She roams maternal hills and bright,
  Dark valleys safe and deep.
Into that tender breast at night
  The chastest stars may peep.
She walks—the lady of my delight—
  A shepherdess of sheep.

She holds her little thoughts in sight,
  Though gay they run and leap.
She is so circumspect and right;
  She has her soul to keep.
She walks—the lady of my delight—
  A shepherdess of sheep.

OF DEATH

Francis Bacon

Men fear death as children fear to go in the dark. And as that natural fear in children is increased with tales, so is the other. Certainly, the contemplation of death, as the wages of sin and passage to another world, is holy and religious. But the fear of it, as a tribute due unto Nature, is weak. . . . It is worthy of the observing that there is no passion in the mind of man so weak but it mates and masters the fear of death. And, therefore, death is no such terrible enemy when a man hath so many attendants about him that can win the combat of him. Revenge triumphs over death. Love slights it. Honor aspireth to it. Grief fleeth to it. Fear preoccupateth it. . . . A man would die, though he were neither valiant nor miserable, only upon a weariness to do the same thing so oft over and over. It is no less worthy to observe how little alteration in good spirits the approach of death make. For they appear to be the same men till the last instant. . . . It is as natural to die as to be born; but to a little infant, perhaps, the one is as painful as the other. He that dies in an earnest pursuit is like one that is wounded in hot blood, who, for the time, scarce feels the hurt. And, therefore, a mind fixed and bent upon somewhat that is good doth avert the dolors of death. But above all, believe it, the sweetest canticle is, *Nunc dimittis;* when a man hath obtained worthy ends and expectations. Death hath this also: that it openeth the gate to good fame and extinguisheth envy.

GRAMMAR IN A NUTSHELL

Anonymous

Three little words you often see
Are Articles—A, An, and The.

A Noun's the name of anything,
As School, or Garden, Hoop or Swing.

Adjectives tell the kind of Noun,
As Great, Small, Pretty, White or Brown.

Instead of Nouns the Pronouns stand—
Her head, His face, Your arm, My hand.

Verbs tell something being done—
To Read, Count, Laugh, Sing, Jump or Run.

How things are done the Adverbs tell,
As Slowly, Quickly, Ill, or Well.

Conjunctions join the words together,
As men And women, wind Or weather.

The preposition stands before
A Noun, as In or Through a door.

The Interjection shows surprise,
As Oh! how pretty! Ah! how wise!

The Whole are called Nine Parts of Speech,
Which reading, writing, speaking teach.

MONEY

My friends, money is not all. It is not money that will mend a
broken heart or reassemble the fragments of a dream. Money cannot brighten the hearth nor repair the portals of a shattered home.
I refer, of course, to Confederate money.
                    (Attributed to Judge Kelly of Chicago)

A PRAYER FOUND IN CHESTER CATHEDRAL

Anonymous

Give me a good digestion, Lord,
And also something to digest;
Give me a healthy body, Lord,
With sense to keep it at its best.

Give me a healthy mind, Lord,
To keep the good and pure in sight;
Which, seeing sin, is not appalled,
But finds a way to set it right.

Give me a mind that is not bored,
That does not whimper, whine or sigh;
Don't let me worry overmuch,
About the fussy thing called "I."

Give me a sense of humour, Lord;
Give me the grace to see a joke;
To get some happiness from life,
And pass it on to other folk.

EVEN SUCH IS TIME

Sir Walter Raleigh

Even such is Time, that takes in trust our youth, our joys, our all
    we have,
And pays us but with earth and dust;
Who in the dark and silent grave,
When we have wandered all our ways,
Shuts up the story of our days;
But from this earth, this grave, this dust,
My God shall raise me up, I trust.

                    (From his History of the World)

LONDON, 1802

William Wordsworth

Milton! thou should'st be living at this hour;
England hath need of thee: she is a fen
Of stagnant waters: altar, sword, and pen,
Fireside, the heroic wealth of hall and bower,
Have forfeited their ancient English dower
Of inward happiness. We are selfish men;
Oh! raise us up, return to us again;
And give us manners, virtue, freedom, power.
Thy soul was like a Star, and dwelt apart:
Thou hadst a voice whose sound was like the sea:
Pure as the naked heavens, majestic, free,
So didst thou travel on life's common way,
In cheerful godliness; and yet thy heart
The lowliest duties on herself did lay.

HERACLITUS

William (Johnson) Cory

They told me, Heraclitus, they told me you were dead,
They brought me bitter news to hear and bitter tears to shed
I wept as I remember'd how often you and I
Had tired the sun with talking and sent him down the sky.

And now that thou art lying, my dear old Carian guest,
A handful of gray ashes, long, long ago at rest,
Still are thy pleasant voices, thy nightingales, awake;
For Death, he taketh all away, but them he cannot take.

CALLICLES' EXHORTATION

Plato

(TRANSLATOR: Benjamin Jowett)

Now I, Callicles, am persuaded of the truth of these things, and I consider how I shall present my soul whole and undefiled before the judge in that day. Renouncing the honors at which the world aims, I desire only to know the truth, and to live as well as I can, and, when I die, to die as well as I can. And to the utmost of my power, I exhort all other men to do the same. And, in return for your exhortation of me, I exhort you also to take part in the great combat, which is the combat of life, and greater than every other earthly conflict.

(From *Gorgias*)

INSCRIPTION ON THE CROSS

Holy Bible, John 19:19–22

And Pilate wrote a title, and put it on the cross. And the writing was JESUS OF NAZARETH THE KING OF THE JEWS.

This title then read many of the Jews; for the place where Jesus was crucified was nigh to the city: and it was written in Hebrew, and Greek, and Latin.

Then said the chief priests of the Jews to Pilate, Write not, The King of the Jews; but that he said, I am the King of the Jews.

Pilate answered, What I have written I have written.

ZEST FOR LIFE

William Allen White

I have never been bored an hour in my life. I get up every morning wondering what new strange glamorous thing is going to happen and it happens at fairly regular intervals. Lady Luck has been good to me and I fancy she has been good to every one. Only some people are dour, and when she gives them the come hither with her eyes, they look down or turn away and lift an eyebrow. But me, I give her the wink and away we go.

TODAY

Mary F. Butts

Build a little fence of trust
Around Today,
Fill the space with loving work
And therein stay.
Look not through the sheltering bars
Upon Tomorrow;
God will help thee bear what comes
Of joy or sorrow.

JOHN HAY, PRESIDENT LINCOLN'S SECRETARY, RECORDS IN HIS DIARY THE OCCASION OF THE GETTYSBURG ADDRESS

In the morning of the 19th, I got a beast and rode out with the President and suite to the Cemetery in procession. The procession formed itself in an orphanly sort of way, and moved out with very little help from anybody; and after a little delay Mr. Everett took his place on the stand—and Mr. Stockton made a prayer which thought it was an oration—and Mr. Everett spoke as he always does, perfectly, and the President, in a firm free way, with more grace than is his wont, said a half-dozen lines of consecration—and the music wailed, and we went home through crowded and cheering streets.

(November, 1863)

IN FLANDERS FIELDS

Captain John D. McCrae

In Flanders fields the poppies blow
Between the crosses, row on row,
That mark our place; and in the sky
The larks, still bravely singing, fly
Scarce heard amid the guns below.

We are the Dead. Short days ago
We lived, felt dawn, saw sunset glow,
Loved and were loved, and now we lie
    In Flanders fields.

Take up our quarrel with the foe!
To you from failing hands, we throw
The torch— Be yours to hold it high!
If ye break faith with us who die
We shall not sleep, though poppies grow
    In Flanders fields.

THE WEST WIND

John Masefield

It's a warm wind, the west wind, full of birds' cries;
I never hear the west wind, but tears are in my eyes.
For it comes from the west lands, the old brown hills,
And April's in the west wind, and daffodils.

It's a fine land, the west land, for hearts as tired as mine;
Apple orchards blossom there, and the air's like wine.
There is cool green grass there, where men may lie at rest;
And the thrushes are in song there, fluting from the nest.

"Will you not come home, brother? You have been long away.
It's April, and blossom time, and white is the spray:
And bright is the sun, brother, and warm is the rain;
Will you not come home, brother, home to us again?

"The young corn is green, brother, where the rabbits run;
It's blue sky, and white clouds, and warm rain and sun.
It's song to a man's soul, brother, fire to a man's brain,
To hear the wild bees and see the merry spring again.

"Larks are singing in the west, brother, above the green wheat,
So will you not come home, brother, and rest your tired feet?
I've a balm for bruised hearts, brother, sleep for aching eyes,"
Says the warm wind, the west wind, full of birds' cries.

It's the white road westwards is the road I must tread
To the green grass, the cool grass, and rest for heart and head,
To the violets and the brown brooks and the thrushes' song
In the fine land, the west land, the land where I belong.

THAT NANTUCKET LIMERICK, AND
WHAT FOLLOWED

There once was a man from Nantucket
Who kept all his cash in a bucket;
But his daughter, named Nan,
Ran away with a man,
And as for the bucket, Nantucket.

(Princeton Tiger)

But he followed the pair to Pawtucket—
The man and the girl with the bucket;
And he said to the man
He was welcome to Nan,
But as for the bucket, Pawtucket.

(Chicago Tribune)

Then the pair followed Pa to Manhasset,
Where he still held the cash as an asset;
But Nan and the man
Stole the money and ran,
And as for the bucket, Manhasset.

(New York Press)

* * *

Opinion is a species of property that I am always desirous
of sharing with my friends.

—Charles Lamb

NOW I LAY ME DOWN TO TAKE MY SLEEP

Now I lay me down to take my sleep,
I pray The Lord my soul to keep;
If I should die before I wake
I pray The Lord my soul to take.
(From the New England Primer 1777 ed.) *

MARK TWAIN DISCUSSES SATAN

Of course, Satan has some kind of a case, it goes without saying. It may be a poor one, but that is nothing; that can be said about any one of us.—We may not pay him reverence for that would be indiscreet; but we can at least respect his talents. A person who has for untold centuries maintained the imposing position of spiritual head of four fifths of the human race, and political head of the whole of it, must be granted the possession of executive abilities of the loftiest order.—I would like to see him. I would rather see him and shake him by the tail than any other member of the European Concert.

UPON WESTMINSTER BRIDGE

William Wordsworth

Earth has not anything to show more fair:
Dull would he be of soul who could pass by
A sight so touching in its majesty:
This City now doth, like a garment, wear
The beauty of the morning; silent, bare,
Ships, towers, domes, theatres and temples lie
Open unto the fields, and to the sky;
All bright and glittering in the smokeless air.
Never did sun more beautifully steep
In his first splendour, valley, rock, or hill;
Ne'er saw I, never felt, a calm so deep!
The river glideth at his own sweet will:
Dear God! the very houses seem asleep;
And all that mighty heart is lying still!

---

* The first record of this prayer is said to be found in the *Enchiridion Leonis*, A.D. 1160.

BABY

George Macdonald

Where did you come from, Baby dear?
Out of the everywhere into here.

Where did you get your eyes so blue?
Out of the sky as I came through.

What makes the light in them sparkle and spin?
Some of the starry spikes left in.

Where did you get that little tear?
I found it waiting when I got here.

What makes your forehead so smooth and high?
A soft hand stroked it as I went by.

What makes your cheek like a warm white rose?
I saw something better than anyone knows.

Whence that three-cornered smile of bliss?
Three angels gave me at once a kiss.

Where did you get this pearly ear?
God spoke, and it came out to hear.

Where did you get those arms and hands?
Love made itself into hooks and bands.

Feet, whence did you come, you darling things?
From the same box as the cherubs' wings.

How did they all come to be you?
God thought about me, and so I grew.

But how did you come to us, you dear?
God thought about you, and so I am here.

MANDALAY

Rudyard Kipling

By the old Moulmein Pagoda, lookin' eastward to the sea,
There's a Burma girl a-settin', an' I know she thinks o' me;
For the wind is in the palm-trees, an' the temple-bells they say:
"Come you back, you British soldier; come you back to Mandalay!"
       Come you back to Mandalay,
       Where the old Flotilla lay:
       Can't you 'ear their paddles chunkin' from Rangoon to
         Mandalay?
       On the road to Mandalay,
       Where the flyin'-fishes play,
       An' the dawn comes up like thunder outer China 'crost
         the Bay!

'Er petticoat was yaller an' 'er little cap was green,
An' 'er name was Supi-yaw-let—jes' the same as Theebaw's Queen,
An' I seed her fust a-smokin' of a whackin' white cheroot,
An' a-wastin' Christian kisses on an 'eathen idol's foot:
       Bloomin' idol made o' mud—
       What they called the Great Gawd Budd—
       Plucky lot she cared for idols when I kissed 'er where she
         stud!
       On the road to Mandalay—

When the mist was on the rice-fields an' the sun was droppin' slow,
She'd git 'er little banjo an' she'd sing *"Kulla-lo-lo!"*
With 'er arm upon my shoulder an' her cheek agin my cheek
We useter watch the steamers an' the *hathis* pilin' teak.
       Elephints a-pilin' teak
       In the sludgy, squdgy creek,
       Where the silence 'ung that 'eavy you was 'arf afraid to
         speak!
       On the road to Mandalay—

But that's all shove be'ind me—long ago an' fur away,
An' there ain't no 'busses runnin' from the Bank to Mandalay;
An' I'm learnin' 'ere in London what the ten-year soldier tells:
"If you've 'eard the East a-callin', why, you won't 'eed naught
   else."

No! you won't 'eed nothin' else
But them spicy garlic smells
An' the sunshine an' the palm-trees an' the tinkly temple
    bells;
On the road to Mandalay—

I am sick o' wastin' leather on these gritty pavin'-stones,
An' the blasted Henglish drizzle wakes the fever in my bones;
Tho' I walks with fifty 'ousemaids outer Chelsea to the Strand,
An' they talks a lot o' lovin', but wot do they understand?
    Beefy face an' grubby 'and—
    Law! wot *do* they understand?
    I've a neater, sweeter maiden in a cleaner, greener land!
    On the road to Mandalay—

Ship me somewheres east of Suez where the best is like the worst,
Where there aren't no Ten Commandments, an' a man can raise
  a thirst;
For the temple-bells are callin', an' it's there that I would be—
By the old Moulmein Pagoda, lookin' lazy at the sea—
    On the road to Mandalay,
    Where the old Flotilla lay,
    With our sick beneath the awnings when we went to
      Mandalay!
    Oh, the road to Mandalay,
    Where the flyin'-fishes play,
    An' the dawn comes up like thunder outer China 'crost
      the Bay!

APPOINTMENT IN SAMARRA

Somerset Maugham

DEATH SPEAKS:
    There was a merchant in Bagdad who sent his servant to market
to buy provisions and in a little while the servant came back,
white and trembling, and said, "Master, just now when I was in
the market place I was jostled by a woman in the crowd and when
I turned I saw it was Death that jostled me. She looked at me and
made a threatening gesture; now, lend me your horse and I will
ride away from this city and avoid my fate. I will go to Samarra
and there Death will not find me." The merchant lent him his

438

horse, and he dug his spurs in its flanks and as fast as the horse could gallop he went. Then the merchant went down to the market place and he saw me standing in the crowd and he came to me and said, "Why did you make a threatening gesture to my servant when you saw him this morning?" "That was not a threatening gesture," I said, "it was only a start of surprise. I was astonished to see him in Bagdad, for I had an appointment with him tonight in Samarra."

(From Sheppy)

REVEILLE

A. E. Housman

Wake: the silver dusk returning
Up the beach of darkness brims,
And the ship of sunrise burning
Strands upon the eastern rims.

Wake: the vaulted shadow shatters,
Trampled to the floor it spanned,
And the tent of night in tatters
Strews the sky-pavilioned land.

Up, lad, up, 'tis late for lying:
Hear the drums of morning play;
Hark, the empty highways crying
"Who'll beyond the hills away?"

Towns and countries woo together,
Forelands beacon, belfries call;
Never lad that trod on leather
Lived to feast his heart with all.

Up, lad: thews that lie and cumber
Sunlit pallets never thrive;
Morns abed and daylight slumber
Were not meant for man alive.

Clay lies still, but blood's a rover;
Breath's a ware that will not keep.
Up, lad: when the journey's over
There'll be time enough to sleep.

FINNIGIN TO FLANNIGAN

Strickland Gillilan

Superintindint wuz Flannigan;
Boss av the siction wuz Finnigin;
Whiniver the kyars got offen th' thrack
An' muddled up things t' th' divil an' back
Finnigin writ it to Flannigan,
Afther the wrick wuz all on agin:
That is, this Finnigin
Repoorted to Flannigan.

Whin Finnigin furst writ to Flannigan,
He writ tin pages—did Finnigin.
An' he tould jist how the smash occurred;
Full minny a tajus, blunderin' wurrd
Did Finnigin write to Flannigan
Afther the cars had gone on agin.
That's th' way Finnigin
Repoorted to Flannigan.

Now Flannigan knowed more than Finnigin—
He'd more idjucation—had Flannigan;
An' it wore 'm clane an' complately out
To tell what Finnigin writ about
In his writin' to Muster Flannigan.
So he writed this here: Masther Finnigin:
Don't do sich a sin agin;
Make 'em brief, Finnigin!"

Whin Finnigin got this from Flannigan,
He blushed rosy rid—did Finnigin;
An' he said: "I'll gamble a whole month's pa-ay
That it'll be minny an' minny a da-ay
Befoore Sup'rintindint—that's Flannigan—
Gits a whack at that very same sin agin.
From Finnigin to Flannigan
Repoorts won't be so long agin."

Wan da-ay on the siction av Finnigin,
On the road sup'rintinded be Flannigan,

440

A rail give way on a bit av a curve
An' some kyars went off as they made th' shwerrve.
"There's nobody hurted," sez Finnigin,
"But repoorts must be made to Flannigan,"
An' he winked at Mike Corrigan,
As married a Finnigin.

He wuz shantyin' thin, wuz Finnigin,
As minny a railroader's been agin,
An' his shmoky ol' lamp wuz burnin' bright
In Finnigin's shanty all that night—
Bilin' down his repoort was Finnigin
An' he writed this here: "Muster Flannigan:
Off agin, on agin,
Gone agin.—Finnigin."

THE THINGS THAT ARE CAESAR'S

Holy Bible, Matthew 22:15-22

15 Then went the Pharisees, and took counsel how they might entangle him in his talk.

16 And they sent out unto him their disciples with the Herodians, saying, Master, we know that thou art true, and teachest the way of God in truth, neither carest thou for any man: for thou regardest not the person of men.

17 Tell us therefore, What thinkest thou? Is it lawful to give tribute unto Caesar, or not?

18 But Jesus perceived their wickedness, and said, Why tempt ye me, ye hypocrites?

19 Shew me the tribute money. And they brought unto him a penny.

20 And he saith unto them, Whose is this image and superscription?

21 They say unto him, Caesar's. Then saith he unto them, Render therefore unto Caesar the things which are Caesar's; and unto God the things that are God's.

22 When they had heard these words, they marvelled, and left him, and went their way.

ROBERT E. LEE'S FAREWELL TO HIS ARMY

Headquarters Army of Northern Virginia
April 10, 1865

After four years of arduous service marked by unsurpassed courage and fortitude, the Army of Northern Virginia has been compelled to yield to overwhelming numbers and resources.

I need not tell the survivors of so many hard-fought battles who have remained steadfast to the last that I have consented to this result from no distrust of them; but feeling that valor and devotion could accomplish nothing that would compensate for the loss that must have attended the continuance of the contest, I determined to avoid the useless sacrifice of those whose past services have endeared them to their countrymen. By the terms of the agreement, officers and men can return to their homes and remain until exchanged.

You may take with you the satisfaction that proceeds from the consciousness of duty faithfully performed, and I earnestly pray that a merciful God will extend to you His blessing and protection.

With an unceasing admiration of your constancy and devotion to your country, and a grateful remembrance of your kind and generous consideration of myself, I bid you all an affectionate farewell.

R. E. LEE, *General*

T.R. ON WAR VETERANS

A man who is good enough to shed his blood for his country is good enough to be given a square deal afterward. More than that no man is entitled to, and less than that no man shall have.
—Theodore Roosevelt, Springfield, Ill., 1903

I CAN STAND ANY SOCIETY

Mark Twain

I'm quite sure that . . . I have no race prejudices, and I think I have no color prejudices nor creed prejudices. Indeed, I know it. I can stand any society. All I care to know is that a man is a human being— that is enough for me; he can't be any worse.

THE BOWERY

Charles H. Hoyt

Oh! the night that I struck New York,
I went out for a quiet walk;
Folks who are "on to" the city say,
Better by far that I took Broadway;
But I wasn't out to enjoy the sights,
There was the Bowery ablaze with lights;
I had one of the devil's own nights!
I'll never go there anymore!

Chorus:

The Bowery, the Bowery! They say such things, and they **do**
strange things on
The Bowery! The Bowery! I'll never go there anymore!

I had walked but a block or two,
When up came a fellow and me he knew;
Then a policeman came walking by,
Chased him away, and I asked him why?
"Wasn't he pulling your leg," said he;
Said I, "He never laid hands on me!"
"Get off the Bowery, you Yap!" said he,
I'll never go there anymore! (*Chorus.*)

I went into an auction store,
I never saw any thieves before;
First he sold me a pair of socks,
Then said he how much for the box?
Someone said "Two dollars!" I said "Three!"
He emptied the box and gave it to me,
"I sold you the box, not the socks," said he,
I'll never go there anymore! (*Chorus.*)

I went into a concert hall,
I didn't have a good time at all;
Just the minute that I sat down,
Girls began singing, "New Coon in town."
I got up mad and spoke out free,
"Somebody put that man out," said she;
A man called a bouncer attended to me,
I'll never go there anymore! (*Chorus.*)

I struck a place that they called a "dive,"
I was in luck to get out alive;
When the policeman heard my woes,
Saw my black eyes and my battered nose;
"You've been held up!" said the "copper" fly!
"No, sir! but I've been knocked down!" said I,
Then he laughed, though I couldn't see why!
I'll never go there anymore! (*Chorus.*)

THIS WAS THEIR FINEST HOUR

Winston Churchill

What General Weygand called the Battle of France is over.
The Battle of Britain is about to begin. On this battle depends
the survival of Christian civilization.

Upon it depends our own British life and the long continuity
of our institutions and our empire. The whole fury and might of
the enemy must very soon be turned upon us. Hitler knows he
will have to break us in this island or lose the war.

If we stand up to him all Europe may be freed and the life of
the world may move forward into broad sunlit uplands; but if
we fail, the whole world, including the United States and all that
we have known and cared for, will sink into the abyss of a new
dark age made more sinister and perhaps more prolonged by the
lights of a perverted science.

Let us therefore brace ourselves to our duty and so bear ourselves that if the British Commonwealth and Empire last for a
thousand years, men will still say, "This was their finest hour."

(From the Speech of June 18, 1940)

THE WOODPECKER

Coleman Cox

Even the woodpecker owes his success to the fact that he uses his
head and keeps pecking away until he finishes the job he starts.

THE LAKE ISLE OF INNISFREE

William Butler Yeats

I will arise and go now, and go to Innisfree,
And a small cabin build there, of clay and wattles made:
Nine bean rows will I have there, a hive for the honey bee,
And live alone in the bee-loud glade.

And I shall have some peace there, for peace comes dropping slow,
Dropping from the veils of the morning to where the cricket sings;
There midnight's all a glimmer, and noon a purple glow,
And evening full of the linnet's wings.

I will arise and go now, for always night and day
I hear lake water lapping with low sounds by the shore;
While I stand on the roadway, or on the pavements gray,
I hear it in the deep heart's core.

CLEOPATRA AND HER BARGE

William Shakespeare

The barge she sat in, like a burnish'd throne,
Burn'd on the water: the poop was beaten gold;
Purple the sails, and so perfumed that
The winds were love-sick with them; the oars were silver,
Which to the tune of flutes kept stroke, and made
The water which they beat to follow faster,
As amorous of their strokes. For her own person,
It beggar'd all description: she did lie
In her pavilion—cloth-of-gold of tissue—
O'er-picturing that Venus where we see
The fancy outwork nature: on each side her
Stood pretty dimpled boys, like smiling Cupids,
With divers-colour'd fans, whose wind did seem
To glow the delicate cheeks which they did cool,
And what they undid did.

Age cannot wither her, nor custom stale
Her infinite variety: other women cloy

The appetites they feed; but she makes hungry
Where most she satisfies: for vilest things
Become themselves in her; that the holy priests
Bless her when she is riggish.

(From Antony and Cleopatra)

SAY NOT THE STRUGGLE NOUGHT AVAILETH

Arthur Hugh Clough

Say not the struggle nought availeth,
    The labour and the wounds are vain,
The enemy faints not, nor faileth,
    And as things have been they remain.

If hopes were dupes, fears may be liars;
    It may be, in yon smoke concealed,
Your comrades chase e'en now the fliers,
    And, but for you, possess the field.

For while the tired waves, vainly breaking,
    Seem here no painful inch to gain,
Far back, through creeks and inlets making,
    Comes silent, flooding in, the main.

And not by eastern windows only,
    When daylight comes, comes in the light;
In front, the sun climbs slow, how slowly,
    But westward, look, the land is bright.

THE SULTAN'S HAREM

Anonymous

The sultan got sore on his harem,
And invented a scheme to scare 'em;
He caught him a mouse
Which he loosed in the house;
(The confusion is called harem scarem.)

SO WE SAUNTER TOWARD THE HOLY LAND

Henry David Thoreau

The sun sets on some retired meadow, where no house is visible, with all the glory and splendor that is lavished on cities, and, perchance, as it has never set before—where there is but a solitary marsh-hawk to have his wings gilded by it, or only a musquash looks out from his cabin, and there is some little black-veined brook in the midst of the marsh, just beginning to meander, winding slowly round a decaying stump. We walked in so pure and bright a light, gilding the withered grass and leaves, so softly and serenely bright, I thought I had never bathed in such a golden flood, without a ripple or a murmur to it. The west side of every wood and rising ground gleamed like a boundary of Elysium, and the sun on our backs seemed like a gentle herdsman driving us home at evening.

So we saunter toward the Holy Land, till one day the sun shall shine more brightly than ever he has done, shall perchance shine into our minds and hearts, and light up our whole lives with a great awakening light, as warm and serene and golden as on a bank-side in autumn.

COURAGE

Sydney Smith

A great deal of talent is lost in the world for want of a little courage. Every day sends to their graves obscure men whom timidity prevented from making a first effort; who, if they could have been induced to begin, would in all probability have gone great lengths in the career of fame. The fact is, that to do anything in the world worth doing, we must not stand back shivering and thinking of the cold and danger, but jump in and scramble through as well as we can. It will not do to be perpetually calculating risks and adjusting nice chances; it did very well before the Flood, when a man would consult his friends upon an intended publication for a hundred and fifty years, and live to see his success afterwards; but at present, a man waits, and doubts, and consults his brother, and his particular friends, till one day he finds he is sixty years old and that he has lost so much time in consulting cousins and friends that he has no more time to follow their advice.

TREES

Joyce Kilmer

I think that I shall never see
A poem lovely as a tree.

A tree whose hungry mouth is prest
Against the earth's sweet flowing breast;

A tree that looks at God all day
And lifts her leafy arms to pray;

A tree that may in summer wear
A nest of robins in her hair;

Upon whose bosom snow has lain;
Who intimately lives with rain.

Poems are made by fools like me,
But only God can make a tree.

OFT HAVE I SEEN AT SOME CATHEDRAL DOOR

Oft have I seen at some cathedral door,
A laborer, pausing in the dust and heat,
Lay down his burden, and with reverent feet
Enter, and cross himself, and on the floor
Kneel to repeat his paternoster o'er;
Far off the noises of the world retreat;
The loud vociferations of the street
Become an indistinguishable roar.
So, as I enter here from day to day,
And leave my burden at this minster gate,
Kneeling in prayer, and not ashamed to pray,
The tumult of the time disconsolate
To inarticulate murmurs dies away,
While the eternal ages watch and wait.
          (From Divina Commedia, transl. Longfellow)

ANNABEL LEE

Edgar Allan Poe

It was many and many a year ago,
  In a kingdom by the sea,
That a maiden there lived, whom you may know
  By the name of Annabel Lee;
And this maiden she lived with no other thought
  Than to love, and be loved by me.

I was a child and she was a child,
  In this kingdom by the sea;
But we loved with a love that was more than love,
  I and my Annabel Lee,—
With a love that the wingèd seraphs of heaven
  Coveted her and me.

And this was the reason that long ago,
  In this kingdom by the sea,
A wind blew out of a cloud, chilling
  My beautiful Annabel Lee;
So that her high-born kinsmen came,
  And bore her away from me,
To shut her up in a sepulchre,
  In this kingdom by the sea.

The angels, not so happy in heaven,
  Went envying her and me.
Yes! that was the reason (as all men know)
  In this kingdom by the sea,
That the wind came out of the cloud by night,
  Chilling and killing my Annabel Lee.

But our love it was stronger by far than the love
  Of those who were older than we,
  Of many far wiser than we;
And neither the angels in heaven above,
  Nor the demons down under the sea,
Can ever dissever my soul from the soul
  Of the beautiful Annabel Lee.

For the moon never beams without bringing me dreams
   Of the beautiful Annabel Lee,
And the stars never rise but I feel the bright eyes
   Of the beautiful Annabel Lee.
And so, all the night-tide I lie down by the side
Of my darling, my darling, my life, and my bride,
   In her sepulchre there by the sea,
   In her tomb by the sounding sea.

BREAK, BREAK, BREAK

Alfred, Lord Tennyson

Break, break, break,
On thy cold gray stones, O Sea!
And I would that my tongue could utter
The thoughts that arise in me.

O, well for the fisherman's boy,
That he shouts with his sister at play!
O, well for the sailor lad,
That he sings in his boat on the bay!

And the stately ships go on
To the haven under the hill;
But O, for the touch of a vanish'd hand,
And the sound of a voice that is still!

Break, break, break,
At the foot of thy crags, O Sea!
But the tender grace of a day that is dead
Will never come back to me.

WHOLE DUTY OF CHILDREN

Robert Louis Stevenson

A child should always say what's true,
And speak when he is spoken to,
And behave mannerly at table;
At least as far as he is able.

NEARER, MY GOD, TO THEE

Sarah Flower Adams

Nearer, my God, to Thee,
Nearer to Thee!
E'en though it be a cross
That raiseth me;
Still all my song shall be,
Nearer, my God, to Thee,
Nearer to Thee!

Though like the wanderer,
The sun gone down,
Darkness be over me,
My rest a stone;
Yet in my dreams I'd be
Nearer, my God, to Thee,
Nearer to Thee!

There let the way appear
Steps unto Heaven,
All that Thou send'st me
In mercy given;
Angels to beckon me
Nearer, my God, to Thee,
Nearer to Thee!

Then, with my waking thoughts
Bright with Thy praise,
Out of my stony griefs,
Bethel I'll raise;
So by my woes to be
Nearer, my God, to Thee,
Nearer to Thee!

Or if, on joyful wing,
Cleaving the sky,
Sun, moon and stars forgot,
Upward I fly,
Still all my song shall be,
Nearer, my God, to Thee,
Nearer to Thee!

WE HAVE LIVED AND LOVED TOGETHER

Charles Jefferys

We have lived and loved together
  Through many changing years;
We have shared each other's gladness
  And wept each other's tears;
I have known ne'er a sorrow
  That was long unsoothed by thee;
For thy smiles can make a summer
  Where darkness else would be.

Like the leaves that fall around us
  In autumn's fading hours,
Are the traitor's smiles, that darken
  When the cloud of sorrow lowers;
And though many such we've known, love,
  Too prone, alas, to range,
We both can speak of one love
  Which time can never change.

We have lived and loved together
  Through many changing years;
We have shared each other's gladness
  And wept each other's tears.
And let us hope the future
  As the past has been will be:
  I will share with thee my sorrows,
  And thou thy joys with me.

THE SOUL SELECTS

Emily Dickinson

The soul selects her own society,
Then shuts the door;
On her divine majority
Obtrude no more.

Unmoved, she notes the chariot's pausing
At her low gate;
Unmoved, an emperor is kneeling
Upon her mat.
I've known her from an ample nation
Choose one;
Then close the valves of her attention
Like stone.

POWER FROM GOD

Holy Bible, Isaiah 40:28–31

Hast thou not known? hast thou not heard, that the everla:
God, the Lord, the Creator of the ends of the earth, fainteth
neither is weary? there is no searching of his understanding.

He giveth power to the faint; and to them that have no migł
increaseth strength.

Even the youths shall faint and be weary, and the young
shall utterly fall; But they that wait upon the Lord shall renew
strength; they shall mount up with wings as eagles; they shall
and not be weary; and they shall walk, and not faint.

TO ONE WHO HAS BEEN LONG IN CITY PENT

John Keats

To one who has been long in city pent,
   'Tis very sweet to look into the fair
   And open face of heaven,—to breathe a prayer
Full in the smile of the blue firmament.
Who is more happy, when, with heart's content,
   Fatigued he sinks into some pleasant lair
   Of wavy grass, and reads a debonair
And gentle tale of love and languishment?
Returning home at evening, with an ear
   Catching the notes of Philomel,—an eye
Watching the sailing cloudlet's bright career,
   He mourns that day so soon has glided by:
E'en like the passage of an angel's tear
   That falls through the clear ether silently.

FATHER FORGETS

William Livingston Larned

Listen, son, I am saying this to you as you lie asleep, one little paw crumpled under your cheek and the blond curls stickily wet on your damp forehead. I have stolen into your room alone. Just a few moments ago, as I sat reading my paper in the library, a hot, stifling wave of remorse swept over me. I could not resist it. Guiltily I came to your bedside.

These were the things I was thinking, son: I had been cross to you. I scolded you as you were dressing for school because you gave your face merely a dab with a towel. I took you to task for not cleaning your shoes. I called out angrily when I found you had thrown some of your things on the floor.

At breakfast, I found fault, too. You spilled things. You gulped down your food. You put your elbows on the table. You spread butter too thick on your bread. And as you started off to play and I made for my train, you turned and waved a little hand and called, "Good-by, Papa!" and I frowned and said in reply, "Hold your shoulders back!"

Then it began all over again in the late afternoon. As I came up the hill road, I spied you, down on your knees, playing marbles. There were holes in your stocking. I humiliated you before your boy friends, by making you march on ahead of me, back to the house. Stockings were expensive—and if *you* had to buy them you would be more careful. Imagine that, son, from a father! It was such a stupid, silly logic.

But do you remember, later, when I was reading in the library, how you came in softly, timidly, with a sort of hurt, hunted look in your eyes? When I glanced up, over my paper, impatient at the interruption, you hesitated at the door.

"What is it you want?" I snapped.

You said nothing, but you ran across, gathering all your childish courage, in one tempestuous plunge, and threw your arms around my neck, and kissed me, again and again, and your small arms tightened with an affection that God had set blooming in your heart and which even neglect could not wither. And then you were gone, pattering up the stairs.

Well, son, it was shortly afterwards that my paper slipped from my hands and a terrible, sickening fear came over me. Suddenly I saw myself as I really was, in all my horrid selfishness, and I felt sick at heart.

What had habit been doing to me? The habit of complaining, of finding fault, of reprimanding—all these were my rewards to you for being a boy. It was not that I did not love you; it was that I expected so terribly much of youth. I was measuring you by the yardstick of my own years.

And there is so much that is good, and fine, and true in your character. You did not *deserve* my treatment of you, son. The little heart of you was as big as the dawn itself, over wide hills. All this was shown by your spontaneous impulse to rush in and kiss me goodnight. Nothing else matters, tonight, son. I have come to your bedside in the darkness, and I have knelt here, choking with emotion and so ashamed!

It is a feeble atonement. I know you would not understand these things if I told them to you during your waking hours. Yet I must say what I am saying. I must burn sacrificial fires, alone, here in your own bedroom, and make free confession.

And I have prayed God to strengthen me in my new resolve. Tomorrow I will be a *real* daddy! I will chum with you and suffer when you suffer and laugh when you laugh. I will bite my tongue when impatient words come. I will keep saying, as if it were a ritual: "He is nothing but a boy—a little boy!"

I am afraid I have visualized you as a man. Yet as I see you now, son, crumpled and weary in your cot, I see that you are still a baby. Yesterday you were in your mother's arms, your head on her shoulder. I have asked too much, too much!

Dear boy! Dear little son! A penitent kneels at your infant shrine, here in the moonlight. I kiss the little fingers, and the damp forehead, and the yellow curls, and, if it were not for waking you, I would snatch you up and crush you to my breast.

Tears came and heartache and remorse and, I think, a greater, deeper love, when you ran through the library door and *wanted* to kiss me!

THE WORDS OF THE PREACHER

Holy Bible, Ecclesiastes 1:2–11

Vanity of vanities, saith the Preacher, vanity of vanities; all is vanity. What profit hath a man of all his labour which he taketh under the sun? One generation passeth away, and another generation cometh: but the earth abideth for ever. The sun also ariseth, and the sun goeth down, and hasteth to his place where he arose. The wind goeth toward the south, and turneth about unto the north; it whirleth about continually, and the wind returneth again according to his circuits. All the rivers run into the sea; yet the sea is not full; unto the place from whence the rivers come, thither they return again. All things are full of labour; man cannot utter it: the eye is not satisfied with seeing, nor the ear filled with hearing. The thing that hath been, it is that which shall be; and that which is done is that which shall be done: and there is no new thing under the sun. Is there any thing whereof it may be said, See, this is new? It hath been already of old time, which was before us. There is no remembrance of former things; neither shall there be any remembrance of things that are to come with those that shall come after.

SONG OF THE OPEN ROAD

Ogden Nash

I think that I shall never see
A billboard lovely as a tree.
Indeed, unless the billboards fall
I'll never see a tree at all.

EXPLANATION

Josh Billings

I hate to be a kicker,
    I always long for peace,
But the wheel that does the squeaking,
    Is the one that gets the grease.

FAITH OF OUR FATHERS

Frederick W. Faber

Faith of our fathers, living still
  In spite of dungeon, fire and sword,
O how our hearts beat high with joy
  Whene'er we hear that glorious word!
Faith of our fathers, holy faith,
  We will be true to thee till death.

Our fathers, chained in prisons dark,
  Were still in heart and conscience free,
And blest would be their children's fate,
  If they, like them, should die for thee:
Faith of our fathers, holy faith,
  We will be true to thee till death.

Faith of our fathers, we will strive
  To win all nations unto thee;
And through the truth that comes from God
  Mankind shall then indeed be free:
Faith of our fathers, holy faith,
  We will be true to thee till death.

Faith of our fathers, we will love
  Both friend and foe in all our strife,
And preach thee, too, as love knows how,
  By kindly words and virtuous life:
Faith of our fathers, holy faith,
  We will be true to thee till death.

MARTHA

Walter de la Mare

"Once . . . once upon a time . . ."
  Over and over again,
Martha would tell us stories,
  In the hazel glen.

Hers were those clear grey eyes
  You watch, and the story seems
Told by their beautifulness
  Tranquil as dreams.

She would sit with her two slim hands
    Clasped round her bended knees;
While we on our elbows lolled,
    And stared at ease.

Her voice and her narrow chin,
    Her grave small lovely head,
Seemed half the meaning
    Of the words she said.

"Once . . . once upon a time . . ."
    Like a dream you dream in the night,
Fairies and gnomes stole out
    In the leaf-green light.

And her beauty far away
    Would fade, as her voice ran on,
Till hazel and summer sun
    And all were gone:

All fordone and forgot;
    And like clouds in the height of the sky,
Our hearts stood still in the hush
    Of an age gone by.

THE LAUGHTER OF A CHILD

Robert G. Ingersoll

The laugh of a child will make the holiest day more sacred still. Strike with hand of fire, O weird musician, thy harp strung with Apollo's golden hair; fill the vast cathedral aisles with symphonies sweet and dim, deft toucher of the organ keys; blow, bugler, blow, until thy silver notes do touch and kiss the moonlit waves, and charm lovers wandering 'mid the vine-clad hills. But know, your sweetest strains are discords all, compared with childhood's happy laugh—the laugh that fills the eyes with light and every heart with joy. O rippling river of laughter, thou art the blessed boundary line between the beasts and men; and every forward wave of thine doth drown some fretful fiend of care. O Laughter, rose-lipped daughter of joy, there are dimples enough in thy cheeks to catch and hold and glorify all the tears of grief.

O TO BE UP AND DOING

Robert Louis Stevenson

O to be up and doing,
Unfearing and unashamed to go
In all the uproar and the press
About my human business!
My undissuaded heart I hear
Whisper courage in my ear.
With voiceless calls, the ancient earth
Summons me to a daily birth,
Thou, O my love, ye, O my friends—
The gist of life, the end of ends—
To laugh, to love, to live, to die
Ye call me by the ear and eye!

CRABBÈD AGE AND YOUTH

Anonymous

Crabbèd Age and Youth
Cannot live together:
Youth is full of pleasance,
Age is full of care;
Youth like summer morn,
Age like winter weather;
Youth like summer brave,
Age like winter bare.
Youth is full of sport,
Age's breath is short;
Youth is nimble, Age is lame;
Youth is hot and bold,
Age is weak and cold;
Youth is wild, and Age is tame.
Age, I do abhor thee;
Youth, I do adore thee;
O, my Love, my Love is young!
Age, I do defy thee:
O, sweet shepherd, hie thee!
For methinks thou stay'st too long.
        (Usually attributed to William Shakespeare)

ALL MEN SHOULD WORK

Abraham Lincoln

I hold that if the Almighty had ever made a set of men that should do all the eating and none of the work, He would have made them with mouths only and no hands; and if He had ever made another class that He intended should do all the work and no eating, He would have made them with hands only and no mouths.

CHAUCER

Artemus Ward

Some kind person has sent me Chaucer's poems. Mr. C. had talent, but he couldn't spel. No man has a right to be a lit-rary man onless he knows how to spel. It is a pity that Chaucer, who had a geneyus, was so unedicated. He's the wus speller I know of.

UP-HILL

Christina Georgina Rossetti

Does the road wind up-hill all the way?
   Yes, to the very end.
Will the day's journey take the whole long day?
   From morn to night, my friend.

Shall I meet other way-farers at night?
   Those who have gone before.
Then must I knock, or call when just in sight?
   They will not keep you standing at that door.

Shall I find comfort, travel-sore and weak?
   Of labour you shall find the sum.
Will there be beds for me and all who seek?
   Yea, beds for all who come.

But is there for the night a resting-place?
    A roof for when the slow dark hours **begin.**
May not the darkness hide it from my face?
    You cannot miss that inn.

EVENTIDE

Caroline Atherton Briggs Mason

At cool of day, with God I walk
    My garden's grateful shade;
I hear His voice among the trees,
    And I am not afraid.

He speaks to me in every wind,
    He smiles from every star;
He is not deaf to me, nor blind,
    Nor absent, nor afar.

His hand that shuts the flowers to sleep,
    Each in its dewy fold,
Is strong my feeble life to keep,
    And competent to hold.

The powers below and powers above,
    Are subject to His care—
I cannot wander from His love
    Who loves me everywhere.

Thus dowered, and guarded thus, with Him
    I walk this peaceful shade;
I hear His voice among the trees,
    And I am not afraid.

FROM PARADISE LOST

John Milton

Invocation to the Heavenly Muse

Of Man's first disobedience, and the fruit
Of that forbidden tree whose mortal taste
Brought death into the World, and all our woe,
With loss of Eden, till one greater Man
Restore us, and regain the blissful Seat,
Sing, Heavenly Muse, that, on the secret top
Of Oreb, or of Sinai, didst inspire
That Shepherd who first taught the chosen seed
In the beginning how the heavens and earth
Rose out of Chaos: or, if Sion hill
Delight thee more, and Siloa's brook that flowed
Fast by the oracle of God, I thence
Invoke thy aid to my adventrous song,
That with no middle flight intends to soar
Above the Aonian mount, while it pursues
Things unattempted yet in prose or rhyme.
And chiefly Thou, O Spirit, that dost prefer
Before all temples the upright heart and pure,
Instruct me, for Thou know'st; Thou from the first
Wast present, and, with mighty wings outspread,
Dove-like sat'st brooding on the vast Abyss,
And mad'st it pregnant: what in me is dark
Illumine, what is low raise and support;
That, to the highth of this great argument,
I may assert Eternal Providence,
And justify the ways of God to men.

Satan Ponders His Fallen State

"Is this the region, this the soil, the clime,"
Said then the lost Archangel, "this the seat
That we must change for Heaven?—this mournful gloom
For that celestial light? Be it so, since he
Who now is sovran can dispose and bid
What shall be right: fardest from him is best,
Whom reason hath equalled, force hath made supreme

Above his equals. Farewell, happy fields,
Where joy for ever dwells! Hail, horrors! hail,
Infernal World! and thou, profoundest Hell,
Receive thy new possessor—one who brings
A mind not to be changed by place or time.
The mind is its own place, and in itself
Can make a Heaven of Hell, a Hell of Heaven.
What matter where, if I be still the same,
And what I should be, all but less than he
Whom thunder hath made greater? Here at least
We shall be free; the Almighty hath not built
Here for his envy, will not drive us hence:
Here we may reign secure; and, in my choice,
To reign is worth ambition, though in Hell:
Better to reign in Hell than serve in Heaven.

Satan Looks upon Adam and Eve in Paradise

Two of far nobler shape, erect and tall,
God-like erect, with native honour clad
In naked majesty, seemed lords of all,
And worthy seemed; for in their looks divine
The image of their glorious Maker shon,
Truth, wisdom, sanctitude severe and pure—
Severe, but in true filial freedom placed,
Whence true authority in men: though both
Not equal, as their sex not equal seemed;
For contemplation he and valour formed,
For softness she and sweet attractive grace;
He for God only, she for God in him.
His fair large front and eye sublime declared
Absolute rule; and Hyacinthin locks
Round from his parted forelock manly hung
Clustering, but not beneath his shoulders broad:
She, as a veil down to the slender waist,
Her unadornèd golden tresses wore
Dishevelled, but in wanton ringlets waved
As the vine curls her tendrils—which implied
Subjection, but required with gentle sway,
And by her yielded, by him best received
Yielded, with coy submission, modest pride,

And sweet, reluctant, amorous delay.
Nor those mysterious parts were then concealed;
Then was not guilty shame. Dishonest shame
Of Nature's works, honour dishonourable,
Sin-bred, how have ye troubled all mankind
With shews instead, mere shews of seeming pure,
And banished from man's life his happiest life,
Simplicity and spotless innocence!
So passed they naked on, nor shunned the sight
Of God or Angel, for they thought no ill:
So hand in hand they passed, the loveliest pair
That ever since in love's imbraces met—
Adam the goodliest man of men since born
His sons; the fairest of her daughters Eve.

Night Falls on Eden

Now came still Evening on, and Twilight gray
Had in her sober livery all things clad;
Silence accompanied; for beast and bird,
They to their grassy couch, these to their nests
Were slunk, all but the wakeful nightingale.
She all night long her amorous descant sung:
Silence was pleased. Now glowed the firmament
With living Saphirs; Hesperus, that led
The starry host, rode brightest, till the Moon,
Rising in clouded majesty, at length
Apparent queen, unveiled her peerless light,
And o'er the dark her silver mantle threw.

Eve to Adam

"With thee conversing, I forget all time,
All seasons, and their change; all please alike.
Sweet is the breath of Morn, her rising sweet,
With charm of earliest birds; pleasant the Sun,
When first on this delightful land he spreads
His orient beams, on herb, tree, fruit, and flower,
Glistering with dew; fragrant the fertil Earth
After soft showers; and sweet the coming on
Of grateful Evening mild, then silent Night,
With this her solemn bird, and this fair Moon,

And these the gems of Heaven, her starry train:
But neither breath of Morn, when she ascends
With charm of earliest birds; nor rising Sun
On this delighful land; nor herb, fruit, flower,
Glistering with dew; nor fragrance after showers;
Nor grateful Evening mild; nor silent Night,
With this her solemn bird; nor walk by moon,
Or glittering star-light, without thee is sweet."

Banishment from Paradise

Descended, Adam to the bower where Eve
Lay sleeping ran before, but found her waked;
And thus with words not sad she him received:—
"Whence thou return'st and whither went'st I know;
For God is also in sleep, and dreams advise,
Which he hath sent propitious, some great good
Presaging, since, with sorrow and heart's distress
Wearied, I fell asleep. But now lead on;
In me is no delay; with thee to go
Is to stay here; without thee here to stay
Is to go hence unwilling; thou to me
Art all things under Heaven, all places thou,
Who for my wilful crime art banished hence.
This further consolation yet secure
I carry hence: though all by me is lost,
Such favour I unworthy am voutsafed,
By me the Promised Seed shall all restore."
So spake our mother Eve; and Adam heard
Well pleased, but answered not; for now too nigh
The Archangel stood, and from the other hill
To their fixed station, all in bright array,
The Cherubim descended, on the ground
Gliding metéorous, as evening mist
Risen from a river o'er the marish glides,
And gathers ground fast at the labourer's heel
Homeward returning. High in front advanced,
The brandished sword of God before them blazed,
Fierce as a comet; which with torrid heat,
And vapour as the Libyan air adust,
Began to parch that temperate clime; whereat
In either hand the hastening Angel caught

Our lingering Parents, and to the eastern gate
Led them direct, and down the cliff as fast
To the subjected plain—then disappeared.
They, looking back, all the eastern side beheld
Of Paradise, so late their happy seat,
Waved over by that flaming brand; the gate
With dreadful faces thronged and fiery arms.
Some natural tears they dropped, but wiped them soon;
The world was all before them, where to choose
Their place of rest, and Providence their guide.
They, hand in hand, with wandering steps and slow,
Through Eden took their solitary way.

"TO THE VICTOR BELONGS THE SPOILS"

U. S. Senator William L. Marcy, of New York

It may be, sir, that the politicians of New York are not so fastidi-
ous as some gentlemen are, as to disclosing the principles on which
they act. They boldly preach what they practice. When they are
contending for victory, they avow their intentions of enjoying the
fruits of it. If they are defeated, they expect to retire from office.
If they are successful, they claim, as a matter of right, the advantages of success. They see nothing wrong in the rule that to the
VICTOR belongs the spoils of the ENEMY.

(Defending Van Buren's appointment
as Minister to England, 1832.)

EPITAPH PLACED ON HIS DAUGHTER'S TOMB

Warm summer sun,
Shine kindly here.
Warm southern wind,
Blow softly here.

Green sod above,
Lie light, lie light.
Good night, dear heart,
Good night, good night.

(Mark Twain, adapted from
Robert Richardson)

THE FIRST CHRISTMAS

Holy Bible, Luke 2:1–19

And it came to pass in those days, that there went out a decree from Caesar Augustus, that all the world should be taxed. (And this taxing was first made when Cyrenius was governor of Syria.) And all went to be taxed, every one into his own city. And Joseph also went up from Galilee, out of the city of Nazareth, into Judaea, unto the city of David, which is called Bethlehem; (because he was of the house and lineage of David:) To be taxed with Mary his espoused wife, being great with child. And so it was, that, while they were there, the days were accomplished that she should be delivered. And she brought forth her firstborn son, and wrapped him in swaddling clothes, and laid him in a manger; because there was no room for them in the inn. And there were in the same country shepherds abiding in the field, keeping watch over their flock by night. And, lo, the angel of the Lord came upon them, and the glory of the Lord shone round about them: and they were sore afraid. And the angel said unto them, Fear not: for, behold, I bring you good tidings of great joy, which shall be to all people. For unto you is born this day in the city of David a Saviour, which is Christ the Lord. And this shall be a sign unto you; Ye shall find the babe wrapped in swaddling clothes, lying in a manger. And suddenly there was with the angel a multitude of the heavenly host praising God, and saying, Glory to God in the highest, and on earth peace, good will toward men. And it came to pass, as the angels were gone away from them into heaven, the shepherds said one to another, Let us now go even unto Bethlehem, and see this thing which is come to pass, which the Lord hath made known unto us. And they came with haste, and found Mary, and Joseph, and the babe lying in a manger. And when they had seen it, they made known abroad the saying which was told them concerning this child. And all they that heard it wondered at those things which were told them by the shepherds. But Mary kept all these things, and pondered them in her heart.

* * *

There is only one class in the community that thinks more about money than the rich, and that is the poor.
—Oscar Wilde

WHAT I LIVE FOR

George Linnaeus Banks

I live for those who love me,
  Whose hearts are kind and true;
For the Heaven that smiles above me,
  And awaits my spirit too;
For all human ties that bind me,
For the task by God assigned me,
For the bright hopes yet to find me,
  And the good that I can do.

I live to learn their story
  Who suffered for my sake;
To emulate their glory,
  And follow in their wake;
Bards, patriots, martyrs, sages,
The heroic of all ages,
Whose deeds crowd History's pages,
  And Time's great volume make.

I live to hold communion
  With all that is divine,
To feel there is a union
  Twixt Nature's heart and mine;
To profit by affliction,
Reap truth from fields of fiction,
Grow wiser from conviction,
  And fulfil God's grand design.

I live to hail that season
  By gifted ones foretold,
When men shall live by reason,
  And not alone by gold;
When man to man united,
And every wrong thing righted,
The whole world shall be lighted
  As Eden was of old.

I live for those who love me,
  For those who know me true,
For the Heaven that smiles above me,

And awaits my spirit too;
For the cause that lacks assistance,
For the wrong that needs resistance,
For the future in the distance,
    And the good that I can do.

MIA CARLOTTA

T. A. Daly

Giuseppe, da barber, ees greata for "mash,"
He gotta da bigga, da blacka moustache,
Good clo'es an' good styla an' playnta good cash.

W'enevra Giuseppe ees walk on da street,
Da peopla dey talka, "How nobby! how neat!
How softa da handa, how smalla da feet."

He leefta hees hat an' he shaka hees curls,
An' smila weeth teetha so shiny like pearls;
Oh, manny da heart of da seelly young girls

        He gotta.
    Yes, playnta he gotta—
        But notta
        Carlotta!

Giuseppe, da barber, he maka da eye,
An' lika da steam engine puffa an' sigh,
For catch Carlotta w'en she ees go by.

Carlotta she walka weeth nose in da air,
An' look through Giuseppe weeth far-away stare,
As eef she no see dere ees som'body dere.

Giuseppe, da barber, he gotta da cash,
He gotta da clo'es an' da bigga moustache,
He gotta da seelly young girl for da "mash,"

        But notta—
    You bat my life, notta—
        Carlotta
        I gotta!

469

Holy Bible, John 8:12-32

Then spake Jesus again unto them, saying, I am the light of the world: he that followeth me shall not walk in darkness, but shall have the light of life. The Pharisees therefore said unto him, Thou bearest record of thyself; thy record is not true. Jesus answered and said unto them, Though I bear record of myself, yet my record is true: for I know whence I came, and whither I go; but ye cannot tell whence I come, and whither I go. Ye judge after the flesh; I judge no man. And yet if I judge, my judgment is true: for I am not alone, but I and the Father that sent me. It is also written in your law, that the testimony of two men is true. I am one that bear witness of myself, and the Father that sent me beareth witness of me. Then said they unto him, Where is thy Father? Jesus answered, Ye neither know me, nor my Father: if ye had known me, ye should have known my Father also. These words spake Jesus in the treasury, as he taught in the temple: and no man laid hands on him; for his hour was not yet come. Then said Jesus again unto them, I go my way, and ye shall seek me, and shall die in your sins: whither I go, ye cannot come. Then said the Jews, Will he kill himself? because he saith, Whither I go, ye cannot come. And he said unto them, Ye are from beneath; I am from above: ye are of this world; I am not of this world. I said therefore unto you, that ye shall die in your sins: for if ye believe not that I am he, ye shall die in your sins. Then said they unto him, Who art thou? And Jesus saith unto them, Even the same that I said unto you from the beginning. I have many things to say and to judge of you: but he that sent me is true; and I speak to the world those things which I have heard of him. They understood not that he spake to them of the Father. Then said Jesus unto them, When ye have lifted up the Son of man, then shall ye know that I am he, and that I do nothing of myself; but as my Father hath taught me, I speak these things. And he that sent me is with me: the Father hath not left me alone; for I do always those things that please him. As he spake these words, many believed on him. Then said Jesus to those Jews which believed on him, If ye continue in my word, then ye are my disciples indeed; And ye shall know the truth, and the truth shall make you free.

COME, LET US KISS AND PART

Michael Drayton

Since there's no help, come, let us kiss and part,
Nay, I have done; you get no more of me.
And I am glad, yea, glad with all my heart
That thus so cleanly I myself can free.
Shake hands for ever; cancel all our vows;
And when we meet at any time again,
Be it not seen in either of our brows
That we one jot of former love retain.
Now at the last gasp of Love's latest breath,
When, his pulse failing, Passion speechless lies,
When Faith is kneeling by his bed of death,
And Innocence is closing up his eyes—
   Now, if thou wouldst, when all have given
      him over,
  From death to life thou might'st him yet
      recover.

A LITTLE SONG OF LIFE

Lizette Woodworth Reese

Glad that I live am I;
That the sky is blue;
Glad for the country lanes,
And the fall of dew.

After the sun the rain,
After the rain the sun;
This is the way of life,
Till the work be done.

All that we need to do,
Be we low or high,
Is to see that we grow
Nearer the sky.

OLD FOLKS AT HOME

Stephen Foster

'Way down upon de Swanee ribber,
Far, far away,
Dere's wha' my heart is turning ebber,
Dere's wha' de old folks stay.
All up and down de whole creation,
Sadly I roam,
Still longing for de old plantation,
And for de old folks at home.

All round de little farm I wander'd
When I was young,
Den many happy days I squander'd,
Many de songs I sung.

When I was playing wid my brudder,
Happy was I.
Oh! take me to my kind old mudder,
Dere let me live and die.

One little hut among de bushes,
One dat I love,
Still sadly to my mem'ry rushes,
No matter where I rove.
When will I see the bees a-humming,
All round de comb?
When will I hear de banjo tumming,
Down in my good old home?

Chorus:

    All de world am sad and dreary,
    Ebrywhere I roam,
    Oh! darkies how my heart grows weary,
    Far from de old folks at home.

JUSTICE HOLMES UPHOLDS FREEDOM OF SPEECH

Persecution for the expression of opinions seems to me perfectly logical. If you have no doubt of your premises or your power and want a certain result with all your heart you naturally express your wishes in law and sweep away all opposition. To allow opposition by speech seems to indicate that you think the speech impotent, as when a man says that he has squared the circle, or that you do not care whole-heartedly for the result, or that you doubt either your power or your premises. But when men have realized that time has upset many fighting faiths, they may come to believe even more than they believe the very foundations of their own conduct that the ultimate good desired is better reached by free trade in ideas—that the best test of truth is the power of the thought to get itself accepted in the competition of the market, and that truth is the only ground upon which their wishes safely can be carried out. That at any rate is the theory of our Constitution. It is an experiment, as all life is an experiment. Every year if not every day we have to wager our salvation upon some prophecy based upon imperfect knowledge. While that experiment is part of our system I think that we should be eternally vigilant against attempts to check the expression of opinions that we loathe and believe to be fraught with death, unless they so imminently threaten immediate interference with the lawful and pressing purposes of the law that an immediate check is required to save the country.

(Dissenting Opinion, Abrams vs.
United States, 250 U.S. 616, 1919)

AT DAY'S END

Anonymous

Now that day doth end,
My spirit I commend,
To Thee, my Lord, my Friend.
Into Thy hands, yea, Thine,
Those glorious hands benign,
Those human hands divine
My spirit I resign.

473

"HOW SWEET THE MOONLIGHT SLEEPS UPON THIS BANK!"

William Shakespeare

Lorenzo. How sweet the moonlight sleeps upon this bank!
Here will we sit, and let the sounds of music
Creep in our ears: soft stillness and the night
Become the touches of sweet harmony.
Sit, Jessica. Look how the floor of heaven
Is thick inlaid with patines of bright gold:
There's not the smallest orb which thou behold'st
But in his motion like an angel sings,
Still quiring to the young-eyed cherubins;
Such harmony is in immortal souls;
But whilst this muddy vesture of decay
Doth grossly close it in, we cannot hear it.
     [Enter Musicians]
Come, ho, and wake Diana with a hymn!
With sweetest touches pierce your mistress' ear,
And draw her home with music.
 Jessica. I am never merry when I hear sweet music.
 Lorenzo. The reason is, your spirits are attentive:
For do but note a wild and wanton herd,
Or race of youthful and unhandled colts,
Fetching mad bounds, bellowing and neighing loud,
Which is the hot condition of their blood;
If they but hear perchance a trumpet sound,
Or any air of music touch their ears,
You shall perceive them make a mutual stand,
Their savage eyes turn'd to a modest gaze
By the sweet power of music: therefore the poet
Did feign that Orpheus drew trees, stones and floods;
Since nought so stockish, hard and full of rage,
But music for the time doth change his nature.
The man that hath no music in himself,
Nor is not moved with concord of sweet sounds,
Is fit for treasons, stratagems and spoils;
The motions of his spirit are dull as night,
And his affections dark as Erebus:
Let no such man be trusted. Mark the music.
      (From The Merchant of Venice)

AS I'D NOTHING ELSE TO DO

Herbert Fry

'Twas a pleasant summer's morning—
  Just the day I like t' enjoy,
When I woke, and looked out early,
  Puzzled how my time t' employ;
In such fine and splendid weather
  I don't care for work—do you?
So I went to see my sweetheart,
  As I'd nothing else to do.

Off I started thro' the meadow,
  Where the dew-beads pearled the pray,
And responsive to the song-birds,
  I kept singing all the way;
Quite surprised she was to see me
  Come so early there to woo,
Till I said I'd just walked over,
  'Cause I'd nothing else to do.

Then we rambled forth together,
  Down the lane beneath the trees,
While so gentle stirred the shadow
  Of their branches in the breeze;
And whenever our conversation
  Languished for a word or two,
Why, of course I kindly kissed her,
  As I'd nothing else to do.

But before the day was over,
  I'd somehow made up my mind,
That I'd pop the question to her,
  If to me her heart inclined;
So I whispered "Sweet, my darling,
  Will you have me, Yes or No?"
"Well," said she, "perhaps I may my dear,
  When I've nothing else to do."

DO YOU FEAR THE WIND?

Hamlin Garland

Do you fear the force of the wind,
The slash of the rain?
Go face them and fight them,
Be savage again.
Go hungry and cold like the wolf,
   Go wade like the crane;
The palms of your hands will thicken,
The skin of your cheek will tan,
You'll grow ragged and weary and swarthy,
   But you'll walk like a man!

GATHER YE ROSES

Robert Louis Stevenson

Gather ye roses while ye may,
   Old time is still a-flying;
A world where beauty fleets away
   Is no world for denying.
Come lads and lasses, fall to play
   Lose no more time in sighing.

The very flowers you pluck to-day
   To-morrow will be dying;
   And all the flowers are crying,
And all the leaves have tongues to say,—
Gather ye roses while ye may.

THINK ON THESE THINGS

Holy Bible, Phillippians 4:8

   Finally, brethren, whatsoever things are true, whatsoever things are honest, whatsoever things are just, whatsoever things are pure, whatsoever things are lovely, whatsoever things are of good report; if there be any virtue, and if there be any praise, think on these things.

THE CHARIOT

Emily Dickinson

Because I could not stop for Death,
He kindly stopped for me;
The carriage held but just ourselves
And Immortality.

We slowly drove, he knew no haste,
And I had put away
My labor, and my leisure too,
For his civility.

We passed the school where children played
At wrestling in a ring;
We passed the field of grazing grain,
We passed the setting sun.

We paused before a house that seemed
A swelling of the ground;
The roof was scarcely visible,
The cornice but a mound.

Since then 'tis centuries; but each
Feels shorter than the day
I first surmised the horses' heads
Were toward eternity.

MARK ANTONY'S LAMENT

William Shakespeare

O mighty Caesar! dost thou lie so low?
Are all thy conquests, glories, triumphs, spoils,
Shrunk to this little measure? Fare thee well.
I know not, gentlemen, what you intend,
Who else must be let blood, who else is rank:
If I myself, there is no hour so fit
As Caesar's death hour, nor no instrument
Of half that worth as those your swords, made rich
With the most noble blood of all this world.

I do beseech ye, if you bear me hard,
Now, whilst your purpled hands do reek and smoke,
Fulfil your pleasure. Live a thousand years,
I shall not find myself so apt to die:
No place will please me so, no mean of death,
As here by Caesar, and by you cut off,
The choice and master spirits of this age.

* * *

O, pardon me, thou bleeding piece of earth,
That I am meek and gentle with these butchers!
Thou art the ruins of the noblest man
That ever lived in the tide of times.
Woe to the hand that shed this costly blood!
Over thy wounds now do I prophesy,—
Which, like dumb mouths, do ope their ruby lips,
To beg the voice and utterance of my tongue—
A curse shall light upon the limbs of men;
Domestic fury and fierce civil strife
Shall cumber all the parts of Italy;
Blood and destruction shall be so in use,
And dreadful objects so familiar,
That mothers shall but smile when they behold
Their infants quarter'd with the hands of war;
All pity choked with custom of fell deeds;
And Caesar's spirit ranging for revenge,
With Ate by his side come hot from hell,
Shall in these confines with a monarch's voice
Cry "Havoc," and let slip the dogs of war
That this foul deed shall smell above the earth
With carrion men, groaning for burial.

(From Julius Caesar)

FAMILY PRAYER

Book of Common Prayer

O Lord, support us all the day long, until the shadows lengthen
and the evening comes, and the busy world is hushed, and the fever
of life is over, and our work is done. Then in Thy mercy grant us a
safe lodging, and a holy rest, and peace at the last.

THE LOVER'S RESOLUTION

George Wither

Shall I, wasting in despair,
Die because a woman's fair?
Or make pale my cheeks with care
'Cause another's rosy are?
Be she fairer than the day,
Or the flow'ry meads in May,
    If she think not well of me,
    What care I how fair she be?

Shall my silly heart be pined
'Cause I see a woman kind?
Or a well-disposèd nature
Joinèd with a lovely feature?
Be she meeker, kinder, than
Turtle-dove or pelican,
    If she be not so to me,
    What care I how kind she be?

Shall a woman's virtues move
Me to perish for her love?
Or her well-deservings known
Make me quite forget my own?
Be she with that goodness blest
Which may merit name of Best,
    If she be not such to me,
    What care I how good she be?

'Cause her fortune seems too high,
Shall I play the fool and die?
She that bears a noble mind,
If not outward helps she find,
Thinks what with them he would do
That without them dares her woo;
    And unless that mind I see,
    What care I how great she be?

Great, or good, or kind, or fair,
I will ne'er the more despair;
If she love me, this believe,
I will die ere she shall grieve;
If she slight me when I woo,
I can scorn and let her go;
   For if she be not for me,
   What care I for whom she be?

STOPPING BY WOODS ON A SNOWY EVENING

Robert Frost

Whose woods these are I think I know.
His house is in the village though;
He will not see me stopping here
To watch his woods fill up with snow.

The little horse must think it queer
To stop without a farmhouse near
Between the woods and frozen lake
The darkest evening of the year.

He gives his harness bells a shake
To ask if there is some mistake.
The only other sound's the sweep
Of easy wind and downy flake.

The woods are lovely, dark and deep.
But I have promises to keep,
And miles to go before I sleep,
And miles to go before I sleep.

LITTLE WILLIE

Anonymous

Little Willie hung his sister;
She was dead before we missed her.
Willie's always up to tricks!
Ain't he cute? He's only six!

BENJAMIN FRANKLIN'S METHOD OF "DOING A GREAT DEAL OF GOOD WITH A LITTLE MONEY"

Passy, France, 22 April, 1784

Dear Sir:

Your situation grieves me and I send you herewith a banknote for ten louis d'ors. I do not pretend to give such a sum; I only lend it to you. When you shall return to your country, you cannot fail of getting into some business that will in time enable you to pay all your debts. In that case, when you meet with another honest man in similar distress, you must pay by lending this sum to him, enjoining him to discharge the debt by a like operation when he shall be able and shall meet with another such opportunity. I hope it may thus go through many hands before it meets with a knave that will stop its progress. This is a trick of mine for doing a great deal of good with a little money. I am not rich enough to afford much in good works, and so am obliged to be cunning and make the most of a little. With best wishes for your future prosperity, I am, dear sir, your most obedient servant,

B. FRANKLIN (letter to Benjamin Webb)

THE MULE DEFINED BY SAMUEL JOHNSON

Without pride of ancestry or hope of posterity.

THE COMPANY ONE KEEPS

Aimor R. Dickson

One night in late October,
When I was far from sober,
Returning with my load with manly pride,
My feet began to stutter
So I lay down in the gutter,
And a pig came near and lay down by my side,
A lady passing by was then heard plain to say,
"You can tell a man who boozes,
By the company he chooses."
At which the pig got up and slowly walked away.

THE HOUSE BY THE SIDE OF THE ROAD

Sam Walter Foss

There are hermit souls that live withdrawn
In the place of their self-content;
There are souls like stars, that dwell apart,
In a fellowless firmament;
There are pioneer souls that blaze their paths
Where highways never ran—
But let me live by the side of the road
And be a friend to man.

Let me live in a house by the side of the road,
Where the race of men go by—
The men who are good and the men who are bad,
As good and as bad as I.
I would not sit in the scorner's seat,
Or hurl the cynic's ban—
Let me live in a house by the side of the road
And be a friend to man.

I see from my house by the side of the road,
By the side of the highway of life,
The men who press with the ardor of hope,
The men who are faint with the strife.
But I turn not away from their smiles nor their tears,
Both parts of an infinite plan—
Let me live in a house by the side of the road
And be a friend to man.

I know there are brook-gladdened meadows ahead,
And mountains of wearisome height;
That the road passes on through the long afternoon
And stretches away to the night.
But still I rejoice when the travelers rejoice,
And weep with the strangers that moan,
Nor live in my house by the side of the road
Like a man who dwells alone.

Let me live in my house by the side of the road,
It's here the race of men go by—
They are good, they are bad, they are weak, they are strong,
Wise, foolish—so am I;
Then why should I sit in the scorner's seat,
Or hurl the cynic's ban?
Let me live in my house by the side of the road
And be a friend to man.

THE BRIDGE BUILDER

(Miss) Will Allen Dromgoole

An old man, going a lone highway,
Came at the evening, cold and gray,
To a chasm, vast and deep and wide,
Through which was flowing a sullen tide.
The old man crossed in the twilight dim—
That sullen stream had no fears for him;
But he turned, when he reached the other side,
And built a bridge to span the tide.
"Old man," said a fellow pilgrim near,
"You are wasting strength in building here.
Your journey will end with the ending day;
You never again must pass this way.
You have crossed the chasm, deep and wide,
Why build you the bridge at the eventide?"

The builder lifted his old gray head.
"Good friend, in the path I have come," he said,
"There followeth after me today
A youth whose feet must pass this way.
This chasm that has been naught to me
To that fair-haired youth may a pitfall be.
He, too, must cross in the twilight dim;
Good friend, I am building the bridge for *him*."

*   *   *

Every man complains of his memory but no man complains of
his judgment.—Anonymous

PROSPECTUS OF THE FAMOUS LACON, ILLINOIS, CAT-AND-RAT RANCH

Anonymous

GLORIOUS OPPORTUNITY TO GET RICH—We are starting a cat ranch in Lacon with 100,000 cats. Each cat will average twelve kittens a year. The cat skins will sell for thirty cents each. One hundred men can skin 5,000 cats a day. We figure a daily net profit of over $10,000. Now what shall we feed the cats? We will start a rat ranch next door with 1,000,000 rats. The rats will breed twelve times faster than the cats. So we will have four rats to feed each day to each cat. Now what shall we feed the rats? We will feed the rats the carcasses of the cats after they have been skinned. Now Get This! We feed the rats to the cats and the cats to the rats and get the skins for nothing.

(This hoax was carried by every newspaper in the United States, in 1875)

O COME ALL YE FAITHFUL

(ADESTE FIDELES)

Anonymous

O come, all ye faithful, joyful and triumphant;
O come ye, O come ye to Bethlehem.
Come and behold Him, born the King of angels;
O come, let us adore Him, O come, let us adore Him,
O come, let us adore Him, Christ the Lord.

Sing, choirs of angels, sing in exultation,
Sing, all ye citizens of heav'n above:
Glory to God, in the highest:
    O come, etc.

Yea, Lord, we greet Thee, born this happy morning,
Jesus, to Thee be glory giv'n;
Word of the Father, now in flesh appearing:
    O come, etc.

In Latin
Adeste fideles, laeti triumphantes;
Venite, venite in Bethlehem;
Natum videte, Regem angelorum;
Venite adoremus, Venite adoremus,
Venite adoremus, Dominum.

LOVE IS A SICKNESS

Samuel Daniel

Love is a sickness full of woes,
    All remedies refusing;
A plant that with most cutting grows,
    Most barren with best using.
        Why so?
More we enjoy it, more it dies;
If not enjoy'd, it sighing cries—
        Heigh ho!

Love is a torment of the mind,
    A tempest everlasting;
And Jove hath made it of a kind
    Not well, nor full nor fasting.
        Why so?
More we enjoy it, more it dies;
If not enjoy'd, it sighing cries—
        Heigh ho!

*   *   *

Give me a lever long enough, and a fulcrum strong enough,
and single-handed I can move the world.—Archimedes

THE DEATH OF DEATH

William Shakespeare

Poor soul, the centre of my sinful earth,
Press'd by these rebel powers that thee array,
Why dost thou pine within and suffer dearth,
Painting thy outward walls so costly gay?
Why so large cost, having so short a lease,
Dost thou upon thy fading mansion spend?
Shall worms, inheritors of this excess,
Eat up thy charge? is this thy body's end?

Then, soul, live thou upon thy servant's loss,
And let that pine to aggravate thy store;
Buy terms divine in selling hours of dross;
Within be fed, without be rich no more;
  So shalt thou feed on Death, that feeds on men,
  And Death once dead, there's no more dying then.

THE AHKOOND OF SWAT

"The Ahkoond of Swat is dead."—London papers of Jan. 22, 1878.

George Thomas Lanigan

What, what, what,
  What's the news from Swat?
  Sad news,
  Bad news,
Comes by the cable led
Through the Indian Ocean's bed,
Through the Persian Gulf, the Red
Sea and the Med-
Iterranean—he's dead;
The Ahkoond is dead!

For the Ahkoond I mourn,
  Who wouldn't?
He strove to disregard the message stern,
  But he Ahkoodn't.
Dead, dead, dead:
  (Sorrow, Swats!)
Swats wha hae wi' Ahkoond bled,
Swats whom he hath often led
Onward to a gory bed,
  Or to victory,
  As the case might be.
    Sorrow, Swats!
Tears shed,
  Shed tears like water.
Your great Ahkoond is dead!
  That Swat's the matter!

Mourn, city of Swat,
Your great Ahkoond is not,
But laid 'mid worms to rot.
His mortal part alone, his soul was caught
  (Because he was a good Ahkoond)
  Up to the bosom of Mahound.
Though earthly walls his frame surround
(Forever hallowed by the ground!)

And skeptics mock the lowly mound
And say "He's now of no Ahkoond!"
  His soul is in the skies—
The azure skies that bend above his loved
  Metropolis of Swat.
  He sees with larger, other eyes,
  Athwart all earthly mysteries—
  He knows what's Swat.

Let Swat bury the great Ahkoond
  With a noise of mourning and of lamentation!

LIVE JOYFULLY

Holy Bible, Ecclesiastes 9:7–11

Go thy way, eat thy bread with joy, and drink thy wine with a merry heart; for God now accepteth thy works. Let thy garments be always white; and let thy head lack no ointment. Live joyfully with the wife whom thou lovest all the days of the life of thy vanity, which he hath given thee under the sun, all the days of thy vanity: for that is thy portion in this life, and in thy labour which thou takest under the sun. Whatsoever thy hand findeth to do, do it with thy might; for there is no work, nor device, nor knowledge, nor wisdom, in the grave, whither thou goest.

I returned, and saw under the sun, that the race is not to the swift, nor the battle to the strong, neither yet bread to the wise, nor yet riches to men of understanding, nor yet favour to men of skill; but time and chance happeneth to them all.

FLOWER IN THE CRANNIED WALL

Alfred, Lord Tennyson

Flower in the crannied wall,
I pluck you out of the crannies,
I hold you here, root and all, in my hand,
Little flower—but *if* I could understand
What you are, root and all, and all in all,
I should know what God and man is.

ASPIRATION

Henry David Thoreau

Did you ever hear of a man who had striven all his life faithfully and singly toward an object and in no measure obtained it? If a man constantly aspires, is he not elevated? Did ever a man try heroism, magnanimity, truth, sincerity, and find that there was no advantage in them,—that it was a vain endeavor?

THE WRECK OF THE "JULIE PLANTE"

A Legend of Lac St. Pierre

William Henry Drummond

On wan dark night on Lac St. Pierre,
  De win' she blow, blow, blow,
An' de crew of de wood scow *Julie Plante*
  Got scar't an' run below—

For de win' she blow lak hurricane
  Bimeby she blow some more,
An' de scow bus' up on Lac St. Pierre
  Wan arpent from de shore.

De captinne walk on de fronte deck,
  An' walk de hin' deck too—
He call de crew from up de hole
  He call de cook also.
De cook she's name was Rosie,
  She come from Montreal,
Was chambre maid on lumber barge,
  On de Grande Lachine Canal.

De win' she blow from nor'-eas'-wes',—
  De sout' win' she blow too,
W'en Rosie cry "Mon cher captinne,
  Mon cher, w'at I shall do?"
Den de captinne t'row de big ankerre,
  But still the scow she dreef,
De crew he can't pass on de shore,
  Becos' he los' hees skeef.

De night was dark lak wan black cat,
  De wave run high an' fas',
W'en de captinne tak de Rosie girl
  An' tie her to de mas'.
Den he also tak' de life preserve,
  An' jomp off on de lak',
An' say, "Good-bye, ma Rosie dear,
  I go drown for your sak'."

Nex' morning very early
  'Bout ha'f-pas' two-t'ree-four—
De captinne—scow—an' de poor Rosie
  Was corpses on de shore,
For de win' she blow lak hurricane
  Bimeby she blow some more,
An' de scow bus' up on Lac St. Pierre,
  Wan arpent from de shore.

Moral

Now all good wood scow sailor man
  Tak' warning by dat storm
An' go an' marry some nice French girl
  An' leev on wan beeg farm.
De win' can blow lak hurricane
  An' s'pose she blow some more,
You can't get drown on Lac St. Pierre
  So long you stay on shore.

TO NIGHT

Joseph Blanco White

Mysterious Night! when our first parent knew
Thee from report divine, and heard thy name,
Did he not tremble for this lovely frame,
This glorious canopy of light and blue?
Yet 'neath the curtain of translucent dew,
Bathed in the rays of the great setting flame,
Hesperus with the host of heaven came,
And lo! creation widened on man's view.
Who could have thought such darkness lay concealed
Within thy beams, O Sun! or who could find,
While fly, and leaf, and insect stood revealed,
That to such countless orbs thou mad'st us blind!
  Why do we, then, shun Death with anxious strife?—
  If Light can thus deceive, wherefore not Life?

DEPARTURE

Coventry Patmore

It was not like your great and gracious ways!
Do you, that have naught other to lament,
Never, my Love, repent
Of how, that July afternoon,
You went,
With sudden, unintelligible phrase,
And frightened eye,
Upon your journey of so many days
Without a single kiss, or a good-bye?
I knew, indeed, that you were parting soon;
And so we sate, within the low sun's rays,
You whispering to me, for your voice was weak,
Your harrowing praise.
Well, it was well
To hear such things speak,
And I could tell
What made your eyes a growing gloom of love,
As a warm South wind sombres a March grove.
And it was like your great and gracious ways
To turn your talk on daily things, my Dear,
Lifting the luminous, pathetic lash
To let the laughter flash,
Whilst I drew near,
Because you spoke so low that I could scarcely hear.
But all at once to leave me at the last,
More at the wonder than the loss aghast,
With huddled, unintelligible phrase,
And frightened eye,
And go your journey of all days
With not one kiss, or a good-bye,
And the only loveless look the look with which
    you passed:
'Twas all unlike your great and gracious ways.

JOHN RANDOLPH'S OPINION OF HENRY CLAY

This being, so brilliant yet so corrupt, like a rotten mackerel
by moonlight, shines and stinks.

UPON THE DEATH OF SIR ALBERT MORTON'S WIFE

Sir Henry Wotton

> He first deceased; she for a little tried
> To live without him, liked it not, and died.

THE PEACE OF CHRIST

Holy Bible, John 14:1–27

Let not your heart be troubled: ye believe in God, believe also in me. In my Father's house are many mansions: if it were not so, I would have told you. I go to prepare a place for you. And if I go and prepare a place for you, I will come again, and receive you unto myself; that where I am, there ye may be also. And whither I go ye know, and the way ye know. Thomas saith unto him, Lord, we know not whither thou goest; and how can we know the way? Jesus saith unto him, I am the way, the truth, and the life: no man cometh unto the Father, but by me. If ye had known me, ye should have known my Father also: and from henceforth ye know him, and have seen him. Philip saith unto him, Lord, shew us the Father, and it sufficeth us. Jesus saith unto him, Have I been so long time with you, and yet hast thou not known me, Philip? he that seen me hath seen the Father; and how sayest thou then, Shew us the Father? Believest thou not that I am in the Father, and the Father in me? the words that I speak unto you I speak not of myself: but the Father that dwelleth in me, he doeth the works. Believe me that I am in the Father, and the Father in me: or else believe me for the very works' sake. Verily, verily, I say unto you, He that believeth on me, the works that I do shall he do also; and greater works than these shall he do; because I go unto my Father. And whatsoever ye shall ask in my name, that will I do, that the Father may be glorified in the Son. If ye shall ask any thing in my name, I will do it.

If ye love me, keep my commandments. And I will pray the Father, and he shall give you another Comforter, that he may abide with you for ever; Even the Spirit of truth; whom the world cannot receive, because it seeth him not, neither knoweth him; but ye know him; for he dwelleth with you, and shall be in you. I will not leave you comfortless; I will come to you. Yet a little while, and the world seeth me no more; but ye see me: because I live, ye shall live also. At that day ye shall know that I am in my

Father, and ye in me, and I in you. He that hath my commandments, and keepeth them, he it is that loveth me. And he that loveth
me shall be loved of my Father, and I will love him, and will manifest myself in him. Judas saith unto him, not Iscariot, Lord, how
is it that thou wilt manifest thyself unto us, and not unto the
world? Jesus answered and said unto him, If a man love me, he
will keep my words: and my Father will love him, and we will
come unto him, and make our abode with him. He that loveth me
not keepeth not my sayings: and the word which ye hear is not
mine, but the Father's which sent me. These things have I spoken
unto you, being yet present with you. But the Comforter, which is
the Holy Ghost, whom the Father will send in my name, he shall
teach you all things, and bring all things to your remembrance,
whatsoever I have said unto you. Peace I leave with you, my peace
I give unto you: not as the world giveth, give I unto you. Let not
your heart be troubled, neither let it be afraid.

A CREED

Edwin Markham

There is a destiny that makes us brothers;
None goes his way alone:
All that we send into the lives of others
Comes back into our own.

I care not what his temples or his creeds,
One thing holds firm and fast—
That into his fateful heap of days and deeds
The soul of man is cast.

DIOGENES TO ALEXANDER THE GREAT

ARISTIPPUS:
    You send me word that Alexander, King of Macedonia, has a
great desire to see me. You did well to give him that title, for
whatever the Macedonians may be, you know I am subject to
nobody. If that prince has a mind to be acquainted with me, and
my manner of life, let him come hither, for I shall always think
Athens as far distant from Macedon as Macedon is from Athens.
                                    Farewell.

DANNY DEEVER

Rudyard Kipling

"What are the bugles blowin' for?" said Files-on-Parade.
"To turn you out, to turn you out," the Colour-Sergeant said.
"What makes you look so white, so white?" said Files-on-Parade.
"I'm dreadin' what I've got to watch," the Colour-Sergeant said.
  For they're hangin' Danny Deever, you can hear the Dead March
    play,
  The regiment's in 'ollow square—they're hangin' him today;
  They've taken of his buttons off an' cut his stripes away.
  An' they're hangin' Danny Deever in the mornin'.

"What makes the rear-rank breathe so 'ard?" said Files-on-Parade.
"It's bitter cold, it's bitter cold," the Colour-Sergeant said.
"What makes that front-rank man fall down?" says Files-on-Parade.
"A touch o' sun, a touch o' sun," the Colour-Sergeant said.
  They are hangin' Danny Deever, they are marchin' of 'im round,
  They 'ave 'alted Danny Deever by 'is coffin on the ground;
  An' 'e'll swing in 'arf a minute for a sneakin' shootin' hound—
  O they're hangin' Danny Deever in the mornin'!

"'Is cot was right-'and cot to mine," said Files-on-Parade.
"'E's sleepin' out an' far to-night," the Colour-Sergeant said.
"I've drunk 'is beer a score o' times," said Files-on-Parade.
"'E's drinkin' bitter beer alone," the Colour-Sergeant said.
  They are hangin' Danny Deever, you must mark 'im to 'is place,
  For 'e shot a comrade sleepin'—you must look 'im in the face;
  Nine 'undred of 'is county an' the regiment's disgrace,
  While they're hangin' Danny Deever in the mornin'.

"What's that so black agin the sun?" said Files-on-Parade.
"It's Danny fightin' 'ard for life," the Colour-Sergeant said.
"What's that that whimpers over'ead?" said Files-on-Parade.
"It's Danny's soul that's passin' now," the Colour-Sergeant said.
  For they're done with Danny Deever, you can 'ear the quickstep
    play,
  The regiment's in column, an' they're marchin' us away;
  Ho! the young recruits are shakin', an' they'll want their beer
    to-day,
  After hangin' Danny Deever in the mornin'.

A FAMOUS BUT SPURIOUS DESCRIPTION
OF JESUS CHRIST

There has appeared in these our days, a man of great virtue, named Jesus Christ, who is living among us, and of the Gentiles is accepted as a Prophet, but his disciples call him the "Son of God." He raiseth the dead, and cures all manner of diseases; a man of stature somewhat tall and comely, with very revered countenance, such as the beholders both love and fear; his hair the color of chestnut, full ripe, plain to his ears, whence downwards it is more orient, curling and waving about his shoulders.

In the midst of his head is a seam or partition of his hair after the manner of Nazarites, his forehead plain and very delicate; his face without a spot or wrinkle, beautiful with a most lovely red; his nose and mouth so formed that nothing can be reprehended; his beard thickish, in color like his hair, not very long but forked; his look, innocent and mature; his eyes, gray, clear and quick. In reproving he is terrible; in admonishing, courteous and fair-spoken; pleasant in conversation, mixed with gravity. It cannot be remarked that any one saw him laugh, but many have seen him weep. In proportion of body, most excellent, his hands and arms most delicate to behold. In speaking, very temperate, modest and wise. A man, for his singular beauty, surpassing the children of men.

(This is supposed to have been a letter sent by Publius Lentulus to the Emperor Tiberius and the Roman senate. But authorities have repeatedly rejected its authenticity, some of them attributing it to an unnamed 14th century monk, possibly adapted from a letter found in one of works of a credulous and not very critical Greek historian.)

SAMUEL JOHNSON'S COMMENT ON POVERTY

When I was running about this town a very poor fellow, I was a great arguer for the advantages of poverty; but I was, at the same time, very sorry to be poor. Sir, all the arguments which are brought to represent poverty as no evil, show it to be evidently a great evil. You never find people laboring to convince you that you may live very happily upon a plentiful fortune.

WHEN YOU ARE OLD

William Butler Yeats

When you are old and grey and full of sleep,
And nodding by the fire, take down this book,
And slowly read, and dream of the soft look
Your eyes had once, and of their shadows deep;

How many loved your moments of glad grace,
And loved your beauty with love false or true;
But one man loved the pilgrim soul in you,
And loved the sorrows of your changing face.

And bending down beside the glowing bars,
Murmur, a little sadly, how love fled
And paced upon the mountains overhead
And hid his face amid a crowd of stars.

THE IRON CURTAIN

Winston S. Churchill

From Stettin to the Baltic to Trieste in the Adriatic, an iron
curtain has descended across the Continent. Behind that line lie
all the capitals of the ancient states of central and eastern Europe.
Warsaw, Berlin, Prague, Vienna, Budapest, Belgrade, Bucharest
and Sofia, all of these famous cities and the populations around
them lie in what I might call the Soviet Sphere, and all are subject, in one form or another, not only to Soviet influence but to
very high and in some cases increasing measure of control from
Moscow.

Police governments are pervading from Moscow. But Athens
alone, with its immortal glories, is free to decide its future at an
election under British, American and French observation. . . .

This is certainly not the liberated Europe we fought to build
up. Nor is it one which contains the essentials of permanent peace.

The safety of the world requires a unity in Europe from which
no nation should be permanently outcast.

(From the address at Fulton, Mo., March 5, 1946)

"NO COWARD SOUL IS MINE"

Emily Brontë

No coward soul is mine,
No trembler in the world's storm-troubled sphere:
  I see Heaven's glories shine,
And Faith shines equal, arming me from Fear.

O God within my breast,
Almighty, ever-present Deity!
  Life, that in me has rest,
As I, undying Life, have power in Thee!

Vain are the thousand creeds
That move men's hearts, unutterably vain,
  Worthless as withered weeds,
Or idle froth amid the boundless main,

To waken doubt in one
Holding so fast by Thine infinity,
  So surely anchored on
The steadfast rock of Immortality.

With wide-embracing love
Thy spirit animates eternal years,
  Pervades and broods above,
Changes, sustains, dissolves, creates, and rears.

Though earth and moon were gone,
And suns and universes ceased to be,
  And Thou were left alone,
Every existence would exist in Thee.

There is not room for Death,
Nor atom that his might could render void:
  Thou—THOU art Being and Breath,
And what THOU art may never be destroyed.

"THERE IS NO GOD," THE WICKED SAITH

Arthur Hugh Clough

"There is no God," the wicked saith,
  "And truly it's a blessing,
For what He might have done with us
  It's better only guessing."

"There is no God," a youngster thinks,
  "Or really, if there may be,
He surely did not mean a man
  Always to be a baby."

"There is no God, or if there is,"
  The tradesman thinks, " 'twere funny
If He should take it ill in me
  To make a little money."

"Whether there be," the rich man says,
  "It matters very little,
For I and mine, thank somebody,
  Are not in want of victual."

Some others, also, to themselves,
  Who scarce so much as doubt it,
Think there is none, when they are well
  And do not think about it.

But country folks who live beneath
  The shadow of the steeple;
The parson and the parson's wife,
  And mostly married people;

Youths green and happy in first love,
  So thankful for illusion;
And men caught out in what the world
  Calls guilt, in first confusion;

And almost everyone when age,
   Disease, or sorrows strike him,
Inclines to think there is a God,
   Or something very like Him.

* * *

The rung of a ladder was never meant to rest upon, but only to hold a man's foot long enough to enable him to put the other somewhat higher.—Thomas Henry Huxley

JULIET'S YEARNING

William Shakespeare

Spread thy close curtain, love-performing night,
That runaways' eyes may wink, and Romeo
Leap to these arms, untalk'd of and unseen.
Lovers can see to do their amorous rites
By their own beauties; or, if love be blind,
It best agrees with night. Come, civil night,
Thou sober-suited matron, all in black,
And learn me how to lose a winning match,
Play'd for a pair of stainless maidenhoods:
Hood my unmann'd blood bating in my cheeks
With thy black mantle, till strange love grown bold
Think true love acted simple modesty.
Come, night, come, Romeo, come, thou day in night;
For thou wilt lie upon the wings of night
Whiter than new snow on a raven's back.
Come, gentle night, come, loving, black-brow'd night,
Give me my Romeo; and, when he shall die,
Take him and cut him out in little stars,
And he will make the face of heaven so fine,
That all the world will be in love with night,
And pay no worship to the garish sun.
O, I have bought the mansion of a love,
But not possess'd it, and, though I am sold,
Not yet enjoy'd; so tedious is this day
As is the night before some festival
To an impatient child that hath new robes
And may not wear them.

(From Romeo and Juliet)

499

HAMLET'S INSTRUCTIONS TO THE PLAYERS

William Shakespeare

Speak the speech, I pray you, as I pronounced it to you, trippingly on the tongue: but if you mouth it, as many of your players do, I had as lief the town-crier spoke my lines. Nor do not saw the air too much with your hand, thus; but use all gently: for in the very torrent, tempest, and, as I may say, the whirlwind of passion, you must acquire and beget a temperance that may give it smoothness. O, it offends me to the soul to hear a robustious periwig-pated fellow tear a passion to tatters, to very rags, to split the ears of the groundlings, who for the most part are capable of nothing but inexplicable dumb-shows and noise: I would have such a fellow whipped for o'erdoing Termagant; it out-herods Herod: pray you, avoid it.

Be not too tame neither, but let your own discretion be your tutor. Suit the action to the word, the word to the action; with this special observance, that you o'erstep not the modesty of nature: for any thing so overdone is from the purpose of playing, whose end, both at the first and now, was and is, to hold, as 'twere, the mirror up to nature; to show virtue her own feature, scorn her own image, and the very age and body of the time his form and pressure. Now this overdone, or come tardy off, though it make the unskilful laugh, cannot but make the judicious grieve; the censure of the which one must in your allowance o'erweigh a whole theatre of others. O, there be players that I have seen play, and heard others praise, and that highly, not to speak it profanely, that, neither having the accent of Christians nor the gait of Christian, pagan, nor man, have so strutted and bellowed that I have thought some of nature's journeymen had made men, and not made them well, they imitated humanity so abominably.

(From Hamlet)

COME WHERE MY LOVE LIES DREAMING

Stephen C. Foster

Come where my love lies dreaming,
   Dreaming the happy hours away,
In visions bright redeeming
   The fleeting joys of day;
Dreaming the happy hours,
Dreaming the happy hours away.

Come where my love lies dreaming,
   Come with a lute-toned lay;
Come where my love lies dreaming,
   Dreaming the happy hours away;
Come with a lute, come with a lay,
Dreaming the happy hours away.

Soft is her slumber, thoughts bright and free
Dance through her dreams like a gushing melody,
Light is her young heart, light may it be,
Come where my love lies dreaming,
Dreaming the happy hours away.

THE TRICKS OF IMAGINATION

William Shakespeare

The lunatic, the lover and the poet
Are of imagination all compact:
One sees more devils than vast hell can hold,
That is, the madman: the lover, all as frantic,
Sees Helen's beauty in a brow of Egypt:
The poet's eye, in a fine frenzy rolling,
Doth glance from heaven to earth, from earth to heaven;
And as imagination bodies forth
The forms of things unknown, the poet's pen
Turns them to shapes, and gives to airy nothing
A local habitation and a name.
Such tricks hath strong imagination,
That, if it would but apprehend some joy,
It comprehends some bringer of that joy;
Or in the night, imagining some fear,
How easy is a bush supposed a bear!

            (From A Midsummer-Night's Dream)

THE HIGHWAYMAN

Alfred Noyes

Part One

The wind was a torrent of darkness among the gusty trees,
The moon was a ghostly galleon tossed upon cloudy seas,
The road was a ribbon of moonlight over the purple moor,
And the highwayman came riding—
   Riding—riding—
The highwayman came riding, up to the old inn-door.

He'd a French cock-hat on his forehead, a bunch of lace at his chin,
A coat of the claret velvet, and breeches of brown doe-skin;
They fitted with never a wrinkle: his boots were up to the thigh!
And he rode with a jeweled twinkle,
   His pistol butts a-twinkle,
His rapier hilt a-twinkle, under the jeweled sky.

Over the cobbles he clattered and clashed in the dark inn-yard,
And he tapped with his whip on the shutters, but all was locked
    and barred;
He whistled a tune to the window, and who should be waiting
    there
But the landlord's black-eyed daughter,
   Bess, the landlord's daughter,
Plaiting a dark red love-knot into her long black hair.

And dark in the dark old inn-yard, a stable-wicket creaked
Where Tim the ostler listened; his face was white and peaked;
His eyes were hollows of madness, his hair like mouldy clay,
But he loved the landlord's daughter,
   The landlord's red-lipped daughter,
Dumb as a dog he listened, and he heard the robber say—

"One kiss, my bonny sweetheart, I'm after a prize to-night,
But I shall be back with the yellow gold before the morning light;
Yet, if they press me sharply, and harry me through the day,
Then look for me by moonlight,
   Watch for me by moonlight,
I'll come to thee by moonlight, though hell should bar the way."

He rose upright in his stirrups; he scarce could reach her hand,
But she loosened her hair i' the casement! His face burnt like a
   brand
As the black cascade of perfume came tumbling over his breast;
And he kissed its waves in the moonlight,
   (Oh, sweet black waves in the moonlight!)
Then he tugged at his reins in the moonlight, and galloped away
   to the West.

Part Two

He did not come in the dawning; he did not come at noon;
And out o' the tawny sunset, before the rise o' the moon,
When the road was a gipsy's ribbon, looping the purple moor,
A red-coat troop came marching—
   Marching—marching—
King George's men came marching, up to the old inn-door.

They said no word to the landlord, they drank his ale instead,
But they gagged his daughter and bound her to the foot of her
   narrow bed;
Two of them knelt at her casement, with muskets at their side!
There was death at every window;
   And hell at one dark window;
For Bess could see, through her casement, the road that *he* would
   ride.

They had tied her up to attention, with many a sniggering jest;
They had bound a musket beside her, with the barrel beneath her
   breast!
"Now keep good watch!" and they kissed her.
   She heard the dead man say—
Look for me by moonlight;
   Watch for me by moonlight;
I'll come to thee by moonlight, though hell should bar the way!

She twisted her hands behind her; but all the knots held good!
She writhed her hands till her fingers were wet with sweat or
   blood!
They stretched and strained in the darkness, and the hours crawled
   by like years,

Till, now, on the stroke of midnight,
    Cold, on the stroke of midnight,
The tip of one finger touched it! The trigger at least was hers!

The tip of one finger touched it; she strove no more for the rest!
Up, she stood up to attention, with the barrel beneath her breast,
She would not risk their hearing; she would not strive again;
For the road lay bare in the moonlight;
And the blood of her veins in the moonlight throbbed to her love's
    refrain.

Tlot-tlot; tlot-tlot! Had they heard it? The horse-hoofs ringing
    clear;
Tlot-tlot, tlot-tlot, in the distance? Were they deaf that they did
    not hear?
Down the ribbon of moonlight, over the brow of the hill,
The highwayman came riding,
    Riding, riding!
The red-coats looked to their priming! She stood up, straight and
    still!

Tlot-tlot, in the frosty silence! *Tlot-tlot,* in the echoing night!
Nearer he came and nearer! Her face was like a light!
Her eyes grew wide for a moment; she drew one last deep breath,
Then her finger moved in the moonlight,
    Her musket shattered the moonlight,
Shattered her breast in the moonlight and warned him—with her
    death.

He turned; he spurred to the West; he did not know who stood
Bowed, with her head o'er the musket, drenched with her own red
    blood!
Not till the dawn he heard it, his face grew gray to hear
How Bess, the landlord's daughter,
    The landlord's black-eyed daughter,
Had watched for her love in the moonlight, and died in the dark-
    ness there.

Back he spurred like a madman, shrieking a curse to the sky,
With the white road smoking behind him and his rapier bran-
    dished high!
Blood-red were his spurs i' the golden noon; wine-red was his
    velvet coat,

When they shot him down in the highway,
   Down like a dog in the highway,
And he lay in his blood on the highway, with the bunch of lace at
   his throat.

.   .   .   .

And still of a winter's night, they say, when the wind is in the
   trees,
When the moon is a ghostly galleon tossed upon cloudy seas,
When the road is a ribbon of moonlight over the purple moor,
A highwayman comes riding—
   Riding—riding—
A highwayman comes riding, up to the old inn-door.

Over the cobbles he clatters and clangs in the dark inn-yard;
He taps with his whip on the shutters, but all is locked and barred;
He whistles a tune at the window, and who should be waiting there
But the landlord's black-eyed daughter,
   Bess, the landlord's daughter,
Plaiting a dark red love-knot into her long black hair.

"FULL MANY A GLORIOUS MORNING HAVE I SEEN"

William Shakespeare

Full many a glorious morning have I seen
Flatter the mountain-tops with sovereign eye,
Kissing with golden face the meadows green,
Gilding pale streams with heavenly alchemy;
Anon permit the basest clouds to ride
With ugly rack on his celestial face,
And from the forlorn world his visage hide,
Stealing unseen to west with his disgrace:
Even so my sun one early morn did shine
With all-triumphant splendour on my brow;
But, out, alack! he was but one hour mine,
The region cloud hath mask'd him from me now.
   Yet him for this my love no whit disdaineth;
   Suns of the world may stain when heaven's sun staineth.
                                        (Sonnet XXXIII)

A NEWSPAPER HOAX THAT FOOLED THE NATION

Popular Young Couple Married This Week

The groom is a popular young bum who hasn't done a lick of work since he got shipped in the middle of his junior year at college. He manages to dress well and to keep a supply of spending money because his dad is a soft-hearted old fool who takes up his bad checks instead of letting him go to jail where he belongs.

The bride is a skinny, fast little idiot who has been kissed and handled by every boy in town since she was twelve years old. She paints like a Sioux Indian, sucks cigarettes in secret, and drinks mean corn-liquor when she is out joy-riding in her dad's car at night. She doesn't know how to cook, sew or keep house.

The groom wore a rented dinner suit over athletic underwear of imitation silk. His pants were held up by pale green suspenders. His number eight patent-leather shoes matched his state in tightness and harmonized nicely with the axle-grease polish of his hair. In addition to his jag he carried a pocket-knife, a bunch of keys, a dun for the ring and his usual look of imbecility.

The bride wore some kind of white thing that left most of her legs sticking out at one end and her bony upper end sticking out at the other. The young people will make their home with the bride's parents, which means they will sponge on the old man until he dies and then she will take in washing. The happy couple anticipate a great event in about five months.

Postscript.—This may be the last issue of *The Tribune*, but my life ambition has been to write up one wedding and tell the unvarnished truth. Now that it is done, death can have no sting.

(By Robert E. Quillen in the Fountain Inn, S. C., *Tribune*)

TEARS

Lizette Woodworth Reese

When I consider Life and its few years—
A wisp of fog betwixt us and the sun;
A call to battle, and the battle done
Ere the last echo dies within our ears;
A rose choked in the grass; an hour of fears;
The gusts that past a darkening shore do beat;
The burst of music down an unlistening street,—

I wonder at the idleness of tears.
Ye old, old dead, and ye of yesternight,
Chieftains, and bards, and keepers of the sheep,
By every cup of sorrow that you had,
Loose from me my tears, and make me see aright
How each hath back what once he stayed to weep:
Homer his sight, David his little lad!

DIFFERENCES

Paul Laurence Dunbar

My neighbor lives on the hill,
　And I in the valley dwell,
My neighbor must look down on me,
　Must I look up?—ah, well,
My neighbor lives on the hill,
　And I in the valley dwell.

My neighbor reads, and prays,
　And I—I laugh, God wot,
And sing like a bird when the grass is green
　In my small garden plot;
But ah, he reads and prays,
　And I—I laugh, God wot.

His face is a book of woe,
　And mine is a song of glee;
A slave he is to the great "They say,"
　But I—I am bold and free;
No wonder he smacks of woe,
　And I have the tang of glee.

My neighbor thinks me a fool,
　"The same to yourself," says I;
"Why take your books and take your prayers,
　Give me the open sky;"
My neighbor thinks me a fool,
　"The same to yourself," says I.

TO AUTUMN

John Keats

Season of mists and mellow fruitfulness,
　　Close bosom-friend of the maturing sun;
Conspiring with him how to load and bless
　　With fruit the vines that round the thatch-eaves run;
To bend with apples the moss'd cottage-trees,
　　And fill all fruit with ripeness to the core;
　　　　To swell the gourd, and plump the hazel shells
　　With a sweet kernel; to set budding more,
And still more, later flowers for the bees,
Until they think warm days will never cease,
　　　　For Summer has o'er-brimmed their clammy cells.

Who hath not seen thee oft amid thy store?
　　Sometimes whoever seeks abroad may find
Thee sitting careless on a granary floor,
　　Thy hair soft-lifted by the winnowing wind;
Or on a half-reap'd furrow sound asleep,
　　Drows'd with the fume of poppies, while thy hook
　　　　Spares the next swath and all its twined flowers:
And sometimes like a gleaner thou dost keep
　　Steady thy laden head across a brook;
　　Or by a cider-press, with patient look,
　　　　Thou watchest the last oozings hours by hours.

Where are the songs of Spring? Ay, where are they?
　　Think not of them, thou hast thy music too,—
While barred clouds bloom the soft-dying day,
　　And touch the stubble-plains with rosy hue;
Then in a wailful choir the small gnats mourn
　　Among the river sallows, borne aloft
　　　　Or sinking as the light wind lives or dies;
And full-grown lambs loud bleat from hilly bourn;
　　Hedge-crickets sing; and now with treble soft
　　The red-breast whistles from a garden-croft;
　　　　And gathering swallows twitter in the skies.

* * *

Nothing except a battle lost can be half so melancholy as a
battle won.—Duke of Wellington

HUCK FINN'S OLD MAN CONDEMNS
THE GOVERNMENT

Mark Twain

While I was cooking supper the old man took a swig or two and got sort of warmed up, and went to ripping again. He had been drunk over in town, and laid in the gutter all night, and he was a sight to look at. A body would have thought he was Adam—he was just all mud. Whenever his liquor began to work he most always went for the government! This time he says:

"Call this a govment! why just look at it and see what it's like. Here's the law a-standing ready to take a man's son away from him—a man's own son, which he has had all the trouble and all the anxiety and all the expense of raising. Yes, just as that man has got that son raised at last, and ready to go to work and begin to do sumthin' for *him* and give him a rest, the law up and goes for him. And they call *that* govment! That ain't all, nuther. The law backs that old Judge Thatcher up and helps him to keep me out o' my property. Here's what the law does: The law takes a man worth six thousand dollars and up'ards, and jams him into an old trap of a cabin like this, and lets him go round in clothes that ain't fitten for a hog. They call that govment! A man can't get his rights in a govment like this. Sometime's I've a mighty notion to just leave the country for good and all. Yes, and I *told* 'em so; I told old Thatcher so to his face. Lots of 'em heard me, and can tell what I said. Says I, for two cents I'd leave the blamed country and never come a-near it ag'in. Them's the very words. I says, look at my hat—if you call it a hat—but the lid raises up and the rest of it goes down till it's below my chin, and then it ain't rightly a hat at all, but more like my head was shoved up through the jint o' stove-pipe. Look at it, says I—such a hat for me to wear—one of the wealthiest men in this town if I could git my rights.

"Oh, yes, this is a wonderful govment, wonderful. Why looky here. There was a free nigger there from Ohio—a mulateer, most as white as a white man. He had the whitest shirt on you ever see, too, and the shinest hat; and there ain't a man in that town that's got as fine clothes as what he had; and he had a gold watch and chain, and a silver-headed cane—the awfulest old gray-headed nabob in the state. And what do you think? They said he was a p'fessor in a college, and could talk all kinds of languages, and knowed everything. And that ain't the wust. They said he could *vote* when he was at home. Well, that let me out. Thinks I, what is the country a-coming to? It was 'lection day, and I was about to go and vote myself if I warn't too drunk to get there; but when they told me there was a state in this country where they'd let that nigger vote, I drawed up. I says I'll never vote ag'in. Them's the very words I said; they all heard me; and the country may rot for all me—I'll never vote ag'in as long as I live. And to see the cool way of that nigger—why he wouldn't a' give me the road if I hadn't shoved him out o' the way. I says to the people, why ain't this nigger put up at auction and sold?—that's what I want to know. And what do you reckon they said? Why they said he couldn't be sold till he's been in the state six months, and he hadn't been there that long yet. There, now—that's a specimen. They call that a govment that can't sell a free nigger till he's been in the state six months. Here's a govment that calls itself a govment, and lets on to be a govment, and thinks it is a govment, and yet's got to set stock still for six whole months before it can take a-hold of a prowling, thieving, infernal, white-shirted free nigger, and—"

Pap was a-going on so he never noticed where his old limber legs were taking him to, so he went head over heels over the tub of salt pork and barked both shins, and the rest of his speech was all the hottest kind of language—mostly hove at the nigger and the govment, though he give the tub some too, all along, here and there.

THE GREAT COMMANDMENT

Holy Bible, Matthew 22:34–40

But when the Pharisees had heard that he had put the Sadducees to silence, they were gathered together.

Then one of them, which was a lawyer, asked him a question, tempting him, and saying,

Master, which is the great commandment in the law?

Jesus said unto him, Thou shalt love the Lord thy God with all thy heart, and with all thy soul, and with all thy mind.

This is the first and great commandment.

And the second is like unto it. Thou shalt love thy neighbor as thyself.

On these two commandments hang all the law and the prophets.

MY LIFE CLOSED TWICE

Emily Dickinson

My life closed twice before its close;
It yet remains to see
If Immortality unveil
A third event to me,

So huge, so hopeless to conceive,
    As these that twice befell:
Parting is all we know of heaven,
    And all we need of hell.

A BALLOT

Benjamin R. Tucker

What is a ballot? It is neither more nor less than a paper representative of the bayonet, the billy, and the bullet. It is a labor-saving device for ascertaining on which side force lies and bowing to the inevitable. The voice of the majority saves bloodshed, but it is no less the arbitrament of force than is the decree of the most absolute of despots backed by the most powerful of armies.

FOUR THINGS

Henry Van Dyke

Four things a man must learn to do
If he would make his record true:
To think without confusion clearly;
To love his fellow man sincerely;
To act from honest motives purely;
To trust in God and Heaven securely.

SELF-ESTIMATE

Sir Isaac Newton

I do not know what I may appear to the world; but to myself I seem to have been only like a boy playing on the seashore, and diverting myself in now and then finding a smoother pebble or a prettier shell than ordinary, whilst the great ocean of truth lay all undiscovered before me.

"THE PROPER STUDY OF MAN"

Alexander Pope

Know then thyself, presume not God to scan;
The proper study of Mankind is Man.
Plac'd on this isthmus of a middle state,
A Being darkly wise, and rudely great:
With too much knowledge for the Sceptic side,
With too much weakness for the Stoic's pride,
He hangs between; in doubt to act, or rest;
In doubt to deem himself a God, or Beast;
In doubt his Mind or Body to prefer;
Born but to die, and reas'ning but to err;
Alike in ignorance, his reason such,
Whether he thinks too little, or too much:
Chaos of Thought and Passion, all confus'd;
Still by himself abus'd, or disabus'd;
Created half to rise, and half to fall;
Great lord of all things, yet a prey to all;
Sole judge of Truth, in endless Error hurl'd:
The glory, jest, and riddle of the world!

(From An Essay on Man)

ILL FARES THE LAND

Oliver Goldsmith

Ill fares the land, to hastening ills a prey,
Where wealth accumulates, and men decay;
Princes and lords may flourish or may fade;

A breath can make them, as a breath has made;
But a bold peasantry, their country's pride,
When once destroy'd, can never be supplied.

BRIGHT STAR, WOULD I WERE STEADFAST AS THOU ART!

John Keats

Bright star, would I were steadfast as thou art!
　　Not in lone splendour hung aloft the night,
And watching, with eternal lids apart,
　　Like Nature's patient, sleepless Eremite,
The moving waters at their priestlike task
　　Of pure ablution round earth's human shores,
Or gazing on the new soft fallen mask
　　Of snow upon the mountains and the moors:
No—yet still steadfast, still unchangeable,
　　Pillow'd upon my fair love's ripening breast,
To feel for ever its soft fall and swell,
　　Awake for ever in a sweet unrest,
Still, still to hear her tender-taken breath,
And so live ever—or else swoon to death.

TAXES

Benjamin Franklin

Taxes are indeed very heavy; but if those laid on by the government were the only ones we had to pay, we might more easily discharge them; but we have many others, and much more grievous ones to some of us. We are taxed quite as heavily by idleness, three times as much by our pride, and four times as much by our folly; and from these taxes the commissioners cannot easily deliver us by allowing an abatement.

*　　*　　*

The heart has its reasons, which reason does not know.
　　　　　　　　　　　　　　　　—Blaise Pascal

LINCOLN'S GETTYSBURG ADDRESS

November 19, 1863

Fourscore and seven years ago our fathers brought forth upon this continent a new nation, conceived in liberty, and dedicated to the proposition that all men are created equal. Now we are engaged in a great civil war, testing whether that nation, or any nation so conceived and so dedicated, can long endure. We are met on a great battlefield of that war. We have come to dedicate a portion of that field as a final resting-place for those who here gave their lives that that nation might live. It is altogether fitting and proper that we should do this. But in a larger sense we cannot dedicate, we cannot consecrate, we cannot hallow this ground. The brave men, living and dead, who struggled here, have consecrated it far above our poor power to add or detract. The world will little note, nor long remember, what we say here; but it can never forget what they did here. It is for us, the living, rather to be dedicated here to the unfinished work which they who fought here have thus far so nobly advanced. It is rather for us to be here dedicated to the great task remaining before us, that from these honored dead we take increased devotion to that cause for which they gave the last full measure of devotion; that we here highly resolve that these dead shall not have died in vain; that this nation, under God, shall have a new birth of freedom, and that government of the people, by the people, and for the people, shall not perish from the earth.

From THE AMERICAN CRISIS

Thomas Paine

I have as little suspicion in me as any man living, but my secret opinion has ever been, and still is, that God Almighty will not give up a people to military destruction, or leave them unsupported to perish, who have so earnestly and so repeatedly sought to avoid the calamities of war, by every decent method which wisdom could invent. Neither have I so much of the infidel in me, as to suppose that He has relinquished the government of the world, and given us up to the care of devils.

(From The American Crisis, No. 1)

WILLY LOMAN, SALESMAN

Arthur Miller

(*Linda Loman is defending her husband, to her two grown sons:*)

I don't say he's a great man. Willy Loman never made a lot of money. His name was never in the paper. He's not the finest character that ever lived. But he's a human being, and a terrible thing is happening to him. So attention must be paid. He's not to be allowed to fall into his grave like an old dog. Attention, attention must be finally paid to such a person. You called him crazy . . . A lot of people think he's lost his—balance. But you don't have to be very smart to know what his trouble is. The man is exhausted. . . . A small man can be just as exhausted as a great man. He works for a company thirty-six years this March, opens up unheard-of-territories to their trademark, and now in his old age they take his salary away. . . . For five weeks he's been on straight commission, like a beginner, an unknown! . . . When he brought them business, when he was young, they were glad to see him. But now his old friends, the old buyers that loved him so and always found some order to hand him in a pinch—they're all dead, retired. He used to be able to make six, seven calls a day in Boston. Now he takes his valises out of the car and puts them back and takes them out again and he's exhausted. Instead of walking he talks now. He drives seven hundred miles, and when he gets there no one knows him any more, no one welcomes him. . . . How long can that go on? How long? You see what I'm sitting here and waiting for? And you tell me he has no character? The man who never worked a day but for your benefit. When does he get a medal for that? . . .

(*After Willy Loman's suicide, an old business friend speaks to the dead man's sons:*)

Nobody dast blame this man. You don't understand: Willy was a salesman. And for a salesman, there is no rock bottom to the life. He don't put a bolt to a nut, he don't tell you the law or give you medicine. He's a man way out there in the blue riding on a smile and a shoeshine. And when they start not smiling back—that's an earthquake. And then you get yourself a couple of spots on your hat, and you're finished. Nobody dast blame this man. A salesman is got to dream, boy. It comes with the territory.

(From *The Death of a Salesman*)

From RABBI BEN EZRA

Robert Browning

Grow old along with me!
The best is yet to be,
The last of life, for which the first was made:
Our times are in his hand
Who saith: "A whole I planned,
Youth shows but half; trust God, see all, nor be afraid."

Ah, but a man's reach should exceed his grasp,
Or what's a heaven for?

RUSSIA

Winston S. Churchill

I cannot forecast to you the action of Russia. It is a riddle
wrapped in a mystery inside an enigma; but perhaps there is a key.
That key is Russian national interest.
(October 1, 1939, four days after Russia occupied Eastern Poland)

COME, SLEEP

Sir Philip Sidney

Come, Sleep! O Sleep, the certain knot of peace,
The baiting-place of wit, the balm of woe,
The poor man's wealth, the prisoner's release,
The indifferent judge between the high and low;
With shield of proof shield me from out the prease
Of those fierce darts Despair at me doth throw;
O make in me those civil wars to cease.
I will good tribute pay, if thou do so.
Take thou of me smooth pillows, sweetest bed,
A chamber deaf to noise and blind to light,
A rosy garland and a weary head;
And if these things, as being thine by right,
Move not thy heavy grace, thou shalt in me,
Livelier than elsewhere, Stella's image see.
                                    (From Astrophel and Stella)

LINCOLN'S LETTER TO EDWARD EVERETT, WRITTEN THE DAY AFTER THE GETTYSBURG ADDRESS

(Everett, a noted orator of his day, spoke for two hours and ostensibly made the principal address. He was followed by Lincoln who spoke only a few but immortal words)

Executive Mansion, Washington, November 20, 1863.

HON. EDWARD EVERETT:

MY DEAR SIR: Your kind note of to-day is received. In our respective parts yesterday, you could not have been excused to make a short address, nor I a long one. I am pleased to know that, in your judgment, the little I did say was not entirely a failure. Of course I knew Mr. Everett would not fail, and yet, while the whole discourse was eminently satisfactory, and will be of great value, there were passages in it which transcended my expectations. The point made against the theory of the General Government being only an agency whose principals are the States, was new to me, and, as I think, is one of the best arguments for the national supremacy. The tribute to our women for their angel ministering to the suffering soldiers surpasses in its way, as do the subjects of it, whatever has gone before.

Our sick boy, for whom you kindly inquire. we hope is past the worst.

Your obedient servant,
A. Lincoln

ON POLITICIANS

Jonathan Swift

And he gave it for his opinion that whoever could make two ears of corn, or two blades of grass, to grow upon a spot of ground where only one grew before, would deserve better of mankind, and do more essential service to his country, than the whole race of politicians put together.

(From Gulliver's Travels)

* * *

The imagination gallops but judgment goes on foot.—Anonymous

WHY BOOKS ARE WRITTEN

Robert J. Burdette

The appearance of a new book is an indication that another man has found a mission, has entered upon the performance of a lofty duty, activated by the noblest impulses that can spur the soul of man to action. It is the proudest boast of the profession of literature, that no man ever published a book for selfish purposes or with ignoble aim. Books have been published for the consolation of the distressed; for the guidance of the wandering; for the relief of the destitute; for the hope of the penitent; for uplifting the burdened soul above its sorrows and fears; for the general amelioration of the condition of all mankind; for the right against wrong; for the good against bad; for the truth. This book is published for two dollars per volume.

(Preface to The Rise and Fall of the Mustache, 1877)

SALUTATION OF THE DAWN

Listen to the Exhortation of the Dawn!
Look to this Day!
For it is Life, the very Life of Life.
In its brief course lie all the
Verities and Realities of your Existence:
    The Bliss of Growth,
    The Glory of Action,
    The Splendor of Beauty,
For Yesterday is but a Dream,
And To-morrow is only a Vision:
But Today well-lived makes
Every Yesterday a Dream of Happiness,
And every To-morrow a Vision of Hope.
Look well therefore to this Day!
Such is the Salutation of the Dawn!
        (From the Sanskrit,
sometimes attributed to Kalidasa)

*   *   *

Most of the shadows of this life are caused by standing in one's own sunshine.—Ralph Waldo Emerson

OH, THE WILD JOY OF LIVING

Robert Browning

Oh, the wild joy of living! the leaping from rock up to rock,
The strong rending of boughs from the fir-tree, the cool silver shock
Of the plunge in the pool's living water, the hunt of the bear,
And the sultriness showing the lion couched in his lair.
And the meal, the rich dates yellowed over the gold dust divine,
And the locust-flesh steeped in the pitcher, the full draft of wine,
And the sleep in the dried river-channel where bulrushes tell
That the water was wont to go marbling so softly and well.
How good is man's life, the mere living! how fit to employ
All the heart and the soul and the senses forever in joy!

THE THINKING REED

Blaise Pascal

Man is but a reed—the weakest thing in nature—but he is a reed
that thinks. It is not necessary that the whole universe should arm'
itself to crush him. A vapor, a drop of water, is enough to kill
him. But if the universe should crush him, man would still be
nobler than that which slays him, for he knows that he dies; but
of the advantage which it has over him the universe knows nothing.
Our dignity consists, then, wholly in thought. Our elevation must
come from this, not from space and time, which we cannot fill. Let
us, then, labor to think well: that is the fundamental principle of
morals.

* * *

Don't cheer, boys; the poor devils are dying.—Capt. John W.
Philip, U.S.N., at the battle of Santiago, 1898.

ON HEARING A LADY PRAISE A CERTAIN
REVEREND DOCTOR'S EYES

George Outram

I cannot praise the Doctor's eyes;
I never saw his glance divine;
He always shuts them when he prays,
And when he preaches he shuts mine.

From TO A HIGHLAND GIRL

William Wordsworth

Sweet Highland Girl, a very shower
Of beauty is thy earthly dower!
Twice seven consenting years have shed
Their utmost bounty on thy head:
And these grey rocks; that household lawn;
Those trees, a veil just half withdrawn;
This fall of water that doth make
A murmur near the silent lake;
This little bay; a quiet road
That holds in shelter thy Abode—
In truth together do ye seem
Like something fashioned in a dream. . . .
   With earnest feeling I shall pray
For thee when I am far away:
For never saw I mien, or face,
In which more plainly I could trace
Benignity and home-bred sense
Ripening in perfect innocence. . . .
   Now thanks to Heaven! that of its grace
Hath led me to this lonely place.
Joy have I had; and going hence
I bear away my recompense.
In spots like these it is we prize
Our Memory, feel that she hath eyes:
Then, why should I be loth to stir?

I feel this place was made for her;
To give new pleasure like the past,
Continued long as life shall last.
Nor am I loth, though pleased at heart,
Sweet Highland Girl! from thee to part:
For I, methinks, till I grow old,
As fair before me shall behold,
As I do now, the cabin small,
The lake, the bay, the waterfall;
And Thee, the Spirit of them all!

THE ASS AND THE LAP-DOG

Aesop
(Translator: Thomas James)

There was an Ass and a Lap-dog that belonged to the same master. The Ass was tied up in the stable, and had plenty of corn and hay to eat, and was as well off as Ass could be. The little Dog was always sporting and gamboling about, caressing and fawning upon his master in a thousand amusing ways, so that he became a great favorite, and was permitted to lie in his master's lap. The Ass, indeed, had enough to do; he was drawing wood all day, and had to take his turn at the mill at night. But while he grieved over his own lot, it galled him more to see the Lap-dog living in such ease and luxury; so thinking that if he acted a like part to his master, he should fare the same, he broke one day from his halter, and rushing into the hall began to kick and prance about in the strangest fashion; then swishing his tail and mimicking the frolics of the favorite, he upset the table where his master was at dinner, breaking it in two and smashing all the crockery; nor would he leave off till he jumped upon his master, and pawed him with his rough-shod feet. The servants, seeing their master in no little danger, thought it was now high time to interfere, and having released him from the Ass's caresses, they so belabored the silly creature with sticks and staves, that he never got up again; and as he breathed his last, exclaimed: "Why could not I have been satisfied with my natural position, without attempting, by tricks and grimaces, to imitate one who was but a puppy after all!"

WHEN EARTH'S LAST PICTURE IS PAINTED

Rudyard Kipling

When Earth's last picture is painted and the tubes are twisted and
  dried,
When the oldest colours have faded, and the youngest critic has
  died,
We shall rest, and, faith, we shall need it—lie down for an aeon or
  two,
Till the Master of All Good Workmen shall put us to work anew.

And those that were good shall be happy: they shall sit in a golden
  chair;
They shall splash at a ten-league canvas with brushes of comets'
  hair;
They shall find real saints to draw from—Magdalene, Peter, and
  Paul;
They shall work for an age at a sitting and never be tired at all!
And only the Master shall praise us, and only the Master shall
  blame;
And no one shall work for money, and no one shall work for fame,
But each for the joy of the working, and each, in his separate star,
Shall draw the Things as he sees It for the God of Things as They
  are!

OTHELLO'S FAREWELL

William Shakespeare

Soft you; a word or two before you go.
I have done the state some service, and they know't.
No more of that. I pray you, in your letters,
When you shall these unlucky deeds relate,
Speak of me as I am; nothing extenuate,
Nor set down aught in malice; then must you speak
Of one that loved not wisely but too well;
Of one not easily jealous, but, being wrought,
Perplex'd in the extreme; of one whose hand,
Like the base Indian, threw a pearl away
Richer than all his tribe; of one whose subdued eyes,
Albeit unused to the melting mood,

Drop tears as fast as the Arabian trees
Their medicinal gum. Set you down this;
And say besides, that in Aleppo once,
Where a malignant and a turban'd Turk
Beat a Venetian and traduced the state,
I took by the throat the circumcised dog
And smote him, thus.

              [Stabs himself]
                (From Othello)

"IF THOU MUST LOVE ME, LET IT BE FOR NOUGHT"

Elizabeth Barrett Browning

If thou must love me, let it be for nought
Except for love's sake only. Do not say
"I love her for her smile—her look—her way
Of speaking gently,—for a trick of thought
That falls in well with mine, and certes brought
A sense of pleasant ease on such a day"—
For these things in themselves, Belovèd, may
Be changed, or change for thee,—and love, so wrought,
May be unwrought so. Neither love me for
Thine own dear pity's wiping my cheeks dry,—
A creature might forget to weep, who bore
Thy comfort long, and lose thy love thereby!
But love me for love's sake, that evermore
Thou mayest love on, through love's eternity.

HOW THE MONEY ROLLS IN

Anonymous

My sister she works in a laundry,
My father he fiddles for gin,
My mother she takes in washing,
My God, how the money rolls in.

THE GOVERNMENT OF ALL

Chief Justice John Marshall

If any one proposition could command the universal assent of mankind, we might expect it would be this: that the government of the Union, though limited in its powers, is supreme within its sphere of action. This would seem to result necessarily from its nature. It is the government of all; its powers are delegated by all; it represents all, and acts for all. Though any one State may be willing to control its operations, no State is willing to allow others to control them. The nation, on those subjects on which it can act, must necessarily bind its component parts. But this question is not left to mere reason: the people have, in express terms, decided it, by saying, "this Constitution, and the laws of the United States, which shall be made in pursuance thereof," "shall be the supreme law of the land," and by requiring that the members of the State legislatures, and the officers of the executive and judicial departments of the States, shall take the oath of fidelity to it.

The government of the United States, then, though limited in its powers, is supreme; and its laws, when made in pursuance of the Constitution, form the supreme law of the land, "anything in the constitution or laws of any State to the contrary notwithstanding."

(*M'Culloch v. Maryland,* 1819)

From ON FRIENDSHIP

William Cowper

The man that hails you Tom or Jack,
And proves, by thumping on your back,
His sense of your great merit,
Is such a friend that one had need
Be very much his friend indeed
To pardon or to bear it.

HIGHLAND MARY

Robert Burns

Ye banks, and braes, and streams around
   The castle o' Montgomery,
Green be your woods, and fair your flowers,
   Your waters never drumlie!
There simmer first unfauld her robes
   And there the langest tarry;
For there I took the last fareweel
   O' my sweet Highland Mary.

How sweetly bloom'd the gay green birk,
   How rich the hawthorn's blossom,
As underneath their fragrant shade
   I clasp'd her to my bosom!
The golden hours, on angel wings,
   Flew o'er me and my dearie;
For dear to me, as light and life,
   Was my sweet Highland Mary.

Wi' monie a vow, and lock'd embrace,
   Our parting was fu' tender;
And, pledging aft to meet again,
   We tore oursels asunder;
But oh! fell death's untimely frost
   That nipt my flower sae early!
Now green's the sod, and cauld's the clay,
   That wraps my Highland Mary!

O pale, pale now, those rosy lips,
   I aft hae kiss'd sae fondly!
And closed for ay the sparking glance
   That dwelt on me sae kindly!
And mold'ring now in silent dust,
   That heart that lo'ed me dearly!
But still within my bosom's core
   Shall live my Highland Mary.

SONNET ON CHILLON

Lord Byron

Eternal Spirit of the chainless Mind!
  Brightest in dungeons, Liberty! thou art,
  For there thy habitation is the heart—
The heart which love of thee alone can bind;
And when thy sons to fetters are consign'd—
  To fetters, and the damp vault's dayless gloom,
  Their country conquers with their martyrdom,
And Freedom's fame finds wings on every wind.
Chillon! thy prison is a holy place,
  And thy sad floor an altar—for 'twas trod,
Until his very steps have left a trace
  Worn, as if thy cold pavement were a sod,
By Bonnivard!—May none those marks efface!
  For they appeal from tyranny to God.

OF GARDENS

Francis Bacon

God Almighty first planted a garden. And indeed it is the purest of human pleasures. It is the greatest refreshment to the spirits of man. . . . I do hold . . . there ought to be gardens for all the months in the year; in which . . . things of beauty may be then in season.

FRET NOT THYSELF BECAUSE OF EVIL DOERS

Holy Bible, Psalm 37:1–4, 7

Fret not thyself because of evil doers, neither be thou envious against the workers of iniquity:

For they shall soon be cut down like the grass, and wither as the green herb.

Trust in the Lord, and do good: so shalt thou dwell in the land, and verily thou shalt be fed.

Delight thyself also in the Lord; and he shall give thee the desires of thine heart. . . .

Rest in the Lord, and wait patiently for him: fret not thyself because of him who prospereth in his way, because of the man who bringeth wicked devices to pass.

BURIAL OF THE DEAD

The Book of Common Prayer

Man, that is born of a woman, hath but a short time to live, and is full of misery. He cometh up, and is cut down, like a flower; he fleeth as it were a shadow, and never continueth in one stay.

In the midst of life we are in death: of whom may we seek for succour, but of thee, O Lord, who for our sins art justly displeased?

Yet, O Lord God most holy, O Lord most mighty, O holy and most merciful Saviour, deliver us not into the bitter pains of eternal death.

Thou knowest, Lord, the secrets of our hearts; shut not thy merciful ears to our prayer; but spare us, Lord most holy, O God most mighty, O holy and merciful Saviour, thou most worthy Judge eternal, suffer us not, at our last hour, for any pains of death, to fall from thee.

A BIRTHDAY

Christina Georgina Rossetti

My heart is like a singing bird
  Whose nest is in a water'd shoot;
My heart is like an apple-tree
  Whose boughs are bent with thick-set fruit;
My heart is like a rainbow shell
  That paddles in a halcyon sea;
My heart is gladder than all these,
  Because my love is come to me.

Raise me a dais of silk and down;
  Hang it with vair and purple dyes;
Carve it in doves and pomegranates,
  And peacocks with a hundred eyes;
Work it in gold and silver grapes,
  In leaves and silver fleurs-de-lys;
Because the birthday of my life
  Is come, my love is come to me.

KUBLA KHAN

Samuel Taylor Coleridge

In Xanadu did Kubla Khan
A stately pleasure-dome decree:
Where Alph, the sacred river, ran
Through caverns measureless to man
   Down to a sunless sea.
So twice five miles of fertile ground
With walls and towers were girdled round:
And here were gardens bright with sinuous rills,
Where blossom'd many an incense-bearing tree;
And here were forests ancient as the hills,
Enfolding sunny spots of greenery.

But oh! that deep romantic chasm which slanted
Down the green hill athwart a cedarn cover!
A savage place! as holy and enchanted
As e'er beneath a waning moon was haunted
By woman wailing for her demon-lover!
And from this chasm, with ceaseless turmoil seething,
As if this earth in fast thick pants were breathing,
A mighty fountain momently was forced;
Amid whose swift half-intermitted burst
Huge fragments vaulted like rebounding hail,
Or chaffy grain beneath the thresher's flail:
And 'mid these dancing rocks at once and ever
It flung up momently the sacred river.
Five miles meandering with a mazy motion
Through wood and dale the sacred river ran,
Then reach'd the caverns measureless to man,
And sank in tumult to a lifeless ocean:
And 'mid this tumult Kubla heard from far
Ancestral voices prophesying war!

  The shadow of the dome of pleasure
  Floated midway on the waves;
  Where was heard the mingled measure
  From the fountain and the caves.
It was a miracle of rare device,
A sunny pleasure-dome with caves of ice!

A damsel with a dulcimer
In a vision once I saw:
It was an Abyssinian maid,
And on her dulcimer she play'd,
Singing of Mount Abora.
Could I revive within me,
Her symphony and song,

To such a deep delight 'twould win me,
That with music loud and long,
I would build that dome in air,
That sunny dome! those caves of ice!
And all who heard should see them there,
And all should cry, Beware! Beware!
His flashing eyes, his floating hair!
Weave a circle round him thrice,
And close your eyes with holy dread,
For he on honey-dew hath fed,
And drunk the milk of Paradise.

A WAND'RING MINSTREL

W. S. Gilbert

A wand'ring minstrel I,
    A thing of shreds and patches,
    Of ballads, songs and snatches,
And dreamy lullaby!

My catalogue is long,
    Through ev'ry passion ranging,
    And to your humours changing
I tune my supple song!
I tune my supple song!

Are you in sentimental mood?
    I'll sigh with you, Oh, sorrow!
On maiden's coldness do you brood?
    I'll do so too, Oh, sorrow, sorrow!
I'll charm your willing ears
With songs of lovers' fears,
While sympathetic tears
    My cheeks bedew, Oh, sorrow, sorrow!

But if patriotic sentiment is wanted,
   I've patriotic ballads cut and dried;
For where'er our country's banner may be planted,
   All other local banners are defied!
Our warriors, in serried ranks assembled,
   Never quail, or they conceal it if they do,
And I shouldn't be surprised if nations trembled
   Before the mighty troops, the troops of Titipu!

And if you call for a song of the sea,
   We'll heave the capstan round,
With a yeo heave-ho, for the wind is free,
Her anchor's a-trip and her helm's a-lee,
   Hurrah for the homeward bound!
   Yeo heave-ho, hurrah for the homeward bound!

To lay aloft in a howling breeze
   May tickle a landsman's taste,
But the happiest hour a sailor sees
   Is when he's down at an inland town,
With his Nancy on his knees, yeo-ho!
   And his arm around her waist!

A wand'ring minstrel I,
   A thing of shreds and patches,
   Of ballads, songs and snatches,
And dreamy lullaby,
And dreamy lulla-lullaby, lullaby!

WHAT ONE MAY AND MAY NOT CALL A WOMAN

Anonymous

You may call a woman a kitten, but you must not call her a cat.
You may call her a mouse, but you must not call her a rat.
You may call her a chicken, but you must not call her a hen.
You may call her a duck, but you must not call her a goose.
You may call her a vision, but you must not call her a sight.

BENJAMIN FRANKLIN, AT THE CONSTITUTIONAL CONVENTION, SUPPORTS THE CONSTITUTION

I confess that there are several parts of this Constitution which I do not at present approve, but I am not sure I shall never approve them. For, having lived long, I have experienced many instances of being obliged, by better information or fuller consideration, to change opinions, even on important subjects, which I once thought right, to be found otherwise. It is therefore that, the older I grow, the more apt I am to doubt my own judgment, and to pay more respect to the judgment of others. Most men, indeed, as well as most sects in religion, think themselves in possession of all truth, and that wherever others differ from them, it is so far error. Steele, a Protestant, in a dedication, tells the Pope, that the only difference between our churches, in their opinions of the certainty of their doctrines, is "the Church of Rome is infallible, and the Church of England is never in the wrong." But though many private persons think almost as highly of their own infallibility as of that of their sect, few express it so naturally as a certain French lady, who, in a dispute with her sister, said, "I don't know how it happens, sister, but I meet with nobody but myself that is always in the right."

In these sentiments, Sir, I agree to this Constitution, with all its faults, if they are such; . . . I doubt, too, whether any other Convention we can obtain may be able to make a better Constitution. For, when you assemble a number of men to have the advantage of their joint wisdom, you inevitably assemble with those men all their prejudices, their passions, their errors of opinion, their local interests, and their selfish views. From such an assembly can a perfect production ever be expected? It therefore astonishes, me, sir, to find this system approaching so near to perfection as it does. . . . Thus I consent, sir, to this Constitution because I expect no better, and because I am not sure that it is not the best. The opinions I have had of its errors I sacrifice to the public good. I have never whispered a syllable of them abroad. Within these walls they were born, and here they shall die.

(September 17, 1787)

THE TWELVE DAYS OF CHRISTMAS

Anonymous

The first day of Christmas,
My true love sent to me
A partridge in a pear tree.

The second day of Christmas,
My true love sent to me
Two turtle doves, and
A partridge in a pear tree.

The third day of Christmas,
My true love sent to me
Three French hens,
Two turtle doves, and
A partridge in a pear tree.

The fourth day of Christmas,
My true love sent to me
Four colly birds,
Three French hens,
Two turtle doves, and
A partridge in a pear tree.

The fifth day of Christmas,
My true love sent to me
Five gold rings,
Four colly birds,
Three French hens,
Two turtle doves, and
A partridge in a pear tree.

The sixth day of Christmas,
My true love sent to me
Six geese a-laying,
Five gold rings,
Four colly birds,
Three French hens,
Two turtle doves, and
A partridge in a pear tree.

The seventh day of Christmas
My true love sent to me
Seven swans a-swimming,
Six geese a-laying,
Five gold rings,
Four colly birds,
Three French hens,
Two turtle doves, and
A partridge in a pear tree.

The eighth day of Christmas
My true love sent to me
Eight maids a-milking,
Seven swans a-swimming,
Six geese a-laying,
Five gold rings,
Four colly birds,
Three French hens,
Two turtle doves, and
A partridge in a pear tree.

The ninth day of Christmas
My true love sent to me
Nine drummers drumming,
Eight maids a-milking,
Seven swans a-swimming,
Six geese a-laying,
Five gold rings,
Four colly birds,
Three French hens,
Two turtle doves, and
A partridge in a pear tree.

The tenth day of Christmas
My true love sent to me
Ten pipers piping,
Nine drummers drumming,
Eight maids a-milking,
Seven swans a-swimming,
Six geese a-laying,
Five gold rings,
Four colly birds,
Three French hens,

Two turtle doves, and
A partridge in a pear tree.

The eleventh day of Christmas
My true love sent to me
Eleven ladies dancing,
Ten pipers piping,
Nine drummers drumming,
Eight maids a-milking,
Seven swans a-swimming,
Six geese a-laying,
Five gold rings,
Four colly birds,
Three French hens,
Two turtle doves, and
A partridge in a pear tree.

The twelfth day of Christmas
My true love sent to me
Twelve lords a-leaping,
Eleven ladies dancing,
Ten pipers piping,
Nine drummers drumming,
Eight maids a-milking,
Seven swans a-swimming,
Six geese a-laying,
Five gold rings,
Four colly birds,
Three French hens,
Two turtle doves, and
A partridge in a pear tree.

PORTIA'S PLEA FOR MERCY

William Shakespeare

The quality of mercy is not strain'd,
It droppeth as the gentle rain from heaven
Upon the place beneath: it is twice blest;
It blesseth him that gives and him that takes:
'Tis mightiest in the mightiest: it becomes
The throned monarch better than his crown;
His sceptre shows the force of temporal power,
The attribute to awe and majesty,

Wherein doth sit the dread and fear of kings;
But mercy is above this sceptred sway;
It is enthroned in the hearts of kings,
It is an attribute to God himself;
And earthly power doth then show likest God's
When mercy seasons justice. Therefore, Jew,
Though justice be thy plea, consider this,
That, in the course of justice, none of us
Should see salvation: we do pray for mercy;
And that same prayer doth teach us all to render
The deeds of mercy. I have spoke thus much
To mitigate the justice of thy plea;
Which if thou follow, this strict court of Venice
Must needs give sentence 'gainst the merchant there.

(From The Merchant of Venice)

ONE SOLITARY LIFE

Anonymous

Here is a man who was born in an obscure village, the child of a peasant woman. He grew up in another obscure village. He worked in a carpenter shop until he was thirty, and then for three years he was an itinerant preacher.

He never wrote a book. He never held an office. He never owned a home. He never had a family. He never went to college. He never traveled two hundred miles from the place where he was born. He never did one of the things that usually accompany greatness. . . . While still a young man, the tide of popular opinion turned against him. His friends ran away. One of them denied him. He was turned over to his enemies. He went through the mockery of a trial. He was nailed upon a cross between two thieves. His executioners gambled for the only piece of property he had on earth while he was dying— his coat. When he was dead he was taken down and laid in a borrowed grave through the pity of a friend.

Nineteen wide centuries have come and gone; today he is the centerpiece of the human race and the Leader of the column of progress.

I am far within the mark when I say that all the armies that ever marched, and all the navies that ever were built, and all the parliaments that ever sat, and all the kings that ever reigned, put together, have not affected the life of man upon this earth as powerfully as has that one solitary life.

OLD GRIMES

Albert Gorton Greene

Old Grimes is dead; that good old man
  We never shall see more:
He used to wear a long black coat,
  All buttoned down before.

His heart was open as the day,
  His feelings all were true;
His hair was some inclined to gray—
  He wore it in a queue.

Whene'er he heard the voice of pain,
  His breast with pity burned;
The large, round head upon his cane
  From ivory was turned.

Kind words he had for all;
  He knew no base design:
His eyes were dark and rather small,
  His nose was aquiline.

He lived at peace with all mankind,
  In friendship he was true;
His coat had pocket-holes behind,
  His pantaloons were blue.

Unharmed, the sin which earth pollutes
  He passed securely o'er,
And never wore a pair of boots
  For thirty years or more.

But good old Grimes is now at rest,
  Nor fears misfortune's frown:
He wore a double-breasted vest—
  The stripes ran up and down.

He modest merit sought to find,
  And pay it its desert:
He had no malice in his mind,
  No ruffles on his shirt.

His neighbors he did not abuse—
  Was sociable and gay:
He wore large buckles on his shoes,
  And changed them every day.

His knowledge, hid from public gaze,
  He did not bring to view,
Nor made a noise, town-meeting days,
  As many people do.

His worldly goods he never threw
  In trust to fortune's chances,
But lived (as all his brothers do)
  In easy circumstances.

Thus undisturbed by anxious cares,
  His peaceful moments ran;
And everybody said he was
  A fine old gentleman.

JINGLE BELLS

J. Pierpont

Dashing thro' the snow in a one-horse open sleigh,
O'er the fields we go, laughing all the way;
Bells on bob-tail ring, making spirits bright;
What fun it is to ride and sing a sleighing song tonight!

Chorus:
  Jingle bells! Jingle bells! Jingle all the way!
  Oh! what fun it is to ride in a one-horse open sleigh!

A day or two ago I thought I'd take a ride,
And soon Miss Fanny Bright was seated by my side;
The horse was lean and lank, misfortunes seemed his lot,
He got into a drifted bank, and we, got upsot. (*Chorus.*)

Now the ground is white, go it while you're young,
Take the girls tonight, and sing this sleighing song;
Just get a bob-tailed nag, two-forty for his speed,
Then hitch him to an open sleigh, and crack! you'll take the lead.
                                        (*Chorus.*)

IF I SHOULD DIE TO-NIGHT

Ben King

If I should die to-night,
And you should come to my cold corpse and say,
Weeping and heartsick o'er my lifeless clay—
If I should die to-night,
And you should come in deepest grief and woe—
And say: "Here's that ten dollars that I owe,"
I might arise in my large white cravat
And say, "What's that?"

If I should die to-night,
And you should come to my cold corpse and kneel,
Clasping my bier to show the grief you feel,
I say, if I should die to-night,
And you should come to me, and there and then
Just even hint at paying me that ten,
I might arise the while,
But I'd drop dead again.

"CARE-CHARMER SLEEP, SON OF THE SABLE NIGHT"

Samuel Daniel

Care-charmer Sleep, son of the sable Night,
Brother to Death, in silent darkness born:
Relieve my anguish, and restore the light;
With dark forgetting of my care, return!
And let the day be time enough to mourn
The shipwreck of my ill-adventured youth:
Let waking eyes suffice to wail their scorn,
Without the torment of the night's untruth.
Cease, dreams, the images of day-desires,
To model forth the passions of the morrow;
Never let rising sun approve you liars,
To add more grief to aggravate my sorrow.
   Still let me sleep, embracing clouds in vain;
   And never wake to feel the day's disdain.

THE SPHYNX

Alexander W. Kinglake

And near the Pyramids, more wondrous, and more awful than all else in the land of Egypt, there sits the lonely Sphynx. Comely the creature is, but the comeliness is not of this world; the once worshipped beast is a deformity and a monster to this generation, and yet you can see that those lips, so thick and heavy, were fashioned according to some ancient mould of beauty—some mould of beauty now forgotten—forgotten because that Greece drew forth Cytherea, from the flashing foam of the Aegean, and in her image created new forms of beauty, and made it a law among men that the short and proudly wreathed lips should stand for a sign and the main condition of loveliness through all generations to come. Yet still there lives on the race of those who were beautiful in the fashion of the elder world, and Christian girls of Coptic blood will look on you with the sad, serious gaze, and kiss your charitable hand with the big pouting lips of the very Sphynx.

Laugh and mock if you will at the worship of stone idols, but mark ye this, ye breakers of images, that in one regard, the stone idol bears awful semblance of Deity—unchangefulness in the midst of change—the same seeming will, and intent for ever and ever inexorable! Upon ancient dynasties of Ethiopians and Egyptian kings—upon Greek and Roman, upon Arab and Ottoman conquerors—upon Napoleon dreaming of an Eastern Empire—upon battle and pestilence—upon the ceaseless misery of the Egyptian race—upon keen-eyed travellers—Herodotus yesterday, and Warburton today—upon all and more this unworldly Sphynx has watched, and watched like a Providence with the same earnest eyes, the same sad, tranquil mien. And we, we shall die, and Islam will wither away, and the Englishman straining far over to hold his loved India, will plant a firm foot on the banks of the Nile, and sit in the seats of the Faithful, and still that sleepless rock will lie watching and watching the works of the new busy race, with those same sad, earnest eyes, and the same tranquil mien everlasting. You dare not mock at the Sphynx.

INSCRIPTION ON THE STATUE OF LIBERTY

THE NEW COLOSSUS

Not like the brazen giant of Greek fame,
With conquering limbs astride from land to land,
Here at our sea-washed, sunset gates shall stand
A mighty woman with a torch, whose flame
Is the imprisoned lightning, and her name
Mother of Exiles. From her beacon-hand
Glows world-wide welcome; her mild eyes command
The air-bridged harbor that twin cities frame.
"Keep, ancient lands, your storied pomp!" cries she
With silent lips. "Give me your tired, your poor,
Your huddled masses yearning to breathe free,
The wretched refuse of your teeming shore.
Send these, the homeless, tempest-tost to me,
I lift my lamp beside the golden door!"

This tablet, with her Sonnet to the Bartholdi Statue
of Liberty engraved upon it, is placed upon these walls
in loving memory of
Emma Lazarus
born in New York City, July 22, 1849
Died November 18, 1887

PRAYER IN THE MORNING

From *The Book of Common Prayer*

O God, the King Eternal, who dividest the day from the darkness,
and turnest the shadow of death into the morning; Drive far off
from us all wrong desires, incline our hearts to keep thy law, and
guide our feet into the way of peace; that having done thy will
with cheerfulness while it was day, we may, when the night
cometh, rejoice to give thee thanks; through Jesus Christ our
Lord. *Amen.*

Almighty God, who alone gavest us the breath of life, and alone
canst keep alive in us the holy desires thou dost impart; We beseech
thee, for thy compassion's sake, to sanctify all our thoughts and
endeavours; that we may neither begin an action without a pure
intention nor continue it without thy blessing. And grant that,
having the eyes of the mind opened to behold things invisible and

unseen, we may in heart be inspired by thy wisdom, and in wo be upheld by thy strength, and in the end be accepted of thee thy faithful servants; through Jesus Christ our Saviour. *Amen.*

OLD BLACK JOE

Stephen C. Foster

Gone are the days when my heart was young and gay,
Gone are my friends from the cotton fields away;
Gone from the earth to a better land I know,
I hear their gentle voices calling "Old Black Joe."

Chorus:
> I'm coming, I'm coming, for my head is bending low;
> I hear their gentle voices calling "Old Black Joe."

Why do I weep when my heart should feel no pain?
Why do I sigh that my friends come not again?
Grieving for forms now departed long ago,
I hear their gentle voices calling "Old Black Joe."

Where are the hearts once so happy and so free?
The children so dear that I held upon my knee?
Gone to the shore where my soul has longed to go,
I hear their gentle voices calling "Old Black Joe."

SONG

Hartley Coleridge

She is not fair to outward view
  As many maidens be,
Her loveliness I never knew
  Until she smiled on me;
O, then I saw her eye was bright,
A well of love, a spring of light!

But now her looks are coy and cold,
  To mine they ne'er reply,
And yet I cease not to behold

541

The love-light in her eye:
Her very frowns are fairer far
Than smiles of other maidens are.

THE INNER GLEAM

Ralph Waldo Emerson

A man should learn to detect and watch that gleam of light which
flashes across his mind from within, more than the lustre of the
firmament of bards and sages. Yet he dismisses without notice his
thought, because it is his. In every work of genius we recognize our
own rejected thoughts: they come back to us with a certain alienated
majesty.

"THE TIMES THAT TRIED MEN'S SOULS ARE OVER"

Thomas Paine

"The times that tried men's souls" are over—and the greatest
and completest revolution the world has ever known, gloriously
and happily accomplished.

But to pass from the extremes of danger to safety—from the
tumult of war to the tranquillity of peace, though sweet in contemplation, requires a gradual composure of senses to receive it.
Even calmness has the power of stunning, when it opens too instantly upon us. The long and raging hurricane that should cease
in a moment, would leave us in a state rather of wonder than
enjoyment; and some moments of recollection must pass, before
we could be capable of tasting the felicity of repose. There are
but few instances, in which the mind is fitted for sudden transi-
tions: it takes in its pleasures by reflection and comparison and
those must have time to act, before the relish for new scenes is
complete. . . .

To see it in our power to make a world happy—to teach mankind in the art of being so—to exhibit, on the theater of the universe, a character hitherto unknown—and to have, as it were, a new

creation intrusted to our hands, are honours that command reflection, and can neither be too highly estimated, nor too gratefully received.

(From Thoughts on Peace)

LET ME LIVE BUT FROM YEAR TO YEAR

Henry van Dyke

Let me but live from year to year,
    With forward face and unreluctant soul;
    Not hurrying to, nor turning from the goal;
Not mourning for the things that disappear
In the dim past, nor holding back in fear
    From what the future veils; but with a whole
    And happy heart, that pays its toll
To Youth and Age, and travels on with cheer.

So let the way wind up the hill or down
    O'er rough or smooth, the journey will be joy;
    Still seeking what I sought when but a boy,
New friendship, high adventure, and a crown,
    My heart will keep the courage of the quest,
    And hope the road's last turn will be the best.

THIS IS MY LETTER TO THE WORLD

Emily Dickinson

This is my letter to the world,
    That never wrote to me,—
The simple news that Nature told,
    With tender majesty.

Her message is committed
    To hands I cannot see;
For love of her, sweet countrymen,
    Judge tenderly of me.

543

THE DEATH OF CAPTAIN WASKOW

Ernie Pyle

AT THE FRONT LINES IN ITALY, Jan. 10 [1944] (by Wireless).—In this war I have known a lot of officers who were loved and respected by the soldiers under them. But never have I crossed the trail of any man as beloved as Capt. Henry T. Waskow of Belton, Tex.

Capt. Waskow was a company commander in the 36th Division. He was very young, only in his middle twenties, but he carried in him a sincerity and gentleness that made people want to be guided by him.

"After my own father, he comes next," a sergeant told me.

"He always looked after us," a soldier said. "He'd go to bat for us every time."

"I've never known him to do anything unkind," another one said.

I was at the foot of the mule trail the night they brought Capt. Waskow down. The moon was nearly full, and you could see far up the trail, and even part way across the valley. Soldiers made shadows as they walked.

Dead men had been coming down the mountain all evening, lashed onto the backs of mules. They came lying belly down across the wooden packsaddles, their heads hanging down on the left side of the mules, their stiffened legs sticking awkwardly from the other side, bobbing up and down as the mule walked.

The Italian mule skinners were afraid to walk beside the dead men, so Americans had to lead the mules down that night. Even the Americans were reluctant to unlash and lift off the bodies when they got to the bottom, so an officer had to do it himself and ask others to help.

The first one came early in the morning. They slid him down from the mule, and stood him on his feet for a moment. In the half light he might have been merely a sick man standing there leaning on the other. Then they laid him on the ground in the shadow of the stone wall alongside the road.

I don't know who that first one was. You feel small in the presence of dead men and you don't ask silly questions.

We left him there beside the road, that first one, and we all went back into the cowshed and sat on watercans or lay on the straw, waiting for the next batch of mules.

Somebody said the dead soldier had been dead for four days, and then nobody said anything more about him. We talked for an

544

hour or more; the dead man lay all alone, outside in the shadow of the wall.

Then a soldier came into the cowshed and said there were some more bodies outside. We went out into the road. Four mules stood there in the moonlight, in the road where the trail came down off the mountain. The soldiers who led them stood there waiting.

"This one is Capt. Waskow," one of them said quickly.

Two men unlashed his body from the mule and lifted it off and laid it in the shadow beside the stone wall. Other men took the other bodies off. Finally there were five lying end to end in a long row. You don't cover up dead men in the combat zone. They just lie there in the shadows until somebody else comes after them.

The uncertain mules moved off to their olive groves. The men in the road seemed reluctant to leave. They stood around, and gradually I could sense them moving, one by one, close to Capt. Waskow's body. Not so much to look, I think, as to say something in finality to him and to themselves. I stood close by and I could hear.

One soldier came and looked down, and he said out loud:

"God damn it!"

That's all he said, and then he walked away.

Another one came, and he said, "God damn it to hell, anyway!" He looked down for a few last moments and then turned and left.

Another man came. I think he was an officer. It was hard to tell officers from men in the dim light, for everybody was grimy and dirty. The man looked down into the dead captain's face and then spoke directly to him, as though he were alive:

"I'm sorry, ol' man."

Then a soldier came in and stood beside the officer and bent over, and he too spoke to his dead captain, not in a whisper but awfully tenderly, and he said:

"I sure am sorry, sir."

Then the first man squatted down, and he reached down and took the captain's hand, and he sat there for a full five minutes holding the dead hand in his own and looking intently into the dead face. And he never uttered a sound all the time he sat there.

Finally he put the hand down. He reached up and gently straightened the points of the captain's shirt collar, and then he sort of rearranged the tattered edges of his uniform around the wound, and then he got up and walked away down the road in the moonlight, all alone.

The rest of us went back into the cowshed, leaving the five dead men lying in a line end to end in the shadow of the low stone wall. We lay down on the straw in the cowshed, and pretty soon we were all asleep.

THE SWEETEST STORY EVER TOLD

R. M. Stults

O, answer me a question, Love, I pray;
My heart for thee is pining day by day.
O, answer me, my dearest, answer true;
Hold me close as you were wont to do.
Whisper once again, the story old,
The dearest, sweetest story ever told;
Whisper once again the story old;
The dearest, sweetest story ever told.

Chorus:
    Tell me, do you love me?
    Tell me softly, sweetly, as of old!
    Tell me that you love me,
    For that's the sweetest story ever told.
    Tell me, do you love me?
    Whisper softly, sweetly, as of old!
    Tell me that you love me,
    For that's the sweetest story ever told.

O, tell me that your heart to me is true;
Repeat to me the story, ever new.
O, take my hand in yours and tell me, dear,
Is it joy to thee when I am near?
Whisper o'er and o'er the story old,
The dearest, sweetest story ever told.
Whisper o'er and o'er the story old,
The dearest, sweetest story ever told.

ABRAHAM LINCOLN ON DOING RIGHT

I do the very best I know how—the very best I can; and I mean to keep doing so until the end. If the end brings me out all right, what is said against me won't amount to anything. If the end brings me out wrong, ten angels swearing I was right would make no difference.

GEORGE WASHINGTON AND THE CHERRY-TREE

Mason Locke ("Parson") Weems

The following anecdote is a case in point. It is too valuable to be lost, and too true to be doubted; for it was communicated to me by the same excellent lady to whom I am indebted for the last.

"When George," said she, "was about six years old, he was made the wealthy master of a hatchet! of which, like most little boys, he was immoderately fond, and was constantly going about chopping every thing that came in his way. One day, in the garden, where he often amused himself hacking his mother's pea-sticks, he unluckily tried the edge of his hatchet on the body of a beautiful young cherry-tree, which he barked so terribly, that I don't believe the tree ever got the better of it. The next morning the old gentleman, finding out what had befallen his tree, which, by the by, was a great favourite, came into the house; and with much warmth asked for the mischievous author, declaring at the same time, that he would not have taken five guineas for his tree. Nobody could tell him anything about it. Presently George and his hatchet made their appearance. 'George,' said his father, 'do you know who killed that beautiful little cherry-tree yonder in the garden?' This was a tough question; and George staggered under it for a moment; but quickly recovered himself; and looking at his father, with the sweet face of youth brightened with the inexpressible charm of all-conquering truth, he bravely cried out, 'I can't tell a lie. I did cut it with my hatchet.'—'Run to my arms, you dearest boy,' cried his father in transports, 'run to my arms; glad am I, George, that you killed my tree; for you have paid me for it a thousand fold. Such an act of heroism in my son is more worth than a thousand trees, though blossomed with silver, and their fruits of purest gold.' "

(From The Life of George Washington)

RHYMING RIDDLE

The beginning of eternity, the end of time and space,
The beginning of every end, and the end of every place.
(Answer: The Letter *E*)

DON'T COPY CAT

Mark Twain

Don't, like the cat, try to get more out
of an experience than there is in it.
The cat, having sat upon a hot stove lid,
Will not sit upon a hot stove lid again.
Nor upon a cold stove lid.

HEALTH COUNSEL

Sir John Harrington

Use three physicians still: first Doctor Quiet,
Next Doctor Merry-man, and Doctor Diet.

Joy, Temperance and Repose
Slam the door on the doctor's nose.

TWO SIDES OF WAR

Grantland Rice

All wars are planned by old men
   In council rooms apart,
Who plan for greater armament
   And map the battle chart.

But out along the shattered fields
   Where golden dreams turned gray,
How very young their faces were
   Where all the dead men lay.

Portly and solemn, in their pride
   The elders cast their vote
For this or that, or something else,
   That sounds the warlike note.

But where their sightless eyes stare out
Beyond life's vanished joys,
I've noticed nearly all the dead
Were hardly more than boys.

CLOTHES

Henry David Thoreau

It is an interesting question how far men would retain their relative rank if they were divested of their clothes. Could you in such a case tell surely of any company of civilized men which belong to the respected class?

COMMONPLACE

Susan Coolidge

"A commonplace life," we say, and we sigh,
But why should we sigh as we say?
The commonplace sun in the commonplace sky
Makes up the commonplace day;
The moon and the stars are commonplace things,
And the flower that blooms, and the bird that sings,
But dark were the world, and sad our lot,
If the flowers failed, and the sun shone not;
And God, who studies each separate soul,
Out of commonplace lives makes His beautiful whole.

ONE DAY AT A TIME

Ralph Waldo Emerson

Finish every day and be done with it. You have done what you could. Some blunders and absurdities no doubt crept in; forget them as soon as you can. Tomorrow is a new day; begin it well and serenely and with too high a spirit to be cumbered with your old nonsense. This day is all that is good and fair. It is too dear, with its hopes and invitations, to waste a moment on the yesterdays.

MORNING HYMN

Thomas Ken

Awake, my soul, and with the sun
Thy daily stage of duty run;
Shake off dull sloth, and joyful rise
To pay thy morning sacrifice.

'Wake, and lift up thyself, my heart,
And with the angels bear thy part,
Who all night long unwearied sing
High praise to the Eternal King.

All praise to Thee, Who safe hast kept
And hast refreshed me while I slept!
Grant, Lord, when I from death shall wake,
I may of endless life partake!

Lord, I my vows to Thee renew;
Disperse my sins as morning dew:
Guard my first springs of thought and will,
And with Thyself my spirit fill.

Direct, control, suggest this day
All I design, or do, or say;
That all my powers, with all their might,
In Thy sole glory may unite.

Praise God, from Whom all blessings flow!
Praise Him, all creatures here below!
Praise Him above, ye heavenly host!
Praise Father, Son, and Holy Ghost!

MIKE O'DAY

Anonymous

This is the grave of Mike O'Day
Who died maintaining his right of way.
His right was clear, his will was strong,
But he's just as dead as if he'd been wrong.

KISSIN'

Some say kissin's ae sin,
    But I say, not at a';
For it's been in the warld
    Ever sin' there were twa.
If it werena lawfu',
    Lawyers wadna' 'low it;
If it werena haly,
    Meenisters wadna' dae it;
If it werena modest,
    Maidens wadna' taste it;
If it werena plenty,
    Puir folk couldna' hae it.
       (A Scottish saying)

THE DECLARATION OF INDEPENDENCE

When in the Course of human Events, it becomes necessary for one People to dissolve the Political Bands which have connected them with another, and to assume among the Powers of the Earth, the separate and equal Station to which the Laws of Nature and of Nature's God entitle them, a decent Respect to the Opinions of Mankind requires that they should declare the causes which impel them to the Separation.

WE hold these Truths to be self-evident, that all Men are created equal, that they are endowed by their Creator with certain unalienable Rights, that among these are Life, Liberty, and the Pursuit of Happiness—That to secure these Rights, Governments are instituted among Men, deriving their just Powers from the Consent of the Governed, that whenever any Form of Government becomes destructive of these Ends, it is the Right of the People to alter or to abolish it, and to institute new Government, laying its Foundation on such Principles, and organizing its Powers in such Form, as to them shall seem most likely to effect their Safety and Happiness. Prudence, indeed, will dictate that Governments long established should not be changed for light and transient Causes; and accordingly all Experience hath shewn, that Mankind are more disposed to suffer, while Evils are sufferable, than to right themselves by abolishing the Forms to which they are accustomed. But when a long Train of Abuses and Usurpations, pursuing invariably the same Object, evinces a Design to reduce them under absolute Despotism, it is their Right, it is their Duty, to throw off such Government, and to provide new Guards for their future Security. Such has been the patient Sufferance of these Colonies; and such is now the Necessity which constrains them to alter their former Systems of Government. The History of the present King of Great-Britain is a History of repeated Injuries and Usurpations, all having in direct Object the Establishment of an absolute Tyranny over these States. To prove this, let Facts be submitted to a candid World.

HE has refused his Assent to Laws, the most wholesome and necessary for the public Good.

HE has forbidden his Governors to pass Laws of immediate and pressing Importance, unless suspended in their Operation till his Assent should be obtained; and when so suspended, he has utterly neglected to attend to them.

HE has refused to pass other Laws for the Accommodation of large Districts of People, unless those People would relinquish the Right of Representation in the Legislature, a Right inestimable to them, and formidable to Tyrants only.

HE has called together Legislative Bodies at Places unusual, uncomfortable, and distant from the Depository of their public Records, for the sole Purpose of fatiguing them into Compliance with his Measures.

HE has dissolved Representative Houses repeatedly, for opposing with manly Firmness his Invasions on the Rights of the People.

HE has refused for a long Time, after such Dissolutions, to cause others to be elected; whereby the Legislative Powers, incapable of Annihilation, have returned to the People at large for their exercise; the State remaining in the mean time exposed to all the Dangers of Invasion from without, and Convulsions within.

HE has endeavoured to prevent the Population of these States; for that Purpose obstructing the Laws for Naturalization of Foreigners; refusing to pass others to encourage their Migrations hither, and raising the Conditions of new Appropriations of Lands.

HE has obstructed the Administration of Justice, by refusing his Assent to Laws for establishing Judiciary Powers.

HE has made Judges dependent on his Will alone, for the Tenure of their Offices, and the Amount and Payment of their Salaries.

HE has erected a Multitude of new Offices, and sent hither Swarms of Officers to harass our People, and eat out their Substance.

HE has kept among us, in Times of Peace, Standing Armies, without the consent of our Legislatures.

HE has affected to render the Military independent of and superior to the Civil Power.

HE has combined with others to subject us to a Jurisdiction foreign to our Constitution, and unacknowledged by our Laws; giving his Assent to their Acts of pretended Legislation:

FOR quartering large Bodies of Armed Troops among us:

FOR protecting them, by a mock Trial, from Punishment for any Murders which they should commit on the Inhabitants of these States:

FOR cutting off our Trade with all Parts of the World:

FOR imposing Taxes on us without our Consent:

FOR depriving us, in many Cases, of the Benefits of Trial by Jury:

FOR transporting us beyond Seas to be tried for pretended Offences:

FOR abolishing the free System of English Laws in a neighbouring Province, establishing therein an arbitrary Government, and enlarging its Boundaries, so as to render it at once an Example and fit Instrument for introducing the same absolute Rule into these Colonies:

FOR taking away our Charters, abolishing our most valuable Laws, and altering fundamentally the Forms of our Governments:

FOR suspending our own Legislatures, and declaring themselves invested with Power to legislate for us in all Cases whatsoever.

HE has abdicated Government here, by declaring us out of his Protection and waging War against us.

HE has plundered our Seas, ravaged our Coasts, burnt our Towns, and destroyed the Lives of our People.

HE is, at this Time, transporting large Armies of foreign Mercenaries to compleat the Works of Death, Desolation, and Tyranny, already begun with circumstances of Cruelty and Perfidy, scarcely paralleled in the most barbarous Ages, and totally unworthy the Head of a civilized Nation.

HE has constrained our fellow Citizens taken Captive on the high Seas to bear Arms against their Country, to become the Executioners of their Friends and Brethren, or to fall themselves by their Hands.

HE has excited domestic Insurrections amongst us, and has endeavoured to bring on the Inhabitants of our Frontiers, the merciless Indian Savages, whose known Rule of Warfare, is an undistinguished Destruction, of all Ages, Sexes and Conditions.

IN every stage of these Oppressions we have Petitioned for Redress in the most humble Terms: Our repeated Petitions have been answered only by repeated Injury. A Prince, whose Character is thus marked by every act which may define a Tyrant, is unfit to be the Ruler of a free People.

Nor have we been wanting in Attentions to our British Brethren. We have warned them from Time to Time of Attempts by their Legislature to extend an unwarrantable Jurisdiction over us. We have reminded them of the Circumstances of our Emigration and Settlement here. We have appealed to their native Justice and Magnanimity, and we have conjured them by the Ties of our common Kindred to disavow these Usurpations, which, would inevitably interrupt our Connections and Correspondence. They too have been deaf to the Voice of Justice and of Consanguinity. We must, therefore, acquiesce in the Necessity, which denounces our Separation, and hold them, as we hold the rest of Mankind, Enemies in War, in Peace, Friends.

We, therefore, the Representatives of the UNITED STATES OF AMERICA, in General Congress, Assembled, appealing to the Supreme Judge of the World for the Rectitude of our Intentions, do, in the Name, and by Authority of the good People of these Colonies, solemnly Publish and Declare, That these United Colonies are, and of Right ought to be, Free and Independent States; that they are absolved from all Allegiance to the British Crown, and that all political Connection between them and the State of Great-Britain, is and ought to be totally dissolved; and that as Free and Independent States, they have full Power to levy War, conclude Peace, contract Alliances, establish Commerce, and to do all other Acts and things which Independent States may of right do. And for the support of this Declaration, with a firm Reliance on the Protection of divine Providence, we mutually pledge to each other our Lives, our Fortunes, and our sacred Honor.

Signed by Order *and in* Behalf *of the* Congress,
JOHN HANCOCK, President.

Attest.
Charles Thomson, Secretary.

SIGNERS OF THE DECLARATION OF INDEPENDENCE

ACCORDING TO THE AUTHENTICATED LIST PRINTED BY
ORDER OF CONGRESS OF JANUARY 18, 1777 *

John Hancock.

NEW-HAMPSHIRE.
{ Josiah Bartlett,
W^m. Whipple,
Matthew Thornton.†

DELAWARE.
{ Cæsar Rodney,
Geo. Read,
(Tho M:Kean.) ‡

MASSACHUSETTS-
BAY.
{ Saml. Adams,
John Adams,
Robt. Treat Paine,
Elbridge Gerry.

MARYLAND.
{ Samuel Chase,
W^m. Paca,
Thos. Stone,
Charles Carroll, of
    Carrollton.

RHODE-ISLAND AND
PROVIDENCE, &C.
{ Step. Hopkins,
William Ellery.

CONNECTICUT.
{ Roger Sherman,
Saml. Huntington,
W^m. Williams,
Oliver Wolcott.

VIRGINIA.
{ George Wythe,
Richard Henry Lee,
Th^s. Jefferson,
Benj^a. Harrison,
Thos. Nelson, j^r.
Francis Lightfoot Lee,
Carter Braxton.

NEW-YORK.
{ W^m. Floyd,
Phil. Livingston,
Fran^s. Lewis,
Lewis Morris.

NORTH-CAROLINA.
{ W^m. Hooper,
Joseph Hewes,
John Penn.

NEW-JERSEY.
{ Rich^d. Stockton,
Jno. Witherspoon,
Fra^s. Hopkinson,
John Hart,
Abra. Clark.

SOUTH-CAROLINA.
{ Edward Rutledge,
Thos. Heyward, jun^r.
Thomas Lynch, jun^r.
Arthur Middleton.

GEORGIA.
{ Button Gwinnett,
Lyman Hall,
Geo. Walton.

PENNSYLVANIA.
{ Robt. Morris,
Benjamin Rush,
Benja. Franklin,
John Morton,
Geo. Clymer,
Ja^s. Smith,
Geo. Taylor,
James Wilson,
Geo. Ross.

* Braces, spelling, and abbreviation of names conform to original printed list.

† Matthew Thornton's name was signed on the engrossed copy following the Connecticut Members, but was transferred in the printed copy to its proper place with the other New Hampshire Members.

‡ Thomas McKean's name was not included in the list of signers printed by order of Congress on January 18, 1777, as he did not sign the engrossed copy until some time thereafter, probably in 1781.

EVENSONG

Robert Louis Stevenson

The embers of the day are red
Beyond the murky hill.
The kitchen smokes; the bed
In the darkling house is spread:
The great sky darkens overhead,
And the great woods are shrill.
So far have I been led,
Lord, by Thy will:
So far have I followed, Lord, and wondered still.
The breeze from the embalmed land
Blows sudden towards the shore,
And claps my cottage door.
I hear the signal, Lord—I understand.
The night at Thy command
Comes. I will eat and sleep and will not question more.

PRAYER FOR A LITTLE HOUSE

Florence Bone

God send us a little home
To come back to when we roam—
Low walls and fluted tiles,
Wide windows, a view for miles;
Red firelight and deep chairs;
Small white bed upstairs;
Great talk in little nooks;
Dim color, rows of books;
One picture on each wall;
Not many things at all.
God send us a little ground—
Tall trees standing round,
Homely flowers in brown sod,
Overhead thy stars, O God!
God bless when winds blow
Our home and all we know.

EULOGY OF THE DOG

George G. Vest

Gentlemen of the jury, the best friend a man has in this world may turn against him and become his enemy. His son or daughter whom he has reared with loving care may prove ungrateful. Those who are nearest and dearest to us—those whom we trust with our happiness and our good name—may become traitors to their faith. The money that a man has he may lose. It flies away from him, perhaps when he needs it most. A man's reputation may be sacrificed in a moment of ill-considered action. The people who are prone to fall on their knees to do us honor when success is with us may be the first to throw the stone of malice when failure settles its clouds upon our heads. The one absolutely unselfish friend that man can have in this selfish world—the one that never deserts him, the one that never proves ungrateful or treacherous—is his dog.

Gentlemen of the jury, a man's dog stands by him in prosperity and in poverty, in health and sickness. He will sleep on the cold ground, where the wintry winds blow and the snow drives fiercely, if only he can be near his master's side. He will kiss the hand that has no food to offer, he will lick the wounds and sores that come in encounter with the roughness of the world. He guards the sleep of his pauper master as if he were a prince. When all other friends desert, he remains. When riches take wings and reputation falls to pieces he is as constant in his love as the sun in its journey through the heavens. If fortune drives the master forth an outcast in the world, friendless and homeless, the faithful dog asks no higher privilege than that of accompanying him to guard against danger, to fight against his enemies. And when the last scene of all comes, and death takes the master in its embrace, and his body is laid away in the cold ground, no matter if all other friends pursue their way, there by his graveside will the noble dog be found, his head between his paws, his eyes sad but open in alert watchfulness, faithful and true even to death.

* * *

The louder he talked of his honor, the faster we counted our spoons.

—Ralph Waldo Emerson

THE ROAD NOT TAKEN

Robert Frost

Two roads diverged in a yellow wood,
And sorry I could not travel both
And be one traveler, long I stood
And looked down one as far as I could
To where it bent in the undergrowth;

Then took the other, as just as fair,
And having perhaps the better claim,
Because it was grassy and wanted wear;
Though as for that the passing there
Had worn them really about the same.

And both that morning equally lay
In leaves no step had trodden black.
Oh, I kept the first for another day!
Yet knowing how way leads on to way,
I doubted if I should ever come back.

I shall be telling this with a sigh
Somewhere ages and ages hence:
Two roads diverged in a wood, and I—
I took the one less traveled by,
And that has made all the difference.

ENGLISH AIR-RAID SHELTER PRAYER

Anonymous

Increase, O God, the spirit of neighborliness among us, that in peril we may uphold one another, in calamity serve one another, in suffering tend one another and in homelessness and loneliness in exile befriend one another. Grant us brave and enduring hearts that we may strengthen one another, till the disciplines and testing of these days be ended, and Thou dost give again peace in our time, through Jesus Christ, our Lord, Amen.

*   *   *

In a calm sea every man is a pilot.—Anonymous

SWEET ADELINE

Richard H. Gerard

In the evening when I sit alone a-dreaming
Of days gone by love—to me so dear,
There's a picture that in fancy 'oft appearing
Brings back the time love—when you were near;
It is then I wonder where you are my darling,
And if your heart to me is still the same,
For the sighing wind and the nightingale a-singing
Are breathing only your sweet name.

Chorus
Sweet Adeline, My Adeline,
At night, dear heart, for you I pine,
In all my dreams your fair face beams;
You're the flower of my heart,
Sweet Adeline.

THE BEGINNING OF THE NUCLEAR AGE

Albert Einstein
Old Grove Road
Nassau Point
Peconic, Long Island
August 2, 1939

F. D. Roosevelt
President of the United States
White House
Washington, D. C.

SIR:
  Some recent work by E. Fermi and L. Szilard, which has been communicated to me in manuscript, leads me to expect that the element uranium may be turned into a new and important source of energy in the immediate future. Certain aspects of the situation seem to call for watchfulness and, if necessary, quick action on the part of the Administration. I believe, therefore, that it is my duty

to bring to your attention the following facts and recommendations.

In the course of the last four months, it has been made probable—through the work of Joliot in France as well as Fermi and Szilard in America—that it may become possible to set up nuclear chain reactions in a large mass of uranium, by which vast amounts of power and large quantities of new radium-like elements would be generated. Now it appears almost certain that this could be achieved in the immediate future.

This new phenomenon would also lead to the construction of bombs and it is conceivable—though much less certain—that extremely powerful bombs of a new type may thus be constructed. A single bomb of this type, carried by boat or exploded in a port, might very well destroy the whole port together with some of the surrounding territory. However, such bombs might very well prove to be too heavy for transportation by air.

(The letter from which the above is a quotation was delivered to President Roosevelt on October 11, 1939, by Alexander Sachs.)

GOD

John Banister Tabb

I see Thee in the distant blue;
But in the violet's dell of dew,
Behold, I *breathe and touch* Thee too.

THE SPIRIT OF LIBERTY

Judge Learned Hand

We have gathered here to affirm a faith, a faith in a common purpose, a common conviction, a common devotion. Some of us have chosen America as the land of our adoption; the rest have come from those who did the same. For this reason we have some right to consider ourselves a picked group, a group of those who had the courage to break from the past and brave the dangers and loneliness of a strange land.

What was the object that nerved us, or those who went before us, to this choice? We sought liberty; freedom from oppression, freedom from want, freedom to be ourselves. This we then sought. This we now believe that we are by way of winning.

What do we mean when we say that first of all we seek liberty? I often wonder whether we do not rest our hopes too much upon constitutions, upon laws and upon courts. These are false hopes; believe me, these are false hopes. Liberty lies in the hearts of men and women. When it dies there, no constitution, no law, no court can save it. No constitution, no law, no court can even do much to help it. While it lies there, it needs no constitution, no law, no court to save it.

And what is this liberty which must lie in the hearts of men and women? It is not the ruthless, the unbridled will. It is not freedom to do as one likes. That is the denial of liberty, and leads straight to its overthrow. A society in which men recognize no check upon their freedom soon becomes a society where freedom is the possession of only a savage few; as we have learned to our sorrow.

What then is the spirit of liberty? I cannot define it; I can only tell you my own faith. The spirit of liberty is the spirit which is not too sure that it is right. The spirit of liberty is the spirit which seeks to understand the minds of other men and women. The spirit of liberty is the spirit which weighs their interests alongside its own without bias. The spirit of liberty remembers that not even a sparrow falls to earth unheeded. The spirit of liberty is the spirit of Him who, near two thousand years ago, taught mankind that lesson it has never learned, but has never quite forgotten: that there may be a kingdom where the least shall be heard and considered side by side with the greatest.

And now in that spirit, that spirit of an America which has never been, and which may never be; nay, which never will be, except as the conscience and courage of Americans create it; yet in the spirit of that America which lies hidden in some form in the aspirations of us all; in the spirit of that America for which our young men are at this moment fighting and dying; in that spirit of liberty and of America I ask you to rise and with me to pledge our faith in the glorious *destiny* of our beloved country—with liberty and justice for all.

(Address on "I Am an American Day"—
Central Park, New York City, May, 1944)

A LETTER FROM FRA GIOVANNI
TO THE CONTESSINA

To the Most Illustrious
The Contessina Allagia
degli Aldobrandeschi,
on the Via de' Martelli, Firenze.

Most Noble Contessina:

I salute you. Believe me your most humble servant.

The rascal who carries this letter, if he devour them not on the way, will crave your acceptance of some of the fruits of our garden. Would that the peace of heaven might reach you through such things of earth!

Contessina, forgive an old man's babble. But I am your friend, and my love for you goes deep. There is nothing I can give you which you have not got; but there is much, very much, that, while I cannot give it, you can take. No heaven can come to us unless our hearts find rest in it today. Take heaven! No peace lies in the future which is not hidden in this present little instant. Take peace!

The gloom of the world is but a shadow. Behind it, yet within our reach, is joy. There is radiance and glory in the darkness, could we but see; and to see, we have only to look. Contessina, I beseech you to look.

Life is so generous a giver, but we, judging its gifts by their covering, cast them away as ugly or heavy or hard. Remove the covering, and you will find beneath it a living splendor, woven of love, by wisdom, with power. Welcome it, grasp it, and you touch the Angel's hand that brings it to you. Everything we call a trial, a sorrow, or a duty: believe me, that Angel's hand is there; the gift is there, and the wonder of an overshadowing presence. Our joys, too: be not content with them as joys. They, too, conceal diviner gifts.

Life is so full of meaning and of purpose, so full of beauty: beneath its covering: that you will find earth but cloaks your heaven. Courage, then, to claim it: that is all! But courage you have; and the knowledge that we are pilgrims together, wending, through unknown country, home.

And so, at this Christmas time, I greet you: not quite as the world sends greetings, but with profound esteem, and with the prayer that for you, now and for ever, the day breaks and the shadows flee away.

I have the honor to be your servant, though the least of them.
Fra Giovanni.
Christmas Eve, Anno Domini MDXIII. Pontassieve.
(Actually written by Ernest Temple Hargrove, who died in 1939)

FALSE WITNESSES

Henry Ward Beecher

Life would be a perpetual flea hunt if a man were obliged to run down all the innuendos, inveracities, insinuations and misrepresentations which are uttered against him.

GOOD AND BAD

There is so much good in the worst of us,
And so much bad in the best of us,
That it hardly becomes any of us
To talk about the rest of us.
(Attributed to Edward Wallis Hoch)

LINES COMPOSED A FEW MILES
ABOVE TINTERN ABBEY

William Wordsworth

               For I have learned
To look on nature, not as in the hour
Of thoughtless youth; but hearing often-times
The still, sad music of humanity,
Nor harsh, nor grating, though of ample power
To chasten and subdue. And I have felt
A presence that disturbs me with the joy
Of elevated thoughts; a sense sublime
Of something far more deeply interfused,
Whose dwelling is the light of setting suns,
And the round ocean and the living air,
And the blue sky, and in the mind of man;
A motion and a spirit, that impels
All thinking things, all objects of all thought,
And rolls through all things. Therefore am I still
A lover of the meadows and the woods,
And mountains; and of all that we behold
From this green earth; of all the mighty world
Of eye, and ear,—both what they half create,
And what perceive; well pleased to recognise
In nature and the language of the sense,
The anchor of my purest thoughts, the nurse,
The guide, the guardian of my heart, and soul
Of all my moral being.
                   Nor perchance,
If I were not thus taught, should I the more
Suffer my genial spirits to decay:
For thou art with me here upon the banks
Of this fair river; thou my dearest Friend.
My dear, dear Friend; and in thy voice I catch
The language of my former heart, and read
My former pleasures in the shooting lights
Of thy wild eyes. Oh! yet a little while
May I behold in thee what I was once,
My dear, dear Sister! and this prayer I make,
Knowing that Nature never did betray
The heart that loved her; 'tis her privilege,

Through all the years of this our life, to lead
From joy to joy: for she can so inform
The mind that is within us, so impress
With quietness and beauty, and so feed
With lofty thoughts, that neither evil tongues,
Rash judgments, nor the sneers of selfish men,
Nor greetings where no kindness is, nor all
The dreary intercourse of daily life,
Shall e'er prevail against us, or disturb
Our cheerful faith, that all which we behold
Is full of blessings. Therefore let the moon
Shine on thee in thy solitary walk;
And let the misty mountain-winds be free
To blow against thee: and, in after years,
When these wild ecstasies shall be matured
Into a sober pleasure; when thy mind
Shall be a mansion for all lovely forms,
Thy memory be as a dwelling-place
For all sweet sounds and harmonies; oh! then,
If solitude, or fear, or pain, or grief,
Should be thy portion, with what healing thoughts
Of tender joy wilt thou remember me,
And these my exhortations! Nor, perchance—
If I should be where I no more can hear
Thy voice, nor catch from thy wild eyes these gleams
Of past existence—wilt thou then forget
That on the banks of this delightful stream
We stood together; and that I, so long
A worshipper of Nature, hither came
Unwearied in that service: rather say
With warmer love—oh! with far deeper zeal
Of holier love. Nor wilt thou then forget,
That after many wanderings, many years
Of absence, these steep woods and lofty cliffs,
And this green pastoral landscape, were to me
More dear, both for themselves and for thy sake!

*   *   *

Adam and Eve had many advantages, but the principal one was
that they escaped teething.—Mark Twain

LOVELIEST OF TREES

A. E. Housman

Loveliest of trees, the cherry now
Is hung with bloom along the bough,
And stands about the woodland ride
Wearing white for Eastertide.

Now, of my threescore years and ten,
Twenty will not come again,
And take from seventy springs a score,
It only leaves me fifty more.

And since to look at things in bloom
Fifty springs are little room,
About the woodlands I will go
To see the cherry hung with snow.

LOVE THE BEAUTIFUL

Moses Mendelssohn

Love the beautiful,
Seek out the true,
Wish for the good,
And the best do.

YOUR FRIEND

Anonymous

If your friend has got a heart,
There is something fine in him;
Cast away his darkest part,—
Cling to what's divine in him.

DEATH BE NOT PROUD

John Donne

Death be not proud, though some have called thee
Mighty and dreadfull, for thou art not soe,
For those whom thou think'st thou dost overthrow
Die not, poore death, nor yet canst thou kill mee.
From rest and sleepe, which but thy pictures bee,
Much pleasure, then from thee, much more must flow,
And soonest our best men with thee doe goe,
Rest of their bones, and soules deliverie.
Thou art slave to Fate, Chance, kings, and desperate men,
And dost with poyson, warre, and sicknesse dwell,
And poppie, or charmes can make us sleepe as well,
And better than thy stroake; why swell'st thou then?
One short sleepe past, wee wake eternally,
And death shall be no more; death, thou shalt die.

ABRAHAM LINCOLN MEDITATES ON THE WILL OF GOD

The will of God prevails. In great contests each party claims to act in accordance with the will of God. Both *may* be and one *must* be wrong. God cannot be *for* and *against* the same thing at the same time. In the present civil war it is quite possible that God's purpose is something different from the purpose of either party; and yet the human instrumentalities, working just as they do, are ready to say that this is probably true; that God wills this contest, and wills that it shall not end yet. By His mere great power on the minds of the now contestants, He could have either *saved* or *destroyed* the Union without a human contest. Yet the contest began. And having begun, He could give the final victory to either side any day. Yet the contest proceeds.

(September 30, 1862)

THE HERO AND THE SAINT

Felix Adler

The hero is one who kindles a great light in the world, who sets up blazing torches in the dark streets of life for men to see by. The saint is the man who walks through the dark paths of the world, himself a "light".

THE MARRIED LOVER

Coventry Patmore

Why, having won her, do I woo?
   Because her spirit's vestal grace
Provokes me always to pursue,
   But, spirit-like, eludes embrace;
Because her womanhood is such
   That, as on court-days subjects kiss
The Queen's hand, yet so near a touch
   Affirms no mean familiarness;
Nay, rather marks more fair the height
   Which can with safety so neglect
To dread, as lower ladies might,
   That grace could meet with disrespect;
Thus she with happy favour feeds
   Allegiance from a love so high
That thence no false conceit proceeds
   Of difference bridged, or state put by;
Because, although in act and word
   As lowly as a wife can be,
Her manner, when they call me lord,
   Remind me 'tis by courtesy;
Not with her least consent of will.
   Which would my proud affection hurt,
But by the noble style that still
   Imputes an unattained desert;
Because her hair and lofty brows,
   When all is won which hope can ask,
Reflect a light of hopeless snows
   That bright in virgin ether bask;
Because, though free of the outer court
   I am, this Temple keeps its shrine
Sacred to heaven; because, in short,
   She's not and never can be mine.

"WITH WHOM IS NO VARIABLENESS, NEITHER SHADOW OR TURNING"

Arthur Hugh Clough

It fortifies my soul to know
That, though I perish, Truth is so:
That, howso'er I stray and range,
Whate'er I do Thou dost not change.
I steadier step when I recall
That, if I slip, Thou dost not fall.

"LO, THE POOR INDIAN!"

Alexander Pope

Lo, the poor Indian! whose untutor'd mind
Sees God in clouds, or hears him in the wind;
His soul proud Science never taught to stray
Far as the solar walk or milky way;
Yet simple nature to his hope has giv'n,
Behind the cloud-topt hill, an humbler Heav'n,
Some safer world in depth of woods embraced,
Some happier island in the wat'ry waste,
Where slaves once more their native land behold,
No fiends torment, no Christians thirst for gold.
To be, contents his natural desire;
He asks no Angel's wing, no Seraph's fire;
But thinks, admitted to that equal sky,
His faithful dog shall bear him company.

(From An Essay on Man)

SHELLEY

Francis Thompson

Enchanted child, born into a world unchildlike; spoiled darling of Nature, playmate of her elemental daughters; 'pard-like spirit, beautiful and swift,' laired amidst the burning fastnesses of his own fervid mind; bold foot along the verges of precipitous dream; light leaper from crag to crag of inaccessible fancies; towering Genius, whose soul rose like a ladder between heaven and earth with the angels of song ascending and descending it;—he is shrunken into the little vessel of death, and sealed with the unshatterable seal of doom, and cast down deep below the rolling tides of Time.

Mighty meat for little guests, when the heart of Shelley was laid in the cemetery of Caius Cestius! Beauty, music, sweetness, tears— the mouth of the worm has fed them all. Into that sacred bridal-gloom of death where he holds his nuptials with eternity let not our rash speculations follow him; let us hope rather that as, amidst material nature, where our dull eyes see only ruin, the finer eye of science has discovered life in putridity and vigour in decay, seeing dissolution even and disintegration, which in the mouth of man symbolize disorder, to be in the works of God undeviating order, and the manner of our corruption to be no less wonderful than the manner of our health,—so, amidst the supernatural universe, some tender undreamed surprise of life in doom awaited that wild nature, which, worn by warfare with itself, its Maker, and all the world, now

> Sleeps, and never palates more the dug,
> The beggar's nurse, and Caesar's.

EPITAPH

> As I was, so be ye;
> As I am, ye shall be;
> That I gave, that I have;
> That I spent, that I had;
> Thus I end all my cost;
> What I left, that I lost.
>   (Churchyard, Leek, Derbyshire, England, on
>   the grave of Thomas Osborne, died 1749)

* * *

Here's to the banker, who lends you an umbrella when the sun is shining and demands it back as soon as it starts to rain.
—Anonymous

THE STAR

Jane Taylor

Twinkle, twinkle, little star,
How I wonder what you are!
Up above the world so high,
Like a diamond in the sky.

When the blazing sun is set,
When the grass with dew is wet,
Then you show your little light,
Twinkle, twinkle, all the night.

Then the traveler in the dark,
Thanks you for your tiny spark;
He could not see which way to go
If you did not twinkle so.

In the dark blue sky you keep,
And often through my curtains peep,
For you never shut your eye
Till the sun is in the sky.

As your bright and shiny spark,
Lights the traveler in the dark,
Though I know not what you are,
Twinkle, twinkle, little star.

* * *

The blood of the martyrs is the seed of the Church.
—Tertullian

CHOOSE LIFE

Holy Bible, Deuteronomy 30:15–19

See, I have set before thee this day life and good, and death and evil:
In that I command thee this day to love the Lord thy God, to walk
in his ways, and to keep his commandments and his statutes and his

judgments, that thou mayest live and multiply: and the Lord thy God shall bless thee in the land whither thou goest to possess it.

But if thine heart turn away, so that thou wilt not hear, but shalt be drawn away, and worship other gods, and serve them:

I denounce unto you this day, that ye shall surely perish, and that ye shall not prolong your days upon the land, whither thou passest over Jordan to go to possess it.

I call heaven and earth to record this day against you, that I have set before you life and death, blessing and cursing: therefore choose life, that both thou and thy seed may live.

PLUTARCH RELATES HOW ANTONY FELL UNDER THE SPELL OF CLEOPATRA

(TRANSLATOR: John Dryden)

The last and crowning mischief that could befall him [Antony] came in the love of Cleopatra, to awaken and kindle to fury passions that as yet lay still and dormant in his nature, and to stifle and finally corrupt any elements that yet made resistance in him of goodness and a sound judgment. He fell into the snare thus. When making preparation for the Parthian war, he sent to command her to make her personal appearance in Cilicia, to answer an accusation, that she had given great assistance, in the late wars, to Cassius. Dellius, who was sent on this message, had no sooner seen her face, and remarked her adroitness and subtlety in speech, but he felt convinced that Antony would not so much as think of giving any molestation to a woman like this; on the contrary, she would be the first in favor with him. So he set himself at once to pay his court to the Egyptian, and gave her his advice, "to go," in the Homeric style, to Cilicia, "in her best attire," and bade her fear nothing from Antony, the gentlest and kindest of soldiers. She had some faith in the words of Dellius, but far more in her own attractions; which, having formerly recommended her to Caesar and the young Cnaeus Pompey, she did not doubt might prove yet more successful with Antony. Their acquaintance was with her when a girl, young and ignorant of the world, but she was to meet Antony in the time of life when women's beauty is most splendid, and their intellects are in full maturity. She made great preparations for her journey, of money, gifts, and ornaments of value, such as so wealthy a kingdom might afford, but she brought with her, her surest hopes in her own magic arts and charms.

She received several letters, both from Antony and from his friends, to summon her, but she took no account of these orders; and at last, as if in mockery of them, she came sailing up the river Cydnus, in a barge with gilded stern and outspread sails of purple, while oars of silver beat time to the music of flutes and fifes and harps. She herself lay all alone under a canopy of cloth of gold, dressed as Venus in a picture, and beautiful young boys, like painted Cupids, stood on each side to fan her. Her maids were dressed like sea nymphs and graces, some steering at the rudder, some working at the ropes. The perfumes diffused themselves from the vessel to the shore, which was covered with multitudes, part following the galley up the river on either bank, part running out of the city to see the sight. The market-place was quite emptied, and Antony was at last left alone, sitting upon the tribunal; while the word went through all the multitude that Venus was come to feast with Bacchus, for the common good of Asia. On her arrival, Antony sent to invite her to supper. She thought it fitter he should come to her; so, willing to show his good-humor and courtesy, he complied, and went. He found the preparations to receive him magnificent beyond expression, but nothing so admirable as the great number of lights; for on a sudden there was let down altogether so great a number of branches with lights in them so ingeniously disposed, some in squares, and some in circles, that the whole thing was a spectacle that has seldom been equalled for beauty.

The next day Antony invited her to supper, and was very desirous to outdo her in magnificence as well as contrivance; but he found he was altogether beaten in both, and was so well convinced of it that he was himself the first to jest and mock at his poverty of wit and his rustic awkwardness. She perceiving that his raillery was broad and gross, and savored more of the soldier than the courtier, rejoined in the same taste, and fell into it at once, without any sort of reluctance or reserve. For her actual beauty, it is said, was not in itself so remarkable that none could be compared with her, or that no one could see her without being struck by it, but the contact of her presence, if you lived with her, was irresistible; the attraction of her person, joining with the charm of her conversation, and the character that attended all she said or did, was something bewitching. It was a pleasure merely to hear the sound of her voice, with which, like an instrument of many strings, she could pass from one language to another; so that there were few of the barbarian nations that she answered by an interpreter; to most of them she spoke herself, as to the Ethiopians, Troglodytes, Hebrews, Arabians, Syrians, Nedes, Parthians, and many others, whose languages she had learnt; which was all the more surprising because most of the kings, her predecessors, scarcely gave themselves the trouble to acquire the Egyptian tongue, and several of them quite abandoned the Macedonian.

Antony was so captivated by her that, while Fulvia his wife maintained his quarrels in Rome against Caesar by actual force of arms, and the Parthian troops, commanded by Lebienus (the king's general having made him commander-in-chief), were assembled in Mesopotamia, and ready to enter Syria, he could yet suffer himself to be carried away by her to Alexandria, there to keep holiday, like a boy, in play and diversion, squandering and fooling away in enjoyments that most costly, as Antiphon says, of all valuables, time. . . .

To return to Cleopatra. Plato admits four sorts of flattery, but she had a thousand. Were Antony serious or disposed to mirth, she had at any moment some new delight or charm to meet his wishes; at every turn she was upon him, and let him escape her neither by day nor by night. She played at dice with him, drank with him, hunted with him; and when he exercised in arms, she was there to see. At night she would go rambling with him to disturb and torment people at their doors and windows, dressed like a servant-woman, for Antony also went in servant's disguise, and from these expeditions he often came home very scurvily answered, and sometimes even beaten severely, though most people guessed who it was. However, the Alexandrians in general liked it all well enough, and joined good-humoredly and kindly in his frolics and play, saying they were much obliged to Antony for acting his tragic parts at Rome, and keeping his comedy for them. It would be trifling without end to be particular in his follies, but his fishing must not be forgotten. He went out one day to angle with Cleopatra, and being so unfortunate as to catch nothing in the presence of his mistress, he gave secret orders to the fishermen to dive under water, and put fishes that had already been taken upon his hooks; and these he drew so fast that the Egyptian perceived it. But, feigning great admiration, she told everybody how dexterous Antony was, and invited them next day to come and see him again. So, when a number of them had come on board the fishing boats, as soon as he had let down his hook, one of her servants was beforehand with his divers, and fixed upon his hook a salted fish from Pontus. Antony, feeling his line give, drew up the prey, and when, as may be imagined, great laughter ensued, "Leave," said Cleopatra, "the fishing-rod, general, to us poor sovereigns of Pharos and Canopus; your game is cities, provinces, and kingdoms."

POLITICAL SKILL

Abraham Lincoln, asked what he thought was the best attribute for a politician, said he thought it "would be the ability to raise a cause which would produce an effect and then fight the effect."

THE HAPPIEST MAN

Seneca

The longest space of time exhibits only what may be found in one day—light and darkness, with their vicissitudes and alternations. Every day should be therefore so ordered and disposed, as if it closed the series, and were the measure and completion of our existence. . . .

He is the happiest man—the secure possessor of himself, who waits for the morrow without solicitude;—he who can go to bed at night saying, "I have lived," in the full sense of the phrase, rises every morning with a day gained.

THE TRUE TEACHER

James A. Garfield

I am not willing that this discussion should close without mention of the value of a true teacher. Give me a log hut, with only a simple bench, Mark Hopkins on one end and I on the other, and you may have all the buildings, apparatus and libraries without him.

THE GARDEN YEAR

Sara Coleridge

January brings the snow,
Makes our feet and fingers glow.

February brings the rain,
Thaws the frozen lake again.

March brings breezes, loud and shrill,
To stir the dancing daffodil.

April brings the primrose sweet,
Scatters daisies at our feet.

May brings flocks of pretty lambs,
Skipping by their fleecy dams.

June brings tulips, lilies, roses,
Fills the children's hands with posies.

Hot July brings cooling showers,
Apricots, and gillyflowers.

August brings the sheaves of corn,
Then the harvest home is borne.

Warm September brings the fruit;
Sportsmen then begin to shoot.

Fresh October brings the pheasant;
Then to gather nuts is pleasant.

Dull November brings the blast;
Then the leaves are whirling fast.

Chill December brings the sleet,
Blazing fire, and Christmas treat.

THE MISTLETOE BOUGH

Thomas Haynes Bayly

The mistletoe hung in the castle hall,
The holly branch shone on the old oak wall;
And the baron's retainers were blithe and gay,
And keeping their Christmas holiday.
The baron beheld with a father's pride
His beautiful child, young Lovell's bride;
While she with her bright eyes seemed to be
The star of the goodly company.

"I'm weary of dancing now," she cried;
"Here, tarry a moment—I'll hide, I'll hide!
And, Lovell, be sure thou'rt first to trace
The clew to my secret lurking place."
Away she ran—and her friends began
Each tower to search, and each nook to scan;
And young Lovell cried, "O where dost thou hide?
I'm lonesome without thee, my own dear bride."

They sought her that night, and they sought her next day,
And they sought her in vain while a week passed away;
In the highest, the lowest, the loneliest spot,
Young Lovell sought wildly—but found her not.
And years flew by, and their grief at last
Was told as a sorrowful tale long past;
And when Lovell appeared the children cried,
"See! the old man weeps for his fairy bride."

At length an oak chest, that had long lain hid,
Was found in the castle—they raised the lid,
And a skeleton form lay moldering there
In the bridal wreath of that lady fair!
O sad was her fate!—in sportive jest
She hid from her lord in the old oak chest.
It closed with a spring!—and, dreadful doom,
The bride lay clasped in her living tomb!

THE FATAL WEDDING

W. H. Windom

The wedding bells were ringing on a moonlight winter's night,
The church was decorated, all within was gay and bright.
A mother with her baby came and saw the lights aglow,
She thought of how these same bells chimed for her three years
    ago!
"I'd like to be admitted, sir," she told the sexton old,
"Just for the sake of baby, to protect him from the cold."
He told her that the wedding there was for the rich and grand,
And with the eager watching crowd outside she'd have to stand.
While the wedding bells were ringing, while the bride and groom
    were there,
Marching up the aisle together, as the organ pealed an air;
Telling tales of fond affection, vowing never more to part,
Just another fatal wedding; just another broken heart.

She begged the sexton once again to let her pass inside.
"For baby's sake you may step in," the gray-haired man replied.
"If any one knows reason why this couple should not wed,
Speak now, or hold your peace forever," soon the preacher said!
"I must object," the woman cried, with voice so meek and mild,
"The bridegroom is my husband, sir, and this our little child."
"What proof have you?" the preacher asked. "My infant," she
    replied.
She raised her babe, then knelt to pray, the little one had died.

The parents of the bride then took the outcast by the arm,
"We'll care for you through life," they said, "you've save our child
    from harm."
The outcast wife, the bride and parents, quickly drove away,
The husband died by his own hand, before the break of day.
No wedding feast was spread that night; two graves were made
    next day,
One for the little baby, and in the other the father lay.
The story has been often told by firesides warm and bright,
Of bride and groom, of outcast, and the fatal wedding night.

LET ME LIVE OUT MY YEARS

John G. Neihardt

Let me live out my years in heat of blood!
  Let me die drunken with the dreamer's wine!
Let me not see this soul-house built of mud
  Go toppling to the dust—a vacant shrine!

Let me go quickly like a candle-light
  Snuffed out just at the heyday of its glow!
Give me high-noon—and let it then be night!
  Thus would I go.

And grant me when I face this grisly Thing,
  One haughty cry to pierce the gray Perhaps!
Let me be as a tune-swept fiddle-string
  That feels the Master Melody—and snaps!

OF LOVE OF SILENCE AND OF SOLITUDE

Thomas À Kempis

Seek a convenient time to take heed to thyself and think oft-times of the benefits of God.

Leave curious things and read such matters that rather give compunction than occupation.

If thou withdraw thyself from void speakings and idle circuits and from vanities and hearing of tidings thou shalt find time sufficient and convenient to have sweet meditations.

The great holy men where they might, fled men's fellowship and chose to live to God in secret places.

One said 'as ofttimes as I was among men I came back a less man' that is to say less holy: this we find by experience when we talk any while.

It is easier for a man always to be still than not to exceed in words. It is easier for a man to abide privily at home than well to keep himself being away from home.

Wherefore whoever purposeth to come to inward and to spiritual things it behoveth him to decline from the company of people —with Jesu.

No man appeareth safely away from home but he that loveth gladly to abide at home.

No man speaketh safely but he that is glad to hold his peace.

No man is safe above but he that will gladly be beneath.

No man commandeth safely but he that hath learned to obey.

No man rejoiceth safely but he that hath the witness of a good conscience.

Nevertheless the safety of holy men was never without dread of God; nor were they the less busy and meek in themselves though they had great virtues and grace.

The safety of shrews (wicked men) groweth from pride and presumption and in the end it turneth into deceit.

Promise thyself safety in this world never, though thou seem a good religious man or a devout hermit: Ofttimes they that are best in man's estimation fall most perilously for their trust in themselves.

Wherefore it is not profitable that they lack temptations utterly but they should ofttimes be attacked lest they be too secure and lest they be left up by pride and lightly decline to outer consolations.

O he that never sought transitory gladness, he that never occupied him in the world, how good a conscience would he keep.

O he that would cut away all manner of vain business and would think all only on ghostly and godly things and set all his hope in God how great peace and quiet should he have.

There is no man worthy heavenly comfort unless he diligently exercise himself in holy compunction. If thou heartily be sorry enter into thy closet, exclude all worldly noise as it is written 'Be ye sorry in your chambers'; thou shalt find there what outside thou shalt ofttimes lose.

The cell well continued waxeth sweet and the cell evil kept engendreth weariness. If in the beginning of thy conversion thou keep thy cell and dwell well therein it shall be to thee afterwards as a dear and well beloved friend and most pleasant solace.

In silence and quiet the devout soul profiteth and learneth the secrets of the scriptures: there he findeth the flood of tears wherewith every night he may wash and cleanse himself that he may be the more familiar to his creator the more he withdraweth him far from secular noise.

He that withdraweth himself from friends and known men, God shall come nigh unto him with his holy angels.

Better it is for a man to be hid and take care of himself than, taking no heed of himself, to work wonders.

It is commendable for a man of religion seldom to go out, to fly from being seen and not wish to see men; why wilt thou see what is not lawful for thee to have?

The world passeth and his concupiscence.

The desires of sensuality draw men to walk about; but when the hour is past what cometh thereof but grudging (murmuring) of conscience and dispersion of heart?

A glad going out ofttimes bringeth forth a sorrowful coming home and a glad watching over evening bringeth forth a sorry morning; so every fleshly joy entereth in pleasantly but in the end he biteth and slayeth.

What canst thou see elsewhere that thou canst not see here? Lo here heaven earth and all elements and of these all things are made.

What canst thou see elsewhere that may long abide under the sun? peradventure thou waitest to be filled; but thou shalt never come thereto.

If thou sawest all things that are present what were that but a vain sight? Lift up thine eyes to God on high and pray God for thy sins and negligence; leave vain things to the vain and take thou heed to the things that God commandeth thee.

Shut thy door upon thee and call to thee Jesu thy love: dwell with him in thy cell for thou shalt not find elsewhere so great peace.

If thou hadst not gone out nor heard no tidings thou wouldst the better have abided in peace; and since it delighteth thee sometimes to hear new tidings it behoveth, following this, that thou suffer turbation of heart.

(From Imitation of Christ)

* * *

Young men think old men fools, and old men know young men to be so.

—Anonymous

WHY SO PALE AND WAN, FOND LOVER?

Sir John Suckling

Why so pale and wan, fond lover?
   Prithee, why so pale?
Will, when looking well can't move her,
   Looking ill prevail?
   Prithee, why so pale?

Why so dull and mute, young sinner?
   Prithee, why so mute?
Will, when speaking well can't win her,
   Saying nothing do 't?
   Prithee, why so mute?

Quit, quit for shame! This will not move,
   This cannot take her.
If of herself she will not love,
   Nothing can make her:
   The devil take her!

MR. DOOLEY ON NEW YEAR'S RESOLUTIONS

Finley Peter Dunne

Mr. Hennessy looked out at the rain dripping down in Archey Road, and sighed, "A-ha, 'tis a bad spell iv weather we're havin' ".

"Faith, it is," said Mr. Dooley, "or else we mind it more thin we did. I can't remimber wan day fr'm another. Whin I was young, I niver thought iv rain or snow, cold or heat. But now th' heat stings and th' cold wrenches me bones; an', if I go out in th' rain with less on me thin a ton iv rubber, I'll pay dear f'r it in achin' j'ints, so I will. That's what old age means; an' now another year has been put on to what we had befur, an' we're expected to be gay. 'Ring out th' old, ring in th' new,' says a guy at th' Brothers' School. 'Ring out th' old, ring in th' new,' he says. 'Ring out th' false, ring in th' true,' says he. It's a pretty sintimint, Hinnissy; but how ar-re we goin' to do it? Nawthin'd please me betther thin to turn me back on th' wicked an' ingloryous past, rayform me life, an' live at peace with th' wurruld to th' end iv me days. But how th' divvle can I do it? As th' fellow says, 'Can the leopard change his spots,' or can't he?

"You know Dorsey, iv coorse, th' cross-eyed May-o man that comes to this counthry about wan day in advance iv a warrant f'r stealin'? Ye know what he done to me, tellin' people I was caught in me cellar poorin' wather into a bar'l? Well, last night says I to mesilf, thinkin' iv Dorsey, I says: 'I swear that henceforth I'll keep me temper with me fellow-men. I'll not let anger or jealousy get the betther iv me,' I says. 'I'll lave off all me old feuds; an' if I meet me inimy goin' down th' sthreet, I'll go up an' shake him by th' hand, if I'm sure he hasn't a brick in th' other hand.' Oh, I was mighty compliminthry to mesilf. I set by th' stove dhrinkin' hot wans, an' ivry wan I dhrunk made me more iv a pote. 'Tis th' way with th' stuff. Whin I'm in dhrink, I have a fine thought; an' if I wasn't too comfortable to go an' look f'r th' ink-bottle, I cud write pomes that'd make Shakespeare an' Mike Scanlan think they were wur-rkin' on a dredge. 'Why,' says I, 'carry into th' new year th' hathreds iv th' old?' I says. 'Let the dead past bury its dead,' says I. 'Tur-rn ye'er lamps up to th' blue sky,' I says. (It was rainin' like the divvile, an' th' hour was midnight, but I give no heed to that, bein' comfortable with the hot wans.) An' I wint to th' dure, an', whin Mike Duffy came by on number wan hundherd an' five, ringin' th' gong iv th' ca-ar, I hollered to him: 'Ring out th' old, ring in th' new.' 'Go back into ye-er stall,' he says, 'an' wring ye-ersilf out,' he says. 'Ye-er wet through,' he says.

"Whin I woke up this mornin', th' pothry had all disappeared, an' I begun to think th' las' hot wan I took had something wrong with it. Besides, th' lumbago was grippin' me till I cud hardly put wan foot befure th' other. But I remembered me promises to mesilf, an' wint out on th' sthreet, intindin' to wish ivry wan a 'Happy New Year!' an' hopin' in me hear-rt that th' first wan I wished it to'd tell me to go to th' divvle, so I cud hit him in th' eye. I hadn't gone half a block befure I spied Dorsey acrost the sthreet. I picked up half a brick an' put it in me pocket, an' Dorsey done th' same. Thin we wint up to each other. 'A Happy New Year,' says I. 'Th' same to you!' says he. 'An' manny iv thim,' he says. 'Ye have a brick in ye-er hand,' says I. 'I was thinkin' iv givin' ye a New Year's gift,' says he. 'Th' same to you, an' manny iv thim,' says I, fondlin' me own ammunition. ' 'Tis even all around,' says he. 'It is,' says I. 'I was thinkin' las' night I'd give up me gredge again ye,' says he. 'I had th' same thought mesilf,' says I. 'But, since I seen ye-er face,' he says, 'I've concluded that I'd be more comfortable hatin' ye thin havin' ye f'r a frind,' says he. 'Ye-er a man iv taste,' says I. An' we backed away fr'm each other. He's a Tip, an' can throw a stone like a rifleman; an' Hinnissy, I'm somethin' iv an amachoor shot with a half-brick mesilf.

"Well, I've been thinkin' it over, and I've argied it out that life'd not be worth livin' if we didn't keep our inimies. I can have all th' frinds I need. Anny man can that keeps a liquor sthore. But a rale sthrong inimy, specially a May-o inimy—wan that hates ye ha-ard, an' that ye'd take th' coat off yer back to do a bad tur-rn to—is a luxury that I can't go without in me ol' days. Dorsey is the right sort. I can't go by his house without bein' in fear he'll spill the chimbly down on me head; an', whin he passes my place, he walks in th' middle iv th' sthreet, an' crosses himsilf. I'll swear off anything but Dorsey. He's a good man, an' I despise him. Here's long life to him."

WOLSEY'S REGRETS

William Shakespeare

Cromwell, I did not think to shed a tear
In all my miseries; but thou hast forced me,
Out of thy honest truth, to play the woman.
Let's dry our eyes: and thus far hear me, Cromwell;
And, when I am forgotten, as I shall be,
And sleep in dull cold marble, where no mention
Of me more must be heard of, say, I taught thee;
Say, Wolsey, that once trod the ways of glory,
And sounded all the depths and shoals of honour,
Found thee a way, out of his wreck, to rise in;
A sure and safe one, though thy master miss'd it.
Mark but my fall and that that ruin'd me.
Cromwell, I charge thee, fling away ambition:
By that sin fell the angels; how can man then,
The image of his Maker, hope to win by it?
Love thyself last: cherish those hearts that hate thee;
Corruption wins not more than honesty.
Still in thy right hand carry gentle peace,
To silence envious tongues. Be just, and fear not:
Let all the ends thou aim'st at be thy country's,
Thy God's, and truth's; then if thou fall'st, O Cromwell,
Thou fall'st a blessed martyr! Serve the king;
And prithee, lead me in:

There take an inventory of all I have,
To the last penny; 'tis the king's: my robe,
And my integrity to heaven, is all
I dare now call mine own. O Cromwell, Cromwell!
Had I but served my God with half the zeal
I served my king, he would not in mine age
Have left me naked to mine enemies.

(From King Henry VIII)

SO NIGH IS GRANDEUR

Ralph Waldo Emerson

In an age of fops and toys,
Wanting wisdom, void of right,
Who shall nerve heroic boys
To hazard all in Freedom's fight,—
Break sharply off their jolly games,
Forsake their comrades gay
And quit proud homes and youthful dames
For famine, toil and fray?
Yet on the nimble air benign
Speed nimbler messages,
That waft the breath of grace divine
To hearts in sloth and ease.
So nigh is grandeur to our dust,
So near is God to man,
When Duty whispers low, *Thou must*,
The youth replies, *I can*.

THE BROOKSIDE

Richard Monckton Milnes (Lord Houghton)

I wandered by the brookside,
    I wandered by the mill;
I could not hear the brook flow,—
    The noisy wheel was still.
There was no burr of grasshopper,
    No chirp of any bird,

But the beating of my own heart
   Was all the sound I heard.

I sat beneath the elm tree;
   I watched the long, long shade,
And, as it grew still longer,
   I did not feel afraid;
For I listened for a footfall,
   I listened for a word,
But the beating of my own heart
   Was all the sound I heard.

He came not,—no, he came not,—
   The night came on alone,—
The little stars sat, one by one,
   Each on his golden throne;
The evening air passed by my cheek,
   The leaves above were stirred,
But the beating of my own heart
   Was all the sound I heard.

Fast silent tears were flowing,
   When something stood behind;
A hand was on my shoulder,—
   I knew its touch was kind:
It drew me nearer—nearer—
   We did not speak one word,
For the beating of our own hearts
   Was all the sound we heard.

TO F. C.

Mortimer Collins

Fast falls the snow, O lady mine,
Sprinkling the lawn with crystals fine,
But by the gods we won't repine
   While we're together,
We'll chat and rhyme and kiss and dine,
   Defying weather.

So stir the fire and pour the wine,
And let those sea-green eyes divine
Pour their love-madness into mine:
    I don't care whether
'Tis snow or sun or rain or shine
    If we're together.

FARE THEE WELL

Lord Byron

Fare thee well! and if for ever,
    Still for ever, fare *thee well*:
Even though unforgiving, never
    'Gainst thee shall my heart rebel.
Would that breast were bared before thee
    Where thy head so oft hath lain,
While that placid sleep came o'er thee
    Which thou ne'er canst know again:
Would that breast, by thee glanced over,
    Every inmost thought could show!
Then thou wouldst at last discover
    'Twas not well to spurn it so.
Though the world for this commend thee—
    Though it smile upon the blow,
Even its praises must offend thee,
    Founded on another's woe:
Though my many faults defaced me,
    Could no other arm be found,
Than the one which once embraced me,
    To inflict a cureless wound?
Yet, oh yet, thyself deceive not—
    Love may sink by low decay,
But by sudden wrench, believe not
    Hearts can thus be torn away:
Still thine own its life retaineth—
    Still must mine, though bleeding, beat;
And the undying thought which paineth
    Is—that we no more may meet.
These are words of deeper sorrow

Than the wail above the dead;
  Both shall live—but every morrow
    Wake us from a widowed bed.
And when thou wouldst solace gather,
    When our child's first accents flow
Wilt thou teach her to say "Father!"
    Though his care she must forego?
When her little hands shall press thee,
    When her lip to thine is pressed,
Think of him whose prayer shall bless thee,
    Think of him thy love *had* blessed!
Should her lineaments resemble
    Those thou never more mayst see,
Then thy heart will softly tremble
    With a pulse yet true to me.
All my faults perchance thou knowest,
    All my madness none can know;
All my hopes—where'er thou goest—
    Wither, yet with *thee* they go.
Every feeling hath been shaken;
    Pride—which not a world could bow—
Bows to thee—by thee forsaken.
    Even my soul forsakes me now.
But 'tis done—all words are idle—
    Words from me are vainer still;
But the thoughts we cannot bridle
    Force their way without the will.
Fare thee well! thus disunited,
    Torn from every nearer tie,—
Sear'd in heart, and lone, and blighted,
    More than this I scarce can die.

THE SPIDER AND THE FLY

Mary Howitt

"Will you walk into my parlor?" said the Spider to the Fly,
" 'Tis the prettiest little parlor that ever you did spy;
The way into my parlor is up a winding stair,
And I have many curious things to show when you are there."
"Oh no, no," said the little Fly, "to ask me is in vain;
For who goes up your winding stair can ne'er come down again."

"I'm sure you must be weary, dear, with soaring up so high;
Will you rest upon my little bed?" said the Spider to the Fly.
"There are pretty curtains drawn around, the sheets are fine and
   thin;
And if you like to rest awhile, I'll snugly tuck you in!"
"Oh no, no," said the little Fly, "for I've often heard it said
They never wake again, who sleep upon your bed!"

Said the cunning Spider to the Fly, "Dear friend, what can I do
To prove the warm affection I've always felt for you?
I have within my pantry, good store of all that's nice;
I'm sure you're very welcome—will you please to take a slice?"
"Oh no, no," said the little Fly, "kind sir, that cannot be,
I've heard what's in your pantry, and I do not wish to see!"

"Sweet creature," said the Spider, "you're witty and you're wise;
How handsome are your gauzy wings, how brilliant are your eyes!
I have a little looking-glass upon my parlor shelf;
If you'll step in one moment, dear, you shall behold yourself."
"I thank you, gentle sir," she said, "for what you're pleased to say,
And bidding you good-morning now, I'll call another day."

The Spider turned him round about, and went into his den,
For well he knew the silly Fly would soon be back again;
So he wove a subtle web in a little corner sly,
And set his table ready to dine upon the Fly.
Then he came out to his door again, and merrily did sing,
"Come hither, hither, pretty Fly, with the pearl and silver wing;
Your robes are green and purple, there's a crest upon your head;
Your eyes are like the diamond bright, but mine are dull as lead."

Alas, alas! how very soon this silly little Fly,
Hearing his wily, flattering words, came slowly flitting by;
With buzzing wings she hung aloft, then near and nearer drew,—
Thinking only of her brilliant eyes, and green and purple hue;
Thinking only of her crested head—poor foolish thing! At last,
Up jumped the cunning Spider, and fiercely held her fast.
He dragged her up his winding stair, into his dismal den
Within his little parlor—but she ne'er came out again!

And now, dear little children, who may this story read,
To idle, silly, flattering words, I pray you ne'er give heed;
Unto an evil counsellor close heart, and ear, and eye,
And take a lesson from this tale of the Spider and the Fly.

Most of those who have spoken here before me have commended the lawgiver who added this oration to our other funeral customs; it seemed to them a worthy thing that such an honor should be given at their burial to the dead who had fallen on the field of battle. But I should have preferred that, when men's deeds have been brave, they should be honored in deed only, and with such an honor as this public funeral, which you are now witnessing. Then the reputation of many would not have been imperilled on the eloquence or want of eloquence of one, and their virtues believed or not, as he spoke well or ill. For it is difficult to say neither too little or too much; and even moderation is apt not to give the impression of truthfulness. The friend of the dead who knows the facts is likely to think that the words of the speaker fall short of his knowledge and of his wishes; another who is not so well informed, when he hears of anything which surpasses his own powers, will be envious and will suspect exaggeration. Mankind is tolerant of the praises of others so long as each hearer thinks that he can do as well or nearly as well himself; but, when the speaker rises above him, jealousy is aroused, and he begins to be incredulous. However, since our ancestors have set the seal of their approval upon the practice, I must obey, and to the utmost of my power shall endeavor to satisfy the wishes and beliefs of all who hear me. . . .

I have dwelt upon the greatness of Athens because I want to show you that we are contending for a higher prize than those who enjoy none of these privileges, and to establish by manifest proof the merit of these men whom I am now commemorating. Their loftiest praise has been already spoken. For in magnifying the city I have magnified them, and men like them whose virtues made her glorious. And of how few Hellenes can it be said, as of them, that their deeds when weighed in the balance have been found equal to their fame! Methinks that a death such as theirs has been gives the true measure of a man's worth; it may be the first revelation of his virtues, but is at any rate their final seal. For even those who come short in other ways may justly plead the valor with which they fought for their country; they have blotted out the evil with the good, and have benefited the State more by their public services than they have injured her by their private actions. None of these men were enervated by wealth or hesitated to resign the pleasures of life; none of them put off the evil day in the hope, natural to poverty, that a man, though poor, may one day become rich. But deeming that the punishment of their enemies was sweeter than any of these things, and that they could fall in no nobler cause, they determined at the hazard of their lives to be honorably avenged, and to leave the rest. They resigned to hope their unknown chance of happiness; but in the face of death they resolved to rely upon themselves alone. And when the moment came they were minded to resist and suffer, rather than to fly and save their lives; they ran away from the world of dishonor, but on the battlefield their feet stood fast, and in an instant, at the height of their fortune, they passed away from the scene, not of their fear, but of their glory.

Such was the end of these men; they were worthy of Athens, and the living need not desire to have a more heroic spirit, although they may pray for a less fatal issue. The value of such a spirit is not to be expressed in words. Anyone can discourse to you forever about the advantages of a brave defense which you know already. But instead of listening to him I would have you day by day fix your eyes upon the greatness of Athens, until you become filled with the love of her; and when you are impressed by the spectacle of her glory, reflect that this empire has been acquired by men who knew their duty and had the courage to do it, who in the hour of conflict had the fear of dishonor always present to them, and who, if they ever failed in an enterprise, would not allow their virtues to be lost to their country, but freely gave their lives to her as the fairest offering which they could present at her feast. The sacrifice which they collectively made was individually repaid to them; for they received again each one for himself a praise which grows not old, and the noblest of all sepulchres—I speak not of that in which their remains are laid, but of that in which their glory survives and is proclaimed always and on every fitting occasion both in word and deed. For the whole earth is the sepulchre of famous men; not only are they commemorated by famous columns and inscriptions in their own country, but in foreign lands there dwells also an unwritten memorial to them, graven, not on stone, but in the hearts of men. Make them your examples, and, esteeming courage to be freedom and freedom to be happiness, do not weigh too nicely the perils of war. The unfortunate who has no hope of a change for the better has less reason to throw away his life than the prosperous who, if he survives, is always liable to a change for the worse, and to whom any accidental fall makes the most serious difference. To a man of spirit, cowardice and disaster coming together are far more bitter than death striking him unperceived at a time when he is full of courage and animated by the general hope.

Wherefore I do not now commiserate the parents of the dead who stand here; I would rather comfort them. You know that your life has been passed amid manifold vicissitudes; and that they may be deemed fortunate who have gained most honor, whether an honorable death like theirs, or an honorable sorrow like yours, and whose days have been so ordered that the term of their happiness is likewise the term of their life. I know how hard it is to make you feel this, when the good fortunes of others will too often remind you of the gladness which once lightened your hearts. And sorrow is felt at the want of those blessings, not which a man never knew, but which were a part of his life before they were taken from him. Some [of you] are of an age at which they may hope to have other children, and they ought to bear their sorrow better; not only will the children who may hereafter be born make them forget their own lost ones, but the city will be doubly a gainer. She will not be left desolate, and she will be safer. For a man's counsel cannot have equal weight or worth, when he alone has no children to risk in the general danger. To those of you who have passed their prime, I say: Congratulate yourselves that you have been happy during the greater part of your days; remember that your life of sorrow will not last long, and be comforted by the glory of those who are gone. For the love of honor alone is ever young, and not riches, as some say, but honor is the delight of men when they are old and useless.

To you who are the sons and brothers of the departed, I see that the struggle to emulate them will be an arduous one. For all men praise the dead, and, however preeminent your virtues may be, hardly will you be thought, I do not say equal, but even to approach them. The living have their rivals and detractors, but when a man is out of the way, the honor and good-will which he receives is unalloyed. And, if I am to speak of womanly virtues to those of you who will henceforth be widows, let me sum them up in one short admonition: To a woman not to show more weakness than is natural to her sex is a great glory, and not to be talked about for good or for evil among men. I have paid the required tribute, in obedience to the law, making use of such fitting words as I had. The tribute in deeds has been paid in part; for the dead have been honorably interred, and it remains only that their children should be maintained at the public charge until they are grown up; this is the solid prize with which, as with a garland,

Athens crowns her sons living and dead, after a struggle like theirs. For where the rewards of virtue are greatest, there the noblest citizens are enlisted in the service of the State. And now, when you have duly lamented, every one his own dead, you may depart.

MAUD MULLER

John Greenleaf Whittier

Maud Muller on a summer's day
Raked the meadows sweet with hay.

Beneath her torn hat glowed the wealth
Of simple beauty and rustic health.

Singing, she wrought, and her merry glee
The mock-bird echoed from his tree.

But when she glanced to the far-off town,
White from its hill-slope looking down,

The sweet song died, and a vague unrest
And a nameless longing filled her breast,—

A wish that she hardly dared to own,
For something better than she had known.

The Judge rode slowly down the lane,
Smoothing his horse's chestnut mane.

He drew his bridle in the shade
Of the apple-trees, to greet the maid,

And ask a draught from the spring that flowed
Through the meadow across the road.

She stooped where the cool spring bubbled up,
And filled for him her small tin cup,

And blushed as she gave it, looking down
On her feet so bare, and her tattered gown.

"Thanks!" said the Judge, "a sweeter draught
From a fairer hand was never quaffed."

He spoke of the grass and flowers and trees,
Of the singing birds and humming bees;

Then talked of the haying, and wondered whether
The cloud in the west would bring foul weather.

And Maud forgot her brier-torn gown,
And her graceful ankles bare and brown;

And listened, while a pleased surprise
Looked from her long-lashed hazel eyes.

At last, like one who for delay
Seeks a vain excuse, he rode away.

Maud Muller looked and sighed: "Ah me!
That I the Judge's bride might be!

"He would dress me up in silks so fine,
And praise and toast me at his wine.

"My father should wear a broadcloth coat,
My brother should sail a painted boat.

"I'd dress my mother so grand and gay,
And the baby should have a new toy each day.

"And I'd feed the hungry and clothe the poor,
And all should bless me who left our door."

The Judge looked back as he climbed the hill,
And saw Maud Muller standing still.

"A form more fair, a face more sweet,
Ne'er hath it been my lot to meet.

"And her modest answer and graceful air
Show her wise and good as she is fair.

"Would she were mine, and I to-day,
Like her, a harvester of hay:

"No doubtful balance of rights and wrongs,
Nor weary lawyers with endless tongues,

"But low of cattle and song of birds,
And health and quiet and loving words."

But he thought of his sister, proud and cold,
And his mother, vain of her rank and gold.

So, closing his heart, the Judge rode on,
And Maud was left in the field alone.

But the lawyers smiled that afternoon,
When he hummed in court an old love tune;

And the young girl mused beside the well,
Till the rain on the unraked clover fell.

He wedded a wife of richest dower,
Who lived for fashion, as he for power.

Yet oft, in his marble hearth's bright glow,
He watched a picture come and go;

And sweet Maud Muller's hazel eyes
Looked out in their innocent surprise.

Oft, when the wine in his glass was red,
He longed for the wayside well instead;

And closed his eyes on his garnished rooms,
To dream of meadows and clover-blooms.

And the proud man sighed, with a secret pain,
"Ah, that I were free again!

"Free as when I rode that day
Where the barefoot maiden raked her hay."

She wedded a man unlearned and poor,
And many children played round her door.

But care and sorrow, and child-birth pain,
Left their traces on heart and brain.

And oft, when the summer sun shone hot,
On the new-mown hay in the meadow lot,

And she heard the little spring brook fall
Over the roadside, through the wall,

In the shade of the apple-tree again
She saw a rider draw his rein;

And, gazing down with a timid grace,
She felt his pleased eyes read her face.

Sometimes her narrow kitchen walls
Stretched away into stately halls;

The weary wheel to a spinnet turned,
The tallow candle an astral burned,

And for him who sat by the chimney lug,
Dozing and grumbling o'er pipe and mug,

A manly form at her side she saw,
And joy was duty and love was law.

Then she took up her burden of life again,
Saying only, "It might have been."

Alas for maiden, alas for judge,
For rich repiner and household drudge!

God pity them both! and pity us all,
Who vainly the dreams of youth recall.

For of all sad words of tongue or pen,
The saddest are these: "It might have been!"

Ah, well! for us all some sweet hope lies
Deeply buried from human eyes;

And, in the hereafter, angels may
Roll the stone from its grave away!

COUNT THAT DAY LOST

George Eliot

If you sit down at set of sun
And count the acts that you have done,
    And, counting, find
One self-denying deed, one word
That eased the heart of him who heard,
    One glance most kind
That fell like sunshine where it went—
Then you may count that day well spent.

But if, through all the livelong day,
You've cheered no heart, by yea or nay—
    If, through it all
You've nothing done that you can trace
That brought the sunshine to one face—
    No act most small
That helped some soul and nothing cost—
Then count that day as worse than lost.

597

"I AM THE BREAD OF LIFE"

Holy Bible, John 6:35–40

And Jesus said unto them, I am the bread of life: he that cometh to me shall never hunger; and he that believeth on me shall never thirst. But I said unto you, That ye also have seen me, and believe not. All that the Father giveth me shall come to me; and him that cometh to me I will in no wise cast out. For I came down from heaven, not to do mine own will, but the will of him that sent me. And this is the Father's will which hath sent me, that of all which he hath given me I should lose nothing, but should raise it up again at the last day. And this is the will of him that sent me, that every one which seeth the Son, and believeth on him, may have everlasting life: and I will raise him up at the last day.

ROSE AYLMER

Walter Savage Landor

Ah, what avails the sceptred race,
   Ah, what the form divine!
What every virtue, every grace!
   Rose Aylmer, all were thine.

Rose Aylmer, whom these wakeful eyes
   May weep, but never see,
A night of memories and of sighs
   I consecrate to thee.

From AUGURIES OF INNOCENCE

William Blake

To see a World in a Grain of Sand
And a Heaven in a Wild Flower,
Hold Infinity in the palm of your hand
And Eternity in an hour.

LEAD, KINDLY LIGHT

John Henry Newman

Lead, kindly Light, amid the encircling gloom,
Lead Thou me on!
The night is dark, and I am far from home—
Lead Thou me on!
Keep Thou my feet; I do not ask to see
The distant scene,—one step enough for me.

I was not ever thus, nor prayed that Thou
Shouldst lead me on.
I loved to choose and see my path; but now
Lead Thou me on!
I loved the garish day, and, spite of fears,
Pride ruled my will: Remember not past years.

So long Thy power has blest me, sure it still
Will lead me on
O'er moor and fen, o'er crag and torrent, till
The night is gone;
And with the morn those angel faces smile
Which I have loved long since, and lost awhile!

THREE GATES

Beth Day

If you are tempted to reveal
A tale to you someone has told
About another, make it pass,
Before you speak, three gates of gold.
These narrow gates: First, "Is it true?"
Then, "Is it needful?" In your mind
Give truthful answer. And the next
Is last and narrowest, "Is it kind?"

599

And if to reach your lips at last
It passes through these gateways three,
Then you may tell the tale, nor fear
What the result of speech may be.

(From the Arabian)

HORSE SENSE

Anonymous

A horse can't pull while kicking.
This fact I merely mention.
And he can't kick while pulling,
Which is my chief contention.

Let's imitate the good old horse
And lead a life that's fitting;
Just pull an honest load, and then
There'll be no time for kicking.

THE LORD IS MY LIGHT AND MY SALVATION

Holy Bible, Psalm 27:1, 4, 14

The Lord is my light and my salvation; whom shall I fear? the Lord is the strength of my life; of whom shall I be afraid? . . .
One thing have I desired of the Lord, that will I seek after; that I may dwell in the house of the Lord all the days of my life, to behold the beauty of the Lord, and to inquire in his temple. . . .
Wait on the Lord; be of good courage, and he shall strengthen thine heart: wait, I say, on the Lord.

* * *

The only thing necessary for the triumph of evil is for good men to do nothing.

—Edmund Burke

THE BIVOUAC OF THE DEAD

Theodore O'Hara

The muffled drum's sad roll has beat
  The soldier's last tattoo!
No more on life's parade shall meet
  The brave and fallen few.
On Fame's eternal camping ground
  Their silent tents are spread,
And glory guards with solemn round
  The bivouac of the dead.

No rumor of the foe's advance
  Now swells upon the wind,
Nor troubled thought of midnight haunts,
  Of loved ones left behind;
No vision of the morrow's strife
  The warrior's dreams alarms,
No braying horn or screaming fife
  At dawn to call to arms.

Their shivered swords are red with rust,
  Their plumèd heads are bowed,
Their haughty banner, trailed in dust,
  Is now their martial shroud—
And plenteous funeral tears have washed
  The red stains from each brow,
And the proud forms by battle gashed
  Are free from anguish now.

The neighing troop, the flashing blade,
  The bugle's stirring blast,
The charge,—the dreadful cannonade,
  The din and shout, are passed;
Nor war's wild notes, nor glory's peal
  Shall thrill with fierce delight
Those breasts that nevermore shall feel
  The rapture of the fight.

Like the fierce Northern hurricane
  That sweeps the great plateau,

Flushed with the triumph yet to gain,
    Come down the serried foe,
Who heard the thunder of the fray
    Break o'er the field beneath,
Knew the watchword of the day
    Was "Victory or death!"

Rest on, embalmed and sainted dead,
    Dear is the blood you gave—
No impious footstep here shall tread
    The herbage of your grave.
Nor shall your glory be forgot
    While Fame her record keeps,
Or honor points the hallowed spot
    Where valor proudly sleeps.

Yon marble minstrel's voiceless stone
    In deathless song shall tell,
When many a vanquished year hath flown,
    The story how you fell.
Nor wreck nor change, nor winter's blight,
    Nor time's remorseless doom,
Can dim one ray of holy light
    That gilds your glorious tomb.

A LITTLE LEARNING IS A DANGEROUS THING

Alexander Pope

A *little learning* is a dangerous thing;
Drink deep, or taste not the Pierian spring:
There shallow draughts intoxicate the brain,
And drinking largely sobers us again.
Fired at first sight with what the muse imparts,
In fearless youth we tempt the heights of arts,
While from the bounded level of our mind,
Short views we take, nor see the lengths behind;
But more advanced, behold with strange surprise

New distant scenes of endless science rise!
So pleased at first the towering Alps we try,
Mount o'er the vales and seem to tread the sky,
The eternal snows appear already pass'd,
And the first clouds and mountains seem the last:
But, those attain'd, we tremble to survey
The growing labours of the lengthen'd way,
The increasing prospect tires our wandering eyes,
Hills peep o'er hills, and Alps on Alp arise!
(From An Essay on Criticsm)

THE FLYING TRAPEZE

George Lebourne

O once I was happy but now I'm forlorn,
Like an old coat that is tatter'd and torn,
Left on this wide world to fret and to mourn,
Betray'd by a maid in her teens.
The girl that I lov'd she was handsome,
I tried all I knew, her to please.
But I could not please her one quarter so well,
Like that man upon the Trapeze.

Chorus:

> He'd fly through the air with the greatest of ease,
> A daring young man on the flying Trapeze,
> His movements were graceful all girls he could please,
> And my love he purloin'd away.

This young man by name was Signor Bona Slang.
Tall, big, and handsome, as well made as Chang,
Where'er he appeared, the Hall loudly rang
With ovation from all people there.
He'd smile from the bar on the people below
And one night he smil'd on my love
She wink'd back on him and shouted *Bravo!*
As he hung by his nose up above!

603

Her father and mother were both on my side,
And very hard tried to make her my own bride,
Her father he sigh'd, and her mother she cried,
To see her throw herself away.
'Twas all no avail, she went there ev'ry night,
And would throw him Bouquets on the stage.
Which caus'd him to meet her, how he ran me down,
To tell you would take a whole page.

One night I as usual went to her dear home,
Found there her father and mother alone,
I asked for my love, and soon they made known
To my horror, that she'd run away,
She'd pack'd up her box, and elop'd in the night
With him, with the greatest of ease,
From two stories high, he had lower'd her down
To the ground, on his flying Trapeze!

Some months after this I went to a Hall,
Was greatly surprised to see on the Wall
A bill in red letters, which did my heart gall,
That she was appearing with him.
He taught her gymnastics and dress'd her in tights
To help him to live at his ease,
And made her assume a masculine name,
And now she goes on the Trapeze.

Second Chorus:
> She floats through the air with the greatest of ease,
> You'd think her a man on the flying Trapeze,
> She does all the work, while he takes his ease,
> And that's what's become of my love.

WHEN LOVELY WOMAN STOOPS TO FOLLY

Oliver Goldsmith

When lovely woman stoops to folly
And finds too late that men betray,—
What charm can soothe her melancholy,
What art can wash her guilt away?

ABRAHAM LINCOLN'S LETTER TO JOHNSTON, HIS STEP-BROTHER

Dear Johnston: Your request for eighty dollars I do not think it best to comply with now. At the various times when I have helped you a little you have said to me, "We can get along very well now"; but in a very short time I find you in the same difficulty again. Now this can only happen by some defect in your conduct. What that defect is, I think I know. You are not lazy, and still you are an idler. I doubt whether, since I saw you, you have done a good whole day's work in any one day. You do not very much dislike to work, and still you do not work much, merely because it does not seem to you that you could get much for it. This habit of uselessly wasting time is the whole difficulty; it is vastly important to you, and still more so to your children, that you should break the habit. It is more important to them, because they have longer to live, and can keep out of an idle habit before they are in it, easier than they can get out of it after they are in.

You are now in need of some money; and what I propose is, that you shall go to work, "tooth and nail," for somebody who will give you money for it. Let father and your boys take charge of your things at home, prepare for a crop, and make a crop, and you go to work for the best money wages, or in discharge of any debt you owe, that you can get; and, to secure you a fair reward for your labor, I now promise you, that for every dollar you will, between this and the first of May, get for your own labor, either in money or as your own indebtedness, I will then give you one other dollar. By this, if you hire yourself at ten dollars a month, from me you will get ten more, making twenty dollars a month for your work. In this I do not mean you shall go off to St. Louis, or the lead mines, or the gold mines in California, but I mean for you to go at it for the best wages you can get close to home in Coles County Now, if you will do this, you will soon be out of debt, and, what is better, you will have a habit that will keep you from getting in debt again. But if I should now clear you out of debt, next year you would be just as deep in as ever. You say you would almost give your place in heaven for seventy or eighty dollars. Then you value your place in heaven very cheap, for I am sure you can, with the offer I make, get the seventy or eighty dollars for four or five months' work. You say if I will furnish you the money you will deed me the land, and, if you don't pay the money back, you will deliver possession. Nonsense! If you can't live with the land, how will you then live without it? You have always been kind to me,

and I do not mean to be unkind to you. On the contrary, if you
will but follow my advice, you will find it worth more than eighty
times eighty dollars to you.

Affectionately your brother,

A. Lincoln

FROM IN MEMORIAM

Alfred, Lord Tennyson

Strong Son of God, immortal Love,
  Whom we, that have not seen thy face,
  By faith, and faith alone, embrace,
Believing where we cannot prove;

Thine are these orbs of light and shade;
  Thou madest Life in man and brute;
  Thou madest Death; and lo, thy foot
Is on the skull which thou hast made.

Thou wilt not leave us in the dust;
  Thou madest man, he knows not why,
  He thinks he was not made to die;
And thou hast made him: thou art just.

Thou seemest human and divine,
  The highest, holiest manhood, thou.
  Our wills are ours, we know not how;
Our wills are ours, to make them thine.

Our little systems have their day;
  They have their day and cease to be;
  They are but broken lights of thee,
And thou, O Lord, art more than they.

We have but faith: we cannot know,
  For knowledge is of things we see;

And yet we trust it comes from thee,
A beam in darkness: let it grow.

Let knowledge grow from more to more,
　But more of reverence in us dwell;
　That mind and soul, according well,
May make one music as before,

But vaster. We are fools and slight;
　We mock thee when we do not fear:
　But help thy foolish ones to bear;
Help thy vain worlds to bear thy light.

Forgive what seem'd my sin in me,
　What seem'd my worth since I began;
　For merit lives from man to man,
And not from man, O Lord, to thee.

Forgive my grief for one removed,
　Thy creature, whom I found so fair.
　I trust he lives in thee, and there
I find him worthier to be loved.

Forgive these wild and wandering cries,
　Confusions of a wasted youth;
　Forgive them where they fail in truth,
And in thy wisdom make me wise.

AN ELEGY ON THE DEATH OF A MAD DOG

Oliver Goldsmith

Good people all, of every sort,
　Give ear unto my song;
　And if you find it wondrous short—
It cannot hold you long.

In Islington there was a man,
Of whom the world might say
That still a godly race he ran—
Whene'er he went to pray.

A kind and gentle heart he had,
To comfort friends and foes;
The naked every day he clad—
When he put on his clothes.

And in that town a dog was found,
As many dogs there be,
Both mongrels, puppy, whelp, and hound,
And curs of low degree.

This dog and man at first were friends;
But when a pique began,
The dog, to gain some private ends,
Went mad, and bit the man.

Around from all the neighboring streets,
The wondering neighbors ran,
And swore the dog had lost his wits
To bite so good a man!

The wound it seemed both sore and sad
To every Christian eye;
And while they swore the dog was mad,
They swore the man would die.

But soon a wonder came to light,
That showed the rogues they lied;
The man recovered of the bite,
The dog it was that died!

* * *

I knew a very wise man that believed that if a man were permitted to make all the ballads, he need not care who should make the laws of a nation.—Andrew Fletcher of Saltoun, in Letter to Marquis of Montrose

PRAYER

Alfred, Lord Tennyson

More things are wrought by prayer
Than this world dreams of. Wherefore, let thy voice
Rise like a fountain for me night and day.
For what are men better than sheep or goats
That nourish a blind life within the brain,
If, knowing God, they lift not hands of prayer
Both for themselves and those who call them friend?
For so the whole round earth is every way
Bound by gold chains about the feet of God.

(From Idylls of the King)

WHY I WENT TO THE WOODS

Henry David Thoreau

When first I took up my abode in the woods, that is, began to
spend my nights as well as days there, which, by accident, was on
Independence Day, on the 4th of July, 1845, my house was not
finished for winter, but was merely a defence against the rain,
without plastering or chimney, the walls being of rough weather-
stained boards, with wide chinks, which made it cool at night.
The upright white hewn studs and freshly planed door and win-
dow-casings gave it a clean and airy look, especially in the morning, when its timbers were saturated with dew, so that I fancied
that by noon some sweet gum would exude from them. To my
imagination it retained throughout the day more or less of this
auroral character, reminding me of a certain house on a mountain
which I had visited the year before. This was an airy, an unplas-
tered cabin, fit to entertain a travelling god, and where a goddess
might trail her garments. The winds which passed over my dwelling were such as sweep over the ridges of mountains, bearing the
broken strains, or celestial parts only, of terrestrial music. The
morning wind forever blows, the poem of creation is uninterrupted; but few are the ears that hear it. Olympus is but the outside of the earth everywhere.

The only house I had been the owner of before, if I except a boat, was a tent, which I used occasionally when making excursions in the summer, and this is still rolled up in my garret; but the boat, after passing from hand to hand, has gone down the stream of time. With this more substantial shelter about me, I had made some progress toward settling in the world. This frame, so slightly clad, was a sort of crystallisation around me, and reacted on the builder. It was suggestive somewhat as a picture in outlines. I did not need to go out doors to take the air, for the atmosphere within had lost none of its freshness. It was not so much within doors as behind a door where I sat, even in the rainiest weather. The Harivansa says: 'An abode without birds is like a meat without seasoning.' Such was not my abode, for I found myself suddenly neighbour to the birds; not by having imprisoned one, but having caged myself near them. I was not only nearer to some of those which commonly frequent the garden and the orchard, but to those wilder and more trilling songsters of the forest which never, or rarely, serenade a villager—the woodthrush, the veery, the scarlet tanager, the field-sparrow, the whip-poor-will, and many others.

I was seated by the shore of a small pond, about a mile and a half south of the village of Concord and somewhat higher than it, in the midst of an extensive wood between that town and Lincoln, and about two miles south of that our only field known to fame, Concord battle ground; but I was so low in the woods that opposite shore, half a mile off, like the rest, covered with wood, was my most distant horizon. For the first week, whenever I looked out on the pond, it impressed me like a tarn high up on the one side of a mountain, its bottom far above the surface of other lakes, and as the sun arose, I saw it throwing off its nightly clothing of mist, and here and there, by degrees, its soft ripples or its smooth reflecting surface was revealed, while the mists, like ghosts, were stealthily withdrawing in every direction into the woods, as at the breaking up of some nocturnal conventicle. The very dew seemed to hang upon the trees later into the day than usual, as on the sides of mountains.

This small lake was of most value as a neighbour in the intervals of a gentle rain-storm in August, when, both air and water being perfectly still, but the sky overcast, mid-afternoon had all the serenity of evening, and the woodthrush sang around, and was heard from shore to shore. A lake like this is never smoother than at such a time; and the clear portion of the air above it being shallow and darkened by clouds, the water, full of light and reflections, becomes a lower heaven itself so much the more important. From a hill-top near by, where the wood had been recently cut off, there was a pleasing vista southward across the pond, through a wide indentation in the hills which form the shore there, where their opposite sides sloping toward each other suggested a stream flowing out in that direction through a wooded valley, but stream there was none. That way I looked between and over the near green hills to some distant and higher ones in the horizon, tinged with blue. Indeed, by standing on tiptoe I could catch a glimpse of some of the peaks of the still bluer and more distant mountain ranges in the northwest, those true-blue coins from heaven's own mint, and also of some portion of the village. But in other directions, even from this point, I could not see over or beyond the woods which surrounded me. It is well to have some water in your neighbourhood, to give buoyancy to and float the earth. One value even of the smallest well is, that when you look into it you see that earth is not continent but insular. This is as important as that it keeps butter cool. When I looked across the pond from this peak toward the Sudbury meadows, which in time of flood I distinguished elevated perhaps by a mirage in their seething valley, like a coin in a basin, all the earth beyond the pond appeared like a thin crust insulated and floated even by this small sheet of intervening water, and I was reminded that this on which I dwelt was but dry land.

Though the view from my door was still more contracted, I did not feel crowded or confined in the least. There was pasture enough for my imagination. The low shrub-oak plateau to which the opposite shore arose, stretched away toward the prairies of the West and the steppes of Tartary, affording ample room for all the roving families of men. 'There are none happy in the world but beings who enjoy freely a vast horizon,' said Damodara, when his herds required new and larger pastures.

I went to the woods because I wish to live deliberately, to front only the essential facts of life, and see if I could not learn what it had to teach, and not, when I came to die, discover that I had not lived. I did not wish to live what was not life, living is so dear; nor did I wish to practise resignation, unless it was quite necessary. I wanted to live deep and suck out all the marrow of life, to live so sturdily and Spartan-like as to put to rout all that was not life, to cut a broad swath and shave close, to drive life into a corner, and reduce it to its lowest terms, and, if it proved to be mean, why then to get the whole and genuine meanness of it, and publish its meanness to the world; or if it were sublime, to know it by experience, and be able to give a true account of it in my next excursion. For most men, it appears to me, are in a strange uncertainty about it, whether it is of the devil or of God, and have somewhat hastily concluded that it is the chief end of man here to 'glorify God and enjoy Him forever.'

Still we live meanly, like ants; though the fable tells us that we were long ago changed into men; like pygmies we fight with cranes; it is error upon error, and clout upon clout, and our best virtue has for its occasion a superfluous and evitable wretchedness. Our life is frittered away by detail. An honest man has hardly need to count more than his ten fingers, or in extreme cases he may add his ten toes, and lump the rest. Simplicity, simplicity, simplicity! I say, let your affairs be as two or three, and not a hundred or a thousand; instead of a million count half-a-dozen, and keep your accounts on your thumb-nail. In the midst of this chopping sea of civilised life, such are the clouds and storms and quicksands and thousand-and-one items to be allowed for, that a man has to live, if he would not founder and go to the bottom and not make his port at all, by dead reckoning, and he must be a great calculator indeed who succeeds. Simplify, simplify. Instead of three meals a-day, if it be necessary eat but one; instead of a hundred dishes, five; and reduce other things in proportion. Our life is like a German Confederacy, made up of petty states, with its boundary forever fluctuating, so that even a German cannot tell you how it is bounded at any moment. The nation itself, with all its so-called internal improvements, which, by the way, are all external and superficial, is just such an unwieldy and overgrown establishment, cluttered with furniture and tripped up by its own traps, ruined by luxury and heedless expense, by want of calculation and a worthy aim, as the million households in the land; and the only cure for it as for them is in a rigid economy, a stern and more than Spartan simplicity of life and elevation of purpose. It lives too fast. Men think that it is essential that the Nation have commerce, and export ice, and talk through a telegraph, and ride thirty miles an hour, without a doubt, whether they do or not; but whether we should live like baboons or like men, is a little uncertain. If we do not get out sleepers and forge rails, and devote days and nights to the work, but go to tinkering upon our lives to improve them, who will build railroads? And if railroads are not built, how shall we get to heaven in season? But if we stay at home and mind our business, who will want railroads? We do not ride on the railroad; it rides upon us. Did you ever think what those sleepers are that underlie the railroad? Each one is a man, an Irishman or a Yankee man. The rails are laid on them and they are covered with sand, and the cars run smoothly over them. They are sound sleepers, I assure you. And every few years a new lot is laid down and run over; so that, if some have the pleasure of riding on a rail, others have the misfortune to be ridden upon. And when they run over a man that is walking in his sleep, a supernumerary sleeper in the wrong position, and wake him up, they suddenly stop the cars, and make a hue and cry about it, as if this were an exception. I am glad to know that it takes a gang of men for every five miles to keep the sleepers down and level in their beds as it is, for this is a sign that they may sometime get up again.

Why should we live with such hurry and waste of life? We are determined to be starved before we are hungry. Men say that a stitch in time saves nine, and so they take a thousand stitches to-day to save nine to-morrow. As for work, we haven't any of any consequence. We have the Saint Vitus' dance, and cannot possibly keep our heads still. If I should only give a few pulls at the parish bell-rope, as for a fire, that is, without setting the bell, there is hardly a man on his farm in the outskirts of Concord, not withstanding that press of engagements which was his excuse so many times this morning, nor a boy, nor a woman, I might almost say, but would forsake all and follow that sound, not mainly to save property from the flames, but, if we will confess the truth, much more to see it burn, since burn it must, and we, be it known, did not set it on fire—or to see it put out, and have a hand in it, if that is done as handsomely; yes, even if it were the parish church itself. Hardly a man takes a half-hour's nap after dinner, but when he wakes he holds up his head and asks 'What's the news?' as if the rest of mankind had stood his sentinels. Some give directions to be waked every half-hour, doubtless for no other purpose; and then to pay for it, they tell what they have dreamed. After a night's sleep the news is as indispensable as the breakfast. 'Pray, tell me anything new that has happened to a man anywhere on this globe'—and he reads it over his coffee and rolls, that a man has had his eyes gouged out this morning on the Wachito River; never dreaming the while that he lives in the dark unfathomed mammoth cave of this world, and has but the rudiment of an eye himself.

For my part, I could easily do without the post office. I think that there are very few important communications made through it. To speak critically, I never received more than one or two letters in my life—I wrote this some years ago—that were worth the postage. The penny-post is commonly an institution through which you seriously offer a man that penny for his thoughts which is so often safely offered in jest. And I am sure that I never read any memorable news in a newspaper. If we read of one man robbed, or murdered, or killed by accident, or one house burned, or one vessel wrecked, or one steam-boat blown-up or one cow run over on the Western Railroad, or one mad dog killed, or one lot of grass-hoppers in the winter—we never need read of another. One is enough. If you are acquainted with the principle, what do you care for a myriad instances and applications? To a philosopher all news, as it is called, is gossip, and they who edit and read it are old women over their tea. Yet not a few are greedy after this gossip. There was such a rush, as I hear, the other day at one of the offices to learn the foreign news by the last arrival, that several large squares of plate glass belonging to the establishment were broken by the pressure—news which I seriously think a ready wit might write a twelvemonth or twelve years beforehand with sufficient accuracy. As for Spain, for instance, if you know how to throw in Don Carlos and the Infanta, and Don Pedro and Seville and Granada, from time to time in the right proportions—they may have changed the names a little since I saw the papers—and serve up a bull-fight when other entertainments fail, it will be true to the letter, and give us as good an idea of the exact state or ruin of things in Spain as the most succinct and lucid reports under this head in the newspapers; and as for England, almost the last significant scrap of news from that quarter was the Revolution of 1649; and if you have learned the history of her crops for an average year, you never need attend to that thing again, unless your speculations are of a merely pecuniary character. If one may judge who rarely looks into the newspapers, nothing new does ever happen in foreign parts, a French Revolution not excepted.

Let us spend one day as deliberately as Nature, and not be thrown off the track by every nutshell and mosquito's wing that falls on the rails. Let us rise early and fast, or break fast, gently and without perturbation; let company come and let company go, let the bells ring and the children cry—determined to make a day of it. Why should we knock under and go with the stream? Let us not be upset and overwhelmed in that terrible rapid and whirlpool called a dinner, situated in the meridian shallows. Weather this danger and you are safe, for the rest of the way is down hill. With unrelaxed nerves, with morning vigour, sail by it, looking another way, tied to the mast like Ulysses. If the engine whistles, let it whistle till it is hoarse for its pains. If the bell rings, why should we run? We will consider what kind of music they are like. Let us settle ourselves, and work and wedge our feet downward through the mud and slush of opinion, and prejudice, and tradition, and delusion, and appearance, that alluvion which covers the globe, through Paris and London, through New York and Boston and Concord, through church and state, through poetry and philosophy and religion, till we come to a hard bottom and rocks in place, which we call reality, and say, This is, and no mistake; and then begin, having a point d'appui, below freshet and frost and fire, a place where you might found a wall or a state, or set a lamp-post safely, or perhaps a gauge, not a Nilometer, but a Realometer, that future ages might know how deep a freshet of shams and appearances had gathered from time to time. If you stand right fronting and face to face to a fact, you will see the sun glimmer on both its surfaces, as if it were a cimeter, and feel its sweet edge dividing you through the heart and marrow, and so you will happily conclude your mortal career. Be it life or death, we crave only reality. If we are really dying, let us hear the rattle in our throats and feel cold in the extremities; if we are alive, let us go about our business.

Time is but the stream I go a-fishing in. I drink at it; but while I drink I see the sandy bottom and detect how shallow it is. Its thin current slides away, but eternity remains. I would drink deeper; fish in the sky, whose bottom is pebbly with stars. I cannot count one. I know not the first letter of the alphabet. I have always been regretting that I was not as wise as the day I was born. The intellect is a cleaver; it discerns and rifts its way into the secret of things. I do not wish to be any more busy with my hands than is necessary. My head is hands and feet. I feel all my best faculties concentrated in it. My instinct tells me that my head is an organ for burrowing, as some creatures use their snout and forepaws, and with it I would mine and burrow my way through these hills. I think that the richest vein is somewhere hereabouts; so by the divining rod and thin rising vapours I judge; and here I will begin to mine.

(From Walden)

"HERE LIES JULIET"

William Shakespeare

Romeo. For here lies Juliet, and her beauty makes
This vault a feasting presence full of light.
Death, lie thou there, by a dead man interr'd.
How oft when men are at the point of death
Have they been merry! which their keepers call
A lightning before death: O, how may I
Call this a lightning? O my love! my wife!
Death, that hath suck'd the honey of thy breath,
Hath had no power yet upon thy beauty:
Thou art not conquer'd; beauty's ensign yet
Is crimson in thy lips and in thy cheeks,
And death's pale flag is not advanced there.
Tybalt, liest thou there in thy bloody sheet?
O, what more favour can I do to thee
Than with that hand that cut thy youth in twain
To sunder his that was thine enemy?
Forgive me, cousin! Ah, dear Juliet,
Why art thou yet so fair? shall I believe
That unsubstantial death is amorous,
And that the lean abhorred monster keeps
Thee here in dark to be his paramour?
For fear of that, I still will stay with thee;
And never from this dim palace of dim night
Depart again: here, here will I remain
With worms that are thy chamber-maids; O, here
Will I set up my everlasting rest,
And shake the yoke of inauspicious stars
From this world-wearied flesh. Eyes, look your last!
Arms, take your last embrace! and lips, O you
The doors of breath, seal with a righteous kiss
A dateless bargain to engrossing death!
Come, bitter conduct, come, unsavoury guide!
Thou desperate pilot, now at once run on
The dashing rocks thy sea-sick weary bark.
Here's to my love! (*Drinks*) O true apothecary!
Thy drugs are quick. Thus with a kiss I die.

(From Romeo and Juliet)

TRAY'S EPITAPH

Peter Pindar (John Wolcot)

Here rest the relics of a friend below,
Blest with more sense than half the folks I know:
Fond of his ease, and to no parties prone,
He damn'd no sect, but calmly gnaw'd his bone;
Perform'd his functions well in ev'ry way—
Blush, *Christians,* if you can, and copy *Tray.*

BARTER

Sara Teasdale

Life has loveliness to sell,
    All beautiful and splendid things,
Blue waves whitened on a cliff,
    Soaring fire that sways and sings,
And children's faces looking up
Holding wonder like a cup.

Life has loveliness to sell,
    Music like a curve of gold,
Scent of pine trees in the rain,
    Eyes that love you, arms that hold,
And for your spirit's still delight,
Holy thoughts that star the night.

Spend all you have for loveliness,
    Buy it and never count the cost;
For one white singing hour of peace
    Count many a year of strife well lost,
And for a breath of ecstasy
Give all you have been, or could be.

* * *

Do good by stealth and blush to find it fame.—Alexander Pope

THE FIRST LORD'S SONG

W. S. Gilbert

When I was a lad I served a term
As office boy to an Attorney's firm;
I cleaned the windows and I swept the floor,
And I polished up the handle of the big front door.
 I polished up that handle so successfulee,
  That now I am the Ruler of the Queen's Navee!

As office boy I made such a mark
That they gave me the post of a junior clerk;
I served the writs with a smile so bland,
And I copied all the letters in a big round hand.
 I copied all the letters in a hand so free,
  That now I am the Ruler of the Queen's Navee!

In serving writs I made such a name
That an articled clerk I soon became;
I wore clean collars and a brand-new suit
For the Pass Examination at the Institute:
 And that Pass Examination did so well for me,
  That now I am the Ruler of the Queen's Navee!

Of legal knowledge I acquired such a grip
That they took me into the partnership,
And that junior partnership, I ween,
Was the only ship that I ever had seen:
 But that kind of ship so suited me,
  That now I am the Ruler of the Queen's Navee!

I grew so rich that I was sent
By a pocket borough into Parliament;
I always voted at my Party's call,
And I never thought of thinking for myself at all.
 I thought so little they rewarded me,
  By making me the Ruler of the Queen's Navee!

Now, landsmen all, whoever you may be,
If you want to rise to the top of the tree—
If your soul isn't fettered to an official stool,
Be careful to be guided by this golden rule—
 Stick close to your desks and *never go to sea,*
  And you all may be Rulers of the Queen's Navee!

THOMAS JEFFERSON UPHOLDS THE VALUE
OF NEWSPAPERS

I am persuaded myself that the good sense of the people will always be found to be the best army. They may be led astray for the moment, but will soon correct themselves. The people are the only censors of their governors; and even their errors will tend to keep these to the true principles of their institution. To punish these errors too severely would be to suppress the only safeguard of the public liberty. The way to prevent these irregular interpositions of the people, is to give them full information of their affairs through the channel of the public papers, and to contrive that those papers should penetrate the whole mass of the people. The basis of our government being the opinion of the people, the very first object would be to keep that right; and were it left to me to decide whether we should have a government without newspapers, or newspapers without a government, I should not hesitate to prefer the latter.

(1787)

THE SNOW-STORM

Ralph Waldo Emerson

Announced by all the trumpets of the sky,
Arrives the snow, and, driving o'er the fields,
Seems nowhere to alight: the whited air
Hides hills and woods, the river and the heaven,
And veils the farm-house at the garden's end.
The sled and traveller stopped, the courier's feet
Delayed, all friends shut out, the housemates sit
Around the radiant fireplace, enclosed
In a tumultuous privacy of storm.
Come see the north wind's masonry.
Out of an unseen quarry evermore
Furnished with tile, the fierce artificer
Curves his white bastions with projected roof
Round every windward stake, or tree, or door.
Speeding, the myriad-handed, his wild work
So fanciful, so savage, nought cares he
For number or proportion. Mockingly,

On coop or kennel he hangs Parian wreaths;
A swan-like form invests the hidden thorn;
Fills up the farmer's lane from wall to wall,
Maugre the farmer's sighs; and at the gate
A tapering turret overtops the work.
And when his hours are numbered, and the world
Is all his own, retiring, as he were not,
Leaves, when the sun appears, astonished Art
To mimic in slow structures, stone by stone,
Built in an age, the mad wind's night-work,
The frolic architecture of the snow.

AWAY IN A MANGER

Martin Luther

Away in a manger, no crib for a bed,
The little Lord Jesus laid down His sweet head.
The stars in the sky looked down where He lay,
The little Lord Jesus, asleep on the hay.

The cattle are lowing, the Baby awakes,
But little Lord Jesus, no crying He makes.
I love Thee, Lord Jesus, look down from the sky,
And stay by my cradle till morning is nigh.

Be near me, Lord Jesus, I ask Thee to stay
Close by me for ever, and love me, I pray.
Bless all the dear children in Thy tender care,
And fit us for heaven to live with Thee there.

EFFECTIVE PRAYER

Holy Bible, Luke 11:9–13

And I say unto you, Ask; and it shall be given you; seek and ye shall find; knock and it shall be opened unto you.

For every one that asketh receiveth; and he that seeketh findeth; and to him that knocketh it shall be opened.

If a son shall ask bread of any of you that is a father, will he give him a stone? or if he ask a fish, will he for a fish give him a serpent?

Or if he shall ask an egg, will he offer him a scorpion?

If ye then, being evil, know how to give good gifts unto your children; how much more shall your heavenly Father give the Holy Spirit to them that ask him?

SEVEN AGES OF MAN

William Shakespeare

All the world's a stage,
And all the men and women merely players:
They have their exits and their entrances;
And one man in his time plays many parts,
His acts being seven ages. At first the infant,
Mewling and puking in the nurse's arms.
And then the whining school-boy, with his satchel
And shining morning face, creeping like snail
Unwillingly to school. And then the lover,
Sighing like furnace, with a woeful ballad
Made to his mistress' eyebrow. Then a soldier,
Full of strange oaths and bearded like the pard,
Jealous in honour, sudden and quick in quarrel,
Seeking the bubble reputation
Even in the cannon's mouth. And then the justice,
In fair round belly with good capon lined,
With eyes severe and beard of formal cut,
Full of wise saws and modern instances;
And so he plays his part. The sixth age shifts
Into the lean and slipper'd pantaloon,
With spectacles on nose and pouch on side,
His youthful hose, well saved, a world too wide
For his shrunk shank; and his big manly voice,
Turning again toward childish treble, pipes
And whistles in his sound. Last scene of all,
That ends this strange eventful history,
Is second childishness and mere oblivion,
Sans teeth, sans eyes, sans taste, sans every thing.

(From As You Like It)

THE FOURTH ESTATE

Thomas Carlyle

Burke said there were three estates in Parliament, but in the reporters' gallery yonder there sat a Fourth Estate more important far than them all.

THE GLORIOUS WHITEWASHER

Mark Twain

Saturday morning was come, and all the summer world was bright and fresh, and brimming with life. There was a song in every heart; and if the heart was young the music issued at the lips. There was cheer in every face and a spring in every step. The locust trees were in bloom and the fragrance of the blossoms filled the air. Cardiff Hill, beyond the village and above it, was green with vegetation, and it lay just far enough away to seem a Delectable Land, dreamy, reposeful, and inviting.

Tom appeared on the sidewalk with a bucket of whitewash and a long-handled brush. He surveyed the fence, and all gladness left him and a deep melancholy settled down upon his spirit. Thirty yards of board fence nine feet high. Life to him seemed hollow, and existence but a burden. Sighing he dipped his brush and passed it along the topmost plank; repeated the operation; did it again; compared the insignificant whitewashed streak with the far-reaching continent of unwhitewashed fence, and sat down on a tree-box discouraged. Jim came skipping out at the gate with a tin pail, and singing "Buffalo Gals." Bringing water from the town pump had always been hateful work in Tom's eyes, before, but now it did not strike him so. He remembered that there was company at the pump. White, mulatto, and Negro boys and girls were always there waiting their turns, resting, trading playthings, quarreling, fighting, skylarking. And he remembered that although the pump was only a hundred and fifty yards off, Jim never got back with a bucket of water under an hour—and even then somebody generally had to go after him. Tom said:

"Say, Jim, I'll fetch the water if you'll whitewash some."

Jim shook his head and said:

"Can't, Mars Tom. Ole missis, she tole me I got to go an' git dis water an' not stop foolin' roun' wid anybody. She says she spec' Mars Tom gwine to ax me to whitewash, an' so she tole me go 'long an' tend to my own business—she 'lowed *she'd* 'tend to de whitewashin'."

"O, never you mind what she said, Jim. That's the way she always talks. Gimme the bucket—I won't be gone only a minute. *She* won't ever know."

"Oh, I dasn't, Mars Tom. Ole missis she'd take an' tar de head off'n me. Deed she would."

"*She!* She never licks anybody—whacks 'em over the head with her thimble—and who cares for that, I'd like to know. She talks awful, but talk don't hurt—anyways it don't if she don't cry. Jim, I'll give you a marvel. I'll give you a white alley!"

Jim began to waver.

"White alley, Jim! And it's a bully taw."

"My! Dat's a mighty gay marvel, I tell you! But Mars Tom I's powerful afraid ole missis—"

"And, besides, if you will I'll show you my sore toe."

Jim was only human—this attraction was too much for him. He put down the pail, took the white alley, and bent over the toe with absorbing interest while the bandage was being unwound. In another moment he was flying down the street with his pail and a tingling rear. Tom was whitewashing with vigor, and Aunt Polly was retiring from the field with a slipper in her hand and triumph in her eye.

But Tom's energy did not last. He began to think of the fun he had planned for this day, and his sorrows multiplied. Soon the free boys would come tripping along on all sorts of delicious expeditions, and they would make a world of fun of him for having to work—the very thought of it burnt him like fire. He got out his worldly wealth and examined it—bits of toys, marbles, and trash; enough to buy an exchange of *work,* maybe, but not half enough to buy so much as half an hour of pure freedom. So he returned his straitened means to his pocket, and gave up the idea of trying to buy the boys. At this dark and hopeless moment an inspiration burst upon him! Nothing less than a great, magnificent inspiration.

He took up his brush and went tranquilly to work. Ben Rogers hove in sight presently—the very boy, of all boys, whose ridicule he had been dreading. Ben's gait was the hop-skip-and-jump— proof enough that his heart was light and his anticipations high. He was eating an apple, and giving a long, melodious whoop, at intervals, followed by a deep-toned ding-dong-dong, for he was personating a steamboat. As he drew near, he slackened speed, took the middle of the street, leaned far over to starboard and rounded to ponderously and with laborious pomp and circumstance—for he was personating the *Big Missouri,* and considered himself to be drawing nine feet of water. He was boat and captain and engine-bells combined, so he had to imagine himself standing on his own hurricane-deck giving the orders and executing them:

"Stop her, sir! Ting-a-ling-ling!" The headway ran almost out and he drew up slowly toward the sidewalk.

"Ship up to back! Ting-a-ling-ling!" His arms straightened and stiffened down his sides.

"Set her back on the starboard! Ting-a-ling-ling! Chow! ch-chow-wow! Chow!" His right hand, meantime, describing stately circles—for it was representing a forty-foot wheel.

"Let her go back on the labboard! Ting-a-ling-ling! Chow-ch-chow-chow!" The left hand began to describe circles.

"Stop the stabboard! Ting-a-ling-ling! Stop the labboard! Come ahead on the stabboard! Stop her! Let your outside turn over slow! Ting-a-ling-ling! Chow-ow-ow! Get out that head-line! *Lively* now! Come—out with your spring-line—what're you about there! Take a turn round that stump with the bight of it! Stand by that stage, now—let her go! Done with the engines, sir! Ting-a-ling-ling! Sh't! Sh't!" (trying the gauge-cocks.)

Tom went on whitewashing—paid no attention to the steamboat. Ben stared a moment and then said:

"Hi-*yi! You're* up a stump, ain't you!"

No answer. Tom surveyed his last touch with the eye of an artist, then he gave his brush another gentle sweep and surveyed the result, as before. Ben ranged up alongside of him. Tom's mouth watered for the apple, but he stuck to his work. Ben said:

"Hello, old chap, you got to work, hey?"

Tom wheeled suddenly and said:

"Why, it's you, Ben! I warn't noticing."

"Say—I'm going in a-swimming, I am. Don't you wish you could? But of course you'd druther *work*—wouldn't you? Course you would!"

Tom contemplated the boy a bit, and said:

"What do you call work?"

"Why, ain't *that* work?"

Tom resumed his whitewashing and answered carelessly:

"Well, maybe it is, and maybe it ain't. All I know is, it suits Tom Sawyer."

"Oh, come now, you don't mean to let on that you *like* it?"

The brush continued to move.

"Like it? Well, I don't see why I oughtn't to like it. Does a boy get a chance to whitewash a fence every day?"

That put the thing in a new light. Ben stopped nibbling his apple. Tom swept his brush daintily back and forth—stepped back to note the effect—added a touch here and there—criticized the effect again—Ben watching every move and getting more and more interested, more and more absorbed. Presently he said:

"Say, Tom, let *me* whitewash a little."

Tom considered, was about to consent; but he altered his mind:

"No—no—I reckon it wouldn't hardly do, Ben. You see, Aunt Polly's awful particular about this fence—right here on the street, you know—but if it was the back fence I wouldn't mind and *she* wouldn't. Yes, she's awful particular about this fence; it's got to be done very careful; I reckon there ain't one boy in a thousand, maybe two thousand, that can do it the way it's got to be done."

"No—is that so? Oh, come, now—lemme just try. Only just a little—I'd let *you*, if you was me, Tom."

"Ben, I'd like to, honest injun; but Aunt Polly—well, Jim wanted to do it, but she wouldn't let him; Sid wanted to do it, and she wouldn't let Sid. Now don't you see how I'm fixed? If you was to tackle this fence and anything was to happen to it—"

"Oh, shucks, I'll be just as careful. Now lemme try. Say—I'll give you the core of my apple."

"Well, here— No, Ben, now don't. I'm afeard—"

"I'll give you *all* of it!"

Tom gave up the brush with reluctance in his face, but alacrity in his heart. And while the late steamer *Big Missouri* worked and sweated in the sun, the retired artist sat on a barrel in the shade close by, dangled his legs, munched his apple, and planned the slaughter of more innocents. There was no lack of material; boys happened along every little while; they came to jeer, but remained to whitewash. By the time Ben was fagged out, Tom had traded the next chance to Billy Fisher for a kite, in good repair; and when *he* played out, Johnny Miller bought in for a dead rat and a string to swing it with—and so on, and so on, hour after hour. And when the middle of the afternoon came, from being a poor poverty-stricken boy in the morning, Tom was literally rolling in wealth. He had beside the things before mentioned, twelve marbles, part of a jew's-harp, a piece of blue bottle-glass to look through, a spool cannon, a key that wouldn't unlock anything, a fragment of chalk, a glass stopper of a decanter, a tin soldier, a couple of tadpoles, six firecrackers, a kitten with only one eye, a brass door-knob, a dog-collar—but no dog—the handle of a knife, four pieces of orange-peel, and a dilapidated old window-sash.

He had had a nice, good, idle time all the while—plenty of company—and the fence had three coats of whitewash on it! If he hadn't run out of whitewash, he would have bankrupted every boy in the village.

Tom said to himself that it was not such a hollow world, after all. He had discovered a great law of human action, without knowing it—namely, that in order to make a man or boy covet a thing, it is only necessary to make the thing difficult to attain. If he had been a great and wise philosopher, like the writer of this book, he would now have comprehended that Work consists of whatever a body is *obliged* to do, and that Play consists of whatever a body is not obliged to do. And this would help him to understand why constructing artificial flowers or performing on a treadmill is work, while rolling tenpins or climbing Mont Blanc is only amusement. There are wealthy gentlemen in England who drive four-horse passenger-coaches twenty or thirty miles on a daily line, in the summer, because the privilege costs them considerable money; but if they are offered wages for the service, that would turn it into work and then they would resign.

The boy mused awhile over the substantial change which had taken place in his worldly circumstances, and then wended toward headquarters to report.

(From The Adventures of Tom Sawyer)

JOHN WESLEY'S RULE

Do all the good you can,
By all the means you can,
In all the ways you can,
In all the places you can,
At all the times you can,
To all the people you can,
As long as ever you can.

RICHARD II'S DEJECTION

William Shakespeare

Let's talk of graves, of worms and epitaphs;
Make dust our paper and with rainy eyes
Write sorrow on the bosom of the earth.
Let's choose executors and talk of wills:
And yet not so, for what can we bequeath
Save our deposed bodies to the ground?
Our lands, our lives and all are Bolingbroke's,
And nothing can we call our own but death,
And that small model of the barren earth
Which serves as paste and cover to our bones.
For God's sake, let us sit upon the ground
And tell sad stories of the death of kings:
How some have been deposed; some slain in war;
Some haunted by the ghosts they have deposed;
Some poison'd by their wives; some sleeping kill'd;
All murder'd: for within the hollow crown
That rounds the mortal temples of a king
Keeps Death his court, and there the antic sits,
Scoffing his state and grinning at his pomp,
Allowing him a breath, a little scene,
To monarchize, be fear'd and kill with looks,
Infusing him with self and vain conceit,
As if this flesh which walls about our life
Were brass impregnable, and humour'd thus
Comes at the last and with a little pin
Bores through his castle wall, and farewell king!
Cover your heads and mock not flesh and blood
With solemn reverence: throw away respect,
Tradition, form and ceremonious duty,
For you have but mistook me all this while:
I live with bread like you, feel want,
Taste grief, need friends: subjected thus,
How can you say to me, I am a king?
                    (From King Richard II)

TRUST THYSELF

Ralph Waldo Emerson

Trust thyself: every heart vibrates to that iron string. . . . Who so would be a man, must be a nonconformist. He who would gather immortal palms must not be hindered by the name of goodness, but must explore if it be goodness. . . .

Insist on yourself; never imitate. Your own gift you can present every moment with the cumulative force of a whole life's cultivation; but of the adopted talent of another you have only an extemporaneous half possession. That which each can do best, none but his Maker can teach him. No man yet knows what it is, nor can, till that person has exhibited it. . . .

Nothing can bring you peace but yourself. Nothing can bring you peace but the triumph of principles.

SLEEP

William Shakespeare

Methought I heard a voice cry "Sleep no more!
Macbeth does murder sleep"—the innocent sleep,
Sleep that knits up the ravell'd sleave of care,
The death of each day's life, sore labour's bath,
Balm of hurt minds, great nature's second course,
Chief nourisher in life's feast.

(From Macbeth)

From THE BALLAD OF EAST AND WEST

Rudyard Kipling

O East is East, and West is West, and never the twain shall meet,
Till Earth and Sky stand presently at God's great Judgment Seat;
But there is neither East nor West, Border, nor Breed, nor Birth,
When two strong men stand face to face, though they come from the
    ends of earth!

628

SAMUEL JOHNSON'S VIEW ON HAPPY MARRIAGES

Boswell: Pray, Sir, do you suppose that there are fifty women in the world, with any one of whom a man may be as happy, as with any one woman in particular?

Johnson: Ay, Sir, fifty thousand.

Boswell: Then, Sir, you are not of opinion with some who imagine that certain men and certain women are made for each other; and that they cannot be happy if they miss their counterpart?

Johnson: To be sure, not, Sir. I believe marriages in general would be as happy, and often more so, if they were all made by the Lord Chancellor, upon a due consideration of characters and circumstances, without the parties having any choice in the matter.

SELF-KNOWLEDGE

Blaise Pascal

(Translator: W. F. Trotter)

It is dangerous to make man see too clearly his equality with the brutes without showing him his greatness. It is also dangerous to make him see his greatness too clearly, apart from his vileness. It is still more dangerous to leave him in ignorance of both. But it is very advantageous to show him both. Man must not think that he is on a level with the brutes or with the angels, nor must he be ignorant of both sides of his nature; but he must know both.

(From Pensées)

I–THOU

Martin Buber

The primary word *I–Thou* can be spoken only with the whole being. Concentration and fusion into the whole being can never take place through my agency, nor can it ever take place without me. I become through my relation to the *Thou;* as I become *I,* I say *Thou.*

All real living is meeting.

YOUNG AND OLD

Charles Kingsley

When all the world is young, lad,
    And all the trees are green;
And every goose a swan, lad,
    And every lass a queen;
Then hey for boot and horse, lad,
    And round the world away;
Young blood must have its course, lad,
    And every dog his day.

When all the world is old, lad,
    And all the trees are brown;
And all the sport is stale, lad,
    And all the wheels run down:
Creep home, and take your place there,
    The spent and maimed among:
God grant you find one face there
    You loved when all was young.

THE LORD IS MY SHEPHERD

Holy Bible, Psalm 23

1 The Lord is my shepherd; I shall not want.

2 He maketh me to lie down in green pastures; he leadeth me beside the still waters.

3 He restoreth my soul; he leadeth me in the paths of righteousness for his name's sake.

4 Yea, though I walk through the valley of the shadow of death, I will fear no evil; for thou art with me; thy rod and thy staff they comfort me.

5 Thou preparest a table before me in the presence of mine enemies: thou anointest my head with oil; my cup runneth over.

6 Surely goodness and mercy shall follow me all the days of my life; and I will dwell in the house of the LORD for ever.

* * *

To recommend thrift to the poor is both grotesque and insulting. It is advising a man who is starving to eat less.
—Oscar Wilde

THE UNKNOWN CITIZEN

(To Js/o7/M 378 This Marble Monument is Erected by the State)

W. H. Auden

He was found by the Bureau of Statistics to be
One against whom there was no official complaint,
And all the reports on his conduct agree
That, in the modern sense of an old-fashioned word, he was a saint,
For in everything he did he served the Greater Community.
Except for the War till the day he retired
He worked in a factory and never got fired,
But satisfied his employers, Fudge Motors Inc.
Yet he wasn't a scab or odd in his views,
For his Union reports that he paid his dues,
(Our report on his Union shows it was sound)
And our Social Psychology workers found
That he was popular with his mates and liked a drink.
The Press are convinced that he bought a paper every day
And that his reactions to advertisements were normal in every way.
Policies taken out in his name prove that he was fully insured,
And his Health-card shows he was once in hospital but left it cured.
Both Producers Research and High-Grade Living declare
He was fully sensible to the advantages of the Installment Plan
And had everything necessary to the Modern Man,
A phonograph, a radio, a car and a frigidaire.
Our researchers into Public Opinion are content
That he held the proper opinions for the time of year;
When there was peace, he was for peace; when there was war,
    he went.
He was married and added five children to the population,
Which our Eugenist says was the right number for a parent of his
    generation,
And our teachers report that he never interfered with their education.
Was he free? Was he happy? The question is absurd:
Had anything been wrong, we should certainly have heard.

A HYMN—O GOD OF EARTH AND ALTAR

G. K. Chesterton

O God of earth and altar,
   Bow down and hear our cry,
Our earthly rulers falter,
   Our people drift and die;

The walls of gold entomb us.
   The swords of scorn divide,
Take not thy thunder from us,
   But take away our pride.

From all that terror teaches,
   From lies of tongue and pen,
From all the easy speeches
   That comfort cruel men,
For sale and profanation
   Of honour and the sword,
From sleep and from damnation,
   Deliver us, good Lord!

Tie in a living tether
   The prince and priest and thrall,
Bind all our lives together,
   Smite us and save us all;
In ire and exultation
   Aflame with faith, and free,
Lift up a living nation,
   A single sword to thee.

LINCOLN'S LETTER TO MAJOR RAMSEY

Executive Mansion
October 17, 1861

My Dear Sir:
   The lady bearer of this says she has two sons who want to work.
Set them at it if possible. Wanting to work is so rare a want that it
should be encouraged.

Yours truly,
A. LINCOLN

SHALL I COMPARE THEE TO A SUMMER'S DAY?

William Shakespeare

Shall I compare thee to a summer's day?
Thou art more lovely and more temperate:
Rough winds do shake the darling buds of May,
And summer's lease hath all too short a date:
Sometimes too hot the eye of heaven shines,
And every fair form from fair sometimes declines,
By chance or nature's changing course untrimm'd;
But thy eternal summer shall not fade,
Nor lose possession of that fair thou owest;
Nor shall Death brag thou wander'st in his shade,
When in eternal lines to time thou grow'st:
  So long as men can breathe, or eyes can see,
  So long lives this, and this gives life to thee.

(From his *Sonnets*)

* * *

As a goose is not frightened by cackling nor a sheep by bleating,
so do not let the clamor of a senseless multitude alarm you.

—Epictetus

GEORGE WASHINGTON

Inscription at Mount Vernon, Virginia

Washington, the brave, the wise, the good,
Supreme in war, in council, and in peace.
Valiant without ambition, discreet without fear, confident without
  assumption.
In disaster calm; in success moderate; in all, himself.
The hero, patriot, the Christian.
The father of nations, the friend of mankind,
Who, when he had won all, renounced all, and sought in the
  bosom of his family and of nature, retirement, and in the hope
  of religion, immortality.

TO HIS COY MISTRESS

Andrew Marvell

Had we but World enough, and Time,
This coyness, Lady, were no crime.
We would sit down, and think this way
To walk, and pass our love's long day.
Thou by the Indian Ganges' side
Should'st rubies find: I by the tide
of Humber should complain. I Would
Love you ten years before the Flood:
And you should if you please refuse
Till the conversion of the Jews.
My vegetable love should grow
Vaster than empires, and more slow.
An hundred years should go to praise
Thine eyes, and on thy forehead gaze.
Two hundred to adore each breast:
But thirty thousand to the rest.
An age at least to every part,
And the last stage should show your heart.
For, Lady, you deserve this state;
Nor would I love at lower rate.

   But at my back I always hear
Time's winged chariot drawing near:
And yonder before us lie
Deserts of vast Eternity.
Thy beauty shall no more be found
Nor, in thy marble vault, shall sound
My echoing song: then worms shall try
That long preserved virginity;
And your quaint honour turn to dust;
And into ashes all my lust.
The grave's a fine and private place,
But none I think do there embrace.

   Now therefore, while the youthful hue
Sits on thy skin by morning dew,
And while thy willing soul transpires
At every pore with instant fires,
Now let us sport us while we may;
And now, like amorous birds of prey,

Rather at once our time devour,
Than languish in his slow-chapt power.
Let us roll all our strength, and all
Our sweetness, up into one ball:
And tear our pleasures with rough strife,
Through the iron gates of life.
Thus, though we cannot make our sun
Stand still, yet we will make him run.

CRITICISM

Samuel Johnson

Criticism is a study by which men grow important and formidable at very small expense. The power of invention has been conferred by nature upon few, and the labor of learning those sciences which may, by mere labor, be obtained is too great to be willingly endured; but every man can exert such judgment as he has upon the works of others; and he whom nature has made weak, and idleness keeps ignorant, may yet support his vanity by the name of Critic. . . .

This profession has one recommendation peculiar to itself, that it gives vent to malignity without real mischief. No genius was ever blasted by the breath of critics. The poison which, if confined, would have burst the heart, fumes away in empty hisses, and malice is set at ease with very little danger to merit. The Critic is the only man whose triumph is without another's pain, and whose greatness does not rise upon another's ruin.

WILLIAM FAULKNER'S RESIGNATION AS POSTMASTER

As long as I live under the capitalistic system I expect to have my life influenced by the demands of moneyed people. But I will be damned if I propose to be at the beck and call of every itinerant scoundrel who has two cents to invest in a postage stamp. This, sir, is my resignation.

LOVE'S PHILOSOPHY

Percy Bysshe Shelley

The fountains mingle with the river
And the rivers with the ocean,
The winds of heaven mix for ever
With a sweet emotion;
Nothing in the world is single,
All things by a law divine
In another's being mingle—
Why not I with thine?

See the mountains kiss high heaven,
And the waves clasp one another;
No sister flower would be forgiven
If it disdained its brother;
And the sunlight clasps the earth,
And the moonbeams kiss the sea—
What are all these kissings worth,
If thou kiss not me?

MACAULAY'S ONE LINE BOOK REVIEW OF ATTERBURY'S "A DEFENSE OF THE LETTERS OF PHALARIS"

The best book ever written by a man on the wrong side of a question of which the author was profoundly ignorant.

MY OWN EPITAPH

John Gay

Life is a jest and all things show it;
I thought so once, but now I know it.

GRADATIM

Josiah Gilbert Holland

Heaven is not reached at a single bound;
   But we build the ladder by which we rise
   From the lowly earth to the vaulted skies,
And we mount to its summit round by round.

I count this thing to be grandly true,
   That a noble deed is a step toward God,
   Lifting the soul from the common sod
To a purer air and a broader view.

We rise by things that are 'neath our feet;
   By what we have mastered of good and gain,
   By the pride deposed and the passion slain,
And the vanquished ills that we hourly meet.

We hope, we aspire, we resolve, we trust,
   When the morning calls us to life and light;
   But our hearts grow weary, and ere the night,
Our lives are trailing the sordid dust.

We hope, we resolve, we aspire, we pray,
   And we think that we mount the air on wings
   Beyond the recall of sensual things,
While our feet still cling to the heavy clay.

Wings for angels, but feet for men!
   We may borrow the wings to find the way;
   We may hope, and resolve, and aspire, and pray;
But our feet must rise, or we fall again.

Only in dreams is a ladder thrown
   From the weary earth to the sapphire walls,
   But the dreams depart, and the vision falls,
And the sleeper wakes on his pillow of stone.

Heaven is not reached at a single bound;
   But we build the ladder by which we rise
   From the lowly earth to the vaulted skies,
And we mount to its summit round by round.

LITTLE LOST PUP *

Arthur Guiterman

He was lost!—not a shade of doubt of that;
For he never barked at a slinking cat,
But stood in the square where the wind blew raw
With a drooping ear and a trembling paw
And a mournful look in his pleading eye
And a plaintive sniff at the passer-by
That begged as plain as a tongue could sue,
"O Mister! please may I follow you?"
A lorn wee waif of a tawny brown
Adrift in the roar of a heedless town.
Oh, the saddest of sights in a world of sin
Is a little lost pup with his tail tucked in!

Now he shares my board and he owns my bed,
And he fairly shouts when he hears my tread;
Then, if things go wrong, as they sometimes do,
And the world is cold and I'm feeling blue,
He asserts his right to assuage my woes
With a warm, red tongue and a nice, cold nose
And a silky head on my arm or knee
And a paw as soft as a paw can be.

When we rove the woods for a league about
He's as full of pranks as a school let out;
For he romps and frisks like a three months' colt,
And he runs me down like a thunderbolt.
Oh, the blithest of sights in the world so fair
Is a gay little pup with his tail in the air!

JUDGMENT

Anonymous

Before God's footstool to confess
A poor soul knelt, and bowed his head;
"I failed," he cried. The Master said,
"Thou didst thy best—that is success!"

WORDS FROM THE FIRST MEN ON THE MOON, NEIL A. ARMSTRONG AND EDWIN A. ALDRIN, JR., AND MICHAEL COLLINS, WHO REMAINED IN THE COMMAND SPACESHIP COLUMBIA

HOUSTON [The Mission Control center] (4 P.M.): *Eagle* [the lunar landing craft, undocked from the command ship *Columbia*], you are go for powered descent. Over. . . .

HOUSTON: Coming up one minute to ignition.

EAGLE (4:05 P.M.): Altitude about 46,000 feet, continuing to descend. Ignition about ten per cent.

HOUSTON: *Eagle*, everything's looking good here. Over. . . .

HOUSTON: We're still go. Altitude 27,000 feet.

EAGLE: Bravo on time. Throttle down better than the simulator.

HOUSTON: Roger. Altitude now 21,000 feet still looking very good. Velocity down now to 1,200 feet per second. You look great to us, *Eagle*. . . .

HOUSTON (4:12 P.M.): Seven minutes 30 seconds into the burn. Altitude 16,300 feet.

HOUSTON: We're go. Altitude 9,200 feet. You're looking great. Descent rate 129 feet per second. *Eagle*, you're looking great, coming up on nine minutes.

HOUSTON: We're now in the approach phase. Everything looking good. Altitude 5,200 feet.

EAGLE: Manual control is good.

HOUSTON: Altitude 4,200 feet. You are go for landing. Over.

EAGLE: Roger go for landing, 3,000 feet. We're go. We're go. Two thousand feet. Into the AGS 47 degrees.

HOUSTON: Roger.

HOUSTON: *Eagle*, looking great. You're go. Altitude 1,600 feet . . . 1,400 feet, still looking very good.

EAGLE: 35 degrees. 35 degrees. 750 coming down to 23; 700 feet 21 down, 33 degrees; 600 feet down to 19; 540 down to 15; 400 feet down at 9 three forward; 350 feet down at 4; 300 feet down 3½; 47 forward; on one a minute 1½ down; 270 . . . 50 down at 2½; 19 forward. Altitude velocity lights down 15 forward, 11 forward; 200 feet 4½ down 5½ down 6½ down, 5½ down, nine forward; 120 feet 100 feet 3½ down, nine forward, 5 per cent 75 feet looking good down ½, six forward.

HOUSTON: Sixty seconds.

EAGLE: Lights on; down 2½. Forward, forward 40 feet down 2½ picking up some dust; 30 feet 2½ down shadow, four forward, four forward, drifting to the right a little.

HOUSTON: Thirty seconds.

EAGLE: Contact light. Okay, engines stop. Engine arm off.

HOUSTON: We copy. You're down, Eagle.

EAGLE: Houston. Tranquillity Base here. The *Eagle* has landed. . . .

HOUSTON: Roger, Tranquillity, we copy you on the ground. You've got a bunch of guys about to turn blue. We're breathing again. Thanks a lot.

TRANQUILLITY BASE: Thank you.

HOUSTON: You're looking good here.

TRANQUILLITY BASE: A very smooth touchdown.

HOUSTON: You are stay for TL [the first step in the lunar operation]. Over.

TRANQUILLITY BASE: Roger. Stay for TL. . . .

COLUMBIA [The command spacecraft]: How do you read me?

HOUSTON: *Columbia*, he has landed Tranquillity Base. *Eagle* is at Tranquillity. I read you five by. Over.

COLUMBIA: Yes, I heard the whole thing.

HOUSTON: Well, it's a good show.

COLUMBIA: Fantastic.

TRANQUILLITY BASE: I'll second that. . . .

HOUSTON: We have an unofficial time for that touchdown of 102 hours, 45 minutes, 42 seconds and we will update that. . . .

TRANQUILLITY BASE: Houston, that may have seemed like a very long final phase but the auto targeting was taking us right into a football field-sized crater with a large number of big boulders and rocks for about one or two craters diameter around it and it required us to fly manually over the rock field to find a reasonably good area.

HOUSTON: We copy. It was beautiful from here, Tranquillity. Over.

TRANQUILLITY BASE: We'll get to the details of what's around here, but it looks like a collection of just about every shape, angularity, granularity, about every variety of rock you could find. The colors are pretty much depending on how you are looking relative to the zero phase length. There doesn't appear to be too much of a general color at all. However, it looks as though some of the rocks and boulders, of which there are quite a few in the near area—it looks as though they're going to have some interesting colors to them. Over. . . .

HOUSTON: Roger. Tranquillity. Be advised there are lots of smiling faces in this room and all over the world. Over. . . .

TRANQUILLITY BASE: Thank you, Houston, the guys that bet that we wouldn't be able to tell precisely where we are are the

640

winners today. We were a little busy worrying about program alarms and things like that in the part of the descent where we would normally be picking out our landing spot; and aside from a good look at several of the craters we came over in the final descent, I haven't been able to pick out the things on the horizon as a reference yet.

HOUSTON: Rog, Tranquillity. No sweat. We'll figure out—we'll figure out. Over.

TRANQUILLITY BASE: You might be interested to know that I don't think we noticed any difficulty at all in adapting to one-sixth G. It seems immediately natural to live in this environment. . . . [Unintelligible] . . . window, with relatively level plain cratered with a large number of craters of the 5-to-50-foot variety. And some ridges small, 20 to 30 feet high, I would guess. And literally thousands of little ones—and two-foot craters around the area. We see some angular blocks out several hundred feet in front of us that are probably two feet in size and have angular edges. There is a hill in view just about on the ground track ahead of us. Difficult to estimate, but might be a half a mile or a mile . . . I'd say the color of the local surface is very comparable to that we observed from orbit at this sun angle—about 10 degrees sun angle or that nature. It's pretty much without color. It's gray and it's very white as you look into the zero phase line. And it's considerably darker grey, more like an ashen grey, as you look out 90 degrees to the sun. Some of the surface rocks in close here that have been fractured or disturbed by the rocket engine plume are coated with this light gray on the outside. But where they have been broken, they display a dark, very dark, gray interior and it looks like it could be country basalt. . . . From the surface we could not see any stars out the window, but on my overhead patch I'm looking at the earth. It's big and bright, beautiful. Buzz [Aldrin] is going to give a try at seeing some stars through the optics. . . .

HOUSTON: We have some heart rates for Neil Armstrong [in command of the craft that landed on the moon] during that powered descent to lunar surface. At the time the burn was initiated, Armstrong's heart rate was 110. At touchdown on the lunar surface, he had a heart rate of 156 beats per minute, and the flight surgeon reports that his heart rate is now in the 90's. We do not have biomedical data on Buzz Aldrin. We have an up date on that touchdown time . . . 102 hours, 45 minutes, 40 seconds, which would have been 12 minutes, 36 seconds after initiating the powered descent. . . . . . . It appears that the spacecraft *Eagle* touched down at 799 degrees north, or just about on the lunar equator, and 23.46 degrees east longitude, which would have put it about four miles from the targeted landing point downrange. . . .

TRANQUILLITY BASE: This is the LM pilot [Buzz Aldrin]. I'd like to take this opportunity to ask every person listening in, whoever, wherever they may be, to pause for a moment and contemplate the events of the past few hours and to give thanks in his or her own way. Over. . . .

HOUSTON: We have an interesting phenomena here in the Mission Control Center, Houston, something we've never seen before. Our visual of the lunar module—our visual display of the lunar module—our visual display standing still, our velocity digitals for our Tranquillity Base now reading zero. Reverting, if we could, to the terminology of an earlier form of transportation—the railroad —what we're witnessing now is man's very first trip into space with a station-stop along the route. . . .

TRANQUILLITY BASE: I think we'll be ready to start EVA [Extra Vehicular Activity—walking on the moon] in about a half hour or so. We are beginning our EVA prep. . . .

TRANQUILLITY BASE (9:45 P.M.): Houston, Tranquillity. You'll find that the area around the ladder is in a complete dark shadow, so we're going to have some problem with TV. But I'm sure you'll see the—you'll get a picture from the lighted horizon. . . . Neil's got his antenna up now. Let's see if he comes through any better now. Okay, Houston, this is Neil [Armstrong]. How do you read?

HOUSTON: Neil, this is Houston, reading you beautifully. . . .

TRANQUILLITY BASE: Houston, this is Tranquillity. We're standing by for a cabin depress.

HOUSTON: You are go for cabin depressureization. . . .

TRANQUILLITY BASE: Okay, the vent window is clear. I remove lever from the engine cover. . . . Lock system, decks, exit check, blue locks are checked, lock locks, red locks, perch locks, and on this side the perch locks and lock locks—both sides, body locks, and the calm. . . .

HOUSTON: In the control center a clock has been set up to record the operating time on Neil's life support system. EVA will be counted from that time.

TRANQUILLITY BASE: Cabin repress closed. Now come the gymnastics. Air pressure going toward zero. Standby LM suit circuit 36 to 43. That's verified. FIT GA pressure about 4.5, 4.75 and coming down. We'll open the hatch when we get to zero. Do you want to bring down one of your visors now or leave them up? We can put them down if we need them. We have visor down.

HOUSTON (10:33 P.M.): Coming up on five minutes of operation of Neil Armstrong's portable life support system now. (10:37 P.M. Neil, this is Houston, what's your status on hatch opening?
TRANQUILLITY BASE: Everything is go here. We're just waiting for the cabin pressure to bleed to a low enough pressure to open the hatch. It's about .1 on our gauge now. I'd hate to tug on that thing. Alternative would be to open that one too.
HOUSTON: We're seeing a relatively static pressure on your cabin. Do you think you can open the hatch at this pressure?
TRANQUILLITY BASE: We're going to try it. The hatch is coming open. [Aldrin] Hold it from going closed and I'll get the valve turner. I'd better get up first.
ALDRIN: Your window cleared yet?
ARMSTRONG: It was, yeah.
ALDRIN: Mine hasn't cleared yet.
[The following is a conversation between Armstrong and Aldrin:] Bical pump secondary circuit breaker open. Back to lean—this way. Radar circuit breakers open. Well, I'm looking head-on at it. I'll get it. Okay. My antenna's out. Right. Okay, now we're ready to hook up the LEC. Okay. Now we need to hook this. Your visor. Yep. Your back is up against the perch. Now you're clear. Over toward me. Straight down, to your left a little bit. Plenty of room. You're lined up nicely.

Toward me a little bit. Down. Okay. Now you're clear. You're catching the first hinge. The what hinge? All right, move. Roll to your left. Okay, now you're clear. You're lined up on the platform. Put your left foot to the right a little bit. Okay that's good. More left. Good.
ARMSTRONG: Okay, Houston, I'm on the porch. . . .
ALDRIN: Halt where you are a minute, Neil.
ARMSTRONG AND ALDRIN: Okay. Everything's nice and straight in here. Okay. can you pull the door open a little more? Right.
HOUSTON: We're getting a picture on TV.
ALDRIN: You've got a good picture, huh?
HOUSTON: There's a great deal of contrast in it and currently it's upside down on monitor. But we can make out a fair amount of detail.
ARMSTRONG: Okay, will you verify the position, the opening I ought to have on the camera.
HOUSTON: The what? We can see you coming down the ladder now.
ARMSTRONG: Okay. I just checked getting back up to that first

643

step. It didn't collapse too far. But it's adequate to get back up. It's a pretty good little jump. I'm at the foot of the ladder. The LM foot beds are only depressed in the surface about one or two inches, although the surface appears to be very, very fine-grained as you get close to it. It's almost like a powder. It's very fine. I'm going to step off the LM now.

That's one small step for a man, one giant leap for mankind.

The surface is fine and powdery. I can pick it up loosely with my toe. It does adhere in fine layers like powdered charcoal to the sole and sides of my boots. I only go in a small fraction of an inch, maybe an eighth of an inch but I can see the footprints of my boots and the treads in the fine sandy particles.

There seems to be no difficulty in moving around this and we suspect that it's even perhaps easier than the simulations of 1/6 G that we performed in various simulations on the ground. Actually no trouble to walk around.

The descent engine did not leave a crater of any size. It has about one foot clearance on the ground. We're essentially on a very level place here. I can see some evidence of rays emanating from the descent engine, but a very insignificant amount.

Okay, Buzz, are we ready to bring down the camera?

ALDRIN: I'm all ready. I think it's squared away and in good shape. But you'll have to play out all the LEC. Looks like it's coming out nice and evenly.

It's quite dark here in the shadow and a little hard for me to see if I have a good footing. I'll work my way over into the sunlight here without looking directly into the sun.

ARMSTRONG: Looking up at the LM, I'm standing directly in the shadow now looking up at . . . in the windows I can see everything quite clearly. The light is sufficiently bright backlighted into the front of the LM that everything is clearly visible.

I'll step out and take some of my first pictures here.

ALDRIN: Are you going to get the contingency sample [from moon's surface]? Okay. That's good.

ARMSTRONG: The contingency sample is down and it's up. Like it's a little difficult to dig through the crust. It's very interesting. It's a very soft surface but here and there where I plug with the contingency sample collector I run into very hard surface but it appears to be very cohesive material of the same sort. I'll try to get a rock in here.

HOUSTON: Oh, that looks beautiful from here, Neil.

ARMSTRONG: It has a stark beauty all its own. It's like much of the high desert of the United States. It's different but it's very pretty out here. Be advised that a lot of the rock samples out here, the hard rock samples have what appears to be vesicles on the surface. This has been about six or eight inches into the surface. It's easy to push on it. I'm sure I could push it in farther, but it's hard for me to bend down farther than that.

ALDRIN: Ready for me to come out?

ARMSTRONG: Yeah. Just stand by for a second, I'll move this over the handrail.

ALDRIN: Okay?

ARMSTRONG: All right, that's got it. Are you ready?

ALDRIN: All set. . . .

ALDRIN: How far are my feet from the . . .

ARMSTRONG: You're right at the edge of the porch.

ALDRIN: Small little foot movement. Porch. Arching of the back . . . without any trouble at all. Now I want to back up and partially close the hatch—making sure not to lock it on my way out.

ARMSTRONG: Good thought.

ALDRIN: That's our home for the next couple of hours; we want to take care of it. I'm on the top step. It's a very simple matter to hop down from one step to the next.

ARMSTRONG: Yes, I found that to be very comfortable, and walking is also very comfortable, Houston. You've got three more steps and then a long one.

ALDRIN: I'm going to leave that one foot up there and both hands down to about the fourth rung up.

ARMSTRONG: A little more. About one inch. There you got it. That's a good step.

ALDRIN: About a three footer. Beautiful view.

ARMSTRONG: Ain't that somethin'? . . .

HOUSTON (1:37 P.M.): You're cleared for take-off.

TRANQUILLITY BASE: Roger. Understand. We're No. 1 on the runway.

HOUSTON (1:38 P.M.): We have confirmation on the ground that the ascent propulsion system propellant has been pressurized. . . .

TRANQUILLITY BASE: Okay. I assume we're go for lift-off and will proceed with the ascent feeds.

HOUSTON (1:44 P.M.): A little less than ten minutes here. Everything looks good. (1:50 P.M.) *Eagle*, you're looking good to us. We'll continue to monitor now at 3 minutes 12 seconds away from ignition as crew of Eagle goes through their pre-launch checklist. Guidance reports both navigation systems on *Eagle* are looking good.

TRANQUILLITY BASE: Nine, eight, seven, six, five, first stage engine on ascent. Proceed. Beautiful. 26, 36 feet per second up.

Little pitch over, very smooth, very quiet ride. There's that one crater down there.

HOUSTON (1:54 P.M.): A thousand feet high, 80 feet per second vertical rise. Twenty-six hundred feet altitude. *Eagle*, Houston. One minute and you're looking good. A hundred thirty feet vertical rise rate.

EAGLE: A little bit of slow wallowing back and forth. Not very much thruster activity.

HOUSTON: Mighty fine. *Eagle*, you're go at three minutes. Everything's looking good.

EAGLE: Right. This is . . . This is H dot max now. Right down U.S. 1.

HOUSTON: Height's now approaching 32,000 feet. *Eagle*, four minutes. You're going right down the track. Everything is great.

EAGLE: Horizontal velocity approaching 2,500 feet per second. We've got Sabine now to our right now.

HOUSTON: Some 120 miles to go until insertion [with command ship *Columbia*]. . . .

EAGLE: *Eagle* is back in orbit, having left Tranquillity Base, and leaving behind a replica from our Apollo patch with an olive branch.

HOUSTON: Roger. We copy. The whole world is proud of you. (3:26 P.M.) Less than a minute away from acquisition of the spacecraft *Columbia* coming around on the near side of the moon, on the 26th revolution. Some three minutes, 11 seconds away from *Eagle*'s appearance on the lunar frontside. We have AOS [Acquisition of Signal] of the spacecraft *Columbia*. Range between *Eagle* and *Columbia* now showing 67.5 nautical miles, Range rate—closure rate—121 feet per second. . . .

EAGLE (4:31 P.M.): Mike [Collins in *Columbia*], if you want our target delta V, I'll give it to you.

COLUMBIA: Ready to copy.

EAGLE: 127 03 3082 plus 22.7 plus 1.1, minus 10.6.

HOUSTON (5:23 P.M.): Less than a minute away from acquisition of the spacecraft *Columbia*. Hopefully flying within a few feet of it will be *Eagle*. Docking should take place about ten minutes from now according to the flight plan. However, this is a crew-option matter. . . .

EAGLE (5:27 P.M.): Okay, Mike. I'll try to get positioned here. Then you got it.

COLUMBIA: How did the roll attitude look? I'll stop. As a matter of fact, I could stop right here, if you like that.

EAGLE (5:30 P.M.): I'm not going to do a thing, Mike. I'm just letting her hold in attitude.

EAGLE (5:36 P.M.): We're all yours, *Columbia*.

COLUMBIA: Okay. . . .

HOUSTON (7:20 P.M.): Hello *Eagle*, Houston. Do you read?

COLUMBIA: Read you loud and clear. We're all three back inside. The hatch is installed. We're ready to . . . Everything's going well.

> (July 21 and 22, 1969)
> (*The historic voyage to the moon terminated with a successful splashdown in the Pacific Ocean on July 24 at 12:50 P.M., Eastern daylight time, 950 miles southwest of Hawaii, and 11 miles from the prime recovery ship, the U.S. aircraft carrier Hornet.*)

CHEERFULNESS

Anonymous

I'm glad the sky is painted blue;
　And the earth is painted green;
And such a lot of nice fresh air
　All sandwiched in between.

TO THE VIRGINS TO MAKE MUCH OF TIME

Robert Herrick

Gather ye rosebuds while ye may,
　Old Time is still a-flying;
And this same flower that smiles today,
　Tomorrow will be dying.

The glorious lamp of heaven, the sun,
　　The higher he's a-getting,
The sooner will his race be run,
　　And nearer he's to setting.

That age is best which is the first,
　　When youth and blood are warmer;
But being spent, the worse and worst
　　Times still succeed the former.

Then be not coy, but use your time,
　　And while ye may, go marry;
For, having lost but once your prime,
　　You may forever tarry.

"LORD, MAKE ME AN INSTRUMENT OF YOUR PEACE"

St. Francis of Assisi

Lord, make me an instrument of Your peace; where there is hatred, let me sow love; where there is injury, pardon; where there is discord, union; where there is doubt, faith; where there is despair, hope; where there is darkness, light; and where there is sadness, joy.

O Divine Master, grant that I may not so much seek to be consoled as to console, to be understood as to understand, to be loved as to love; for it is in giving that we receive, it is in pardoning that we are pardoned, and it is in dying that we are born to eternal life

THE BETTER PATH

Holy Bible, Ecclesiastes 7:1-5

A good name is better than precious ointment; and the day of death better than the day of one's birth. It is better to go to the house of mourning, than to go to the house of feasting: for that is the end of all men; and the living will lay it to his heart. Sorrow is better than laughter: for by the sadness of the countenance the heart is made better. The heart of the wise is in the house of mourning; but the heart of fools is in the house of mirth. It is better to hear the rebuke of the wise, than for a man to hear the song of fools.

THE MODERN HIAWATHA

Anonymous

He killed the noble Mudjokivis.
Of the skin he made him mittens,
Made them with the fur side inside,
Made them with the skin side outside.
He, to get the warm side inside,
Put the inside skin outside;
He, to get the cold side outside,
Put the warm side fur side inside.
That's why he put the fur side inside,
Why he put the skin side outside,
Why he turned them inside outside.

RUMORS

Reginald Arkell

Actual evidence I have none,
But my aunt's charwoman's sister's son
Heard a policeman, on his beat,
Say to a housemaid in Downing Street
That he had a brother, who had a friend,
Who knew when the war was going to end.

WHO LOVE THE RAIN

Frances Wells Shaw

Who loves the rain,
And loves his home,
And looks on life with quiet eyes,
  Him will I follow through the storm;
  And at his hearth-fire keep me warm;
Nor hell nor heaven shall that soul surprise,
Who loves the rain,
And loves his home,
And looks on life with quiet eyes.

THE HOUSE BEAUTIFUL

Anonymous

The Crown of the house is Godliness.
The Beauty of the house is Order.
The Glory of the house is Hospitality.
The Blessing of the house is Contentment.

COURAGE

Mark Twain

Courage is resistance to fear, mastery of fear—not absence of fear. Except a creature be part coward it is not a compliment to say it is brave; it is merely a loose misapplication of the word. Consider the flea!—incomparably the bravest of all the creatures of God, if ignorance of fear were courage. Whether you are asleep or awake he will attack you, caring nothing for the fact that in bulk and strength you are to him as are the massed armies of the earth to a sucking child; he lives both day and night and all days and nights in the very lap of peril and the immediate presence of death, and yet is no more afraid than is the man who walks the streets of a city that was

threatened by an earthquake ten centuries before. When we speak of
Clive, Nelson and Putnam as men who "didn't know what fear was,"
we ought always to add the flea—and put him at the head of the
procession.

IN ALL THESE TURNING LIGHTS I FIND NO CLUE

Maxwell Anderson

*The following is the conclusion of the play "Winterset." Miriamne
and Mio, poor young lovers, have just been murdered by gangsters,
Miriamne deliberately exposing herself to the murderer's gun.
Esdras, a venerable rabbi and Miriamne's father, witnessed the crime.*

> ESDRAS: Miriamne—Miriamne—yes, and Mio,
> one breath shall call you now—forgive us both—
> forgive this ancient evil of the earth
> that brought you here—
> GARTH: Why must she be a fool?
> ESDRAS: Well, they were wiser than you and I. To die
> when you are young and untouched, that's beggary
> to a miser of years, but the devils locked in synod
> shake and are daunted when men set their lives
> at hazard for the heart's love, and lose. And these,
> who were yet children, will weigh more than all
> a city's elders when the experiment
> is reckoned up in the end. Oh Miriamne,
> and Mio—Mio, my son—know this where you lie,
> this is the glory of earthborn men and women,
> not to cringe, never to yield, but standing,
> take defeat implacable and defiant,
> die unsubmitting. I wish that I'd died so,
> long ago; before you're old you'll wish
> that you had died as they have. On this star,
> in this hard star-adventure, knowing not
> what the fires mean to right and left, not whether
> a meaning was intended or presumed,
> man can stand up, and look out blind, and say:
> in all these turning lights I find no clue,
> only a masterless night, and in my blood

no certain answer, yet is my mind my own,
yet is my heart a cry toward something dim
in distance, which is higher than I am
and makes me emperor of the endless dark
even in seeking! What odds and ends of life
men may live otherwise, let them live, and then
go out, as I shall go, and you. Our part
is only to bury them. Come, take her up.
They must not lie here.

FRIENDSHIP IS LOVE WITHOUT HIS WINGS

Lord Byron

Why should my anxious breast repine,
  Because my youth is fled?
Days of delight may still be mine;
  Affection is not dead.
In tracing back the years of youth,
One firm record, one lasting truth
  Celestial consolation brings;
Bear it, ye breezes, to the seat
Where first my heart responsive beat,—
  "Friendship is Love without his wings!"

EXCEPT THE LORD BUILD THE HOUSE

Holy Bible, Psalm 127

Except the Lord build the house, they labor in vain that build it; except the Lord keep the city, the watch waketh but in vain.

It is vain for you to rise up early, to sit up late, to eat the bread of sorrows: for so he giveth his beloved sleep.

Lo, children are an heritage of the Lord: and the fruit of the womb is his reward.

As arrows are in the hand of a mighty man; so are children of the youth.

Happy is the man that hath his quiver full of them: they shall not be ashamed, but they shall speak with the enemies in the gate.

THE LIGHT OF OTHER DAYS

Thomas Moore

Oft in the stilly night
  Ere slumber's chain has bound me,
Fond Memory brings the light
  Of other days around me:
    The smiles, the tears,
    Of boyhood's years,
  The words of love then spoken;
    The eyes that shone,
    Now dimmed and gone,
  The cheerful hearts now broken!
Thus in the stilly night
  Ere slumber's chain has bound me,
Sad Memory brings the light
  Of other days around me.

When I remember all
  The friends so linked together
I've seen around me fall
  Like leaves in wintry weather,
    I feel like one
    Who treads alone
  Some banquet-hall deserted,
    Whose lights are fled,
    Whose garlands dead,
  And all but he departed!
Thus in the stilly night
  Ere slumber's chain has bound me,
Sad Memory brings the light
  Of other days around me.

TRUTH, THE INVINCIBLE

William Cullen Bryant

Truth crushed to earth shall rise again,—
The eternal years of God are hers;
But Error, wounded, writhes with pain,
And dies among his worshippers.

A TOWN'S TRIBUTE TO ITS FRIEND

William Allen White

The other day in Emporia [Kansas], the longest funeral procession that has formed in ten years followed the Rev. John Jones three long miles in the hot July sun out to Dry Creek Cemetery. Now, a funeral procession may mean little or much. When a rich and powerful man dies, the people play politics and attend his funeral for various reasons. But here was the body of a meek, gentle little old man—a man "without purse or scrip." It won't take twenty minutes to settle his estate in probate court. He was a preacher of the gospel—but preachers have been buried before this in Emporia without much show of sorrow.

The reason so many people lined up behind the hearse that held the kind old man's mortality was simple: they loved him. He devoted his life to helping people. In a very simple way, without money or worldly power, he gave of the gentleness of his heart to all around him. . . . When others gave money—which was of their store—he gave prayers and hard work and an inspiring courage. He helped. In his sphere he was a power. And so when he lay down to sleep hundreds of friends trudged out to bid him good-by with moist eyes and with cramped throats to wish him sweet slumber.

GOD AND THE SOLDIER

God and the soldier
All men adore
In time of trouble,
And no more;
For when war is over
And all things righted,
God is neglected—
The old soldier slighted.

(Said to have been found on an old stone sentry-box at Gibraltar. Sometimes the lines are adapted to read "God and the doctor.")

ON THE COUNTESS OF PEMBROKE

William Browne

Underneath this sable hearse
Lies the subject of all verse:
Sidney's sister, Pembroke's mother:
Death, ere thou hast killed another,
Fair, and learn'd, and good as she,
Time shall throw a dart at thee.

AN AMERICAN

Daniel Webster

I was born an American; I will live an American; I shall die an American; and I intend to perform the duties incumbent upon me in that character to the end of my career. I mean to do this with absolute disregard of personal consequences. What are the personal consequences? What is the individual man, with all the good or evil that may betide him, in comparison with the good or evil which may befall a great country, and in the midst of great transactions which concern that country's fate? Let the consequences be what they will, I am careless. No man can suffer too much, and no man can fall too soon, if he suffer, or if he fall, in the defense of the liberties and constitution of his country.

(July 17, 1850)

WHAT CAN I DO?

Horace Traubel

What can I do? I can talk out when others are silent. I can say man when others say money. I can stay up when others are asleep. I can keep on working when others have stopped to play. I can give life big meanings when others give life little meanings. I can say love when others say hate. I can say every man when others say one man. I can try events by a hard test when others try it by an easy test.

What can I do? I can give myself to life when other men refuse themselves to life.

AGAINST OBLIVION

Percy Bysshe Shelley

Peace, peace! he is not dead, he doth not sleep—
He hath awaken'd from the dream of life—
'Tis we, who, lost in stormy visions, keep
With phantoms an unprofitable strife,
And in mad trance strike with our spirit's knife
Invulnerable nothings.—*We* decay
Like corpses in a charnel; fear and grief
Convulse us and consume us day by day,
And cold hopes swarm like worms within our living clay.

He has outsoar'd the shadow of our night;
Envy and calumny, and hate and pain,
And that unrest which men miscall delight,
Can touch him not and torture not again;
From the contagion of the world's slow stain
He is secure, and now can never mourn
A heart grown cold, a head grown grey in vain;
Nor, when the spirit's self has ceased to burn,
With sparkless ashes load an unlamented urn. . . .

He is made one with Nature; there is heard
His voice in all her music, from the moan
Of thunder, to the song of night's sweet bird;
He is a presence to be felt and known
In darkness and in light, from herb and stone,
Spreading itself where'er that Power may move
Which has withdrawn its being to its own;
Which wields the world with never-wearied love,
Sustains it from beneath, and kindles it above.

He is a portion of the loveliness
Which once he made more lovely; he doth bear
His part, while the one Spirit's plastic stress
Sweeps through the dull dense world, compelling there
All new successions to the forms they wear;
Torturing th' unwilling dross that checks its flight
To its own likeness, as each mass may bear;
And bursting in its beauty and its might
From trees and beasts and men into the Heaven's light.

The splendours of the firmament of time
May be eclipsed but are extinguish'd not;
Like stars to their appointed height they climb,
And death is a low mist which cannot blot
The brightness it may veil. When lofty thought
Lifts a young heart above its mortal lair,
And love and life contend in it, for what
Shall be its earthly doom, the dead live there
And move like winds of light on dark and stormy air. . . .

The One remains, the many change and pass;
Heaven's light for ever shines, Earth's shadows fly;
Life, like a dome of many-colour'd glass,
Stains the white radiance of Eternity,
Until Death tramples it to fragments.—Die,
If thou wouldst be with that which thou dost seek!
Follow where all is fled!—Rome's azure sky,
Flowers, ruins, statues, music, words, are weak
The glory they transfuse with fitting truth to speak. . . .

The breath whose might I have invoked in song
Descends on me; my spirit's bark is driven
Far from the shore, far from the trembling throng
Whose sails were never to the tempest given;
The massy earth and sphered skies are riven!
I am borne darkly, fearfully, afar;
Whilst burning through the inmost veil of Heaven,
The soul of Adonais, like a star,
Beacons from the abode where the Eternal are.

                                        (From Adonais)

TO BE MISUNDERSTOOD

Ralph Waldo Emerson

Misunderstood! It is a right fool's word. Is it so bad then to be misunderstood? Pythagoras was misunderstood, and Socrates and Jesus, and Luther, and Copernicus, and Galileo and Newton and every pure and wise spirit that ever took flesh. To be great is to be misunderstood.

ACRES OF DIAMONDS

Russell H. Conwell

When going down the Tigris and Euphrates rivers many years ago with a party of English travelers I found myself under the direction of an old Arab guide whom we hired up at Bagdad, and I have often thought how that guide resembled our barbers in certain mental characteristics. He thought that it was not only his duty to guide us down those rivers, and do what he was paid for doing, but also to entertain us with stories curious and weird, ancient and modern, strange and familiar. Many of them I have forgotten, and I am glad I have, but there is one I shall never forget. . . .

The old guide told me that there once lived not far from the River Indus an ancient Persian by the name of Ali Hafed. He said that Ali Hafed owned a very large farm, that he had orchards, grain-fields, and gardens; that he had money at interest, and was a wealthy and contented man. He was contented because he was wealthy, and wealthy because he was contented. One day there visited that old Persian farmer one of those ancient Buddhist priests, one of the wise men of the East. He sat down by the fire and told the old farmer how this world of ours was made. He said that this world was once a mere bank of fog and that the Almighty thrust His finger into this bank of fog, and began slowly to move His finger around, increasing the speed until at last He whirled this bank of fog into a solid ball of fire. Then it went rolling through the universe, burning its way through other banks of fog, and condensed the moisture without, until it fell in floods of rain upon its hot surface, and cooled the outward crust. Then the internal fires bursting outward through the crust threw up the mountains and hills, the valleys, the plains and prairies of this wonderful world of ours. If this internal molten mass came bursting out and cooled very quickly it became granite; less quickly copper, less quickly silver, less quickly gold, and, after gold, diamonds were made.

Said the old priest, "A diamond is a congealed drop of sunlight." Now that is literally scientifically true, that a diamond is an actual deposit of carbon from the sun. The old priest told Ali Hafed that if he had one diamond the size of his thumb he could purchase the county, and if he had a mine of diamonds he could place his children upon thrones through the influence of their great wealth.

Ali Hafed heard all about diamonds, how much they were

worth, and went to his bed that night a poor man. He had not lost anything, but he was poor because he was discontented, and discontented because he feared he was poor. He said, "I want a mine of diamonds," and he lay awake all night.

Early in the morning he sought out the priest. I know by experience that a priest is very cross when awakened early in the morning, and when he shook the old priest out of his dreams, Ali Hafed said to him:

"Will you tell me where I can find diamonds?"

"Diamonds! What do you want with diamonds?" "Why, I wish to be immensely rich." "Well, then, go along and find them. That is all you have to do; go and find them, and then you have them." "But I don't know where to go." "Well, if you will find a river that runs through white sand, between high mountains, in those white sands you will always find diamonds." "I don't believe there is any such river." "Oh, yes, there are plenty of them. All you have to do is to go and find them, and then you have them." Said Ali Hafed, "I will go."

So he sold his farm, collected his money, left his family in charge of a neighbor, and away he went in search of diamonds. He began his search, very properly to my mind, at the Mountains of the Moon. Afterwards he came around into Palestine, and then wandered on into Europe, and at last when his money was all spent and he was in rags, wretchedness, and poverty, he stood on the shore of that bay at Barcelona, in Spain, when a great tidal wave came rolling in between the pillars of Hercules, and the poor, afflicted, suffering, dying man could not resist the awful temptation to cast himself into that incoming tide, and he sank beneath its foaming crest, never to rise in this life again. . . .

The man who purchased Ali Hafed's farm one day led his camel into the garden to drink, and as that camel put its nose into the shallow water of that garden brook, Ali Hafed's successor noticed a curious flash of light from the white sands of the stream. He pulled out a black stone having an eye of light reflecting all the hues of the rainbow. He took the pebble into the house and put it on the mantel which covers the central fires, and forgot all about it.

A few days later this same old priest came in to visit Ali Hafed's successor, and the moment he opened that drawing-room door he saw that flash of light on the mantel, and he rushed up to it, and shouted: "Here is a diamond! Has Ali Hafed returned?" "Oh no, Ali Hafed has not returned, and that is not a diamond. That is nothing but a stone we found right out here in our own garden."

"But," said the priest, "I tell you I know a diamond when I see it. I know positively that is a diamond."

Then together they rushed out into that old garden and stirred up the white sands with their fingers, and lo! there came up other more beautiful and valuable gems than the first. "Thus," said the guide to me, and, friends, it is historically true, "was discovered the diamond-mine of Golconda, the most magnificent diamond-mine in all the history of mankind, excelling the Kimberley itself. The Kohinoor, and the Orloff of the crown jewels of England and Russia, the largest on earth, came from that mine."

When that old Arab guide told me the second chapter of his story, he then took off his Turkish cap and swung it around in the air again to get my attention to the moral. Those Arab guides have morals to their stories, although they are not always moral. As he swung his hat, he said to me, "Had Ali Hafed remained at home and dug in his own cellar, or underneath his own wheatfields, or in his own garden, instead of wretchedness, starvation, and death by suicide in a strange land, he would have had 'acres of diamonds.' For every acre of that old farm, yes, every shovelful, afterwards revealed gems which since have decorated the crowns of monarchs."

When he added the moral to his story I saw why he had reserved it for "his particular friends." But I did not tell him I could see it. It was that mean old Arab's way of going around a thing like a lawyer, to say indirectly what he did not dare say directly, that "in his private opinion there was a certain young man then traveling down the Tigris River that might better be at home in America."

* * * *

Let every man or woman here, if you never hear me again, remember this, that if you wish to be great at all, you must begin where you are and what you are—now. He that can give to his city any blessing, he who can be a good citizen while he lives here, he that can make better homes, he that can be a blessing whether he works in a shop or sits behind the counter or keeps house, whatever be his life, he who would be great anywhere must first be great in his own town.

* * *

Be thine own palace, or the world's thy gaol.—John Donne

LINCOLN ON SWAPPING HORSES

I have not permitted myself, gentlemen, to conclude that I am the best man in the country, but I am reminded in this connection of an old Dutch farmer who remarked it was not best to swap horses while crossing a stream.

(June 9, 1864)

HE HEARS WITH GLADDENED HEART THE THUNDER

Robert Louis Stevenson

He hears with gladdened heart the thunder
   Peal, and loves the falling dew;
He knows the earth above and under—
   Sits and is content to view.

He sits beside the dying ember,
   God for hope and man for friend,
Content to see, glad to remember,
   Expectant of the certain end.

INSCRIPTION ON THE CHRIST OF THE ANDES

(Erected on the Chile-Argentina Border)

Sooner shall these mountains crumble into dust
than the people of Argentina and Chile break the
peace they have sworn to maintain at the feet of
Christ the Redeemer

OLD ENGLISH PRAYER

Anonymous

Take time to work—
    It is the price of success.
Take time to think—
    It is the source of power.
Take time to play—
    It is the secret of perpetual youth.
Take time to read—
    It is the fountain of wisdom.
Take time to be friendly—
    It is the road to happiness.
Take time to dream—
    It is hitching your wagon to a star.
Take time to love and to be loved—
    It is the privilege of the gods.
Take time to look around—
    It is too short a day to be selfish.
Take time to laugh—
    It is the music of the soul.

JEAN

Robert Burns

Of a' the airts the wind can blaw,
    I dearly like the west,
For there the bonnie lassie lives,
    The lassie I lo'e best:
There wild woods grow, and rivers row
    And monie a hill between;
But day and night my fancy's flight
    Is ever wi' my Jean.

I see her in the dewy flowers,
    I see her sweet and fair:
I hear her in the tunefu' birds,
    I hear her charm the air:

There's not a bonnie flower that springs
    By fountain, shaw, or green;
There's not a bonnie bird that sings,
    But minds me o' my Jean.

THE NIGHT HAS A THOUSAND EYES

F. W. Bourdillon

The night has a thousand eyes,
And the day but one;
Yet the light of the bright world dies
With the dying sun.

The mind has a thousand eyes,
And the heart but one;
Yet the light of a whole life dies
When love is done.

*   *   *

An expert is one who knows more and more about less and less.
        —Nicholas Murray Butler

I WILL LIFT UP MINE EYES UNTO THE HILLS

Holy Bible, Psalm 121

1 I will lift up mine eyes unto the hills, from whence cometh my help.

2 My help cometh from the Lord, which made heaven and earth.

3 He will not suffer thy foot to be moved: he that keepeth thee will not slumber.

4 Behold, he that keepeth Israel shall neither slumber nor sleep.

5 The Lord is thy keeper: the Lord is thy shade upon thy right hand.

6 The sun shall not smite thee by day, nor the moon by night.

7 The Lord shall preserve thee from all evil: he shall preserve thy soul.

8 The Lord shall preserve thy going out and thy coming in from this time forth, and even for evermore.

NEVER THE SPIRIT WAS BORN

Bhagavad Gita

(TRANSLATOR: Sir Edwin Arnold)

Never the spirit was born;
the spirit shall cease to be never;
Never was time it was not; End
and Beginning are dreams!
Birthless and deathless and changeless
remaineth the spirit for ever;
Death hath not touched it at all,
dead though the house of it seems!
Nay, but as when one layeth
his worn-out robes away,
And, taking new ones, sayeth,
"These will I wear today!"
So putteth by the spirit
lightly its garb of flesh,
And passeth to inherit
a residence afresh.

LITTLE BUTTERCUP

W. S. Gilbert

For I'm called Little Buttercup—dear Little Buttercup,
    Though I could never tell why,
But still I'm called Buttercup—poor Little Buttercup,
    Sweet Little Buttercup I!

I've snuff and tobaccy, and excellent jacky,
    I've scissors, and watches, and knives;
I've ribbons and laces to set off the faces
    Of pretty young sweethearts and wives.

I've treacle and toffee, I've tea and I've coffee,
    Soft tommy and succulent chops;
I've chickens and conies, and pretty polonies.
    And excellent peppermint drops.

Then buy of your Buttercup—dear Little Buttercup;
    Sailors should never be shy;
So, buy of your Buttercup—poor Little Buttercup;
    Come, of your Buttercup buy!

THE BLADES OF GRASS

Stephen Crane

In Heaven,
Some little blades of grass
Stood before God.
"What did you do?"
Then all save one of the little blades
Began eagerly to relate
The merits of their lives.
This one stayed a small way behind,
Ashamed.
Presently, God said,
"And what did you do?"
The little blade answered, "Oh, my Lord,
Memory is bitter to me,
For, if I did good deeds,
I know not of them."
Then God, in all His splendor,
Arose from His throne,
"Oh, best little blade of grass!" He said.

SPARTACUS TO THE GLADIATORS AT CAPUA

E. Kellogg

Ye call me chief; and ye do well to call him chief who, for twelve long years, has met upon the arena every shape of man or beast the broad Empire of Rome could furnish, and who never yet lowered his arm. If there be one among you who can say that ever, in public fight or private brawl, my actions did belie my tongue, let him stand forth and say it. If there be three in all your company dare face me on the bloody sands, let them come on. And yet I was not always thus—a hired butcher, a savage chief of still more savage men!

My ancestors came from old Sparta, and settled among the vine-clad rocks and citron groves of Cyrasella. My early life ran quiet as the brooks by which I sported; and when, at noon, I gathered the sheep beneath the shade, and played upon the shepherd's flute, there was a friend, the son of a neighbor, to join me in the pastime. We led our flocks in the same pasture, and partook together our rustic meal.

One evening, after the sheep were folded, and we were all seated beneath the myrtle which shaded our cottage, my grandsire, an old man, was telling of Marathon and Leuctra; and how, in ancient times, a little band of Spartans, in a defile of the mountains, had withstood a whole army. I did not then know what war was; but my cheeks burned, I knew not why, and I clasped the knees of that venerable man until my mother, parting the hair from off my forehead, kissed my throbbing temples, and bade me go to rest, and think no more of those old tales and savage wars. That very night the Romans landed on our coast. I saw the breast that had nourished me trampled by the hoof of the war-horse; the bleeding body of my father flung amid the blazing rafters of our dwelling!

Today I killed a man in the arena; and when I broke his helmet-clasps, behold! he was my friend. He knew me, smiled faintly, gasped, and died—the same sweet smile upon his lips that I had marked when, in adventurous boyhood, we scaled the lofty cliff to pluck the first ripe grapes and bear them home in childish triumph! I told the pretor that the dead man had been my friend, generous and brave; and I begged him that I might bear away the body, to burn it on the funeral pile, and mourn over its ashes. Ay! upon my knees, amid the dust and blood of the arena, I begged that poor boon, while all the assembled maids and matrons, and the holy virgins they call Vestals, and the rabble shouted in derision, deeming it rare sport, forsooth, to see Rome's fiercest gladiator turn pale and tremble at sight of that piece of bleeding clay! And the pretor drew back as if I were pollution, and sternly said—"Let the carrion rot; there are no noble men but Romans!" And so, fellow-gladiators, must you, and so must I, die like dogs.

O Rome! Rome! thou hast been a tender nurse to me. Ay! thou has given to that poor, gentle, timid shepherd-lad, who never knew a harsher tone than a flute-note, muscles of iron and a heart of flint; taught him to drive the sword through a plaited mail and links of rugged brass, and warm it in the marrow of his foe:—to gaze into the glaring eye-balls of the fierce Numidian lion even as a boy upon a laughing girl! And he shall pay thee back, until the yellow Tiber is red as frothing wine, and in its deepest ooze thy life-blood lies curdled.

Ye stand here now like giants, as ye are! The strength of brass is in your toughened sinews; but tomorrow some Roman Adonis, breathing sweet perfume from his curly locks, shall with his lily fingers pat your red brawn, and bet his sesterces upon your blood. Hark! hear ye yon lion roaring in his den? 'Tis three days since he tasted flesh; but tomorrow he shall break his fast upon yours—and a dainty meal for him ye will be!

If ye are beasts, then stand here like fat oxen, waiting for the butcher's knife! If ye are men—follow me! Strike down yon guard, gain the mountain passes, and there do bloody work, as did your sires at old Thermopylae! Is Sparta dead? Is the old Grecian spirit frozen in your veins, that you do couch and cower like a belabored hound beneath his master's lash? O comrades! warriors! Thracians! —if we must fight, let us fight for ourselves! If we must slaughter, let us slaughter our oppressors! If we must die, let it be under the clear sky, by the bright waters, in noble, honorable battle!

THE CREMATION OF SAM McGEE

Robert W. Service

There are strange things done in the midnight sun
By the men who moil for gold;
The Arctic trails have their secret tales
That would make your blood run cold;
The Northern Lights have seen queer sights,
But the queerest they ever did see

Was that night on the marge of Lake Lebarge
I cremated Sam McGee.

Now Sam McGee was from Tennessee, where the cotton blooms
and blows.
Why he left his home in the South to roam 'round the Pole, God
only knows.
He was always cold, but the land of gold seemed to hold him like
a spell;
Though he'd often say in his homely way that "he'd sooner live
in hell."

On a Christmas day we were mushing our way over the Dawson
trail.
Talk of your cold! through the parka's fold it stabbed like a
driven nail.
If our eyes we'd close, then the lashes froze till sometimes we
couldn't see;
It wasn't much fun, but the only one to whimper was Sam McGee.

And that very night, as we lay packed tight in our robes beneath
the snow,
And the dogs were fed, and the stars o'erhead were dancing heel
and toe,
He turned to me, and "Cap," says he, "I'll cash in this trip, I
guess;
And if I do, I'm asking that you won't refuse my last request."

Well, he seemed so low that I couldn't say no; then he says with
a sort of moan:
"It's the cursed cold, and it's got right hold till I'm chilled clean
through to the bone.
Yet 'taint being dead—it's my awful dread of the icy grave that
pains;
So I want you to swear that, foul or fair, you'll cremate my last
remains."

A pal's last need is a thing to heed, so I swore I would not fail;
And we started on at the streak of dawn; but God! he looked
ghastly pale.
He crouched on the sleigh, and he raved all day of his home in
Tennessee;
And before nightfall a corpse was all that was left of Sam McGee.

There wasn't a breath in that land of death, and I hurried, horror-driven,
With a corpse half-hid that I couldn't get rid, because of a promise given;
It was lashed to the sleigh, and it seemed to say: "You may tax your brawn and brains,
But you promised true, and it's up to you to cremate these last remains."

Now a promise made is a debt unpaid, and the trail has its own stern code.
In the days to come, though my lips were dumb, in my heart how I cursed that load.
In the long, long night, by the lone firelight, while the huskies, round in a ring,
Howled out their woes to the homeless snows—O God! how I loathed the thing.

And every day that quiet clay seemed to heavy and heavier grow;
And on I went, though the dogs were spent and the grub was getting low;
The trail was bad, and I felt half mad, but I swore I would not give in;
And I'd often sing to the hateful thing, and it harkened with a grin.

Till I came to the marge of Lake Lebarge, and a derelict there lay;
It was jammed in the ice, but I saw in a trice it was called the "Alice May."
And I looked at it, and I thought a bit, and I looked at my frozen chum;
Then "Here," said I, with a sudden cry, "is my cre-ma-to-re-um."

Some planks I tore from the cabin floor, and I lit the boiler fire;
Some coal I found that was lying around, and I heaped the fuel higher;
The flames just soared, and the furnace roared—such a blaze you seldom see;
And I burrowed a hole in the glowing coal, and I stuffed in Sam McGee.

Then I made a hike, for I didn't like to hear him sizzle so;

669

And the heavens scowled, and the huskies howled, and the wind
    began to blow.
It was icy cold, but the hot sweat rolled down my cheeks, and I
    don't know why;
And the greasy smoke in an inky cloak went streaking down the
    sky.

I do not know how long in the snow I wrestled with grisly fear;
But the stars came out and they danced about ere again I ventured
    near;
I was sick with dread, but I bravely said: "I'll just take a peep
    inside.
I guess he's cooked, and it's time I looked"; . . . then the door I
    opened wide.

And there sat Sam, looking cool and calm, in the heart of the
    furnace roar;
And he wore a smile you could see a mile, and he said: "Please
    close that door.
It's fine in here, but I greatly fear you'll let in the cold and storm—
Since I left Plumtree down in Tennessee, it's the first time I've
    been warm."

There are strange things done in the midnight sun
By the men who moil for gold;
The Arctic trails have their secret tales
That would make your blood run cold;
The Northern Lights have seen queer sights,
But the queerest they ever did see
Was that night on the marge of Lake Lebarge
I cremated Sam McGee.

* * *

We should all be concerned about the future because we
will have to spend the rest of our lives there.
                             —Charles F. Kettering

THREE LITTLE MAIDS FROM SCHOOL

Sir William S. Gilbert

Three little maids from school are we,
Pert as a school girl well can be,
Filled to the brim with girlish glee,
    Three little maids from school!

Everything is a source of fun.
Nobody's safe for we care for none!
Life is a joke that's just begun!
    Three little maids from school!

Three little maids, who, all unwary,
Come from a ladies' seminary,
Freed from its genius tutelary—
    Three little maids from school!

One little maid is a bride, Yum-Yum—
Two little maids in attendance come—
Three little maids is the total sum.
    Three little maids from school!

From three little maids take one away.
Two little maids remain and they—
Won't have to wait very long, they say—
    Three little maids from school!

Three little maids, who, all unwary,
Come from a ladies' seminary,
Freed from its genius tutelary—
    Three little maids from school!

* * *

Bad officials are elected by good citizens who do not vote.
        —George Jean Nathan

FRIENDSHIP

Mark Twain

The holy passion of Friendship is of so sweet and steady and loyal and enduring a nature that it will last through a whole lifetime, if not asked to lend money.

AH, FADING JOY

John Dryden

Ah, fading joy, how quickly art thou past!
    Yet we thy ruine haste:
As if the cares of Humane Life were few,
    We seek out new,
And follow Fate that does too fast pursue.

See how on ev'ry Bough the Birds express
    In their sweet notes their happiness.
They all enjoy and nothing spare;
But on their Mother Nature lay their care:
Why then should Man, the Lord of all below,
    Such troubles chuse to know,
As none of all his Subjects undergo?

IT PAYS TO ADVERTISE

Anonymous

The codfish lays ten thousand eggs,
    The homely hen lays one.
The codfish never cackles
    To tell you what she's done.
And so we scorn the codfish,
    While the humble hen we prize,
Which only goes to show you
    That it pays to advertise.

PARENTS

Francis Bacon

The joys of parents are secret; and so are their griefs and fears. They cannot utter the one; nor will they utter the other. Children sweeten labors; but they make misfortunes more bitter. They increase the cares of life; but they mitigate the remembrance of death. The perpetuity by generation is common to beasts; but memory, merit, and noble works are proper to men.

TO KNOW ALL IS TO FORGIVE ALL

Nixon Waterman

If I knew you and you knew me—
If both of us could clearly see,
And with an inner sight divine
The meaning of your heart and mine—
I'm sure that we would differ less
And clasp our hands in friendliness;
Our thought would pleasantly agree
If I knew you, and you knew me.

If I knew you and you knew me,
As each one knows his own self, we
Could look each other in the face
And see therein a truer grace.
Life has so many hidden woes,
So many thorns for every rose;
The "Why" of things our hearts would see,
If I knew you and you knew me.

INSCRIPTION TO SPARTANS DEAD
AT THERMOPYLAE

Go, tell the Spartans, thou that passeth by,
That here obedient to their laws we lie.

"PIPING DOWN THE VALLEYS WILD"

William Blake

Piping down the valleys wild,
Piping songs of pleasant glee,
On a cloud I saw a child,
And he laughing said to me:

"Pipe a song about a Lamb!"
So I piped with a merry chear.
"Piper, pipe that song again":
So I piped: he wept to hear.

"Drop thy pipe. thy happy pipe;
Sing thy songs of happy chear":
So I sung the same again,
While he wept with joy to hear.

"Piper, sit thee down and write
In a book, that all may read."
So he vanish'd from my sight,
And I pluck'd a hollow reed,

And I made a rural pen,
And I stain'd the water clear,
And I wrote my happy songs
Every child may joy to hear.

IF THIS BE TREASON

Patrick Henry

Caesar had his Brutus; Charles the First his Cromwell; and
George the Third ("Treason!" cried the Speaker)—may profit by
their example. If *this* be treason, make the most of it!

(In the Virginia Convention, 1765)

ROBERT E. LEE'S RESIGNATION FROM THE U.S. ARMY

Arlington, Va., April 20, 1861

General:

Since my interview with you on the 18th inst. I have felt that I ought no longer to retain my commission in the Army. I therefore tender my resignation, which I request you will recommend for acceptance. I would have presented it at once, but for the struggle it has cost me to separate myself from a service to which I have devoted all the best years of my life and all the ability I possessed.

During the whole of that time—more than a quarter of a century—I have experienced nothing but kindness from my superiors and a most cordial friendship from my comrades. To no one, General, have I been so much indebted as to yourself for uniform kindness and consideration, and it has always been my ardent desire to meet your approbation. I shall carry to the grave the most grateful recollections of your kind consideration, and your name and fame will always be dear to me.

Save in defense of my native State, I never desire again to draw my sword.

Be pleased to accept my most earnest wishes for the continuance of your happiness and prosperity, and believe me, most truly yours,

R. E. LEE

(Letter to Gen. Winfield Scott)

LAWYER LINCOLN ANSWERS AN INQUIRY CONCERNING THE FINANCIAL STANDING OF A FELLOW TOWNSMAN

First of all, he has a wife and baby; together they ought to be worth $500,000 to any man. Secondly, he has an office in which there is a table worth $1.50, and three chairs, worth, say $1.00. Last of all, there is in one corner a large rathole, which will bear looking into.

Respectfully,
A. Lincoln

MACBETH'S WORDS BEFORE MURDERING

William Shakespeare

Is this a dagger which I see before me,
The handle toward my hand? Come, let me clutch thee.
I have thee not, and yet I see thee still.
Art thou not, fatal vision, sensible
To feeling as to sight? or art thou but
A dagger of the mind, a false creation,
Proceeding from the heat-oppressed brain?
I see thee yet, in form as palpable
As this which now I draw.
Thou marshall'st me the way that I was going;
And such an instrument I was to use.
Mine eyes are made the fools o' the other senses,
Or else worth all the rest: I see thee still;
And on thy blade and dudgeon gouts of blood,
Which was not so before. There's no such thing:
It is the bloody business which informs
Thus to mine eyes. Now o'er the one half-world
Nature seems dead, and wicked dreams abuse
The curtain'd sleep; witchcraft celebrates
Pale Hecate's offerings; and wither'd murder,
Alarum'd by his sentinel, the wolf,
Whose howl's his watch, thus with his stealthy pace,
With Tarquin's ravishing strides, towards his design
Moves like a ghost. Thou sure and firm-set earth,
Hear not my steps, which way they walk, for fear
Thy very stones prate of my whereabout,
And take the present horror from the time,
Which now suits with it. Whiles I threat, he lives:
Words to the heat of deeds too cold breath gives.
                                        [*A bell rings.*]
I go, and it is done: the bell invites me.
Hear it not, Duncan, for it is a knell
That summons thee to heaven, or to hell.

                    *   *   *

Who builds a church to God, and not to fame,
Will never mark the marble with his name.
                                        Alexander Pope

WALTZ ME AROUND AGAIN, WILLIE

Will D. Cobb

Willie Fitzgibbons who used to sell ribbons,
And stood up all day on his feet,
Grew very spooney on Madeline Mooney,
Who'd rather be dancing than eat.
Each evening she'd tag him, to some dance hall drag him,
And when the band started to play,
She'd up like a silly and grab tired Willie,
Steer him on the floor and she'd say:

"Waltz me around again, Willie, a-round, a-round, a-round,
The music it's dreamy, it's peaches and creamy,
Oh! don't let my feet touch the ground.
I feel like a ship on an ocean of joy,
I just want to holler out loud, 'Ship ahoy!'
Oh, waltz me around again, Willie, a-round, a-round, a-round."

Willie De Vere was a dry goods cashier,
At his desk he would sit all the day,
Till his doctor advised him to start exercising,
Or else he would soon fade away.
One night this poor looney met Madeline Mooney,
Fitzgibbons then shouted with joy,
"She's a good health regainer, you've got a great trainer,
Just wait till she hollers, my boy, (*Chorus.*)

COLLEGE AGE

Finley Peter Dunne

"If ye had a boy wud ye sind him to colledge?" asked Mr.
Hennessy.

"Well," said Mr. Dooley, "at th' age whin a boy is fit to be in
colledge I wudden't have him around th' house."

677

THE BILL OF RIGHTS

(Adopted as the first ten amendments to the Constitution)

1. Congress shall make no law respecting an establishment of religion, or prohibiting the free exercise thereof; or abridging the freedom of speech, or of the press; or the right of the people peaceably to assemble, and to petition the Government for a redress of grievances.

2. A well regulated Militia, being necessary to the security of a free State, the right of the people to keep and bear Arms, shall not be infringed.

3. No Soldier shall, in time of peace be quartered in any house, without the consent of the Owner, nor in time of war, but in a manner to be prescribed by law.

4. The right of the people to be secure in their persons, houses, papers, and effects, against unreasonable searches and seizures, shall not be violated, and no Warrants shall issue, but upon probable cause, supported by Oath or affirmation, and particularly describing the place to be searched, and the persons or things to be seized.

5. No person shall be held to answer for a capital, or otherwise infamous crime, unless on a presentment or indictment of a Grand Jury, except in cases arising in the land or naval forces, or in the Militia, when in actual service in time of War or public danger; nor shall any person be subject for the same offense to be twice put in jeopardy of life or limb; nor shall be compelled in any criminal case to be a witness against himself, nor be deprived of life, liberty, or property, without due process of law; nor shall private property be taken for public use, without just compensation.

6. In all criminal prosecutions, the accused shall enjoy the right to a speedy and public trial, by an impartial jury of the State and district wherein the crime shall have been committed, which district shall have been previously ascertained by law, and to be informed of the nature and cause of the accusation; to be confronted with the witnesses against him; to have compulsory process for obtaining witnesses in his favor, and to have the Assistance of Counsel for his defense.

7. In Suits at common law, where the value in controversy shall exceed twenty dollars, the right of trial by jury shall be preserved, and no fact tried by a jury shall be otherwise re-examined in any Court of the United States, than according to the rules of the common law.

8. Excessive bail shall not be required, nor excessive fines imposed, nor cruel and unusual punishments inflicted.

9. The enumeration in the Constitution of certain rights shall not be construed to deny or disparage others retained by the people.

10. The powers not delegated to the United States by the Constitution, nor prohibited by it to the States, are reserved to the States respectively, or to the people.

JOY, SHIPMATE, JOY!

Walt Whitman

Joy, shipmate, joy!
 (Pleased to my soul at death I cry;)
 Our life is closed, our life begins;
The long, long, anchorage we leave,
The ship is clear at last, she leaps!
She swiftly courses from the shore;
Joy, shipmate, joy!

ALL FOR LOVE

Lord Byron

O talk not to me of a name great in story;
The days of our youth are the days of our glory;
And the myrtle and ivy of sweet-two-and-twenty
Are worth all your laurels, though ever so plenty.

What are garlands and crowns to the brow that is wrinkled?
'Tis but as a dead flower with May-dew besprinkled:
Then away with all such from the head that is hoary—
What care I for the wreaths that can only give glory?

O Fame!—If I e'er took delight in thy praises,
'Twas less for the sake of thy high-sounding phrases,
Than to see the bright eyes of the dear one discover
She thought that I was not unworthy to love her.

There chiefly I sought thee, there only I found thee;
Her glance was the best of the rays that surround thee;
When it sparkled o'er aught that was bright in my story,
I knew it was love, and I felt it was glory.

THE BALCONY SCENE

William Shakespeare

Enter ROMEO

Rom.   He jests at scars that never felt a wound.
                       [Juliet appears above at a window.
But, soft! what light through yonder window breaks?
It is the east, and Juliet is the sun.
Arise, fair sun, and kill the envious moon,
Who is already sick and pale with grief,
That thou her maid art far more fair than she:
Be not her maid, since she is envious;
Her vestal livery is but sick and green
And none but fools do wear it; cast it off.
It is my lady, O, it is my love!
O, that she knew she were!
She speaks, yet she says nothing: what of that?
Her eye discourses; I will answer it.
I am too bold, 'tis not to me she speaks:
Two of the fairest stars in all the heaven,
Having some business, do entreat her eyes
To twinkle in their spheres till they return.
What if her eyes were there, they in her head?
The brightness of her cheek would shame those stars,
As daylight doth a lamp; her eyes in heaven
Would through the airy region stream so bright
That birds would sing and think it were not night.
See, how she leans her cheek upon her hand!
O, that I were a glove upon that hand,
That I might touch that cheek!
    Jul.   Ay me!
    Rom.   She speaks:
O, speak again, bright angel! for thou art
As glorious to this night, being o'er my head,
As is a winged messenger of heaven
Unto the white-upturned wondering eyes
Of mortals that fall back to gaze on him
When he bestrides the lazy-pacing clouds
And sails upon the bosom of the air.
    Jul.   O Romeo, Romeo! wherefore art thou Romeo?
Deny thy father and refuse thy name;
Or, if thou wilt not, be but sworn my love,

And I'll no longer be a Capulet.

Rom. [*Aside*] Shall I hear more, or shall I speak at this?

Jul. 'Tis but thy name that is my enemy;
Thou art thyself, though not a Montague.
What's Montague? it is nor hand, nor foot,
Nor arm, nor face, nor any other part
Belonging to a man. O, be some other name!
What's in a name? that which we call a rose
By any other name would smell as sweet;
So Romeo would, were he not Romeo call'd,
Retain that dear perfection which he owes
Without that title. Romeo, doff thy name,
And for that name which is no part of thee
Take all myself.

Rom.   I take thee at thy word:
Call me but love, and I'll be new baptized;
Henceforth I never will be Romeo.

Jul. What man art thou that thus bescreen'd in night
So stumblest on my counsel?

Rom.   By a name
I know not how to tell thee who I am:
My name, dear saint, is hateful to myself,
Because it is an enemy to thee;
Had I it written, I would tear the word.

Jul. My ears have not yet drunk a hundred words
Of that tongue's utterance, yet I know the sound:
Art thou not Romeo and a Montague?

Rom. Neither, fair saint, if either thee dislike.

Jul. How camest thou hither, tell me, and wherefore?
The orchard walls are high and hard to climb,
And the place death, considering who thou art,
If any of my kinsmen find thee here.

Rom. With love's light wings did I o'erperch these walls;
For stony limits cannot hold love out,
And what love can do that dares love attempt;
Therefore thy kinsmen are no let to me.

Jul. If they do see thee, they will murder thee.

Rom. Alack, there lies more peril in thine eye
Than twenty of their swords: look thou but sweet,
And I am proof against their enmity.

Jul. I would not for the world they saw thee here.

Rom. I have night's cloak to hide me from their sight;
And but thou love me, let them find me here:

My life were better ended by their hate,
Than death prorogued, wanting of thy love.
   Jul. By whose direction found'st thou out this place?
   Rom. By love, who first did prompt me to inquire;
He lent me counsel and I lent him eyes.
I am no pilot; yet, wert thou as far
As that vast shore wash'd with the farthest sea,
I would adventure for such merchandise.
   Jul. Thou know'st the mask of night is on my face,
Else would a maiden blush bepaint my cheek
For that which thou hast heard me speak to-night.
Fain would I dwell on form, fain, fain deny
What I have spoke: but farewell compliment!
Dost thou love me? I know thou wilt say 'Ay,'
And I will take thy word: yet, if thou swear'st,
Thou mayst prove false; at lovers' perjuries,
They say, Jove laughs. O gentle Romeo,
If thou dost love, pronounce it faithfully:
Or if thou think'st I am too quickly won,
I'll frown and be perverse and say thee nay,
So thou wilt woo; but else, not for the world.
In truth, fair Montague, I am too fond,
And therefore thou mayst think my haviour light:
But trust me, gentleman, I'll prove more true
Than those that have more cunning to be strange.
I should have been more strange, I must confess,
But that thou overheard'st, ere I was ware,
My true love's passion: therefore pardon me,
And not impute this yielding to light love,
Which the dark night hath so discovered.
   Rom. Lady, by yonder blessed moon I swear
That tips with silver all these fruit-tree tops—
   Jul. O, swear not by the moon, the inconstant moon,
That monthly changes in her circled orb,
Lest that thy love prove likewise variable.
   Rom. What shall I swear by?
   Jul.   Do not swear at all;
Or, if thou wilt, swear by thy gracious self,
Which is the god of my idolatry,
And I'll believe thee.
   Rom.   If my heart's dear love—
   Jul. Well, do not swear: although I joy in thee,
I have no joy of this contract to-night:

It is too rash, too unadvised, too sudden;
Too like the lightning, which doth cease to be
Ere one can say 'It lightens.' Sweet, good night!
This bud of love, by summer's ripening breath,
May prove a beauteous flower when next we meet.
Good night, good night! as sweet repose and rest
Come to thy heart as that within my breast!
    Rom.   O, wilt thou leave me so unsatisfied?
    Jul.   What satisfaction canst thou have to-night?
    Rom.   The exchange of thy love's faithful vow for mine.
    Jul.   I gave thee mine before thou didst request it:
And yet I would it were to give again.
    Rom.   Wouldst thou withdraw it? for what purpose, love?
    Jul.   But to be frank, and give it thee again.
And yet I wish but for the thing I have:
My bounty is as boundless as the sea,
My love as deep; the more I give to thee,
The more I have, for both are infinite.

                              [Nurse calls within.

I hear some noise within; dear love, adieu!
Anon, good nurse! Sweet Montague, be true.
Stay but a little, I will come again.

                              [Exit, above.

    Rom.   O blessed, blessed night! I am afeard,
Being in night, all this is but a dream,
Too flattering-sweet to be substantial.

               Re-enter JULIET, *above*

    Jul.   Three words, dear Romeo, and good night indeed.
If that thy bent of love be honourable,
Thy purpose marriage, send me word to-morrow,
By one that I'll procure to come to thee,
Where and what time thou will perform the rite;
And all my fortunes at thy foot I'll lay
And follow thee my lord throughout the world.
    Nurse.   [*Within*] Madam!
    Jul.   I come, anon.—But if thou mean'st not well,
I do beseech thee—
    Nurse.   [*Within*] Madam!
    Jul.   By and by, I come:—
To cease thy suit, and leave me to my grief:
To-morrow will I send.

Rom. So thrive my soul—
Jul. A thousand times good night!

[*Exit, above.*

Rom. A thousand times the worse, to want thy light.
Love goes toward love, as schoolboys from their books,
But love from love, toward school with heavy looks.

[*Retiring.*

Re-enter JULIET, *above*

Jul. Hist! Romeo, hist! O, for a falconer's voice,
To lure this tassel-gentle back again!
Bondage is hoarse, and may not speak aloud;
Else would I tear the cave where Echo lies,
And make her airy tongue more hoarse than mine,
With repetition of my Romeo's name.
Rom. It is my soul that calls upon my name:
How silver-sweet sound lovers' tongues by night,
Like softest music to attending ears!
Jul. Romeo!
Rom. My dear?
Jul. At what o'clock to-morrow
Shall I send to thee?
Rom. At the hour of nine.
Jul. I will not fail: 'tis twenty years till then.
I have forgot why I did call thee back.
Rom. Let me stand here till thou remember it.
Jul. I shall forget, to have thee still stand there,
Remembering how I love thy company.
Rom. And I'll still stay, to have thee still forget,
Forgetting any other home but this.
Jul. 'Tis almost morning; I would have thee gone:
And yet no further than a wanton's bird;
Who lets it hop a little from her hand,
Like a poor prisoner in his twisted gyves,
And with a silk thread plucks it back again,
So loving-jealous of his liberty.
Rom. I would I were thy bird.
Jul. Sweet, so would I:
Yet I should kill thee with much cherishing.
Good night, good night! parting is such sweet sorrow,
That I shall say good night till it be morrow.

[*Exit above.*

Rom. Sleep dwell upon thine eyes, peace in thy breast!
Would I were sleep and peace, so sweet to rest!

Hence will I to my ghostly father's cell,
His help to crave, and my dear hap to tell.

[*Exit.*
(From Romeo and Juliet)

I HAVE A GOODLY HERITAGE

Holy Bible, Psalm 16:5–9

The Lord is the portion of mine inheritance and of my cup: thou maintainest my lot.

The lines are fallen unto me in pleasant places; yea, I have a goodly heritage.

I will bless the Lord, who hath given me counsel; my reins also instruct me in the night seasons.

I have set the Lord always before me: because he is at my right hand, I shall not be moved.

Therefore my heart is glad, and my glory rejoiceth: my flesh also shall rest in hope.

From SLEEP AND POETRY

John Keats

Stop and consider! life is but a day,
A fragile dewdrop on its perilous way
From a tree's summit; a poor Indian's sleep
While his boat hastens to the monstrous steep
of Montmorenci. Why so sad a moan?
Life is the rose's hope while yet unblown;
The reading of an ever-changing tale;
The light uplifting of a maiden's veil;
A pigeon tumbling in clear summer air;
A laughing school-boy, without grief or care,
Riding the springy branches of an elm.

Brother, you say there is but one way to worship and serve the Great Spirit. If there is but one religion, why do you white people differ so much about it? Why are not all agreed, as you can all read the Book?

Brother, we do not understand these things. We are told that your religion was given to your forefathers and has been handed down from father to son. We also have a religion which was given to our forefathers and has been handed down to us, their children. We worship in that way. It teaches us to be thankful for all the favors we receive, to love each other, and to be united. We never quarrel about religion.

Brother, the Great Spirit has made us all, but He has made a great difference between His white and His red children. He has given us different complexions and different customs. To you He has given the arts. To these, He has not opened our eyes. We know these things to be true. Since He has made so great a difference between us in other things, why may we not conclude that He has given us a different religion according to our understanding? The Great Spirit does right. He knows what is best for His children; we are satisfied.

Brother, we do not wish to destroy your religion or take it from you. We only want to enjoy our own.

UNITY OF MANKIND

Holy Bible, Psalm 133

Behold how good and pleasant it is for brethren to dwell together in unity!
It is like the precious ointment upon the head, that ran down upon the beard, even Aaron's beard: that went down to the skirts of his garment:
As the dew of Hermon, and as the dew that descended upon the mountains of Zion: for there the Lord commanded the blessing, even life for evermore.

WEDDING SIGNS

Anonymous

Married in white, you have chosen all right.
Married in gray, you will go far away.
Married in black, you will wish yourself back.
Married in red, you will wish yourself dead.
Married in green, ashamed to be seen.
Married in blue, he will always be true.
Married in pearl, you will live in a whirl.
Married in yellow, ashamed of your fellow.
Married in brown, you will live out of town.
Married in pink, your fortune will sink.

I THINK CONTINUALLY OF THOSE WHO WERE TRULY GREAT

Stephen Spender

I think continually of those who were truly great
Who, from the womb, remembered the soul's history
Through corridors of light where the hours are suns,
Endless and singing. Whose lovely ambition
Was that their lips, still touched with fire,
Should tell of the spirit clothed from head to foot in song.
And who hoarded from the spring branches
The desires falling across their bodies like blossoms.

What is precious is never to forget
The delight of the blood drawn from ageless springs
Breaking through rocks in worlds before our earth;
Never to deny its pleasure in the simple morning light,
Nor its grave evening demand for love;
Never to allow gradually the traffic to smother
With noise and fog the flowering of the spirit.

Near the snow, near the sun, in the highest fields
See how these names are feted by the waving grass,
And by the streamers of white cloud,

And whispers of wind in the listening sky;
The names of those who in their lives fought for life,
Who wore at their hearts the fire's center.
Born of the sun they traveled a short while towards the sun,
And left the vivid air signed with their honour.

THE LAST TEMPTATION

T. S. Eliot

Now is my way clear, now is the meaning plain:
Temptation shall not come in this kind again.
The last temptation is the greatest treason:
To do the right deed for the wrong reason.
           (From *Murder in the Cathedral*)

TOLERANCE

Jeremy Taylor

When Abraham sat at his tent door, according to his custom, waiting to entertain strangers, he espied an old man, stooping and leaning on his staff, weary with age and travail, coming towards him, who
was a hundred years of age; he received him kindly, washed his feet,
provided supper, caused him to sit down; but, observing that the old
man ate and prayed not, nor begged a blessing on his meat, he asked
him why he did not worship the God of heaven. The old man told
him that he worshipped the fire only, and acknowledged no other
God. At which answer Abraham grew so zealously angry, that he
threw the old man out of his tent, and exposed him to all the evils
of the night and an unguarded condition. When the old man was
gone, God called Abraham, and asked him where the stranger was.
"I thrust him away, because he did not worship thee." God answered
him, "I have suffered him these hundred years, though he dishonored
me; and wouldst thou not endure him one night, when he gave thee
no trouble?"

A THING OF BEAUTY IS A JOY FOREVER

John Keats

A thing of beauty is a joy forever:
Its loveliness increases; it will never
Pass into nothingness; but still will keep
A bower quiet for us, and a sleep
Full of sweet dreams, and health, and quiet breathing.
Therefore, on every morrow, are we wreathing
A flowery band to bind us to the earth,
Spite of despondence, of the human dearth
Of noble natures, of the gloomy days,
Of all the unhealthy and o'er-darken'd ways
Made for our searching: yes, in spite of all,
Some shape of beauty moves away the pall
From our dark spirits. Such the sun, the moon,
Trees old and young, sprouting a shady boon
For simple sheep; and such are daffodils
With the green world they live in and clear rills
That for themselves a cooling covert make
'Gainst the hot season; the mid-forest brake,
Rich with a sprinkling of fair musk-rose blooms:
And such too is the grandeur of the dooms
We have imagined for the mighty dead;
All lovely tales that we have heard or read:
An endless fountain of immortal drink,
Pouring unto us from the heaven's brink.

Nor do we merely feel these essences
For one short hour; no, even as the trees
That whisper round a temple become soon
Dear as the temple's self, so does the moon,
The passion poesy, glories infinite,
Haunt us till they become a cheering light
Unto our souls, and bound to us so fast,
That, whether there be shine, or gloom o'ercast,
They always must be with us, or we die.

(From Endymion)

* * *

You can't make a silk purse out of a sow's ear.
—Jonathan Swift

WISDOM FROM WILLIAM PENN

They that love beyond the world cannot be separated by it.

Death cannot kill what never dies.

Nor can spirits ever be divided, that love and live in the same principle: the root and record of their friendship.

If absence be not death, neither is theirs.

Death is but crossing the world, as friends do the seas; they live in one another still.

For they must needs be present, that love and live in that which is omnipresent.

In this divine glass they see face to face; and their converse is free.

This is the comfort of friends, that though they may be said to die, yet their friendship and society are, in the best sense, ever present, because immortal.

THE GAME OF LIFE

Thomas H. Huxley

The chess board is the world, the pieces are the phenomena of the universe, the rules of the game are what we call the laws of Nature. The player on the other side is hidden from us. We know that his play is always fair, just, and patient. But we also know, to our cost, that he never overlooks a mistake, or makes the smallest allowance for ignorance.

EPITAPH ON THE POLITICIAN

Hilaire Belloc

Here, richly, with ridiculous display,
The Politician's corpse was laid away.
While all of his acquaintance sneered and slanged,
I wept: for I had longed to see him hanged.

RULES FOR THE ROAD

Edwin Markham

Stand straight;
Step firmly, throw your weight;
The heaven is high above your head
And the good road is faithful to your tread.

Be strong:
Sing to your heart a battle song:
Though hidden foemen lie in wait,
Something is in you that can smile at Fate.

Press through:
Nothing can harm if you are true.
And when the night comes rest:
The earth is friendly as a mother's breast.

ON HIS BOOKS

Hilaire Belloc

When I am dead, I hope it may be said:
'His sins were scarlet, but his books were read.'

FAITH

Anonymous

Fear knocked at the door.
Faith answered.
There was no one there.

> (From a sign over an
> old inn at Bray, England)

HE WAS FROM MISSOURI

Willard Duncan Vandiver

I come from a state that raises corn and cotton and cockleburs and Democrats, and frothy eloquence neither convinces nor satisfies me. I am from Missouri. You have got to show me.

DIOGENES TO THE PEOPLE OF SYNOPE, HIS NATIVE CITY

My countrymen:

You have banished me, my countrymen, and I on the contrary desire that you be confined to your homes, for while you inhabit Synope, I live at Athens. You spend your time with none but mercenary traders, while I converse daily with philosophers. You deal in nothing but vile merchandise, while I continually read both men and books. Pity me not then, but rather envy me in that being removed from you, I lead a much happier life than when I was with you. I then wallowed in all kinds of sloth and luxury; I now am obliged to labor for my living; I then lived at large, but now am confined to rules. What then hinders me from pitying you in your condition, men of Synope, in that having so great wealth you want knowledge, and in wanting that, want everything?

Your banishing me, I look upon with favour, and value your threats so little, that I had rather be accused than applauded by you. In a word, I would choose to be a vagabond all over the earth, before I would consent to live a wealthy, but unknown citizen of Synope.

Farewell.

LINES WRITTEN ON THE ANTIQUITY OF MICROBES

Strickland Gillilan

Adam
Had 'em.

MARIE ANTOINETTE

Edmund Burke

It is now sixteen or seventeen years since I saw the Queen of France, then the dauphiness, at Versailles; and surely never lighted on this orb, which she hardly seemed to touch, a more delightful vision. I saw her just above the horizon, decorating and cheering the elevated sphere she just began to move in—glittering like the morning-star, full of life, and splendour, and joy. Oh! what a revolution! and what a heart must I have, to contemplate without emotion that elevation and that fall! Little did I dream when she added titles of veneration to those of enthusiastic, distant, respectful love, that she should ever be obliged to carry the sharp antidote against disgrace concealed in that bosom; little did I dream that I should live to see such disasters fallen upon her in a nation of gallant men, in a nation of men of honour, and of cavaliers. I thought ten thousand swords must have leaped from their scabbards to avenge even a look that threatened her with insult. But the age of chivalry is gone. That of sophisters, economists, and calculators has succeeded; and the glory of Europe is extinguished for ever. Never, never more shall we behold that generous loyalty to rank and sex, that proud submission, that dignified obedience, that subordination of the heart, which kept alive, even in servitude itself, the spirit of an exalted freedom. The unbought grace of life, the cheap defence of nations, the nurse of manly sentiment and heroic enterprise is gone! It is gone, that sensibility of principle, that chastity of honour, which felt a stain like a wound, which inspired courage whilst it mitigated ferocity, which ennobled whatever it touched, and under which vice itself lost half its evil, by losing all its grossness.

(From Reflections on the Revolution in France)

* * *

Thrice is he armed that hath his quarrel just;
And four times he who gets his fist in fust.

—Josh Billings

MR. DOOLEY'S TRIUMPHAL ARCH

Finley Peter Dunne

When ye build yer triumphal arch to yer conquerin' hero, Hinnissey, build it out of bricks so the people will have somethin' convanient to throw at him as he passes through.

IN DEFENSE OF YOUTH'S EXCESSES

Robert Louis Stevenson

When the old man waggles his head and says, "Ah, so I thought when I was your age," he has proved the youth's case. Doubtless, whether from growth of experience or decline of animal heat, he thinks so no longer; but he thought so while he was young; and all men have thought so while they were young, since there was dew in the morning or hawthorn in May; and here is another young man adding his vote to those of previous generations and riveting another link to the chain of testimony. It is as natural and as right for a young man to be imprudent and exaggerated, to live in swoops and circles, and beat about his cage like any other wild thing newly captured, as it is for old men to turn grey, or mothers to love their offspring, or heroes to die for something worthier than their lives. . . .

You need repent none of your youthful vagaries. They may have been over the score on one side, just as those of age are probably over the score on the other. But they had a point; they not only befitted your age and expressed its attitude and passions, but they had a relation to what was outside of you, and implied criticisms on the existing state of things, which you need not allow to have been undeserved, because you now see that they were partial. All error, not merely verbal, is a strong way of stating that the current truth is incomplete. The follies of youth have a basis in sound reason, just as much as the embarrassing questions put by babes and sucklings. Their most antisocial acts indicate the defects of our society. When the torrent sweeps the man against a boulder, you must expect him to scream, and you need not be surprised if the scream is sometimes a theory. Shelley, chafing at the Church of England, discovered the cure of all evils in universal atheism. Generous lads irritated at the injustices of society, see nothing for it but the abolishment of everything and Kingdom Come of anarchy. Shelley was a young fool; so are these cock-sparrow revolutionaries. But it is better to be a fool than to be dead. It is better to emit a scream in the shape of a theory than to be entirely insensible to the jars and incongruities of life and take everything as it comes in a forlorn stupidity. Some people swallow the universe like a pill; they travel on through the world, like smiling images pushed from behind. For God's sake give me the young man who has brains enough to make a fool of himself!

FOR A DEAD LADY

Edwin Arlington Robinson

No more with overflowing light
Shall fill the eyes that now are faded,
Nor shall another's fringe with night
Their woman-hidden world as they did.
No more shall quiver down the days
The flowing wonder of her ways,
Whereof no language may requite
The shifting and the many-shaded.

The grace, divine, definitive,
Clings only as a faint forestalling;
The laugh that love could not forgive
Is hushed, and answers to no calling;
The forehead and the little ears
Have gone where Saturn keeps the years;
The breast where roses could not live
Has done with rising and with falling.

The beauty, shattered by the laws
That have creation in their keeping,
No longer trembles at applause,
Or over children that are sleeping;
And we who delve in beauty's lore
Know all that we have known before
Of what inexorable cause
Makes Time so vicious in his reaping.

THE FOOL'S PRAYER

Edward Rowland Sill

The royal feast was done; the King
Sought some new sport to banish care,
And to his jester cried: "Sir Fool,
Kneel now, and make for us a prayer!"

The jester doffed his cap and bells,
And stood the mocking court before;
They could not see the bitter smile
Behind the painted grin he wore.

He bowed his head, and bent his knee
Upon the monarch's silken stool;
His pleading voice arose: "O Lord,
Be merciful to me, a fool!

"No pity, Lord, could change the heart
From red with wrong to white as wool;
The rod must heal the sin; but, Lord,
Be merciful to me, a fool!

" 'Tis not by guilt, the onward sweep
Of truth and right, O Lord, we stay;
'Tis by our follies that so long
We hold the earth from heaven away.

"These clumsy feet, still in the mire,
Go crushing blossoms without end;
These hard, well-meaning hands we thrust
Among the heart-strings of a friend.

"The ill-timed truth we might have kept—
Who knows how sharp it pierced and stung!
The words we had not sense to say—
Who knows how grandly it had rung!

"Our faults no tenderness should ask,
The chastening strips must cleanse them all;
But for our blunders—oh, in shame
Before the eyes of heaven we fall.

"Earth bears no balsam for mistakes;
Men crown the knave, and scourge the tool
That did his will; but Thou, O Lord,
Be merciful to me, a fool!"

The room was hushed; in silence rose
The King, and sought his gardens cool,
And walked apart, and murmured low,
"Be merciful to me, a fool!"

OBSTACLES

Boethius

(TRANSLATOR: W. V. Cooper)

When the stars are hidden by black clouds, no light can they afford.
When the boisterous south wind rolls along the sea and stirs the
surge, the water, now as clear as glass, bright as the fair sun's light is
dark, impenetrable to sight, with stirred and scattered sand. The
stream, that wanders down the mountain's side, must often find a
stumbling-block, a stone within its path torn from the hill's own
rock. So too shalt thou: if thou wouldst see the truth in undimmed
light, choose the straight road, the beaten path; away with passing
joys! away with fear! put vain hopes to flight! and grant no place to
grief! Where these distractions reign, the mind is clouded o'er, the
soul is bound in chains.

DAY DEFINED

Lewis Carroll

The day is the same length of time
as anything that is the same length
as *it*.

FOR MY BROTHER

Sgt. John Paul Merton, R.C.A.F.
Reported Missing in Action, 1943

Thomas Merton

Sweet brother, if I do not sleep
My eyes are flowers for your tomb;
And if I cannot eat my bread,
My fasts shall live like willows where you died.
If in the heat I find no water for my thirst,
My thirst shall turn to springs for you, poor traveller.

Where, in what desolate and smoky country,
Lies your poor body, lost and dead?
And in what landscape of disaster
Has your unhappy spirit lost its road?

Come, in my labor find a resting place
And in my sorrows lay your head,
Or rather take my life and blood
And buy yourself a better bed—
Or take my breath and take my death
And buy yourself a better rest.

When all the men of war are shot
And flags have fallen into dust,
Your cross and mine shall tell men still
Christ died on each, for both of us.

For in the wreckage of your April Christ lies slain,
And Christ weeps in the ruins of my spring;
The money of Whose tears shall fall
Into your weak and friendless hand,
And buy you back to your own land:
The silence of Whose tears shall fall
Like bells upon your alien tomb.
Hear them and come: they call you home.

RIENZI TO THE ROMANS

Mary R. Mitford

Friends!
I came not here to talk. Ye know too well
The story of our thraldom. We are slaves!
The bright sun rises to his course, and lights
A race of slaves! he sets, and his last beam
Falls on a slave! Not such as, swept along
By the full tide of power, the conqueror leads
To crimson glory and undying fame,
But base, ignoble slaves!—slaves to a horde
Of petty tyrants, feudal despots; lords
Rich in some dozen paltry villages,
Strong in some hundred spearmen, only great
In that strange spell,—a name! Each hour, dark fraud,
Or open rapine, or protected murder,
Cries out against them. But this very day
An honest man, my neighbor,—there he stands—
Was struck—struck like a dog—by one who wore
The badge of Ursini! because, forsooth,
He tossed not high his ready cap in air,
Nor lifted up his voice in servile shouts,
At sight of that great ruffian! Be we men,
And suffer such dishonor? men, and wash not
The stain away in blood? such shames are common.
I have known deeper wrongs. I, that speak to ye—
I had a brother once, a gracious boy,
Full of gentleness, of calmest hope,
Of sweet and quiet joy; there was the look
Of Heaven upon his face which limners give
To the beloved disciple. How I loved
That gracious boy! younger by fifteen years,
Brother at once and son! He left my side,—
A summer bloom on his fair cheeks, a smile
Parting his innocent lips. In one short hour
The pretty, harmless boy was slain! I saw
The corse, the mangled corse, and then I cried
For vengeance! Rouse ye, Romans! Rouse ye, slaves!
Have ye brave sons?—Look in the next fierce brawl
To see them die! Have ye fair daughters?—Look

To see them live, torn from your arms, distained,
Dishonored; and, if ye dare call for justice,
Be answered by the lash! Yet this is Rome,
That sate on her seven hills, and from her throne
Of beauty ruled the world! Yet we are Romans!
Why, in that elder day, to be a Roman
Was greater than a king! And once again—
Hear me, ye walls, that echoed to the tread
Of either Brutus!—once again, I swear,
The eternal city shall be free! her sons shall walk with princes.

OPTIMIST AND PESSIMIST

McLandburgh Wilson

Twixt optimist and pessimist,
  The difference is droll;
The optimist sees the doughnut
  The pessimist sees the hole.

ENJOY THE GOOD

Holy Bible, Ecclesiastes 5:18–20

Behold that which I have seen: it is good and comely for one to eat and to drink, and to enjoy the good of all his labor that he taketh under the sun all the days of his life, which God giveth him; for it is his portion.

Every man also to whom God hath given riches and wealth, and hath given him power to eat thereof, and to take his portion, and to rejoice in his labor: this is the gift of God.

For he shall not much remember the days of his life; because God answereth him in the joy of his heart.

THERE WAS A ROARING IN THE WIND ALL NIGHT

William Wordsworth

There was a roaring in the wind all night;
The rain came heavily and fell in floods;
But now the sun is rising calm and bright;
The birds are singing in the distant woods;
Over his own sweet voice the Stock-dove broods;
The Jay makes answer as the Magpie chatters;
And all the air is filled with pleasant noise of waters.

All things that love the sun are out of doors;
The sky rejoices in the morning's birth;
The grass is bright with rain-drops;—on the moors
The hare is running races in her mirth;
And with her feet she from the plashy earth
Raises a mist, that, glittering in the sun,
Runs with her all the way, wherever she doth run.

BROTHERHOOD

Holy Bible, First John 2:9–11; 4:20–21

He that saith he is in the light, and hateth his brother, is in darkness even until now.

He that loveth his brother abideth in the light, and there is none occasion of stumbling in him.

But he that hateth his brother is in darkness, and walketh in darkness, and knoweth not whither he goeth, because that darkness hath blinded his eyes. . . .

If a man say, I love God, and hateth his brother, he is a liar: for he that loveth not his brother whom he hath seen, how can he love God whom he hath not seen?

And this commandment have we from him, That he who loveth God love his brother also.

ULALUME

Edgar Allan Poe

The skies they were ashen and sober;
  The leaves they were crispèd and sere,
  The leaves they were withering and sere;
It was night in the lonesome October
  Of my most immemorial year;
It was hard by the dim lake of Auber,
  In the misty mid region of Weir:
It was down by the dank tarn of Auber,
  In the ghoul-haunted woodland of Weir.

Here once, through an alley Titanic
  Of cypress, I roamed with my Soul—
  Of cypress, with Psyche, my Soul.
These were days when my heart was volcanic
  As the scoriac rivers that roll,
  As the lavas that restlessly roll
Their sulphurous currents down Yaanek
  In the ultimate climes of the pole,
That groan as they roll down Mount Yaanek
  In the realms of the boreal pole.

Our talk had been serious and sober,
  But our thoughts they were palsied and sere,
  Our memories were treacherous and sere,
For we knew not the month was October,
  And we marked not the night of the year,
  (Ah, night of all nights in the year!)
We noted not the dim lake of Auber
  (Though once we had journeyed down here),
Remembered not the dank tarn of Auber
  Nor the ghoul-haunted woodland of Weir.

And now, as the night was senescent
  And star-dials pointed to morn,
  As the star-dials hinted of morn,
At the end of our path a liquescent
  And nebulous lustre was born,

Out of which a miraculous crescent
   Arose with a duplicate horn,
Astarte's bediamonded crescent
   Distinct with its duplicate horn.

And I said—"She is warmer than Dian:
   She rolls through an ether of sighs,
   She revels in a region of sighs:
She has seen that the tears are not dry on
   These cheeks, where the worm never dies,
And has come past the stars of the Lion
   To point us the path to the skies,
   To the Lethean peace of the skies:
Come up, in despite of the Lion,
   To shine on us with her bright eyes:
Come up through the lair of the Lion,
   With love in her luminous eyes."

But Psyche, uplifting her finger,
   Said—"Sadly this star I mistrust,
   Her pallor I strangely mistrust:
Oh, hasten!—oh, let us not linger!
   Oh, fly!—let us fly!—for we must."
In terror she spoke, letting sink her
   Wings until they trailed in the dust;
In agony sobbed, letting sink her
   Plumes till they trailed in the dust,
   Till they sorrowfully trailed in the dust.

I replied—"This is nothing but dreaming:
   Let us on by this tremulous light!
   Let us bathe in this crystalline light!
Its sibyllic splendor is beaming
   With hope and in beauty to-night:
   See, it flickers up the sky through the night!
Ah, we safely may trust to its gleaming,
   And be sure it will lead us aright:
We safely may trust to a gleaming
   That cannot but guide us aright,
   Since it flickers up to Heaven through the night."

Thus I pacified Psyche and kissed her,
   And tempted her out of her gloom,
   And conquered her scruples and gloom;

And we passed to the end of the vista,
    But were stopped by the door of a tomb,
    By the door of a legended tomb;
And I said—"What is written, sweet sister,
    On the door of this legended tomb?"
    She replied—"Ulalume—Ulalume—
    'Tis the vault of thy lost Ulalume!"

Then my heart it grew ashen and sober
    As the leaves that were crispèd and sere,
    As the leaves that were withering and sere,
And I cried—"It was surely October
    On this very night of last year
    That I journeyed—I journeyed down here,
    That I brought a dread burden down here:
    On this night of all nights in the year,
    Ah, what demon has tempted me here?
Well I know, now, this dim lake of Auber,
    This misty mid region of Weir:
Well I know, now, this dank tarn of Auber,
    This ghoul-haunted woodland of Weir."

THE KID'S LAST FIGHT

Anonymous

Us two was pals, the Kid and me;
'Twould cut no ice if some gayzee,
As tough as hell jumped either one,
We'd both light in and hand him some.

Both of a size, the Kid and me,
We tipped the scales at thirty-three;
And when we'd spar 'twas give and take,
I wouldn't slug for any stake.

One day we worked out at the gymn,
Some swell guy hangin' round called "Slim,"
Watched us and got stuck on the Kid,
Then signed him up, that's what he did.

This guy called "Slim" he owned a string
Of lightweights, welters, everything;
He took the Kid out on the road,
And where they went none of us knowed.

I guessed the Kid had changed his name,
And fightin' the best ones in the game.
I used to dream of him at night,
No letters came—he couldn't write.

In just about two months or three
I signed up with Bucktooth McGee.
He got me matched with Denver Brown,
I finished him in half a round.

Next month I fought with Brooklyn Mike,
As tough a boy who hit the pike;
Then Frisco Jim and Battlin' Ben,
And knocked them all inside of ten.

I took 'em all and won each bout,
None of them birds could put me out;
The sportin' writers watched me slug,
Then all the papers run my mug.

"He'd rather fight than eat," they said,
"He's got the punch, he'll knock 'em dead."
There's only one I hadn't met,
That guy they called "The Yorkshire Pet."

He'd cleaned 'em all around in France,
No one in England stood a chance;
And I was champ in U. S. A.,
And knocked 'em cuckoo every day.

Now all McGee and me could think
Was how we'd like to cross the drink,
And knock this bucko for a row,
And grab a wagon load of dough.

At last Mac got me matched all right,
Five thousand smackers for the fight;
Then me and him packed up our grip,
And went to grab that championship.

I done some trainin' and the night
Set for the battle sure was right;
The crowd was wild, for this here bout
Was set to last till one was out.

The mob went crazy when the Pet
Came in, I'd never seen him yet;
And then I climbed up through the ropes,
All full of fight and full of hopes.

The crowd gave me an awful yell,
('Twas even money at the bell)
They stamped their feet and shook the place;
The Pet turned 'round, I saw his face!

My guts went sick, that's what they did,
For Holy Gee, it was the Kid!
We just had time for one good shake,
We meant it, too, it wasn't fake.

Whang! went the bell, the fight was on,
I clinched until the round was gone,
A-beggin', that he'd let me take
The fall for him—he wouldn't fake.

Hell, no, the Kid was on the square,
And said we had to fight it fair,
The crowd had bet their dough on us—
We had to fight (the honest cuss).

The referee was yellin' "break,"
The crowd was sore and howlin' "fake."
They'd paid their dough to see a scrap.
And so far we'd not hit a tap.

The second round we both begin.
I caught a fast one on my chin;
And stood like I was in a doze,
Until I got one on the nose.

I started landin' body blows,
He hooked another on my nose,
That riled my fightin' blood like hell,
And we was sluggin' at the bell.

The next round started, from the go
The millin' we did wasn't slow,
I landed hard on him, and then,
He took the count right up to ten.

He took the limit on one knee,
A chance to get his wind and see;
At ten he jumped up like a flash
And on my jaw he hung a smash.

I'm fightin', too, there, toe to toe,
And hittin' harder, blow for blow,
I damn soon knowed he couldn't stay,
He rolled his eyes—you know the way.

The way he staggered made me sick,
I stalled, McGee yelled "cop him quick!"
The crowd was wise and yellin' "fake,"
They'd seen the chance I wouldn't take.

The mob kept tellin' me to land,
And callin' things I couldn't stand;
I stepped in close and smashed his chin,
The Kid fell hard; he was all in.

I carried him into his chair,
And tried to bring him to for fair,
I rubbed his wrists, done everything,
A doctor climbed into the ring.

And I was scared as I could be,
The Kid was starin' and couldn't see;
The doctor turned and shook his head,
I looked again—the Kid was dead!

* * *

Old men are fond of giving good advice to console themselves for their inability to give bad examples.
                                        —La Rochefoucauld

PRIDE, THE NEVER-FAILING VICE OF FOOLS

Alexander Pope

Of all the Causes which conspire to blind
Man's erring judgment, and misguide the mind,
What the weak head with strongest bias rules,
Is *Pride*, the never-failing vice of fools.

MAN WILL PREVAIL

William Faulkner

Our tragedy today is a general and universal physical fear so long sustained by now that we can even bear it. There are no longer problems of the spirit. There is only the question: when will I be blown up? Because of this, the young man or woman writing today has forgotten the problems of the human heart in conflict with itself which alone can make good writing because only that is worth writing about, worth the agony and the sweat.

He must learn them again. He must teach himself that the basest of all things is to be afraid; and teaching himself that, forget it forever, leaving no room in his workshop for anything but the old verities and truths of the heart, the old universal truths lacking which any story is ephemeral and doomed—love and honor and pity and pride and compassion and sacrifice. Until he does so he labors under a curse. He writes not of love but of lust, of defeats in which nobody loses anything of value, of victories without hope and worst of all without pity or compassion. His griefs grieve on universal bones, leaving no scars. He writes not of the heart, but of the glands.

Until he relearns these things he will write as though he stood among and watched the end of man. It is easy to say that man is immortal simply because he will endure; but when the last ding-dong of doom has clanged and faded from the last worthless rock hanging tideless in the last red and dying evening, that even then there will still be one more sound: that of his puny inexhaustible voice, still talking. I refuse to accept this. I believe that man will not merely endure: he will prevail. He is immortal, not because he alone among creatures has an inexhaustible voice, but because he has a soul, a spirit capable of compassion and sacrifice and endurance. The poet's, the writer's, duty is to write about these things. It is his privilege to help man endure by lifting his heart, by reminding him of the courage and honor and hope and pride and compassion and pity and sacrifice which have been the glory of his past. The poet's voice need not merely be the record of man, it can be one of the props, the pillars to help him endure and prevail.

(From Nobel Prize Speech, January, 1951)

WISE WASTING OF DAYS

Thomas Dekker

To awaken each morning with a smile brightening my face, to greet the day with reverence, for the opportunities it contains; to approach my work with a clean mind; to hold ever before me, even in the doing of little things, the Ultimate Purpose toward which I am working; to meet men and women with laughter on my lips and love in my heart, to be gentle, kind and courteous through all the hours; to approach the night with weariness that ever woos sleep and the joy that comes from work well done—this is how I desire to waste wisely my days.

PEOPLE WILL TALK

Anonymous

We may go through the world, but it will be slow,
If we listen to all that is said as we go.
We will be worried and fretted and kept in a stew;
Too meddlesome tongues must have something to do.
    For people will talk, you know, people will talk;
    Oh, yes, they must talk, you know.

If quiet and modest, you'll have it presumed
Your humble position is only assumed—
You're a wolf in sheep's clothing, or else you're a fool;
But don't get excited, keep perfectly cool,
    For people will talk, etc.

If generous and noble, they'll vent out their spleen—
You'll hear some loud hints that you're selfish and mean;
If upright and honest and fair as the day,
They'll call you a rogue in a sly, sneaking way.
    For people will talk, etc.

And then if you show the least boldness of heart,
Or slight inclination to take your own part,
They'll call you an upstart, conceited and vain;
But keep straight ahead, and don't stop to complain.
    For people will talk, etc.

If threadbare your coat, and old-fashioned your hat,
Some one of course will take notice of that,
And hint rather strong that you can't pay your way,
But don't get excited, whatever you say.
    For people will talk, etc.

If you dress in the fashion, don't think to escape,
For they will criticize then in a different shape;
You're ahead of your means, or your tailor's unpaid;
But mind your own business, there's nought to be made,
    For people will talk, etc.

They'll talk fine before you; but then at your back,
Of venom and slander there's never a lack;
How kind and polite in all that they say,
But bitter as gall when you are away.
    For people will talk, etc.

The best way to do is to do as you please,
For your mind (if you have one) will then be at ease;
Of course you will meet with all sorts of abuse,
But don't think to stop them, it isn't any use,
    For people will talk, you know, people will talk;
    Oh, yes, they must talk, you know.

* * *

Now that is the wisdom of a man, in every instance of his labour,
to hitch his wagon to a star, and see his chore done by the gods
themselves.

—R. W. Emerson

MY OWN MIND IS MY CHURCH

Thomas Paine

I believe in one God, and no more; and I hope for happiness beyond this life.

I believe in the equality of man; and I believe that religious duties consist in doing justice, loving mercy, and endeavoring to make our fellow-creatures happy. . . .

My own mind is my own church. . . .

It is necessary to the happiness of man, that he be mentally faithful to himself. Infidelity does not consist in believing, or in disbelieving; it consists in professing to believe what he does not believe. . . .

The belief of a God, so far from having anything of mystery in it, is of all beliefs the most easy, because it arises to us out of necessity. And the practice of moral truth, or, in other words, a practical imitation of the moral goodness of God, is no other than our acting toward each other as he acts benignly toward all. . . .

The only idea we can have of serving God, is that of contributing to the happiness of the living creation that God has made. This cannot be done by retiring ourselves from the society of the world and spending a recluse life in selfish devotion. . . .

I trouble not myself about the manner of future existence. I content myself with believing even to positive conviction, that the Power that gave me existence is able to continue it, in any form and manner he pleases, either with or without this body; and it appears more probable to me that I shall continue to exist hereafter, than that I should have had existence, as I now have, before that existence began.

(From *The Age of Reason*)

THE STERN PARENT

Harry Graham

Father heard his children scream,
So he threw them in the stream,
Saying, as he drowned the third,
"Children should be seen, *not* heard!"

711

THE THINGS I PRIZE

Henry van Dyke

These are the things I prize
And hold of dearest worth:
Light of the sapphire skies,
Peace of the silent hills,
Shelter of the forests, comfort of the grass,
Music of birds, murmurs of little rills,
Shadows of cloud that swiftly pass,
And, after showers,
The smell of flowers
And of the good brown earth,—
And best of all, along the way, friendship and mirth.

EPITAPH OF SARAH SEXTON

Here lies the body of Sarah Sexton,
Who never did aught to vex one.
Not like the woman under the next stone.
(Thomas Sexton's first wife was buried under the
next stone. Church-yard, Newmarket, England)

HIAWATHA'S WOOING

Henry Wadsworth Longfellow

"As unto the bow the cord is,
So unto the man is woman;
Though she bends him, she obeys him,
Though she draws him, yet she follows;
Useless each without the other!"
Thus the youthful Hiawatha

Said within himself and pondered,
Much perplexed by various feelings,
Listless, longing, hoping, fearing,
Dreaming still of Minnehaha,
Of the lovely Laughing Water,
In the land of the Dacotahs.
　　"Wed a maiden of your people,"
Warning said the old Nokomis;
"Go not eastward, go not westward,
For a stranger, whom we know not!
Like a fire upon the hearth-stone
Is a neighbor's homely daughter,
Like the starlight or the moonlight
Is the handsomest of strangers!"
　　Thus dissuading spake Nokomis:
And my Hiawatha answered
Only this: "Dear old Nokomis,
Very pleasant is the firelight,
But I like the starlight better,
Better do I like the moonlight!"
　　Gravely then said old Nokomis:
"Bring not here an idle maiden,
Bring not here a useless woman,
Hands unskilful, feet unwilling:
Bring a wife with nimble fingers,
Heart and hand that move together,
Feet that run on willing errands!"
　　Smiling answered Hiawatha:
"In the land of the Dacotahs
Lives the Arrow-maker's daughter,
Minnehaha, Laughing Water,
Handsomest of all the women.
I will bring her to your wigwam,
She shall run upon your errands,
Be your starlight, moonlight, firelight,
Be the sunlight of my people!"
　　Still dissuading said Nokomis:
"Bring not to my lodge a stranger
From the land of the Dacotahs!
Very fierce are the Dacotahs,
Often is there war between us,
There are feuds yet unforgotten,
Wounds that ache and still may open!"

Laughing answered Hiawatha:
"For that reason, if no other,
Would I wed the fair Dacotah,
That our tribes might be united,
That old feuds might be forgotten,
And old wounds be healed forever!"
    Thus departed Hiawatha
To the lands of the Dacotahs,
To the land of handsome women;
Striding over moor and meadow,
Through interminable forests,
Through uninterrupted silence.
    With his moccasins of magic,
At each stride a mile he measured;
Yet the way seemed long before him,
And his heart outran his footsteps;
And he journeyed without resting,
Till he heard the cataract's laughter,
Heard the Falls of Minnehaha
Calling to him through the silence,
"Pleasant is the sound!" he murmured,
"Pleasant is the voice that calls me!"
    On the outskirts of the forests,
'Twixt the shadow and the sunshine,
Herds of fallow deer were feeding,
But they saw not Hiawatha;
To his bow, he whispered, "Fail not!"
To his arrow whispered, "Swerve not!"
Sent it singing on its errand,
To the red heart of the roebuck;
Threw the deer across his shoulder,
And sped forward without pausing.
    At the doorway of his wigwam
Sat the ancient Arrow-maker,
In the land of the Dacotahs,
Making arrow-heads of jasper,
Arrow-heads of chalcedony.
At his side, in all her beauty,
Sat the lovely Minnehaha,
Sat his daughter, Laughing Water,
Plaiting mats of flags and rushes;
Of the past the old man's thoughts were,
And the maiden's of the future.

He was thinking, as he sat there.
Of the days when with such arrows
He had struck the deer and bison,
On the Muskoday, the meadow;
Shot the wild goose, flying southward,
On the wing, the clamorous Wawa;
Thinking of the great war-parties,
How they came to buy his arrows,
Could not fight without his arrows.
Ah, no more such noble warriors
Could be found on earth as they were!
Now the men were all like women,
Only used their tongues for weapons!
    She was thinking of a hunter,
From another tribe and country,
Young and tall and very handsome,
Who one morning, in the Spring-time,
Came to buy her father's arrows,
Sat and rested in the wigwam,
Lingered long about the doorway,
Looking back as he departed.
She had heard her father praise him,
Praise his courage and his wisdom;
Would he come again for arrows
To the Falls of Minnehaha?
On the mat her hands lay idle,
And her eyes were very dreamy.
    Through their thoughts they heard a footstep,
Heard a rustling in the branches,
And with glowing cheek and forehead,
With the deer upon his shoulders,
Suddenly from out the woodlands
Hiawatha stood before them.
    Straight the ancient Arrow-maker
Looked up gravely from his labor,
Laid aside the unfinished arrow,
Bade him enter at the doorway,
Saying as he rose to meet him.
"Hiawatha, you are welcome!"
    At the feet of Laughing Water
Hiawatha laid his burden,
Threw the red deer from his shoulders;
And the maiden looked up at him,

Looked up from her mat of rushes,
Said with gentle look and accent,
"You are welcome, Hiawatha!"
   Very spacious was the wigwam,
Made of deer-skins dressed and whitened,
With the Gods of the Dacotahs
Drawn and painted on its curtains,
And so tall the doorway, hardly
Hiawatha stooped to enter,
Hardly touched his eagle-feathers
As he entered at the doorway.
   Then uprose the Laughing Water,
From the ground fair Minnehaha,
Laid aside her mat unfinished,
Brought forth food and set before them,
Water brought them from the brooklet,
Gave them food in earthen vessels,
Gave them drink in bowls of basswood,
Listened while the guest was speaking,
Listened while her father answered,
But not once her lips she opened,
Not a single word she uttered.
   Yes, as in a dream she listened
To the words of Hiawatha,
As he talked of old Nokomis,
Who had nursed him in his childhood,
As he told of his companions,
Chibiabos, the musician,
And the very strong man, Kwasind,
And of happiness and plenty
In the land of the Ojibways,
In the pleasant land and peaceful.
   "After many years of warfare,
Many years of strife and bloodshed,
There is peace between the Ojibways
And the tribe of the Dacotahs."
Thus continued Hiawatha,
And then added, speaking slowly,
"That this peace may last forever,
And our hands be clasped more closely,
And our hearts be more united,
Give me as my wife this maiden,
Minnehaha, Laughing Water,

Loveliest of Dacotah women!"
    And the ancient Arrow-maker
Paused a moment ere he answered,
Smoked a little while in silence,
Looked at Hiawatha proudly.
Fondly looked at Laughing Water,
And made answer very gravely:
"Yes, if Minnehaha wishes;
Let your heart speak, Minnehaha!"
    And the lovely Laughing Water
Seemed more lovely as she stood there,
Neither willing nor reluctant,
As she went to Hiawatha,
Softly took the seat beside him,
While she said, and blushed to say it,
"I will follow you, my husband!"
    This was Hiawatha's wooing!
Thus it was he won the daughter
Of the ancient Arrow-maker.
In the land of the Dacotahs!
    From the wigwam he departed,
Leading with him Laughing Water;
Hand in hand they went together,
Through the woodland and the meadow,
Left the old man standing lonely
At the doorway of his wigwam,
Heard the Falls of Minnehaha
Calling to them from the distance,
Crying to them from afar off,
"Fare thee well, O Minnehaha!"
    And the ancient Arrow-maker
Turned again unto his labor,
Sat down by his sunny doorway,
Murmuring to himself, and saying:
"Thus it is our daughters leave us,
Those we love, and those who love us!
Just when they have learned to help us,
When we are old and lean upon them,
Comes a youth with flaunting feathers,
With his flute of reeds, a stranger
Wanders piping through the village,
Beckons to the fairest maiden,
And she follows where he leads her,

717

Leaving all things for the stranger!"
  Pleasant was the journey homeward,
Through interminable forests,
Over meadow, over mountain,
Over river, hill, and hollow.
Short it seemed to Hiawatha,
Though they journeyed very slowly,
Though his pace he checked and slackened
To the steps of Laughing Water.
  Over wide and rushing rivers
In his arms he bore the maiden;
Light he thought her as a feather,
As the plume upon his head-gear;
Cleared the tangled pathway for her.
Bent aside the swaying branches,
Made at night a lodge of branches,
And a bed with boughs of hemlock,
And a fire before the doorway
With the dry cones of the pine-tree.
  All the travelling winds went with them,
O'er the meadows, through the forest;
All the stars of night looked at them,
Watched with sleepless eyes their slumber;
From his ambush in the oak-tree
Peeped the squirrel, Adjidaumo,
Watched with eager eyes the lovers;
And the rabbit, the Wabasso,
Scampered from the path before them,
Peering, peeping from his burrow,
Sat erect upon his haunches,
Watched with curious eyes the lovers.
  Pleasant was the journey homeward!
All the birds sang loud and sweetly
Songs of happiness and heart's-ease;
Sang the bluebird, the Owaissa,
"Happy are you, Hiawatha,
Having such a wife to love you!"
Sang the robin, the Opechee,
"Happy are you, Laughing Water,
Having such a noble husband!"
  From the sky the sun benignant
Looked upon them through the branches,
Saying to them, "O my children,

Love is sunshine, hate is shadow,
Life is checkered shade and sunshine,
Rule by love, O Hiawatha!"
   From the sky the moon looked at them,
Filled the lodge with mystic splendors,
Whispered to them, "O my children,
Day is restless, night is quiet,
Man imperious, woman feeble;
Half is mine, although I follow;
Rule by patience, Laughing Water!"
   Thus it was they journeyed homeward;
Thus it was that Hiawatha
To the lodge of old Nokomis
Brought the moonlight, starlight, firelight,
Brought the sunshine of his people,
Minnehaha, Laughing Water,
Handsomest of all the women
In the land of the Dacotahs,
In the land of handsome women.

THE HARE AND THE TORTOISE

   A Hare insulted a Tortoise upon account of his slowness, and vainly boasted of her own great speed in running. "Let us make a match," replied the Tortoise; "I will run with you five miles for five pounds, and the fox yonder shall be the umpire of the race." The Hare agreed; and away they both started together. But the Hare, by reason of her exceeding swiftness, outran the Tortoise to such a degree, that she made a jest of the matter; and, finding herself a little tired, squatted in a tuft of fern that grew by the way, and took a nap; thinking that, if the Tortoise went by, she could at any time fetch him up with all the ease imaginable. In the meantime while the Tortoise came jogging on with slow but continued motion and the Hare, out of a too great security and confidence of victory, oversleeping herself, the Tortoise arrived at the end of the race first.

                                            (From Aesop's Fables)

"LET US MOVE FORWARD . . . INTO THE STORM AND THROUGH THE STORM"

Winston S. Churchill

Tonight I speak to you at home, I speak to you in Australia and New Zealand, for whose safety we will strain every nerve; to our loyal friends in India and Burma; to our gallant allies, the Dutch and Chinese; and to our kith and kin in the United States. I speak to you all under the shadow of a heavy and far-reaching military defeat.

It is a British and Imperial defeat. Singapore has fallen. All the Malay Peninsula has been overrun. Other dangers gather about out there and none of the dangers which we have hitherto successfully withstood at home and in the East are in any way diminished.

This, therefore, is one of those moments when the British race and nation can show their quality and their genius. This is one of those moments when they can draw from the heart of misfortune the vital impulses of victory.

Here is the moment to display that calm and poise combined with grim determination which not so long ago brought us out of the very jaws of death. Here is another occasion to show, as so often in our long story, that we can meet reverses with dignity and with renewed accessions of strength.

We must remember that we are no longer alone. We are in the midst of a great company. Three quarters of the human race are now moving with us. The whole future of mankind may depend upon our conduct. So far we have not failed. We shall not fail now. Let us move forward steadfastly together into the storm and through the storm.

(February 1942)

WHEN THE HOUNDS OF SPRING

Algernon Charles Swinburne

When the hounds of spring are on winter's traces,
    The mother of months in meadow or plain
Fills the shadows and windy places
    With lisp of leaves and ripple of rain;

And the brown bright nightingale amorous
Is half assuaged for Itylus,
For the Thracian ships and the foreign faces;
    The tongueless vigil, and all the pain.

Come with bows bent and with emptying of quivers,
    Maiden most perfect, lady of light,
With a noise of winds and many rivers,
    With a clamor of waters, and with might;
Bind on thy sandals, O thou most fleet,
Over the splendor and speed of thy feet;
For the faint east quickens, the wan west shivers,
    Round the feet of the day and the feet of the night.

Where shall we find her, how shall we sing to her,
    Fold our hands round her knees, and cling?
O that man's heart were as fire and could spring to her,
    Fire, or the strength of the streams that spring!
For the stars and the winds are unto her
As raiment, as songs of the harp-player;
For the risen stars and the fallen cling to her,
    And the southwest-wind and the west-wind sing.

For winter's rains and ruins are over,
    And all the season of snows and sins;
The days dividing lover and lover,
    The light that loses, the night that wins;
And time remember'd is grief forgotten,
And frosts are slain and flowers begotten,
And in green underwood and cover
    Blossom by blossom the spring begins.

The full streams feed on flower of rushes,
    Ripe grasses trammel a travelling foot,
The faint fresh flame of the young year flushes
    From leaf to flower and flower to fruit;
And fruit and leaf are as gold and fire,
And the oat is heard above the lyre,
And the hooféd heel of a satyr crushes
    The chestnut-husk at the chestnut-root.

And Pan by noon and Bacchus by night,
    Fleeter of foot than the fleet-foot kid,

Follows with dancing and fills with delight
　　The Mænad and the Bassarid;
And soft as lips that laugh and hide
The laughing leaves of the trees divide,
And screen from seeing and leave in sight
　　The god pursuing, the maiden hid.

The ivy falls with the Bacchanal's hair
　　Over her eyebrows hiding her eyes;
The wild vine slipping down leaves bare
　　Her bright breast shortening into sighs;
The wild vine slips with the weight of its leaves,
But the berried ivy catches and cleaves
To the limbs that glitter, the feet that scare
　　The wolf that follows, the fawn that flies.
　　　　　　　　(First Chorus of Atalanta in Calydon)

SELF-RELIANCE

Ralph Waldo Emerson

I do not wish to expiate, but to live. My life is not an apology, but a life. It is for itself and not for a spectacle. I much prefer that it should be a lower strain, so it be genuine and equal, than that it should be glittering and unsteady. . . .

What I must do is all that concerns me, not what the people think. This rule, equally arduous in actual, and in intellectual life, may serve for the whole distinction between greatness and meanness. It is the harder because you will always find those who think they know what is your duty better than you know it. It is easy in the world to live after the world's opinion; it is easy in solitude to live after our own; but the great man is he who in the midst of the crowd keeps with perfect sweetness the independence of solitude.

* * *

He who lies down with dogs rises with fleas.—Anonymous

THE PHARISEE AND THE PUBLICAN

Holy Bible, Luke 18:9–14

And he spake this parable unto certain which trusted in themselves that they were righteous, and despised others:

Two men went up into the temple to pray; one a Pharisee, and the other a publican.

The Pharisee stood and prayed thus with himself: God, I thank thee that I am not as other men are, extortioners, unjust, adulterers, or even as this publican:

I fast twice in the week, I give tithes of all that I possess.

And the publican, standing afar off, would not lift up so much as his eyes unto heaven, but smote his breast, saying, God be merciful to me a sinner.

I tell you, this man went down to his house justified rather than the other: for every one that exalteth himself shall be abased; and he that humbleth himself shall be exalted.

WILL YOU LOVE ME IN DECEMBER
AS YOU DO IN MAY?

James J. Walker

Now in the summer of life, sweetheart,
You say you love but me,
Gladly I give all my heart to you,
Throbbing with ecstasy.
But last night I saw while a-dreaming,
The future old and gray,
And I wondered if you'll love me then dear,
Just as you do today.

Chorus
    Will you love me in December as you do in May,
Will you love me in the good old fashioned way?
When my hair has all turned gray,
Will you kiss me then, and say,
That you love me in December as you do in May?

You say the glow on my cheek, sweetheart,
Is like the rose so sweet;
But when the bloom of fair youth has flown,
Then will our lips still meet?
When life's setting sun fades away dear,
And all is said and done,
Will your arms still entwine and caress me,
Will our hearts beat as one?

NOW IS THE DAY

Phillips Brooks

You who are letting miserable misunderstandings run from year to year, meaning to clear them up someday; you who are keeping wretched quarrels alive because you cannot quite make up your minds that now is the day to sacrifice your pride and kill them; you who are passing men sullenly upon the street, not speaking to them out of some silly spite, and yet knowing that it would fill you with shame and remorse if you heard that one of them were dead tomorrow morning; you who are letting your neighbor starve, till you hear that he is dying of starvation; or letting your friend's heart ache for a word of appreciation or sympathy, which you mean to give him someday; if you could only know and see and feel, all of a sudden, that "the time is short," how it would break the spell! How you would go instantly and do the thing which you might never have another chance to do!

A LESSON

Sa'di

(TRANSLATOR: Sir Edwin Arnold)

Never did I complain of the chances of fortune, nor make a wry face at the resolution of fate, but once, when I was brought to the pass of going barefooted, and had nothing with which to buy shoes. Just then I entered the mosque at Kusa with a heavy heart, and there I observed a person who had no feet at all. At this I offered up praise and thanks to the Almighty God, and gladly submitted to this accident of being shoeless.

SPRING

John Milton

In those vernal seasons of the year, when the air is calm and pleasant, it were an injury and sullenness against nature not to go out and see her riches, and partake in her rejoicing with heaven and earth.

THE FOX AND THE ROOSTER

Aesop

A Fox came toward a Rooster and said to him: "I would fain know if thou canst as well sing as thy father did." And then the Rooster shut his eyes and began to cry and sing. And the Fox took and bare him away. And the people of the town cried: "The Fox beareth away the Rooster!" And then the Rooster said thus to the Fox: "My lord, understandest thou not what the people saith, that thou bearest away their rooster? Tell to them that is thine and not theirs." And as the Fox said, "It is not yours, but it is mine," the Rooster escaped from the Fox's mouth and flew upon a tree.

And then the Rooster said to the Fox: "Thou liest; for I am theirs and not thine." And the Fox began to hit the earth with his mouth and head, saying: "Mouth, thou hast spoken too much! Thou shouldest have eaten the Rooster had not thy words been over many."

And therefore over much talking harmeth, and too much crowing smarteth. Therefore keep thyself from over many words, to the end that thou repentest not.

PERSEVERANCE

Anonymous

If a task is once begun
Never leave it till it's done.
Be the labor great or small,
Do it well or not at all.

THE DOG IN THE MANGER

A Dog was lying upon a manger full of hay. An Ox, being hungry, came near, and offered to eat of the hay; but the envious, ill-natured cur, getting up and snarling at him, would not suffer him to touch it. Upon which the Ox, in the bitterness of his heart, said, "A curse light on thee, for a malicious wretch, who wilt neither eat hay thyself, nor suffer others to do it."

(From Aesop's Fables)

JUST A WEARYIN' FOR YOU

Frank L. Stanton

Just a wearyin' for you,
All the time a-feelin' blue,
Wishin' for you, wonderin' when
You'll be comin' home again,
Restless, don't know what to do,
Just a wearyin' for you,

Mornin' comes, the birds awake,
Used to sing so for your sake,
But there's sadness in the notes
That come thrillin' from their throats.
Seem to feel your absence, too,
Just a wearyin' for you,

* * *

It is magnificent, but it is not war.
(From François Canrobert, on seeing the
charge of the Light Brigade at Balaklava)

DESTINY

John Oliver Hobbes

Men heap together mistakes of their lives, and create a monster which they call Destiny. Some take a mournful pleasure in contemplating the ugliness of the idol: these are called Stoics. Others build it a temple like Solomon's, and worship the temple. These are called Epicureans.

A FATEFUL MESSAGE AND AN ANNOUNCEMENT
THAT SHOOK THE WORLD

August 6, 1945

TO THE PRESIDENT
FROM THE SECRETARY OF WAR

Big bomb dropped on Hiroshima August 5 at 7.15 P.M. Washington time. First reports indicate complete success which was even more conspicuous than earlier test.

Hiroshima bombed visibly with only one tenth cover at 052315A. There was no fighter opposition and no flak. Parsons reports 15 minutes after drop as follows: "Results clear cut successful in all respects. Visible effects greater than in any test. Conditions normal in airplane following delivery."

HARRY S TRUMAN ANNOUNCES THE FIRST
ATOMIC BOMB

Sixteen hours ago an American airplane dropped one bomb on Hiroshima. . . . It is a harnessing of the basic power of the universe. The force from which the sun draws its powers has been loosed against those who brought war to the Far East. We have spent two billion dollars on the greatest scientific gamble in history—and won.

(August 6, 1945)

PRESIDENT TRUMAN TO CONGRESS, JANUARY 7, 1953

Recently in the thermonuclear tests at Eniwetok, we have entered another stage in the world-shaking development of atomic energy. From now on man moves into a new era of destructive power, capable of creating explosions of a new order of magnitude, dwarfing the mushroom clouds of Hiroshima and Nagasaki.

* * *

If a nation expects to be ignorant and free, in a state of civilization, it expects what never was and never will be.

(Thomas Jefferson, 1816)

SING WHILE YOU DRIVE

Anonymous

At 45 miles per hour, sing—"Highways are Happy Ways."
At 55 miles, sing—"I'm But a Stranger Here, Heaven is My Home."
At 65 miles, sing—"Nearer, My God, to Thee!"
At 75 miles, sing—"When the Roll is Called Up Yonder, I'll Be There."
At 85 miles, sing—"Lord, I'm Coming Home."

THE GEORGIA FUNERAL

Henry W. Grady

I attended a funeral once in Pickens County in my State [Georgia]. A funeral is not usually a cheerful object to me unless I could select the subject. I think I could, perhaps, without going a hundred miles from here, find the material for one or two cheerful funerals. Still, this funeral was peculiarly sad. It was a poor "one gallus" fellow, whose breeches struck him under the armpits and hit him at the other end about the knee. . . . They buried him in the midst of a marble quarry: they cut through solid marble to make his grave: and yet a little tombstone they put above him was from Vermont. They buried him in the heart of a pine forest, and yet the pine coffin was imported from Cincinnati. They buried him within touch of an iron mine, and yet the nails in his coffin and the iron in the shovel that dug his grave was imported from Pittsburgh. They buried him by the side of the best sheep-grazing country on earth, and yet the wool in the coffin bands and the coffin bands themselves were brought from the North. The South didn't furnish a thing on earth for that funeral but the corpse and the hole in the ground. There they put him away and the clods rattled down on his coffin, and they buried him in a New York coat and a Boston pair of shoes and a pair of breeches from Chicago and a shirt from Cincinnati, leaving him nothing to carry into the next world with him to remind him of the country in which he lived, and for which he fought for four years, but the chill of blood in his veins and the marrow in his bones.

(1889)

ON THE ROAD TO EMMAUS

Holy Bible, Luke 24:13–36

And, behold, two of them [that is, two of the disciples on the day of Christ's resurrection] went that same day to a village called Emmaus, which was from Jerusalem about threescore furlongs. And they talked together of all these things which had happened. And it came to pass, that, while they communed together and reasoned, Jesus himself drew near, and went with them. But their eyes were holden that they should not know him. And he said unto them, What manner of communications are these that ye have one to another, as ye walk, and are sad? And the one of them, whose name was Cleopas, answering said unto him, Art thou only a stranger in Jerusalem, and hast not known the things which are come to pass there in these days? And he said unto them, What things? And they said unto him, Concerning Jesus of Nazareth, which was a prophet mighty in deed and word before God and all the people: And how the chief priests and our rulers delivered him to be condemned to death, and have crucified him. But we trusted that it had been he which should have redeemed Israel: and beside all this, today is the third day since these things were done. Yea, and certain women also of our company made us astonished, which were early at the sepulchre; And when they found not his body, they came, saying, that they had also seen a vision of angels, which said that he was alive. And certain of them which were with us went to the sepulchre, and found it even so as the women had said: but him they saw not. Then he said unto them, O fools, and slow of heart to believe all that the prophets have spoken: Ought not Christ to have suffered these things, and to enter into his glory? And beginning at Moses and all the prophets, he expounded unto them in all the scriptures the things concerning himself. And they drew nigh unto the village, whither they went: and he made as though he would have gone further. But they constrained him, saying, Abide with us: for it is toward evening, and the day is far spent. And he went in to tarry with them. And it came to pass, as he sat at meat with them, he took bread, and blessed it, and brake, and gave to them. And their eyes were opened, and they knew him; and he vanished out of their sight. And they said one to another, Did not our heart burn within us, while he talked with us by the way, and while he opened to us the scriptures? And they rose up the same hour, and returned to Jerusalem, and found the eleven gathered together, and them that were with them, saying, The Lord is risen indeed, and hath appeared to Simon. And they told what things were done in the way, and how he was known of them in breaking of bread. And as they thus spake, Jesus himself stood in the midst of them, and saith unto them, Peace be unto you.

WHEN I HAVE FEARS THAT I MAY CEASE TO BE

John Keats

When I have fears that I may cease to be
  Before my pen has glean'd my teeming brain,
Before high piled books, in charactry,
  Hold like rich garners the full-ripen'd grain;
When I behold, upon the night's starr'd face,
  Huge cloudy symbols of a high romance,
And think that I may never live to trace
  Their shadows, with the magic hand of chance;
And when I feel, fair creature of an hour!
  That I shall never look upon thee more,
Never have relish in the faery power
  Of unreflecting love;—then on the shore
  Of the wide world I stand alone, and think
  Till Love and Fame to nothingness do sink.

LESSON OF THE BUMBLEBEE

Anonymous

According to the theory of aerodynamics and as may be readily demonstrated through wind tunnel experiments, the bumblebee is unable to fly. This is because the weight, size and shape of his body in relation to the total wingspread makes flying impossible.

BUT THE BUMBLEBEE, BEING IGNORANT OF THESE SCIENTIFIC TRUTHS, GOES AHEAD AND FLIES ANYWAY —AND MAKES A LITTLE HONEY EVERY DAY.

From the *Charter of the United Nations*

We, the people of the United Nations, determined to save succeeding generations from the scourge of war, which twice in our lifetime
has brought untold sorrow to mankind, and to reaffirm faith in
fundamental human rights, in the dignity and worth of the human
person, in the equal right of men and women and of nations large
and small. . . .

And for these ends to practice tolerance and live together in peace
with one another as good neighbors . . .

Have resolved to combine these efforts to accomplish our aims.

(June, 1945)

THE YARN OF THE *NANCY BELL*

W. S. Gilbert

'Twas on the shores that round our coast
   From Deal to Ramsgate span,
That I found alone on a piece of stone
   An elderly naval man.

His hair was weedy, his beard was long,
   And weedy and long was he,
And I heard this wight on the shore recite,
   In a singular minor key:

"Oh, I am a cook and a captain bold,
   And the mate of the *Nancy* brig,
And a bo'sun tight, and a midshipmite,
   And the crew of the captain's gig."

And he shook his fists and he tore his hair,
   Till I really felt afraid,
For I couldn't help thinking the man had been drinking,
   And so I simply said:

"Oh, elderly man, it's little I know
   Of the duties of men of the sea,
But I'll eat my hand if I understand
   How you can possibly be

731

"At once a cook, and a captain bold,
 And the mate of the *Nancy* brig,
And a bo'sun tight, and a midshipmite,
 And the crew of the captain's gig."

Then he gave a hitch to his trousers, which
 Is a trick all seamen larn,
And having got rid of a thumping quid,
 He spun this painful yarn:

"'Twas in the good ship *Nancy Bell*
 That we sailed to the Indian sea,
And there on a reef we come to grief,
 Which has often occurred to me.

"And pretty nigh all o' the crew was drowned
 (There was seventy-seven o' soul),
And only ten of the *Nancy's* men
 Said 'Here!' to the muster-roll.

"There was me and the cook and the captain bold,
 And the mate of the *Nancy* brig,
And the bo'sun tight, and a midshipmite,
 And the crew of the captain's gig.

"For a month we'd neither wittles nor drink,
 Till a-hungry we did feel,
So we drawed a lot, and accordin' shot
 The captain for our meal.

"The next lot fell to the *Nancy's* mate,
 And a delicate dish he made;
Then our appetite with the midshipmite
 We seven survivors stayed.

"And then we murdered the bo'sun tight,
 And he much resembled pig;
Then we wittled free, did the cook and me,
 On the crew of the captain's gig.

"Then only the cook and me was left,
 And the delicate question, 'Which
Of us two goes to the kettle?' arose
 And we argued it out as sich.

"For I loved that cook as a brother, I did,
   And the cook he worshipped me;
But we'd both be blowed if we'd either be stowed
   In the other chap's hold, you see.

" 'I'll be eat if you dines off me,' says Tom,
   'Yes, that,' says I, 'you'll be,'—
'I'm boiled if I die, my friend,' quoth I,
   And 'Exactly so,' quoth he.

"Says he, 'Dear James, to murder me
   Were a foolish thing to do,
For don't you see that you can't cook *me*,
   While I can—and will—cook *you*!'

"So he boils the water, and takes the salt
   And the pepper in portions true
(Which he never forgot), and some chopped shalot,
   And some sage and parsley too.

" 'Come here,' says he, with a proper pride,
   Which his smiling features tell,
' 'Twill soothing be if I let you see,
   How extremely nice you'll smell.'

"And he stirred it round and round and round,
   And he sniffed at the foaming froth;
When I ups with his heels, and smothers his squeals
   In the scum of the boiling broth.

"And I eat that cook in a week or less,
   And—as I eating be
The last of his chops, why, I almost drops,
   For a wessel in sight I see!

* * *

"And I never grin, and I never smile,
   And I never larf nor play,
But I sit and croak, and a single joke
   I have—which is to say:

"Oh, I am a cook and a captain bold,
   And the mate of the *Nancy* brig,
And a bo'sun tight, *and* a midshipmite,
   And the crew of the captain's gig!"

WHAT IS AN AMERICAN?

Michel Guillaume Jean de Crèvecœur

What then is the American, this new man? He is either an European, or the descendant of an European, hence that strange mixture of blood, which you will find in no other country. I could point out to you a family whose grandfather was an Englishman, whose wife was Dutch, whose son married a French woman, and whose present four sons now have four wives of different nations. *He* is an American, who, leaving behind him all his ancient prejudices and manners, receives new ones from the new mode of life he has embraced, the new government he obeys, and the new rank he holds. He becomes an American by being received in the broad lap of our great *Alma Mater*. Here individuals of all nations are melted into a new race of men, whose labor and posterity will one day cause great changes in the world. Americans are the western pilgrims, who are carrying along with them that great mass of arts, sciences, vigor, and industry which began long since in the east; they will finish the great circle. The Americans were once scattered all over Europe; here they are incorporated into one of the finest systems of population which has ever appeared, and which will hereafter become distinct by the power of the different climates they inhabit. The American ought therefore to love his country much better than that wherein either he or his forefathers were born. Here the rewards of his industry follow with equal steps the progress of his labor; his labor is founded on the basis of nature, *self-interest;* can it want a stronger allurement? Wives and children, who before in vain demanded of him a morsel of bread, now, fat and frolicsome, gladly help their father to clear those fields whence exuberant crops are to arise to feed and to clothe them all; without any part being claimed, either by a despotic prince, a rich abbot, or a mighty lord. Here religion demands but little of him; a small voluntary salary to the minister, and gratitude to God; can he refuse these? The American is a new man, who acts upon new principles; he must therefore entertain new ideas, and form new opinions. From involuntary idleness, servile dependence, penury, and useless labor, he has passed to toils of a very different nature, rewarded by ample subsistence.—This is an American.

(From Letters of an American Farmer, 1782)

THE VOICE OF GOD

Louis I. Newman

I sought to hear the voice of God,
And climbed the topmost steeple.
But God declared: "Go down again,
I dwell among the people."

OUT OF THE CRADLE ENDLESSLY ROCKING

Walt Whitman

Out of the cradle endlessly rocking,
Out of the mocking-bird's throat, the musical shuttle,
Out of the Ninth-month midnight,
Over the sterile sands, and the fields beyond, where the child,
    leaving his bed, wander'd alone, bare-headed, barefoot,
Down from the shower'd halo,
Up from the mystic play of shadows, twining and twisting as if they
    were alive,
Out from the patches of briers and blackberries,
From the memories of the bird that chanted to me,
From your memories, sad brother—from the fitful risings and
    fallings I heard,
From under that yellow half-moon, late-risen, and swollen as if
    with tears,
From those beginning notes of sickness and love, there in the trans-
    parent mist,
From the thousand responses of my heart, never to cease,
From the myriad thence-arous'd words,
From the word stronger and more delicious than any,
From such, as now they start, the scene revisiting,
As a flock, twittering, rising, or overhead passing,
Borne hither—ere all eludes me, hurriedly,
A man—yet by these tears a little boy again,
Throwing myself on the sand, confronting the waves,
I, chanter of pains and joys, uniter of here and hereafter,
Taking all hints to use them—but swiftly leaping beyond them,
A reminiscence sing.

Once, Paumanok,
When the snows had melted—when the lilac-scent was in the air,
    and the Fifth-month grass was growing,
Up this sea-shore, in some briers,
Two guests from Alabama—two together,
And their nest, and four light-green eggs, spotted with brown,
And every day the he-bird, to and fro, near at hand,
And every day the she-bird, crouch'd on her nest, silent, with
    bright eyes,
And every day I, a curious boy, never too close, never disturbing
    them,
Cautiously peering, absorbing, translating.

3

Shine! shine! shine!
Pour down your warmth, great Sun!
While we bask—we two together.

Two together!
Winds blow South, or winds blow North,
Day come white, or night come black,
Home, or rivers and mountains from home,
Singing all time, minding no time,
While we two keep together.

4

Till of a sudden,
May-be kill'd, unknown to her mate,
One forenoon the she-bird crouch'd not on the nest,
Nor return'd that afternoon, nor the next,
Nor ever appear'd again.
And thenceforward, all summer, in the sound of the sea,
And at night, under the full of the moon, in calmer weather,
Over the hoarse surging of the sea,
Or flitting from brier to brier by day,
I saw, I heard at intervals, the remaining one, the he-bird,
The solitary guest from Alabama.

5

Blow! blow! blow!
Blow up, sea-winds, along Paumanok's shore!
I wait and I wait, till you blow my mate to me.

Yes, when the stars glisten'd,
All night long, on the prong of a moss-scallop'd stake,
Down, almost amid the slapping waves,
Sat the lone singer, wonderful, causing tears.

He call'd on his mate;
He pour'd forth the meanings which I, of all men, know.

Yes, my brother, I know;
The rest might not—but I have treasur'd every note;
For once, and more than once, dimly, down to the beach gliding,
Silent, avoiding the moonbeams, blending myself with the shad-
    ows,
Recalling now the obscure shapes, the echoes, the sounds and sights
    after their sorts,
The white arms out in the breakers tirelessly tossing,
I, with bare feet, a child, the wind wafting my hair,
Listen'd long and long.

Listen'd, to keep, to sing—now translating the notes,
Following you, my brother.

7

Soothe! soothe! soothe!
Close on its wave soothes the wave behind,
And again another behind, embracing and lapping, every one
    close,
But my love soothes not me, not me.

Low hangs the moon—it rose late;
O it is lagging—O I think it is heavy with love, with love,

O madly the sea pushes, pushes upon the land,
With love—with love.

O night! do I not see my love fluttering out there among the
    breakers?
What is that little black thing I see there in the white?

Loud! loud! loud!
Loud I call to you, my love!

High and clear I shoot my voice over the waves;
Surely you must know who is here, is here;
You must know who I am, my love.

Low-hanging moon!
What is that dusky spot in your brown yellow?

O it is the shape, the shape of my mate!
O moon, do not keep her from me any longer.

Land! land! O land!
Whichever way I turn, O I think you could give me my mate back
    again, if you only would;
For I am almost sure I see her dimly whichever way I look.

O rising stars!
Perhaps the one I want so much will rise, will rise with some of
    you.

O throat! O trembling throat!
Sound clearer through the atmosphere!
Pierce the woods, the earth;
Somewhere listening to catch you, must be the one I want.

Shake out, carols!
Solitary here—the night's carols!
Carols of lonesome love! Death's carols!
Carols under that lagging, yellow, waning moon!
O, under that moon, where she droops almost down into the sea!
O reckless, despairing carols.

But soft! sink low;
Soft! let me just murmur;
And do you wait a moment, you husky-noised sea;
For somewhere I believe I heard my mate responding to me,
So faint—I must be still, be still to listen;
But not altogether still, for then she might not come immediately
    to me.

Hither, my love!
Here I am! Here!

With this just-sustain'd note I announce myself to you;
This gentle call is for you, my love, for you.

Do not be decoy'd elsewhere!
That is the whistle of the wind—it is not my voice;
That is the fluttering, the fluttering of the spray;
Those are the shadows of leaves.

O darkness! O in vain!
O I am very sick and sorrowful.

O brown halo in the sky, near the moon, drooping upon the sea!
O troubled reflection in the sea!
O throat! O throbbing heart!
O all—and I singing uselessly, uselessly all the night.

Yet I murmur, murmur on!
O murmurs—you yourselves make me continue to sing, I know
   not why.

O past! O life! O songs of joy!
In the air—in the woods—over fields;
Loved! loved! loved! loved! loved!
But my love no more, no more with me!
We two together no more.

8

The aria sinking,
All else continuing—the stars shining,
The winds blowing—the notes of the bird continuous echoing,
With angry moans the fierce old mother incessantly moaning,
On the sands of Paumanok's shore, gray and rustling;
The yellow half-moon enlarged, sagging down, drooping, the face
   of the sea almost touching;
The boy ecstatic—with his bare feet the waves, with his hair the
   atmosphere dallying,
The love in the heart long pent, now loose, now at last tumultu-
   ously bursting,
The aria's meaning, the ears, the Soul, swiftly depositing,
The strange tears down the cheeks coursing,
The colloquy there—the trio—each uttering,
The undertone—the savage old mother, incessantly crying.
To the boy's Soul's questions sullenly timing—some drown'd se-
   cret hissing,
To the outsetting bard of love.

Demon or bird! (said the boy's soul,)
Is it indeed toward your mate you sing? or is it mostly to me?
For I, that was a child, my tongue's use sleeping,
Now I have heard you,
Now in a moment I know what I am for—I awake,
And already a thousand singers—a thousand songs, clearer, louder
  and more sorrowful than yours,
A thousand warbling echoes have started to life within me, never
  to die.
O you singer, solitary, singing by yourself—projecting me;
O solitary me, listening—never more shall I cease perpetuating
  you;
Never more shall I escape, never more the reverberations,
Never more the cries of unsatisfied love be absent from me,
Never again leave me to be the peaceful child I was before what
  there, in the night,
By the sea, under the yellow and sagging moon,
The messenger there arous'd—the fire, the sweet hell within,
The unknown want, the destiny of me.

O give me the clew! (it lurks in the night here somewhere;)
O if I am to have so much, let me have more!
O a word! O what is my destination? (I fear it is henceforth
  chaos;)
O how joys, dreads, convolutions, human shapes, and all shapes,
  spring as from graves around me!
O phantoms! you cover all the land and all the sea!
O I cannot see in the dimness whether you smile or frown upon
  me;
O vapor, a look, a word! O well-beloved!
O you dear women's and men's phantoms!

A word then, (for I will conquer it,)
The word final, superior to all,
Subtle, sent up—what is it?—I listen;
Are you whispering it, and have been all the time, you seawaves?
Is that it from your liquid rims and wet sands?

10

Whereto answering, the sea,
Delaying not, hurrying not,

Whisper'd me through the night, and very plainly before daybreak,
Lisp'd to me the low and delicious word DEATH,
And again Death—ever Death, Death, Death,
Hissing melodious, neither like the bird, nor like my arous'd
    child's heart,
But edging near, as privately for me, rustling at my feet,
Creeping thence steadily up to my ears, and laving me softly all
    over,
Death, Death, Death, Death, Death.

Which I do not forget,
But fuse the song of my dusky demon and brother,
That he sang to me in the moonlight on Paumanok's gray beach,
With the thousand responsive songs, at random,
My own songs, awaked from that hour;
And with them the key, the word up from the waves,
The word of the sweetest song, and all songs,
That strong and delicious word which, creeping to my feet,
The sea whisper'd me.

STANDING ALONE ON A HILL

Thomas Hardy

    To persons standing alone on a hill during a clear mid-night such
as this, the roll of the world eastward is almost a palpable movement.
The sensation may be caused by the panoramic glide of the stars past
earthly objects, which is perceptible in a few minutes of stillness, or
by the better outlook upon space a hill affords, or by the wind, or by
the solitude; but whatever be its origin, the impression of riding
along is vivid and abiding. The poetry of motion is a phrase much in
use, and to enjoy the epic form of that gratification it is necessary to
stand on a hill at a small hour of the night, and, having first expanded
with a sense of difference from the mass of civilized mankind, who
are dreamwrapt and disregardful of all such proceedings at this time,
long and quietly watch your stately progress through the stars. After
such a nocturnal reconnoitre it is hard to get back to earth, and to
believe that the consciousness of such majestic speeding is derived
from a tiny human frame.

741

THE TREASURER'S REPORT

Robert Benchley

The report is delivered by an Assistant Treasurer who has been called in to pinch-hit for the regular Treasurer, who is ill. He is not a very good public-speaker, but after a few minutes of confusion is caught up by the spell of his own oratory and is hard to stop.

I shall take but a very few moments of your time this evening, for I realize that you would much rather be listening to this interesting entertainment than to a dry financial statement . . . but I am reminded of a story—which you have probably all of you heard.

It seems that there were two Irishmen walking down the street when they came to a—oh, I should have said in the first place that the parrot which was hanging out in front of the store—or rather belonging to one of these two fellows—the first Irishman, that is—we—well, anyway, this parrot.—

(After a slight cogitation, he realizes that, for all practical purpose, the story is as good as lost; so he abandons it entirely and, stepping forward, drops his facile, story-telling manner and assumes a quite spurious businesslike air.)

Now, in connection with reading this report, there are one or two points which Dr. Murnie wanted brought up in connection with it, and he asked me to bring them up in connec—to bring them up.

In the first place, there is the question of the work which we are trying to do up there at our little place at Silver Lake, a work which we feel not only fills a very definite need in the community but also fills a very definite need—er—in the community. I don't think that many members of the Society realize just how big the work is that we are trying to do up there. For instance, I don't think that it is generally known that most of our boys are between the age of fourteen. We feel that, by taking the boy at this age, we can get closer to his real nature—for a boy has a very real nature, you may be sure—and bring him into closer touch not only with the school, the parents, and with each other, but also the town in which they live, the country to whose flag they pay allegiance, and to the— ah— (trailing off) town in which they live.

Now the fourth point which Dr. Murnie wanted brought up was that in connection with the installation of the new furnace last Fall. There seems to have been considerable talk going around about this not having been done quite as economically as it might—have—been —done, when, as a matter of fact, the whole thing was done just as economically as possible—in fact, even more so. I have here a report of the Furnace Committee, showing just how the whole thing was handled from start to finish.

(*Reads from report, with considerable initial difficulty with the stiff cover.*)

Bids were submitted by the following firms of furnace contractors, with a clause stating that if we did not engage a firm to do the work for us we should pay them nothing for submitting the bids. This clause alone saved us a great deal of money.

The following firms, then, submitted bids:

Merkle, Wybigant Co., the Eureka Dust Bin and Shaker Co., the Elite Furnace Shop, and Harris, Birnbauer and Harris. The bid of Merkle, Wybignant being the lowest, Harris, Birnbauer were selected to do the job.

(*Here a page is evidently missing from the report, and a hurried search is carried on through all the pages, without result.*)

Well, that pretty well clears up that end of the work.

Those of you who contributed so generously last year to the floating hospital have probably wondered what became of the money.

I was speaking on this subject only last week at our up-town branch, and, after the meeting, a dear little old lady, dressed all in lavender, came up on the platform, and laying her hand on my arm, said: "Mr. So-and-so (calling me by name), Mr. So-and-so, what the hell did you do with all the money we gave you last year?" Well, I just laughed and pushed her off the platform, but it has occurred to the committee that perhaps some of you, like that little old lady, would be interested in knowing the disposition of the funds.

Now, Mr. Rossiter, unfortunately our treasurer—or rather Mr. Rossiter our *treasurer, unfortunately* is confined at his home tonight with a bad head-cold and I have been asked (*he hears someone whispering at him from the wings, but decides to ignore it*) and I have been asked if I would (*the whisperer will not be denied, so he goes over to the entrance and receives a brief message, returning beaming and laughing to himself*).

Well the joke seems to be on *me*! Mr. Rossiter has *pneumonia*!

Following, then, is a summary of the Treasurer's report:

(*Reads in a very business-like manner*).

During the year 1929—and by that is meant 1928—the Choral Society received the following in donations:

B.L.G. $500
G.K.M. 500
Lottie and Nellie W. 500
In memory of a happy summer at Rye Beach ..   10
Proceeds of a sale of coats and hats left in the
   boat house 1.55
And then the Junior League gave a perform-
   ance of "Pinafore" for the benefit of the
   Fund which, unfortunately, resulted in a
   deficit of $300
Then, from dues and charges 2,354.75
And, following the installation of the new furnace, a saving in coal
amounting to $374.75—which made Dr. Murnie very happy, you
may be sure. Making a total of receipts amounting to $3,645.75.
This is all, of course, reckoned as of June.

In the matter of expenditures, the Club has not been so fortunate.
There was the unsettled condition of business, and the late Spring,
to contend with, resulting in the following—er—rather discouraging
figures, I am afraid.

Expenditures $23,574.85
Then there was a loss, owing to—
   several things—of 3,326.70
Car-fare 4,452.25
And then, Mrs. Rawlin's expense account,
   when she went down to see the work
   they are doing in Baltimore, came to
   $256.50, but I am sure that you will all
   agree that it was worth it to find out—er
   —what they are doing in Baltimore.
And then, Mrs. Rawlin's expense account
   and Ends 2,537.50
Making a total disbursement of (hurriedly)
                      $416,546.75
   or a net deficit of—ah—several thousand
   dollars.

Now these figures bring us down only to October. In October
my sister was married, and the house was all torn up, and in the
general confusion we lost track of the figures for May and August.
All those wishing to approximate figures for May and August, however, may obtain them from me in the vestry after the dinner, where
I will be with pledge cards for those of you who wish to subscribe
over and above your annual dues, and I hope that each and every
one of you here tonight will look deep into his heart and (archly)

into his pocketbook, and see if he cannot find it there to help us put this thing over with a bang (accompanied by a wholly ineffectual gesture representing a bang) and to help and make this just the biggest and best year the Armenians have ever had—I thank you.

(Exits, bumping into proscenium.)

THE OLD STOIC

Emily Brontë

Riches I hold in light esteem,
   And Love I laugh to scorn;
And lust of fame was but a dream
   That vanished with the morn:

And, if I pray, the only prayer
   That moves my lips for me
Is, "Leave the heart that now I bear,
   And give me liberty!"

Yea, as my swift days near their goal,
   'Tis all that I implore:
In life and death a chainless soul
With courage to endure.

OBITUARY

William Allen White

Frank Munsey, the great publisher, is dead. Frank Munsey contributed to the journalism of his day the great talents of a meat packer, the morals of a money changer and the manners of an undertaker. He and his kind have about succeeded in transforming a once noble profession into an eight per-cent security. May he rest in trust!

(*Emporia Gazette*, December 23, 1925)

THE LATEST DECALOGUE

Arthur Hugh Clough

Thou shalt have one God only; who
Would be at the expense of two?
No graven image may be
Worshipped, except the currency.
Swear not at all; for, for thy curse
Thine enemy is none the worse.
At Church on Sunday to attend
Will serve to keep the world thy friend.
Honor thy parents; that it, all
From whom advancement may befall.
Thou shalt not kill; but needst not strive
Officiously to keep alive.
Do not adultery commit;
Advantage rarely comes of it.
Thou shalt not steal; an empty feat,
When it's so lucrative to cheat.
Bear not false witness; let the lie
Have time on its own wings to fly.
Thou shalt not covet, but tradition
Approves all forms of competition.

ADVERTISE!

Mark Twain

(When Mark Twain edited a paper in Missouri, one of his subscribers wrote him that he had found a spider in the paper and wanted to know whether it meant good luck or bad. Mark Twain replied:) "Old Subscriber: Finding a spider in your paper was neither good luck nor bad luck for you. The spider was merely looking over our paper to see which merchant is not advertising so that he can go to that store, spin his web across the door and lead a life of undisturbed peace ever afterward."

NOTICE

/

Persons attempting to find a motive in this narrative will be prosecuted; persons attempting to find a moral in it will be banished; persons attempting to find a plot in it will be shot.
By Order of the Author,
Per G.G., Chief of Ordnance
(From Mark Twain's *Huckleberry Finn*)

ON AN OLD SUN DIAL

Time flies,
Suns rise
And shadows fall.
Let time go by.
Love is forever over all.

THE STARS

Ralph Waldo Emerson

If a man would be alone, let him look at the stars. The rays that come from those heavenly worlds will separate between him and what he touches.

One might think the atmosphere was made transparent with this design, to give man, in the heavenly bodies, the perpetual presence of the sublime. Seen in the streets of cities, how great they are!

WAR

John Dryden

War, he sung, is Toil and Trouble;
Honour but an empty Bubble.
     Never ending, still beginning,
Fighting still, and still destroying,
     If the World be worth thy Winning,
Think, O think, it worth Enjoying.
          (From Alexander's Feast)

747

PEACE

Victor Hugo

Have courage for the great sorrows of life and patience for the small ones; and when you have laboriously accomplished your daily tasks, go to sleep in peace. God is awake.

BENJAMIN FRANKLIN'S LETTER OF INTRODUCTION FOR ONE LEAVING EUROPE FOR THE UNITED STATES

Sir:—the bearer of this, who is going to America, presses me to give him a letter of recommendation, though I know nothing of him, not even his name. This may seem extraordinary, but I assure you it is not uncommon here. Sometimes, indeed, one unknown person brings another equally unknown, to recommend him; and sometimes they recommend one another!

As to this gentleman, I must refer you to himself for his character and merits, with which he is certainly better acquainted than I can possibly be. I recommend him, however, to those civilities which every stranger, of whom one knows no harm, has a right to; and I request you will do him all the favor that, on further acquaintance, you shall find him to deserve. I have the honor, to be etc.—

(Paris, April 2, 1777)

HABEAS CORPUS

That every Englishman who is imprisoned by any authority whatsoever, has an undoubted right, by his agents, or friends, to apply for, and obtain a write of *habeas corpus,* in order to procure his liberty by due course of law.

(Resolution of The House of Lords, 1679)

HOME ON THE RANGE

Anonymous

Oh, give me a home where the buffalo roam,
Where the deer and the antelope play;
Where seldom is heard a discouraging word,
And the skies are not cloudy all day.

Chorus:
Home, home on the range;
Where the deer and the antelope play;
Where seldom is heard a discouraging word,
And the skies are not cloudy all day.

Where the air is so pure, the zephyrs so free,
The breezes so balmy and light,
That I would not exchange my home on the range
For all the cities so bright.

The red man was pressed from this part of the West,
He's likely no more to return
To the banks of the Red River where seldom if ever
Their flickering campfires burn.

How often at night when the heavens are bright
With the light of the glittering stars,
Have I stood here amazed and asked as I gazed
If their glory exceeds that of ours.

Oh, I love these wild flowers in this dear land of ours;
The curlew I love to hear scream;
And I love the white rocks and the antelope flocks
That graze on the mountain-tops green.

Oh, give me a land where the bright diamond sand
Flows leisurely down the stream;
Where the graceful white swan goes gliding along
Like a maid in a heavenly dream.

Then I would not exchange my home on the range,
Where the deer and the antelope play;
Where seldom is heard a discouraging word,
And the skies are not cloudy all day.

From THE EVERLASTING MERCY

John Masefield

O Christ who holds the open gate,
O Christ who drives the furrow straight,
O Christ, the plough, O Christ, the laughter
Of holy white birds flying after,
Lo, all my heart's field red and torn,
And Thou wilt bring the young green corn,
The young green corn divinely springing,
The young green corn forever singing;
And when the field is fresh and fair
Thy blessèd feet shall glitter there,
And we will walk the weeded field,
And tell the golden harvest's yield,
The corn that makes the holy bread
By which the soul of man is fed,
The holy bread, the food unpriced,
Thy everlasting mercy, Christ.

MY LAST DUCHESS

Robert Browning

That's my last Duchess painted on the wall,
Looking as if she were alive. I call
That piece a wonder, now: Frà Pandolf's hands
Worked busily a day, and there she stands.
Will 't please you sit and look at her? I said
"Frà Pandolf" by design, for never read
Strangers like you that pictured countenance,
The depth and passion of its earnest glance,
But to myself they turned (since none puts by
The curtain I have drawn for you, but I)
And seemed as they would ask me, if they durst,
How such a glance came there; so not the first
Are you to turn and ask thus. Sir, 't was not
Her husband's presence only, called that spot
Of joy into the Duchess' cheek: perhaps
Frà Pandolf chanced to say, "Her mantle laps
Over my lady's wrist too much," or "Paint

Must never hope to reproduce the faint
Half-flush that dies along her throat:" such stuff
Was courtesy, she thought, and cause enough
For calling up that spot of joy. She had
A heart—how shall I say?—too soon made glad.
Too easily impressed: she liked whate'er
She looked on, and her looks went everywhere.
Sir, 't was all one! My favor at her breast,
The dropping of the daylight in the West,
The bough of cherries some officious fool
Broke in the orchard for her, the white mule
She rode with round the terrace—all and each
Would draw from her alike the approving speech,
Or blush, at least. She thanked men,—good! but thanked
Somehow—I know not how—as if she ranked
My gift of a nine-hundred-years-old name
With anybody's gift. Who'd stoop to blame
This sort of trifling? Even had you skill
In speech—(which I have not)—to make your will
Quite clear to such an one, and say, "Just this
Or that in you disgusts me; here you miss,
Or there exceed the mark"—and if she let
Herself be lessoned so, nor plainly set
Her wits to yours, forsooth, and made excuse,
—E'en then would be some stooping; and I choose
Never to stoop. Oh, sir, she smiled, no doubt,
Whene'er I passed her; but who passed without
Much the same smile? This grew; I gave commands;
Then all smiles stopped together. There she stands
As if alive. Will 't please you rise? We'll meet
The company below, then. I repeat,
The Count your master's known munificence
Is ample warrant that no just pretense
Of mine for dowry will be disallowed;
Though his fair daughter's self, as I avowed
At starting, is my object. Nay, we'll go
Together down, sir. Notice Neptune, though,
Taming a sea-horse, thought a rarity,
Which Claus of Innsbruck cast in bronze for me!

THE DEATH OF LITTLE NELL

Charles Dickens

She was dead. No sleep so beautiful and calm, so free from trace of pain, so fair to look upon. She seemed a creature fresh from the hand of God, and waiting for the breath of life; not one who had lived, and suffered death. Her couch was dressed with here and there some winter berries and green leaves, gathered in a spot she had been used to favor. "When I die, put near me something that has loved the light, and had the sky above it always." These were her words.

She was dead. Dear, gentle, patient, noble Nell was dead. Her little bird, a poor, slight thing the pressure of a finger would have crushed, was stirring nimbly in its cage, and the strong heart of its child-mistress was mute and motionless forever! Where were the traces of her early cares, her sufferings, and fatigues? All gone. Sorrow was dead, indeed, in her; but peace and perfect happiness were born, imaged in her tranquil beauty and profound repose.

And still her former self lay there, unaltered in this change. Yes! the old fireside had smiled upon that same sweet face; it had passed, like a dream, through haunts of misery and care; at the door of the poor schoolmaster on the summer evening, before the furnace fire upon the cold wet night, at the still bedside of the dying boy, there had been the same mild and lovely look. So shall we know the angels, in their majesty, after death.

The old man held one languid arm in his, and had the small hand tight folded to his breast for warmth. It was the hand she had stretched out to him with her last smile; the hand that had led him on through all their wanderings. Ever and anon he pressed it to his lips; then hugged it to his breast again, murmuring that it was warmer now, and as he said it, he looked in agony to those who stood around, as if imploring them to help her.

She was dead, and past all help, or need of help. The ancient rooms she had seemed to fill with life, even while her own was waning fast, the garden she had tended, the eyes she had gladdened, the noiseless haunts of many a thoughtful hour, the paths she had trodden, as it were, but yesterday, could know her no more.

"It is not," said the schoolmaster, as he bent down to kiss her on the cheek, and gave his tears free vent, "It is not in *this* world that heaven's justice ends. Think what earth is, compared with the world to which her young spirit has winged its early flight, and say, if one deliberate wish, expressed in solemn tones above this bed, could call her back to life, which of us would utter it?"

She had been dead two days. They were all about her at the time, knowing that the end was drawing on. She died soon after day-break. They had read and talked to her in the earlier portion of the night; but, as the hours crept on, she sank to sleep. They could tell by what she faintly uttered in her dreams, that they were of her journeyings with the old man; they were of no painful scenes, but of the people who had helped them, and used them kindly; for she often said "God bless you!" with great fervor.

Waking, she had never wandered in her mind but once, and that was at beautiful music, which, she said, was in the air. God knows. It may have been. Opening her eyes, at last, from a very quiet sleep, she begged that they would kiss her once again. That done, she turned to the old man, with a lovely smile upon her face, such, they said, as they had never seen, and could never forget, and clung, with both her arms, about his neck. She had never murmured or complained; but, with a quiet mind, and manner quite unaltered, save that she every day became more earnest and more grateful to them, faded like the light upon the summer's evening.

(From The Old Curiosity Shop)

WHEN LOVELY WOMAN

Phoebe Cary

When lovely woman wants a favor,
    And finds, too late, that man won't bend,
What earthly circumstance can save her
    From disappointment in the end?

The only way to bring him over,
    The last experiment to try,
Whether a husband or a lover,
    If he have a feeling is—to cry.

* * *

How sad it is to think that eyes that are too old to see are yet not too old to shed tears.—François René de Chateaubriand

ECHOES
To W. A.

William Ernest Henley

Or ever the knightly years were gone
  With the old world to the grave,
I was a King in Babylon
  And you were a Christian Slave.

I saw, I took, I cast you by,
  I bent and broke your pride.
You loved me well, or I heard them lie,
  But your longing was denied.
Surely I knew that by and by
  You cursed your gods and died.

And a myriad suns have set and shone
  Since then upon the grave
Decreed by the King of Babylon
  To her that had been his Slave.

The pride I trampled is now my scathe,
  For it tramples me again.
The old resentment lasts like death,
  For you love, yet you refrain.
I break my heart on your hard unfaith,
  And I break my heart in vain.

Yet not for an hour do I wish undone
  The deed beyond the grave,
When I was a King in Babylon
  And you were a Virgin Slave.

EPITAPH

Anonymous

Within this grave do lie
Back to back, my wife and I;
When the last trump the air shall fill,
If she gets up, I'll just lie still.

BRAHMA

Ralph Waldo Emerson

If the red slayer think he slays,
  Or if the slain think he is slain,
They know not well the subtle ways
  I keep, and pass, and turn again.

Far or forgot to me is near;
  Shadow and sunlight are the same;
The vanished gods to me appear;
  And one to me are shame and fame.

They reckon ill who leave me out;
  When me they fly, I am the wings;
I am the doubter and the doubt,
  And I the hymn the Brahmin sings.

The strong gods pine for my abode,
  And pine in vain the sacred Seven;
But thou, meek lover of the good!
  Find me, and turn thy back on heaven.

* * *

It is better to have no ideas than false ones.
                              —Thomas Jefferson

A FOREIGN RULER

Walter Savage Landor

He says, *My reign is peace,* so slays
  A thousand in the dead of night.
Are you all happy now? he says,
  And those he leaves behind cry *quite.*
He swears he will have no contention,
  And sets all nations by the ears;
He shouts aloud, *No intervention!*
  Invades, and drowns them all in tears.

IS THERE A SANTA CLAUS?

We take pleasure in answering at once and thus prominently the communication below, expressing at the same time our great gratification that its faithful author is numbered among the friends of THE SUN:

Dear Editor—I am 8 years old.

Some of my little friends say there is no Santa Claus.

Papa says, "If you see it in THE SUN it's so."

Please tell me the truth, is there a Santa Claus? Virginia O'Hanlon 115 West ninety-fifth street.

Virginia, your little friends are wrong. They have been affected by the skepticism of a skeptical age. They do not believe except they see. They think that nothing can be which is not comprehensible by their little minds. All minds, Virginia, whether they be men's or children's, are little. In this great universe of ours man is a mere insect, an ant, in his intellect, as compared with the boundless world about him, as measured by the intelligence capable of grasping the whole of truth and knowledge.

Yes, Virginia, there is a SANTA CLAUS. He exists as certainly as love and generosity and devotion exist, and you know that they abound and give to your life its highest beauty and joy. Alas! how dreary would be the world if there were no SANTA CLAUS! It would be as dreary as if there were no Virginias. There would be no child-like faith then, no poetry, no romance to make tolerable this existence. We should have no enjoyment, except in sense and sight. The eternal light with which childhood fills the world would be extinguished.

Not believe in SANTA CLAUS! You might as well not believe in fairies! You might get your papa to hire men to watch in all the chimneys on Christmas Eve to catch SANTA CLAUS, but even if they did not see SANTA CLAUS coming down, what would that prove? Nobody sees SANTA CLAUS, but that is no sign there is no SANTA CLAUS. The most real things in the world are those that neither children nor men can see. Did you ever see fairies dancing on the lawn? Of course not, but that's no proof that they are not there. Nobody can conceive or imagine all the wonders there are unseen and unseeable in the world.

You tear apart a baby's rattle and see what makes the noise inside, but there is a veil covering the unseen world which not the strongest man, nor even the united strength of all the strongest men that ever lived, could tear apart. Only faith, fancy, poetry, love, romance, can push aside that curtain and view and picture the supernal beauty and glory beyond. Is it all real? Ah, Virginia, in all this world there is nothing else real and abiding.

No SANTA CLAUS! Thank GOD! he lives, and he lives for- ever. A thousand years from now, Virginia, nay, ten times ten thousand years from now, he will continue to make glad the heart of childhood.

(Editorial in the New York SUN,
Sept. 21, 1897, by Francis P. Church)

THE HOUSE ON THE HILL

Edwin Arlington Robinson

They are all gone away,
   The House is shut and still,
There is nothing more to say.

Through broken walls and gray
   The winds blow bleak and shrill;
They are all gone away.

Nor is there one today
   To speak them good or ill:
There is nothing more to say.

Why is it then we stray
   Around that sunken sill?
They are all gone away,

And our poor fancy-play
   For them is wasted skill:
There is nothing more to say.

There is ruin and decay
   In the House on the Hill:

They are all gone away,
There is nothing more to say.

*   *   *

Men are not hanged for stealing horses, but that horses may not be stolen.

—George Savile, Marquess of Halifax

ASK AND HAVE

Samuel Lover

"Oh, 'tis time I should talk to your mother,
  Sweet Mary," says I;
"Oh, don't talk to my mother," says Mary,
  Beginning to cry:
"For my mother says men are deceivers,
  And never, I know, will consent;
She says girls in a hurry to marry,
  At leisure repent."

"Then, suppose I would talk to your father,
  Sweet Mary," says I;
"Oh, don't talk to my father," says Mary,
  Beginning to cry:
"For my father he loves me so dearly,
  He'll never consent I should go—
If you talk to my father," says Mary,
  "He'll surely say, 'No.' "

"Then how shall I get you, my jewel?
  Sweet Mary," says I;
"If your father and mother's so cruel,
  Most surely I'll die!"
"Oh, never say die, dear," says Mary;
  "A way now to save you I see;
Since my parents are both so contrary—
  You'd better ask me!"

GOD WITH US

Anonymous

God be in my head,
And in my understanding;
God be in mine eyes,
And in my looking;
God be in my mouth
And in my speaking;
God be in my heart,
And in my thinking;
God be at my end and at my departing.

AMERICA IS GREAT BECAUSE—

I sought for the greatness
and genius of America
in her commodious harbors
and her ample rivers,
and it was not there;

in the fertile fields
and boundless prairies,
and it was not there;

in her rich mines
and her vast world commerce,
and it was not there.

Not until I went
into the churches of America
and heard her pulpits
aflame with righteousness,
did I understand the secret
of her genius and power.

America is great
because she is good,
and if America ever ceases to be good,
America will cease to be great.
>   —Attributed to de Tocqueville
>   but not found in his works.

MEET ME IN ST. LOUIS

Andrew B. Sterling

When Louis came home to the flat,
He hung up his coat and his hat,
He gazed all around, but no wifey he found,
So he said "Where can Flossie be at?"
A note on the table he spied,
He read it just once, then he cried.
It ran, "Louis dear, it's too slow for me here,
So I think I will go for a ride."

Chorus
"Meet me in St. Louis, Louis,
Meet me at the fair,
Don't tell me the lights are shining any place but there;
We will dance the Hoochee Koochee,
I will be your tootsie wootsie,
If you will meet me in St. Louis, Louis,
Meet me at the fair."

The dresses that hung in the hall,
Were gone, she had taken them all;
She took all his rings
And the rest of his things;
A picture he missed from the wall.

"What! Moving?" the janitor said,
Your rent is paid three months ahead."
"What good is the flat?" said poor Louis,
"Read that." And the janitor smiled as he read.
(Chorus)

THE DROP OF HONEY

Thousand and One Nights

(TRANSLATOR: Richard Burton)

A certain hunter used to chase wild beast in wold, and one day he came upon a grotto in the mountains, where he found a hollow full of bees' honey. So he took somewhat thereof in a waterskin he had with him and, throwing it over his shoulder, carried it to the city, followed by a hunting dog which was dear to him. He stopped at the shop of an oilman and offered him the honey for sale and he bought it. Then he emptied out the skin, that he might see it, and in the act a drop fell to the ground, whereupon the flies flocked to it and a bird swooped down upon the flies. Now the oilman had a cat, which sprang upon the bird, and the huntsman's dog, seeing the cat, sprang upon it and slew it; whereupon the oilman sprang upon the dog and slew it, and the huntsman in turn sprang upon the oilman and slew him. Now the oilman was of one village and the huntsman of another; and when the people of the two places heard what had passed, they took up arms and weapons and rose one on the other in wrath and the two lines met; nor did the sword leave its play amongst them, till there died of them much people, none knoweth their number saye Almighty Allah.

THE MAN WHO TALKED PROSE

Molière

M. JOURDAIN—I must tell you something in complete confidence. I am in love with a woman of great quality, and I'd like you to help me write a small note which I can drop at her feet.

THE PROFESSOR—Very well. You wish to send her some verses?

M. JOURDAIN—No,—no verses.

THE PROFESSOR—Just prose, then?

M. JOURDAIN—Neither prose nor verses.

THE PROFESSOR—It must be one or the other.

M. JOURDAIN—Why so?

THE PROFESSOR—Simply because to express oneself, one must do it in either verse or prose.

M. JOURDAIN—There's nothing but verse or prose?

THE PROFESSOR—No, sir. Everything that is not prose is verse, and everything that is not verse is prose.

M. JOURDAIN—What is it then when we speak?

THE PROFESSOR—Prose.

M. JOURDAIN—What! When I say "Nicole, bring me my slippers and give me my night-cap"—is that prose?

THE PROFESSOR—Yes, sir.

M. JOURDAIN—Upon my word! Here I have been speaking prose for more than forty years, and never knew it till now!

(From *The Bourgeois Gentleman*, 1670)

STAND TO YOUR GLASSES *

Anonymous

We meet 'neath the sounding rafter,
  And the walls around are bare;
As they shout back our peals of laughter
  It seems that the dead are there.
Then stand to your glasses, steady!
  We drink in our comrades' eyes:
One cup to the dead already—
  Hurrah for the next that dies!

Not here are the goblets glowing,
  Not here is the vintage sweet;
'Tis cold as our hearts are growing,
  And dark as the doom we meet.
But stand to your glasses, steady!
  And soon shall our pulses rise:
A cup to the dead already—
  Hurrah for the next that dies!

There's many a hand that's shaking,
  And many a cheek that's sunk;
But soon, though our hearts are breaking,
  They'll burn with the wine we've drunk.
Then stand to your glasses, steady!
  'Tis here the revival lies:
Quaff a cup to the dead already—
  Hurrah for the next that dies!

Time was when we laughed at others;
  We thought we were wiser then;
Ha! Ha! Let them think of their mothers,
  Who hope to see them again.
No! stand to your glasses, steady!
  The thoughtless here is the wise:
One cup to the dead already—
  Hurrah for the next that dies!

Not a sigh for the lot that darkles,
  Not a tear for the friends that sink;

* Supposed to have been written in India at the time of the plague; attributed
to both Alfred Domett and Bartholomew Dowling.

We'll fall, midst the wine-cup's sparkles,
  As mute as the wine we drink.
Come, stand to your glasses, steady!
  'Tis this that the respite buys:
A cup to the dead already—
  Hurrah for the next that dies!

There's a mist on the glass congealing,
  'Tis the hurricane's sultry breath;
And thus does the warmth of feeling
  Turn ice in the grasp of Death.
But stand to your glasses, steady!
  For a moment the vapor flies:
Quaff a cup to the dead already—
  Hurrah for the next that dies!

Who dreads to the dust returning?
  Who shrinks from the sable shore,
Where the high and haughty yearning
  Of the soul can sting no more?
No, stand to your glasses, steady!
  The world is a world of lies:
A cup to the dead already—
  And hurrah for the next that dies!

Cut off from the land that bore us,
  Betrayed by the land we find,
When the brightest have gone before us,
  And the dullest are most behind—
Stand, stand to your glasses, steady!
  'Tis all we have left to prize:
One cup to the dead already—
  Hurrah for the next that dies!

THE MAN AND HIS GOOSE

A certain Man had a Goose, which laid him a golden egg every day. But, not contented with this, which rather increased than abated his avarice, he was resolved to kill the Goose, and cut up her belly, that so he might come at the inexhaustible treasure which he fancied she had within her. He did so; and, to his great sorrow and disappointment, found nothing.

(From Aesop's Fables)

763

THE DEATH OF THE FLOWERS

William Cullen Bryant

The melancholy days are come, the saddest of the year,
Of wailing winds, and naked woods, and meadows brown and sere.
Heaped in the hollows of the grove, the autumn leaves lie dead;
They rustle to the eddying gust, and to the rabbit's tread;
The robin and the wren are flown, and from the shrubs the jay,
And from the wood-top calls the crow through all the gloomy day.

Where are the flowers, the fair young flowers, that lately sprang
   and stood
In brighter light and softer airs, a beauteous sisterhood?
Alas! they all are in their graves, the gentle race of flowers
Are lying in their lowly beds, with the fair and good of ours.
The rain is falling where they lie but the cold November rain
Calls not from out the gloomy earth the lovely ones again.

The wind-flower and the violet, they perished long ago,
And the brier-rose and the orchis died amid the summer glow;
But on the hill the golden-rod, and the aster in the wood,
And the yellow sun-flower by the brook in autumn beauty stood,
Till fell the frost from the clear cold heaven, as falls the plague
   on men,
And the brightness of their smile was gone, from upland, glade,
   and glen.

And now, when comes the calm mild day, as still such days will
   come,
To call the squirrel and the bee from out their winter home;
When the sound of dropping nuts is heard, though all the trees
   are still,
And twinkle in the smoky light the waters of the rill,
The south-wind searches for the flowers whose fragrance late he
   bore,
And sighs to find them in the wood and by the stream no more.

And then I think of one who in her youthful beauty died,
The fair meek blossom that grew up and faded by my side.
In the cold moist earth we laid her, when the forests cast the leaf,
And we wept that one so lovely should have a life so brief:
Yet not unmeet it was that one, like that young friend of ours,
So gentle and so beautiful, should perish with the flowers.

SHE IS MORE TO BE PITIED THAN CENSURED

William B. Gray

At the old concert hall on the Bowery
Round the table were seated one night
A crowd of young fellows carousing;
With them life seemed cheerful and bright.
At the very next table was seated
A girl who had fallen to shame.
All the young fellows jeered at her weakness
Till they heard an old woman exclaim:

Chorus:
> She is more to be pitied than censured,
> She is more to be helped than despised,
> She is only a lassie who ventured
> On life's stormy path ill-advised.
> Do not scorn her with words fierce and bitter,
> Do not laugh at her shame and downfall;
> For a moment just stop and consider
> That a man was the cause of it all.

There's an old-fashioned church round the corner,
Where the neighbors all gathered one day
While the parson was preaching a sermon
O'er a soul that had just passed away.
'Twas the same wayward girl from the Bow'ry,
Who a life of adventure had led—
Did the clergyman jeer at her downfall?
No—he asked for God's mercy and said: (*Chorus.*)

THE BRIDGE

Henry Wadsworth Longfellow

I stood on the bridge at midnight,
As the clocks were striking the hour,
And the moon rose o'er the city,
Behind the dark church-tower.

I saw her bright reflection
In the waters under me,
Like a golden goblet falling
And sinking into the sea.

And far in the hazy distance
Of that lovely night in June,
The blaze of the flaming furnace
Gleamed redder than the moon.

Among the long, black rafters
The wavering shadows lay,
And the current that came from the ocean
Seemed to lift and bear them away;

As sweeping and eddying through them,
Rose the belated tide,
And, streaming into the moonlight,
The seaweed floated wide.

And like those waters rushing
Among the wooden piers,
A flood of thoughts came o'er me,
That filled my eyes with tears.

How often, oh, how often,
In the days that had gone by,
I had stood on the bridge at midnight
And gazed on that wave and sky!

How often, oh, how often,
I had wished that the ebbing tide
Would bear me away on its bosom
O'er the ocean wild and wide!

For my heart was hot and restless,
And my life was full of care,
And the burden laid upon me
Seemed greater than I could bear.

But now it has fallen from me,
It is buried in the sea;
And only the sorrow of others
Throws its shadow over me.

Yet whenever I cross the river
On its bridge with wooden piers,
Like the odor of brine from the ocean
Come the thought of other years.

And I think how many thousands
Of care-encumbered men,
Each bearing his burden of sorrow,
Have crossed the bridge since then.

I see the long procession
Still passing to and fro,
The young heart hot and restless,
And the old subdued and slow!

And forever and forever,
As long as the river flows,
As long as the heart has passions,
As long as life has woes.

The moon and its broken reflection
And its shadows shall appear,
As the symbol of love in heaven,
And its wavering image here.

A TERRIBLE INFANT

Frederick Locker-Lampson

I recollect a nurse called Ann,
    Who carried me about the grass;
And one fine day, a fine young man
Came up and kiss'd the pretty lass;
She did not make the least objection!
    Thinks I, *Aha!*
When I can talk I'll tell mama;
And that's my earliest recollection.

LETTER FROM GEORGE WASHINGTON
WHEN HE ACCEPTED COMMAND

It has been determined in Congress, that the whole army raised for the defense of the American cause shall be put under my care, and that it is necessary for me to proceed immediately to Boston to take upon me the command of it.

I have been called upon by the unanimous voice of the Colonies to the command of the Continental Army. It is an honor I by no means aspired to. It is an honor I wished to avoid, as well from an unwillingness to quit the peaceful enjoyment of my family, as from a thorough conviction of my own incapacity and want of experience in the conduct of so momentous a concern; but the partiality of the Congress, added to some political motives, left me without a choice. May God grant, therefore, that my acceptance of it, may be attended with some good to the common cause, and without injury (from want of knowledge) to my own reputation. I can answer but for three things: a firm belief in the justice of our cause, close attention in the prosecution of it, and the strictest integrity.

(Letter to Mrs. Martha Washington, June, 1775)

THE MINSTREL BOY

Thomas Moore

The minstrel boy to the war is gone,
　In the ranks of death you'll find him,
His father's sword he has girded on,
　And his wild harp slung behind him.
"Land of song!" said the warrior bard,
　"Though all the world betrays thee,
One sword, at least, thy rights shall guard,
　One faithful harp shall praise thee!"

The minstrel fell!—but the foeman's chain
　Could not bring his proud soul under;
The harp he loved ne'er spoke again,
　For he tore its chords asunder,

And said, "No chains shall sully thee,
  Thou soul of love and bravery!
Thy songs were made for the pure and free,
  They shall never sound in slavery!"

MAN PROPOSES

Man proposes, but God disposes.
When he is out of sight, quickly also is he out of mind.
Of two evils, the less is always to be chosen.
            (From Thomas à Kempis' Imitation of Christ)

CARDINAL WOLSEY'S FAREWELL

William Shakespeare

Farewell! a long farewell, to all my greatness!
This is the state of man: to-day he puts forth
The tender leaves of hopes; to-morrow blossoms,
And bears his blushing honours thick upon him;
The third day comes a frost, a killing frost,
And, when he thinks, good easy man, full surely
His greatness is a-ripening, nips his root,
And then he falls, as I do. I have ventured,
Like little wanton boys that swim on bladders,
This many summers in a sea of glory,
But far beyond my depth: my high-blown pride
At length broke under me and now has left me,
Weary and old with service, to the mercy
Of a rude stream, that must for ever hide me.
Vain pomp and glory of this world, I hate ye:
I feel my heart new open'd. O, how wretched
Is that poor man that hangs on princes' favours!
There is, betwixt that smile we would aspire to,
That sweet aspect of princes, and their ruin,
More pangs and fears than wars or women have:
And when he falls, he falls like Lucifer,
Never to hope again.
                (From King Henry VIII)

MARY WHITE

William Allen White

The Associated Press reports carrying the news of Mary White's death declared that it came as the result of a fall from a horse. How she would have hooted at that! She never fell from a horse in her life. Horses have fallen on her and with her—"I'm always trying to hold 'em in my lap," she used to say. But she was proud of few things, and one was that she could ride anything that had four legs and hair. Her death resulted not from a fall, but from a blow on the head which fractured her skull, and the blow came from the limb of an overhanging tree on the parking.

The last hour of her life was typical of its happiness. She came home from a day's work at school, topped off by a hard grind with the copy on the High School Annual, and felt that a ride would refresh her. She climbed into her khakis, chattering to her mother about the work she was doing, and hurried to get her horse and be out on the dirt roads for the country air and the radiant green fields of the spring. As she rode through the town on an easy gallop she kept waving at passers-by. She knew everyone in town. For a decade the little figure with the long pig-tail and the red hair ribbon has been familiar on the streets of Emporia, and she got in the way of speaking to those who nodded at her. She passed the Kerrs, walking the horse, in front of the Normal Library, and waved at them; passed another friend a few hundred feet further on, and waved at her. The horse was walking and as she turned into North Merchant street she took off her cowboy hat, and the horse swung into a lope. She passed the Tripletts and waved her cowboy hat at them, still moving gaily north on Merchant street. A Gazette carrier passed—a High School boy friend—and she waved at him, but with her bridle hand; the horse veered quickly, plunged into the parking where the low-hanging limb faced her, and, while she still looked back waving, the blow came. But she did not fall from the horse; she slipped off, dazed a bit, staggered and fell in a faint. She never quite recovered consciousness.

But she did not fall from the horse, neither was she riding fast. A year or so ago she used to go like the wind. But that habit was broken, and she used the horse to get into the open to get fresh, hard exercise, and to work off a certain surplus energy that welled up in her and needed a physical outlet. That need has been in her heart for years. It was back of the impulse that kept the dauntless, little brown-clad figure on the streets and country roads of this community and built into a strong, muscular body what had been a frail and sickly frame during the first years of her life. But the riding gave her more than a body. It released a gay and hardy soul. She was the happiest thing in the world. And she was happy because she was enlarging her horizon. She came to know all sorts and conditions of men; Charley O'Brien, the traffic cop, was one of her best friends. W. L. Holtz, the Latin teacher, was another. Tom O'Connor, farmer-politician, and Rev. J. H. J. Rice, preacher and police judge, and Frank Beach, music master, were her special friends, and all the girls, black and white, above the track and below the track, in Pepville and Stringtown, were among her acquaintances. And she brought home riotous stories of her adventures. She loved to rollick; persiflage was her natural expression at home. Her humor was a continual bubble of joy. She seemed to think in hyperbole and metaphor. She was mischievous without malice, as full of faults as an old shoe. No angel was Mary White, but an easy girl to live with, for she never nursed a grouch five minutes in her life.

With all her eagerness for the out-of-doors, she loved books. On her table when she left her room were a book by Conrad, one by Galsworthy, "Creative Chemistry" by E. E. Slossen, and a Kipling book. She read Mark Twain, Dickens and Kipling before she was 10—all of their writings. Wells and Arnold Bennett particularly amused and diverted her. She was entered as a student in Wellesley in 1922; was assistant editor of the High School Annual this year, and in line for election to the editorship of the Annual next year. She was a member of the executive committee of the High School Y. W. C. A.

Within the last two years she had begun to be moved by an ambition to draw. She began as most children do by scribbling in her school books, funny pictures. She bought cartoon magazines and took a course—rather casually, naturally, for she was, after all, a child with no strong purposes—and this year she tasted the first fruits of success by having her pictures accepted by the High School Annual. But the thrill of delight she got when Mr. Ecord, of the Normal Annual, asked her to do the cartooning for that book this spring, was too beautiful for words. She fell to her work with all her enthusiastic heart. Her drawings were accepted, and her pride—always repressed by a lively sense of the ridiculousness of the figure she was cutting—was a really gorgeous thing to see. No successful artist ever drank a deeper draught of satisfaction than she took from the little fame her work was getting among her schoolfellows. In her glory, she almost forgot her horse—but never her car.

For she used the car as a jitney bus. It was her social life. She never had a "party" in all her nearly seventeen years—wouldn't have one; but she never drove a block in the car in her life that she didn't begin to fill the car with pick-ups! Everybody rode with Mary White—white and black, old and young, rich and poor, men and women. She liked nothing better than to fill the car full of long-legged High School boys and an occasional girl, and parade the town. She never had a "date," nor went to a dance, except once with her brother, Bill, and the "boy proposition" didn't interest her—yet. But young people—great, spring-breaking, varnish-cracking, fender-bending, door-sagging carloads of "kids"—gave her great pleasure. Her zests were keen. But the most fun she ever had in her life was acting as chairman of the committee that got up the big turkey dinner for the poor folks at the county home; scores of pies, gallons of slaw; jam, cakes, preserves, oranges and a wilderness of turkeys were loaded in the car and taken to the county home. And, being of a practical turn of mind, she risked her own Christmas dinner by staying to see that the poor folks actually got it all. Not that she was a cynic; she just disliked to tempt folks. While there she found a blind colored uncle, very old, who could do nothing but make rag rugs, and she rustled up from her school friends rags enough to keep him busy for a season. The last engagement she tried to make was to take the guests at the county home out for a car ride. And the last endeavor of her life was to try to get a rest room for colored girls in the High School. She found one girl reading in the toilet, because there was no better place for a colored girl to loaf, and it inflamed her sense of injustice and she became a nagging harpy to those who—she thought—could remedy the evil. The poor she had always with her, and was glad of it. She hungered and thirsted for righteousness; and was the most impious creature in the world. She joined the Congregational Church without consulting her parents; not particularly for her soul's good. She never had a thrill of piety in her life, and would have hooted at a "testimony." But even as a little child she felt the church was an agency for helping people to more of life's abundance, and she wanted to help. She never wanted help for herself. Clothes meant little to her. It was a fight to get a new rig on her; but eventually a harder fight to get it off. She never wore a jewel and had no ring but her High School class ring, and never asked for anything but a wrist watch. She refused to have her hair up; though she was nearly 17. "Mother," she protested, "you don't know how much I get by with, in my braided pigtails that I could not, with my hair up." Above every other passion of her life was her passion not to grow up, to be a child. The tom-boy in her, which was big, seemed to loathe to be put away forever in skirts. She was a Peter Pan, who refused to grow up.

Her funeral yesterday at the Congregational Church was as she would have wished it; no singing, no flowers save the big bunch of red roses from her brother Bill's Harvard classmen—Heavens, how proud that would have made her! and the red roses from the Gazette force—in vases at her head and feet. A short prayer, Paul's beautiful essay on "Love" from the Thirteenth Chapter of First Corinthians, some remarks about her democratic spirit by her friend, John H. J. Rice, pastor and police judge, which she would have deprecated if she could, a prayer sent down for her by her friend, Carl Nau, and opening the service the slow, poignant movement from Beethoven's Moonlight Sonata, which she loved, and closing the service a cutting from the joyously melancholy first movement of Tschaikowski's Pathetic Symphony, which she liked to hear in certain moods on the phonograph; then the Lord's Prayer by her friends in the High School.

That was all.

For her pallbearers only her friends were chosen; her Latin teacher, W. L. Holtz; her High School principal, Rice Brown; her doctor, Frank Foncannon; her friend, W. W. Finney; her pal at the Gazette office, Walter Hughes; and her brother Bill. It would have made her smile to know that her friend, Charley O'Brien, the traffic cop, had been transferred from Sixth and Commerical to the corner near the church to direct her friends who came to bid her goodbye.

A rift in the clouds in a gray day threw a shaft of sunlight upon her coffin as her nervous, energetic little body sank to its last sleep. But the soul of her, the glowing, gorgeous, fervent, soul of her, surely was flaming in eager joy upon some other dawn.

BENJAMIN FRANKLIN'S RELIGIOUS BELIEFS

I believe in one God, the Creator of the universe. That he governs it by his providence. That he ought to be worshipped. That the most acceptable service we render him is doing good to his other children. That the soul of man is immortal, and will be treated with justice in another life respecting its conduct in this.

THE BAREFOOT BOY

John Greenleaf Whittier

Blessings on thee, little man,
Barefoot boy, with cheek of tan!
With thy turned-up pantaloons,
And thy merry whistled tunes;
With thy red lip, redder still
Kissed by strawberries on the hill;
With the sunshine on thy face,
Through thy torn brim's jaunty grace;
From my heart I give thee joy,—
I was once a barefoot boy!

Prince thou art,—the grown-up man
Only is republican.
Let the million-dollared ride!
Barefoot, trudging at his side,
Thou hast more than he can buy
In the reach of ear and eye,—
Outward sunshine, inward joy:
Blessings on thee, barefoot boy!

Oh for boyhood's painless play,
Sleep that wakes in laughing day,
Health that mocks the doctor's rules,
Knowledge never learned of schools,
Of the wild bee's morning chase,
Of the wild-flower's time and place,
Flight of fowl and habitude
Of the tenants of the wood;
How the tortoise bears his shell,
How the woodchuck digs his cell,
And the ground-mole sinks his well;
How the robin feeds her young,
How the oriole's nest is hung;
Where the whitest lilies blow,
Where the freshest berries grow,
Where the ground-nut trails its vine,
Where the wood-grape's clusters shine;

Of the black wasp's cunning way,
Mason of his walls of clay,
And the architectural plans
Of gray hornet artisans!
For, eschewing books and tasks,
Nature answers all he asks;
Hand in hand with her he walks,
Face to face with her he talks,
Part and parcel of her joy,—
Blessings on the barefoot boy!

Oh for boyhood's time of June,
Crowding years in one brief moon,
When all things I heard or saw,
Me, their master, waited for.
I was rich in flowers and trees,
Humming-birds and honey-bees;
For my sport the squirrel played,
Plied the snouted mole his spade;
For my taste the blackberry cone
Purpled over hedge and stone;
Laughed the brook for my delight
Through the day and through the night,
Whispering at the garden wall,
Talked with me from fall to fall;
Mine the sand-rimmed pickerel pond,

Mine the walnut slopes beyond,
Mine, on bending orchard trees,
Apples of Hesperides!
Still as my horizon grew,
Larger grew my riches too;
All the world I saw or knew
Seemed a complex Chinese toy,
Fashioned for a barefoot boy!

Oh for festal dainties spread,
Like my bowl of milk and bread;
Pewter spoon and bowl of wood,
On the door-stone, gray and rude!
O'er me, like a regal tent,
Cloudy-ribbed, the sunset bent,

Purple-curtained, fringed with gold,
Looped in many a wind swung fold;
While for music came the play
Of the pied frogs' orchestra;
And, to light the noisy choir,
Lit the fly his lamp of fire.
I was monarch: pomp and joy
Waited on the barefoot boy!

Cheerily, then, my little man,
Live and laugh, as boyhood can!
Though the flinty slopes be hard,
Stubble-speared the new-mown sward,
Every morn shall lead thee through
Fresh baptisms of the dew;
Every evening from thy feet
Shall the cool wind kiss the heat:
All too soon these feet must hide
In the prison cells of pride,
Lose the freedom of the sod,
Like a colt's for work be shod,
Made to tread the mills of toil,
Up and down in ceaseless moil:
Happy if their track be found
Never on forbidden ground;
Happy if they sink not in
Quick and treacherous sands of sin.
Ah! that thou couldst know thy joy,
Ere it passes, barefoot boy!

THE TWO MATCHES

Robert Louis Stevenson

One day there was a traveller in the woods in California, in the
dry season, when the Trades were blowing strong. He had ridden
a long way, and was tired and hungry, and dismounted from his

horse to smoke a pipe. But when he felt in his pocket he found but two matches. He struck the first, and it would not light.

"Here is a pretty state of things!" said the traveller. "Dying for a smoke; only one match left; and that certain to miss fire!

"Was there ever so unfortunate a creature? And yet," thought the traveller, "suppose I light this match, and smoke my pipe, and shake out the dottle here in the grass—the grass might catch on fire, for it is dry like tinder; and while I snatch out the flames in front, they might evade and run behind me, and seize upon yon bush of poison oak; before I could reach it, that would have blazed up; over the bush I see a pine tree hung with moss; that too would fly in fire upon the instant to its topmost bough; and the flame of that long torch—how would that trade wind take and brandish that through the inflammable forest! I hear this dell roar in a moment with the joint voice of wind and fire, I see myself gallop for my soul, and the flying conflagration chase and outflank me through the hills; I see this pleasant forest burn for days, and the cattle roasted, and the springs dried up, and the farmer ruined, and his children cast upon the world. What a world hangs upon this moment!"

With that he struck the match and it missed fire.

"Thank God!" said the traveller, and put his pipe in his pocket.

GOING TO THE DOGS

Anonymous

My granddad, viewing earth's worn cogs,
Said things were going to the dogs;
His granddad in his house of logs,
Said things were going to the dogs;
His granddad in the Flemish bogs,
Said things were going to the dogs;
His granddad in his old skin togs,
Said things were going to the dogs;
There's one thing that I have to state—
The dogs have had a good long wait.

THE BIRTH OF A NATION

John Adams

Yesterday, the greatest question was decided, which ever was debated in America, and a greater, perhaps, never was nor will be decided among men. A resolution was passed without one dissenting colony, "that these United Colonies are, and of right ought to be, free and independent States, and as such they have, and of right ought to have, full power to make war, conclude peace, establish commerce, and to do all other acts and things which other States may rightfully do." You will see in a few days a Declaration setting forth the causes which have impelled us to this mighty revolution, and the reasons which will justify it in the sight of God and man. A plan of confederation will be taken up in a few days.

You will think me transported with enthusiasm, but I am not. I am well aware of the toil, and blood, and treasure, that it will cost us to maintain this declaration, and support and defend these States. Yet, through all the gloom, I can see the rays of ravishing light and glory. I can see that the end is more than worth all the means, and that posterity will triumph in that day's transaction, even although we should rue it, which I trust in God we shall not.

(From a letter to his wife, July 3, 1776)

TO LUCASTA, GOING TO THE WARS

Richard Lovelace

Tell me not, Sweet, I am unkind,
    That from the nunnery
Of thy chaste breast and quiet mind
    To war and arms I fly.

True, a new mistress now I chase,
    The first foe in the field;
And with a stronger faith embrace
    A sword, a horse, a shield.

Yet this inconstancy is such
    That thou too shalt adore;
I could not love thee, Dear, so much,
    Loved I not honour more.

DREAM-PEDLARY

Thomas Lovell Beddoes

If there were dreams to sell,
  What would you buy?
Some cost a passing bell;
  Some a light sigh,
That shakes from Life's fresh crown
Only a rose-leaf down.

If there were dreams to sell,
Merry and sad to tell,
And the crier rang the bell,
  What would you buy?

A cottage lone and still,
  With bowers nigh,
Shadowy, my woes to still,
  Until I die.
Such pearl from Life's fresh crown
Fain would I shake me down,
Were dreams to have at will,
This would best heal my ill,
  This would I buy.

THIRTY WORDS

The Ten Most Beautiful Words in English, as suggested by Wilfred Funk:
  dawn, lullaby, hush, luminous, murmuring, tranquil,
      mist, chimes, golden, melody.

The Ten Ugliest Words, as suggested by The National Association of Teachers of Speech:
  phlegmatic, crunch, flatulent, cacophony, treachery, sap,
      jazz, plutocrat, gripe, plump.

The Ten Most Over-Worked Words, as suggested by Wilfred Funk:
  okay, terrific, lousy, contact, definitely, gal,
      racket, swell, impact, honey.

BOSWELL DESCRIBES HIS FIRST MEETING
WITH SAMUEL JOHNSON

Mr. Thomas Davies the actor, who then kept a bookseller's shop in Russell Street, Covent Garden, told me that Johnson was very much his friend, and came frequently to his house, where he more than once invited me to meet him; but by some unlucky accident or other he was prevented from coming to us.

Mr. Thomas Davies was a man of good understanding and talents, with the advantage of a liberal education. Though somewhat pompous, he was an entertaining companion; and his literary performances have no inconsiderable share of merit. He was a friendly and very hospitable man. Both he and his wife (who had been celebrated for her beauty), though upon the stage for many years, maintained an uniform decency of character; and Johnson esteemed them, and lived in as easy an intimacy with them as with any family which he used to visit. Mr. Davies recollected several of Johnson's remarkable sayings, and was one of the best of the many imitators of his voice and manner, while relating them. He increased my impatience more and more to see the extraordinary man whose work I highly valued, and whose conversation was reported to be so peculiarly excellent.

At last, on Monday the 16th of May, when I was sitting in Mr. Davies' back-parlor, after having drunk tea with him and Mrs. Davies, Johnson unexpectedly came into the shop; and Mr. Davies having perceived him through the glass door in the room in which we were sitting, advancing towards us, he announced his awful approach to me, somewhat in the manner of an actor in the part of Horatio, when he addresses Hamlet on the appearance of his father's ghost, "Look, my Lord, it comes." I found that I had a very perfect idea of Johnson's figure, from the portrait of him painted by Sir Joshua Reynolds soon after he had published his *Dictionary*, in the attitude of sitting in his easy chair in deep meditation; which was the first picture his friend did for him, which Sir Joshua very kindly presented to me, and from which an engraving has been made for this work. Mr. Davies mentioned my name, and respectfully introduced me to him. I was much agitated; and recollecting his prejudice against the Scotch, of which I had heard much, I said to Davies, "Don't tell where I come from."—"From Scotland," cried Davies, roguishly. "Mr. Johnson," said I, "I do indeed come from Scotland, but I cannot help it." I am willing to flatter myself that I meant this as light pleasantry to soothe and conciliate him, and not as an humiliating abasement at the expense of my country. But however that might be, this speech was somewhat unlucky; for with that quickness of wit for which he was so remarkable, he seized the expression "come from Scotland," which I used in sense of being of that country; and, as if I had said that I had come away from it, or left it, retorted, "That, Sir, I find is what a very great many of your countrymen cannot help." This stroke stunned me a good deal; and when we had sat down, I felt myself not a little embarrassed, and apprehensive of what might come next. He then addressed himself to Davies: "What do you think of Garrick? He has refused me an order for the play for Miss Williams, because he knows the house will be full, and that an order would be worth three shillings." Eager to take any opening to get into conversation with him, I ventured to say, "O Sir, I cannot think Mr. Garrick would grudge such a trifle to you." "Sir," said he, with a stern look, "I have known David Garrick longer than you have done; and I know no right you have to talk to me on the subject." Perhaps I deserved this check; for it was rather presumptuous in me, an entire stranger, to express any doubt of the justice of his animadversion upon his old acquaintance and pupil. I now felt myself much mortified, and began to think that the hope which I had long indulged of obtaining his acquaintance was blasted. And, in truth, had not my ardor been uncommonly strong, and my resolution uncommonly persevering, so rough a reception might have deterred me forever from making any further attempts. Fortunately, however, I remained upon the field not wholly discomfited; and was soon rewarded by hearing some of his conversation. . . .

I was highly pleased with the extraordinary vigor of his conversation, and regretted that I was drawn away from it by an engagement at another place. I had, for a part of the evening, been left alone with him, and had ventured to make an observation now and then, which he received very civilly; so that I was satisfied that though there was a roughness in his manner, there was no ill-nature in his disposition. Davies followed me to the door, and when I complained to him a little of the hard blows which the great man had given me, he kindly took upon him to console me by saying, "Don't be uneasy. I can see he likes you very well."

* * *

Censure is the tax a man pays to the public for being eminent.
—Jonathan Swift

TO ALTHEA, FROM PRISON

Richard Lovelace

When Love with unconfinèd wings
   Hovers within my gates,
And my divine Althea brings
   To whisper at the grates;
When I lie tangled in her hair
   And fettered to her eye,
The birds that wanton in the air
   Know no such liberty.

When flowing cups run swiftly round
   With no allaying Thames,
Our careless heads with roses bound,
   Our hearts with loyal flames;
When thirsty grief in wine we steep,
   When healths and draughts go free,
Fishes that tipple in the deep
   Know no such liberty.

When, like committed linnets, I
   With shriller throat will sing
The sweetness, mercy, majesty,
   And glories of my king;
When I shall voice aloud how good
   He is, how great should be,
Enlargèd winds, that curl the flood,
   Know no such liberty.

Stone walls do not a prison make,
   Nor iron bars a cage;
Minds innocent and quiet take
   That for an hermitage;
If I have freedom in my love
   And in my soul am free,
Angels alone, that soar above,
   Enjoy such liberty.

JUST WORDS

Lewis Carroll

"I quite agree with you," said the Duchess, "and the moral of this is—'Be what you would seem to be'—or if you'd like it put more simply—Never imagine yourself not to be otherwise than what it might appear to others that that that you were or might have been was not otherwise than what you had been would have appeared to them to be otherwise."

THE HORRORS OF SPRING

Ambrose Bierce

Spring is with us with its oldtime stock of horrors—birds blaspheming in the trees; flowers loading the lukewarm air with odious exhalations; grass with snakes in it; matronly cows to gore the unwary. The blue of the sky and the green of the earth renew their immemorial feud, murdering one another in cold blood all along the line of the horizon. Hideous ferns erect themselves in the gulches where the poison oak unsheathes his leaves to work his ghastly joke upon the culler of simples. Fleas call the roll and perfect their organization; spiders hang their poddy carcasses face-high above the trail. 'Come, gentle spring, ethereal mildness, come.' Come with lute, come with clamor of geese, yelling of dogs, deep diapason of the strolling bull, and frequent thud of country asses falling over their own feet.

CAUSE AND EFFECT

Anonymous

For want of a nail the shoe was lost;
For the want of a shoe the horse was lost;
For the want of a horse the rider was lost;
For the want of a rider the battle was lost;
For the want of a battle the kingdom was lost—
And all for the want of a horseshoe nail.

FOR THIS IS WISDOM

Laurence Hope

For this is Wisdom; to love, to live,
To take what Fate, or the Gods, may give,
To ask no question, to make no prayer,
To kiss the lips and caress the hair,
Speed passion's ebb as you greet its flow,—
To have,— to hold,— and,— in time,— let go!

HERE MEN FROM THE PLANET EARTH
FIRST SET FOOT ON THE MOON.
JULY 1969 A.D.
WE CAME IN PEACE FOR ALL MANKIND.
(Inscription on a stainless steel plaque attached
to the landing vehicle left on the moon)

DAYS

Ralph Waldo Emerson

Daughters of Time, the hypocritic Days,
Muffled and dumb like barefoot dervishes,
And marching single in an endless file,
Bring diadems and fagots in their hands.
To each they offer gifts after his will,
Bread, kingdoms, stars, and sky that holds them all.
I, in my pleached garden, watched the pomp,
Forgot my morning wishes, hastily
Took a few herbs and apples, and the Day
Turned and departed silently. I, too late,
Under her solemn fillet saw the scorn.

"THERE IS A LADY SWEET AND KIND"

Anonymous

There is a lady sweet and kind,
Was never face so pleased my mind;
I did but see her passing by,
And yet I love her till I die.

Her gesture, motion, and her smiles,
Her wit, her voice my heart beguiles,
Beguiles my heart, I know not why,
And yet I love her till I die.

Her free behaviour, winning looks,
Will make a lawyer burn his books;
I touched her not, alas! not I,
And yet I love her till I die.

Had I her fast betwixt mine arms,
Judge you that think such sports were harms
Were't any harm? no, no, fie, fie,
For I will love her till I die.

Should I remain confinèd there
So long as Phoebus in his sphere,
I to request, she to deny,
Yet would I love her till I die.

Cupid is wingèd and doth range,
Her country so my love doth change:
But change she earth, or change she sky,
Yet will I love her till I die.

* * *

When I was a boy of fourteen, my father was so ignorant I could
hardly stand to have the old man around. But when I got to be
twenty-one I was astonished at how much the old man had learned
in seven years.
                                                    —Mark Twain

LIFE'S UNCERTAINTY

Holy Bible, Ecclesiastes 11

Cast thy bread upon the waters: for thou shalt find it after many days. Give a portion to seven, and also to eight; for thou knowest not what evil shall be upon the earth. If the clouds be full of rain, they empty themselves upon the earth: and if the tree fall toward the south, or toward the north, in the place where the tree falleth, there shall it be. He that observeth the wind shall not sow; and he that regardeth the clouds shall not reap. As thou knowest not what is the way of the spirit, nor how the bones do grow in the womb of her that is with child: even so thou knowest not the works of God who maketh all. In the morning sow thy seed, and in the evening withhold not thine hand: for thou knowest not whether shall prosper, either this or that, or whether they both shall be alike good. Truly the light is sweet, and a pleasant thing it is for the eyes to behold the sun: But if a man live many years, and rejoice in them all; yet let him remember the days of darkness; for they shall be many. All that cometh is vanity.

Rejoice, O young man, in thy youth; and let thy heart cheer thee in the days of thy youth, and walk in the ways of thine heart, and in the sight of thine eyes: but know thou, that for all these things God will bring thee into judgment. Therefore remove sorrow from thy heart, and put away evil from thy flesh: for childhood and youth are vanity.

THE POWER TO TAX

Chief Justice John Marshall

That the power of taxing [the bank] by the States may be exercised so as to destroy it, is too obvious to be denied . . . That the power to tax involves the power to destroy [is] not to be denied.

This spot is the sweetest I've seen inmy life,
For it raises my flowers and covers my wife.
—Anonymous

THE CANDID FRIEND

George Canning

Give me the avowed, the erect, the manly foe;
Bold I can meet, perhaps return his blow;
But of all plagues, good Heaven, thy wrath can send,
Save, save, oh! save me from the Candid Friend!

GRATITUDE

Charles Kingsley

Thank God every morning when you get up that you have something to do which must be done, whether you like it or not. Being forced to work, and forced to do your best, will breed in you temperance and self-control, diligence and strength of will, cheerfulness and content, and a hundred virtues which the idle never know.

TWO CAREFREE DAYS

Robert J. Burdette

There are two days in the week about which and upon which I never worry. Two carefree days, kept sacredly free from fear and apprehension. One of these days is Yesterday. Yesterday with all its cares and frets, with all its pains and aches, all its faults, and its mistakes and blunders, has passed forever beyond the reach of my recall. I cannot undo an act that I wrought. I cannot unsay a word that I said, on Yesterday. All that it holds of my life, of wrong, regret and sorrow, is in the hands of the Mighty Love that can bring honey out of the rock and sweet waters out of the bitterest desert. And the other day I do not worry about is Tomorrow. Tomorrow with all its possible adversities, its burdens, its perils, its large promise and poor performance, its failures and mistakes is as far beyond the reach of my mastery as its dead sister, Yesterday.

A HEALTH

Edward Coote Pinkney

I fill this cup to one made up of loveliness alone,
A woman, of her gentle sex the seeming paragon;
To whom the better elements and kindly stars have given
A form so fair, that, like the air, 'tis less of earth than heaven.

Her every tone is music's own, like those of morning birds,
And something more than melody dwells ever in her words;
The coinage of her heart are they, and from her lips each flows
As one may see the burthened bee forth issue from the rose.

Affections are as thoughts to her, the measure of her hours;
Her feelings have the fragrancy, the freshness of young flowers;
And lovely passions, changing oft, so fill her, she appears
The image of themselves by turns,—the idol of past years!

Of her bright face one glance will trace a picture on the brain,
And of her voice in echoing hearts a sound must long remain,
But memory such as mine of her so very much endears,
When death is nigh my latest sigh will not be life's but hers.

I fill this cup to one made up of loveliness alone,
A woman, of her gentle sex the seeming paragon—
Her health! and would on earth there stood some more of such a
    frame,
That life might be all poetry, and weariness a name.

LOVE TRIUMPHANT

Frederic Lawrence Knowles

Helen's lips are drifting dust;
Ilion is consumed with rust;
All the galleons of Greece
Drink the ocean's dreamless peace;
Lost was Solomon's purple show
Restless centuries ago;

Stately empires wax and wane—
Babylon, Barbary, and Spain:—
Only one thing, undefaced,
Lasts, though all the worlds lie waste,
And the heavens are overturned.
Dear, how long ago we learned!

There's a sight that blinds the sun,
Sound that lives when sounds are done,
Music that rebukes the birds,
Language lovelier than words,
Hue and scent that shame the rose,
Wine no earthly vineyard knows,
Silence stiller than the shore
Swept by Charon's stealthy oar,
Ocean more divinely free
Than Pacific's boundless sea,—
Ye who love have learned it true.
Dear, how long ago we knew!

A GLASS OF BEER

James Stephens

The lanky hank of a she in the inn over there
Nearly killed me for asking the loan of a glass of beer:
May the devil grip the whey-faced slut by the hair,
And beat bad manners out of her skin for a year.

That parboiled ape, with the toughest jaw you will see
On virtue's path, and a voice that would rasp the dead,
Came roaring and raging the minute she looked at me,
And threw me out of the house on the back of my head!

If I asked her master he'd give me a cask a day;
But she, with the beer at hand, not a gill would arrange!
May she marry a ghost and bear him a kitten, and may
The High King of Glory permit her to get the mange.

WAR IS HELL

General William Tecumseh Sherman

I am sick and tired of war. Its glory is all moonshine. It is only those who have never fired a shot nor heard the shrieks and groans of the wounded who cry aloud for blood, more vengeance, more desolation. War is hell.

THE EDUCATED MAN

Socrates

Whom do I call educated? First, those who manage well the circumstances which they encounter day by day and those who possess a judgment which is accurate in meeting occasions as they arise and rarely miss the expedient course of action. Next, those who are decent and honorable in their intercourse with all men, bearing easily and good-naturedly what is unpleasant and offensive in others, and being as agreeable and reasonable to their associates as it is humanly possible to be. Furthermore, those who hold their pleasures always under control and are not ultimately overcome by their misfortunes, bearing up under them bravely and in a manner worthy of our common nature. Finally, and most important of all, those who are not spoiled by their successes, who do not desert their true selves, but hold their ground steadfastly as wise and sober-minded men, rejoicing no more in the good things that have come to them through chance than in those which, through their own nature and intelligence, are theirs since birth. Those who have a character which is in accord, not with one of these things, but with all of them—these I maintain are educated and whole men possessed of all the virtues of a man.

TAKE MY LIFE AND LET IT BE

Frances R. Havergal

Take my life and let it be
Consecrated, Lord, to Thee;
Take my hands and let them move
At the impulse of Thy love,
At the impulse of Thy love.

Take my feet and let them be
Swift and beautiful for Thee;
Take my voice, and let me sing
Always, only, for my King.
Always, only, for my King.

Take my will and make it Thine
It shall be no longer mine;
Take my heart, it is Thine own.
It shall be Thy royal throne.
It shall be Thy royal throne.

HOW DOTH THE LITTLE CROCODILE

Lewis Carroll

How doth the little crocodile
Improve his shining tail,
And pour the waters of the Nile
On every golden scale!

How cheerfully he seems to grin,
How neatly spreads his claws,
And welcomes little fishes in
With gently smiling jaws!

JESUS CHRIST

Ralph Waldo Emerson

Jesus Christ belonged to the true race of prophets. He saw with open eyes the mystery of the soul. Drawn by its severe harmony, ravished with its beauty, he lived in it, and had his being there. Alone in all history he estimated the greatness of man. One man was true to what is in you and me. He saw that God incarnates himself in man, and evermore goes forth anew to take possession of his World.

MY LAST WALK WITH THE SCHOOLMISTRESS

Oliver Wendell Holmes

I can't say how many walks she and I had taken together before this one. I found the effect of going out every morning was decidedly favorable on her health. Two pleasing dimples, the places for which were just marked when she came, played, shadowy, in her freshening cheeks when she smiled and nodded good-morning to me from the school-house steps.

I am afraid I did the greater part of the talking. At any rate, if I should try to report all that I said during the first half-dozen walks we took together, I fear that I might receive a gentle hint from my friends the publishers, that a separate volume, at my own risk and expense, would be the proper method of bringing them before the public.

I would have a woman as true as Death. At the first real lie which works from the heart outward, she should be tenderly chloroformed into a better world, where she can have an angel for a governess, and feed on strange fruits which will make her all over again, even to her bones and marrow.—Whether gifted with the accident of beauty or not, she should have been moulded in the rose-red clay of Love, before the breath of life made a moving mortal of her. Love-capacity is a congenital endowment; and I think, after a while, one gets to know the warm-hued natures it belongs to from the pretty pipe-clay counterfeits of them.—Proud she may be, in the sense of respecting herself; but pride, in the sense of contemning others less gifted than herself, deserves the two lowest circles of a vulgar woman's Inferno, where the punishments are Smallpox and Bankruptcy.—She who nips off the end of a brittle courtesy, as one breaks the tips of an icicle, to bestow upon those whom she ought cordially and kindly to recognize, proclaims the fact that she comes not merely of low blood, but of bad blood. Consciousness of unquestioned position makes people gracious in proper measure to all; but if a woman put on airs with her real equals, she has something about herself, or her family she is ashamed of, or ought to be. Middle, and more than middle-aged people, who know family histories, generally see through it. An official of standing was rude to me once. Oh, that is the maternal grandfather,—said a wise old friend to me,—he was a boor. Better too few words from the woman we love, than too many; while she is silent, Nature is working for her; while she talks, she is working for herself.—Love is sparingly soluble in the words of men; therefore they speak much of it; but one syllable of woman's speech can dissolve more of it than a man's heart can hold.

Whether I said any or all of these things to the schoolmistress, or not,—whether I stole them out of Lord Bacon,—whether I cribbed them from Balzac,—whether I dipped them from the ocean of Tupperian wisdom,—or whether I have just found them in my head, laid there by that solemn fowl, Experience (who, according to my observation, cackles oftener than she drops real live eggs), I cannot say. Wise men have said more foolish things,—and foolish men, I don't doubt, have said as wise things. Anyhow, the schoolmistress and I had pleasant walks and long talks, all of which I do not feel bound to report. . . .

Books we talked about, and education. It was her duty to know something of these, and of course she did. Perhaps I was somewhat more learned than she, but I found that the difference between her reading and mine was like that of a man's and a woman's dusting a library. The man flaps about with a bunch of feathers; the woman goes to work softly with a cloth. She does not raise half the dust, nor fill her own eyes and mouth with it,—but she goes into all the corners and attends to the leaves as much as to the covers.—Books are the *negative* pictures of thought, and the more sensitive the mind that receives their images, the more nicely the finest lines are reproduced. A woman (of the right kind), reading after a man, follows him as Ruth followed the reapers of Boaz, and her gleanings are often the finest of the wheat.

But it was in talking of Life that we came most nearly together. I thought I knew something about that,—that I could speak or write about it somewhat to the purpose.

To take up this fluid earthly being of ours as a sponge sucks up water,—to be steeped and soaked in its realities as a hide fills its pore lying seven years in a tan-pit,—to have winnowed every wave of it as a mill-wheel works up the stream that runs through the flume upon its float-boards,—to have curled up in the keenest spasms and flattened out in the laxest languors of this breathing-sickness, which keeps certain parcels of matter uneasy for three or four score years,—to have fought all the devils and clasped all the angels of its delirium,—and then, just at the point when the white-hot passions have cooled down to a cherry-red, plunge our experience into the ice-cold stream of some human language or other, one might think would end in a rhapsody with something of spring and temper in it. All this I thought my power and province.

The schoolmistress had tried life, too. Once in a while one meets with a single soul greater than all the living pageant which passes before it. As the pale astronomer sits in his study with sunken eyes and thin fingers, and weighs Uranus or Neptune as in a balance, so there are meek, slight women who have weighed all which this planetary life can offer, and hold it like a bauble in the palm of their slender hands. This was one of them. Fortune had left her, sorrow had baptized her; the routine of labor and the loneliness of almost friendless city-life were before her. Yet, as I looked upon her tranquil face, gradually regaining a cheerfulness which was often sprightly, as she became interested in the various matters we talked about and places we visited, I saw that eye and lip and every shifting lineament were made for love,—unconscious of their sweet office as yet, and meeting the cold aspect of Duty with the natural graces which were meant for the reward of nothing less than the Great Passion.

I never addressed one word of love to the schoolmistress in the course of these pleasant walks. It seemed to me we talked of everything but love on that particular morning. There was, perhaps, a little more timidity and hesitancy on my part than I have commonly shown among our people at the boarding-house. In fact, I considered myself the master at the breakfast-table; but, somehow,

I could not command myself just then so well as usual. The truth is, I had secured a passage to Liverpool in the steamer which was to leave at noon,—with the condition, however, of being released in case circumstances occurred to detain me. The schoolmistress knew nothing of all this, of course, as yet.

It was on the Common that we were walking. The *mall*, or boulevard of our Common, you know, has various branches leading from it in different directions. One of these runs down from opposite Joy Street southward across the whole length of the Common to Boylston Street. We called it the long path, and were fond of it.

I felt very weak indeed (though of a tolerably robust habit) as we came opposite the head of this path on that morning. I think I tried to speak twice without making myself distinctly audible. At last I got out the question,—Will you take the long path with me?—Certainly,—said the schoolmistress,—with much pleasure.— Think,—I said—before you answer; if you take the long path with me now, I shall interpret it that we are to part no more!—The schoolmistress stepped back with a sudden movement, as if an arrow had struck her.

One of the long granite blocks used as seats was hard by,—the one you may still see close by the Gingko-tree.—Pray, sit down,— I said.—No, no, she answered, softly,—I will walk the *long path* with you!

The old gentleman who sits opposite met us walking, arm in arm, about the middle of the long path, and said, very charmingly,—"Good morning, my dears!"

(From the Autocrat of the Breakfast Table)

VANZETTI TO JUDGE THAYER

If it had not been for these things, I might have live out my life, talking at street corners to scorning men. I might have die, unmarked, unknown, a failure. Now we are not a failure. This is our career and our triumph. Never in our full life can we hope to do such work for tolerance, for joostice, for man's onderstanding of man, as now we do by an accident. Our words—our lives—our pains—nothing! The taking of our lives—lives of a good shoemaker and a poor fish peddler—all! That last moment belong to us—that agony is our triumph!

SANCHO PANZA PRAISES SLEEP

Miguel De Cervantes

(TRANSLATOR: P. A. Matteux)

Now blessings light on him that first invented this same sleep! It covers a man all over, thoughts and all, like a cloak; 'tis meat for the hungry, drink for the thirsty, heat for the cold, and cold for the hot. 'Tis the current coin that purchases all the pleasures of the world cheap; and the balance that sets the king and the shepherd, the fool and the wise man even. There is only one thing, which somebody once put into my head, that I dislike in sleep: it is, that it resembles death; there is very little difference between a man in his first sleep and a man in his last sleep.

WHERE LIES THE LAND?

Arthur Hugh Clough

Where lies the land to which the ship would go?
Far, far ahead, is all her seamen know.
And where the land she travels from? Away,
Far, far behind, is all that they can say.

On sunny noons upon the deck's smooth face,
Linked arm in arm, how pleasant here to pace;
Or, o'er the stern reclining, watch below
The foaming wake far widening as we go.

On stormy nights, when wild north-westers rave,
How proud a thing to fight with wind and wave!
The dripping sailor on the reeling mast
Exults to bear, and scorns to wish it past.

Where lies the land to which the ship would go?
Far, far ahead, is all her seamen know.
And where the land she travels from? Away,
Far, far behind, is all that they can say.

WEATHER WISDOM

Anonymous

A sunshiny shower
Won't last half an hour.

Rain before seven,
Fair by eleven.

The South wind brings wet weather,
The North wind wet and cold together;
The West wind always brings us rain,
The East wind blows it back again.

March winds and April showers
Bring forth May flowers.

Evening red and morning gray
Set the traveler on his way;
But evening gray and morning red
Bring the rain upon his head.

Rainbow at night is the sailor's delight;
Rainbow at morning, sailors, take warning.

If bees stay at home,
Rain will soon come;
If they fly away,
Fine will be the day.

When clouds appear like rocks and towers,
The earth's refreshed by frequent showers.

*   *   *

Defend me from my friends; I can defend myself from my enemies.
—Villars

*   *   *

And so no force, however great, can stretch a cord, however fine,
into a horizontal line which shall be absolutely straight.—William
Whewell (Elementary Treatise on Mechanics)

THE GLOVE AND THE LIONS

James Henry Leigh Hunt

King Francis was a hearty king, and loved a royal sport,
And one day, as his lions fought, sat looking on the court.
The nobles filled the benches, with the ladies in their pride,
And 'mongst them sat the Count de Lorge, with one for whom he
    sighed:
And truly 'twas a gallant thing to see that crowning show,
Valor and love, and a king above, and the royal beasts below.

Ramped and roared the lions, with horrid laughing jaws;
They bit, they glared, gave blows like beams, a wind went with
    their paws;
With wallowing might and stifled roar they rolled on one another,
Till all the pit with sand and mane was in a thunderous smother;
The bloody foam above the bars came whisking through the air;
Said Francis then, "Faith, gentlemen, we're better here than there."

De Lorge's love o'erheard the King, a beauteous lively dame,
With smiling lips and sharp bright eyes, which always seemed the
    same;
She thought, The Count my lover is brave as brave can be;
He surely would do wondrous things to show his love of me;
King, ladies, lovers, all look on; the occasion is divine;
I'll drop my glove, to prove his love; great glory will be mine.

She dropped her glove, to prove his love, then looked at him and
    smiled;
He bowed, and in a moment leaped among the lions wild:
The leap was quick, return was quick, he has regained his place,
Then threw the glove, but not with love, right in the lady's face.
"By Heaven," said Francis, "rightly done!" and he rose from
    where he sat;
"No love," quoth he, "but vanity, sets love a task like that."

*   *   *

The house of everyone is to him as his castle and fortress, as well
for his defense against injury and violence as for his repose.
        —Sir Edward Coke (1552–1634)

SPOONERISMS

Reverend W. A. Spooner (1844–1930), the Warden of New College, was famous for his habitual metathesis—transposing the initial sound of words so as to form some laughable combination. These are some of the best that are attributed to him.

Upon dismissing a student: You have deliberately tasted two worms; you can leave Oxford by the town drain.

We all know what it is to have a half-warmed fish within us [for "half-formed wish"].

Yes, indeed, the Lord is a shoving leopard.

Rebuking his congregation for its small attendance, and meaning to refer to the weary benches, *he said:* I am tired of addressing these beery wenches.

Sir, I believe you are under the affluence of incahol.

Now, Rabbabbas was a bobber.

He referred to a blushing crow *instead of a* crushing blow.

It is kisstomary to cuss the bride.

And perhaps most famous of all, he said, Mardon me, Padam, but I am afraid that you are occupewing the wrong pie. May I sew you to another sheet?

IF I WERE KING

Justin Huntly McCarthy

If I were king—ah, love, if I were king—
  What tributary nations would I bring
To stoop before your sceptre and to swear
Allegiance to your lips and eyes and hair;
Beneath your feet what treasures I would fling:—
The stars should be your pearls upon a string,
The world a ruby for your finger ring,
And you should have the sun and moon to wear,
    If I were king.
Let these wild dreams and wilder words take wing,
Deep in the woods I hear a shepherd sing
A simple ballad, to a sylvan air,
Of love that ever finds your face more fair;
I could not give you any goodlier thing
    If I were king.

SOLOMON JUDGES BETWEEN TWO WOMEN
DISPUTING OVER A CHILD

Holy Bible, I Kings 3:16–27

Then came there two women, that were harlots, unto the king, and stood before him.

And the one woman said, O my lord, I and this woman dwell in one house; and I was delivered of a child with her in the house.

And it came to pass, the third day after that I was delivered, that this woman was delivered also: and we were together: there was no stranger with us in the house, save we two in the house.

And this woman's child died in the night; because she overlaid it.

And she arose at midnight, and took my son from beside me, while thine handmaid slept, and laid it in her bosom, and laid her dead child in my bosom.

And when I arose in the morning to give my child suck, behold, it was dead; but when I had considered it in the morning, behold, it was not my son which I did bear.

And the other woman said, Nay; but the living is my son, and the dead is thy son. And this said, No; but the dead is thy son, and the living is my son. Thus they spake before the king.

Then said the king, The one saith, This is my son that liveth, and thy son is the dead; and the other saith, Nay; but thy son is the dead, and my son is the living.

And the king said, Bring me a sword. And they brought a sword before the king.

And the king said, Divide the living child in two, and give half to one, and half to the other.

Then spake the woman whose the living child was unto the king, for her bowels yearned upon her son, and she said, O my lord, give her the living child, and in no wise slay it. But the other said, Let it be neither mine nor thine, but divide it.

Then the king answered and said, Give her the living child, and in no wise slay it: she is the mother thereof.

ON FIRST LOOKING INTO CHAPMAN'S HOMER

John Keats

Much have I travell'd in the realms of gold,
And many goodly states and kingdoms seen;
Round many western islands have I been

Which bards in fealty to Apollo hold.
Oft of one wide expanse had I been told
　　That deep-brow'd Homer ruled as his demesne:
　　Yet did I never breathe its pure serene
Till I heard Chapman speak out loud and bold:
Then felt I like some watcher of the skies
　　When a new planet swims into his ken;
Or like stout Cortez when with eagle eyes
　　He star'd at the Pacific—and all his men
Look'd at each other with a wild surmise—
　　Silent, upon a peak in Darien.

THE FACE

Anthony Euwer

As a beauty I'm not a great star,
There are others more handsome by far,
But my face I don't mind it,
Because I'm behind it—
'Tis the folks in the front that I jar.

　　(Woodrow Wilson's favorite limerick)

THE OPTIMIST

Anonymous

The optimist fell ten stories;
At each window bar
He shouted to his friend
"All right so far."

WHERE THERE'S A WILL THERE'S A WAY

Eliza Cook

We have faith in old proverbs full surely,
　　For Wisdom has traced what they tell,
And Truth may be drawn up as purely
　　From them, as it may from "a well."

Let us question the thinkers and doers,
   And hear what they honestly say;
And you'll find they believe, like bold wooers,
   In "Where there's a will there's a way."

The hills have been high for man's mounting,
   The woods have been dense for his axe,
The stars have been thick for his counting,
   The sands have been wide for his tracks,
The sea has been deep for his diving,
   The poles have been broad for his sway,
But bravely he's proved in his striving,
That "Where there's a will there's a way."

Have ye vices that ask a destroyer?
   Or passions that need your control?
Let Reason become your employer,
   And your body be ruled by your soul.
Fight on, though ye bleed in the trial,
   Resist with all strength that ye may;
Ye may conquer Sin's host by denial;
   For "Where there's a will there's a way."

WHAT WE MAY LIVE WITHOUT

Owen Meredith

We may live without poetry, music and art;
We may live without conscience and live without heart;
We may live without friends; we may live without books;
But civilized man cannot live without cooks.

He may live without books,—what is knowledge but grieving?
He may live without hope,—what is hope but deceiving?
He may live without love,—what is passion but pining?
But where is the man that can live without dining?
           (From Lucile, Pt. I, Canto II)

THE LADIES

Rudyard Kipling

I've taken my fun where I've found it;
    I've rogued an' I've ranged in my time;
I've 'ad my pickin' o' sweet'earts,
    An' four o' the lot was prime.
One was an 'arf-caste widow,
    One was a woman at Prome,
One was the wife of a *jemedar-sais,* *
    And one is a girl at 'ome.

Now I aren't no 'and with the ladies,
    For, takin' 'em all along,
You never can say till you've tried 'em,
    An' then you are like to be wrong.
There's time when you'll think that you mightn't,
    There's times when you'll know that you might;
But the things you will learn from the Yellow an' Brown,
    They'll 'elp you a lot with the White!

I was a young un at 'Oogli,
    Shy as a girl to begin;
Aggie de Castrer she made me,
    An' Aggie was clever as sin;
Older than me, but my first un—
    More like a mother she were—
Showed me the way to promotion and pay,
    An' I learned about women from 'er!

Then I was ordered to Burma,
    Actin' in charge o' Bazar,
An' I got me a tiddy live 'eathen
    Through buyin' supplies off 'er pa.
Funny an' yellow an' faithful—
    Doll in a teacup she were,
But we lived on the square, like a true-married pair,
    An' I learned about women from 'er!

* Head-groom

Then we was shifted to Neemuch
 (Or I might ha' been keepin' 'er now),
An' I took with a shiny she-devil,
 The wife of a nigger at Mhow;
Taught me the gipsy-folks' *bolee;**
 Kind of volcano she were,
For she knifed me one night 'cause I wished she was white,
 An' I learned about women from 'er!

Then I come 'ome in a trooper,
 'long of a kid of sixteen—
Girl from a convent at Meerut,
 The straightest I ever 'ave seen.
Love at first sight was 'er trouble,
 She didn't know what it were;
An' I wouldn't do such, 'cause I loved 'er too much,
 But—I learned about women from 'er!

I've taken my fun where I've found it,
 An' now I must pay for my fun,
For the more you 'ave known o' the others
 The less will you settle to one;
An' the end of it's sittin' and thinkin',
 An' dreamin' Hell-fires to see;
So be warned by my lot (which I know you will not),
 An' learn about women from me!

What did the Colonel's Lady think?
 Nobody ever knew.
Somebody asked the Sergeant's wife,
 An' she told 'em true!
When you get to a man in the case,
 They're like as a row of pins—
For the Colonel's Lady an' Judy O'Grady
 Are sisters under their skins!

* Slang

HOW SLEEP THE BRAVE

William Collins

How sleep the brave, who sink to rest
By all their country's wishes blest!
When Spring, with dewy fingers cold,
Returns to deck their hallowed mould,
She there shall dress a sweeter sod
Than Fancy's feet have ever trod.

By fairy hands their knell is rung;
By forms unseen their dirge is sung;
There Honour comes, a pilgrim grey,
To bless the turf that wraps their clay;
And Freedom shall awhile repair
To dwell, a weeping hermit, there!

NIKITA KHRUSHCHEV'S BOAST

About the capitalist states, it doesn't depend on you whether or
not we exist. If you don't like us, don't accept our invitations, and
don't invite us to come and see you. Whether you like it or not,
history is on our side. We will bury you.

(November, 1956)

OUR COMMON NATURE

Ralph Waldo Emerson

In all conversation between two persons, tacit reference is made
as to a third party, to a common nature. That third party or common
nature is not social; it is impersonal; it is God.

THE HIPPOCRATIC OATH

I swear by Apollo Physician, by *Asclepius*, by Health, by Heal-All, and by all the gods and goddesses, that, according to my ability and judgment, I will keep this oath and stipulation; to reckon him who taught me this art equally dear to me as my parents, and share my substance with him and relieve his necessities if required. To regard his offspring as on the same footing with my own brothers and to teach them this art if they should wish to learn it, without fee or stipulation; and that by precept, lecture and every other mode of instruction I will impart a knowledge of the art to my own sons and to those of my teachers and to disciples bound by a stipulation and oath, according to the law of medicine, but to none others.

I will follow that method of treatment which, according to my ability and judgment, I consider for the benefit of my patients, and abstain from whatever is deleterious and mischievous. I will give no deadly medicine to anyone if asked, nor suggest any such counsel. Furthermore, I will not give to a woman an instrument to produce an abortion.

With Purity and with Holiness I will pass my life and practice my art. I will not cut a person who is suffering with a stone, but will leave this to be done by practitioners of this work. Into whatever houses I enter I will go into them for the benefit of the sick and will abstain from every voluntary act of mischief and corruption; and further from the seduction of females or males, bond or free.

Whatever, in connection with my professional practice, or not in connection with it, I may see or hear in the lives of men which ought not to be spoken abroad, I will not divulge, as reckoning that all such should be kept secret.

While I continue to keep this oath unviolated, may it be granted to me to enjoy life and the practice of the art, respected by all men, at all times, but should I trespass and violate this oath, may the reverse be my lot.

DEMOCRACY

Abraham Lincoln

As I would not be a slave, so I would not be a master. This expresses my idea of democracy. Whatever differs from this, to the extent of the difference is no democracy.

SOMETIMES

Thomas S. Jones, Jr.

Across the fields of yesterday
　He sometimes comes to me,
A little lad just back from play—
　The lad I used to be.

And yet he smiles so wistfully
　Once he has crept within,
I wonder if he hopes to see
　The man I might have been.

THE WIT OF WINSTON CHURCHILL

On Stanley Baldwin, when the latter was Prime Minister: Baldwin occasionally stumbles over the truth, but he always hastily picks himself up and hurries on as if nothing happened.

On Sir Stafford Cripps: There but for the grace of God goes God.

On Charles Beresford: When my Right Honorable friend rose to his feet a few minutes ago, he had not the least idea of what he was going to say. Moreover, he did not know what he was saying when speaking. And when he sat down, he was doubtless unable to remember what he had said.

On Clement Atlee: A modest man, and I know of no one with more to be modest about.

When the Nazis invaded Russia, Churchill pledged aid to Russia: If Hitler invaded Hell, I would make at least a favorable reference to the devil in the House of Commons.

Referring to Stanley Baldwin, known for his honesty: It is a fine thing to be honest, but it is also very important to be right.

Referring to Ramsay Macdonald, in the House of Commons, January, 1931: I remember, when I was a child, being taken to the celebrated Barnum's Circus, which contained an exhibition of freaks and monstrosities, but the exhibit on the program which I most desired to see was . . . "The Boneless Wonder." My parents judged that that spectacle would be too revolting and demoralizing for youthful eyes, and I have waited fifty years to see The Boneless Wonder sitting on the Treasury Bench.

On R. H. S. Crossman: The Honorable Member is never lucky in the coincidence of his facts with the truth.

Broadcast, October 21, 1940: We are waiting for the long-promised invasion. So are the fishes.

On his 75th Birthday (1949): I am ready to meet my Maker. Whether my Maker is prepared for the great ordeal of meeting me is another matter.

From an address at the Convocation of the Massachusetts Institute of Technology, March 20, 1949: The Dean of the humanities spoke with awe "of an approaching scientific ability to control men's thoughts with precision."—I shall be very content to be dead before that happens.

THE MULTIPLICATION OF BOOKS

Samuel Johnson

One of the peculiarities which distinguish the present age is the multiplication of books. Every day brings new advertisements of literary undertakings, and we are flattered with repeated promises of growing wise on easier terms than our progenitors.

How much either happiness or knowledge is advanced by this multitude of authors, is not very easy to decide. He that teaches us anything which we knew not before, is undoubtedly to be reverenced as a master. He that conveys knowledge by more pleasing ways, may very properly be loved as a benefactor; and he that supplies life with innocent amusement will be certainly caressed as a pleasing companion. But few of those who fill the world with books have any pretensions to the hope either of pleasing or instructing. They often have no other task than to lay two books before them, out of which they compile a third, without any new materials of their own, and with very little application of judgment to those which former authors have supplied.

EARTH IS ENOUGH

Edwin Markham

We men of Earth have here the stuff
Of Paradise—we have enough!
We need no other stones to build
The stairs into the Unfulfilled—
No other ivory for the doors—
No other marble for the floors—
No other cedar for the beam
And dome of man's immortal dream.

Here on the paths of every-day—
Here on the common human way
Is all the stuff the gods would take
To build a Heaven, to mold and make
New Edens. Ours the stuff sublime
To build Eternity in time!

THE BOYS AND THE FROG

Aesop

A troop of boys were playing at the edge of a pond, when, perceiving a number of Frogs in the water, they began to pelt them with stones. They had already killed many of the poor creatures, when one Frog more hardy than the rest put his head above the water and cried: "Stop your cruel sport, my lads; consider, what is Play to you, is Death to us."

THANKSGIVING PROCLAMATION

State of Connecticut

By His Excellency Wilbur L. Cross, Governor

Time out of mind at this turn of the seasons when the hardy oak leaves rustle in the wind and the frost gives a tang to the air and the dusk falls early and the friendly evenings lengthen under the heel of Orion, it has seemed good to our people to join together in praising the Creator and Preserver, who has brought us by a way that we did not know to the end of another year. In observance of this custom, I appoint Thursday, the twenty-sixth of November as a day of

PUBLIC THANKSGIVING

for the blessings that have been our common lot and have placed our beloved State with the favored regions of earth—for all the creature comforts; the yield of the soil that has fed us and the richer yield from labor of every kind that has sustained our lives— and for all those things, as dear as breath to the body, that quicken man's faith in his manhood, that nourish and strengthen his spirit to do the great work still before him: for the brotherly word and act; for honor held above price; for steadfast courage and zeal in the long, long search after truth; for liberty and for justice freely granted by each to his fellow and so as freely enjoyed; and for the crowning glory and mercy of peace upon our land—that we may humbly take heart of these blessings as we gather once again with solemn and festive rites to keep our Harvest Home.

Given under my hand and seal of the State at the Capitol, in Hartford, this twelfth day of November, in the year of our Lord one thousand nine hundred and thirty-six and of the independence of the United States the one hundred and sixty-first.

WILBUR L. CROSS

AWAY WITH FUNERAL MUSIC

Robert Louis Stevenson

Away with funeral music—set
    The pipe to powerful lips—
The cup of life's for him that drinks
    And not for him that sips.

810

"O LORD, HOW EXCELLENT IS THY NAME"

Holy Bible, Psalm 8

O Lord our Lord, how excellent is thy name in all the earth! who
hast set thy glory above the heavens.

Out of the mouths of babes and sucklings hast thou ordained
strength because of thine enemies, that thou mightest still the
enemy and the avenger.

When I consider thy heavens, the work of thy fingers, the moon
and the stars, which thou hast ordained;

What is man, that thou art mindful of him? and the son of man,
that thou visitest him?

For thou hast made him a little lower than the angels, and hast
crowned him with glory and honour.

Thou madest him to have dominion over the works of thy hands:
thou hast put all things under his feet:

All sheep and oxen, yea, and the beasts of the field;

The fowl of the air, and the fish of the sea, and whatsoever passeth
through the paths of the seas.

O Lord our Lord, how excellent is thy name in all the earth!

REALISM AND DUTY

Ralph Waldo Emerson

There is a time in every man's education when he arrives at the
conviction that envy is ignorance; that imitation is suicide; that he
must take himself, for better or for worse, as his portion; that,
though the wide universe is full of good, no kernel of nourishing
corn can come to him but through his toil bestowed on that plot of
ground which is given him to till.

THE SATISFIED TIGER

Cosmo Monkhouse

There was a young lady of Niger
Who smiled as she rode on a tiger;
They returned from the ride
With the lady inside,
And the smile on the face of the tiger.

"NOW IS THE HIGH-TIDE OF THE YEAR"

James Russell Lowell

Now is the high-tide of the year,
   And whatever of life hath ebbed away
Comes flooding back with a ripply cheer,
   Into every bare inlet and creek and bay;
Now the heart is so full that a drop overfills it,
We are happy now because God wills it;
No matter how barren the past may have been,
'Tis enough for us now that the leaves are green;
We sit in the warm shade and feel right well
How the sap creeps up and the blossoms swell;
We may shut our eyes, but we cannot help knowing
That skies are clear and grass is growing;
The breeze comes whispering in our ear,
That dandelions are blossoming near,
   That maize has sprouted, that streams are flowing,
That the river is bluer than the sky,
That the robin is plastering his house hard by;
And if the breeze kept the good news back,
For other couriers we should not lack;
   We could guess it all by yon heifer's lowing,—
And hark! how clear bold chanticleer,
Warmed with the new wine of the year,
   Tells all in his lusty crowing!

Joy comes, grief goes, we know not how;
Everything is happy now,
   Everything is upward striving;
'Tis as easy now for the heart to be true
As for grass to be green or skies to be blue,—
   'Tis the natural way of living:
Who knows whither the clouds have fled?
   In the unscarred heaven they leave no wake;
And the eyes forget the tears they have shed,
   The heart forgets its sorrow and ache;
The soul partakes the season's youth,
   And the sulphurous rifts of passion and woe

Lie deep 'neath a silence pure and smooth,
Like burnt-out craters healed with snow.

(From the Prelude to Part First,
The Vision of Sir Launfal)

EPITAPH ON SIR JOHN VANBRUGH, ARCHITECT

Abel Evans

Under this stone, Reader, survey
Dead Sir John Vanbrugh's house of clay.
Lie heavy on him, Earth! for he
Laid many heavy loads on thee!

HISTORY REPEATS

Charles Dickens

It was the best of times, it was the worst of times, it was the age
of wisdom, it was the age of foolishness, it was the epoch of belief,
it was the epoch of incredulity, it was the season of Light, it was the
season of Darkness, it was the spring of hope, it was the winter of
despair, we had everything before us, we had nothing before us, we
were all going direct to Heaven, we were all going direct the other
way—in short, the period was so far like the present period, that some
of its noisiest authorities insisted on its being received, for good or
for evil, in the superlative degree of comparison only.

(From *A Tale of Two Cities*)

OFFICE SEEKERS

Harried night and day by office seekers, President Lincoln once
said, "This human struggle and scramble for office, for a way to live
without work, will finally test the strength of our institutions."

How long, O Catiline, wilt thou abuse our patience! How long shalt thou baffle justice in thy mad career? To what extreme wilt thou carry thy audacity? Art thou nothing daunted by the nightly watch, posted to secure the Palatium? Nothing, by the city guards? Nothing, by the rally of all good citizens? Nothing, by the assembling of the Senate in this fortified place? Nothing, by the averted looks of all here present? Seest thou not that all thy plots are exposed? that thy wretched conspiracy is laid bare to every man's knowledge, here in the Senate? that we are all well aware of thy proceedings of last night; of the night before;—the place of meeting, the company convoked, the measures concerted? Alas, the times! Alas, the public morals? The Senate understands all this. The consul sees it. Yet the traitor lives! Lives? Ay, truly, and confronts us here in Council, takes part in our deliberations, and, with his measuring eye, marks out each man of us for slaughter. And we, all this while, strenuous that we are, think we have amply discharged our duty to the State, if we but shun this madman's sword and fury.

Long since, O Catiline, ought the consul to have ordered thee to execution, and brought upon thine own head the ruin thou hast been meditating against others. There was that virtue once in Rome, that a wicked citizen was held more execrable than the deadliest foe. We have a law still, Catiline, for thee. Think not that we are powerless, because forbearing. We have a decree,—though it rests among our archives like a sword in its scabbard—a decree by which thy life would be made to pay the forfeit of thy crimes. And should I order thee to be instantly seized and put to death, I make just doubt whether all good men would not think it done rather too late than any man too cruelly.

But, for good reasons, I will yet defer the blow long since deserved. Then will I doom thee, when no man is found so lost, so wicked, nay, so like thyself, but shall confess that it was justly dealt. While there is one man that dares defend thee, live! But thou shalt live so beset, so surrounded, so scrutinized, by the vigilant guards that I have placed around thee, that thou shalt not stir a foot against the Republic without my knowledge. Proceed, plot, conspire, as thou wilt; there is nothing you can contrive, nothing you can propose, nothing you can attempt, which I shall not know, hear, and promptly understand. Thou shalt soon be made aware that I am even more active in providing for the preservation of the State, than thou in plotting its destruction.

JOHN KEATS' FAREWELL LETTER TO FANNY BRAWNE

Wednesday Morng. (Kentish Town, 1820)

MY DEAREST GIRL,

I have been a walk this morning with a book in my hand, but as usual I have been occupied with nothing but you: I wish I could say in an agreeable manner. I am tormented day and night. They talk of my going to Italy. 'Tis certain I shall never recover if I am to be so long separate from you: yet with all this devotion to you I cannot persuade myself into any confidence of you.

Past experience connected with the fact of my long separation from you gives me agonies which are scarcely to be talked of. When your mother comes I shall be very sudden and expert in asking her whether you have been to Mrs. Dilke's, for she might say no to make me easy. I am literally worn to death, which seems my only recourse. I cannot forget what has pass'd. What? nothing with a man of the world, but to me dreadful.

I will get rid of this as much as possible. When you were in the habit of flirting with Brown you would have left off, could your own heart have felt one half of one pang mine did. Brown is a good sort of Man—he did not know he was doing me to death by inches. I feel the effect of every one of those hours in my side now; and for that cause, though he had done me many services, though I know his love and friendship for me, though at this moment I should be without pence were it not for his assistance, I will never see or speak to him until we are both old men, if we are to be. I will resent my heart having been made a football. You will call this madness. I have heard you say that it was not unpleasant to wait a few years—you have amusements—your mind is away—you have not brooded over one idea as I have, and how should you?

You are to be an object intensely desirable—the air I breathe in a room empty of you is unhealthy. I am not the same to you—no—you can wait—you have a thousand activities—you can be happy without me. Any party, any thing to fill up the day has been enough.

How have you pass'd this month? Who have you smil'd with? All this may seem savage in me. You do not feel as I do—you do not know what it is to love—one day you may—your time is not come.

Ask yourself how many unhappy hours Keats has caused you in Loneliness. For myself I have been a Martyr the whole time, and for this reason I speak, the confession is forc'd from me by the torture.

I appeal to you by the blood of that Christ you believe in; Do not write to me if you have done anything this month which it would have pained me to have seen. You may have altered—if you have not—if you still behave in dancing rooms and other societies as I have seen you—I do not want to live—if you have done so I wish this coming night may be my last.

I cannot live without you, and not only you but chaste you; virtuous you. The Sun rises and sets, the day passes, and you follow the bent of your inclination to a certain extent—you have no conception of the quantity of miserable feeling that passes through me in a day.—Be serious! Love is not a plaything—and again do not write unless you can do it with a crystal conscience. I would sooner die for want of you than—

Yours for ever

J. Keats

(A few months after this letter was written, Keats died of tuberculosis.)

DEMOSTHENES' FAREWELL

(TRANSLATOR: Rufus Choate)

(When the Macedonians finally conquered Greece after forty years of struggle, Demosthenes, who strove desperately to save his country, was forced to flee to the temple of Poseidon. The Thracian soldiers who pursued him dared not violate the temple, but tried to tempt Demosthenes to surrender by promising his pardon. This was Demosthenes' reply. After responding, he took poison and died.)

I dread the clemency you offer more than the torture and death which I had reason to expect, for I cannot bear that it be reported that the king had corrupted me by the promise of life to desert the ranks of Greece and stand in those of Macedon. Glorious and beautiful I should have thought if it my life could have been guarded by my country; by the fleet; by the walls which I have built; by the treasury which I have filled; by her constitution giving liberty to her people; by her ancestral glory; by her assemblies of freemen; by the love of my brother Athenians who so often have crowned me; by Greece which hitherto I have been able to save. But since this may not be, since this temple, these altars and sanctities cannot keep me from the court of the king of Macedon; a spectacle—a slave—I, Demosthenes, whom Nature never formed for disgrace—I who have drunk in from Xenophon and Plato the hope of immortality—I, for the honor of Athens, prefer death to bondage and thus wrap myself in liberty, the finest winding sheet.

MUSIC, WHEN SOFT VOICES DIE

Percy Bysshe Shelley

Music when soft voices die,
Vibrates in the memory—
Odours, when sweet violets sicken,
Live within the sense they quicken.

Rose leaves, when the rose is dead,
Are heaped for the beloved's bed;
And so thy thoughts, when thou art gone,
Love itself shall slumber on.

SYDNEY SMITH'S STORY OF MRS. PARTINGTON

I do not mean to be disrespectful, but the attempt of the Lords to stop the progress of reform reminds me very forcibly of the great storm of Sidmouth, and of the conduct of the excellent Mrs. Partington on that occasion. In the winter of 1824 there set in a great flood upon that town—the tide rose to an incredible height—the waves rushed in upon the houses—and everything was threatened with destruction. In the midst of this sublime storm, Dame Partington, who lived upon the beach, was seen at the door of her house with mop and pattens, trundling her mop, and squeezing out the seawater, and vigorously pushing away the Atlantic Ocean. The Atlantic was roused. Mrs. Partington's spirit was up; but I need not tell you that the contest was unequal. The Atlantic Ocean beat Mrs. Partington. She was excellent at slop or a puddle, but she should not have meddled with a tempest. (1831)

GOD'S WORK

Charlotte Cushman

God conceived the world, that was poetry;
He formed it, that was sculpture;
He colored it, that was painting;
He peopled it with living beings, that was the
    grand, divine, eternal drama.

LOUIS PASTEUR PROCLAIMS THE EXISTENCE OF THE INFINITE

He who proclaims the existence of the Infinite—and none can avoid it—accumulates in that affirmation more of the supernatural than is to be found in all the miracles of all the religions; for the notion of the Infinite presents that double character that forces itself upon us and yet is incomprehensible. When this notion seizes upon our understanding we can but kneel. . . . I see everywhere the inevitable expression of the Infinite in our world: through it the supernatural is at the bottom of every heart. The idea of God is a form of the idea of the Infinite. As long as the mystery of the Infinite weighs on human thought, temples will be erected for the worship of the Infinite, whether God is called Brahma, Allah, Jehovah or Jesus, and on the pavement of those temples men will be seen kneeling, prostrated, annihilated in the thought of the Infinite. Blessed is he who carries within himself a God, an ideal, and who obeys it: ideal of art, ideal of science, ideal of the gospel virtues, therein lie the springs of great thoughts and great actions; they all reflect light from the Infinite.

THE SOUND OF THE SEA

Henry Wadsworth Longfellow

The sea awoke at midnight from its sleep,
And round the pebbly beaches far and wide
I heard the first wave of the rising tide
Rush onward with uninterrupted sweep;
A voice out of the silence of the deep,
A sound mysteriously multiplied
As of a cataract from the mountain's side,
Or roar of winds upon a wooded steep.
So comes to us at times, from the unknown
And inaccessible solitudes of being,
The rushing of the sea-tides of the soul;
And inspirations, that we deem our own,
Are some divine foreshadowing and foreseeing
Of things beyond our reason or control.

LA BELLE DAME SANS MERCI

John Keats

O what can ail thee, knight-at-arms,
   Alone and palely loitering?
The sedge has wither'd from the lake,
   And no birds sing.

O what can ail thee, knight-at-arms,
   So haggard and so woe-begone?
The squirrel's granary is full,
   And the harvest's done.

I see a lily on thy brow
   With anguish moist and fever dew;
And on thy cheeks a fading rose
   Fast withereth too.

I met a lady in the meads,
   Full beautiful—a faëry's child,
Her hair was long, her foot was light,
   And her eyes were wild.

I made a garland for her head,
   And bracelets too, and fragrant zone;
She look'd at me as she did love,
   And made sweet moan.

I set her on my pacing steed,
   And nothing else saw all day long,
For sidelong would she bend, and sing
   A faëry's song.

She found me roots of relish sweet,
   And honey wild, and manna dew,
And sure in language strange she said,
   "I love thee true!"

She took me to her elfin grot,
   And there she wept and sigh'd full sore,
And there I shut her wild, wild eyes
   With kisses four.

And there she lulled me asleep,
  And there I dream'd,—ah! woe betide!
The latest dream I ever dream'd
  On the cold hill's side.

I saw pale kings and princes too,
  Pale warriors, death-pale were they all;
They cried—"La Belle Dame sans Merci
  Hath thee in thrall!"

I saw their starved lips in the gloam,
  With horrid warning gaped wide,
And I awoke and found me here,
  On the cold hill's side.

And this is why I sojourn here,
  Alone and palely loitering,
Though the sedge is wither'd from the lake,
  And no birds sing.

* * *

Those who make peaceful revolution impossible will
make violent revolution inevitable.
                    (John F. Kennedy, March 12, 1962)

ONE WEPT WHOSE ONLY CHILD WAS DEAD

Alice Meynell

One wept whose only child was dead,
New-born, ten years ago.
"Weep not; he is in bliss," they said.
She answered, "Even so,

"Ten years ago was born in pain
A child, not now forlorn.
But oh, ten years ago, in vain,
A mother, a mother was born."

THE DEATH OF CLEOPATRA

William Shakespeare

Cleopatra. Give me my robe, put on my crown; I have
Immortal longings in me: now no more
The juice of Egypt's grape shall moist this lip:
Yare, yare, good Iras; quick. Methinks I hear
Antony call; I see him rouse himself
To praise my noble act; I hear him mock
The luck of Caesar, which the gods give men
To excuse their after wrath. Husband, I come:
Now to that name my courage prove my title!
I am fire and air; my other elements
I give to baser life. So; have you done?
Come then and take the last warmth of my lips.
Farewell, kind Charmian; Iras, long farewell.

                              [Kisses them. Iras falls and dies.
Have I the aspic in my lips? Dost fall?
If thou and nature can so gently part,
The stroke of death is as a lover's pinch,
Which hurts, and is desired. Dost thou lie still?
If thus thou vanishest, thou tell'st the world
It is not worth leave-taking.
    Charmian. Dissolve, thick cloud, and rain, that I may say
The gods themselves do weep!
    Cleopatra.   This proves me base:
If she first meet the curled Antony,
He'll make demand of her, and spend that kiss
Which is my heaven to have. Come, thou mortal wretch,
             [To an asp which she applies to her breast
With thy sharp teeth this knot intrinsicate
Of life at once untie: poor venomous fool,
Be angry, and dispatch. O, couldst thou speak,
That I might hear thee call great Caesar ass
Unpolicied!
    Charmian. O eastern star!
    Cleopatra.   Peace, peace!
Dost thou not see my baby at my breast,
That sucks the nurse asleep?

                          (From Antony and Cleopatra)

"WHEN TO THE SESSIONS OF SWEET SILENT THOUGHT"

William Shakespeare

When to the sessions of sweet silent thought
I summon up remembrance of things past,
I sigh the lack of many a thing I sought,
And with old woes new wail my dear time's waste:
Then can I drown an eye, unused to flow,
For precious friends hid in death's dateless night,
And weep afresh love's long since cancell'd woe,
And moan the expense of many a vanish'd sigh:
Then can I grieve at grievances foregone,
And heavily from woe to woe tell o'er
The sad account of fore-bemoaned moan,
Which I new pay as if not paid before.
    But if the while I think on thee, dear friend,
    All losses are restored and sorrows end.

(Sonnet XXX)

"O ELOQUENT, JUST AND MIGHTY DEATH!"

Sir Walter Raleigh

O eloquent, just and mighty Death! whom none could advise, thou hast persuaded; what none hath dared, thou hast done; and whom all the world hath flattered, thou only hast cast out of the world and despised; thou hast drawn together all the far-stretched greatness, all the pride, cruelty, and ambition of man, and covered it all over with these two narrow words, *Hic jacet.*

(From The History of the World)

LINCOLN REPARTEE

A foreign diplomat unexpectedly walked in on Abraham Lincoln when he was shining his shoes.

"I am astonished, Mr. President," he said, "to find you blacking your own shoes."

"Whose shoes do you shine?" asked Lincoln.

RUTH

Thomas Hood

She stood breast high among the corn,
Clasped by the golden light of morn,
Like the sweetheart of the sun,
Who many a glowing kiss had won.

On her cheek an autumn flush,
Deeply ripened;—such a blush
In the midst of brown was born,
Like red poppies grown with corn.

Round her eyes her tresses fell,
Which were blackest none could tell.
But long lashes veiled a light,
That had else been all too bright.

And her hat, with shady brim,
Made her tressy forehead dim;
Thus she stood amid the stooks,
Praising God with sweetest looks.—

Sure, I said, Heav'n did not mean,
Where I reap thou shouldst but glean,
Lay thy sheaf adown and come,
Share my harvest and my home.

THE PLACE OF PEACE

Edwin Markham

At the heart of the cyclone tearing the sky
And flinging the clouds and towers by,
    Is a place of central calm;
So here in the roar of mortal things,
I have a place where my spirit sings,
    In the hollow of God's Palm.

GIVE ME LIBERTY, OR GIVE ME DEATH

Patrick Henry

MR. PRESIDENT:

No man thinks more highly than I do of the patriotism, as well as abilities, of the very worthy gentlemen who have just addressed the House. But different men often see the same subjects in different lights; and, therefore, I hope that it will not be thought disrespectful to those gentlemen, if entertaining as I do, opinions of a character very opposite to theirs, I shall speak forth *my* sentiments freely and without reserve. This is no time for ceremony. The question before the House is one of awful moment to this country. For my own part I consider it as nothing less than a question of freedom or slavery. And in proportion to the magnitude of the subject ought to be the freedom of debate. It is only in this way that we can hope to arrive at truth, and fulfil the great responsibility which we hold to God and our country. Should I keep back my opinions at such a time, through fear of giving offense, I should consider myself as guilty of treason toward my country, and of an act of disloyalty toward the majesty of Heaven, which I revere above all earthly kings.

Mr. President, it is natural to man to indulge in the illusions of hope. We are apt to shut our eyes against a painful truth,—and listen to the song of that siren, till she transforms us into beasts. Is this the part of wise men, engaged in a great and arduous struggle for liberty? Are we disposed to be of the number of those who, having eyes, see not, and having ears, hear not, the things which so nearly concern their temporal salvation? For my part, whatever anguish of spirit it may cost, I am willing to know the whole truth; to know the worst and to provide for it. I have but one lamp by which my feet are guided, and that is the lamp of experience. I know of no way of judging of the future but by the past. And judging by the past, I wish to know what there has been in the conduct of the British ministry for the last ten years, to justify those hopes with which gentlemen have been pleased to solace themselves and the House. Is it that insidious smile with which our petition has been lately received? Trust it not, sir; it will prove a snare to your feet. Suffer not yourselves to be betrayed with a kiss. Ask yourselves how this gracious reception of our petition comports with these warlike preparations which cover our waters and darken our land. Are fleets and armies necessary to a work of love and reconciliation? Have we shown ourselves so unwilling to be reconciled, that force must be called in to win back our love? Let us not deceive ourselves, sir. These are the implements of war and subjugation—the last arguments to which kings resort. I ask gentlemen, sir, what means this martial array, if its purpose be not to force us to submission? Can gentlemen assign any other possible motive for it? Has Great Britain any enemy, in this quarter of the world, to call for all this accumulation of navies and armies? No, sir, she has none. They are meant for us; they can be meant for no other. They are sent over to bind and rivet upon us those chains which the British ministry have been so long forging. And what have we to oppose them? Shall we try argument? Sir, we have been trying that for the last ten years. Have we anything new to offer on the subject? Nothing. We have held the subject up in every light of which it is capable; but it has been all in vain. Shall we resort to entreaty and humble supplication? What terms shall we find, which have not been already exhausted? Let us not, I beseech you, sir, deceive ourselves longer. Sir, we have done everything that could be done, to avert the storm which is now coming on. We have petitioned—we have remonstrated—we have supplicated—we have prostrated ourselves before the throne, and have implored its interposition to arrest the tyrannical hands of the ministry and parliament. Our petitions have been slighted; our remonstrances have produced additional violence and insult; our supplications have been disregarded; and we have been spurned with contempt, from the foot of the throne. In vain, after these things, may we indulge the fond hope of peace and reconciliation. There is no longer any room for hope. If we wish to be free—if we mean to preserve inviolate those inestimable privileges for which we have been so long contending—if we mean not basely to abandon the noble struggle in which we have been so long engaged, and which we have pledged ourselves never to abandon until the glorious object of our contest shall be obtained, we must fight! I repeat it, sir, we must fight! An appeal to arms and to the God of Hosts is all that is left us!

They tell us, sir, that we are weak—unable to cope with so formidable an adversary. But when shall we be stronger? Will it be the next week, or the next year? Will it be when we are totally disarmed, and when a British guard shall be stationed in every house? Shall we gather strength by irresolution and inaction? Shall we acquire the means of effectual resistance by lying supinely on our backs, and hugging the delusive phantom of Hope, until our enemies shall have bound us hand and foot? Sir, we are not weak, if we make a proper use of those means which the God of nature hath placed in our power. Three millions of people, armed in the holy cause of liberty, and in such a country as that which we possess, are invincible by any force which our enemy can send against us. Besides, sir, we shall not fight our battles alone. There is a just God who presides over the destinies of nations; and who will raise up friends to fight our battles for us. The battle, sir, is not to the strong alone; it is to the vigilant, the active, the brave. Besides, sir, we have no election. If we, the brave, were base enough to desire it, it is now too late to retire from the contest. There is no retreat, but in submission and slavery! Our chains are forged, their clanking may be heard on the plains of Boston! The war is inevitable,— and let it come! I repeat it, sir, let it come!

It is in vain, sir, to extenuate the matter. Gentlemen may cry, peace, peace—but there is no peace. The war is actually begun! The next gale that sweeps from the north will bring to our ears the clash of resounding arms! Our brethren are already in the field! Why stand we here idle? What is it that gentlemen wish? What would they have? Is life so dear, or peace so sweet, as to be purchased at the price of chains and slavery? Forbid it, Almighty God! I know not what course others may take; but as for me, give me liberty, or give me death!

March 23, 1775

SOURCE OF NEWS

Anonymous

Absolute knowledge I have none,
But my niece's washerwoman's son
Heard a policeman on his beat
Say to a laborer in the street
That he had a letter last week
Written in the finest Greek,
From a Chinese coolie in Timbuctoo,
Who said that the niggers in Cuba knew
Of a colored man in a Texas town,
Who got it straight from a circus clown,
That a man in the Klondike heard the news

From a gang of South American Jews,
Who heard of a society female rake,
Whose mother-in-law will undertake
To prove that her husband's sister knows,
As stated in a printed piece,
That she has a son, who has a friend
Who knows when the war is going to end!

WARREN'S ADDRESS AT BUNKER HILL

John Pierpont

Stand! the ground's your own, my braves!
Will ye give it up to slaves?
Will ye look for greener graves?
    Hope ye mercy still?
What's the mercy despots feel?
Hear it in that battle-peal!
Read it on yon bristling steel!
    Ask it,—ye who will.

Fear ye foes who kill for hire?
Will ye to your *homes* retire?
Look behind you!—they're afire!
    And, before you, see
Who have done it! From the vale
On they come!—and will ye quail?
Leaden rain and iron hail
    Let their welcome be!

In the God of battles trust!
Die we may,—and die we must:
But, O, where can dust to dust
    Be consigned so well,
As where heaven its dews shall shed
On the martyred patriot's bed,
And the rocks shall raise their head,
    Of his deeds to tell?

LOGAN'S SPEECH

I appeal to any white man to say if ever he entered Logan's cabin hungry, and he gave him not meat; if he ever came cold and naked, and he clothed him not. During the course of the last long and bloody war, Logan remained idle in his cabin, an advocate for peace. Such was my love for the whites, that my countrymen pointed as they passed, and said, "Logan is the friend of the white men." I had even thought to live with you, but for the injuries of one man. Colonel Cresap, last spring, in cold blood, and unprovoked, murdered all the relatives of Logan, not sparing even my women and children. There runs not a drop of my blood in the veins of any living creature. This called on me for revenge. I have sought it. I have killed many. I have fully glutted my vengeance. For my country, I rejoice at the beam of peace: but do not harbor a thought that mine is the joy of fear. Logan never felt fear. He will not turn on his heel to save his life. Who is there to mourn for Logan? Not one.

(Logan, a Mingo chief, to Lord Dunmore, Governor of Virginia, in 1774. Colonial forces had defeated several Indian tribes. Logan refused to join the pleas for peace, but sent this speech to be read to the Governor lest his absence harm the negotiations.)

* * *

I never could believe that Providence sent a few men into the world, ready booted and spurred to ride, and millions ready saddled and bridled to be ridden.—Richard Rumbold, on the scaffold, 1685.

THEY ARE NOT LONG

Ernest Dowson

They are not long, the weeping and the laughter,
 Love and desire and hate:
I think they have no portion in us after
 We pass the gate.

They are not long, the days of wine and roses:
 Out of a misty dream
Our path emerges for awhile, then closes
 Within a dream.

THE SIN OF OMISSION

Margaret E. Sangster

It isn't the thing you do, dear,
   It's the thing you leave undone
That gives you a bit of a heartache
   At setting of the sun.
The tender word forgotten,
   The letter you did not write,
The flowers you did not send, dear,
   Are your haunting ghosts at night.

The stone you might have lifted
   Out of a brother's way;
The bit of heartsome counsel
   You were hurried too much to say;
The loving touch of the hand, dear,
   The gentle, winning tone
Which you had no time nor thought for
   With troubles enough of your own.

Those little acts of kindness
   So easily out of mind,
Those chances to be angels
   Which we poor mortals find—
They come in night and silence,
   Each sad, reproachful wraith,
When hope is faint and flagging,
   And a chill has fallen on faith.

For life is all too short, dear,
   And sorrow is all too great,
To suffer our slow compassion
   That tarries until too late;
And it isn't the thing you do, dear,
   It's the thing you leave undone
Which gives you a bit of a heartache
   At the setting of the sun.

*   *   *

The greatest pleasure I know is to do a good action by stealth,
and to have it found out by accident.—Charles Lamb

THE SIDEWALKS OF NEW YORK

Charles B. Lawlor

Down in front of Casey's old brown wooden stoop,
On a summer's evening we formed a merry group.
Boys and girls together, we would sing and waltz
While the Ginnie played the organ on the sidewalks of New York.

Chorus:
East-side, West-side, all around the town,
The tots sang Ring-a-Rosie, London Bridge is falling down.
Boys and girls together, me and Mamie Rorke,
Tripped the light fantastic on the sidewalks of New York.

That's where Johnny Casey and little Jimmy Crowe,
With Jakey Krause, the baker, who always had the dough,
Pretty Nelly Shannon with a dude as light as cork,
First picked up the waltz-step on the sidewalks of New York.

Things have changed since those times; some are up in G.
Others, they are on the hog, but they all feel just like me.
They would part with all they've got could they but once more
    walk
With their best girl and have a twirl on the sidewalks of New York.

LIVING

Anonymous

To touch the cup with eager lips and taste, not drain it;
To woo and tempt and court a bliss—and not attain it;
To fondle and caress a joy, yet hold it lightly,
Lest it become necessity and cling too tightly;
To watch the sun set in the west without regretting;
To hail its advent in the east—the night forgetting;
To smother care in happiness and grief in laughter;
To hold the present close—not questioning hereafter;
To have enough to share—to know the joy of giving;
To thrill with all the sweets of life—is living.

DOVER BEACH

Matthew Arnold

The sea is calm to-night.
The tide is full, the moon lies fair
Upon the straits;—on the French coast the light
Gleams and is gone; the cliffs of England stand,
Glimmering and vast, out in the tranquil bay.
Come to the window, sweet is the night-air!
Only, from the long line of spray
Where the sea meets the moon-blanch'd land,
Listen! you hear the grating roar
Of pebbles which the waves draw back, and fling,
At their return, up the high strand,
Begin, and cease, and then again begin,
With tremulous cadence slow, and bring
The eternal note of sadness in.

Sophocles long ago
Heard it on the Aegean, and it brought
Into his mind the turbid ebb and flow
Of human misery; we
Find also in the sound a thought,
Hearing it by this distant northern sea.

The Sea of Faith
Was once, too, at the full, and round earth's shore
Lay like the folds of a bright girdle furl'd.
But now I only hear
Its melancholy, long, withdrawing roar,
Retreating, to the breath
Of the night-wind, down the vast edges drear
And naked shingles of the world.

Ah, love, let us be true
To one another! for the world, which seems
To lie before us like a land of dreams,
So various, so beautiful, so new,
Hath really neither joy, nor love, nor light,

Nor certitude, nor peace, nor help for pain;
And we are here as on a darkling plain
Swept with confused alarms of struggle and flight,
Where ignorant armies clash by night.

LINDBERGH FLIES ALONE

Harold MacDonald Anderson

Alone?

Is he alone at whose right side rides Courage, with Skill within the cockpit and Faith upon the left? Does solitude surround the brave when Adventure leads the way and Ambition reads the dials? Is there no company with him, for whom the air is cleft by Daring and the darkness made light by Emprise?

True, the fragile bodies of his fellows do not weigh down his plane; true, the fretful minds of weaker men are lacking from his crowded cabin; but as his airship keeps her course he holds communion with those rare spirits that inspire to intrepidity and by their sustaining potency give strength to arm, resource to mind, content to soul.

Alone? With what other companions would man fly to whom the choice were given?

(Editorial in the New York Sun, 1927)

HALLUCINATION

Lewis Carroll

"I see nobody on the road," said Alice.

"I only wish I had such eyes," the White King remarked in a fretful tone. "To be able to see Nobody! And at that distance, too! Why it's as much as I can do to see real people by this light!"

THE TEN COMMANDMENTS

Holy Bible, Exodus 20:1–17

1 And God spake all these words, saying,

2 I am the Lord thy God, which have brought thee out of the land of Egypt, out of the house of bondage.

3 Thou shalt have no other gods before me.

4 Thou shalt not make unto thee any graven image, or any likeness of any thing that is in heaven above, or that is in the earth beneath, or that is in the water under the earth:

5 Thou shalt not bow down thyself to them, nor serve them: for I the Lord thy God am a jealous God, visiting the iniquity of the fathers upon the children unto the third and fourth generation of them that hate me;

6 And shewing mercy unto thousands of them that love me, and keep my commandments.

7 Thou shalt not take the name of the Lord thy God in vain; for the Lord will not hold him guiltless that taketh his name in vain.

8 Remember the sabbath day, to keep it holy.

9 Six days shalt thou labour, and do all thy work:

10 But the seventh day is the sabbath of the Lord thy God: in it thou shalt not do any work, thou, nor thy son, nor thy daughter, thy manservant, nor thy maidservant, nor thy cattle, nor thy stranger that is within thy gates:

11 For in six days the Lord made heaven and earth, the sea, and all that in them is, and rested the seventh day: wherefore the Lord blessed the sabbath day, and hallowed it.

12 Honour thy father and thy mother: that thy days may be long upon the land which the Lord thy God giveth thee.

13 Thou shalt not kill.

14 Thou shalt not commit adultery.

15 Thou shalt not steal.

16 Thou shalt not bear false witness against thy neighbour.

17 Thou shalt not covet thy neighbour's house, thou shalt not covet thy neighbour's wife, nor his manservant, nor his maidservant, nor his ox, nor his ass, nor any thing that is thy neighbour's.

THE WIDOW'S MITE

Holy Bible, Luke 21:1–4

And he looked up, and he saw the rich men casting their gifts into the treasury.

And he saw also a certain poor widow casting in thither two mites.

And he said, Of a truth I say unto you, that this poor widow hath cast in more than they all.

For all these have of their abundance cast in unto the offerings of God: but she of her penury hath cast in all the living that she had.

QUO VADIS, DOMINE?

Henry K. Sienkiewicz

(TRANSLATOR: J. Curtin)

At dawn . . . two dark figures were stealing along the Appian Way towards the valley of the Campania. One of them was Nazarius, the other the Apostle, Peter, who was leaving Rome and his distracted brethren. In the East the sky was already assuming a slight tinge of green, which changed gradually into a saffron color. From out the shadows appeared trees with silvery foliage, white marble villas and the arches of aqueducts stretching along the plain toward the city. The green tinge of the sky was becoming shot with gold. Soon the rays began to redden and illuminate the Alban Hills, which appeared as if wrapped in a violet frame. The dawn was mirrored in drops of dew trembling on the leaves of trees. The haze grew thinner and unveiled a wider view of the plain, the houses that dotted it, the cemeteries, towns and groups of trees, among which gleamed the white columns of temples.

The road was deserted. The peasants who brought vegetables to the city had evidently not yet harnessed their horses. The blocks of stone with which the road was paved as far as the mountains echoed from the wooden-soled shoes of the wayfarers.

The sun rose over the hills, and then a wonderful vision burst upon the Apostle. It seemed to him that the golden disc, instead of rising higher in the sky, came gliding down from the heights and moved along the road. Then Peter stopped and said: "Didst thou see the brightness approaching us?"

"I see nothing," replied Nazarius.

Peter, shading his eyes with his hands, continued:

"Some figure is approaching us in the gleam of the sun."

But no sound of footsteps reached their ears. Nazarius saw only that the trees in the distance were trembling as if shaken, and that the light was spreading more widely over the valley. With amazement in his eyes he looked at the Apostle.

"Rabbi, what troubles thee?" he cried in alarm.

Peter dropped his staff; his eyes looked straight ahead, his mouth was open, his face expressed wonder, delight, ecstasy.

Suddenly he fell upon his knees, with his hands stretched out, and cried:

"O Christ! O Christ!" and he pressed his face towards the earth, as though kissing someone's feet. Then the voice of the old man was heard, choked with tears.

"Quo Vadis, Domine?" ("Whither goest Thou, O Lord?")

Nazarius did not catch the answer, but to Peter's ears came the sad, sweet voice, which said: "As thou art deserting my people, I go to Rome to be crucified a second time."

The Apostle lay on the ground, his face in the dust, motionless and silent. It seemed to Nazarius that he had fainted, or perhaps even that he was dead. But suddenly he arose, and without a word, turned back toward the City of the Seven Hills.

The lad, seeing this, repeated like an echo:

"Quo Vadis, Domine?"

"To Rome," replied the Apostle.

And he returned.

THE ETERNAL GOODNESS

John Greenleaf Whittier

I know not what the future hath
Of marvel or surprise;
Assured alone that life and death
His mercy underlies.

And if my heart and flesh are weak
  To bear an untried pain,
The bruisèd reed He will not break,
  But strengthen and sustain.

No offerings of my own I have,
  No works my faith to prove;
I can but give the gifts He gave,
  And plead His love for love.

And so, beside the silent sea,
  I wait the muffled oar;
No harm from Him can come to me
  On ocean or on shore.

I know not where His islands lift
  Their fronded palms in air;
I only know I cannot drift
  Beyond His love and care.

THOMAS BAILEY ALDRICH WRITES A LETTER TO PROFESSOR EDWARD S. MORSE

My Dear Morse: It was very pleasant to receive a letter from you the other day. Perhaps I should have found it pleasanter if I had been able to decipher it. I don't think I mastered anything beyond the date, which I knew, and the signature, at which I guessed. There is a singular and perpetual charm in a letter of yours; it never grows old, and it never loses its novelty. One can say every morning, as one looks at it: "Here's a letter of Morse's I haven't read yet. I think I shall take another shy at it today; and maybe I shall be able in the course of years to make out what he means by those "t's" that look like "w's" and those "i's" that haven't any eyebrows." Other letters are read, and thrown away and forgotten; but yours are kept forever—unread. One of them will last a reasonable man a lifetime.

FRANCIS BACON TO SIR EDWARD COKE

Mr. Attorney, I respect you, I fear you not; and the less you speak of your own greatness, the more I will think of it.

BEFORE SEDAN

Austin Dobson

"The dead hand clasped a letter."
                    —Special Correspondence

Here in this leafy place
    Quiet he lies,
Cold with his sightless face
    Turned to the skies;
'Tis but another dead;
All you can say is said.

Carry his body hence,—
    Kings must have slaves;
Kings climb to eminence
    Over men's graves:
So this man's eye is dim;—
Throw the earth over him.

What was the white you touched,
    There, at his side?
Paper his hand had clutched
    Tight ere he died;—
Message or wish, may be;
Smooth the folds out and see.

Hardly the worst of us
    Here could have smiled!
Only the tremulous
Prattle, that has for stops
Just a few ruddy drops.

Look. She is sad to miss,
    Morning and night,
His—her dead father's—kiss;
    Tries to be bright,
Good to mamma, and sweet.
That is all. "Marguerite."

Ah, if beside the dead
    Slumbered the pain!

Ah, if the hearts that bled
  Slept with the slain!
If the grief died;—but no,
Death will not have it so.

THE TIME I'VE LOST IN WOOING

Thomas Moore

The time I've lost in wooing,
In watching and pursuing
  The light that lies
  In woman's eyes,
Has been my heart's undoing.
Tho' Wisdom oft has sought me,
I scorn'd the lore she brought me,
  My only books
  Were women's looks,
And folly's all they taught me.

Her smile when Beauty granted,
I hung with gaze enchanted,
  Like him the Sprite
  Whom maids by night
Oft meet in glen that's haunted.
Like him, too, Beauty won me;
But when the spell was on me,
  If once their ray
  Was turn'd away,
O! winds could not outrun me.

And are those follies going?
And is my proud heart growing
  Too cold or wise
  For brilliant eyes
Again to set it glowing?

No—vain, alas! th' endeavour
From bonds so sweet to sever;—
  Poor Wisdom's chance
  Against a glance
Is now as weak as ever.

EPITAPH ON CHARLES II

John Wilmot, Earl of Rochester

Here lies our Sovereign Lord the King,
    Whose word no man relies on,
Who never said a foolish thing,
    Nor ever did a wise one.

ON HIS BLINDNESS

John Milton

When I consider how my light is spent
Ere half my days in this dark world and wide,
And that one talent which is death to hide
Lodged with me useless, though my soul more bent

To serve therewith my Maker, and present
My true account, lest he returning chide,
'Doth God exact day-labor, light denied?'
I fondly ask. But Patience, to prevent

That murmur, soon replies, 'God doth not need
Either man's work or his own gifts. Who best
Bear his mild yoke, they serve him best. His state
Is kingly: thousands at his bidding speed,
And post o'er land and ocean without rest;
They also serve who only stand and wait.'

Saturn and Love their long repose
    Shall burst, more bright and good
Than all who fell, than One who rose,
    Than many unsubdued:
Not gold, not blood, their altar dowers,
But votive tears and symbol flowers.

Oh, cease! must hate and death return?
  Cease! must men kill and die?
Cease! drain not to its dregs the urn
  Of bitter prophecy.
The world is weary of the past,
Oh, might it die or rest at last!

(From Hellas)

LINCOLN TO GREELEY ON SAVING THE UNION

Executive Mansion, Washington
August 22, 1862
Hon. Horace Greeley:

Dear Sir: I have just read yours of the 19th, addressed to myself through THE N.Y. TRIBUNE. If there be in it any statements or assumptions of fact which I may know to be erroneous, I do not now and here controvert them. If there be in it any inferences which I may believe to be falsely drawn, I do not now here argue against them. If there be perceptible in it an impatient and dictatorial tone, I waive it in deference to an old friend, whose heart I have always supposed to be right.

As to the policy "I seem to be pursuing," as you say, I have not meant to leave any one in doubt.

I would save the Union. I would save it in the shortest way under the Constitution. The sooner the National authority can be restored, the nearer the Union will be "the Union as it was." If there be those who would not save the Union unless they could at the same time *save* Slavery, I do not agree with them. If there be those who would not save the Union unless they could at the same time *destroy* Slavery, I do not agree with them. My paramount object in this struggle is to save the Union, and is *not* either to save or destroy Slavery. If I could save the Union without freeing *any* slave, I would do it; and if I could save it by freeing *all* the slaves, I would do it; and if I could save it by freeing some and leaving others alone, I would also do that. What I do about Slavery and the colored race, I do because I believe it helps to save this Union and what I forbear, I forbear because I do not believe it would help to save the Union. I shall do *less* whenever I shall believe what I am doing hurts the cause, and I shall do *more*

840

whenever I shall believe doing more will help the cause. I shall try to correct errors when shown to be errors; and I shall adopt new views so fast as they shall appear to be true views. I have here stated my purpose according to my view of *official* duty; and I intend no modification of my oft-expressed *personal* wish that all men, everywhere, could be free.

Yours,
A. Lincoln

MY BED IS A BOAT

Robert Louis Stevenson

My bed is like a little boat;
   Nurse helps me when I embark;
She girds me in my sailor's coat
   And starts me in the dark.

At night, I go on board and say
   Good-night to all my friends on shore;
I shut my eyes and sail away
   And see and hear no more.

And sometimes things to bed I take,
   As prudent sailors have to do;
Perhaps a slice of wedding cake,
   Perhaps a toy or two.

EARLY DEATH

Hartley Coleridge

She passed away, like morning dew,
   Before the sun was high;
So brief her time, she scarcely knew
   The meaning of a sigh.

As round the rose its soft perfume,
  Sweet love around her floated;
Admired she grew—while mortal doom
  Crept on, unfeared, unnoted.

Love was her guardian Angel here,
  But love to death resigned her;
Tho' love was kind, who should we fear,
  But holy death is kinder?

"A WET SHEET AND A FLOWING SEA"

Allan Cunningham

A wet sheet and a flowing sea,
  A wind that follows fast
And fills the white and rustling sail
  And bends the gallant mast;
And bends the gallant mast, my boys,
  While like the eagle free
Away the good ship flies, and leaves
  Old England on the lee.

O for a soft and gentle wind!
  I heard a fair one cry;
But give to me the snoring breeze
  And white waves heaving high;
And white waves heaving high, my lads,
  The good ship tight and free—
The world of waters is our home,
  And merry men are we.

There's tempest in yon hornèd moon,
  And lightning in yon cloud;
But hark the music, mariners!
  The wind is piping loud;
The wind is piping loud, my boys,
  The lightning flashes free—
While the hollow oak our palace is,
  Our heritage of the sea.

THE TEMPEST

James T. Fields

We were crowded in the cabin,
  Not a soul would dare to sleep,—
It was midnight on the waters
  And a storm was on the deep.

'Tis a fearful thing in winter
  To be shattered by the blast,
And to hear the rattling trumpet
  Thunder, "Cut away the mast!"

So we shuddered there in silence,—
  For the stoutest held his breath,
While the hungry sea was roaring,
  And the breakers talked with Death.

As thus we sat in darkness,
  Each one busy in his prayers,
"We are lost!" the captain shouted
  As he staggered down the stairs.

But his little daughter whispered,
  As she took his icy hand,
"Isn't God upon the ocean
  Just the same as on the land?"

Then we kissed the little maiden,
  And we spoke in better cheer,
And we anchored safe in harbor
  When the morn was shining clear.

* * *

They have learned nothing, and forgotten nothing.
  —Talleyrand (referring to the Bourbons)

ON THE BANKS OF THE WABASH, FAR AWAY

Paul Dresser

'Round my Indiana homestead wave the corn fields,
In the distance loom the woodlands clear and cool,
Often times my thoughts revert to scenes of childhood,
Where I first received my lessons—Nature's school.
But one thing there is missing in the picture,
Without her face it seems so incomplete,—
I long to see my mother in the doorway,
As she stood there years ago, her boy to greet.

Chorus:
Oh, the moonlight's fair tonight along the Wabash,
From the fields there comes the breath of new-mown hay,
Through the sycamores the candelights are gleaming,
On the banks of the Wabash, far away.

Many years have passed since I strolled by the river
Arm in arm, with sweetheart Mary by my side.
It was there I tried to tell her that I loved her,
It was there I begged of her to be my bride.
Long years have passed since I strolled through the churchyard,
She's sleeping there, my angel, Mary dear;
I loved her but she thought I didn't mean it,
Still I'd give my future were she only here.

CONCERNING THE U.S.A.

Thomas Babington Macaulay

Either some Caesar or Napoleon will seize the reins of government with a strong hand, or your republic will be as fearfully plundered and laid waste by barbarians in the Twentieth Century as the Roman Empire was in the Fifth; with this difference, that the Huns and Vandals who ravaged the Roman Empire came from without, and that your Huns and Vandals will have been engendered within your own country by your own institutions.

(From a letter to H. S. Randall, May 23, 1857)

FROM DOUGLAS MACARTHUR'S ADDRESS TO A JOINT MEETING OF CONGRESS

I do not stand here as advocate for any partisan cause, for the issues are fundamental and reach quite beyond the realm of partisan considerations. They must be resolved on the highest plane of national interest if our course is to prove sound and our future protected. . . .

The issues are global, and so interlocked that to consider the problems of one sector oblivious to those of another is to court disaster for the whole. While Asia is commonly referred to as the gateway to Europe, it is no less true that Europe is the gateway to Asia, and the broad influence of the one cannot fail to have its impact upon the other.

There are those who claim our strength is inadequate to protect on both fronts, that we cannot divide our effort. I can think of no greater expression of defeatism.

If a potential enemy can divide his strength on two fronts, it is for us to counter his efforts. The Communist threat is a global one. Its successful advance in one sector threatens the destruction of every other sector. You cannot appease or otherwise surrender to Communism in Asia without simultaneously undermining our efforts to halt its advance in Europe. . . .

I know war as few other men now living know it, and nothing to me is more revolting. I have long advocated its complete abolition, as its very destructiveness on both friend and foe has rendered it useless as a means of settling international disputes.

Indeed, on the second day of September, 1945, just following the surrender of the Japanese nation on the battleship *Missouri*, I formally cautioned as follows:

"Men since the beginning of time have sought peace. Various methods through the ages have been attempted to devise an international process to prevent or settle disputes between nations. From the very start workable methods were found in so far as individual citizens were concerned, but the mechanics of an instrumentality of larger international scope have never been successful.

"Military alliances, balances of power, league of nations, all in turn failed, leaving the only path to be by way of the crucible of war. The utter destructiveness of war now blocks out this alternative. We have had our last chance. If we will not devise some greater and more equitable system, our Armageddon will be at our door. The problem basically is theological and involves a spiritual recrudescence, an improvement of human character that will synchronize with our almost matchless advances in science, art, literature and all material and cultural developments of the past 2,000 years. It must be of the spirit if we are to save the flesh.

But once war it forced upon us, there is no other alternative than to apply every available means to bring it to a swift end. War's very object is victory, not prolonged indecision.

In war there is no substitute for victory." . . .

I am closing my fifty-two years of military service. When I joined the Army, even before the turn of the century, it was the fulfillment of all my boyish hopes and dreams.

The world has turned over many times since I took the oath on the plains at West Point, and the hopes and dreams have long since vanished, but I still remember the refrain of one of the most popular barrack ballads of that day which proclaimed that old soldiers never die; they just fade away.

And like the old soldier of that ballad, I now close my military career and just fade away, an old soldier who tried to do his duty as God gave him the light to see that duty. Good-bye.

(April 19, 1951)

ODE TO DUTY

William Wordsworth

Stern Daughter of the Voice of God!
O Duty! if that name thou love
Who art a light to guide, a rod
To check the erring, and reprove;
Thou, who art victory and law
When empty terrors overawe;
From vain temptations dost set free;
And calm'st the weary strife of frail humanity!

There are who ask not if thine eye
Be on them; who, in love and truth,
Where no misgiving is, rely
Upon the genial sense of youth:
Glad Hearts! without reproach or blot
Who do thy work, and know it not:

Oh! if through confidence misplaced
They fail, thy saving arms, dread Power! around them cast.

Serene will be our days and bright,
And happy will our nature be,
When love is an unerring light,
And joy its own security.
And they a blissful course may hold
Even now, who, not unwisely bold,
Live in the spirit of this creed;
Yet seek thy firm support, according to their need.

I, loving freedom, and untried;
No sport of every random gust,
Yet being to myself a guide,
Too blindly have reposed my trust:
And oft, when in my heart was heard
Thy timely mandate, I deferred
The task, in smoother walks to stray;
But thee I now would serve more strictly, if I may.

Through no disturbance of my soul,
Or strong compunction in me wrought,
I supplicate for thy control;
But in the quietness of thought:
Me this unchartered freedom tires;
I feel the weight of chance-desires:
My hopes no more must change their name,
I long for a repose that ever is the same.

Stern Lawgiver! yet thou dost wear
The Godhead's most benignant grace;
Nor know we anything so fair
As is the smile upon thy face:
Flowers laugh before thee on their beds
And fragrance in thy footing treads;
Thou dost preserve the stars from wrong;
And the most ancient heavens, through Thee, are fresh and strong.

To humbler functions, awful Power!
I call thee: I myself commend
Unto thy guidance from this hour;

Oh, let my weakness have an end!
Give unto me, made lowly wise,
The spirit of self-sacrifice;
The confidence of reason give;
And in the light of truth thy Bondman let me live!

OBLIVION

Sir Thomas Browne

Oblivion is not to be hired: the greater part must be content to
be as though they had not been; to be found in the register of God,
not in the record of man. Twenty-seven names make up the first
story before the flood, and the recorded names ever since contain
not one living century. The number of the dead long exceedeth
all that shall live. The night of time far surpasseth the day, and
who knows when was the equinox? Every hour adds unto that
current arithmetick, which scarce stands one moment. And since
death must be the Lucina of life, and even Pagans could doubt
whether thus to live were to die; since our longest sun sets at right
descensions, and makes but winter arches, and therefore it cannot
be long before we lie down in darkness, and have our light in
ashes; since the brother of death daily haunts us with dying me-
mentos, and time, that grows old in itself, bids us hope no long
duration: Diuturnity is a dream and folly of expectation.

Darkness and light divide the course of time, and oblivion shares
with memory a great part even of our living beings; we slightly
remember our felicities, and the smartest strokes of affliction leave
but short smart upon us. Sense endureth no extremities, and sorrows destroy us or themselves. To weep into stones are fables.
Afflictions induce callosities; miseries are slippery, or fall like snow
upon us, which notwithstanding is no unhappy stupidity. To be
ignorant of evils to come, and forgetful of evils past, is a merciful
provision in nature, whereby we digest the mixture of our few and
evil days; and our delivered senses not relapsing into cutting re-
membrances, our sorrows are not kept raw by the edge of repetitions. A great part of antiquity contented their hopes of subsistency
with a transmigration of their souls: a good way to continue their
memories, while, having the advantage of plural successions, they

could not but act something remarkable in such variety of beings, and enjoying the fame of their past selves, make accumulation of glory unto their last durations. Others, rather than be lost in the uncomfortable night of nothing, were content to recede into the common being, and make one particle of the public soul of all things, which was no more than to return into their unknown and divine original again. Egyptian ingenuity was more unsatisfied, contriving their bodies in sweet consistencies to attend the return of their souls. But all was vanity, feeding the wind, and folly. The Egyptian mummies, which Cambyses or time hath spared, avarice now consumeth. Mummy is become merchandise, Mizraim cures wounds, and Pharaoh is sold for balsams.

(From Urn Burial)

* * *

Love thy neighbor but do not pull down thy hedge.—Anonymous

GEORGE WASHINGTON

Thomas Jefferson

His mind was great and powerful, without being of the very first order; his penetration strong, though not so acute as that of a Newton, Bacon or Locke; and as far as he saw, no judgment was ever sounder. It was slow in operation, being little aided by invention or imagination, but sure in conclusion. . . . Hearing all suggestions, he selected whatever was best; and certainly no General ever planned his battles more judiciously. But if deranged during the course of the action . . . he was slow in readjustment. . . . He was incapable of fear, meeting personal dangers with the calmest unconcern.

Perhaps the strongest feature in his character was prudence, never acting until every circumstance, every consideration was maturely weighed. . . . His integrity was most pure, his justice the most inflexible I have ever known, no motives of interest or consanguinity, of friendship or hatred, being able to bias his decision. He was, indeed, in every sense of the words, a wise, a good, and a great man. His temper was naturally irritable and high toned; but reflection and resolution had obtained a firm and habitual ascendancy over it. If ever, however, it broke its bonds, he was most tremendous in his wrath.

In his expenses he was honorable, but exact; liberal in contributions to whatever promised utility; but frowning and unyielding on all visionary projects and all unworthy calls on his charity. His heart was not warm in its affections; but he exactly calculated every man's value, and gave him a solid esteem proportioned to it.

His person, you know, was fine, his stature exactly what one would wish, his deportment easy, erect and noble; the best horseman of his age, and the most graceful figure that could be seen on horseback.

Although in the circle of his friends, where he might be unreserved with safety, he took a free share in conversation, his colloquial talents were not above mediocrity, possessing neither copiousness of ideas, nor fluency of words. In public, when called on for a sudden opinion, he was unready, short and embarrassed. Yet he wrote readily, rather diffusely, in an easy and correct style. This he had acquired by conversation with the world, for his education was merely reading, writing and common arithmetic, to which he added surveying at a later day. His time was employed in action chiefly, reading little, and that only in agriculture and English history. . . . His agricultural proceedings occupied most of his leisure hours within doors.

On the whole, his character was, in its mass, perfect, in nothing bad, in few points indifferent; and it may truly be said, that never did nature and fortune combine more perfectly to make a man great, and to place him . . . in an everlasting remembrance.

(1814)

THE FACE OF ABRAHAM LINCOLN

Walt Whitman

I see the President almost every day, as I happen to live where he passes to and from his lodgings out of town. He never sleeps at the White House during the hot season, but has quarters at a healthy location some three miles north of the city, the Soldiers' home, a United States military establishment. I saw him this morning about 8½ coming in to business, riding on Vermont Avenue, near L Street. He always has a company of twenty-five or thirty cavalry, with sabres drawn and held upright over their shoulders. They say this guard was against his personal wish, but he let his counselors have their way. The party makes no great show in uniform or horses. Mr. Lincoln on the saddle generally rides a good-sized, easy-going gray horse, is dressed in plain black, somewhat rusty and dusty, wears a black stiff hat, and looks about as ordinary in attire, etc. as the commonest man. A lieutenant, with yellow straps, rides at his left, and following behind, two by two, come the cavalry men, in their yellow-striped jackets. They are generally going at a slow trot, as that is the pace set them by the one they wait upon. The sabres and accoutrements clank, and the entirely unornamental *cortège* as it trots towards Lafayette Square arouses no sensation, only some curious stranger stops and gazes. I see very plainly Abraham Lincoln's dark brown face, with the deep-cut lines, the eyes, always to me with a deep latent sadness in the expression. We have got so that we exchange bows, and very cordial ones. Sometimes the President goes and comes in an open barouche. The cavalry always accompany him, with drawn sabres. Often I notice as he goes out evening—and sometimes in the morning, when he returns early—he turns off and halts at the large and handsome residence of the Secretary of War, on K Street, and holds conference there. If in his barouche, I can see from my window he does not alight, but sits in his vehicle, and Mr. Stanton comes out to attend him. Sometimes one of his sons, a boy of ten or twelve, accompanies him, riding at his right on a pony. Earlier in the summer I occasionally saw the President and his wife, toward the latter part of the afternoon, out in a barouche, on a pleasure ride through the city. Mrs. Lincoln was dressed in complete black, with a long crepe veil. The equipage is of the plainest kind, only two horses, and they nothing extra. They passed me once very close, and I saw the President in the face fully, as they were moving slowly, and his look, though abstracted, happened to be directed steadily in my eye. He bowed and smiled, but far beneath his smile I noticed well the expression I have alluded to. None of the artists or pictures has caught the deep, though subtle and indirect expression of this man's face. There is something else there. One of the great portrait painters of two or three centuries ago is needed.

(From Specimen Days)

TO THOMAS MOORE

Lord Byron

My boat is on the shore,
　And my bark is on the sea;
But, before I go, Tom Moore,
　Here's a double health to thee!

Here's a sigh to those who love me,
　And a smile to those who hate;
And, whatever sky's above me,
　Here's a heart for every fate.

Though the ocean roar around me,
　Yet it still shall bear me on;
Though a desert should surround me,
　It hath springs that may be won.

Were the last drop in the well,
　As I gasp'd upon the brink,
Ere my fainting spirit fell,
　'Tis to thee that I would drink.

With what water, as this wine,
　The libation I would pour
Should be—Peace with thine and mine
　And a health to thee, Tom Moore.

THE TIDE RISES, THE TIDE FALLS

Henry Wadsworth Longfellow

The tide rises, the tide falls,
The twilight darkens, the curlew calls;
Along the sea-sands damp and brown
The traveller hastens toward the town,
　And the tide rises, the tide falls.

Darkness settles on roofs and walls,
But the sea, the sea in the darkness calls;
The little waves, with their soft, white hands,
Efface the footprints in the sands,
   And the tide rises, the tide falls.

The morning breaks; the steeds in their stalls
Stamp and neigh, as the hostler calls;
The day returns, but nevermore
Returns the traveller to the shore.
   And the tide rises, the tide falls.

BILL NYE'S OBSERVATIONS ON SPACE

Space is very large. It is immense, very immense. A great deal of immensity exists in space. Space has no top, no bottom. In fact, it is bottomless both at the bottom and at the top. Space extends as far backwards as it does forward, and *vice versa*. There is no compass of space, nor points of the compass, and no boxing of the compass. A billion million of miles traveled in space won't bring a man any nearer than one mile or one inch. Consequently, in space, it's better to stay where you are, and let well enough alone.

Conclusion of THE COMMUNIST MANIFESTO

Karl Marx and Friedrich Engels

The Communists disdain to conceal their views and aims. They openly declare that their ends can be attained only by the forcible overthrow of all existing social conditions. Let the ruling classes tremble at a communistic revolution. The proletarians have nothing to lose but their chains. They have a world to win.

Workingmen of the world, unite!

(1848)

THE GOLD RUSH

Mark Twain

Look history over and you will see. The missionary comes after the whiskey—I mean, he arrives after the whiskey has arrived. Next comes the poor immigrant with ax and hoe and rifle; next, the trader, next the miscellaneous rush; next the gambler, the desperado, the highwayman, and all their kindred in sin of both sexes; and next the smart chap who has bought up an old grant that covers all the land; this brings in the lawyer tribe; the vigilance committe brings the undertaker. All these interests bring the newspaper; the newspaper starts up politics and a railroad; all hands turn to and build a church and a jail—and behold, civilization is established forever in the land.

THE TABLE AND THE CHAIR

Edward Lear

Said the Table to the Chair,
"You can hardly be aware
How I suffer from the heat
And from chilblains on my feet.

"If we took a little walk,
We might have a little talk;
Pray let us take the air,"
Said the Table to the Chair.

Said the Chair unto the Table,
"Now you *know* we are not able:
How foolishly you talk,
When you know we *cannot* walk!"

Said the Table with a sigh,
"It can do no harm to try.
I've as many legs as you:
Why can't we walk on two?"

So they both went slowly down,
And walked about the town
With a cheerful bumpy sound
And they toddled round and round;

And everybody cried,
As they hastened to their side,
"See! the Table and the Chair
Have come out to take the air!"

But in going down an alley
To a castle in the valley
They completely lost their way,
And wandered all the day;

Till to see them safely back,
They paid a Ducky-quack,
And a beetle, and a Mouse,
Who took them to their house.

Then they whispered to each other,
"O delightful little brother,
What a lovely walk we've taken!
Let us dine on beans and bacon!"

So the Ducky and the leetle
Browny-Mousy and the Beetle
Dined and danced upon their heads
Till they toddled to their beds.

AN ELEGY ON THAT GLORY OF HER SEX,
MRS. MARY BLAIZE

Oliver Goldsmith

Good people all, with one accord,
   Lament for Madame Blaize,
Who never wanted a good word—
   From those who spoke her praise.

The needy seldom pass'd her door,
   And always found her kind;
She freely lent to all the poor,—
   Who left a pledge behind.

She strove the neighbourhood to please,
   With manners wond'rous winning,
And never followed wicked ways,—
   Unless when she was sinning.

At church, in silks and satins new,
   With hoops of monstrous size,
She never slumber'd in her pew,—
   But when she shut her eyes.

Her love was sought, I do aver,
   By twenty beaux and more;
The king himself has followed her,—
   When she has walk'd before.

But now her wealth and finery fled,
   Her hangers-on cut short all;
The doctors found, when she was dead,—
   Her last disorder mortal.

Let us lament, in sorrow sore,
   For Kent-street well may say,
That had she lived a twelve-month more,—
   She had not died today.

EMPEROR HADRIAN'S DYING ADDRESS TO HIS SOUL

Soul of mine, pretty one, flitting one,
   Guest and partner of my clay,
   Whither wilt thou hie away—
Pallid one, rigid one, naked one,
   Never to play again, never to play?

A LITTLE WHILE

Emily Brontë

A little while, a little while,
   The weary task is put away,
And I can sing and I can smile,
   Alike, while I have holiday.

Where wilt thou go, my harassed heart—
   What thought, what scene invites thee now?
What spot, or near or far apart,
   Has rest for thee, my weary brow?

There is a spot, 'mid barren hills,
   Where winter howls, and driving rain;
But, if the dreary tempest chills,
   There is a light that warms again.

The house is old, the trees are bare,
   Moonless above bends twilight's dome;
But what on earth is half so dear—
   So longed for—as the hearth of home?

The mute bird sitting on the stone,
   The dank moss dripping from the wall,
The thorn trees gaunt, the walks o'ergrown,
   I love them—how I love them all!

Still, as I mused, the naked room,
   The alien firelight died away;
And from the midst of cheerless gloom,
   I passed to bright, unclouded day.

A little and a lone green lane
   That opened on a common wide;
A distant, dreamy, dim blue chain
   Of mountains circling every side.

A heaven so clear, and earth so calm,
   So sweet, so soft, so hushed an air;
And, deepening still the dreamlike charm,
   Wild moor-sheep feeding everywhere.

That was the scene, I knew it well;
   I knew the turfy pathway's sweep,
That, winding o'er each billowy swell,
   Marked out the tracks of wandering sheep.

Could I have lingered but an hour,
   It well had paid a week of toil;
But Truth has banished Fancy's power:
   Restraint and heavy task recoil.

Even as I stood with raptured eye,
   Absorbed in bliss so deep and dear,
My hour of rest had fleeted by,
   And back came labor, bondage, care.

SAMUEL JOHNSON'S TRIBUTE TO DAVID GARRICK

I hoped to have gratified with this character of our common friend: but what are the hopes of man! I am disappointed by that stroke of death, which has eclipsed the gaiety of nations and impoverished the public stock of harmless pleasure.

HORACE GREELEY TO THOMAS DEVYR, WHO ATTACKED HIM IN 1860 FOR ADVOCATING LINCOLN'S ELECTION

The only favor I shall ever ask of you is that you procure and read Benedict Arnold's letter to his betrayed countrymen after he escaped from West Point to the British camp, and then take a steady look at your own face in the mirror. I loathe you too much for your treason to the rights of man to speak to you, but for what you have said or may say about me I care nothing. I remain, glad that you have ceased personally to infest me,

        —Horace Greeley

MY FAMILIAR

John Godfrey Saxe

Again I hear that creaking step—
    He's rapping at the door!
Too well I know the boding sound
    That ushers in a bore.
I do not tremble when I meet
    The stoutest of my foes,
But Heaven defend me from the friend
    Who comes—but never goes!

He drops into my easy-chair,
    And asks about the news;
He peers into my manuscript,
    And gives his candid views;
He tells me where he likes the line,
    And where he's forced to grieve;
He takes the strangest liberties—
    But never takes his leave!

He reads my daily paper through
    Before I've seen a word;
He scans the lyric (that I wrote)
    And thinks it quite absurd;
He calmly smokes my last cigar,
    And coolly asks for more;
He opens everything he sees—
    Except the entry door!

He talks about his fragile health,
    And tells me of the pains
He suffers from a score of ills
    Of which he ne'er complains;
And how he struggled once with death
    To keep the fiend at bay;
On themes like those away he goes—
    But never goes away!

He tells me of the carping words
   Some shallow critic wrote;
And every precious paragraph
   Familiarly can quote;
He thinks the writer did me wrong;
   He'd like to run him through!
He says a thousand pleasant things—
   But never says, "Adieu!"

Whene'er he comes, that dreadful man,
   Disguise it as I may,
I know that, like an Autumn rain,
   He'll last throughout the day.
In vain I speak of urgent tasks;
   In vain I scowl and pout;
A frown is no extinguisher—
   It does not put him out!

I mean to take the knocker off,
   Put crape upon the door,
Or hint to John that I am gone
   To stay a month or more.
I do not tremble when I meet
   The stoutest of my foes,
But Heaven defend me from the friend
   Who never, never goes!

IT'S THE SYME THE WHOLE WORLD OVER

Anonymous

It's the syme the whole world over,
It's the poor what gets the blyme,
W'ile the rich 'as all the plysures.
Now a'nt that a blinkin' shyme?

She was just a parson's daughter,
Pure, unstyned was 'er fyme;
Till a country squire came courtin'—
And the poor girl lorst 'er nyme.

So she went aw'y to Lunnon,
Just to 'ide 'er guilty shyme.
There she met another squire;
Once agine, she lorst her nyme.

Look at 'im with all 'is 'orses,
Drinking champyne in 'is club,
W'ile the wictim of 'is passions
Drinks 'er Guinness in a pub.

Now 'e's in 'is ridin' britches,
'Untin' foxes in the chyse,
W'ile the wictim of 'is folly
Mykes 'er livin' by 'er wice.

So she settled down in Lunnon,
Sinkin' deeper in 'er shyme,
Till she met a lybor leader
And agine she lorst 'er nyme.

Now 'e's in the 'Ouse of Commons
Mykin' laws to put down crime,
W'ile the wictim of 'is plysure
Walks the street each night in shyme.

Then there cyme a bloated bishop.
Marriage was the tyle 'e told.
There was no one else to tyke 'er
So she sold her soul for gold.

See 'er in 'er 'orse and carriage,
Drivin' d'ily through the park.
Though she's myde a wealthy marriage
Still she 'ides a brykin' 'eart.

In a cottage down in Sussex
Lives 'er payrents old and lyme.
And they drink the wine she sends 'em.
But they never speak 'er nyme.

In their poor and humble dwellin',
There 'er grievin' payrents live,
Drinkin' champyne as she sends 'em
But they never can forgive.

It's the syme the whole world over,
It's the poor what gets the blyme,
W'ile the rich 'as all the plysures;
Now, a'nt that a blinkin' shyme!

HAMLET BROODS OVER THE DEATH
OF HIS FATHER

William Shakespeare

O, that this too too solid flesh would melt,
Thaw and resolve into a dew!
Or that the Everlasting had not fix'd
His canon 'gainst self-slaughter! O God! God!
How weary, stale, flat and unprofitable
Seem to me all the uses of this world!
Fie on 't! ah fie! 'Tis an unweeded garden,
That grows to seed; things rank and gross in nature
Possess it merely. That it should come to this!
But two months dead! nay, not so much, not two:
So excellent a king; that was, to this,
Hyperion to a satyr: so loving to my mother,
That he might not beteem the winds of heaven
Visit her face too roughly. Heaven and earth!
Must I remember? why, she would hang on him,
As if increase of appetite had grown
By what it fed on: and yet, within a month—
Let me not think on 't—Frailty, thy name is woman!—
A little month, or ere those shoes were old
With which she follow'd my poor father's body,
Like Niobe, all tears:—why she, even she,—
O God! a beast that wants discourse of reason
Would have mourn'd longer,—married with my uncle,
My father's brother, but no more like my father
Than I to Hercules: within a month;
Ere yet the salt of most unrighteous tears
Had left the flushing in her galled eyes,
She married.

(From Hamlet)

AGAINST CENSORSHIP

John Milton

I deny not, but that it is of greatest concernment in the church and commonwealth, to have a vigilant eye how books demean themselves, as well as men; and thereafter to confine, imprison, and do sharpest justice on them as malefactors; for books are not absolutely dead things, but do contain a potency of life in them to be as active as that soul was whose progeny they are; nay, they do preserve as in a vial the purest efficacy and extraction of that living intellect that bred them. I know they are as lively, and as vigorously productive, as those fabulous dragon's teeth: and being sown up and down, may chance to spring up armed men. And yet, on the other hand, unless wariness be used, as good almost kill a man as kill a good book: who kills a man kills a reasonable creature, God's image; but he who destroys a good book, kills reason itself, kills the image of God, as it were, in the eye. Many a man lives a burden to the earth; but a good book is the precious life-blood of a master-spirit, embalmed and treasured up on purpose to a life beyond life. It is true, no age can restore a life, whereof, perhaps, there is no great loss; and revolutions of ages do not oft recover the loss of a rejected truth, for the want of which whole nations fare the worse. We should be wary, therefore, what persecution we raise against the living labours of public men, how we spill that seasoned life of man, preserved and stored up in books; since we see a kind of homicide may be thus committed, sometimes a martyrdom; and if it extend to the whole impression, a kind of massacre, whereof the execution ends not in the slaying of an elemental life, but strikes at the ethereal and fifth essence, the breath of reason itself; slays an immortality rather than a life.

(From Areopagitica)

FORBEARANCE

Ralph Waldo Emerson

Hast thou named all the birds without a gun?
Loved the wood rose, and left it on its stalk?
At rich men's tables eaten bread and pulse?
Unarmed, faced danger with a heart of trust?
And loved so well a high behavior,
In man or maid, that thou from speech refrained,
Nobility more nobly to repay?
O, be my friend, and teach me to be thine!

"THE WORLD'S GREAT AGE BEGINS ANEW"

Percy Bysshe Shelley

The world's great age begins anew,
  The golden years return,
The earth doth like a snake renew
  Her winter weeds outworn;
Heaven smiles, and faiths and empires gleam,
Like wrecks of a dissolving dream.

A brighter Hellas rears its mountains
  From waves serener far;
A new Peneus rolls his fountains
  Against the morning star.
Where fairer Tempes bloom, there sleep
Young Cyclads on a sunnier deep,

A loftier Argo cleaves the main,
  Fraught with a later prize;
Another Orpheus sings again,
  And loves, and weeps, and dies.
A new Ulysses leaves once more
Calypso for his native shore.

Oh, write no more the tale of Troy,
  If earth Death's scroll must be!
Nor mix with Laian rage the joy
  Which dawns upon the free:
Although a subtler Sphinx renew
Riddles of death Thebes never knew.

Another Athens shall arise,
  And to remoter time
Bequeath, like sunset to the skies,
  The splendour of its prime;
And leave, if naught so bright may live,
All earth can take or Heaven can give.

LITTLE BOY BLUE

Eugene Field

The little toy dog is covered with dust,
  But sturdy and stanch he stands;
And the little toy soldier is red with rust,
  And his musket molds in his hands.
Time was when the little toy dog was new
  And the soldier was passing fair,
And that was the time when our Little Boy Blue
  Kissed them and put them there.

"Now, don't you go till I come," he said,
  "And don't you make any noise!"
So toddling off to his trundle-bed
  He dreamed of the pretty toys.
And as he was dreaming, an angel song
  Awakened our Little Boy Blue—
Oh, the years are many, the years are long,
  But the little toy friends are true.

Aye, faithful to Little Boy Blue they stand,
  Each in the same old place,
Awaiting the touch of a little hand,
  And the smile of a little face.
And they wonder, as waiting these long years through,
  In the dust of that little chair,
What has become of our Little Boy Blue
  Since he kissed them and put them there.

THE UNITED STATES...THE GREATEST POEM

Walt Whitman

The Americans of all nations at any time upon the earth have
probably the fullest poetical nature. The United States themselves
are essentially the greatest poem. In the history of the earth hitherto
the largest and most stirring appear tame and orderly to their ampler
largeness and stir. Here at last is something in the doings of man

865

that corresponds with the broadcast doings of the day and night. Here is not merely a nation but a teeming nation of nations. Here is action untied from strings necessarily blind to particulars and details magnificently moving in vast masses. Here is the hospitality which forever indicates heroes. . . . Here are the roughs and beards and space and ruggedness and nonchalance that the soul loves. Here the performance disdaining the trivial unapproached in the tremendous audacity of its crowds and groupings and the push of its perspective spreads with crampless and flowing breadth and showers its prolific and splendid extravagance. One sees it must indeed own the riches of the summer and winter, and need never be bankrupt while corn grows from the ground or the orchards drop apples or the bays contain fish or men beget children upon woman.

Other states indicate themselves in their deputies . . . but the genius of the United States is not best or most in its executives or legislatures, nor in its ambassadors or authors or colleges or churches or parlors, nor even in its newspapers or inventors . . . but always most in the common people. Their manners speech dress friendships —the freshness and candor of their physiognomy—the picturesque looseness of their carriage . . . their deathless attachment to freedom —their aversion to anything indecorous or soft or mean—the practical acknowledgment of the citizens of one state by the citizens of all other states—the fierceness of their roused resentment—their curiosity and welcome of novelty—their self-esteem and wonderful sympathy—their susceptibility to a slight—the air they have of persons who never knew how it felt to stand in the presence of superiors— the fluency of their speech—their delight in music, the sure symptom of manly tenderness and native elegance of soul . . . their good temper and open-handedness—the terrible significance of their elections—the President's taking off his hat to them not they to him—these too are unrhymed poetry. It awaits the gigantic and generous treatment worthy of it.

(From the Preface of the 1855 edition of *Leaves of Grass*)

PRESIDENT KENNEDY TO THE NATION ON THE CUBAN MISSILE CRISIS, OCTOBER 22, 1962

Within the past week unmistakable evidence has established the fact that a series of offensive missile sites is now in preparation on that imprisoned island.

The purpose of these bases can be none other than to provide a nuclear strike capability against the Western Hemisphere. . . .

Each of these missiles, in short, is capable of striking Washington, D.C., the Panama Canal, Cape Canaveral, Mexico City or any other city in the southeastern part of the United States, in Central America or in the Caribbean area.

Additional sites not yet completed appear to be designed for intermediate-range ballistic missiles capable of traveling more than twice as far, and thus capable of striking most of the major cities in the Western Hemisphere ranging as far north as Hudson's Bay, Canada, and as far south as Lima, Peru.

In addition, jet bombers, capable of carrying nuclear weapons, are now being uncrated and assembled in Cuba while the necessary air bases are being prepared.

This urgent transformation of Cuba into an important strategic base by the presence of these large long-range and clearly offensive weapons of sudden mass destruction constitutes an explicit threat to the peace and security of all the Americas in flagrant and deliberate defiance of the Rio Pact of 1947, the traditions of this nation and hemisphere, the joint resolution of the 87th Congress, the Charter of the United Nations and my own public warnings to the Soviets on September 4 and 13.

This action also contradicts the repeated assurances of Soviet spokesmen both publicly and privately delivered that the arms build-up in Cuba would retain its original defensive character and that the Soviet Union had no need or desire to station strategic missiles on the territory of any other nation.

The size of this undertaking makes clear that it had been planned for some months. . . .

But this secret, swift, extraordinary build-up of Communist missiles in an area well-known to have a special and historical relationship to the United States and the nations of the Western Hemisphere, in violation of Soviet assurances and in defiance of American and hemispheric policy—this sudden, clandestine decision to station strategic weapons for the first time outside of Soviet soil —is a deliberately provocative and unjustified change in the status quo which cannot be accepted by this country if our courage and our commitments are ever to be trusted again, by either friend or foe.

This nation is opposed to war. We are also true to our word.

Our unswerving objective, therefore, must be to prevent the use of these missiles against this or any other country; and to secure their withdrawal or elimination from the Western Hemisphere.

Our policy has been one of patience and restraint, as befits a peaceful and powerful nation which leads a world-wide alliance.

We have been determined not to be diverted from our central concerns by mere irritants, and fanatics. But now further action is required. And it is underway. And these actions may only be the beginning.

We will not prematurely or unnecessarily risk the course of world-wide nuclear war in which even the fruits of victory would be ashes in our mouth, but neither will we shrink from that risk at any time it must be faced.

Acting, therefore, in the defense of our own security and of the entire Western Hemisphere and under the authority entrusted to me by the Constitution as endorsed by the resolution of the Congress, I have directed that the following initial steps be taken immediately:

First, to halt this offensive build-up, a strict quarantine on all offensive military equipment under shipment to Cuba is being initiated. All ships of any kind bound for Cuba from whatever nation or port, where they are found to contain cargoes of offensive weapons, be turned back. This quarantine will be extended if needed to other types of cargo and carriers.

I have directed the armed forces to prepare for any eventualities, and I trust that in the interests of both the Cuban people and the Soviet technicians at the sites, the hazards to all concerned of continuing this threat will be recognized.

Third, it shall be the policy of this nation to regard any nuclear missile launched from Cuba against any nation in the Western Hemisphere as an attack by the Soviet Union on the United States requiring a full retaliatory response upon the Soviet Union.

Finally, I call Chairman Khrushchev to halt and eliminate this clandestine, reckless and provocative threat to world peace and to stable relations between our two nations.

I call upon him further to abandon this course of world domination and to join in an historic effort to end the perilous arms race and to transform the history of man.

He has an opportunity now to move the world back from the

abyss of destruction by returning to his Government's own words that it had no need to station missiles outside its own territory, and withdrawing these weapons from Cuba; by refraining from any action which will widen or deepen the present crisis, and then by participating in a search for peaceful and permanent solutions.

We have no wish to war with the Soviet Union for we are a peaceful people who desire to live in peace with all other peoples.

But it is difficult to settle or even discuss these problems in an atmosphere of intimidation.

That is why this latest Soviet threat or any other threat which is made either independently or in response to our actions this week must and will be met with determination.

Any hostile move anywhere in the world against the safety and freedom of peoples to whom we are committed including in particular the brave people of West Berlin will be met by whatever action is needed.

My fellow citizens, let no one doubt that this is a difficult and dangerous effort on which we have set out. No one can foresee precisely what course it will take, or what course or casualties will be incurred.

Many months of sacrifice and self-discipline lie ahead, months in which both our patience and our will will be tested. Months in which many threats and denunciations will keep us aware of our dangers. But the greatest danger of all would be to do nothing.

The path we have chosen for the present is full of hazards, as all paths are. But it is the one most consistent with our character and courage as a nation and our commitments around the world.

The cost of freedom is always high, but Americans have always paid it.

And one path we shall never choose, and that is the path of surrender, or submission.

Our goal is not the victory of might, but the vindication of right; not peace at the expense of freedom, but both peace and freedom here in this hemisphere, and, we hope, around the world.

RIME OF THE ANCIENT MARINER

IN SEVEN PARTS

Samuel Taylor Coleridge

PART I

An ancient mariner
meeteth three gal-
lants bidden to a
wedding feast, and
detaineth one.

It is an ancient mariner,
And he stoppeth one of three.
"By thy long gray beard and glittering eye,
Now wherefore stopp'st thou me?

The bridegroom's doors are opened wide,
And I am next of kin;
The guests are met, the feast is set,—
May'st hear the merry din."

He holds him with his skinny hand:
"There was a ship," quoth he.
"Hold off! unhand me, graybeard loon!"—
Eftsoons his hand dropt he.

The wedding-guest
is spellbound by the
eye of the old sea-
faring man, and con-
strained to hear
his tale.

He holds him with his glittering eye.—
The wedding-guest stood still;
He listens like a three years' child;
The mariner hath his will.

The wedding-guest sat on a stone,—
He cannot choose but hear;
And thus spake on that ancient man,
The bright-eyed mariner:

"The ship was cheered, the harbor cleared;
Merrily did we drop
Below the kirk, below the hill,
Below the lighthouse top.

The mariner tells
how the ship sailed
southward, with a
good wind and fair
weather, till it
reached the line.

The sun came up upon the left,
Out of the sea came he;
And he shone bright, and on the right
Went down into the sea.

Higher and higher every day,
Till over the mast at noon—"
The wedding-guest here beat his breast,
For he heard the loud bassoon.

The bride hath paced into the hall,—
Red as a rose is she;
Nodding their heads before her goes
The merry minstrelsy.

The wedding-guest
heareth the bridal
music; but the mari-
ner continueth
his tale.

The wedding-guest he beat his breast,
Yet he cannot choose but hear;
And thus spake on that ancient man,
The bright-eyed mariner:

"And now the storm-blast came, and he
Was tyrannous and strong;
He struck with his o'ertaking wings,
And chased us south along.

The ship drawn by
a storm toward the
south pole.

With sloping masts and dipping prow,—
As who pursued with yell and blow
Still treads the shadow of his foe,
And forward bends his head,—
The ship drove fast; loud roared the blast,
And southward aye we fled.

And now there came both mist and snow,
And it grew wondrous cold;
And ice, mast-high, came floating by,
As green as emerald.

And through the drifts the snowy clifts
Did send a dismal sheen;
Nor shapes of men nor beasts we ken,—
The ice was all between.

The land of ice and
of fearful sounds,
where no living
thing was to be
seen.

The ice was here, the ice was there,
The ice was all around;
It cracked and growled, and roared and howled,
Like noises in a swound!

Till a great sea-bird, called the albatross, came through the snow-fog, and was received with great joy and hospitality.

At length did cross an albatross,—
Thorough the fog it came;
As if it had been a Christian soul,
We hailed it in God's name.

It ate the food it ne'er had eat,
And round and round it flew.
The ice did split with a thunder-fit;
The helmsman steered us through!

And lo! the albatross proveth a bird of good omen, and followeth the ship as it returned northward through fog and floating ice.

And a good south wind sprung up behind;
The albatross did follow,
And every day, for food or play,
Came to the mariners' hollo!

In mist or cloud, on mast or shroud,
It perched for vespers nine;
Whiles all the night, through fog-smoke white,
Glimmered the white moonshine."

The ancient mariner inhospitably killed the pious bird of good omen.

"God save thee, ancient mariner!
From the fiends that plague thee thus!—
Why look'st thou so?"—"With my cross-bow
I shot the albatross."

PART II

"The sun now rose upon the right,—
Out of the sea came he,
Still hid in mist, and on the left
Went down into the sea.

And the good south wind still blew behind;
But no sweet bird did follow.
Nor any day for food or play
Came to the mariners' hollo.

His shipmates cry out against the ancient mariner, for killing the bird of good luck.

And I had done a hellish thing,
And it would work 'em woe;
For all averred I had killed the bird
That made the breeze to blow:
Ah, wretch! said they, the bird to slay,
That made the breeze to blow!

872

Nor dim nor red, like God's own head
The glorious sun uprist;
Then all averred I had killed the bird
That brought the fog and mist:
'Twas right, said they, such birds to slay,
That bring the fog and mist.

But when the fog cleared off, they justify the same, and thus make themselves accomplices in the crime.

The fair breeze blew, the white foam flew,
The furrow followed free;
We were the first that ever burst
Into that silent sea.

The fair breeze continues; the ship enters the Pacific Ocean, and sails northward, even till it reaches the line.

Down dropt the breeze, the sails dropt down,—
'Twas sad as sad could be;
And we did speak only to break
The silence of the sea.

The ship hath been suddenly becalmed.

All in a hot and copper sky
The bloody sun, at noon,
Right up above the mast did stand,
No bigger than the moon.

Day after day, day after day,
We stuck,—nor breath nor motion;
As idle as a painted ship
Upon a painted ocean.

Water, water everywhere,
And all the boards did shrink;
Water, water everywhere,
Nor any drop to drink.

And the albatross begins to be avenged.

The very deep did rot: O Christ!
That ever this should be!
Yea, slimy things did crawl with legs
Upon the slimy sea!

About, about, in reel and rout,
The death-fires danced at night;
The water, like a witch's oils,
Burnt green, and blue, and white.

A spirit had followed them,—one of the invisible inhabitants of this planet, neither departed souls nor angels; concerning whom the learned Jew, Josephus, and the Platonic Constantinopolitan, Michael Psellus, may be consulted. They are very numerous, and there is no climate or element without one or more.

And some in dreams assured were
Of the spirit that plagued us so;
Nine fathom deep he had followed us
From the land of mist and snow.

And every tongue, through utter drought,
Was withered at the root;
We could not speak, no more than if
We had been choked with soot.

The shipmates, in their sore distress, would fain throw the whole guilt on the ancient mariner: in sign whereof they hang the dead seabird round his neck.

Ah! well-a-day! what evil looks
Had I from old and young!
Instead of the cross, the albatross
About my neck was hung.

PART III

There passed a weary time. Each throat
Was parched, and glazed each eye,—
A weary time! a weary time!
How glazed each weary eye!—
The ancient mariner beholdeth a sign in the element afar off. When, looking westward, I beheld
A something in the sky.

At first it seemed a little speck,
And then it seemed a mist;
It moved and moved, and took at last
A certain shape, I wist,—

A speck, a mist, a shape, I wist!
And still it neared and neared;
As if it dodged a water-sprite,
It plunged, and tacked, and veered.

At its nearer approach it seemeth him to be a ship; and at a dear ransom he freeth his speech from the bonds of thirst.

With throats unslaked, with black lips baked,
We could not laugh nor wail;
Through utter drought all dumb we stood;
I bit my arm, I sucked the blood,
And cried, A sail! a sail!

With throats unslaked, with black lips baked,
Agape they heard me call;

Gramercy! they for joy did grin,
And all at once their breath drew in,
As they were drinking all.

A flash of joy.

See! see! I cried, she tacks no more!
Hither, to work us weal,—
Without a breeze, without a tide,
She steadies with upright keel!

And horror follows;
for can it be a ship
that comes onward
without wind or
tide?

The western wave was all aflame;
The day was well-nigh done;
Almost upon the western wave
Rested the broad bright sun,—
When that strange shape drove suddenly
Betwixt us and the sun.

And straight the sun was flecked with bars,
(Heaven's mother send us grace!)
As if through a dungeon grate he peered
With broad and burning face.

It seemeth him but
the skeleton of a
ship.

Alas! thought I—and my heart beat loud—
How fast she nears and nears!
Are those her sails that glance in the sun
Like restless gossameres?

Are those her ribs through which the sun
Did peer, as through a grate?
And is that woman all her crew?
Is that a Death? and are there two?
Is Death that woman's mate?

And its ribs are seen
as bars on the face
of the setting sun.
The spectre-woman
and her death-mate,
and no other, on
board the skeleton
ship.

Her lips were red, her looks were free,
Her locks were yellow as gold;
Her skin was as white as leprosy:
The nightmare Life-in-death was she,
Who thicks man's blood with cold.

Like vessel, like
crew!

The naked hulk alongside came,
And the twain were casting dice:
'The game is done! I've won! I've won!'
Quoth she, and whistles thrice.

Death and Life-in-
Death have diced for
the ship's crew, and
she (the latter)
winneth the ancient
mariner,

The sun's rim dips, the stars rush out,
At one stride comes the dark;
With far-heard whisper, o'er the sea
Off shot the spectre bark.

At the rising of the
moon,

We listened, and looked sideways up;
Fear at my heart, as at a cup,
My life-blood seemed to sip;
The stars were dim, and thick the night,—
The steersman's face by his lamp gleamed white;
From the sails the dew did drip,—
Till clomb above the eastern bar
The hornéd moon, with one bright star
Within the nether tip.

One after another

One after one, by the star-dogged moon,
Too quick for groan or sigh,
Each turneth his face, with a ghastly pang,
And cursed me with his eye.

His shipmates drop
down dead;

Four times fifty living men,
(And I heard nor sigh nor groan!)
With heavy thump, a lifeless lump,
They dropped down one by one.

But Life-in-Death
begins her work on
the ancient mariner.

The souls did from their bodies fly,—
They fled to bliss or woe!
And every soul it passed me by,
Like the whiz of my cross-bow!"

PART IV

The wedding-guest
feareth that a spirit
is talking to him;

"I fear thee, ancient mariner!
I fear thy skinny hand!
And thou art long, and lank, and brown,
As is the ribbed sea-sand.

I fear thee and thy glittering eye,
And thy skinny hand so brown."

But the ancient
mariner assureth
him of his bodily
life, and proceedeth
to relate his horrible
penance.

"Fear not, fear not, thou wedding-guest!
This body dropt not down.

876

Alone, alone, all, all alone,
Alone on a wide, wide sea!
And never a saint took pity on
My soul in agony.

The many men, so beautiful!
And they all dead did lie;
And a thousand thousand slimy things
Lived on,—and so did I.

I looked upon the rotting sea,
And drew my eyes away;
I looked upon the rotting deck,
And there the dead men lay.

I looked to heaven and tried to pray;
But or ever a prayer had gusht
A wicked whisper came, and made
My heart as dry as dust.

I closed my lids, and kept them close,
And the balls like pulses beat;
For the sky and the sea, and the sea and the sky
Lay like a load on my weary eye,
And the dead were at my feet.

The cold sweat melted from their limbs,—
Nor rot nor reek did they;
The look with which they looked on me
Had never passed away.

An orphan's curse would drag to hell
A spirit from on high;
But O, more horrible than that
Is the curse in a dead man's eye!
Seven days, seven nights, I saw that curse,—
And yet I could not die.

The moving moon went up the sky,
And nowhere did abide;
Softly she was going up,
And a star or two beside.

877

Her beams bemocked the sultry main,
Like April hoar-frost spread;
But where the ship's huge shadow lay
The charméd water burnt alway
A still and awful red.

Beyond the shadow of the ship
I watched the water-snakes;
They moved in tracks of shining white;
And when they reared, the elfish light
Fell off in hoary flakes.

Within the shadow of the ship
I watched their rich attire,—
Blue, glossy green, and velvet black,
They coiled and swam; and every track
Was a flash of golden fire.

O happy living things! no tongue
Their beauty might declare;
A spring of love gushed from my heart,

And I blessed them unaware,—
Sure my kind saint took pity on me,
And I blessed them unaware.

The selfsame moment I could pray;
And from my neck so free
The albatross fell off, and sank
Like lead into the sea.

PART V

O sleep! it is a gentle thing,
Beloved from pole to pole!
To Mary Queen the praise be given!
She sent the gentle sleep from heaven
That slid into my soul.

The silly buckets on the deck,
That had so long remained,
I dreamt that they were filled with dew;
And when I woke, it rained.

My lips were wet, my throat was cold,
My garments all were dank;
Sure I had drunken in my dreams,
And still my body drank.

I moved, and could not feel my limbs;
I was so light—almost
I thought that I had died in sleep,
And was a blessèd ghost.

And soon I heard a roaring wind,—
It did not come anear;
But with its sound it shook the sails,
That were so thin and sere.

The upper air burst into life;
And a hundred fire-flags sheen,
To and fro they were hurried about;
And to and fro, and in and out,
The wan stars danced between.

And the coming wind did roar more loud,
And the sails did sigh like sedge;
And the rain poured down from one black cloud,—
The moon was at its edge.

The thick black cloud was cleft, and still
The moon was at its side;
Like waters shot from some high crag,
The lightning fell with never a jag,
A river steep and wide.

The loud wind never reached the ship,
Yet now the ship moved on!
Beneath the lightning and the moon
The dead men gave a groan.

They groaned, they stirred, they all uprose,
Nor spake, nor moved their eyes;
It had been strange, even in a dream,
To have seen those dead men rise.

He heareth sounds and seeth strange sights and commotions in the sky and the element.

The bodies of the ship's crew are inspired, and the ship moves on.

The helmsman steered, the ship moved on;
Yet never a breeze upblew;
The mariners all 'gan work the ropes,
Where they were wont to do;
They raised their limbs like lifeless tools,—
We were a ghastly crew.

The body of my brother's son
Stood by me, knee to knee;
The body and I pulled at one rope,
But he said naught to me."

"I fear thee, ancient mariner!"
"Be calm, thou wedding-guest!
'Twas not those souls that fled in pain,
Which to their corses came again,
But a troop of spirits blest.

For when it dawned they dropped their arms,
And clustered round the mast;
Sweet sounds rose slowly through their mouths,
And from their bodies passed.

Around, around flew each sweet sound,
Then darted to the sun;
Slowly the sounds came back again,
Now mixed, now one by one.

Sometimes, a-dropping from the sky,
I heard the skylark sing;
Sometimes all little birds that are,—
How they seemed to fill the sea and air
With their sweet jargoning!

And now 'twas like all instruments,
Now like a lonely flute;
And now it is an angel's song,
That makes the heavens be mute.

It ceased; yet still the sails made on
A pleasant noise till noon,—

A noise like of a hidden brook
In the leafy month of June,
That to the sleeping woods all night
Singeth a quiet tune.

Till noon we quietly sailed on,
Yet never a breeze did breathe;
Slowly and smoothly went the ship,
Moved onward from beneath.

Under the keel nine fathom deep,
From the land of mist and snow,
The spirit slid; and it was he
That made the ship to go.
The sails at noon left off their tune,
And the ship stood still also.

The sun, right up above the mast,
Had fixed her to the ocean;
But in a minute she 'gan to stir,
With a short uneasy motion,—
Backwards and forwards half her length,
With a short uneasy motion.

Then like a pawing horse let go,
She made a sudden bound,—
It flung the blood into my head,
And I fell down in a swound.

How long in that same fit I lay
I have not to declare;
But ere my living life returned
I heard, and in my soul discerned,
Two voices in the air;

'Is it he?' quoth one, 'Is this the man?
By him who died on cross,
With his cruel bow he laid full low
The harmless albatross!

The spirit who bideth by himself
In the land of mist and snow.

The lonesome spirit from the south pole carries on the ship as far as the line in obedience to the angelic troop; but still requireth vengeance.

The polar spirit's fellow-demons, the invisible inhabitants of the element, take part in his wrong; and two of them relate, one to the other, that penance, long and heavy for the ancient mariner, hath been accorded to the polar spirit, who returneth southward.

He loved the bird that loved the man
Who shot him with his bow.'

The other was a softer voice,
As soft as honey-dew:
Quoth he, 'The man hath penance done,
And penance more will do.'

PART VI

FIRST VOICE

'But tell me, tell me! speak again,
Thy soft response renewing,—
What makes that ship drive on so fast?
What is the ocean doing?'

SECOND VOICE

'Still as a slave before his lord,
The ocean hath no blast;
His great bright eye most silently
Up to the moon is cast,—

If he may know which way to go;
For she guides him smooth or grim.
See, brother, see! how graciously
She looketh down on him.

FIRST VOICE

The mariner hath been cast into a trance; for the angelic power causeth the vessel to drive northward faster than human life could endure.

'But why drives on that ship so fast,
Without or wave or wind?'

SECOND VOICE

'The air is cut away before,
And closes from behind.

Fly, brother, fly! more high, more high!
Or we shall be belated;
For slow and slow that ship will go,
When the mariner's trance is abated.'

The supernatural motion is retarded; the mariner awakes, and his penance begins anew.

I woke, and we were sailing on
As in a gentle weather;
'Twas night, calm night,—the moon was high;
The dead men stood together.

882

All stood together on the deck,
For a charnel-dungeon fitter;
All fixed on me their stony eyes,
That in the moon did glitter.

The pang, the curse, with which they died,
Had never passed away;
I could not draw my eyes from theirs,
Nor turn them up to pray.

And now this spell was snapt; once more
I viewed the ocean green,
And looked far forth, yet little saw
Of what had else been seen,—

The curse is finely expiated.

Like one that on a lonesome road
Doth walk in fear and dread,
And, having once turned round, walks on,
And turns no more his head;
Because he knows a frightful fiend
Doth close behind him tread.

But soon there breathed a wind on me,
Nor sound nor motion made;
Its path was not upon the sea,
In ripple or in shade.

It raised my hair, it fanned my cheek,
Like a meadow-gale of spring,—
It mingled strangely with my fears,
Yet it felt like a welcoming.

Swiftly, swiftly flew the ship,
Yet she sailed softly too;
Sweetly, sweetly blew the breeze,—
On me alone it blew.

O dream of joy! is this indeed
The lighthouse top I see?
Is this the hill? is this the kirk?
Is this mine own countree?

And the ancient mariner beholdeth his native country.

We drifted o'er the harbor-bar,
And I with sobs did pray,—
O, let me be awake, my God!
Or let me sleep alway.

The harbor-bay was clear as glass,
So smoothly was it strewn!
And on the bay the moonlight lay,
And the shadow of the moon.

The rock shone bright, the kirk no less,
That stands above the rock;
The moonlight steeped in silentness
The steady weathercock.

The angelic spirits leave the dead bodies.

And the bay was white with silent light,
Till, rising from the same,
Full many shapes, that shadows were,
In crimson colors came.

And appear in their own forms of light.

A little distance from the prow
Those crimson shadows were;
I turned my eyes upon the deck,—
O Christ! what saw I there!

Each corse lay flat, lifeless and flat;
And, by the holy rood!
A man all light, a seraph man,
On every corse there stood.

This seraph band, each waved his hand,—
It was a heavenly sight!
They stood as signals to the land,
Each one a lovely light;

This seraph band each waved his hand;
No voice did they impart,—
No voice; but O, the silence sank
Like music on my heart!

But soon I heard the dash of oars,
I heard the pilot's cheer;

My head was turned perforce away,
And I saw a boat appear.

The pilot and the pilot's boy,
I heard them coming fast;
Dear Lord in heaven! it was a joy
The dead men could not blast.

I saw a third,—I heard his voice;
It is the hermit good!
He singeth loud his godly hymns
That he makes in the wood;
He'll shrieve my soul,—he'll wash away
The albatross's blood.

PART VII

This hermit good lives in that wood   The hermit of the
Which slopes down to the sea.   wood
How loudly his sweet voice he rears!
He loves to talk with marineres
That come from a far countree.

He kneels at morn and noon and eve,—
He hath a cushion plump;
It is the moss that wholly hides
The rotted old oak-stump.

The skiff-boat neared,—I heard them talk:
'Why, this is strange, I trow!
Where are those lights, so many and fair,
That signal made but now?'

'Strange, by my faith!' the hermit said,—   Approacheth the ship
'And they answered not our cheer!   with wonder.
The planks looked warped! and see those sails,
How thin they are and sere!
I never saw aught like to them,
Unless perchance it were

Brown skeletons of leaves that lag
My forest-brook along,

When the ivy-tod is heavy with snow,
And the owlet whoops to the wolf below,
That eats the she-wolf's young.'

'Dear Lord! it hath a fiendish look,'
The pilot made reply,—
'I am a-feared.'—'Push on, push on!'
Said the hermit cheerily.

The boat came closer to the ship,
But I nor spake nor stirred;
The boat came close beneath the ship,
And straight a sound was heard:

The ship suddenly sinketh.

Under the water it rumbled on,
Still louder and more dread;
It reached the ship, it split the bay;
The ship went down like lead.

The ancient mariner is saved in the pilot's boat.

Stunned by that loud and dreadful sound,
Which sky and ocean smote,
Like one that hath been seven days drowned,
My body lay afloat;
But, swift as dreams, myself I found
Within the pilot's boat.

Upon the whirl where sank the ship
The boat spun round and round;
And all was still, save that the hill
Was telling of the sound.

I moved my lips,—the pilot shrieked,
And fell down in a fit;
The holy hermit raised his eyes,
And prayed where he did sit.

I took the oars; the pilot's boy,
Who now doth crazy go,
Laughed loud and long; and all the while
His eyes went to and fro:
'Ha! ha!' quoth he, 'full plain I see,
The Devil knows how to row.'

And now, all in my own countree,
I stood on the firm land!
The hermit stepped forth from the boat,
And scarcely he could stand.

'O, shrieve me, shrieve me, holy man!'—
The hermit crossed his brow:
'Say quick,' quoth he, 'I bid thee say,—
What manner of man art thou?'

The ancient mariner
earnestly entreateth
the hermit to shrieve
him; and the pen-
ance of life falls on
him.

Forthwith this frame of mine was wrenched
With a woful agony,
Which forced me to begin my tale,—
And then it left me free.

Since then, at an uncertain hour,
That agony returns;
And till my ghastly tale is told,
This heart within me burns.

And ever and anon,
throughout his fu-
ture life, an agony
constraineth him to
travel from land to
land.

I pass, like night, from land to land;
I have strange power of speech;
That moment that his face I see
I know the man that must hear me,—
To him my tale I teach.

What loud uproar bursts from that door!
The wedding-guests are there;
But in the garden bower the bride
And bridemaids singing are;
And hark the little vesper bell,
Which biddeth me to prayer!

O wedding-guest! this soul hath been
Alone on a wide, wide sea,—
So lonely 'twas, that God himself
Scarce seemed there to be.

O, sweeter than the marriage-feast,
'Tis sweeter far to me
To walk together to the kirk
With a goodly company!—

To walk together to the kirk,
And all together pray,
While each to his great Father bends,—
Old men, and babes, and loving friends,
And youths and maidens gay!

Farewell! farewell! but this I tell
To thee, thou wedding-guest!
He prayeth well who loveth well
Both man and bird and beast.

He prayeth best who loveth best
All things both great and small;
For the dear God who loveth us,
He made and loveth all."

The mariner, whose eye is bright,
Whose beard with age is hoar,
Is gone. And now the wedding-guest
Turned from the bridegroom's door.

He went like one that hath been stunned,
And is of sense forlorn;
A sadder and a wiser man
He rose the morrow morn.

A FAREWELL

Charles Kingsley

My fairest child, I have no song to give you;
  No lark could pipe to skies so dull and gray;
Yet, ere we part, one lesson I can leave you
  For every day.

Be good, sweet maid, and let who will be clever;
  Do noble things, not dream them, all day long:
And so make life, death, and that vast forever
  One grand, sweet song.

* * *

A conservative government is an organized hypocrisy.
                    —Benjamin Disraeli

AN IRISH WISH

Anonymous

May the road rise to meet you.
May the wind be ever at your back
May the Good Lord keep you
    in the hollow of His hand.
May your heart be as warm
    as your hearthstone.
And when you come to die
    may the wail of the poor
    be the only sorrow
    you'll leave behind.
May God bless you always.

ENVOY

Robert Louis Stevenson

Go, little book, and wish to all
Flowers in the garden, meat in the hall,
A bin of wine, a spice of wit,
A house with lawns enclosing it,
A living river by the door,
A nightingale in the sycamore!

ACKNOWLEDGMENTS

Anderson House, Publishers, J. K. Anderson, Director, for the last eleven lines of *Winterset* by Maxwell Anderson, copyright 1935 by Anderson House, copyright renewed 1963 by Gilda Anderson, all rights reserved, reprinted by permission of Anderson House.

Richard Armour for his "Money" from *An Armoury of Light Verse*, copyright.

A. S. Barnes and Co., Inc. for "Two Sides of War" from *The Final Answer And Other Poems* by Grantland Rice, copyright 1955.

Dodd, Mead and Co., Inc. for "The Dead" and "The Soldier" from *The Collected Poems of Rupert Brooke,* copyright 1915 by Dodd, Mead and Co., Inc., copyright renewed 1943 by Edward Marsh. For "Elegy in a Country Churchyard" from *The Collected Poems of G. K. Chesterton,* copyright 1932 by Dodd, Mead and Co., Inc., copyright renewed 1959 by Oliver Chesterton. For "My Financial Career" by Stephen Leacock from his *Laugh With Leacock,* copyright 1950 by Dodd, Mead and Co., Inc., copyright renewed 1958 by George Leacock. For "The Shooting of Dan McGrew" and "The Cremation of Sam McGee" from *The Collected Poems of Robert W. Service,* copyright 1907, 1909, 1912, 1916 and 1921 by Dodd, Mead and Co., Inc., copyright 1940 by Robert W. Service. All above reprinted by permission of Dodd, Mead and Co., Inc.

Doubleday and Co., Inc. for "If," copyright 1910 by Rudyard Kipling, from *Rudyard Kipling's Verse, Definitive Edition,* reprinted by permission of Doubleday and Co., Inc. For "Baseball's Sad Lexicon" excerpted from *The Column Book* by Franklin P. Adams, copyright 1928 by Doubleday and Co., Inc., reprinted by permission of the publisher. For passages from the R. L. Devonshire translation of *Life of Pasteur* by R. Vallery-Radot.

Fountain Inn (S. C.) *Tribune* for "Popular Young Couple Married This Week," a famous news hoax, by Robert E. Quillen.

Estate of Albert Einstein, Otto Nathan, Trustee, for passages from *Ideas and Opinions* by Albert Einstein, New York, 1954; passage from page 11 reprinted by *Living Philosophies.*

The Emporia Gazette and Mrs. William White for the editorials of William Allen White in *The Emporia Gazette* (Topeka, Kansas), reprinted with the permission of Mrs. William White.

893

My wife, Lillias W. Woods, has given much help on the index.

R. L. W.

900

902

909

INDEX OF FAMILIAR LINES

Note: Many of the selections in this book contain more than one familiar line. But this index includes only one familiar line from each selection. Consequently, the choosing of lines has often been arbitrary, representing only the editor's opinion of what is familiar.

918

INDEX BY AUTHORS

* All Bible passages are from the authorized King James version.

945